The
PROGENY

Justice William J. Brennan's Fight to Preserve the Legacy of *New York Times v. Sullivan*

LEE LEVINE AND STEPHEN WERMIEL

Forum on
Communications Law
AMERICAN BAR ASSOCIATION

Section of
Individual Rights
and Responsibilities

Cover design by Jill Tedhams/ABA Publishing.

The materials contained herein represent the opinions of the authors and/ or the editors, and should not be construed to be the views or opinions of the law firms or companies with whom such persons are in partnership with, associated with, or employed by, nor of the American Bar Association or Communications Law unless adopted pursuant to the bylaws of the Association.

Nothing contained in this book is to be considered as the rendering of legal advice for specific cases, and readers are responsible for obtaining such advice from their own legal counsel. This book is intended for educational and informational purposes only.

Printed in the United States of America.

18 17 16 15 14 5 4 3 2

Library of Congress Cataloging-in-Publication data
Wermiel, Stephen, author.
    The progeny : Justice William J. Brennan's fight to preserve the legacy of New York Times v. Sullivan / By Stephen Wermiel and Lee Levine.
        p. cm.
    Includes bibliographical references and index.
    ISBN 978-1-62722-449-9 (alk. paper)
    1. Brennan, William J., 1906-1997. 2. Judges--United States--Biography. 3. United States. Supreme Court--Biography. 4. Freedom of the press--United States. 5. Press law--United States. 6. Libel and slander--United States. 7. Sullivan, L. B.--Trials, litigation, etc. 8. New York Times Company--Trials, litigation, etc. I. Levine, Lee, author. II. Title.
    KF8745.B68W47 2014
    342.7308'53--dc23
                                                                    2014000996
Discounts are available for books ordered in bulk. Special consideration is given to state bars, CLE programs, and other bar-related organizations. Inquire at Book Publishing, ABA Publishing, American Bar Association, 321 N. Clark Street, Chicago, Illinois 60654-7598.

www.ShopABA.org

CONTENTS

ACKNOWLEDGMENTS

The authors acknowledge the help of many people in the preparation of this book. At the American Bar Association (ABA), we wish to thank Steven Zansberg for the ABA Forum on Communications Law and Tanya Terrell for the ABA Section of Individual Rights & Responsibilities. We also appreciate the support and encouragement of Richard Paszkiet of ABA Publishing, who has been consistently enthusiastic about this project.

For research, we had the benefit of the tireless and invaluable help of Abigail Duggan, American University Washington College of Law Class of 2013; Matthew Schafer, Georgetown University Law Center Class of 2013; and Renata Strause, Yale Law School Class of 2013. Matt and Renata also undertook the thankless but critical work of helping us produce the endnotes for the book.

Many librarians contributed their knowledge and expertise to help with this project. Jeff Flannery at the Manuscript Division of the Library of Congress is a wonderful resource about the collections of justices' papers at the Library of Congress. John Jacob, archivist of the Lewis Powell Papers at Washington and Lee Law School, was always helpful with access to materials and answers to questions. Jill Golden shared her knowledge of the William H. Rehnquist Papers at the Hoover Institution at Stanford University. Amy Taylor at the American University Washington College of Law Pence Law Library answered many questions and dug up hard-to-find articles and transcripts.

We thank the law firm of Levine, Sullivan, Koch & Schulz for supporting this project in innumerable ways, including by permitting Bridgette Simmons—Lee Levine's assistant—to provide invaluable assistance in preparing and formatting the manuscript. We also thank Dean Claudio Grossman of American University

Washington College of Law for the support and encouragement he provided for research, enabling Steve Wermiel to pursue this book.

Before we undertook to write this book, we published two articles that contributed in different ways to it. For the *Communications Lawyer* article, we are grateful to Stephanie Abrutyn of HBO, who is one of the editors of that quarterly publication and who provided significant encouragement and helpful feedback. We are also grateful to the very professional staff of the *Washington Law Review*, which published the other article, especially James Wendell and Kathleen Kline.

For the *Washington Law Review* article, Adam Liptak gave us thoughtful comments on a draft, and Ron Collins provided wise counsel, encouragement, and guidance. Three former Supreme Court law clerks, each for a justice who played a significant part in the story we tell, contributed commentary in the *Washington Law Review*, and we thank them for their thoughtful insights. They are Scott Nelson, Justice White; Robert O'Neil, Justice Brennan; and Paul Smith, Justice Powell.

In addition, we are grateful to several other law clerks, for Justice Brennan and other justices, who made themselves available to us to verify facts about which we were unsure and to prevent us from drawing unwarranted conclusions from source documents. We also thank Michael Sullivan, Celeste Phillips, and Leonard Zeskind for assisting us in tracking down some obscure documents. And finally, we thank Seth Stern, Steve Wermiel's collaborator on *Justice Brennan: Liberal Champion*, who worked closely with Steve on that book's discussion of *Sullivan* itself, from which we draw extensively in chapter 1 of this work.

ABOUT THE AUTHORS

Lee Levine, a founding partner of the Levine Sullivan Koch & Schulz law firm, has represented media clients in First Amendment-related cases for more than three decades. In the United States Supreme Court, he argued for the media defendants in *Harte-Hanks Communications, Inc. v. Connaughton* and *Bartnicki v. Vopper.* Mr. Levine is also an Adjunct Professor at the Georgetown University Law Center. He is the lead author of the treatise *Newsgathering and the Law,* now in its fourth edition, and, along with the late David Kohler, co-authored the casebook *Media and the Law.*

Stephen Wermiel, Professor of Practice at American University Washington College of Law, completed his term as chair of the ABA Section of Individual Rights & Responsibilities (IRR) in August 2013. He is chair of the IRR Publications Committee and is a member of the ABA Committee on Public Education. He is co-author of the biography, *Justice Brennan: Liberal Champion,* published in 2010 by Houghton Mifflin Harcourt and in paperback in 2013 by University Press of Kansas.

AUTHORS' NOTE

In 2010, Steve Wermiel and Seth Stern published their highly acclaimed biography of Justice Brennan. Because Brennan's remarkable tenure on the Supreme Court spanned such a long period in American history, and because he personally influenced the development of constitutional law in so many areas, it was impossible for his biographers to devote concentrated attention to any one of them. Thus, for example, although *Justice Brennan: Liberal Champion* devotes seven pages to *New York Times Co. v. Sullivan*, the Court's groundbreaking decision articulating the "central meaning" of the First Amendment that is the inspiration for this book, the development of the body of constitutional law that followed it is barely mentioned. The biography's inability, as a practical matter, to explore that subject spawned a series of discussions between us about the prospect of a more narrowly focused work devoted to Brennan's role in formulating what we now understand to be the freedom of expression guaranteed by the First Amendment. Ultimately, we determined to embark on such a project, focused on the development of the constitutional law of defamation and related claims following *Sullivan* and targeted for publication in 2014, the fiftieth anniversary of Brennan's opinion for the Court in that landmark case.

The volume that we have produced is, we believe, true to the mission we set for ourselves. Because the biography contains a comparatively detailed discussion of *Sullivan* and because the case itself is the subject of *Make No Law*, the authoritative account of how it came to be by Anthony Lewis, we reprise some of that history here merely to ground the reader and set the stage for our exploration of the decades of constitutional development that have followed it. In addition, like the biography, this work approaches the subject largely from Brennan's perspective.

In short, this is Brennan's story, his take on how the constitutional law of defamation and related claims came to be, based largely on his papers. In that cause, the book also draws on Steve's interviews with Brennan, conducted between 1986 and 1990, and on some of Brennan's materials that Steve had access to before they were deposited with the Library of Congress where access may now be restricted.

Nevertheless, the book is based as well on the papers of other justices, especially in those cases in which one or more of them played a significant role, along with Brennan, in the law's formulation. Some of the papers of other justices were not available when the biography was written but have been opened to researchers since then.

In one instance, we discovered in Brennan's papers a wealth of material about the Court's deliberations in *Dun & Bradstreet v. Greenmoss Builders*, a relatively obscure 1985 decision from which he dissented. That discovery led us to examine the voluminous papers that several other justices had collected about the case, most notably Justices Powell and White, and to memorialize our work in an article published in the *Washington Law Review*. *See* "The Landmark That Wasn't: A First Amendment Play in Five Acts," 88 Wash. L. Rev. 1 (2013). A somewhat abbreviated version of that article appears as a chapter in this book.

Given *Sullivan*'s enormous impact on the development of the Court's First Amendment jurisprudence generally, we found it necessary, at the outset, to make some draws about what cases (and categories of cases) to include in our examination. In the end, we somewhat arbitrarily decided to limit ourselves to those cases addressing the law of defamation directly, as well as those adjudicating closely related tort claims (such as, for example, invasion of privacy and intentional infliction of emotional distress), along with the line of cases examining the impact of *Sullivan* (and the Court's subsequent decision in *Gertz v. Robert Welch, Inc.*) on governmental efforts to impose liability, in the name of protecting individual privacy, on the publication of truthful information about matters of public concern. And, in the book's last chapter, which describes those defamation and closely related cases implicating *Sullivan* that the Court has decided since Brennan left the bench, we do not address *Tory v. Cochran*, a 2005 defamation case in which, after granting review and hearing argument, the justices decided that, in the wake of the death of the plaintiff, renowned criminal defense lawyer Johnnie Cochran, it was both "unnecessary, indeed unwarranted, for us to explore petitioners' basic claims, namely, (1) that the First Amendment forbids the issuance of a permanent injunction in a defamation case, at least when the plaintiff is a public figure, and (2) that the injunction," issued prior to Cochran's death to prevent Tory from picketing Cochran's law office "was not properly tailored and consequently violated the First Amendment."

Another draw we faced was how to refer to the 1964 case that spawned all of the others we address. It appears that, in the years immediately following the decision, most of the justices and the majority of commentators referred to it as *New York Times*. At some point, however, that changed and, for most of the last fifty years, it has been more commonly—but not always—referred to as *Sullivan*. The reason for this change in nomenclature is unclear, but it likely has something to do with the fact that, in 1963, the Court decided *Bantam Books, Inc. v. Sullivan*, another case adjudicating First Amendment rights while, in 1971, it decided *New York Times Co. v. United States*, the famous "Pentagon Papers" case reaffirming the First Amendment's virtually absolute protections against the imposition of prior restraints on publication. Whatever the reason, we opted for *Sullivan* and ask the reader's indulgence on those occasions when our use of that short form is interrupted in the text by a justice's reference to *New York Times*.

Readers will note that, in two instances, the book addresses cases argued before the Court by one of the authors, specifically *Harte-Hanks Communications, Inc. v. Connaughton* and *Bartnicki v. Vopper*. In other instances, Lee and/or his law firm represented either a party to the case at some stage of the litigation or submitted a brief *amicus curiae* to the Court on behalf of other clients. Specifically, in *Anderson v. Liberty Lobby*, his then law firm represented the defendants following the Supreme Court's remand; in *Masson v. New Yorker Magazine*, the firm represented Janet Malcolm (along with her extraordinarily able trial counsel Gary Bostwick) in postremand proceedings in the United States Court of Appeals for the Ninth Circuit and her insurance carrier following the Ninth Circuit's initial decision; and, in *Cohen v. Cowles Media Co.* and *Milkovich v. Lorain Journal Co.*, the firm represented other clients as *amici curiae* in the Supreme Court. In each of these instances, we have endeavored to discuss the cases honestly and accurately, while disclosing here the ever-present potential for bias.

Finally, a word about the book's title. Literally hundreds of reported cases, published books and articles refer to "*New York Times Co. v. Sullivan* and its progeny" or some variation of that phrase. Justice Scalia has railed against this use of the term *progeny* to describe a line of judicial decisions, pronouncing it, on more than one occasion, "hackneyed." If nothing else, however, our research has confirmed our view that Justice Brennan was not only justifiably proud of what he and the Court accomplished in *Sullivan*, but that, in the nearly three decades thereafter, he took a decidedly paternal interest in the cases that followed it. Thus, with all due respect to Justice Scalia, we concluded that, in this instance, the term is appropriately invoked and that, for his part, Justice Brennan would approve.

CHAPTER 1

SULLIVAN

To understand and appreciate what Justice William J. Brennan Jr. accomplished when, on March 9, 1964, he announced and summarized from the bench the United States Supreme Court's decision in *New York Times Co. v. Sullivan*, one needs to return to the beginning, to a new nation's adoption of a Constitution and, shortly thereafter, a bill of those rights reserved to its citizens including, as the first among them, the "freedom of speech or of the press."

The authors of that phrase, contained in the First Amendment to the new Constitution, left no clear explication of what they meant by it, not to mention the import of the language that surrounded it in the constitutional text. That language, which declared simply that the "Congress shall make no law" that "abridg[ed]" those freedoms, raised innumerable questions not only about what the "freedom of speech or of the press" encompasses, but also about what constitutes a law "abridging" that freedom in the first place, whether the freedoms of "speech" and "press" in fact delineate different things, and whether, despite its express limitation to "Congress" and its lawmaking powers, the prohibition in fact extends to actions taken by one of the other branches of the federal government.

The first years of actual experience under the newly amended Constitution yielded some clues but also highlighted the ongoing mystery. While there appeared to be a reasonably strong consensus that the freedom of the press included a broad right to be free from laws prohibiting publication in advance—a so-called prior restraint on expression—the historical signals with respect to the power of the federal government to punish those responsible for such publications after they had been disseminated were decidedly weaker.

1

Most notably, the ink had barely dried on what would come to be known simply as "the First Amendment" when the nation's second president, John Adams, signed legislation, duly enacted by the Congress, that made it a crime, punishable by a fine and up to five years in prison, to "write, print, utter or publish . . . any false, scandalous and malicious writing or writings against the government of the United States, or either house of the Congress . . . , or the President . . . with the intent to defame . . . or to bring them, or either of them, into contempt or disrepute." When it passed a Congress then controlled by Adams's Federalist Party, the Sedition Act of 1798 was vigorously opposed by Thomas Jefferson, Adams's primary political antagonist, who would become his successor as president, and by James Madison, Jefferson's successor and the principal author of the Bill of Rights itself. At the time, they both famously championed the Virginia Resolutions of 1798, in which the general assembly of their home state declared that, in enacting the Sedition Act, the federal government had exercised "a power not delegated by the Constitution, but, on the contrary, expressly and positively forbidden by one of the amendments thereto." When he became president, Jefferson pardoned those who had been convicted of violating the statute, explaining that he had always "considered, and now consider, that law to be a nullity, as absolute and as palpable as if Congress had ordered us to fall down and worship a golden image."

The Sedition Act, which expired by its terms in 1801, was never considered by the Supreme Court, and, in the years that followed, the Court had precious little to say about the scope and meaning of the "freedom of speech or of the press" enshrined in the First Amendment. This was largely because, following the uproar surrounding that statute, the federal government, with a couple of notable exceptions, stayed out of the business of enacting legislation that purported either to prohibit or punish the publication of speech about matters of public concern.

The exceptions largely involved statutes the Congress enacted in the period surrounding World War I to address perceived threats to the national security arising from publicly expressed opposition to that conflict by socialists, anarchists, and other critics as well as later efforts to enforce those laws, and others, against calls for the abolition of the federal government by the adherents of the political philosophy known as "communism." These cases uniformly upheld the enforcement of such laws in the face of challenges grounded in the First Amendment, typically to the consternation of Justices Oliver Wendell Holmes and Louis D. Brandeis, who authored a series of eloquent opinions, frequently in dissent, advocating the view that the First Amendment generally ought to protect speech about matters of public concern. Still, it remained the case that, in the first 150 years after its passage, there were relatively few occasions on which Congress enacted laws that arguably infringed the freedom of speech or press guaranteed by the First Amendment.

The experience in the several states, however, was another matter. State legislatures regularly enacted, and state courts routinely enforced as a matter of common law, a host of measures regulating what their citizens could write and say. Most notably, the states subjected those who published a libel or uttered a slander to both criminal sanctions and awards of civil damages. In addition, their legislatures passed laws prohibiting the dissemination of obscenity and their judges held litigants in contempt for making statements critical of them and their courts. And their executive officials on occasion prosecuted, for "disturbing the peace" and analogous offenses, those citizens who fomented controversy and occasionally violence by virtue of what they said in the public square.

Prior to the Civil War, the Supreme Court could have nothing to say about the constitutional propriety of such "state action" because the First Amendment, on its face, applied only to laws enacted by the federal Congress. As a result of the war, however, the Constitution was amended to bring within its scope some actions undertaken by state governments. In addition to prohibiting slavery in any state in the union in the Thirteenth Amendment, and precluding the states from denying any person the right to vote based on the color of his skin in the Fifteenth, the newly amended Constitution provided, in the Fourteenth Amendment, that no state could lawfully deny the "privileges or immunities" of citizenship or the "equal protection" and "due process of law." The Fourteenth Amendment held the promise that the limitations on the federal government's power enshrined in the Bill of Rights would similarly circumscribe the authority of the states themselves to, among other things, "abridg[e] the freedom of speech or of the press."

That promise, however, took a long time to be realized. Shortly after it became effective, the Supreme Court held that the Fourteenth Amendment's "privileges or immunities" clause, the portion of it that, at least on its face, appeared most likely to "incorporate" the Bill of Rights against the states, did no such thing. In fact, it was not until well after the turn of the next century that the Court slowly began to consider seriously and, one by one, determine that most of the rights guaranteed in the Constitution's initial amendments were part and parcel of the "liberty" that the Fourteenth Amendment established could not be denied by the states without "due process of law." In 1925, the Supreme Court first determined that the "freedom of speech or of the press" constituted such a right and, in 1931, it held that the First Amendment, as incorporated against the states through the Fourteenth, prohibited the state of Minnesota from enforcing a law that authorized its courts to enjoin the publication of a newspaper as a "public nuisance" because it contained defamatory and otherwise inappropriate content. That latter case, *Near v. Minnesota*, recognized that, at the very least, the First Amendment's speech and press clauses were intended to prohibit the government, both federal and state, from imposing a "prior restraint" on publication.

Although the state law before the Court in *Near* purported to restrict the dissemination of "defamatory" newspapers, the decision itself was limited to the prior restraint issue and did not consider the extent to which the states remained free to address through their laws the publication of defamatory statements after the fact, either by criminal statute or by permitting those defamed to bring civil suits to recover money damages. In the years that followed, however, the justices appeared to suggest that the states retained significant authority to do so. In one influential decision, the Court indicated that several species of expression—including words that were obscene, defamatory, or that might incite violence—did not constitute "speech" within the meaning of the First Amendment at all because, historically, they had been deemed to be "of such slight social value as a step to truth that any benefit that may be derived from them is clearly outweighed by the social interest in order and morality." In another, decided in 1952, the Court sustained, largely on that ground, the application of Illinois's criminal libel statute to a publication that allegedly defamed a racial group and was thereby "liable to cause violence and disorder."

Thus, when, on Tuesday, March 29, 1960, the *New York Times* published a full-page advertisement entitled "Heed Their Rising Voices," soliciting contributions to the "Committee to Defend Martin Luther King and the Struggle for Freedom in the South," there was no reason to believe that, if that advertisement contained defamatory falsehoods about an identifiable person as defined by state law, either the *Times* or the advertisement's authors and signatories (which listed more than sixty persons including, in addition to a number of ministers residing in southern states, such celebrities as poet Langston Hughes, baseball player Jackie Robinson, former First Lady Eleanor Roosevelt, and actor Marlon Brando) could look to the First Amendment to protect them from civil liability. This fact was not lost on those in southern states looking for a vehicle to counter and stem the tide of adverse national publicity that had served to fuel the civil rights movement spearheaded by Dr. King and others. They found one such vehicle in the civil defamation laws of Alabama, which were not materially different from those of other states.

Like the laws of most jurisdictions, the common law of Alabama provided that any person who was the subject of a publication that, on its face, was reasonably construed to injure his or her reputation (that was "defamatory") could recover money damages against those responsible for the publication. If the publication was reasonably capable of such a meaning, the law both presumed that it was false and that the plaintiff suffered harm as a result of its dissemination to a third party. Truth was generally deemed to be a defense, but the burden of proving it rested on the defendant publisher. Damages flowing from a defamatory publication were generally presumed and could be awarded in the discretion of the jury, which was called on to value each plaintiff's reputation and determine the extent to which it had been injured. Punitive damages, in Alabama as in most states, could be awarded if there was evidence of malice, even if the defendant otherwise acted with a salutary motive and a good faith belief in the accuracy of its publication.

The body of the advertisement published by the *Times* did not identify a single person, other than Dr. King, by name. Instead, it recounted incidents in which he and his followers had been mistreated or, in the words of the advertisement, "met by an unprecedented wave of terror," for advocating for their civil rights. The ad detailed specific examples of such activities in cities across the South, including in Montgomery, Alabama. In the portion of the advertisement addressing events in that city, its authors wrote:

> In Montgomery, Alabama, after students sang "My Country, 'Tis of Thee" on the State Capitol steps, their leaders were expelled from school, and truckloads of police armed with shotguns and tear-gas ringed the Alabama State College Campus. When the entire student body protested to state authorities by refusing to re-register, their dining hall was padlocked in an attempt to starve them into submission.

The ad referred generally to the perpetrators of these actions as "Southern violators of the Constitution," and asserted that such persons "fear this new, non-violent brand of freedom fighter" and were therefore "determined to destroy the one man who, more than any other, symbolizes the new spirit sweeping the South—the Rev. Dr. Martin Luther King, Jr." According to the ad's text, the "Southern violators" had

> answered Dr. King's protests with intimidation and violence. They have bombed his home almost killing his wife and child. They have assaulted his person. They have arrested him seven times—for "speeding," "loitering" and similar "offenses." And now they have charged him with "perjury"—a *felony* under which they could imprison him for *ten years*.

Following its publication, five separate defamation actions were filed against the *Times* in the state courts of Alabama. The plaintiff in one of them was the state's sitting governor, and in another was the mayor of Montgomery. Three other plaintiffs either were or had been elected city commissioners. In all, the five lawsuits sought more than $3 million in damages. In 2013 dollars, the claimed damages totaled more than $23 million. The entire circulation of the *Times* on March 29, 1960, was approximately 650,000 copies, of which 394 were distributed in Alabama (35 in Montgomery County).

Among the plaintiffs was L. B. Sullivan, one of the elected commissioners. His responsibilities included "supervision of the Police Department, Fire Department, Department of Cemetery and Department of Scales." In his complaint, he sought $500,000 in damages against the *Times* and four Alabama clergymen whose names were listed in the advertisement as among those who "warmly endorse[d]" its appeal for donations. Sullivan alleged that he was the subject of false and defamatory statements in the advertisement—that is, that it was "of and concerning him"—because the word "police" in the paragraph about events in Montgomery necessarily referred to him as the commissioner who supervised the police department. He further alleged that, as a result, the advertisement falsely accused him of, among other things, "ringing" the campus with police and padlocking the student dining facility. And, his complaint contended, the advertisement's references to "Southern violators" would similarly be understood to refer to him and therefore to accuse him, and the Montgomery police, of answering "Dr. King's protests with intimidation and violence."

Commissioner Sullivan asserted that several of the statements published in the advertisement were false. He submitted evidence demonstrating that the students sang the "Star-Spangled Banner," not "My Country, 'Tis of Thee"; that the student leaders were expelled for demanding service at a lunch counter, not for leading the demonstration at the capitol; that only a majority of the student body had boycotted class (and had not refused to register for classes); and that only certain students were refused service in the dining hall, which was never padlocked. In addition, he contended that, although large numbers of police were deployed near the campus on multiple occasions, they at no time "ringed" it. Sullivan also offered evidence that Dr. King had been arrested four times, not seven, and that the police officer that Dr. King accused of assaulting him following his arrest on loitering charges denied having done so. Although he conceded that Dr. King's home had been bombed on two occasions, while his wife and child were there, Sullivan introduced evidence demonstrating that he was not a commissioner at the time and had not participated in those events and that, similarly, he played no role in any of the other actions described in the advertisement as directed specifically at Dr. King.

At trial, Sullivan called several witnesses who testified that they understood the advertisement to refer to him in his capacity as a commissioner. He offered no evidence that he had suffered pecuniary harm as a result of the advertisement's publication, and sponsored the testimony of no witnesses who testified that they believed that he had in fact done any of the things recounted in its text. One witness testified that, if he had believed that Sullivan was responsible for such actions (which he emphasized he did not), he would likely not "want to be associated with anybody who would be a party to such things."

When the case was submitted to the jury, the trial judge charged it in accordance with the common law of Alabama. In relevant part, the jury was instructed that the advertisement was libelous "per se" and, as a result, the defendants were liable if they were responsible for its publication and if the defamatory statements within it were "of and concerning" Sullivan. Because the challenged statements constituted libel per se, the jury was instructed, "the law . . . implies legal injury from the mere fact of publication itself," that "falsity and malice are presumed," that "general damages need not be alleged or proved but are presumed," and that punitive damages could be awarded even if actual damages were "neither found nor shown." To award punitive damages, however, the jury was instructed that it must find that defendants published with "actual malice" which, the jury was informed, requires something more than "mere negligence or carelessness." The trial judge declined to charge the jury that a finding of "actual malice" required evidence of "actual intent" to harm or even "gross negligence or recklessness."

Following two hours and twenty minutes of deliberations, the jury awarded Sullivan $500,000, the full amount he claimed, as did another jury in the case brought by Montgomery Mayor Earl James. The trials in the other three cases had not yet taken place when, in 1962, the Alabama Supreme Court unanimously affirmed the jury verdict in favor of Sullivan in its entirety. When the *Times* and the four individual defendants sought review in the Supreme Court, Sullivan asked his lawyer, M. Roland Nachman (who, among other clients, regularly represented Montgomery's leading daily newspaper), about the chances that the justices would hear the case and take away his jury verdict. Nachman responded, "L.B., for that to happen, they would have to reverse 200 years of settled law." He was not far off the mark.

In 1962, the highest judicial tribunal in the United States was already known to most citizens as the Warren Court, named for its chief justice, Earl Warren. The former governor of California and Republican candidate for vice president (running unsuccessfully in 1948 with fellow governor Thomas Dewey of New York), Warren was appointed the Supreme Court's fourteenth chief justice by President Eisenhower in 1953. Seven months later, under Warren's leadership, the Court unanimously held in *Brown v. Board of Education* that the "separate but equal" regime of public education that then dominated the southern and border states violated the Fourteenth Amendment's equal protection clause. From there, the Warren Court not only spearheaded the desegregation of public schools throughout the South, it issued a series of decisions recognizing and protecting the civil rights of African Americans, accelerated the process of "incorporating" the Bill of Rights against the states (particularly those rights protecting criminal defendants), and insinuated itself into the formerly "political" process of drawing voting districts by declaring that the Constitution required judicial enforcement of the principle of "one man, one vote." Opponents of the Court's decisions, which included most elected officials in the South and a large portion of its citizens, as well as a host of academics, railed against what they described as the Court's "activist" justices.

The Court that decided *Brown v. Board of Education* did indeed include justices, in addition to Warren, who were not afraid to interpret the Constitution, and particularly the Bill of Rights, in a manner that insinuated it into the most controversial issues of the day. First among them were Justices Hugo Black and William O. Douglas, both of whom had been appointed by President Franklin Roosevelt and had seen the Court through the turmoil surrounding the federal government's implementation of Roosevelt's New Deal. For both Black and Douglas, the Bill of Rights had not only been incorporated against the states through the Fourteenth, but the commands of those amendments were to be taken literally. Thus, for example, when the First Amendment said that "Congress shall make no law abridging the freedom of speech or of the press," it meant exactly that—all laws that purported to regulate speech or the press were unconstitutional, regardless of their impact or purpose. After *Brown* and before *New York Times Co. v. Sullivan*, Black and Douglas joined Warren in a series of decisions enforcing the Bill of Rights against the states, including the right to be free from unreasonable searches and seizures at the hands of state law enforcement officers and the right of indigents to have counsel appointed to defend them in criminal cases.

The other justices that comprised the Court that decided *Brown*, however, were decidedly less robust in their embrace of such judicial forays into previously uncharted constitutional territory. Several of them were, with the exception of *Brown*, affirmatively hostile to what they viewed as the Court's notable lack of the kind of "self-restraint" that, in their view, properly circumscribed the role of the Supreme Court in the nation's political affairs. The intellectual and, within the Court itself, operational leader of this faction was Felix Frankfurter, a former professor at Harvard Law School. Until his retirement in 1962, Frankfurter frequently marshaled opposition to the efforts of Warren, Black, and Douglas to expand the Court's role in protecting and enforcing civil and political rights. He was often joined by colleagues such as former attorney general and legendary war crimes prosecutor Robert Jackson, the well-regarded former New York lawyer John Marshall Harlan, and Tom Clark, another former attorney general, who had been appointed both to that position and to the Supreme Court by President Truman.

By 1962, however, the Court's composition had changed in material ways. For one thing, in 1956, two years after *Brown*, President Eisenhower appointed Brennan, a relatively unknown member of the New Jersey Supreme Court, to replace another of President Truman's appointees, the lightly regarded Sherman Minton. Almost from the moment of his appointment, Brennan became a reliable, if more flexible and politically conscious than Black and Douglas, ally of the chief justice. In short order, Brennan helped Warren navigate the Court through a host of important issues, from opening the door to judicial recognition of the "one man, one vote" principle in *Baker v. Carr*, to enforcement of the justices' desegregation decisions in *Cooper v. Aaron*. Brennan and Warren forged a particularly close friendship and professional relationship that, over the years they served together, had a palpable impact on the Court and its work.

For another thing, when the often irascible Frankfurter retired in 1962, he was replaced by Arthur Goldberg, a card-carrying liberal who had served as President Kennedy's labor secretary. With that single appointment, the young president had substituted a justice who served as a reliable fifth vote for Warren's agenda (along with Black, Douglas, and Brennan) for the chief justice's most formidable and uncompromising ideological adversary. With Frankfurter's retirement, his role as the champion of judicial self-restraint fell largely to the decidedly more congenial but nevertheless intellectually impressive Harlan, who often found an ally in Clark.

The other two seats on the iteration of the Warren Court that would be asked to decide *New York Times Co. v. Sullivan* were occupied by Potter Stewart and Byron White. Stewart, another Eisenhower appointee who came to the Court two years after Brennan, was previously a federal appellate judge from Ohio who replaced another of Truman's relatively inconsequential appointees, Harold Burton. Stewart proved to be a mercurial figure on the Court, a justice who aligned himself with none of his colleagues on a regular basis. As a result, especially in later years, securing his vote would become increasingly important to forging a majority.

White was similarly impossible to pigeonhole. Like Goldberg, he came to the Court in 1962, after serving as deputy attorney general under Robert Kennedy. He had previously been a highly acclaimed football player, both at the University of Colorado and in the National Football League. Known during his athletic career as "Whizzer" White (a nickname he reportedly despised), he was also a Rhodes Scholar who had served as a naval intelligence officer during World War II. Despite his credentials as a leading figure in Kennedy's "New Frontier," White was, from the outset of his service on the Court, a less reliable supporter of so-called liberal positions than Goldberg, President Kennedy's only other Supreme Court appointee. Not surprisingly, given his prominent role in Robert Kennedy's Justice Department, White readily joined Warren and Brennan in cases involving desegregation and other aspects of the civil rights movement, but—especially as he became more senior—he came to be viewed, along with Stewart, as a swing vote who, as often as not, went his own way. Even so, he and Brennan developed a warm friendship, one that endured throughout the almost three decades that they served together.

In the First Amendment area, at least with respect to that portion of the amendment that spoke to the "freedom of speech or of the press," perhaps the Warren Court's most noteworthy decision prior to 1962 was *Roth v. United States*. In that case, decided in 1957 in a majority opinion authored by Brennan, the Court for the first time held that the government did not have the unbridled authority to declare speech "obscene" and thereby prohibit its dissemination. Joined by a highly unusual majority composed of Frankfurter, Burton, Clark, and Justice Charles Whittaker (another Eisenhower appointee, who served only five years on the Court before being replaced by White), Brennan wrote that it was up to the Supreme Court to define "obscenity" in a manner consistent with the First Amendment and that legislatures were empowered only to restrict, regulate, or prohibit speech that met that court-ordered definition. For his part, Warren could bring himself only to concur in the Court's judgment. Black and Douglas dissented because, in their view, the literal reading of the First Amendment they deemed to be required absolutely precluded the government from legislating in the name of "obscenity." Harlan also dissented, although his objections were quite different—in his view, the federal government had every right to regulate "obscenity" and to define that term as well.

The Court's decision in *Roth* set in motion a revolution in the degree to which so-called pornographic materials—including books, magazines, and films—could be freely disseminated and, for a number of years, put the Court in a position of reviewing large numbers of such works itself to determine whether the *Roth* test had been satisfied and the book or film at issue in a given case could be regulated. In large sections of the country, including the comparatively conservative southern states, the Court's role in making pornography more freely available was another hot-button example of the Warren Court's judicial activism. Still, the analytical framework that Brennan employed in *Roth*—simultaneously affirming the view that obscenity was not protected by the First Amendment but consigning to the Supreme Court the ultimate authority to define that term—would become significant when, five years later, the justices decided whether to grapple with another category of expression that had previously been declared to be unprotected by the First Amendment—libel or, as it was also often known, defamation.

When *New York Times Co. v. Sullivan* reached the Supreme Court in 1962, Brennan and the other justices recognized that enormous jury awards of the kind Sullivan had secured threatened to drive out of the South reporters from major news organizations, which was of course precisely the goal of Sullivan and his colleagues. Keeping the national press out would deprive the civil rights movement of the valuable media attention needed to fan outrage in the rest of the country and increase political pressure on the southern states to desegregate. The *Times* itself had already pulled its correspondent out of Alabama for a year to avoid being served process as it sought to challenge the state courts' jurisdiction over the paper. All the better, southern politicians thought, if libel judgments also forced the four ministers who had been sued along with the *Times* to give up their cars and property to pay the huge awards, drove some of them out of the state entirely, and forced Dr. King's cash-strapped Southern Christian Leadership Conference to spend a fortune in legal fees. The use of libel suits as a tool of intimidation had already spread beyond the ones targeted at the *Times*. CBS faced a lawsuit of its own for a television program describing difficulties African Americans faced in registering to vote in Montgomery.

In short, Brennan and his colleagues fully understood what was at stake for the civil rights movement they had helped to advance in *Brown* when the Court heard argument in the *Sullivan* case on January 6, 1964. If the Court did not impose some restraints, Brennan believed, the progress toward desegregation that had begun with *Brown* ten years earlier would be seriously retarded. And, if Brennan and his colleagues needed any reminder of the potential consequences of their decision in *New York Times Co. v. Sullivan* as they gathered for oral arguments, they needed only to look out into the gallery, where Dr. King sat among the spectators. Justice Goldberg abandoned any pretense of impartiality when he slipped the civil rights leader a copy of King's book, *Stride Toward Freedom*, for him to sign.

Both at argument and in briefing, the *Times* was represented by Herbert Wechsler, a distinguished law professor and constitutional scholar from Columbia Law School. Wechsler's primary contention was the broad one, designed no doubt to appeal to Black and Douglas, that the First Amendment prohibited all libel suits by public officials based on statements concerning their official conduct. At the very least, Wechsler argued, the Court should define the kinds of "libels" about which public officials could seek legal redress precisely, as it had done with "obscenity" in *Roth*, and that the definition of punishable libel mandated by the First Amendment should exclude all allegedly defamatory statements about public officials that the publisher did not know to be false. Nachman, who represented Sullivan before the Supreme Court as he had at trial and in the Alabama Supreme Court, countered with the justices' unbroken history of deeming libel to be speech unprotected by the First Amendment at all, which, he argued, explained why the common law of defamation and the constitutional guarantee of "freedom of speech or of the press" had peacefully coexisted for nearly two hundred years.

For his part, Brennan was uncharacteristically vocal from the moment the argument began. He and the other justices interrupted Wechsler with so many questions that he could only present his argument in favor of absolute immunity rather than the less robust alternative premised on the defendant's knowledge of falsity. Among other things, Brennan questioned Wechsler closely about the underlying facts, including identifying the specific statements that Sullivan claimed were false and establishing that he had submitted "no proof of actual damages, other than as flows from the supposed presumption" of such injury under Alabama law. After Wechsler turned to the substance of the matter and, to support his contention that the First Amendment is "primarily about" protecting the "criticism of public officials," invoked "the same argument that James Madison made and that Thomas Jefferson made with respect to the validity of the Sedition Act of 1798," Brennan interrupted him again, asking whether the absolute protection Wechsler advocated was limited to criticism "addressed to official conduct" and whether there were "any limits whatever which take it outside the protection of the First Amendment?" In response, Wechsler stood his ground, asserting that he could "see no toying with limits or with exclusions."

When Wechsler continued that, in his view, the "First Amendment was precisely designed to do away with seditious libel, the punishment for criticism of the government and criticism of officials," Goldberg intervened, asking whether the rule Wechsler advocated "applies not only to newspapers but to anybody?" After Wechsler responded "exactly" and "of course," Goldberg confirmed that "in other words, you are not arguing here for the special rule that applies to newspapers," to which Wechsler replied "certainly not."

Later, when the argument turned to consideration of the defense of truth under Alabama law, Brennan questioned the extent to which the jury had considered the issue. When Brennan suggested that to "the extent to which the jury passed on anything, the jury finding I take it was this meant that Sullivan bombed King's home," Wechsler demurred, explaining that "we don't know what the jury thought referred to Sullivan. The jury defined that the statements referred to Sullivan" but did not make explicit "that all statements referred to Sullivan or only some of the statements." And when White asked whether the jury was "free to believe that all of these statements were false," Wechsler responded that "it was free, except that the evidence didn't support such a view."

This contention, and other similar assertions, led Justice Harlan to ask Wechsler whether the Court was "entitled to review the evidence here?" Wechsler responded, without hesitation, "very definitely," and proceeded to assert that "this Court has the responsibility and the duty to satisfy itself that the record sustains the basis on which the constitutional right asserted has been held to be untenable." And, when Goldberg questioned whether Wechsler was "saying that the state fact-finding cannot relieve us of our function of determining whether the constitutional right was abridged," Wechsler quickly responded, "certainly."

Toward the end of Wechsler's argument, Justice White sought to focus his attention on the issue of what he described as "calculated falsehood." Specifically, he asked Wechsler "what is the fact in the record about whether the *Times* knew these statements were true or false?" Wechsler responded that, although the Alabama Supreme Court had purported to conclude otherwise based on contrary information contained "in our files" and in "dispatches, stories from our correspondents," the "exact facts, Mr. Justice, are that at the time when the publication was made, the *New York Times* had nothing by way of information to indicate that the statements were false." To this, White responded, "then if you accept the Supreme Court of Alabama's version, we must deal with your broader first ground."

When Nachman rose to argue, he promptly turned to the facts of the case, reminding the justices that "this case . . . is here after a jury trial, with all that that means in terms of the Seventh Amendment," which both guarantees the right to a jury trial in civil cases and limits the ability of appellate courts to second-guess a jury's evaluation of the evidence and the determinations it makes based on that evidence. He was, however, quickly interrupted by Goldberg, who, despite asserting that he did not wish to disturb Sullivan's counsel, proceeded to challenge what Goldberg described as his "rather provocative statement, . . . you said a jury trial in terms of the Seventh Amendment. Is it your idea," Goldberg continued, that "the Seventh Amendment applies to the States by the Fourteenth? Is that part of your argument?" This, of course, was a reference to the process, in which the Court was then controversially engaged, of considering in a piecemeal fashion which portions of the Bill of Rights had been incorporated against the states through the Fourteenth Amendment's due process clause. Goldberg apparently assumed that the

Court had not yet considered whether the Seventh Amendment was one of those rights. And he was correct that no such case had come before the Warren Court.

Nachman, however, was ready for Goldberg's question. Without hesitation, he cited the Justice to *Chicago B&Q Railroad Co. v. Chicago*, an otherwise obscure 1897 decision in which the Court had in fact held that "the protections of the Seventh Amendment which surround the reexamination of jury verdicts apply equally to State jury verdicts as they do to Federal jury verdicts." Nachman accordingly proceeded to catalogue, at some length, all of the facts that the jury could have found, based on the evidence presented at trial, to support its verdict:

> What I am saying . . . is that there was evidence from the *Times* itself, from the pleadings, from statements of its counsel, from evidence in the case in addition to this, which could justify a jury verdict that the entire ad was false. And, as I began by saying, this case comes here obviously after a jury verdict. And I am saying there is evidence in the record that the entire ad was false.

At this juncture, Brennan posed his first series of questions to Nachman, again asking whether the Court was free to reexamine the evidence on which Nachman claimed the jury had relied. When Nachman insisted that "the Seventh Amendment protects this verdict unless this Court finds there is no reasonable basis whatever for it, no evidence at all to support it," Brennan, like Goldberg, questioned his reference to and reliance on the Seventh Amendment in the context of a "state trial." Once again, Nachman reminded Brennan and the other justices that the Seventh Amendment "protects State verdicts as well as Federal verdicts."

This response led Justice White to approach the issue from a different perspective, asking Nachman to confirm that it was Sullivan's position that "libel falls outside the protection of the First Amendment," a contention that inevitably, as White saw it, required "that someone has to finally decide what libel is that falls outside the protection of the First Amendment." Nachman readily agreed with White's premise—that "libel falls outside the protection of the First Amendment"—but took issue with the justice's further suggestion that "the jury isn't the final arbiter of that" issue. "That," Nachman responded, "is a question of State law." Nachman's last response drew a sharp reaction from Brennan, who skeptically rephrased counsel's contention as advocating "that we can't reexamine here as a constitutional question?"

Toward the end of his argument, Nachman turned to summarizing the evidence placed before the jury on the issue of "malice and deliberateness," asserting "that there was plenty from which the jury could find deliberateness." He then proceeded to catalogue a host of facts in the trial record, including

> the inconsistent treatment of Governor Patterson [who had received a retraction from the *Times*] and this plaintiff, [who had not], the treatment of this plaintiff after investigations showing falsity, the treatment of this plaintiff by the testimony of the [*Times's* Corporate] Secretary telling the jury that it was not substantially incorrect, after his own lawyers couldn't even plead truth, [and] the failure of the *Times* to apply a very rigorous set of advertising acceptability standards.

In response, White again questioned whether, based on Nachman's description of the evidence, "this case unavoidably presents the question of whether or not a person may tell a deliberate lie about a public official." After Nachman first resisted this suggestion, and White nevertheless persisted in his inquiry, Sullivan's counsel shifted gears, agreeing with the justice that "yes, your Honor, we think that the defendant in order to succeed must convince this Court that a newspaper corporation has an absolute immunity from anything it publishes." To this, White responded, "but if it were held here that a newspaper can publish a falsehood which it thought to be true, that would still not save the *Times* here," because, as White understood Nachman's position, "on the facts of this case you say they knew it was false or essentially false." Not surprisingly, Nachman agreed with this formulation as well.

Three days after the argument, when the justices gathered for their weekly conference, they unanimously agreed that the jury's verdict in favor of Sullivan should be overturned. They did not, however, agree on how to do so. A majority favored reversal on the narrowest possible ground—that Sullivan had not proven the ad was talking about him. For his part, Brennan suggested a broader holding—that a public official be required to prove each element of his defamation claim by "clear, convincing and unequivocal" evidence. There was, however, nothing approaching a consensus in support of Brennan's position.

That Brennan would advocate for the *Times* in this manner was, in some senses, surprising. In fact, he harbored ambivalent feelings about the press. On the one hand, he was an avid consumer of journalism, reading at least two newspapers each morning and watching the evening news on television each night. He certainly believed that reporters played a vital role in a democratic society, concurring generally in the views of political philosopher Alexander Meiklejohn, who had long espoused the theory that, even in the absence of the First Amendment, the democracy created by the Constitution necessarily required a broad freedom of expression so that the "citizen-governors" could effectively and intelligently exercise their right to vote and to instruct their elected representatives on matters of governance. "As money is to the economy, so the press is to our political culture," Brennan said in a 1979 speech. And, in addition to all of that, Brennan's wife Marjorie had worked at a newspaper and two of his three children would marry reporters.

Family members aside, Brennan did not particularly enjoy dealing with the press. He quickly came to regret the one time he had given an impromptu press conference during a February 1962 visit to Puerto Rico with fellow justices Warren and Clark. Reporters asked Brennan whether a new statute that required the Supreme Court to review directly the judgments of Puerto Rico's highest court—just as it did with the highest courts of each state—meant that Puerto Rico was a de facto state. Brennan gave a complicated answer about Puerto Rico's status as a territory, but front page headlines in the island's newspapers the next day trumpeted his comments as an important endorsement of statehood. "I did put my foot in my mouth, didn't I?" Brennan wrote Luis Blanco Lugo of the Puerto Rico Supreme Court upon his return to Washington. "Apparently, I should have followed my general practice of keeping quiet on such matters." And that is precisely what he did in the years that followed, declining all interview requests during his campus speaking engagements. As he explained to one college administrator, "there is just too much risk of being misquoted or misunderstood."

Brennan's personal experience with the press notwithstanding, a few days after the argument and the Court's conference, Warren asked him to try his hand at writing a majority opinion that could unite the justices. This was not unusual. Over the years they had served together, the chief justice had increasingly turned to Brennan to draft the Court's opinions in high-profile cases in which the justices were unanimous in the result they wished to reach but did not necessarily agree about how best to get there. Moreover, with his opinion for the Court in *Roth* and other First Amendment cases, Brennan had already carved out something of a niche in cases involving free expression, and several of his colleagues thought his analytical approach in *Roth* might provide a model for how to handle *Sullivan*. By this point in their relationship, Warren also knew from experience that Brennan could build and hold on to a majority—a unanimous one if possible—in a way that he or the other justices could not. In this case, Warren recognized, Brennan's challenge was compounded by the fact that their three most reliable allies—Black, Douglas, and Goldberg—had all made clear at conference that they favored an absolute bar against libel suits involving criticism of public officials, a position that justices like Harlan and Clark were almost certain to reject. In fact, *Sullivan* proved to be a nail-biter in which Brennan and Warren were not sure of the ultimate disposition until the very last minute.

In all, Brennan and his clerks generated eight drafts of an opinion for the Court in the less than two months that passed between the argument and the announcement of the decision. For *Sullivan*, Brennan abandoned his usual practice of having one of his law clerks sketch out a first draft after they talked through what he wanted. Instead, he opted to write it out himself. In that initial draft, Brennan embraced a standard that would bar libel actions by public officials against critics of their official conduct unless there was evidence that a story was published with a reckless disregard for the truth. Mere falsity or negligence would not suffice under this "actual malice" standard, which had previously been adopted by a few states as part of their common law. In addition, Brennan concluded that there was no evidence of actual malice, so defined, in the record Sullivan had amassed at trial, at least not "clear and convincing evidence," which Brennan determined was also necessary in such a case. Indeed, Brennan further concluded that Sullivan had failed to prove, again by the clear and convincing evidence his opinion deemed necessary, either that the allegedly false statements in the ad were defamatory or that they had the necessary connection to the plaintiff. And as Brennan later noted in the term history he and his law clerks prepared annually to recount the Court's internal deliberations in significant cases, the first "draft said nothing about whether the plaintiff could be given a new trial at which he might attempt to adduce the missing evidence."

Years later, Brennan would incorrectly credit his clerks with unearthing the "actual malice" language he included in his initial draft, as well as the Kansas Supreme Court decision on which it was based. In fact, that approach had been in Wechsler's brief all along. Stephen Barnett, Brennan's clerk at the time, later confirmed that is where they found it.

Brennan's initial draft was never circulated to his colleagues. He first shared his work product with the other justices on February 6, after reviewing his maiden effort only with his clerks. The second draft differed from its predecessor principally in that it premised the Court's reversal of the jury's verdict solely on the absence in the trial record of the requisite evidence of actual malice, abandoning the earlier draft's reliance on the deficient proof of the other elements of Sullivan's claim, including whether the advertisement was defamatory or of and concerning the commissioner. In addition, this draft addressed the new trial issue that its predecessor had ignored. Specifically, Brennan wrote, "We think, moreover, that a new trial under the correct rule would not be warranted in this case since the evidence submitted was insufficient to establish actual malice." The opinion then proceeded to analyze the evidence adduced at trial and to demonstrate its insufficiency. As Brennan's term history later recounted, "[t]he reference to 'the evidence submitted' was designed to sidestep the critical question whether a new trial would still be barred if the plaintiff offered to submit additional evidence."

Both Warren and White quickly endorsed Brennan's draft, but his three other usual allies—Black, Douglas, and Goldberg—all responded that they did not believe Brennan had gone far enough. They still favored absolute protection for libel against public officials. But Brennan, who had earned a reputation within the Court (and, more importantly, with Warren) as a skillful and careful vote counter, knew that the absolute view simply could not command a majority even if he were to join Black, Douglas, and Goldberg in embracing it. "In order to get a court for the conclusion we reached, I just had to make it clear that while it was a First Amendment right here, there were other considerations that had to be taken into account," Brennan later said.

More than pragmatism motivated this approach. While Brennan later admitted he had some sympathy for his colleagues' more extreme view, he, too, was uneasy about absolute protections. He had repeatedly eschewed absolutes of the kind advocated by Black and Douglas since joining the Court, favoring instead balancing tests that allowed him to weigh competing values. Brennan believed that "there are circumstances under which a government interest can override a First Amendment interest." In the context of libel, he thought that weight should properly be given to the reputation of the targets of defamatory falsehoods. As Brennan explained in a lecture the following year at Brown University, "At the time the First Amendment was adopted, as today, there were those unscrupulous enough and skillful enough to use the deliberate or reckless falsehood as an effective political tool to unseat the public servant or even topple an administration."

Brennan had ample personal experience with such matters. Not only had he sparred with the infamous Senator Joseph McCarthy during his own confirmation hearings, and witnessed firsthand how the senator had ruined the reputations of conscientious public servants for political gain, he had watched while his own father, himself an elected city commissioner in his native Newark, was attacked in the newspaper by prohibitionists, who accused him of lax enforcement of the Eighteenth Amendment and falsely insinuated that he was a drunk. At sixteen, the future Supreme Court justice turned away from politics. "I saw what it did to my father, and I wanted no part of it," Brennan later recalled. "What a filthy business the whole thing is."

Without his usual trio of allies who, with Warren, would provide a working majority for many decisions expanding civil rights and liberties, Brennan had to pick up support for his approach from among Clark, Harlan, and Stewart, an undertaking that proved difficult. Brennan knew that the normal practice would be for the Supreme Court to allow lower courts to apply a new legal rule—such as his newly minted "actual malice" standard—to the facts of a case. But the justices increasingly had come to lose faith in recalcitrant southern judges. Thus, when Brennan circulated another draft of his opinion on February 17, he expanded the scope of the Court's independent evaluation of the evidence, now finding it to be constitutionally deficient in two respects—in addition to insufficient evidence of actual malice, Brennan wrote that there was not enough proof of a connection between Sullivan and the statements in the advertisement about which he complained.

On February 25, Goldberg circulated a separate concurring opinion. In it, he wrote that while he concurred "in the Court's opinion and judgment," he believed that the First Amendment precluded a public official from maintaining a libel action based on criticism of his official conduct, even when that criticism was published with actual malice. The next day, Black circulated his own concurring opinion, although his agreement was limited to the Court's judgment. Douglas quickly joined Black's opinion, in which he maintained—as had Goldberg—that the First Amendment absolutely protected published criticism of public officials. At the same time, however, Black wrote Brennan privately to tell him, "You know of course that despite my position and what I write, I think you are doing a wonderful job in the *Times* case and however it finally comes out it is bound to be a very long step toward preserving the right to communicate ideas."

Still, without Black and Douglas, Brennan needed one additional vote for his own formulation. Thus, as his term history later recounted, he awaited word from Justice Harlan especially "with some trepidation." He did not, however, have to wait long. The same day that Black circulated his concurring opinion, Harlan sent Brennan a letter. In it, he said that, while he agreed with Brennan's creation and formulation of the actual malice standard, he was not comfortable with the ambiguity that characterized Brennan's evaluation of the evidence in Part III of his then most recent draft. "While I agree that there should not be a new trial," Harlan wrote, "I would not feel able to join Part III of your opinion as presently written without writing something in addition by way of elaboration." In the avowed interest of avoiding such a separate opinion, Harlan had taken a hand at revising Part III. Surprisingly, since Harlan was well known as a strong supporter of federalism, his proposed revision took, as Brennan later described it, "a franker and bolder approach to the new-trial problem." Harlan's revision addressed the issue directly, posing the question "whether we should leave the way open for a new trial or should terminate this litigation." Relying largely on a federal statute that authorizes federal appellate courts to "direct the entry of such appropriate judgment, decree, or order . . . as may be just under the circumstances," Harlan's revised draft explicitly concluded that a new trial was not appropriate "on the basis that respondent would be afforded an opportunity to adduce further and sufficient evidence."

In Harlan's view, no new trial was warranted with respect to the "connection" or "of and concerning" issue because it had been hotly contested at trial and "we may reasonably assume therefore that [Sullivan] had no evidence of different and more substantial quality to offer." With respect to actual malice, which could not have been contested at trial since the Court had not yet created the concept, Harlan wrote that Alabama law required evidence of malice for purposes of supporting an award of punitive damages, which Sullivan had sought and attempted to support by introducing evidence, albeit evidence that Harlan deemed insufficient to satisfy the new constitutional standard. Harlan's approach did not "evoke much enthusiasm" in Brennan's chambers, but, recognizing the importance of securing his vote, Brennan substantially incorporated Harlan's text in Part III of his fourth draft, which he circulated to the other justices on February 28.

That decision proved to be something of a miscalculation for, as Brennan's term history later explained, "difficulties with the Harlan approach soon became painfully apparent." For one thing, the federal statute on which Harlan relied as authority to review the evidence and deny Sullivan a new trial had never been applied to a jury verdict issued by a state court and necessarily raised the question whether Harlan's approach exceeded the court's appellate jurisdiction. Indeed, upon receiving Brennan's new draft, Black sent Brennan a note in which he wrote, "I do not see how John could possibly adhere to that position on mature reflection. I can think of few things that would more violently clash with his ideas of 'federalism'.... Construing the statute as authorizing our Court to *overrule* state laws as to a right to a new trial would undoubtedly raise constitutional questions...." In yet another note to Brennan, Black repeated his concerns about Harlan's approach but hastened to add: "I do think, however, that in getting him to agree to your opinion as it is you have done a great service to the freedoms of the First Amendment. For your opinion I believe will inevitably lead to a later holding that people have complete immunity from having to pay damages for criticism of Government or its officials in the performance of their public duties...."

On a different front, Brennan's revision of Part III to reflect Harlan's views was challenged for its assumption that Sullivan could not adduce sufficient evidence to secure a constitutionally permissible verdict at a new trial. With respect to the "of and concerning" issue, for example, Harlan's analysis was predicated on the absence of evidence that Sullivan himself had participated in any of the police misconduct described in the advertisement. As a result, the testimony of Sullivan's trial witnesses that they understood the text to refer to him was said by Harlan's draft to have been based "not on any evidence that he had in fact" authorized the misconduct described in the advertisement, "but solely on the unsupported assumption" that he had. Even if this were the case, Brennan later explained, the Court had to be prepared to address what would happen "if the plaintiff now offered evidence which precisely remedied this defect," i.e., "if he produced witnesses to testify the plaintiff had in fact participated personally and actively in the police activity in question, and that the witnesses had known this and because of such knowledge—not because of any 'unsupported assumption'—had associated the advertisements allegations with the plaintiff?" According to Brennan's term history, Harlan was forced to concede that, in that event, "he did not know how the State could be precluded from granting a new trial."

On March 2, Brennan and Harlan met, ostensibly to address these objections. Harlan, however, arrived at the meeting having had a change of heart. As Brennan's term history later described their meeting, Harlan "completely retracted his proposal for explicitly forbidding a new trial," and instead now "embraced the quite contrary view that, since a new trial upon additional evidence could not be absolutely prohibited, and since reversal was required in any event because the Alabama courts had not applied the rule requiring actual malice, there was no reason for the Court to concern itself at all with the sufficiency of the evidence submitted." As a practical matter, therefore, Harlan was now proposing that virtually all of Part III of Brennan's draft be abandoned—"that the opinion should merely propound the rule requiring a showing of malice, reverse for failure to apply the rule, and leave for another day all questions of how the rule should be applied to specific evidence."

Harlan's new proposal did not sit well with Brennan. Later that same day, he wrote to Harlan to explain why he felt compelled to reject it:

> I think we should retain the analysis of the constitutional insufficiency of the proofs
> of actual malice and connection even if this has the effect of "chilling" the possibility
> of a new trial. I think we are justified in doing this on two counts: (a) the profession
> should be apprised now that we are going to examine evidence in this area as we
> have in others, and (b) because the analysis of the proofs to demonstrate their insuf-
> ficiency will be both illustrative of how we do this and also informative to the parties
> in this case of a void in the proofs that would have to be filled if a new trial is had.

Brennan did, however, agree to eliminate from the opinion the language, which Harlan had first suggested, explicitly precluding a new trial. Instead, Brennan reverted to his initial formulation, in which he wrote simply that the evidence submitted at trial was insufficient on both the malice and "of and concerning" issues, without any reference to the prospect of additional evidence being presented at a new trial.

The next day, March 3, Brennan circulated his fifth draft, which incorporated these changes. The draft was accompanied by a memorandum to his colleagues, in which he explained why he had jettisoned the Harlan approach that had been incorporated in his previous effort:

> [I]f Alabama should give Sullivan a new trial the parties should know that the evi-
> dence in this record will not support a judgment—that there is a large void to be
> filled. If we said nothing and we later overturned another judgment entered on

this record, we might be rightly accused of having second thoughts because of the implication from our silence here that the application of the valid rule to this evidence would be sustained.

Not surprisingly, Harlan responded to Brennan's memorandum by informing his colleague that he would have to dissent from this portion of the opinion since "the present version of Part III seems to me to add up to the same thing as the earlier one, which I am now satisfied did not wash, minus however the element of frankness which the earlier version at least possessed." Harlan circulated his separate opinion later that afternoon and, as promised, it agreed with Parts I and II of Brennan's opinion as well as with Brennan's assertion that the Court's responsibility in such cases "does not end with the establishment of constitutional ground rules but includes also an obligation to scrutinize the record to ensure that such rules have been constitutionally applied." Nevertheless, Harlan's draft went on to explain that he did "not consider it appropriate for the Court to examine the sufficiency of the evidence at this stage, since other constitutional requirements compel a reversal of these judgments, however that issue is resolved."

With that, Brennan had little choice but to wait and see whether the other justices, especially Stewart, who had not yet been heard from, would agree with him or with Harlan. Stewart ended any suspense on that score quickly, sending Brennan a note joining in his opinion that very afternoon and, as Brennan's term history later reflected, Stewart "never wavered" in his support for Brennan's opinion thereafter. The chief justice also weighed in on Brennan's behalf, asserting to his colleagues that, were they to opt for Harlan's approach, "we will merely be going through a meaningless exercise. The case would be remanded, another improvisation would be devised and it would be back to us in a more difficult posture." Still, with Clark left to weigh in, Brennan believed there remained "a very real doubt" whether his entire opinion "could command a majority of the Court."

Recognizing this, Douglas sent Brennan a note on March 3, in which he asserted that he agreed with the entirety of Brennan's opinion except for that portion establishing the actual malice standard and, then, only because it did not go far enough in precluding libel suits by public officials criticized for the performance of their official duties. Accordingly, Douglas offered to write his own opinion declaring his concurrence in Part III's holding—specifically, that the Court having opted for the actual malice standard, he agreed that it had not been satisfied on the evidence presented. That would provide Brennan with a majority for the entirety of his opinion, albeit a different combination of five justices for Part II (establishing the actual malice standard) and Part III (declaring the evidence insufficient under both that standard and the "of and concerning" requirement). Goldberg then announced that he was prepared to follow Douglas's lead and suggested that the opinion be revised to make clear that (1) the Court unanimously agreed with that much of Brennan's opinion explaining that libel suits brought by public officials were indeed properly subject to scrutiny under the First Amendment; (2) all the justices, except Black, Douglas, and Goldberg, agreed that a verdict in favor of such a plaintiff would satisfy the First Amendment if the alleged libel were published with actual malice; and (3) all the justices, except Harlan and perhaps Clark, agreed that the evidence was constitutionally insufficient to support a finding of the requisite malice in this case.

Despite his private notes of encouragement to Brennan, however, Black vigorously opposed the Douglas/Goldberg proposal. In Black's view, if a finding of actual malice was indeed sufficient to satisfy the First Amendment, then Sullivan had adduced sufficient evidence to prove it. To make matters worse, on March 4, when Brennan paid a visit to Clark's chambers to ascertain his views, he was handed a printed opinion in which, as Brennan's term history later described it, Clark "espoused Justice Harlan's approach with a vengeance." In his draft opinion, Clark asserted that, "[h]aving demolished respondent's theory of the case, it appears to me that we should not go further and condemn respondent's evidence." And, to punctuate his point, Clark added this:

> The action of the Court is a departure from a long-established—and I dare say, never deviating—rule. It may be that the evidence of malice or reckless regard for the truth is insufficient; however, this Court should not now measure the old record by a new standard not available at trial. By so doing the Court forecasts, for all practical purposes, the result of a new trial and thereby forecloses respondent's right to a jury trial. I would leave state courts free to first determine whether the evidence on a retrial is sufficient.
>
> Prejudicing the factual basis of the case places an insurmountable burden upon respondent on remand. In so doing the Court departs from its appellate character and thereby invades the province of Alabama's courts to initially pass upon the facts. And,

unfortunately, by thus impugning the integrity of our dual federalism, the Court fails
to reflect that fairness which has always been the hallmark of our judicial processes.

At this juncture, Brennan appeared to have little choice but to opt for the hybrid
approach offered by Douglas and Goldberg, Justice Black's objections to it notwithstanding. Douglas reaffirmed his willingness to proceed in that manner and
authorized Brennan to include in his opinion a statement reading, "Mr. Justice
Douglas, while believing that the evidence in question is constitutionally inadmis-
sible because the presence or absence of malice is immaterial, would agree that
even by the lesser standard prescribed by this opinion the evidence is deficient."
Meanwhile, however, Justice White entered the debate, suggesting that, because
the Alabama trial court failed to instruct the jury on the definition of malice at
all, even to support an award of punitive damages which the jury's general verdict
may well have included, and because that failure was not necessarily erroneous as
a matter of state law, the Court had no choice but to review the evidence itself to
determine whether sufficient proof of the malice necessary to support an award of
punitive damages was in fact present in the trial record. Although Brennan thought
that White's reasoning was "untenable," he nevertheless included it in the sixth
draft of his opinion, which he circulated on March 4 in the hope of attracting a
true majority for his entire opinion.

Brennan's gambit did not work—Harlan quickly announced that he would stand
on his previously drafted concurrence. Thus, Brennan thought, the "fight" was at
that moment "over, with the unsatisfactory Douglas-Goldberg compromise emerging as the necessary end result." During the afternoon of March 5, however, Clark
abruptly changed his mind and—for reasons unknown to Brennan—informed
his colleague that he had decided to withdraw his separate opinion in its entirety.
Moreover, Clark told Brennan that he would join the entire opinion, including
its analysis of the trial evidence, if Brennan would only agree to justify it in terms
of serving the interest in "effective judicial administration." Brennan wasted little
time in adopting Clark's formulation in the seventh draft of his opinion, which
was circulated that afternoon. It contained, in the same language that appeared in
the final opinion, the following addition to Part III:

Since respondent may seek a new trial, we deem that considerations of effective judicial administration require us to review the evidence in the present record to determine whether it could constitutionally support a judgment for respondent.

Warren, White, and Stewart all promptly signified their agreement with this approach and, at the conference on March 6, this draft was approved for announcement the following Monday, March 9.

On Sunday, March 8, Harlan telephoned Brennan at home and told his colleague that he had decided to withdraw his separate opinion and, as Brennan's term history later characterized it, "to unreservedly join[]" Brennan's opinion. In many respects, this was vintage Harlan. He cared greatly about the Court as an institution and did not want to do anything to detract from what he viewed as a great occasion for the Court and for Justice Brennan. And, just like that, the Court was not only unanimous in its result, but five justices had joined Brennan's opinion in all respects, while three others differed with it only in their view that the Court should have gone further and prohibited defamation actions by public officials entirely.

The following morning, March 9, 1964, Brennan announced the decision of the Court, emphasizing its significance from the very first sentence. "We are required in this case to determine for the first time the extent to which the constitutional protections for speech and press limit a State's power to award damages in a libel action brought by a public official against critics of his official conduct." The opinion itself fundamentally altered the nation's libel laws in virtually every state and gave far greater protection to those accused of defaming public officials. In concrete terms, it shifted the burden of proof in libel cases from defendants, who previously had to demonstrate the truth of their published statements, to the public official plaintiff, who would now have to show that the defendants had not only published a falsehood about him, but had done so either knowingly or recklessly. Not surprisingly, the *Times* itself praised the decision as "a victory of first importance in the long—and never ending—struggle for the rights of a free press."

In many ways, however, the real importance of Brennan's opinion was its articulation and explanation of what it characterized as the "central meaning of the First Amendment" itself. In Part II of his opinion, the relevant portions of which from the outset had enjoyed the support of all eight of his colleagues, Brennan put the Court's unanimous weight behind a theory of free expression in a democracy that literally revolutionized the First Amendment's scope and force. At the outset of that historic portion of his historic opinion, Brennan swept away the Court's previous suggestions that defamatory speech is not protected by the First Amendment at all. "In deciding the question now," Brennan wrote, "we are compelled by neither precedent nor policy to give any more weight to the epithet 'libel' than we have to other 'mere labels' of state law," such as "obscenity." In short, "libel can claim no talismanic immunity from constitutional limitations. It must be measured by standards that satisfy the First Amendment."

Brennan then proceeded not only to articulate those standards, but to explain in clear and often elegant prose how they had been derived. He began from the premise that the "general proposition that freedom of expression upon public questions is secured by the First Amendment has long been settled by our decisions." After recounting such assertions contained in the Court's prior decisions, as well as in eloquent opinions authored by the likes of Brandeis and Hand, Brennan penned perhaps the most memorable and frequently cited passage of his own judicial career:

> Thus we consider this case against the background of a profound national commitment to the principle that debate on public issues should be uninhibited, robust and wide-open, and that it may well include vehement, caustic, and sometimes unpleasantly sharp attacks on government and public officials.

Applying that fundamental principle to the facts of the case, Brennan framed the question before the Court:

> The present advertisement, as an expression of grievance and protest on one of the major public issues of our time, would seem clearly to qualify for the constitutional protection. The question is whether it forfeits that protection by the falsity of some of its factual statements and by its alleged defamation of respondent.

With respect to the first issue—falsity—Brennan explained that "[a]uthoritative interpretations of the First Amendment guarantees have consistently refused to recognize an exception for any test of truth, whether administered by judges, juries, or administrative officials—and especially not one that puts the burden of proving truth on the speaker." Then Brennan proceeded to articulate the principle, now so often quoted that it is easy to forget that, prior to Brennan's opinion in

Sullivan it had never previously been so stated, "that erroneous statement is inevitable in free debate, and that it must be protected if the freedoms of expression are to have the 'breathing space' that they 'need . . . to survive.'" With respect to the second issue—the allegedly defamatory character of the statements contained in the advertisement—Brennan wrote that "[i]njury to official reputation affords no more warrant for repressing speech that would otherwise be free than does factual error." As Brennan explained it, criticism of the official conduct of public officials "does not lose its constitutional protection merely because it is effective criticism and hence diminishes . . . official reputations."

It is at this point in the opinion that Brennan unquestionably changed the face of the Court's First Amendment jurisprudence. He began by stating his conclusion—that "if neither factual error nor defamatory content suffices to remove the constitutional shield from criticism of official conduct, the combination of the two elements is no less adequate." This conclusion, Brennan wrote, "is the lesson to be drawn from the great controversy over the Sedition Act of 1798, which first crystalized a national awareness of the central meaning of the First Amendment." In the sentences that followed, Brennan sketched out the history of the Sedition Act's passage and the "controversy" surrounding it, and squarely aligned the Supreme Court with the views of Jefferson and Madison that the statute violated the First Amendment from its inception: "Although the Sedition Act was never tested in this Court, the attack upon its validity has carried the day in the court of history."

From there, Brennan went on to address the ramifications of that historical verdict for the law of defamation specifically, and for the First Amendment's speech and press clauses more generally. The common law's defense of truth, Brennan wrote in another passage that would come to be invoked regularly by his Court and others, did not "save" it from constitutional infirmity:

A rule compelling the critic of official conduct to guarantee the truth of all his factual assertions—and to do so on pain of libel judgments virtually unlimited in amount—would lead to . . . "self-censorship." Allowance of the defense of truth, with the burden of proving it on the defendant, does not mean that only false speech would be deterred. . . . Under such a rule, would-be critics of official conduct may be deterred from voicing their criticisms, even though it is believed to be true and even though it is in fact true, because of doubt whether it can be proved in court or fear of the expense of having to do so. They tend to make only statements which "steer far wider of the unlawful zone." The rule thus dampens the vigor and limits the variety of public debate. It is inconsistent with the First and Fourteenth Amendments.

In saying all of this, Brennan spoke for a unanimous Court. What followed, however, did not enjoy the support of Brennan's usual allies—Black, Douglas, and Goldberg—who drew from his analysis of the "central meaning of the First Amendment" the more expansive conclusion that a public official could never sue a critic of his official conduct for defamation. Brennan, knowing that his remaining colleagues were not prepared to go that far, drew on the concept that motivated his rejection of the defense of truth as a constitutionally sufficient safeguard—that it would nevertheless deter the citizen-critic of government from making statements "believed to be true"—and determined to remove from constitutional protection in such circumstances only the calculated falsehood, the knowing lie. The First Amendment, Brennan explained, did not protect criticism of public officials published with "actual malice"—"that is, with knowledge that it was false or with reckless disregard of whether it was false or not." Here, Brennan wrote for a Court composed of six justices.

As noted, the intense debate within the Court with respect to Part III of Brennan's opinion yielded a decision in which the Court did indeed review the record evidence and determine that it was insufficient to satisfy the First Amendment in two respects—Sullivan had not carried his burden of proving, by what Brennan declared to be the necessary "clear and convincing" standard, either that the allegedly defamatory falsehoods were about him or that they were published with actual malice. In addition to Clark's language grounding Part III in "considerations of effective judicial administration," Brennan's final opinion contained another justification for the Court's independent review of the record evidence, one that would also have substantial ramifications for the justices and for litigants in defamation cases in the years to follow:

> This Court's duty is not limited to the elaboration of constitutional principles; we must also in proper cases review the evidence to make certain that those principles have been constitutionally applied. This is such a case, particularly since the question is one of alleged trespass across "the line between speech unconditionally guaranteed and speech which may legitimately be regulated." In cases where that line must be drawn, the rule is that we "examine for ourselves the statements in issue and the

circumstances under which they were made to see . . .whether they are of a character which the principles of the First Amendment, as adopted by the Due Process Clause of the Fourteenth Amendment, protect." We must "make an independent examination of the whole record," so as to assure ourselves that the judgment does not constitute a forbidden intrusion on the field of free expression.

And, at the end of that crucial paragraph, Brennan included a footnote, designed to meet the objection to such independent judicial review—grounded in the Seventh Amendment—that Nachman had raised at argument. Acknowledging that the Court had indeed incorporated the relevant provision of the Seventh Amendment against the states in the *Chicago B&Q Railroad* case back before the turn of the century, Brennan wrote that the amendment's "ban on reexamination of facts does not preclude us from determining whether governing rules of federal law have been properly applied to the facts." With that issue disposed of, the opinion proceeded to review the record evidence and, in its final sentence, declare that the "judgment of the Supreme Court of Alabama is reversed and the case is remanded to that court for further proceedings not inconsistent with this opinion."

As Brennan had hoped, in the face of his analysis in Part III, the Alabama courts took no further action in the case. The *Times* and its co-defendants had been spared, not only in Sullivan's case but in the other pending defamation actions against it arising from the advertisement as well. Perhaps more significantly, the ramifications for the First Amendment of Brennan's analysis in Part II were at least equally dramatic. Professor Harry Kalven Jr., a University of Chicago law professor and leading scholar of the First Amendment, quickly predicted that Brennan's handiwork for the Court in *New York Times Co. v. Sullivan* "may prove to be the best and most important opinion it has ever produced in the realm of freedom of speech." And, Kalven reported in a seminal article about the decision he published in the prestigious *Supreme Court Review*, he had had occasion to discuss Brennan's opinion with Alexander Meiklejohn, the renowned political philosopher who, in significant measure, had inspired Brennan's conception of the "central meaning of the First Amendment." Meiklejohn, as Kalven recounted it, had pronounced the decision nothing less than "an occasion for dancing in the streets."

REINFORCING THE "CENTRAL MEANING"

When the dancing was over, the Supreme Court faced myriad questions about the scope and meaning of its decision in *New York Times Co. v. Sullivan* and the actual malice standard it had created. The transformation of libel law from a disparate collection of state rules to a new constitutional regime imposed in the name of the First Amendment brought with it a host of concerns about how that law should fit within the framework of other free speech analysis and what practical changes the new public official and actual malice standards would require for judges and juries. The justices began to tackle many of these issues promptly after *Sullivan*.

In this initial period, Justice Brennan remained the pivotal figure, working assiduously to put muscle on the skeletal structure of the constitutional rule he had created, and navigating, as he had in *Sullivan*, a very tricky path among the disparate views of his colleagues. On one end of the spectrum remained Justices Black, Douglas, and Goldberg, who would have essentially abolished—as inconsistent with core principles of the First Amendment—all defamation laws, civil or criminal, that permitted liability for criticism of government or public officials. At the other end of the spectrum, a variety of justices, including Justices Clark, Harlan, and Abe Fortas, who replaced Goldberg in 1965, believed the states should have more freedom to deal with and provide a civil remedy for defamatory falsehoods. Other members of the Warren Court—Chief Justice Earl Warren himself and Justice Stewart—fell somewhere in the middle. With hindsight, perhaps it should have been obvious that the cases and divisions that immediately followed *Sullivan* presaged an even tougher road ahead, one marked more by struggle than by dancing.

Garrison v. Louisiana

Well before he became known to the nation for his own investigation of the November 1963 assassination of President Kennedy, New Orleans District Attorney Jim Garrison made a name for himself in his home state in a different way. First elected in 1962, he set out to clean up the famous Bourbon Street in the French Quarter, which he deemed to be rife with prostitutes and bar owners who ran scams on customers who bought expensive drinks for women and ended up with huge bar tabs that they could not pay. To carry out his probe, Garrison employed undercover investigators and sought to have their expenses paid from a fund into which fines collected by his office were deposited.

But under local law, any use of the funds had to be approved by a judge of the New Orleans criminal court. The judges believed Garrison was shopping from one to another of them to gain approval of his expenditures. In late 1962, they voted that no further expenditures would be allowed unless approved by five of the eight criminal court judges and that no approval at all would be given for undercover expenses. The judges doubted that Garrison had the legal authority to engage in the Bourbon Street investigations in the first place, which were a matter of police jurisdiction, much less to fund them from the fines. In addition, they were concerned with what they considered a growing backlog of cases in the New Orleans criminal courts, which at least one judge blamed directly on Garrison.

The district attorney fired back in a statement to the press on November 2, 1962, published that afternoon in the New Orleans *States-Item*, a daily newspaper. In it, he faulted the judges for blocking his vice investigations and suggested that the blame for the backlog in untried criminal cases lay with the judges themselves, who he said took excessive amounts of vacation. "Again the message is clear," Garrison wrote. "'Don't rock the boat, son. You are not supposed to investigate anything'. This raises interesting questions about the racketeer influences on our eight vacation-minded judges." In addition, Garrison deemed it "incredible" that "a man could wait 19 months before his case is disposed of, during which period the judge enjoyed over 300 days vacation."

Based on the publication of his letter, Garrison was indicted for and convicted of violating the Louisiana defamation law, a criminal statute that punished a person whose "malicious" communication would "expose any person to hatred, contempt, or ridicule, or to deprive him of the benefit of public confidence or social intercourse." On his conviction, he was ordered to pay a $1,000 fine or spend four months in jail. The Louisiana Supreme Court affirmed the conviction in June 1963, and Garrison appealed to the U.S. Supreme Court.

When the appeal was considered by the justices in November 1963, after the Court had granted review in *Sullivan* and just two months before it was argued, there were six votes to hear the case and three against, according to notes from the files of Justice Douglas. Chief Justice Warren and Justices Black, Douglas, Brennan, White, and Goldberg all voted to decide Garrison's appeal, while Justices Clark, Harlan, and Stewart would have let the Louisiana Supreme Court's judgment stand. The first of what turned out to be two arguments in the case was held on April 22, 1964, little more than a month after the Court announced its decision in *Sullivan*. At the time, the justices apparently thought the case presented straightforward questions that would not be difficult to resolve. Indeed, a month before the argument, they rejected a request by Garrison's lawyer and voted to keep the case on their summary calendar. According to the Court's procedures at the time, this meant only thirty minutes of argument for each side and not the additional time that was made available in those difficult and/or important cases that merited it.

After the first argument, the justices met in conference and voted to reverse Garrison's conviction, over the dissents of Justices Clark, Harlan, and White. The chief justice assigned the opinion to Brennan, fresh from his triumph in *Sullivan*. In doing so, Warren may well have recognized that, as in *Sullivan*, Brennan would face an uphill battle to forge an approach that would command a majority but that, given his success there, he would be able to work the same magic in *Garrison*.

Given the approach that all of his colleagues had embraced in Part II of his opinion for the Court in *Sullivan*, Brennan chose to attack Louisiana's criminal defamation law as one punishing seditious libel. In *Sullivan*, after all, Brennan had powerfully articulated, for a unanimous Court, what he described as the "central meaning of the First Amendment"—the "broad consensus" that the Sedition Act, "because of the restraint it imposed upon criticism of government and public officials, was inconsistent with the First Amendment." Citing liberally to his handiwork in *Sullivan*, the draft opinion Brennan circulated to his colleagues in *Garrison* reminded them that the Court had "only recently reviewed the history of the great controversy" over the Sedition Act, and proceeded to assert that "the similarity between expressions prosecuted under that Act and the statements for which appellant was prosecuted here is significant and should be noted." Proceeding from this premise, Brennan continued:

> Of course, any criticism of the manner in which a public official goes about his
> duties will tend to affect his reputation, but to the extent that the Louisiana statute
> is applied to punish statements made about the official conduct of public officials, it
> must be said to fall within the category of "seditious libel" statutes—which Madison
> said were "acts forbidding every publication that might bring the constituted agents
> [of government] into contempt or disrepute, or that might excite the hatred of the
> people against the authors of unjust or pernicious measures."

Recalling in this manner the history lesson that had been the centerpiece of Part
II of his opinion in *Sullivan*, Brennan concluded that "[p]rosecutions for seditious
libel have not found favor in this country." Moreover, he rejected the Louisiana
Supreme Court's view that Garrison had not merely criticized the work of the
criminal court, but had impugned the personal integrity of the judges as well. At
bottom, Brennan wrote, Garrison's criticism of the judges was directed at their
administration of court business. And, he declared unequivocally, "[o]ur Constitution flatly bars criminal prosecutions based on the mere criticism of public men
for their public conduct."

   This, of course, was a bold step. Brennan was pushing the Court to go beyond
Sullivan, which permitted defamed public officials to recover money damages for
those libels published about them with actual malice, and hold that the several
states were nevertheless powerless to declare even the "calculated falsehood" about
a public official a violation of the criminal law. To explain this dichotomy, Brennan
had to formulate a theory that would meaningfully distinguish civil from criminal
libel. Thus, he argued that, in a civil libel suit brought by a public official, the government serves as little more than an "impartial umpire," providing the remedy of
a lawsuit for private litigants to sort out legal responsibility for injury to a public
official's reputation. In a criminal prosecution, however, the government "predomi-
nantly serves not the interest of the official but the impermissible interest of the
government itself in protecting itself against criticism." As Brennan explained it:

> This historical judgment embodies appreciation of a crucial distinction between civil
> and criminal libel laws in their application to defamatory criticism of the official

conduct of public officials. The civil remedy recognizes the interest of the individual official in the integrity of his reputation; but the overriding interest of the people in free discussion of public affairs secured by the First Amendment limits the remedy to damages for defamatory statements made with actual malice. In contrast, the constitutional consensus since the time of the Sedition Act has been that in light of the importance of the protection for free discussion of public affairs, government itself has no legitimate interest which justifies criminal laws inhibiting mere discussion of it or of its officials.

There was a more practical reason, beyond the analytical imperative he found inherent in *Sullivan*'s treatment of the Sedition Act, that led Brennan to conclude that the Louisiana statute could not constitutionally be applied to Garrison's published criticism of the judges. Specifically, the Louisiana Supreme Court had professed to apply what it described as an actual malice standard when it affirmed Garrison's conviction. By determining that the state law punished a form of seditious libel, Brennan was able to sidestep the question of whether the definition of actual malice used by the Louisiana courts satisfied the standard he coined in *Sullivan*. In short, Brennan's draft opinion made the presence or absence of actual malice irrelevant, since the state law was unconstitutional without regard to Garrison's fault or his state of mind.

Brennan's draft produced substantial reaction within the Court, but not a majority in support of its approach. Douglas prepared a concurring opinion, which Black joined, questioning the logic of holding states may permit civil recovery for the libel of public officials when actual malice is present but may not permit the criminal prosecution for libel of public officials at all, even when published with actual malice as defined in *Sullivan*. Actual malice becomes critical for one kind of case and irrelevant to another, Douglas wrote, "when in truth there is nothing in the Constitution about it." He reiterated his view, first expressed in *Sullivan* itself, that the First Amendment does not permit any libel suits for criticism of government or public officials, whether criminal or civil. Thus, while Black and Douglas agreed that Garrison's conviction should be overturned, they did not endorse Brennan's reasoning, much as they had not supported his approach in *Sullivan*. And, as he had done in *Sullivan*, Goldberg also wrote a brief concurring opinion suggesting that, while he too agreed that the First Amendment precluded application of the Louisiana statute to Garrison's letter, the Court had not gone far enough in blocking civil libel suits based on the conduct of public officials.

Although the reaction of his usual allies was not entirely unexpected, especially after *Sullivan*, Brennan had hoped that the rest of the majority he had assembled just months earlier would hold. Such hopes, however, proved to be unrealistic. Dissenting opinions soon flowed from Clark, joined by Harlan, both of whom had joined Brennan's opinion in *Sullivan* somewhat reluctantly, but also from White, who had steadfastly stood by Brennan throughout the internal debate in the earlier case. Clark, in a nine-page dissent, strongly disagreed that the Louisiana law punished seditious libel and asserted there should be ample room for states to punish words of hatred and contempt that cost a government official the loss of public confidence. Pulling other free speech doctrines into the debate, Clark rejected Brennan's view that Garrison's words were "mere criticism" and said they amounted to "fighting words," which the Court had long held were not entitled to First Amendment protection at all. Noting that he had joined the *Sullivan* decision, Clark—like Black, Douglas, and Goldberg—similarly maintained there was no justification for making it harder to bring criminal prosecutions for defamation than it was to bring civil suits for damages: "If a civil damage suit based on actual malice meets the standards of the First Amendment, then it follows that a criminal prosecution for defamation, with traditional criminal safeguards, should do likewise."

Somewhat surprisingly, White also produced a strongly worded nine-page dissent. Although Brennan had no reason to suspect it at the time, White's analysis presaged his retreat from *Sullivan* a decade later and gave Brennan his first glimpse of the battles he would increasingly face with his good friend over the future of libel law. Like many of his colleagues, White argued that the actual malice standard must be applied to both criminal and civil libels, lest the Court find itself protecting the "malicious lie" from prosecution. Brennan's opinion, White complained, "indiscriminately lumps the known lie with honest criticism and extends to both the cloak of constitutional immunity." White explained that he joined Brennan in *Sullivan* with the understanding that "the calculated falsehood damaging to reputation is not entitled to First Amendment protection. It is therefore difficult to understand how the author of the lie should have his First Amendment defense overruled in a civil action but sustained by the same court in a criminal proceeding."

For White, the proper resolution of Garrison's appeal turned, as in *Sullivan*, on consideration of whether he had been convicted for publishing a calculated falsehood about the judges. In White's view, however, the actual malice standard used by the Louisiana courts was not the same as the one devised in *Sullivan*; the version applied by the trial judge yielded at best the conclusion that Garrison could have no reasonable belief that his statements were true, rather than that they were made with reckless disregard for their truth or falsity. As a result, White concluded, Garrison's conviction should be reversed and the case sent back to the state courts to apply the correct standard.

The three dissents and the separate views of Black, Douglas, and Goldberg meant that, at best, Brennan could only hope for the votes of Chief Justice Warren and Justice Stewart. According to Brennan's narrative history of the Court's deliberations, Stewart informed him late in the term that he remained uncertain of his position. With the Court deeply divided, the justices agreed to try again, setting the case for reargument the following fall.

At the second argument, which was heard on October 19, 1964, Eberhard Deutsch, a prominent New Orleans lawyer whom everyone, including opposing counsel, referred to as "Colonel," argued for Garrison, as he had the previous April. Representing the state was Louisiana Attorney General Jack Gremillion, also making a return appearance. If nothing else, the argument reflected the continuing disarray among the justices.

Brennan, perhaps trying to hold on to the reasoning of his draft opinion from the previous term, pressed Deutsch to take a position as to whether criminal libel laws should be subjected to the actual malice standard of *Sullivan*. Deutsch replied, "I do say the overall rule of the *Times* case does not apply to a criminal prosecution, that there may be no such thing as a criminal prosecution or defamation of a public official under the First and Fourteenth Amendments." Nevertheless, there was much debate in the argument about the contours of actual malice defined in *Sullivan* and as construed by the Louisiana courts in their application of the state's criminal defamation statute against Garrison. In this regard, Brennan pressed the further point that the trial judge had not applied the actual malice standard as defined in *Sullivan*, but rather had considered —as White had noted in his draft dissenting opinion the previous term—whether Garrison had a "reasonable belief" that his statements were true. Brennan asserted, again with agreement from Deutsch, that under the Louisiana law, a defendant whose statements were in fact true could still be prosecuted for criminal libel if those statements were made with "ill will." This,

Brennan suggested, was "on its face inconsistent" with the actual malice standard as formulated in *Sullivan*.

As Deutsch concluded his argument, a final exchange between the advocate and Justices Brennan and White revealed a depth of both feeling and of disagreement that would not later appear in the Court's published opinions:

> Justice White: So really to serve the truth, we should protect the lie also.
>
> Mr. Deutsch: Exactly. I'll go all the way on that.
>
> Justice White: And give constitutional protection to the known deliberate liar—
>
> Mr. Deutsch: I think it was intended by the framers of the First Amendment that that should be the case.
>
> Justice Brennan: You mean, Mr. Deutsch, that's the old notion if you can't stand the heat, stay out of the kitchen.
>
> Mr. Deutsch: Exactly. I think that's part of public life in a democracy, and I think it's a good thing that it is.

For his part, Attorney General Gremillion found himself mired in the contentious issue Brennan first raised with the "Colonel" —whether the statute permitted criminal prosecution even for statements that were true. Gremillion appeared to misunderstand what he was being asked, answering simultaneously that the statute complied fully with *Sullivan*'s actual malice requirement and that it *did* prohibit the utterance of defamatory statements that were true. In one colloquy, the usually even-keeled Brennan seemed to lose his temper, rebuking Gremillion for talking over him and saying, "Let me ask you the questions, alright?" Later, Chief Justice Warren repeated Brennan's question and, when Gremillion said he didn't think he had so characterized the state law, Justice Stewart chimed in, "You said yes to that question at least six times." These exchanges, and Gremillion's inability to satisfy the Court's inquiry about the statute's scope, would prove to be important factors in the decision of the case.

When the justices again met in conference to consider *Garrison v. Louisiana* four days after the argument, a consensus seemed to emerge to reverse Garrison's conviction by applying *Sullivan*'s actual malice standard to criminal libel statutes. According to Justice Douglas's handwritten notes of the Court's closed-door session, Chief Justice Warren set the tone by asserting the Louisiana law should be struck down as facially invalid because it "covers truthful as well as false statements."

Warren added, as Douglas recorded the chief's views, that there should be "the same standard in criminal libel as in the *Times* case." Black and Douglas also voted to reverse, although they stuck to the absolutist approach they had embraced in the previous go-around. Clark said that he would still affirm the conviction but, in a departure from the prior term, allowed that he would consider joining a majority to require a new trial on the issue of actual malice. Harlan then revealed that he had changed his view and was now prepared to reverse the conviction because there was no proof that Garrison had published his letter with actual malice. Like Clark, however, Harlan said he believed Louisiana would be entitled to retry Garrison under that constitutional standard.

Brennan spoke next and at some length, according to Douglas's notes. He said he too had changed his mind, that he now believed "it would be okay" for Louisiana to punish "false statements made with malice." But, like his colleagues, he faulted the state law for punishing true statements as well as false ones made without actual malice. Brennan also raised another question that had come up during the second argument. It seems that Garrison had requested and been denied a jury trial because, under Louisiana law, criminal libel was a misdemeanor and was not tried to a jury. But Brennan asked his colleagues at conference, as he had both lawyers during the argument, whether the Court should decide that Garrison was entitled to a jury trial because his First Amendment rights were at stake.

After Brennan spoke, Justice Stewart said he would also apply the *Sullivan* standard, but he did not see any reason to strike down the entire law. He said he would reverse and, like Harlan and Clark, leave it to Louisiana to decide whether to have a new trial. According to Douglas's notes, Stewart concluded by saying he would be "content" to base the decision on what Justice White had written in his draft dissent the previous spring. Not surprisingly, given that unpublished opinion, White, too, said he would find there was insufficient evidence of actual malice. In addition, White said he doubted whether the Court needed to decide the jury trial issue that Brennan had now raised. Goldberg spoke last, arguing that there was no defamatory statement in the case and that the law should be declared facially invalid for the reasons he, Black, and Douglas had consistently advocated.

With the opinion still in his hands, Brennan saw what seemed to be a clear path to a sizeable majority. He circulated a new draft, "borrowing judiciously," as his term history later described it, from Justice White's draft dissent following the initial argument. Brennan recognized that White had been concerned, both during the second argument and in his draft dissent, that Brennan had not distinguished sufficiently between the "known lie" and honest, if erroneous, criticism. Accordingly, Brennan picked up on that theme in his new opinion and actually lifted portions of White's dissent and included them in his draft. "[T]he malicious falsehood," White had written the previous term, "is at once at odds with the premises of democratic government and with the orderly manner in which change is to be effected, under our Constitution, in our political, economic and social affairs." Brennan's new draft said, "the use of the known lie as a tool is at once at odds with the premises of democratic government and with the orderly manner in which economic, social, or political change is to be effected."

Ever the pragmatist in his quest to get to a majority, in another section of his revised opinion, Brennan actually marked up and edited yet another portion of White's draft dissent. White's June 1964 draft contained the following:

> Under the test laid down by *New York Times*, the malice which must be shown in order to defeat the qualified privilege to make defamatory and false statements about a public servant in his official capacity is related not to the motives of the speaker, but rather to whether the statement was made "with knowledge that it was false or with reckless disregard of whether it was false or not." It would appear that the reasonable belief standard applied by the trial judge is not the same as the reckless disregard of truth standard announced in *New York Times*. According to the trial court's opinion, a reasonable belief is one which "an ordinarily prudent man might be able to assign a just and fair reason for;" the inference is that under this test the privilege of fair comment disappears upon proof that the exercise of ordinary care would have revealed that the statement was false. The test which we laid down in *New York Times* is not keyed to ordinary care; defeasance of the privilege is conditioned not on proof that the speaker's failure to perceive the falsity of his remarks was negligent, but on his reckless disregard for the truth.

Brennan crossed out by hand portions of this passage and edited a few words, so that the conclusion of his final opinion for the Court reads, much as White's dissent had:

> The reasonable-belief standard applied by the trial judge is not the same as the reckless-disregard-of-truth standard. According to the trial court's opinion, a reasonable belief is one which "an ordinarily prudent man might be able to assign a just and

fair reason for"; the suggestion is that under this test the immunity from criminal responsibility in the absence of ill-will disappears on proof that the exercise of ordinary care would have revealed that the statement was false. The test which we laid down in *New York Times* is not keyed to ordinary care; defeasance of the privilege is conditioned, not on mere negligence, but on reckless disregard for the truth.

In his new draft, Brennan remained mindful that a final and important part of the *Sullivan* ruling was the Court's decision to reweigh, itself, the evidence or lack thereof of actual malice and to terminate Sullivan's lawsuit against the *New York Times*. In his new opinion in *Garrison*, Brennan included a four-page section explaining that Louisiana could not retry Garrison because the state's criminal libel law was not sufficiently narrow and specific to satisfy the First Amendment. "So long as this overbroad statute remains available to the State the threat of prosecutions of protected criticism of public officials is a real and substantial one," Brennan wrote. "Even the prospect of ultimate failure of such prosecutions by no means dispels its chilling effect on protected expression." The conclusion that there could be no retrial, Brennan added in a footnote, made it unnecessary to decide whether a jury trial was required, although he nevertheless cited the laws of twenty-five states that referred all criminal libel prosecutions to juries.

As had been the case in *Sullivan* itself, Brennan's addition of this section proved to be another example of nearly snatching defeat from the jaws of victory. Justices Clark and Harlan promptly objected to it. This time around, however, Brennan quickly notified them and his other colleagues that he would delete those pages. According to Brennan's term history, he concluded that politics in Louisiana made it "extremely unlikely" that Garrison would be retried, and he did not want to jeopardize the consensus that had otherwise formed around his revised opinion.

On November 18, 1964, Black suggested a few minor changes to the separate, concurring opinion Douglas had crafted and that he had joined. In a handwritten note to Douglas, Black also inquired whether he should write a short separate opinion, which he decided to do. He wanted, he said, "to do everything needed to emphasize our objection to what is being done to the First Amendment." As a result, Black, Douglas, and Goldberg, in his own one-paragraph concurring opinion, all contended that the First Amendment should tolerate no liability for criticism of government or government officials and predicted that the putative safeguard of the actual malice standard would ultimately have the effect of watering down protection for free speech. The concurrence by Douglas, and its professed concern for undermining the First Amendment, was changed very little from the previous term, even though Brennan's first draft in the spring had purported to strike down all criminal libel statutes when used to prosecute criticism of government, a position that should have been much more to Douglas's liking.

In the end, Garrison's conviction was reversed unanimously in a decision announced by Brennan on November 23, 1964, barely a month after the second argument. Despite much internal wrangling, and many pages of unpublished disagreements, *Garrison* proved to be a ringing reaffirmation of *New York Times Co. v. Sullivan*, holding that neither civil nor criminal defamation actions could be maintained for criticism of public officials without proof of actual malice. The decision was not quite the death knell of criminal libel laws for which Brennan initially strived to find a majority. It was, however, an important first building block on the new *Sullivan* edifice, and it was surely gratifying to Brennan to be able to reinforce the *Sullivan* decision so quickly.

Somewhat ironically, Brennan's opinion for the court in *Garrison* also put some additional flesh on the bones of the actual malice standard that he had reluctantly agreed to apply in the case. In addition to the portion of his opinion that he borrowed from White's draft dissent the previous term, Brennan took pains both to equate actual malice with the "calculated falsehood" and to explain that it required an "intent to inflict harm through falsehood" as distinguished from "an intent merely to inflict harm." In another passage that would be quoted repeatedly in subsequent cases explaining what the Court meant when it defined actual malice to require, at the very least, a "reckless disregard for the truth," Brennan wrote that "only those false statements made with the high degree of awareness of their probable falsity demanded by *New York Times* may be the subject of either civil or criminal sanctions."

At the time, it was undoubtedly somewhat dispiriting to Brennan to have to struggle so hard to advance what he deemed to be basic democratic principles: that people should be free to criticize their government and its public officials. Still, that concept not only survived the Court's internal disagreements in *Garrison,* but Brennan's final opinion included a simple but eloquent articulation of it that would, in the years to come, become as recognizable in the Court's First Amendment jurisprudence as anything he had written in *Sullivan* itself. "[S]peech concerning public affairs is more than self-expression," Brennan wrote to explain why the First Amendment necessarily places limitations on a state's ability to enforce its criminal laws against criticism of public officials, "it is the essence of self-government." Brennan likely had no idea whether that sentence, which captured perfectly his and now the Court's firm allegiance to Professor Meiklejohn's theory of the ineluctable relationship between democracy and free expression, was ever called to the great philosopher's attention. Meiklejohn passed away at the age of ninety-two, barely a month after *Garrison* was decided.

Henry v. Collins

The next case to come before the Court after *Garrison* was itself the by-product of a substantial controversy in Mississippi, one that shared the important civil rights context of *Sullivan*. In the end, however, *Henry v. Collins* required far less effort from the Supreme Court than either of its immediate predecessors had.

Aaron Henry was the president of the Mississippi chapter of the National Association for the Advancement of Colored People (NAACP) in 1962 when he was sued for libel by Clarksdale, Mississippi Chief of Police Ben Collins and Coahoma County District Attorney Thomas Pearson. Henry, who was black, was arrested for disturbing the peace on what he contended was a made-up charge that he had picked up a white man who was hitchhiking and then solicited him for sex. On several occasions, including in media interviews, Henry said the arrest was part of a "diabolical plot" by white leaders to discredit him because of his civil rights activities. Juries in Mississippi awarded the full amount of requested damages against Henry—$15,000 to Collins and $25,000 to Pearson. The Mississippi Supreme Court upheld the verdicts a few months before the U.S. Supreme Court announced its decision in *Sullivan*.

The justices made quick work of the two appeals. On the basis of Henry's petitions and without requiring either full briefing or oral argument, the Court in March 1965 unanimously reversed both rulings of the Mississippi court in an unsigned opinion for the Supreme Court, called a *per curiam*. In it, the Court explained that the instructions to the juries in Mississippi may have conveyed to them the impression that they could award damages based on a definition of actual malice that required evidence only of an "intent to inflict harm, rather than intent to inflict harm through falsehood." Such proof, the Court's brief opinion explained, fell short of the requirements of the actual malice standard, as defined in *Sullivan* and *Garrison*, which required clear and convincing evidence of knowing falsity or reckless disregard for falsity. As they had in the past, Justices Black, Douglas, and Goldberg added a short note that they would reverse the libel judgments both because of the faulty jury instructions and on their broader assertion that the First Amendment bars any liability for criticism of public officials.

Files of the justices do not indicate who wrote the unsigned *per curiam*, but Brennan is certainly the most likely candidate, since the brief opinion relies entirely on *Sullivan* and *Garrison*. The relative ease with which the Court reached its decision, and the unanimity that characterized it, served to punctuate the justices' allegiance to *Sullivan* and the protection it afforded to public debate and criticism of government officials.

Rosenblatt v. Baer

Since both *New York Times Co. v. Sullivan* and *Garrison v. Louisiana* involved the right to criticize government and public officials, it was only a matter of time before the Court would be called upon to confront the question of who was a "public official" within the meaning of those cases. That question, in turn, was a precursor to the larger and much more complicated issue of whether the *Sullivan* rule should apply to people in the public eye or otherwise involved in public controversies even if they did not hold public office. The Court soon confronted these challenges as well. And with them, the disagreements among the justices, which had thus far been largely hidden from public view, emerged into the open.

Frank Baer was the longtime manager of the Belknap County recreation area in New Hampshire, a resort featuring skiing and other activities, which was publicly owned by Belknap County. Alfred Rosenblatt ran a variety store in Laconia, New Hampshire, and contributed a regular daily column to the Laconia *Evening Citizen*, a local newspaper. On January 29, 1960, about six months after Baer had been dismissed as its manager, Rosenblatt's column commented on how the recreation area seemed to be taking in substantially more money and generating more revenue for the county than in previous years, which he said was all the more surprising because there had been little snow that year until late in the season. Rosenblatt urged his readers to "ponder" the question: "What happened to all the money last year? and every other year?" Baer and his son, who had worked for him at the recreation area, filed four separate libel lawsuits, one by each of them against both Rosenblatt and the Laconia newspaper. Some of those claims were settled or not otherwise pursued, leaving only Baer's suit against Rosenblatt. A jury awarded Baer $31,500 in damages. Seven months after *Sullivan*, the New Hampshire Supreme Court upheld that award, finding that the trial court had properly instructed the jury that it was obliged to find what amounted to actual malice as Brennan had defined it in *Sullivan* and *Garrison*.

When Rosenblatt's appeal reached the justices, Brennan again attempted to take the lead, suggesting to his colleagues that, as in *Henry v. Collins*, they rule in a short *per curiam*, without briefing and argument, that Baer was a public official and that the jury instructions at the trial were inadequate because they did not recite the Court's actual malice standard accurately. In fact, those instructions permitted damages to be awarded based solely on an intent to harm without regard to whether Rosenblatt knew that what he wrote was probably false. In March 1965, Brennan sent his colleagues a four-page memorandum describing the case and advocating this approach. At first, there appeared to be majority support for Brennan's proposed disposition of the case and, as a result, he proceeded to draft a two-page *per curiam* opinion. But, according to Brennan's narrative term history, Justice Harlan intervened and sent his own memorandum to his colleagues suggesting that review should simply be denied unless the Court was prepared to use the case as a vehicle to formulate standards defining who is a public official within the meaning of *Sullivan* and *Garrison*. Harlan's memo led Brennan to withdraw his draft *per curium* and to agree with his colleague that the Court should proceed to hear the case the following fall. In its order granting review, the Court specifically asked the lawyers to brief the question whether Baer was a public official. As Brennan's term history later noted, "[a]t that time," he did "not have the slightest idea that this case would become one of the most difficult to resolve during the 1965 Term."

At the argument in October 1965, longtime Laconia lawyer Arthur Nighswander, a prominent civil liberties advocate in the state and partner of one of Brennan's Harvard Law School roommates, William Lord, contended that Baer was a public official and that the state courts had not required that he satisfy that actual malice standard as articulated by the Supreme Court in *Sullivan* and *Garrison*. Perhaps of greater significance, Nighswander foreshadowed the battles that lay ahead when he observed that there were cases in the pipeline extending the *Sullivan* rule to

"matters of public concern," and to "public men" who were not public officials, a
line of demarcation he appeared to suggest would be less difficult than the "public official" rule for litigants and courts to understand and apply. Justice Stewart
quickly asked Nighswander why focusing on matters of public concern would be
an easier test, which led the advocate both to concede that "it would not" and to
emphasize that he was not pressing the argument after all.

Stanley Brown, another prominent New Hampshire lawyer from Manchester,
argued for Baer. He suggested an irony in the positions of the lawyers, explaining
that at trial Rosenblatt's counsel had argued that the disputed newspaper column
was about county commissioners, not about Baer at all, and that Baer himself
could not have been the focus of the column because he was *not* a county official. Responding to a question from Brennan, Brown said of Nighswander, "so his
position was that Baer was not a county official until—until *Times* and *Sullivan*
came in, and then it became very apparent that he was." Brown spent a substantial
portion of his argument describing Baer's duties, including whether there was any
record that he was obliged to take an oath of office, and other details that he contended ought to inform the "public official" inquiry. At one juncture, in response
to Brown's recitation of one or another of these niceties of New Hampshire law,
Justice Black expressed concern about whether the term "public official" should
properly lead to "50 different tests in 50 different states."

Between the justices' decision to scrap the *per curiam* approach in the spring
of 1965 and the argument the following October, the makeup of the Court had
changed in a way that would prove to be significant. Justice Goldberg, who had
served on the Court for only three years, resigned at the behest of President Lyndon Johnson to become United Nations ambassador that July. In *Sullivan*, and in
every case applying it thereafter, Goldberg had taken a position similar to Black
and Douglas, consistently advocating that criticism of government and of public officials was absolutely protected by the First Amendment, even when actual
malice was present. Goldberg was replaced by Abe Fortas, a prominent and highly
respected Washington, D.C., lawyer and close friend of the president, who took
his seat on October 4, 1965, at the start of the new term. It quickly became clear
that the new justice was far less sympathetic to Brennan's conception of the First
Amendment than his predecessor had been.

When the justices gathered for their conference to discuss the *Rosenblatt* case
on October 22, 1965, barely two weeks after Fortas joined the Court, there was

no support for the New Hampshire Supreme Court's judgment in favor of Baer. But, according to handwritten notes of the conference prepared by Justice Douglas, there was also no consensus on an appropriate basis for a U.S. Supreme Court ruling in favor of Rosenblatt. Opening the debate at conference, Chief Justice Warren said he thought Baer was a public official and that the state courts had not properly applied the *Sullivan* actual malice standard. Black and Douglas also voted to reverse, on the by now familiar ground that the First Amendment provided absolute protection to published criticism of government affairs, a position that prompted Douglas to add that he wasn't sure the Court needed to decide whether Baer was or was not a public official at all. For his part, Justice Clark expressed doubts about whether the term "public official" should extend to employees "way down the line," although he said he would agree to a reversal with respect to Baer. Brennan argued that Baer was a public official and, according to Douglas's notes, emphasized that, in deciding that question, the Court should be guided by the principle that the "First Amendment puts a premium on discussion of public affairs."

At this point, however, what had appeared to be an emerging consensus began to break down in significant respects. Stewart voiced concerns about applying the actual malice requirement to Baer, citing the Court's decision the previous spring in *Griswold v. Connecticut*, which found a right of privacy implicit in the provisions of the Bill of Rights. After *Griswold*, Stewart suggested, the Court was obliged to recognize that defamation cases pit an aspect of this right of privacy against the competing First Amendment right of freedom of expression and, according to Douglas's notes, said he was "reluctant to extend the *New York Times* rule because it is Draconian in its effect." White then said the Court should formulate a definition of "public official" and remand the case for the New Hampshire courts to apply the new standard. In addition, as Douglas recorded his views, White wanted to be sure the definition did not "include everyone on the public payroll." Finally, in casting his first votes with respect to the meaning and application of *New York Times Co. v. Sullivan*, Justice Fortas raised a concern about which he had also inquired at argument—specifically, that the record did not make clear whether Baer had taken an oath of office, which Fortas thought significant in determining whether he qualified as a public official.

With no majority for any of the proffered grounds for decision, the justices agreed to consider the case again at their next conference. In the wake of the discussion at the first conference, Brennan became concerned that, as his term history later described it, *Sullivan* not be allowed "to founder on plurality opinions," and, to guard against that possibility, he prepared a memorandum to the other justices, laying out his views. In it, he argued that the Court had no real choice but to decide whether Baer was a public official. If he was, Brennan contended, then the instructions to the jury were improper under *Sullivan* because they permitted Baer to recover damages unless Rosenblatt could persuade a jury that he "believed his statement to be true 'on grounds that would satisfy the ordinary man of average prudence.'" This, Brennan emphasized in his fifteen-page memorandum, was well short of *Sullivan*'s requirement that a public official prove knowledge of falsity or reckless disregard of the truth. And, echoing what he had said at the first conference, Brennan asserted that the public official designation must be applied liberally to protect debate about public affairs and about those responsible for conducting them. Accordingly, Brennan concluded, "I would be willing to say that a person claiming to have been defamed is not a public official, even though he may be linked to some matter of public concern," but only "if his connection is so remote that he appears to have no substantial responsibility for or control over the affairs being discussed." In Brennan's view, that formulation would sweep within the definition of the public official not only those who stood for election, but all those hired by elected officials, candidates for office, and even those who might "appear to the public" as if they had the authority to influence public affairs. And, in a passage of his memorandum that anticipated the controversies that loomed ahead, Brennan added that, in *Rosenblatt*, the court did not need to resolve whether the actual malice standard ought to apply as well to "movie actors, football coaches and others whose conduct may interest the public."

The discussion that followed at the second conference resolved little, but Warren once again assigned the opinion to Brennan, hoping no doubt that he could craft something that would garner a majority as he had in *Sullivan* and *Garrison*. To accomplish that goal, Brennan proceeded to prepare a draft opinion drawing heavily on the memorandum he had shared with his colleagues prior to the second conference. Brennan's opinion contained two separate arguments. In Part II, he invoked another aspect of his opinion for the Court in *Sullivan*, explaining that the New Hampshire jury had improperly been allowed to award damages to Baer, even though he wasn't named in the newspaper column, on the theory that criticism of government activity may be presumed to refer to those who administer the activity and that Baer was part of a small group responsible for operation of the recreation area. In his draft opinion, Brennan wrote that *Sullivan* established the principle that, "in the absence of sufficient evidence that the attack focused on the plaintiff, an otherwise impersonal attack on governmental operations cannot be utilized to establish a libel of those administering the operations." In Part III of his draft, Brennan turned to defining those public officials who were obliged to prove actual malice, and proceeded to formulate a national standard, one that was not subject to variation from state to state. While his draft further asserted that the Court need not draw the precise lines of that definition in the *Rosenblatt* case, he wrote that the *Sullivan* rule must apply whenever the public has an "independent interest in the qualifications and performance" of a person holding a government position. As Brennan explained in a passage that has served ever since as the Court's working definition of the kind of public official who is obliged to prove actual malice in order to recover for defamation:

> Criticism of government is at the very center of the constitutionally protected area of free discussion. Criticism of those responsible for government operations must be free, lest criticism of government itself be penalized. *It is clear, therefore, that the "public official" designation applies at the very least to those among the hierarchy of government employees who have, or appear to the public to have, substantial responsibility for or control over the conduct of governmental affairs.*

Justice Douglas quickly expressed concerns about Brennan's opinion in a memorandum that he circulated privately to Brennan and Fortas on November 19, 1965. In it, Douglas questioned whether the actual malice standard could properly be applied in a case, like *Rosenblatt*, which had gone to trial before *Sullivan* and, as a result, had not afforded the litigants any warning that they ought to present evidence or otherwise address the issue of whether the plaintiff was a public official. He also expressed his concern that it would prove impossible to limit the application of the actual malice standard to public officials. "If free discussion of public issues is the guide, I see no possibility of drawing lines that exclude the night watchman, the file clerk, the typist, or anyone, for that matter, on the public payroll," Douglas wrote. Oddly, given his consistent support for a literal and absolute interpretation of the First Amendment, Douglas also expressed concern that Brennan's approach in effect created a "constitutional right to tell lies" about individuals at every level of government. For all of these reasons, Douglas proposed dismissing the case and putting off the resolution of the public official issue for another day.

Brennan responded to Douglas the next day, also copying Fortas, and suggested that, even if the Court could not resolve the public official issue, it should nevertheless reverse the New Hampshire judgment because of the issue raised in Part II of his draft—that the jury had been allowed to convert a general attack on government into a personal libel of Baer. In addition, Brennan insisted that his draft had not purported to resolve what he and other justices had come to describe as the "little man" problem, the question of how far down the chain of government employment the actual malice rule should apply. Referring back to Douglas's invocation of the night watchman as a putative public official, Brennan countered that the security guard would not generally be among those in the hierarchy of public employees with responsibility for the conduct of public affairs, the standard for defining public officials he had included in Part III of his draft.

At this juncture, Brennan began to pursue a bifurcated strategy, trying to line up support separately for the two parts of his opinion with the hope of achieving a bottom line consensus to reverse the judgment for Baer. He made no headway with Fortas, who responded to both Brennan and Douglas that he would prefer to dismiss the appeal and to await another case. But Douglas and Brennan exchanged numerous handwritten messages over the next several weeks. On December 8, Brennan wrote to his senior colleague on two small memo sheets and advised him that, at that point, he had only Warren and White with him for Part II and Warren, White, and Harlan for Part III, as well as Black's vote for a reversal on his own grounds. That, Brennan wrote, was not "a very desirable result," no doubt hoping to persuade Douglas to at least join Part II of his opinion. Indeed, during that period, Brennan made several such personal appeals to Douglas.

Ultimately, despite the disagreement he had with Brennan over the public official issue addressed in Part III, the exchange of handwritten notes between the two justices showed that Douglas was a hardworking ally in helping Brennan "get a Court" for Part II—the "of and concerning" issue. Following his receipt of one such note from Brennan, Douglas responded that he had "concluded to help 'the team' with its woes and join Part II." In the same note, Douglas advised Brennan that Clark's disagreement seemed to be only about the wording of Part II: "I told him I was sure you would edit it to suit him as his criticisms of Part II do not go to the merits," Douglas wrote. "So I think he is fruit on the tree ripe for the picking."

That prediction, however, proved to be wrong; in the end, Clark concurred only in the Court's judgment and not in Brennan's reasoning.

Even as the votes for Part II of his draft began to fall into place, Brennan had less success with Justice Harlan, who continued to object to Part II but said he was willing to join Part III. Harlan did not believe, as Brennan did, that the trial court had improperly allowed the jury to impute what was a generalized criticism of government to Baer. On December 7, Brennan wrote to Harlan privately, suggesting that because the statements in the newspaper column were at best ambiguous as to whom they referred, too much discretion had therefore been left to the jury, which created the risk that it had improperly imputed the criticism to Baer. The *Sullivan* ruling, Brennan wrote, "requires us to balance that risk by cutting back on the jury's freedom" to decide for itself to whom the column referred.

The stalemate continued, but Brennan persisted. Part II of his opinion now had the support of four justices—himself, Warren, White, and Douglas. Part III had similarly been endorsed by a different group of four—Brennan, Warren, White and Harlan. At this point, however, Justice Stewart weighed in with what Brennan's term history accurately described as an "intense and strongly worded dissent." Stewart's primary concern remained, as he had explained at conference, that the Court was paying too little attention to the privacy interests of individuals in their reputations. In an attempt to satisfy Stewart on this score, Brennan added an observation to his opinion that, along with Stewart's separate concurring opinion, would come back to haunt Brennan, not to mention defendants in defamation actions, more than once in the years ahead. "Society," Brennan wrote, "has a pervasive and strong interest in preventing and redressing attacks upon reputation."

At that moment, however, the sentence appeared to serve its intended purpose—it proved sufficient to satisfy Stewart who changed his dissent to a concurring opinion, suddenly and remarkably giving Brennan a majority for both Parts II and III. In his concurring opinion, Stewart picked up on the sentence that Brennan had added to his own and expanded upon it, writing that:

> The right of a man to the protection of his own reputation from unjustified invasion and wrongful hurt reflects no more than our basic concept of the essential dignity and worth of every human being—a concept at the root of any decent system of ordered liberty. The protection of private personality, like the protection of life itself, is left primarily to the individual States under the Ninth and Tenth Amendments.

But this does not mean that the right is entitled to any less recognition by this Court
as a basic of our constitutional system.

Even with Stewart's vote thus secured, the wrangling was far from over. There were
two more hurdles that Brennan had to clear. First, at the same time the Court
was grappling with *Rosenblatt*, it was also deciding the case of *Linn v. United Plant
Guard Workers*. In *Linn*, the justices addressed the question of whether state libel
laws were preempted by federal labor law when false statements were made during a union organizing campaign. Justice Clark wrote for a narrow 5–4 majority
that state libel laws could coexist with federal regulation of labor relations as long
as, when such suits arose in that context, the plaintiff was obliged to prove actual
malice as defined in *Sullivan*. That standard, Clark explained, was required not by
the First Amendment, but rather by the federal statutes governing labor relations.

The dissenters in *Linn* were Chief Justice Warren and Justices Black, Fortas, and
Douglas, all of whom believed that, by allowing any defamation actions in such circumstances, the majority was in fact undermining the approach to resolving labor
disputes set out by Congress. Black in particular felt very strongly that permitting
libel lawsuits over statements made in the normal course of labor strife, which
were often quite heated, would dramatically alter the landscape of management
and worker relations in a way that would open up all manner of potential liability under state law. To underscore his views, Black penned a handwritten note to
Douglas that said, "[a]fter this decision it would be wise for Martin Luther King
to put no property in his name or that of his organization." This was an apparent
reference to the substantial work Dr. King did with labor unions and organizing
workers as part of his civil rights efforts.

The second hurdle for Brennan involved a pending appeal on which the Court
had not yet acted, but which offered a glimpse at what lay ahead. According to
Brennan's term history, at the same conference at which the justices approved
Linn for final decision and at which Brennan's opinion in *Rosenblatt* was also up
for final approval, the petition for review in *Curtis Publishing Co. v. Butts* (discussed
in chapter 3) was also before the justices. That case raised the question whether
Wally Butts, a prominent college football coach and athletic director at a public
university, was a public official. According to Brennan's narrative history, Chief Justice Warren "became very upset" at the prospect that *Sullivan* might be construed
to establish the principle that a football coach could be a public official and that

Brennan's opinion in *Rosenblatt* might bolster that contention. As the conference ended, therefore, Warren insisted on holding up announcement of the Court's decision in *Rosenblatt* and even threatened to withdraw his vote, which was critical to both parts of Brennan's majority. Later that day, with Brennan standing beside him, Douglas called Warren and attempted to assure him that neither *Sullivan* nor *Rosenblatt* resolved the question presented in *Butts*. In that cause, Douglas reminded the chief justice that Brennan had specifically made that clear in footnote 12 of his opinion in the latter case, which emphasized that the issue before the Court in *Rosenblatt* dealt only with "public position," and not with the situation in which "the subject of discussion has thrust himself into the vortex of the discussion of a question of pressing public concern."

While Warren considered his position, Brennan noticed that a new draft of Justice Black's dissent in *Linn* made reference to *Rosenblatt*, meaning the two cases overlapped and could not be decided separately. When the chief justice was informed of this logistical problem, he withdrew his concern about *Rosenblatt*. As a result, the decisions in *Linn* and *Rosenblatt* were announced on the same day, February 21, 1966. Both reaffirmed the fundamental principles of *New York Times Co. v. Sullivan*, although discerning observers of the Court's work began to perceive that, for the first time, what had been broad support for those principles and their extension had begun to fragment.

Time, Inc. v. Hill

The fragility of Brennan's working majority, which first manifested itself in a decided case in *Rosenblatt v. Baer*, reached an even more critical state in the next case to come before the Court in which *Sullivan* and its reach were placed at issue. *Time, Inc. v. Hill* provided the ingredients for additional drama because it not only placed Richard Nixon in front of the Supreme Court twice as an advocate, its resolution was ultimately influenced by Warren Spahn, a member of the Baseball Hall of Fame, and it saw Brennan go head-to-head with Fortas in an ideological confrontation that changed the case's outcome.

The case involved an article that appeared in *Life* magazine, published by Time, Inc., in 1955. The article described a new Broadway play and soon-to-be movie, *The Desperate Hours*. According to the article, the play and a novel of the same name that preceded it were based on a real-life event in 1952, in which the Hill family, two parents and five children, were held hostage by escaped convicts in their home outside Philadelphia for nineteen hours. In the real incident, the Hill family said that, beyond holding them against their will, the convicts had treated them with courtesy and had not hurt or molested them. In the play, a family of four was held hostage and badly mistreated, the father and son beaten and the daughter insulted sexually. After the real incident, the Hill family moved away and tried to put the episode behind them, purposefully staying out of the limelight. The play and the article in *Life*, however, put them back in the public eye in a way that James Hill contended, in a lawsuit he filed in the New York courts, invaded his family's privacy and depicted them under false circumstances. Indeed, Mr. Hill complained, the *Life* article was accompanied by photographs, staged by the magazine and shot by its own photographer, in which the actors in the play were transported to the Hills' former home, where they re-created scenes from the fictionalized drama.

James Hill sued under a New York law that prohibits the use of a person's name or image for advertising or promotion without the individual's permission. Thus, the case involved not a claim for defamation (which would have required a publication that injured Mr. Hill's reputation), but rather a suit alleging a "false light invasion of privacy," a claim based on the contention that, by depicting him and his family in a false light, Time had caused him to suffer emotional distress. A jury awarded Hill $50,000 in compensatory damages and $25,000 in punitive damages. After an appellate court affirmed the jury's verdict of liability but ordered a new trial on damages, a judge reduced the award to $30,000 in compensatory damages and no punitive damages. The highest state court, the New York Court of Appeals, affirmed that judgment.

When Time sought review in the Supreme Court, according to Brennan's term history, five justices—Black, Douglas, Harlan, Brennan, and White—voted to hear the case. The remaining justices—Chief Justice Warren and Justices Clark, Stewart, and Fortas—would have opted to deny the appeal. When the case was called for argument on April 27, 1966, Time was represented by Harold Medina Jr., a prominent New York lawyer at one of New York's most prestigious law firms and the son of a longtime federal judge. Hill was represented by Richard Nixon, the former vice president, who was two-and-a-half-years away from being elected president of the United States. A key issue at the argument was whether the New York law on which Hill had based his suit permitted liability for any unauthorized

exploitation of a person's name or only when such exploitation was false or fictionalized. Nixon insisted that the law was limited to false or fictionalized accounts
in which the plaintiff was the primary focus and in which the defendant had a
commercial purpose. At argument, Nixon's contention was underscored in an
exchange with Chief Justice Warren, with whom he had maintained a long and
often contentious rivalry dating to the earliest stages of their respective political
careers in California and continuing through their service in the nation's capital:

> Warren: Suppose that *Life* instead of doing this the way it did, said that this play of
> Mr. Hughes' is reminiscent of the Hill incident in Philadelphia which we recalled to
> be as follows. And they then proceed to revive the story substantially as it occurred.
> Would you say that no matter how sensitive these people were to their privacy, no
> matter how hard they had tried to get away from reliving this thing that that would
> be appropriate and *Life* could do that without violating your law?
>
> Nixon: Mr. Chief Justice, cruel as it might be in special circumstances . . . I believe
> that that would not be a violation under New York law. It is required under New
> York law that there'd be fictionalization. . . .

When the justices met in conference after the argument and cast their votes, Nixon
prevailed handily. According to Brennan's term history, the vote was six to three
to affirm the New York judgment, and Chief Justice Warren assigned the opinion
to Fortas. Justices Black, Douglas, and White were the only dissenters. Fortified
by what appeared to be a sizeable majority, Fortas proceeded to draft a strongly
worded condemnation of *Life*, which included, among other expressions of hostility toward the magazine specifically and the press more generally, this sentence:
"'Needless, heedless, wanton injury of the sort inflicted by *Life*'s picture story is
not an essential instrument of responsible journalism.'" Harlan wrote a less vitriolic
concurring opinion in which he advocated a "weighing process," balancing Hill's
privacy interests against the public interest in speech about public affairs, and concluded that, on the facts of this case, the scales tipped in favor of Mr. Hill's privacy.

Sensing that Brennan might be unsettled by the intensity of the Fortas opinion, Justice White, who had voted at conference in favor of the magazine, saw an
opportunity to pick away at Fortas's majority. Accordingly, he shared a draft dissent with Brennan (and later with the full Court), in which he raised an issue that
had not been addressed by Fortas and that, as White hoped it would, became an

important concern for the Court. In his draft dissent, White noted that, when the New York Court of Appeals summarily affirmed an intermediate appellate court's ruling in favor of the Hills, it unusually but expressly purported to affirm *both* the lead opinion and a concurring opinion issued by one member of that court. Significantly, the concurring opinion suggested that the New York statute applied to news accounts that were true as long as they were made for commercial purposes. Since newspapers are published to be sold, the concurring judge's analysis would potentially expose to liability under the New York law news accounts that were entirely accurate but which nevertheless arguably invaded the privacy of persons referenced in them. This construction of the statute was of course contrary to the way Nixon had urged the court to understand the New York law during his exchange with the chief justice at argument.

In response to White's dissenting opinion, Fortas recrafted his own to reflect the view that the New York law and the lower court's ruling only applied, as Nixon had argued, to fictionalized accounts. But, according to Brennan's term history, there was enough uncertainty on this important point that the justices opted to have the case reargued the following term. As a result, Fortas's majority, and the strongly worded condemnation of Time he authored were, at least temporarily, extinguished. In the years to come, the irony that this result was the brainchild of Byron White would become apparent, albeit largely unknown outside the Court.

In its order scheduling reargument, the Court asked the lawyers to clarify the issues by addressing specifically whether a true statement could serve as the basis for a lawsuit under the New York law, whether the concurring opinion in the lower court was correct that an accurate and newsworthy item could be actionable if its purpose was commercial, and whether fictionalization, for purposes of the statute, required at least a finding of reckless disregard for falsity within the meaning of *Sullivan*. If nothing else, the framing of these questions suggested that the case might be moving in a different direction.

The day before the second argument, Justice Black circulated a blistering sixteen-page memorandum criticizing the judicial balancing of free speech against privacy interests that he said Fortas and Harlan had advocated in their draft opinions the previous June. In a classic statement of his absolutism about the meaning of the First Amendment, Black wrote:

This means that the scope of press freedom is not to be decided by what the Founders wrote, but by what a Court majority thinks they should have written had they been writing now. . . . We, the judiciary, are no longer to be crippled and hobbled by the old admonition that "We must always remember it is a Constitution we are *expounding*," but we are to work under the exhilarating new slogan that, "We must always remember that it is a Constitution we are *rewriting* to fit the times." . . . After mature reflection I am unable to recall any prior case in this Court that offers a greater threat to freedom of speech and press than this one does, either in the tone and temper of the Court's opinion or in its resulting holding and judgment.

Although Black's memorandum nowhere mentioned it, he had already made clear in earlier cases that he had much the same view of Brennan's actual malice test, which, he similarly believed, compromised core First Amendment rights and effectively amended the otherwise plain language of the First Amendment.

At the second argument, which spanned October 18 and 19, 1966, Medina grappled with the court's concerns for fifty-one minutes, arguing that the New York law "is so broad that it literally covers anything." Noting that state libel law is not currently limited by the First Amendment except in suits brought by public officials, Medina observed, prophetically, "perhaps you'll extend it to public figures and public issues that will be coming up in other cases, of course." As to whether the New York statute had been interpreted in a manner consistent with *Sullivan's* actual malice rule, Medina argued that *any* showing of intent, whether intentional falsity or recklessness, is "utterly foreign to the question of privacy as interpreted by the New York courts."

When his turn came, Nixon protested that the Court's deliberations had gone far afield from the dispute between the Hill family and *Life* magazine. He argued that it was clear that *Life* had lied about the Hills' ordeal and that it knew it had lied by depicting in its article and the accompanying photographs that the play was an account of the actual incident. Addressing Brennan specifically, Nixon said the case differed from *Sullivan* because the earlier litigation involved an advertisement submitted to the newspaper by someone else, while *Life* had written its own original story and, when it did so, it had information in its files that the play *The Desperate Hours* was not based on any specific hostage incident and that it did not accurately describe what had happened to the Hills.

In a somewhat awkward dynamic at the start of his more than fifty minutes of argument, Nixon spoke for more than nine minutes without any questions or interruptions. But, when the questions eventually flowed, Brennan asked Nixon if he believed that "constitutionally a statute like this has to be limited to intentionally or recklessly false statements." Not exactly answering the question and openly disagreeing with Medina, Nixon stuck to his guns and replied that "as far as the application of the New York statute is concerned, it is limited to intentionally false statements." Nixon argued that, in Mr. Hill's case, the jury charge required such proof of intent because the trial judge told the jury it must determine whether *Life* "altered or changed the true facts." Justice White, for one, seemed skeptical that those instructions imposed any intent requirement at all.

Brennan also questioned Nixon about the vexing concurring opinion in the New York appellate court, which appeared to state that commercial exploitation could lead to liability even in the absence of falsity. Nixon replied that, while that opinion was concededly part of the New York Court of Appeals's affirmance of the result below, the specific discussion of "commercial purpose" in the concurring opinion was "dictum," a Latin phrase meaning that it was not essential to the Court's decision and was therefore not binding in subsequent cases. In response, Brennan acknowledged, "It may very well be a dictum," and got a laugh from the gallery when he added, "indeed if this were an opinion of one of my brethren I would say it was." But Brennan then turned serious and asked Nixon whether the Supreme Court was free to declare that "a state court's interpretation of a state statute" was not essential to its holding. "I wonder," Brennan said, " if we're free to just disregard it as merely dictum." Nixon countered that the Court could safely affirm the decision because the language contained in the concurring opinion had not subsequently been embraced or applied by another New York court.

Brennan appeared to be unpersuaded, and some twenty-five minutes later, he again raised his concern that the statute would allow liability for a truthful, newsworthy item because it was published in a newspaper sold for profit. Brennan told Nixon, "If that's the law of New York, if that's the interpretation of the New York statute which we have to take in deciding this case, then number one I have serious difficulty whether that interpretation can stand in the face of the First Amendment." In addition, Brennan asserted, perhaps Time ought to have standing to ask the court to strike down the statute as overbroad even if the justices were otherwise prepared to accept Nixon's contention that the magazine had knowingly and intentionally published a falsehood in this case.

When, following the second argument, the justices again discussed the case in conference, the world had all but turned upside down. This time, the vote was seven to two to *reverse* the judgment against the magazine, with only Chief Justice Warren and Justice Fortas voting to affirm the New York Court of Appeals. With Warren now in dissent, Justice Black—the senior Justice in the new majority— placed responsibility for crafting the Court's opinion in Brennan's familiar hands.

As he set to putting pen to paper, Brennan quickly received a boost of sorts in trying to sort out the meaning of the previous New York decisions. A week after the second argument, the New York Court of Appeals ruled in a case brought by famed major league pitcher Warren Spahn, who had sued under the same New York law about a purported biography of him that Spahn contended contained falsehoods and exaggerations. As Brennan's term history later characterized that decision, in *Spahn v. Julian Messner, Inc.*, New York's highest court had made "crystal-clear the applicability of the statute to mere falsity, without regard to intent or recklessness." In fact, in *Spahn*, the New York Court of Appeals had explained that, while "[t]he factual reporting of newsworthy persons and events is in the public interest and is protected" under the statute, "[t]he fictitious is not."

For Brennan, the *Spahn* decision eased his task in two respects. For one thing, it indicated that the New York law allowed recovery without a showing of actual malice. By the same token, as Brennan saw it, it showed a degree of respect by the New York Court of Appeals for the news function, suggesting that the statute need not be struck down on its face and that the Supreme Court could trust the state court to apply a new, constitutionally required standard if instructed to do so.

Thus, on December 1, Brennan circulated a draft opinion that construed *Spahn* generously, explaining that, following that decision, "it is not clear whether proof of knowledge of . . . falsity or that the article was prepared with reckless disregard for the truth is required" to ground a finding of liability under the New York statute. If, however, the statute were construed to require such a showing, Brennan continued, it would survive First Amendment scrutiny. Accordingly, he concluded, in the *Hill* case, Time was entitled to a new trial under which the lower courts would be obliged by the First Amendment to apply the actual malice standard as he had defined it in *Sullivan*. Brennan wrote that "the constitutional protections for speech and press preclude the application of the New York statute to redress false reports of matters of public interest in the absence of proof that the defendant published the report with knowledge of its falsity or in reckless disregard of the truth." Then, in a passage that arguably reflected the high point of Brennan's authority to speak for the Court on such matters, he added the following:

> The guarantees for speech and press are not the preserve of political expression or comment upon public affairs, essential as those are to healthy government. One need only pick up any newspaper or magazine to comprehend the vast range of published matter which exposes persons to public view, both private citizens and public officials. Exposure of the self to others in varying degrees is a concomitant of life in a civilized community. The risk of this exposure is an essential incident of life in a society which places a primary value on freedom of speech and of press. . . . We have no doubt that the subject of the *Life* article, the opening of a new play linked to an actual incident, is a matter of public interest.

In other words, Brennan asserted, the protection of a free press afforded by the actual malice standard logically extended beyond suits brought by public officials, and even beyond "political expression or comment on public affairs," to reach all "matter[s] of public interest." In such cases, Brennan asserted, "sanctions against either innocent or negligent misstatement would present a grave hazard of discouraging the press from exercising the constitutional guarantees. Those guarantees," Brennan wrote, "are not for the benefit of the press so much as for the benefit of all of us. A broadly defined freedom of the press assures the maintenance of our political system and an open society."

Initially, Brennan's opinion secured only the support of White, his generally reliable ally in *Sullivan* and the cases that had followed it. White wrote Brennan a note explaining that he was joining his opinion "with a good deal of enthusiasm for the job you have done." Curiously, however, more than a month then passed before another vote was cast. On December 22, Fortas circulated a dissent, similar to but toned down from his putative majority opinion of the previous June. Although his opinion continued to protest what he described as "the reckless and irresponsible assault upon [James Hill] and his family which this article represents," Fortas was very solicitous of Brennan. Before sharing his dissent with anyone else, Fortas sent Brennan a copy with a handwritten note written on the top left corner: "For Brother Brennan—Please let me know if any of this bark is too bitey. I'll change it. I will not circulate it until I hear from you—Abe." When he finally did circulate his draft, Fortas quickly gained the support of both Chief Justice Warren and Justice Clark.

Early in the new year, Justice Harlan proposed to concur only in Brennan's result, rejecting extension of the actual malice standard to suits under the New York statute and advocating instead only a requirement that negligence be proven. This left Brennan once again scrambling for enough votes to form a majority. To avoid a splintered result, Justices Black and Douglas circulated opinions expressing their view that there could be no liability for discussion of public affairs consistent with the First Amendment under any circumstances, but both justices purported to join Brennan's opinion, including its application of the actual malice standard because, they said, it would enable a clear decision of the case. That gave Brennan four votes for his formulation and left only Justice Stewart unaccounted for. To entice Stewart to join him, Brennan included in his opinion a citation to Stewart's newly minted concurrence in *Rosenblatt v. Baer* and added the following:

> Were this a libel action, the distinction which has been suggested between the relative opportunities of the public official and the private individual to rebut defamatory charges might be germane. And the additional state interest in the protection of the individual against damage to his reputation would be involved.

This modification proved enough to satisfy Stewart who, on January 5, 1967, joined Brennan's opinion in its entirety and gave him a five-justice majority, albeit one tenuously held together with the less than complete agreement of Black and Douglas. In fact, Stewart wrote Brennan that, while he had a few "minor" suggestions, "I think you have written a fine opinion and I am glad to join it."

Narrow or not, the decision was yet another reaffirmation and extension of *New York Times Co. v. Sullivan*, this time to say that states could not permit liability for false light invasion of privacy based on reports of newsworthy matters without a showing of actual malice. But *Time, Inc. v. Hill* made it inescapably clear not only to Brennan, but now to those outside the Court as well, that each new application of the *Sullivan* rule threatened to reveal deep divisions within the Court over the proper constitutional accommodation between reputation and privacy on the one hand, and freedom of speech and of the press on the other.

In a somewhat ironic footnote, Nixon's former law partner and later White House counsel, Leonard Garment, wrote in the *New Yorker* magazine in 1989 that Nixon assumed before he took on the case that he had enemies at the Court who would "have their knives out for him." Little did Nixon know that he actually won the case after the first argument, in an opinion written by one of President Johnson's closest friends and joined by the chief justice, his old political enemy, and that it was only when Justice Fortas overplayed his support for Nixon's position, replete with a classic Nixonian hostility for the press, that the case was reargued and the outcome changed.

There was another, less well-known footnote as well. In the fall of 1969, Brennan, his wife Marjorie, and their daughter Nancy, all attended the wedding of long-time family friends. There, Brennan met and chatted with James Hill, the plaintiff in *Time, Inc. v. Hill*, although it is not apparent that Brennan knew who Hill was. "One item of drama may have slipped by you unnoticed," his host later wrote Brennan, informing him to whom he had been talking at the wedding. Brennan wrote back on October 9, 1969, some eight months into the Nixon presidency:

> That is simply fantastic! I often wondered how it was that Mr. Nixon represented the Hills. I gather from what Mr. Hill told me of his business that the Nixon firm must be their General Counsel. The President has twitted me about that case on occasions, and when I have the opportunity I am going to tell him that I had the pleasure of meeting his clients.

CHAPTER 3

OF "PUBLIC FIGURES" AND "ACTUAL MALICE"

After *Garrison, Rosenblatt,* and *Hill,* the flow of defamation cases coming before the justices remained unrelenting. Still, it may not have been readily apparent to those outside the Court just how many unresolved issues this new field of constitutional law raised and how difficult some of them would turn out to be. Inside the Court, however, the justices knew they had been dancing around both the definition of *actual malice,* as they had described their new liability standard in *Sullivan,* and the question of to whom that standard applied with all the finesse of regulars on the popular-at-the-time *American Bandstand.* Production of the Court's already impressive number of post-*Sullivan* decisions had involved a substantial amount of hard work on the part of Brennan and others to make them fit within the framework erected in *Sullivan* without directly confronting questions about its scope and reach. If there was any point of clarity, it seemed to be that the justices understood when state courts had not properly applied the actual malice standard as it was articulated in *Sullivan,* by relying instead on evidence of "ill will" or "intent to injure" in lieu of the knowing or reckless falsity mandated by *Sullivan.*

As the 1960s wore on, however, it became impossible to continue to avoid these difficult issues. Ultimately, the Court not only had to confront continued questions of who was a public official for purposes of *Sullivan* but also tough issues of whether to expand the reach of its actual malice requirement from those officials to "public figures," as well as the challenges of applying that standard to new and different situations. The next round of cases raising these issues, a total of eight in less than four years, provided some answers as well as some insight into Brennan's continuing role in shaping them.

Curtis Publishing Co. v. Butts, Associated Press v. Walker

The issue of expanding the reach of *Sullivan* to persons who were not public officials but who were nevertheless in the public eye first came up during the justices' deliberations in *Rosenblatt v. Baer*, when they received a petition for review in *Curtis Publishing Co. v. Butts*. In both *Rosenblatt* and *Time, Inc. v. Hill*, the Court was able to defer any serious consideration of how to deal with public figures, or "public men," as some of the justices' internal memoranda described them. But as the October 1966 term got under way, the Court could delay no longer. On October 10, 1966, a week before the reargument in *Time, Inc. v. Hill*, they agreed to hear both *Butts* and *Associated Press v. Walker*, another case that appeared to raise the same issue. The cases were argued back-to-back on February 23, 1967, little more than a month after the decision in *Hill* was announced.

In the *Butts* case, the *Saturday Evening Post*, a magazine published by Curtis Publishing Co., had run an article accusing Wally Butts of conspiring to fix a football game in 1962 between the University of Georgia and the University of Alabama. At the time, Butts was the Georgia athletic director and former football coach, widely known in college athletic circles and hoping to land a professional football coaching job. At Georgia, his salary was paid by a private athletic association, not by the state university system, so he was technically not a public official. The magazine's article was based on a telephone call accidentally intercepted by a third party who said he had heard Butts talking to the University of Alabama football coach, Paul "Bear" Bryant. The article reported that the third party, an Atlanta insurance salesman named George Burnett, had overheard Butts sharing with Bryant the plays and strategy that Georgia would use against Alabama in an upcoming game. But at trial, Butts and others testified that the conversation was a general one, and that it included no information of value to Alabama. Nevertheless, the *Post* article concluded, "[t]he chances are that Wally Butts will never help any football team again. . . . A great sport will be permanently damaged. For many people the bloom must pass forever from college football."

Butts sued for libel in federal court in Georgia, asking $5 million in compensa-
tory damages and an additional $5 million in punitive damages. The magazine's main
defense at trial was that the article was substantially true. To prevail on that defense,
the jury was instructed, the *Post* would have to prove that the defamatory sting that
Butts attributed to the article was accurate—that he fixed the Georgia-Alabama
game by sharing plays in a manner intended to give Alabama an advantage. The
jury was also instructed that an award of punitive damages required a finding of
actual malice that, for purposes of Georgia law, could be based on evidence of the
defendant's ill will, spite, reckless indifference, or even negligence.

The jury found in Butts's favor and awarded him $60,000 in compensatory
damages and $3 million in punitive damages. The trial judge reduced the total
award to $460,000. When the decision in *Sullivan* was issued by the Supreme Court,
Curtis Publishing moved for a new trial on the ground that Butts should have
been obliged to prove actual malice as defined by the Supreme Court in that case.
The trial judge, however, denied the motion, concluding both that *Sullivan* was
inapplicable because Butts was not a public official and that there was sufficient
evidence of the magazine's reckless disregard of the article's falsity in any event.

In those days, Georgia was part of the U.S. Court of Appeals for the Fifth Circuit. A three-judge panel of that court ruled two-to-one that Curtis Publishing
could not raise First Amendment-based claims under *Sullivan* because the magazine's lawyers were aware of the constitutional arguments before the Court in
Sullivan during the pendency of Butts's lawsuit and had declined to raise them.
The Fifth Circuit majority even noted that some of the lawyers representing Curtis Publishing had also been assisting the *New York Times* in *Sullivan*. The majority
opinion, written by Judge Adrian Spears, was joined by Judge John Brown. The
panel affirmed the judgment for Butts, finding the compensatory damages consistent with state law and the punitive damages a fair reflection of the jury's sense
of the harm that Butts had sustained. Judge Richard Rives dissented, writing that
the *Sullivan* rule should apply and that its application required that the judgment
in Butts's favor be reversed.

Associated Press v. Walker centered on a news report written by reporter Van Savell
and distributed by the Associated Press (AP). It chronicled events at the University of Mississippi on the night of September 30, 1962, as federal marshals tried
to enforce a court order to have its first African American student, James Mer-
edith, enroll for classes there. The AP report described how retired Army Major

General Edwin Walker, on the campus in his capacity as a private citizen, "assumed command" of an unruly crowd of protesters, urged them to use violence, and led them in a charge on the federal marshals. Walker maintained that he had not "commanded" the crowd and, rather, that he had urged peaceful restraint when he addressed the protesters.

In fact, Walker had been in charge of the federal troops sent by President Eisenhower to help desegregate the schools in Little Rock, Arkansas, in September 1957. But, after leaving the military in 1961, Walker became involved in efforts to resist desegregation and suggested that civil rights demonstrations in some cities had been organized by Communists. After the University of Mississippi riot, Walker was arrested on a federal charge of insurrection, but the charges were dropped after a federal grand jury failed to indict him.

Walker sued the AP in state court in Texas where he lived, seeking $2 million in compensatory and punitive damages. At trial, the jury was instructed that it could award compensatory damages if the story was not substantially true, and punitive damages if it found that the AP was motivated in publishing it by ill will, bad motive, or a lack of care suggesting "conscious indifference" to the subjects of its dispatch. The jury awarded $500,000 in compensatory damages and $300,000 in punitive damages. The trial judge struck the punitive damages, finding that the jury did not have before it sufficient evidence of the kind of actual malice required by state law to support such an award—ill will, bad motive, or a lack of care suggesting conscious indifference.

At the trial, it emerged that there was a discrepancy between the reporter's oral account of what he saw and phoned in to the AP's Atlanta bureau, and the AP dispatch that was ultimately disseminated. The discrepancy involved whether Walker had first addressed the crowd before it marched toward the federal marshals or after it did so. The trial judge concluded this discrepancy was not enough to demonstrate the malice required to justify an award of punitive damages. Nor, the trial judge ruled, was evidence that the AP had assigned a young and relatively inexperienced reporter to cover the story. In addition, the trial judge explained, if *Sullivan* applied, the AP would win the case, but because Walker had retired from the military and was therefore not acting in the capacity of a public official on the day in question, there was no reason to apply the actual malice standard as defined in *Sullivan* in the first place. A Texas appeals court affirmed, agreeing with the trial judge both that *Sullivan* did not apply and that the Texas definition of malice had not been satisfied for purposes of awarding punitive damages. The Texas Supreme Court declined to review the case.

On October 10, 1966, the justices of the U.S. Supreme Court concluded that the time had finally come to confront the reach of *Sullivan*. They granted the petitions for review in both *Butts* and *Walker* and ordered them argued for ninety minutes each in sequence, with *Walker* to go first and *Butts* to follow. According to Brennan's term history, the vote to grant review in *Walker* was unanimous, and the vote to hear *Butts* was eight-to-one, with Justice Clark alone voting otherwise.

At argument, the AP was represented by William P. Rogers, the former attorney general under President Eisenhower and later secretary of state under President Nixon who had served in *Sullivan* as counsel for the four minister defendants. When he addressed the justices at argument, Rogers told them, "this case, I believe, represents one of the most serious attacks ever made on the press in this country. It is but one of the 50 libel cases brought by General Walker against the Associated Press, its members or both. . . . The General has made claims against a significant portion of the press asking for damages totaling more than $33 million." Next, Rogers recounted how Walker had been responsible for a great deal of publicity designed to stir up resistance to desegregation at the University of Mississippi. Given that evidence, Rogers said, "we think that the basic constitutional question is whether the *New York Times* doctrine should be extended to cover people such as General Walker, who thrust themselves into the vortex of a highly involved and inflamed public controversy."

During his argument, Rogers also spent time describing Walker's role during the riot, a recitation of the record evidence that seemed to confuse some of the justices. Justice Fortas, for one, asked Rogers if "whether a man is a public figure for purposes of *New York Times* depends upon what he did . . . ? [I]s this vortex idea . . . an essential part of it [in] the sense that you've got to be part of the violence and commotion of the incident?" No, Rogers replied, "I was making the [separate] argument that the AP dispatches were true." Justice Harlan then asked if a student leader who behaved as Walker had would also be a public figure, to which Rogers responded, "yes, . . . I would think then that [*Sullivan*] would cover him" as well.

Fortas also asked Rogers whether the rule in *Sullivan* would apply to an AP story about Walker's private activities. Rogers responded that the *Sullivan* rule likely would not apply to the private conduct of a public person. But Fortas then asked whether, if an individual, "John Doe," came out of nowhere to be involved in the

events at the University of Mississippi, the *Sullivan* rule would apply to him? To
this question, Rogers replied, "I would hope from the standpoint of the press that
the Court will see fit to go that far," but he hastened to add that the justices did
not need to reach that question in the *Walker* case because of the general's extensive and longstanding involvement in public issues.

As his argument time drew to a close, Rogers and Fortas were still sparring.
Fortas suggested that Rogers was resting everything on the "public official question." Rogers scrambled to say, "I hope that I have not given that impression."
Rather, Rogers said, "I think that I'm pitching my argument here on the facts
in this case because I would like to have the Court rule that the *New York Times*
[rule]. . . extends to Walker."

Clyde J. Watts, an Oklahoma lawyer and military colleague of Walker's, argued his
side of the case and got himself into hot water immediately. He began his presentation by informing the Court that he had known Walker as a classmate and military
colleague for a long time. Justice Black promptly interrupted and said "that hasn't
anything to do with this case." Watts then asserted the issue before the Court was
whether there is "an immunity upon the press in this case [to] falsely . . . accuse
a man of a crime." To this, Justice White responded skeptically, "Is that really the
claim here?" Attempting to regain his footing, Watts contended that the AP report
led directly to Walker's being arrested and charged with a crime. Upon hearing
this, Justice Brennan probed whether there was any effort at the trial "to establish that there was a connection" between the AP report and the criminal charges.
Watts responded only with the fact that Walker had been arrested, adding that the
general had then been sent to a prison mental hospital in Missouri where he was
confined for a few days. The frustration of the justices continued as Justice Clark
asked rhetorically if the Court were hearing a lawsuit against the federal government arising from Walker's arrest and incarceration.

Later in his argument, Watts asserted that the AP was not entitled to receive
First Amendment protection because it was selling a commodity like "other busi-
nessmen who sell food, steel, aluminum or anything else people need or want."
The fact that the AP sold news, Watts contended, should not "afford the publisher
a peculiar constitutional sanctuary in which he can with impunity, violate laws
regulating his business practices." Still later, Watts was questioned at great length by
Justice Black about the reason for Walker's presence at the University that fateful
day. In response, Watts denied that Walker had attempted to encourage resistance to

President Kennedy's order sending federal marshals to enforce desegregation there. But Chief Justice Warren then read a long excerpt from public comments Walker had made before he arrived on campus, at which point he asked what Walker had meant when, in those comments, he urged people to "Rise to stand behind [Mississippi] Governor Ross Barnett," who had led the fight against desegregation in the state. In addition, the chief justice noted, Walker had called for "10,000 strong men" from every state to rally for the cause of freedom in Mississippi. "Isn't that something of a call to arms?" the chief justice asked. When Watts insisted it was not, Brennan picked up on Warren's theme and said, "he was there . . . and this was all going on" and "I just wonder whether that establishes necessarily that the young reporter deliberately lied when he said he led them."

During the argument, there was also substantial debate among the justices and lawyers over whether the AP should have requested an instruction at trial obligating Walker to satisfy the actual malice standard as defined in *Sullivan*. For his part, Rogers suggested during his rebuttal argument that perhaps no such request was made because the trial judge had already said that, while Walker was a public figure, the *Sullivan* rule applied only to public officials. The trial judge, however, had made that assertion in a letter he had written to the lawyers, which Rogers insisted constituted a formal ruling and which Watts maintained was only an advisory statement and not a decision of the trial court.

The argument in the *Butts* case followed immediately. The magazine was represented by Herbert Wechsler, the Columbia Law School professor who had argued on behalf of the *Times* in *Sullivan*. Wechsler, too, had to explain to the justices why no request had been made in the trial court for a jury instruction applying *Sullivan*. His short answer was that the trial had taken place before the Supreme Court's decision, but Wechsler added that "trial counsel representing Curtis, believing in their plea of truth, did not consider that the existing law gave them any claim of constitutional privilege" and did not want to engage in "any legal experimentation in the trial of the case." Turning to the merits of his constitutional argument, Wechsler asserted "that running the athletic operation of a state university" places an individual in a position "where criticism of his official conduct ought to be considered within the scope of the First Amendment and therefore, within the scope of the *New York Times* privilege." Justice Fortas asked if the rule Wechsler advocated would also encompass the quarterback or a substitute off the bench and then suggested that, under Wechsler's theory, there was no limit to application of the *Sullivan* rule. In response, Wechsler conceded that drawing the appropriate line "can be an area of enormous difficulty," but asserted that there were nevertheless limits. "It's less clear to me," Wechsler said, "that the First Amendment is at all concerned with the gossip columns about who slept with whom in what hotel room three nights previously." Nevertheless, Fortas persisted, telling Wechsler that, with the exception of pornography, "the rule that you have just suggested would cover everything that's published."

For Butts, two name partners in an Atlanta firm, Allen Lockerman and William Schroder, divided the argument. Lockerman, who led off, contended that Curtis Publishing had waived the right to raise issues based on *Sullivan*. He contended that lawyers representing the magazine in analogous lawsuits arising from the same article filed by Bear Bryant, the Alabama coach, were the same lawyers who represented the *New York Times* at trial in *Sullivan* and that they knew full well that constitutional arguments were being raised before the U.S. Supreme Court in that case. By failing to raise the same First Amendment issues before the lower courts in the *Butts* case, Lockerman asserted, the lawyers had waived the right to make the arguments for the first time in the Supreme Court. Justice Black asked if *Sullivan* had been decided by the time Lockerman contended the Curtis Publishing lawyers waived their client's First Amendment claims. When Lockerman responded that *Sullivan* had not yet been decided, Black said incredulously, "You are basing your claim for waiver on the ground that they should have anticipated that the Court" might at some time announce new rules for libel cases?

Schroder followed his partner and conceded that, although Butts was not a public official, he was a public figure, whose success as a football coach had made him well known. Moreover, Schroder argued, even assuming the *Sullivan* actual malice standard properly applied as a result, there was sufficient evidence in the trial record that the *Saturday Evening Post* had indeed manifested such a reckless disregard for the truth. In that regard, Schroder described at length what he said were the magazine's questionable reporting practices in putting the story together and outlined for the Court numerous steps he said it could have taken to verify the accuracy of what it reported. Specifically, as Schroder recounted it, the evidence at trial showed that, among other things, the *Post* had relied for its published allegations against Butts and Bryant exclusively on an affidavit procured by its reporter from Burnett, who not only had a criminal record but had provided the affidavit only after having been promised (and eventually paid) $5,000 by the magazine. By

the same token, Schroder told the justices, the magazine had not bothered to ask
for or examine contemporaneous notes that Burnett said he took as he listened to
the two coaches talking; did not interview another man, one Carmichael, who had
been with Burnett at the time and presumably could have confirmed (or rebutted) Burnett's account; did not seek to review film of the allegedly "fixed" game
itself to ascertain if it in fact included the kinds of plays that were purportedly
discussed during the conversation; and did not attempt to interview Butts, Bryant,
or any of the players who had participated in the game for either team, even after
Butts's attorney had sent a letter advising it that Burnett's allegations were false.
And, Schroder said, the Post's failure to take any of these steps was explainable by
its conceded editorial policy of so-called sophisticated muckraking, a quest for
"exposés" that, in Butts's case, would have been upended had it learned information that "might differ from what this fellow put in his affidavit."

On rebuttal, Wechsler argued that, even if Schroder were correct about the facts,
the magazine should nevertheless be allowed to take the case to a jury that has
been properly instructed to apply the correct legal standard—the actual malice
test as set out in Sullivan. Nevertheless, Wechsler also attempted to take issue, in the
few minutes he had remaining, with Schroder's recitation of the facts, asserting for
example that Burnett's notes had not been available to the Post because, according
to Wechsler, the university had taken prior possession of them. As his time expired,
however, Wechsler was constrained simply to call the Court's attention to the specific portions of his brief that addressed the record evidence.

At conference following the arguments, according to Brennan's term history,
the justices were unanimous that the judgment against the Associated Press should
be reversed, but "with little agreement on the grounds." In the Butts case, however,
the Court initially split four-to-four, with Justice Harlan abstaining. Chief Justice
Warren and Justices Clark, Stewart, and Fortas voted to affirm the libel judgment
against Curtis Publishing, while Justices Black, Douglas, Brennan, and White voted
to reverse. At Harlan's request, the cases were held over to be considered again at
the next conference, where Harlan cast the deciding vote against Curtis Publishing. The chief justice assigned both opinions to Harlan, apparently on the theory
that he was in the best position to explain the Court's reasoning in a manner that
would secure his own vote.

What ensued was something of a battle royal within the Court that took no
less than four months to resolve. On May 11, 1967, almost three months after

the arguments, Harlan first circulated a draft opinion, which he introduced with a "prefatory note" that may have unknowingly foreseen the disarray that would come to characterize the Court's effort to resolve the public figure issue in these as well as in future cases. Specifically, Harlan advised his colleagues that his opinion was crafted in an effort to keep the Court in the defamation area from being "divided by the kind of conflicting views that have plagued us in the obscenity area," where the justices had felt themselves constrained to review a large volume of cases applying the constitutional definition of "obscenity" that Brennan had first articulated in *Roth v. United States* to specific books and films. In the libel context, in contrast, Harlan told the other justices that he hoped to put forth a "constitutional rule for 'public interest' libel cases that should be relatively easy to apply in most instances, yet not to put the state and lower federal courts in a straitjacket."

Accordingly, in his initial draft, Harlan proposed a new, First Amendment-driven liability standard to govern defamation actions brought by "public figures," a standard that remained more or less intact in his final opinion. Specifically, Harlan wrote that he "would hold that a 'public figure' who is not a public official may also recover damages for a defamatory falsehood whose substance makes substantial danger to reputation apparent, on a showing of highly unreasonable conduct constituting an extreme departure from the standards of investigation and reporting ordinarily adhered to by responsible publishers." The public figure plaintiff would be obliged to satisfy the more daunting actual malice standard, Harlan wrote, only as a prerequisite to the recovery of punitive damages.

In response, Brennan circulated a four-page partial dissent. In it, he contended that "public men" have the same access to the media to rebut false charges as do public officials and that the actual malice standard should therefore be extended to them as well. Brennan's draft argued that, "[c]onduct and decisions having perhaps critical impact upon the community, and thus of acute interest to its citizens, are not the mantle solely of public office." As a result, Brennan asserted, Harlan's less demanding standard, which made it easier for public men to sue for libel and recover compensatory damages, would lead to precisely the same "chilling effect" on the press that *Sullivan* was intended to prevent. Harlan's new standard, Brennan wrote, constituted a "series of vague and imprecise directives, without any roots in prior law," that will "surely have a stifling effect" on the press. Justice White, who had come to be Brennan's most reliable ally in such matters, also circulated a partial dissent on May 31. In it, he backed Brennan's play. "Without saying so and without offering sound reasons," White complained, "the Court has now retreated from the principles" of *Sullivan* and *Garrison*.

White's draft, however, contained one statement that caused Brennan concern. Specifically, he wrote that, in applying the actual malice standard that they both advocated should govern cases brought by public figures, the necessary "reckless disregard" for the truth had to be based on the "conduct" of a publisher, "not his state of mind." White and Brennan met that same day. At Brennan's request, White agreed to recraft this portion of his opinion in a manner that, as Brennan's term history later described it, "eliminated the negation of 'state of mind' as a basis for 'reckless disregard.'" With that change, which would itself prove to be of great significance in cases to come, Brennan promptly joined White's opinion later that same day, and White, in turn, joined Brennan's.

Justice Harlan, however, just as quickly gained the support of Justices Clark, Stewart, and Fortas for both his opinion and his new liability standard. With Black and Douglas sticking to their view that the First Amendment precluded all defamation actions of the kind instituted by Butts and Walker, without regard to the defendant's conduct or state of mind, it appeared that the chief justice would cast the deciding vote. Accordingly, Brennan discussed the case with Warren on June 1, during what may have been one of their regular weekly private meetings. During their discussion, Brennan discovered that, while Warren was adamant about affirming the verdict for Butts, he was "dissatisfied," as Brennan's term history put it, with Harlan's new liability standard (which Brennan described as a "hodgepodge standard") and preferred to stick with the actual malice rule as set out in *Sullivan*. At about the same time, Douglas informed Brennan that he was prepared to write an opinion, as he had in *Hill*, that would provide a solid five votes for the *Sullivan* standard. But Black refused to do so, saying he would not help facilitate different outcomes in the two cases.

For the next several days, Brennan's term history describes the outcome much like the back-and-forth of a Ping-Pong game, with the chief justice moving from one side of the table to the other and then back again. At the Court's conference on June 2, Warren appeared to waiver in his support for the actual malice standard, telling Harlan that he had not studied his latest draft but that Harlan seemed to have addressed some of his concerns. Then, early the following week, the chief justice told Brennan he planned to write his own opinion, one that embraced the *Sullivan* standard in defamation cases brought by public figures but that affirmed the compensatory damages awarded to Butts under that standard. Warren thereafter wrote to Harlan, essentially turning Harlan's own argument back on him. "[W]hile I agree with your result," Warren explained, "I find it impossible to do so for the reasons you express. I am very much afraid that if we start changing *New York Times v. Sullivan* that we will soon be in the same situation we are in the obscenity cases, if we are not already there." At the same time, Warren shared with Harlan a typed draft of what he proposed to circulate to the other justices, although he apparently did not show it to his close ally, Brennan.

Instead, Warren told Brennan that he would be leaving town the next day to deliver a commencement speech at St. Mary's College in rural Maryland. While Warren was away, the two factions continued to jockey for his support. But, in this race, the critical issue was not who would win the cases themselves—Walker was clearly going to lose and Butts was clearly going to prevail. Rather, the contest was over *Sullivan* and whether it would be extended to libel suits brought by "public men." Warren's proposed opinion, first circulated to the other justices while the chief justice was away, adopted the *Sullivan* standard in such cases in Part I, ruled against Walker in Part II, and for Butts in Part III.

With this development, and while Warren was still out of town, Brennan attempted to consolidate his forces. First, Black was persuaded to agree to join Douglas in a statement supporting the outcome in *Walker*. As in *Hill*, they would engage with Brennan to a sufficient degree to provide him with a majority to extend the reach of *Sullivan*, even though they continued to disagree with his invocation of the actual malice standard. Second, Brennan and White agreed that they would withdraw their separate opinions and simply join Part I of Warren's, thereby creating a five-justice majority, along with Black and Douglas, for applying the *Sullivan* standard in public figure cases. In addition, they would both join Part II of Warren's opinion, reversing the judgment in favor of Walker and against the AP on the ground that the general had not mustered sufficient evidence to satisfy the actual malice requirement. And, finally, they would then write a short, separate dissent in the *Butts* case.

Strategic maneuvering in the Supreme Court is not, however, a one-way street, and the four justices on Harlan's side were also working hard to figure out how to gain Chief Justice Warren's support. In that cause, Fortas tried his hand at drafting a new opinion to be issued in Warren's name that, according to Brennan's narrative account, purported to acknowledge that *Sullivan* articulated the appropriate standard but then had the chief justice describe the Harlan "responsible publisher" construct as merely an "embellishment" of, rather than a substitute for, *Sullivan*'s actual malice requirement. According to Brennan's term history, Fortas actually called Warren while he was at St. Mary's College to propose and describe to him the opinion he had taken the liberty of ghostwriting.

Events then moved very quickly. On June 7, Brennan wrote Warren a two-page letter, advising the Chief that he had discussed the cases with Black and Douglas, that they had written a statement of their views supporting Warren's embrace of the actual malice standard, and suggesting that Warren borrow from the Brennan and White discussions of *Sullivan* in their separate opinions, which they would then join. All of that, Brennan wrote, would yield five votes in *Walker* for an outcome that was based on the *Sullivan* actual malice standard. Once again, Brennan's gambit worked. As Brennan's term history later recounted it, when Warren returned, he rejected the Harlan and Fortas approaches and proceeded to redraft his own opinion to incorporate the unpublished descriptions of the actual malice standard previously crafted by Brennan and White. Referring to the Harlan "responsible publisher" standard and choosing language very close to Brennan's, Warren wrote in his final draft, "I cannot believe that a standard which is based on such an unusual and uncertain formulation could either guide a jury of laymen or afford the protection for speech and debate that is fundamental to our society and guaranteed by the First Amendment."

And Warren similarly incorporated Brennan's draft language extensively in discussing the reasons why public figures must be held to the same liability standard in defamation actions as public officials. Specifically, Warren wrote (the italics are added here to highlight Brennan's words):

> Viewed in this context, then, it is plain that *although they are not subject to the restraints of the political process,* "public figures," *like "public officials," often play an influential role in ordering society.* And *surely as a class* these "public figures" *have as ready access as "public officials" to mass media of communication,* both to influence policy and to counter criticism of their views and activities. Our citizenry has a legitimate and substantial interest in the conduct of such persons, and *freedom of the press to engage in uninhibited debate* about their *involvement in public issues* and events is as crucial as it is in the case of "public officials." The fact that *they are not amenable to the restraints of the political process* only underscores the legitimate and substantial nature of the interest,

since it means *that public opinion may be the only instrument by which society can attempt to influence* their conduct.

Once Warren circulated his new opinion, the final votes fell into place, and the result was somewhat bizarre. In the end, Harlan's decision was labeled as announcing the judgments of the Court in both cases, albeit in an opinion that spoke only for himself, Clark, Stewart, and Fortas. This was immediately followed by a footnote that declared, "Five members of the Court, while concurring in the result" in *Walker* "would rest decision on grounds other than those stated in this opinion." In other words, at the Court's public session on June 12, 1967, Harlan announced only the outcome of the cases—the award of damages reversed and tossed out for Walker, the award of compensatory damages affirmed for Butts.

Brennan, however, had prevailed on the liability standard, which was found within the four corners of Chief Justice Warren's separate opinion. In the end, an overriding concern with consistency and the perceived need to avoid the proliferation of different legal tests was enough to convince a bare majority of the Court to stick with the actual malice standard in defamation cases brought by public figures. Nevertheless, what had previously been the Court's public consensus on such matters had largely disappeared. The five justices who voted for extension of the *Sullivan* standard to public figures really included only two—Brennan and White—who genuinely believed that the actual malice requirement was the constitutionally mandated way to handle libel claims brought by "public men." Chief Justice Warren embraced the actual malice standard with less than complete enthusiasm and, truth be told, largely for the sake of consistency, and Justices Black and Douglas did not embrace it at all other than as a necessary inconvenience on the path to what they hoped would eventually become absolute First Amendment protection for debate about public issues.

There were other aspects of the Court's ultimate disposition of *Butts* and *Walker* that proved noteworthy as well. For one thing, Justice Harlan—effectively speaking on this subject for a majority of the Court—swiftly rejected the notion that the *Post* had waived its right to invoke the constitutional protections crafted in *Sullivan*. In language that would prove useful to those seeking to vindicate their First Amendment rights in other contexts as well, Harlan wrote that the Court would remain skeptical of claims that they had somehow been "waived":

[T]he constitutional protection which Butts contends that Curtis has waived safeguards a freedom which is the "matrix, the indispensable condition, of nearly every
other form of freedom." Where the ultimate effect of sustaining a claim of waiver
might be an imposition on that valued freedom, we are unwilling to find waiver in
circumstances which fall short of being clear and compelling.

For another, the justices' multiple opinions—although difficult to parse—provided
significant insight into the kind of evidence that would constitute the necessary
"clear and convincing" proof of actual malice. Chief Justice Warren's conclusion
that the evidence offered by Butts was sufficient to warrant a finding of liability
under the actual malice standard marked the first time the Court had affirmed
such a finding in an actual case. To be sure, the significance of Warren's evaluation
of the evidence was somewhat obscured at the time, since the four other justices
who joined him in confirming the verdict in Butts's favor had purported to apply
a different, more plaintiff-friendly standard—the "responsible publisher" construct
devised by Justice Harlan. Still, the chief justice undertook to evaluate the record
evidence—largely as described to the justices by Schroder during argument—and
concluded that it demonstrated that the *Post* had published despite a "reckless disregard" for the truth. Warren's evaluation of the record evidence in *Butts* would
become something of a roadmap for defamation plaintiffs in future cases including,
perhaps most notably, the only other case in which the Court would ever affirm
a jury verdict for the plaintiff under the actual malice standard—its 1989 decision
in *Harte-Hanks Communications, Inc. v. Connaughton.*

Finally, the Court's multiple opinions in *Butts* and *Walker* also proved notable for
what they did not contain. Although—as the chief justice took pains to emphasize
in his concurring opinion—a majority of the Court had held that, in addition
to "public officials," "public figures" were now obliged to prove actual malice in
order to recover in a defamation action, none of the justices' several opinions purported to provide a definition of that term. Beyond the fact that it was apparently
obvious to the seven justices that considered it relevant (all of them save Black
and Douglas) that Coach Butts and General Walker both qualified, their opinions
offered at best clues as to how lower courts were supposed to determine whether
a libel plaintiff in a case before them was similarly to be deemed a "public man" or,
presumably, woman. (It is a somewhat curious fact that, in the thirty-odd defamation cases considered on their merits by the Supreme Court since *Sullivan*, only

three of the plaintiffs, the socialite Mary Alice Firestone, the actress Shirley Jones, and the publisher Kathy Keeton, have been women). For his part, Warren limited himself largely to explaining why a distinction between public officials and public figures made little sense. Thus, in the operative portion of his own opinion, the chief justice wrote:

> [I]t is plain that although they are not subject to the restraints of the political process, "public figures," like "public officials," often play an influential role in ordering society. And surely as a class these "public figures" have as ready access as "public officials" to mass media of communication, both to influence policy and to counter criticism of their views and activities. Our citizenry has a legitimate and substantial interest in the conduct of such persons, and freedom of the press to engage in uninhibited debate about their involvement in public issues and events is as crucial as it is in the case of "public officials." The fact that they are not amenable to the restraints of the political process only underscores the legitimate and substantial nature of the interest, since it means that public opinion may be the only instrument by which society can attempt to influence their conduct.

In his own opinion, Justice Harlan touched on some of these same themes, although he too appeared to assume that, when it came to the public figure, the justices, like Justice Stewart in obscenity cases, knew them when they saw them. The most that could reasonably be gleaned from Harlan's opinion was that Butts and Walker both qualified, Butts "by position alone and Walker by his purposeful activity amounting to a thrusting of his personality into the 'vortex' of an important public controversy" (the phrase used by Rogers at argument) such that both of them thereby "commanded sufficient continuing public interest and had sufficient access to the means of counterargument to be able 'to expose through discussion the falsehood and fallacies' of the defamatory statements" published about them. Beyond this, the lower courts were largely on their own, at least for the time being.

After the justices announced their decisions in *Butts* and *Walker*, Tom Clark announced his retirement from the Court, making it possible for his son, Ramsey Clark, to become attorney general. Had Ramsey become head of the Justice Department while his father still sat on the Supreme Court, the senior Clark would have been forced to recuse himself in virtually all cases involving the federal government, a high percentage of the Court's total workload. During their long tenure together, Brennan and Tom Clark had become friends and worked well together, although Clark remained skeptical of the *Sullivan* line of cases down to his last moments on the Court when he sided with Justice Harlan in *Butts*.

Beckley Newspapers Corp. v. Hanks

Five months later, the justices issued another brief, unsigned decision without argument, this one reversing a $5,000 libel judgment for Harold Hanks, the elected court clerk of Raleigh County, West Virginia. Hanks had sued the Beckley Newspapers Corp. for its publication of editorials critical of him in the morning *Post-Herald*, a daily newspaper. He particularly objected to the newspaper's commentary, published during his bid for reelection in 1962, that he and the president of the county board of health, Elinor Hurt, were opposed to fluoridation of the water supply. The editorial said, in relevant part, "[t]he only conclusion to which we can come is that either Hanks and Mrs. Hurt have been in league toward the fanatic end, believing all the wild-eyed ravings against fluoridation despite decades of experience to disprove them, or that perhaps his blustering threats were able to intimidate the lady."

The newspaper appealed the jury award to the U.S. Supreme Court after the West Virginia Court of Appeals declined to consider it. On November 6, 1967, in a single stroke, the justices summarily granted the petition for review and reversed the West Virginia court's judgment, finding that there was not sufficiently clear evidence of actual malice to warrant presenting the issue to the jury in the first place. The Supreme Court's unsigned opinion explained that any failure by the newspaper to investigate its charges did not rise to the requisite level of convincingly clear evidence of reckless disregard for the truth.

The vote was unanimous, with Justices Black and Douglas once again adding a brief paragraph that signified their agreement with the Court's result but explained their view that criticism of public officials cannot be the basis for defamation liability whether or not the publisher was in some sense "reckless." Justice Brennan's files contain no paper trail revealing who wrote the Court's *per curiam* decision or whether the justices' unanimity in the result required any negotiation to achieve. Since the short opinion relies heavily on *Sullivan* and *Garrison*, however, it seems a good bet that Warren would have again turned to Brennan to memorialize the Court's decision in writing.

Although *Beckley Newspapers* has proven to be a rarely cited case of minimal consequence in the development of the Court's post-*Sullivan* jurisprudence, it nevertheless was the product of one extremely significant development—the case marked the first defamation action decided by the Court after Justice Clark left the bench and was replaced by Thurgood Marshall, the legendary civil rights lawyer who had argued *Brown v. Board of Education* and led the fight to desegregate the nation's schools and other public facilities. Marshall had most recently served as a judge on the U.S. Court of Appeals for the Second Circuit and then as solicitor general in the Department of Justice. He joined the Court in October 1967 and would quickly prove to be Brennan's reliable ally across the broad spectrum of controversial cases to come before the Court in the almost quarter century they served together. As Brennan would soon learn, however, Marshall had his own mind when it came to First Amendment restrictions on the reach of the law of defamation and would, in relatively short order, have ample opportunity to express it.

St. Amant v. Thompson

At the justices' conference on January 12, 1968, they were near unanimous in deciding to grant review in *St. Amant v. Thompson*. According to Brennan's count, Justice Stewart was alone in voting not to hear the case. As it turned out, *St. Amant* provided the justices with their first real opportunity to attempt to clear up some of the confusion resulting from their multiple opinions in *Butts* and *Walker* and to shed some light on the meaning of the actual malice standard they had created in *Sullivan*.

Phil St. Amant was a candidate for the United States Senate in the 1962 Louisiana Democratic primary, running against incumbent Senator Russell Long. On June 27, 1962, St. Amant appeared on a Baton Rouge television station, WAFB, where he alleged wrongdoing by the local Teamsters Union head, E.G. Partin, who in turn was said to be connected to Senator Long. In his television appearance, St. Amant read from an affidavit prepared by J.D. Albin, a former Teamster, in which Albin charged that the union local had tried to block a criminal investigation by secreting a safe that contained incriminating documents. The relevant portions of Albin's affidavit, which St. Amant read on the air, asserted it was difficult to know how to stop Partin from hiding the safe because he had close ties to local law enforcement through Captain Herman Thompson of the East Baton Rouge Parish Sheriff's office. The affidavit also alleged that money "had passed hands" from Partin to Thompson. Thompson would later say he visited the Teamsters local to collect contributions for charitable events.

Thompson sued St. Amant for defamation, seeking $150,000 in damages. After a nonjury trial in May 1964, some two months after the Supreme Court's decision in *Sullivan*, a Louisiana court entered a judgment of liability in favor of Thompson and awarded him $5,000. St. Amant's lawyer asked the trial judge to reconsider the verdict in light of *Sullivan* and its newly minted actual malice requirement, but the judge denied the request, ruling that St. Amant's statements had been made with the requisite actual malice in any event. In a unanimous ruling in February 1966, an appeals court determined the trial judge had misunderstood and therefore misapplied the actual malice standard:

> The statement of the Trial Judge that Mr. St. Amant did not have any interest in Captain Thompson and did not know what the money was for, which the Judge said is evidence that he made no attempt to investigate whether his statements were true in order to justify his charge that Captain Thompson was being paid off and that he gave no consideration as to what effect the remarks might have on Captain Thompson's reputation and character but was content to let the public draw whatever inference it desired, would not place the case under the *New York Times* rule of proving he acted with reckless and wanton disregard for whether the statement was false or not.

One year later, the Louisiana Supreme Court reversed, albeit over two dissents. The state's highest court conceded that Thompson was a public official because the public would perceive that he had authority over government affairs. Nevertheless, it held that St. Amant had made the defamatory statement about Thompson with actual malice; his reckless disregard for truth or falsity, the court said, was manifested by his reliance on and reading of the Albin affidavit without first undertaking any investigation to determine whether Albin's statements were true or reliable. One dissenting judge simply wrote a one-sentence opinion asserting that the appeals court had gotten it right. But the other, Justice E. Howard McCaleb, wrote a longer opinion allowing that St. Amant's reliance on the affidavit might have been negligent, but stressing that the actual malice standard as set out in *Sullivan* required more:

[T]he majority opinion, in holding St. Amant liable for damages, deduces that the alleged defamatory remarks concerning Thompson were uttered by St. Amant with "a reckless disregard as to whether the statements concerning Thompson were true or not." In reaching this conclusion the majority feels that St. Amant could not rely on the verity of the statements of fact contained in the affidavit; that it was incumbent on him to make an investigation of the truth of the statements before publication; and that his failure to do so renders him liable as he necessarily utters the defamatory statement with reckless disregard of its truth or falsity. This pronouncement effectually implies malice for it places ignorance of falsity on a parity with knowledge of falsity and in the same category with actual malice by holding that failure to make an independent investigation of truth constitutes a reckless disregard of truth or falsity. But this is exactly contrary to the view of the United States Supreme Court in the *New York Times* case.

Once the case reached the U.S. Supreme Court, it was decided with remarkable speed. It was heard on April 4, 1968, and the decision was issued on April 29, barely three weeks later. At the argument, Justice White was the most active of the justices in questioning St. Amant's lawyer, Russell Schonekas of New Orleans. During his presentation, Schonekas emphasized that St. Amant knew Albin personally. To this, Justice White skeptically observed, "so . . . anybody who gets an affidavit from anybody else with scandalous charges in it about a third person may publish it . . . freely?" Schonekas replied that "the burden is upon the party that brings the suit to show that they acted with malice." Still, White persisted, responding "well, I know but the party who brings the suits says this does amount to reckless disregard when all you've done is taken an affidavit from some person, this contains a scandalous charge." Justice Brennan stepped in a few minutes later to try to synthesize the issue, saying, "I guess this really for us narrows down to the single question whether there was evidence upon which there could have been—a finding . . . that this was done with reckless disregard of whether it was true or false."

Robert Kleinpeter, a Baton Rouge attorney, argued the case for Thompson. In his first opportunity to question a lawyer appearing before the Court in a defamation action, Justice Marshall asked whether the trial judge had relied on *Sullivan*. Kleinpeter said he had, which led Brennan to ask, "is there anything for us to decide but whether this evidence is sufficient to satisfy the *New York Times* test?" Kleinpeter replied that he did not concede that Thompson, a police captain, was a public official in the first instance. Upon hearing that, White interjected, "but your Supreme Court said he was a public official for the *New York Times* purposes." In response, Kleinpeter conceded that the elected sheriff would be a public official, but argued that all of the officers below the sheriff, including Thompson, should not be so characterized.

For his part, Justice Black seemed surprised that a police captain would not be considered a public official, and his skepticism with respect to Kleinpeter's contention led Brennan to add, "well, isn't a captain of the uniform police at least a public man?" To this, Kleinpeter replied, "I guess he's a public man just like a lawyer would be sir." Brennan then countered, "well, if he is, didn't in the *Butts* cases, didn't we apply the *New York Times* test to the public man as well as to the public official?" Kleinpeter acknowledged that was true, but reminded Brennan that the Court had upheld the verdict for Butts. At this juncture, Justice Marshall sparred with Kleinpeter about his position that only the elected sheriff and not his appointed deputies could be public officials. "You surely don't mean that," Marshall said. Kleinpeter conceded there were others who were higher ranked than a captain who would fit the description of a public official contemplated by *Sullivan*. And, in an apparent if misguided effort to punctuate his point, Kleinpeter added, "this man is a close friend . . . a neighbor, a drinking buddy and everything else. And I just never considered him a public official."

At the conference, the outcome appeared at first to be somewhat uncertain. Chief Justice Warren seemed perturbed by St. Amant's conduct and his lawyer's defense of it. According to notes taken by Justice Douglas, Warren gave a "qualified answer." Specifically, Douglas's notes show Warren saying only that St. Amant's "lawyer said does the record show this was false or reckless? He has not read the record." Brennan's vote chart, however, lists the chief justice as voting to reverse. Not surprisingly, Black and Douglas voted to reverse as well. Harlan also voted to reverse saying, according to Douglas's notes, that the Louisiana Supreme Court had "misconstrue[d]" *Sullivan* and had therefore "applied wrong standard of review." Justice Stewart reportedly "agreed with" Harlan and, as Douglas recorded his views, asserted that a public official "must show that there was malice" and the Louisiana Supreme Court had "put burden of proof on [the] wrong party." Stewart further suggested that the Court might reverse in another unsigned *per curiam* opinion, as it had done in *Henry v. Collins* and *Beckley Newspapers Corp. v. Hanks*.

When it came his turn to speak, Justice White reportedly echoed Stewart's views, asserting that the Louisiana Supreme had wrongly determined that recklessness "might be proved merely from what [St. Amant] said or from failure to inquire," but "on these facts, [the] *Times* case was not satisfied." Douglas's notes further indicate that Marshall also voted to reverse and that Fortas provided the lone vote to affirm. Brennan's own vote log shows the outcome as eight-to-one to reverse. Warren assigned the opinion to White, Brennan's steady ally in such matters.

The speed with which the case was decided suggests there was little negotiation or change in the opinions and, indeed, Brennan's files contain no evidence of internal horse-trading or multiple drafts. On April 29, less than a month after the argument, the justices announced their decision reversing the Louisiana Supreme Court and used the opportunity to instruct lower courts and future litigants about the meaning of the actual malice requirement that they had adopted in cases brought by public officials in *Sullivan* and extended, albeit in a muddled and often confusing manner in *Butts* and *Walker*, to public figures. Despite the flurry of questions about it posed at argument, White's opinion for the Court spent virtually no time addressing the issue of whether Thompson was properly classified as a public official; it merely "accepted" the Louisiana Supreme Court's conclusion in that regard and proceeded to address the pivotal issue of actual malice.

In that regard, no doubt drawing on his meeting with Brennan during the Court's deliberations in *Butts*, when Brennan persuaded him to amend his description of actual malice as a concept premised on the defendant's "conduct" rather than his "state of mind," White wrote that actual malice must be proven through evidence that the defendant "in fact entertained serious doubts" about the truth of a defamatory statement but chose to publish it anyway. With this, White left no doubt that actual malice is a subjective standard designed to ferret out the "calculated falsehood," not an objective assessment of highly unreasonable conduct of the kind Harlan had advocated in *Butts*. Relying on Brennan's unveiling of the actual malice concept in *Sullivan* and his later description of it in *Garrison* as requiring a showing of the defendant's "high degree of awareness" of probable falsity, as well as Warren's pivotal concurring opinion in *Butts*, White wrote:

> These cases are clear that reckless conduct is not measured by whether a reasonably prudent man would have published, or would have investigated before publishing. There must be sufficient evidence to permit the conclusion that the defendant in fact

entertained serious doubts as to the truth of his publication. Publishing with such doubts shows reckless disregard for truth or falsity and demonstrates actual malice.

In this manner, White's opinion made it appear as if this approach was a foregone conclusion from the cases he cited, specifically *Garrison* and *Butts*. But, in reality, his *St. Amant* opinion significantly advanced and solidified the notion that a finding of actual malice requires clear and convincing evidence that the defendant had serious, subjective doubts about the truth of the alleged defamation. There is little question that White understood the crucial significance of this conclusion. In another portion of the opinion, he explained:

> It may be said that such a test puts a premium on ignorance, encourages the irresponsible publisher not to inquire, and permits the issue to be determined by the defendant's testimony that he published the statement in good faith and unaware of its probable falsity. Concededly the reckless disregard standard may permit recovery in fewer situations than would a rule that publishers must satisfy the standard of the reasonable man or the prudent publisher.

By the same token, White's opinion recognized the difficulties a plaintiff would necessarily face in securing evidence of a defendant's subjective state of mind, especially proof sufficient to constitute the kind of clear and convincing evidence that Brennan had demanded in *Sullivan*. Thus, White offered the following guidance, which would prove—as he no doubt hoped it would—critical to the lower courts in applying the actual malice standard in the years to come:

> The defendant in a defamation action brought by a public official cannot, however, automatically insure a favorable verdict by testifying that he published with a belief that the statements were true. The finder of fact must determine whether the publication was indeed made in good faith. Professions of good faith will be unlikely to prove persuasive, for example, where a story is fabricated by the defendant, is the product of his imagination, or is based wholly on an unverified anonymous telephone call. Nor will they be likely to prevail when the publisher's allegations are so inherently improbable that only a reckless man would have put them in circulation. Likewise, recklessness may be found where there are obvious reasons to doubt the veracity of the informant or the accuracy of his reports.

As had become their custom, Justices Black and Douglas joined only the Court's judgment to reverse the verdict. In a one-paragraph statement citing their analogous opinions in *Sullivan* and *Garrison*, the two justices made clear that they did not endorse White's reasoning and wanted no part of the actual malice requirement. Still, since there were otherwise six votes for White's opinion, there was no need for the two aging absolutists to join White's opinion as they had been obliged to do to give Brennan a majority in earlier cases.

Alone in dissent, Justice Fortas wrote a short opinion contending that, in his view, *Sullivan* required St. Amant to check the veracity of the affidavit before reading from it on television. In a strong statement of his ongoing disagreement with Brennan and White over the meaning and legacy of *Sullivan* as well as his mounting frustration over his inability to stem the tide of its expansion, Fortas wrote:

> The First Amendment is not so fragile that it requires us to immunize this kind of reckless, destructive invasion of the life, even of public officials, heedless of their interests and sensitivities. The First Amendment is not a shelter for the character assassinator, whether his action is heedless and reckless or deliberate. The First Amendment does not require that we license shotgun attacks on public officials in virtually unlimited open season. The occupation of public officeholder does not forfeit one's membership in the human race. The public official should be subject to severe scrutiny and to free and open criticism. But if he is needlessly, heedlessly, falsely accused of crime, he should have a remedy in law.

At the time he wrote those words, both Fortas and his colleagues were unaware that he would never again have the opportunity to engage them in this debate or that, to a significant extent, the kind of "severe scrutiny and . . . free and open criticism" about which he had written in *St. Amant* would prove to be the reason.

Greenbelt Cooperative Publishing Association v. Bresler

Despite the substantial effort the Court had devoted to explaining the contours of actual malice in *St. Amant*, only a few months elapsed before the justices turned their attention to it once again. On October 20, 1969, the Court granted review in *Greenbelt Cooperative Publishing Association v. Bresler*. According to the notes Justice

Douglas recorded at the Court's conference, the vote to hear the case was unanimous. In fact, the vote was 8–0. That was because, barely six months after the Court announced its decision in *St. Amant*, Abe Fortas resigned as an associate justice of the Supreme Court.

The series of events that led to Fortas's resignation were both complicated and, in the world of the U.S. Supreme Court, unprecedented. With the 1968 presidential election looming, Lyndon Johnson having decided not to seek a second full term, and his longtime nemesis Richard Nixon the presumptive Republican nominee, Earl Warren decided to retire from the Court in June of that year and thereby afford Johnson, rather than Nixon, the opportunity to appoint his successor. Johnson wasted little time announcing his decision to nominate Fortas as the Court's next chief justice and Homer Thornberry, an old Texas friend of the President and a well-regarded federal judge, to succeed Fortas. To put it mildly, things did not work out as Warren, Johnson, and Fortas had planned. First, with only a few months left in his presidency, Johnson underestimated the extent to which his lame duck status would embolden those in the Senate who had long been hostile to "the Warren Court." They mounted a successful filibuster of the Fortas nomination, which, in October 1968, caused the justice to ask Johnson to withdraw his nomination. As a practical matter, that meant that Nixon, who was elected President the following month, would be responsible for appointing Warren's successor as chief justice. Then, to add insult to injury, news reports began to surface about questionable financial dealings between Fortas and Louis Wolfson, a Las Vegas financier and industrialist who had twice been indicted. Ironically, the story chronicling the Fortas-Wolfson connection was broken by *Life* magazine, the publication that Fortas had excoriated in his never published and ill-fated majority opinion in *Time, Inc. v. Hill*, which was itself written in support of now-President Nixon's client, James Hill. In the end, Fortas had no choice but to resign from the Court entirely, which he did on May 14, 1969. As a result, in office barely four months, Nixon had been afforded the opportunity to fill two vacancies on the nation's highest court.

At first blush, Fortas's departure appeared to bode well for Brennan's ongoing efforts within the Court to strengthen and expand the reach of *Sullivan*. After all, Fortas had been a consistent and vehement opponent, Marshall—a likely ally— had only recently replaced Clark, another frequent critic, and, at least until Nixon nominated and the Senate confirmed a successor, Warren—who had most recently

provided the fifth vote for extension of the actual malice standard to public figures in *Butts*—continued to serve as chief. Any cause for optimism on this score,
however, proved to be short lived. In June 1969, four months before the Court
considered the petition for review in *Bresler*, Warren Burger replaced Earl Warren
as chief justice.

The record shows that Warren was never a huge fan of the *Sullivan* line of cases,
but he was a fairly consistent supporter of Brennan's decisions. Warren was also
Brennan's close friend and mentor, and the two enjoyed a special bond of colle-
giality and cooperation. Brennan would not develop the same relationship with
Burger, with whom he had sparred over criminal procedure issues and the rights
of criminal defendants at judicial seminars when Burger was a judge of the U.S.
Court of Appeals for the District of Columbia Circuit. Burger would also prove
much more conservative than Warren, much more imperious in his performance
of the job of chief justice, and much more antagonistic in his views of the press
generally and of *Sullivan* specifically. At least at the outset, however, the departure
of Warren and Fortas, along with the arrival of the new chief justice, appeared to
solidify the Court's support for Brennan's agenda with respect to *Sullivan*.

Harry Blackmun, another federal appellate judge and an old friend of the new
chief justice from their native Minnesota, would eventually be appointed to take
Fortas's seat. He would not, however, take his oath until June 1970, leaving the
Court that decided *Bresler* with only eight members. The delay in Blackmun's confirmation was the result of what, with the successful filibuster of Fortas's nomination
as chief justice, was to become an increasingly politicized process of appointing
and confirming Supreme Court justices. Before confirming Blackmun, the Senate
had rejected two other nominees proffered by President Nixon. A third, respected
Virginia attorney Lewis Powell, had rebuffed Nixon's overtures that he consent to
be the nominee. Two years later, as it turned out, Powell would change his mind
and join the Court. Of all of the machinations that altered the composition of the
Supreme Court in the relatively brief period following Warren's announcement of
his retirement in 1968, for purposes of *New York Times Co. v. Sullivan*, the elevation
of Lewis Powell would prove to be the most significant.

In the fall of 1969, however, as the then eight-member Court turned its attention to *Greenbelt Cooperative Publishing Association v. Bresler*, none of that was, or
could have been, on Brennan's radar screen. The Supreme Court's decision in *Bresler*
arose in the context of a lawsuit against the publisher of the *Greenbelt News Review*,

a weekly newspaper serving the city of Greenbelt, Maryland, northeast of Washington, D.C. The newspaper had written a series of stories about a zoning dispute in 1965 between developer Charles Bresler and Greenbelt city officials. According to court opinions and news accounts, Bresler owned two sizeable parcels of land totaling about 230 acres on which he wanted the zoning changed to allow for more high-density residential development. Some community groups were opposed to the change and objected that it would alter the residential character of the Greenbelt community. At the same time, Greenbelt officials wanted to build a new high school and were trying to purchase land from Bresler to use as the site.

On October 14, 1965, the *News Review* reported that Bresler had agreed to sell the land for the school if the city would agree to rezone his other parcels. Otherwise, the newspaper reported, Bresler had threatened to hold up construction of the school through litigation. The news account included reaction to Bresler's negotiating tactics expressed by those present at a city council meeting, appearing under a subheadline that read, "Blackmail." The article proceeded to quote citizens and councilmembers, one of whom had said at the meeting that Bresler's threat to delay the school land sale was a "slight case of blackmail," while another referred to Bresler's "blackmail scheme." A letter to the editor published the same day urged the city council to reject the "unethical trade."

A week later, the *News Review* published another article, this one reporting the city council's decision to reject any deal with Bresler and the debate at the meeting that preceded that vote. One speaker, according to the news story, referred to the "skullduggery" then taking place and urged the council to "fight Bresler's blackmail." Another speaker was quoted as saying it was not blackmail but rather Bresler's right to develop his property. That same day, the newspaper ran an editorial critical of unnamed developers who do not care how they achieve their goals. There were several subsequent articles and letters to the editor published in the newspaper during the first half of 1966, including a story that Bresler was expected to announce his candidacy for Maryland state comptroller and that he faced lawsuits by the city of Greenbelt and by some homeowners.

Bresler sued the weekly newspaper for libel in July 1966, seeking $1 million each for compensatory and punitive damages. He alleged that the *News Review* had published defamatory stories about him with malice, had subjected him to scorn and hatred, and had imputed to him moral turpitude, fraud, and corrupt motives. After a trial, Bresler was awarded $5,000 in compensatory damages and $12,500 in punitive damages.

The Maryland Court of Appeals, the state's highest court, took an approach to the case that reflected the skepticism in many states about the Supreme Court's constitutionalization of libel law. Specifically, the Maryland court felt compelled to set forth at some length why, purely as a matter of state law, the newspaper would be liable before turning to whether its defamation of Bresler was nevertheless excused by *Sullivan* in the name of the First Amendment. The court of appeals unanimous ruling analyzed at great length Maryland's defamation laws and the history of their invocation, concluding that there was "little doubt that under the Maryland law, apart from the federal constitutional protections which the appellants allege apply, the jury's verdict and subsequent judgment thereon would be held to be supported by the evidence and affirmed." Turning to the aforementioned "federal constitutional protections," the Maryland court said it doubted that Bresler was either a public official or a public figure, despite the fact that he was an elected member of the Maryland House of Delegates, but noted that it did not have to decide the issue because Bresler's lawyer had conceded at trial that his client was required to prove actual malice as defined in *Sullivan*.

As for the arguments actually advanced by the *News Review*, the Maryland court rejected, as a matter of state law, the newspaper's assertion of a "fair report privilege"—a claim by the newspaper that it was privileged to report accurately on what transpired at the city council meetings, even if what was said there turned out to be false. "It is doubtful that there is any privilege of reporting, as items of news, the proceedings at a public meeting of a City Council, as contrasted with the publishing of an official report of the City Council itself," the Maryland Court of Appeals wrote. Even if there were such a privilege, the court added, the city council was not considering whether Bresler had committed the crime of "blackmail" and the newspaper therefore enjoyed no privilege to disseminate those comments, much less to use the word "blackmail" as a subheadline.

Turning to the First Amendment, the appeals court determined that the newspaper had published the "blackmail" allegation with actual malice because the speakers quoted in its news stories had not used the term in the legal sense of a criminal act and that the newspaper knew this to be the case but proceeded to publish what the court characterized as the false accusation that Bresler had engaged in criminal conduct nonetheless. In addition, the appeals court noted, there was evidence that, in publishing its articles, the newspaper intended to injure Bresler's reputation.

At the argument in February 1970, the seat formerly held by Justice Fortas remained empty. Roger Clark, a Washington lawyer, argued for the newspaper that there was no evidence to suggest anyone would read the articles as actually charging Bresler with the crime of blackmail. "You can't establish falsity much less knowing falsity by taking a word out of context and ascribing . . . to it a meaning that is wholly different from that which . . . its context dictates," Clark asserted. Chief Justice Burger then asked, "are you saying that read as a whole, the articles say in effect that Bresler was engaging in high pressure tactics to force the city to do something he wanted done?" To this, Clark replied, "that's exactly right and the use of the word blackmail to characterize that is no more strong and intemperate than you see every day in major metropolitan newspapers, responsible newspapers." Clark also argued that the trial judge's instructions —which permitted the jury to base a finding of actual malice on the defendant's "ill will" and to infer it from the "language used"—were flawed because they did not reflect the definition of actual malice contained in *Sullivan, Garrison,* and *St. Amant,* but he added, "I don't emphasize here these erroneous instructions because as I've pointed out, the three articles upon which the court relied, are clearly insufficient as a matter of law to permit recovery under the *New York Times* rule."

Arguing for Bresler, Abraham Chasanow, a Greenbelt lawyer, contended the case was about more than the word *blackmail.* He pointed out, for example, that one reporter testified that her editors had inserted the word *skullduggery* into one of her stories. Justice Brennan then asked Chasanow if Bresler conceded that he had the burden of proving actual malice. When Chasanow replied that he had indeed conceded that point, Brennan pressed the question again. This time, Chasanow raised what he described as an unsettled issue of law and asserted that none of the newspaper's coverage of Bresler referred to his official conduct as a member of the Maryland House of Delegates. Chasanow's implication seemed to be that, while Bresler might be a public official in his capacity as an elected representative, the alleged defamation was about his role as a private land developer which, he contended, should not trigger application of the *Sullivan* rule. The new chief justice seemed skeptical:

Chief Justice Burger: Must they identify him each time by his office in order to bring themselves under the *Times* and *Sullivan* rule?

Chasanow: No sir, I say this because normally, reference is made to official conduct which has to identify the official. This case has nothing to do with official conduct....

Justices White and Brennan then engaged in some serious sparring with Chasanow as well:

Justice White: Well, are you arguing here—you're arguing here then that even if these instructions don't pass muster under *New York Times* or even if the evidence is insufficient to prove malice under *New York Times* that you're nevertheless home free on a non-*New York Times* basis because this isn't a *New York Times* case, is that your position—

Chasanow: I think that would be one aspect in view of the fact that there are—

Justice Brennan: Well, if it's not a *New York Times* case, then actually that principle doesn't apply and is there anything that this Court's ever said what the federal constitution does about a state's libel action? If he's not either a public official or a public figure, why is the case here at all?

Chasanow: Well, that's a question I asked. Now, let me say this . . .

Justice White: Well, then do you concede that the *New York Times* rules apply to him?

Chasanow: I don't think it would apply to this entire case Mr. Justice White for this reason.

Justice White: Well, it's only one case, one figure?

Chasanow: Yes sir. But I'm saying that there are some of these libels which had no application whatsoever to—his activities as a public figure. For example, the accusations that there had been suits filed against him for violation of county building standards. This had nothing—this was a private enterprise, this had nothing to do with the public issue with—which they were emphasizing land and zoning and we think that it would be carrying the public figure concept too far....

Justice Brennan: But you certainly made no objection—

Chasanow: No sir.

Justice Brennan: —as I read the instructions correctly.

The written record that Brennan maintained of what took place inside the Court in the *Bresler* case is thin. At conference, the justices voted to reverse the Maryland Court of Appeals, and Chief Justice Burger assigned the opinion to Justice Stewart. The chief justice, according to Justice Douglas's notes, said there was insufficient evidence for a jury to find liability. Black and Douglas both voted to reverse as well. Harlan, as Douglas recounted his views, said Bresler was a "public figure or official," and agreed with Burger that there was not enough evidence of actual malice to support the jury's verdict. Brennan too agreed with Burger, while Stewart added that Bresler had conceded that he was a public figure. According to Douglas's notes, White noted that charging blackmail "if used in a criminal sense might be actionable," and added that proper jury instructions might have allowed the jury to make that finding. But, he concluded, the instructions that were actually given did not put that critical question to the jurors and, in effect, allowed them to rule for Bresler without finding that the newspaper had published a false statement of fact about him in the first place. According to Douglas's notes, Justice Marshall also voted to reverse.

Despite what appeared to be unanimity at conference, when Stewart circulated his draft opinion to his fellow justices, Brennan quickly became alarmed. Stewart's draft seemed to Brennan to suggest that the appropriate liability rule in defamation actions brought by public figures was the one advocated by Justice Harlan in *Butts*, a standard that was less protective of the press and that imposed a considerably lighter burden on libel plaintiffs than *New York Times Co. v. Sullivan*. Specifically, Stewart's draft both indicated that the liability standard in cases brought by public figures remained an open question and quoted favorably the "responsible publisher" standard that Harlan had advocated in *Butts*. That standard, Brennan knew, had been rejected by five justices in *Butts* in favor of application of the *Sullivan* actual malice rule in cases brought by public figures. In April, therefore, Brennan circulated a draft one-page opinion. In it, Brennan wrote:

> I disagree with the implication in the Court's opinion that my Brother HARLAN's suggested constitutional restriction in ... *Butts* ... upon libel suits brought by "public figures" constitutes an acceptable standard. A Court of Chief Justice Warren, MR. JUSTICE BLACK, MR. JUSTICE DOUGLAS, MR. JUSTICE WHITE, and I expressly rejected that standard in *Butts* and held that the constitutional restriction upon libel suits brought by "public officials" also applied to such suits brought by "public figures." ... Therefore,

while I join in the judgment of reversal and remand, and join the Court's opinion
in all other respects, I dissent from such implication.

Justice Harlan, too, had concerns about Stewart's opinion, albeit different ones
than motivated Brennan. As Harlan saw it, Stewart was proposing to decide issues
that the Court did not need to reach. Foreshadowing an approach that Brennan
would raise two years later and with which the Court would struggle thereafter,
Harlan wrote in his own brief, concurring paragraph:

> I join the Court's opinion, except for that portion . . . which suggests that libel suits
> arising out of discussions of political issues, but not involving as parties any "public
> official" or "public figure," are subject to some special kind of constitutional limita-
> tions, as yet undefined. No such question need be decided in this case, and I would
> reserve any pronouncements or intimations upon it for a case in which such a ques-
> tion must be addressed.

On April 23, 1970, Stewart wrote to his colleagues that he had "restructured this
opinion somewhat" to address the concerns raised by both Brennan and Harlan.
In his new draft, Stewart removed the specific references to Harlan's responsible
publisher standard to which Brennan had objected and modified another passage
to make clear that the "constitutional prohibition" on basing liability on evidence
of ill will "is no different whether the plaintiff be considered a 'public official' or a
'public figure.'" In addition, Stewart moved the location of one paragraph, which
both described the subject matter of the challenged articles as "reports of public
meetings of the citizens of a community concerned with matters of local governmental interest and importance" and asserted that such reports were "of particular
First Amendment concern," in a manner designed to address Harlan's objection
that he was thereby extending application of the actual malice standard to all such
reports. Harlan quickly accepted Stewart's revised draft and withdrew his separate
concurring opinion. On May 12, Brennan similarly advised Stewart that he too
would withdraw his separate opinion.

That left Black and Douglas to write their separate opinion concurring only
in the judgment. Justice White also wrote separately to say that his agreement was
limited to Stewart's recognition that the trial court's erroneous jury instructions
regarding actual malice required reversal. Specifically, White rejected Stewart's

suggestion that the word *blackmail*, as it appeared in the articles, could not be understood by a reasonable person to be an allegation that Bresler had engaged in criminal conduct.

In the end, Stewart's opinion for the Court, issued on May 18, 1970, reinforced the applicability of the *Sullivan* standard in defamation suits brought by public figures, as well as public officials, and emphasized yet again that, to satisfy the First Amendment, a finding of actual malice cannot be based solely on either evidence of a publisher's ill will, spite, and intent to harm or on an inference drawn from the words used in a news story. The opinion also planted the seeds of two additional concepts that would prove significant in later years. First, despite White's resistance on this score, Stewart's opinion ventured beyond the actual malice standard to indicate that, separate and apart from that constitutional requirement, the judgment in favor of Bresler could not stand for a different reason—the First Amendment precluded defamation liability based on the article's use of the word *blackmail*, which the Court's majority described as a kind of "rhetorical hyperbole" that a reasonable reader would not understand to be an assertion of fact capable of being proven false. As Stewart explained in the portion of his opinion that White declined to join:

> It is simply impossible to believe that a reader who reached the word "blackmail" in either article would not have understood exactly what was meant: it was Bresler's public and wholly legal negotiating proposals that were being criticized. No reader could have thought that either the speakers at the meetings or the newspaper articles reporting their words were charging Bresler with the commission of a criminal offense. On the contrary, even the most careless reader must have perceived that the word was no more than rhetorical hyperbole, a vigorous epithet used by those who considered Bresler's negotiating position extremely unreasonable. Indeed, the record is completely devoid of evidence that anyone in the city of Greenbelt or anywhere else thought Bresler had been charged with a crime.
>
> To permit the infliction of financial liability upon the petitioners for publishing these two news articles would subvert the most fundamental meaning of a free press, protected by the First and Fourteenth Amendments.

More than two decades later, this aspect of the Court's decision in *Bresler* would play a pivotal role in its resolution of the final defamation case on which Brennan would sit as a justice of the Supreme Court.

Second, the Court's opinion in *Bresler* also hinted at the existence of First Amendment protection for accurate reporting on what transpires at public meetings like the Greenbelt city council sessions described in the news accounts before the Court in that case. As Stewart's opinion explained, "[t]he Greenbelt News Review was performing its wholly legitimate function as a community newspaper when it published full reports of these public debates in its news columns." Brennan could not have said it any better. Indeed, he would not have to wait long to observe the significance of that observation. Within five years, the Court would embrace this notion afresh in the context of news reporting about what transpires during the course of judicial proceedings.

Monitor Patriot Co. v. Roy, Time, Inc. v. Pape, and Ocala Star-Banner Co. v. Damron

By the time the Court decided *Bresler*, the justices had already assured that its remarkable and seemingly endless litany of libel cases would continue. On February 24, 1970, the justices granted review in *Monitor Patriot Co. v. Roy*, a defamation action brought by a New Hampshire candidate for the U.S. Senate. On April 27, 1970, the Court agreed to hear *Time, Inc. v. Pape*, a lawsuit by a deputy chief of police detectives in Chicago. And, on May 4, 1970, the justices granted review in *Ocala Star-Banner Co. v. Damron*, a dispute over a Florida newspaper report about a mayor and political candidate. The Court would hear argument in all three cases on two consecutive days in mid-December 1970 and decide them together on February 24, 1971. As in *Bresler*, the majority opinions in all three cases were assigned by Chief Justice Burger to Potter Stewart, an apparent effort by the new chief justice to minimize Brennan's ongoing influence on the evolution of what by now was plainly recognizable as a discrete body of "constitutional" libel law. For Brennan, his failure to garner the assignments to write on behalf of the Court in *Bresler* and in these cases provided the first hint that his role in that process was about to change dramatically.

In *Monitor Patriot Co. v. Roy*, Alphonse Roy, an unsuccessful candidate for the Democratic nomination for the U.S. Senate in New Hampshire in 1960, sued the *Concord Monitor* and the North American Newspaper Alliance (NANA) for libel. Roy's suit was based on allegedly defamatory statements made by the well-known columnist Drew Pearson in his nationally syndicated column "The Washington Merry-Go-Round." Pearson's column referred to Roy as "a former small-time bootlegger," and reported that he had made calls to help get another potential candidate out of jail in time to have his name placed on the ballot. Roy's goal, Pearson suggested, was to take votes away from the strongest Democratic candidate and thereby boost the candidacy of the Republican incumbent, Senator Styles Bridges. Roy sued for defamation and, at trial, the judge instructed the jury that it could decide whether the column's characterization of Roy as a "bootlegger" was about his "private" affairs or whether it addressed his fitness for office and, therefore, his "official" conduct. Only the latter finding, the jury was instructed, would trigger application of the *Sullivan* standard. The jury responded by awarding Roy $20,000. The New Hampshire Supreme Court affirmed the verdict and the *Concord Monitor* appealed to the U.S. Supreme Court.

In *Time, Inc. v. Pape*, Frank Pape, a deputy chief of detectives in the Chicago Police Department, sued Time, Inc. for libel based on an article published in *Time*, its weekly news magazine. In 1961, the U.S. Civil Rights Commission had issued a report that, among other topics, discussed instances of police brutality throughout the country. The report recited the allegations contained in the complaint in a civil lawsuit filed by James Monroe, an African-American, against Pape and others. Monroe's complaint alleged, and the Civil Rights Commission's report recounted, that Chicago Police, including Pape, had broken down doors in his home in the middle of the night in 1958, made him and his wife stand naked before them, harassed and hit them, used racial epithets to taunt them, threatened their six children, and took Monroe to the police station for no apparent reason and held him there for several hours. In its issue published the week after the commission report was released, *Time* published a story about the report, which included the details of what Monroe alleged had been done to him by Pape and other officers. But *Time*'s account did not say that the details reported by the commission were based on the *allegations* of Monroe's complaint or that their inclusion in the commission's report did not reflect any independent verification of their accuracy by the commission or its staff. In a separate decision that would itself prove significant to the civil rights movement, the Supreme Court in 1961 had allowed Monroe's lawsuit for damages to proceed against the police officers under a Civil War-era statute, but further ruled that municipal governments like Chicago could not themselves be sued for damages under the provision (this portion of the decision was over-ruled in 1978). Monroe later won a verdict for damages against Pape.

Pape's libel case was filed in federal district court in Illinois. Judge Edwin A. Robson granted Time's motion to dismiss it on the ground that the magazine was simply engaging in fair comment on a government report, which was privileged under applicable state law. The U.S. Court of Appeals for the Seventh Circuit, how-ever, reversed and sent the case back to Judge Robson, at which point he applied the *Sullivan* actual malice standard and again granted the magazine's request that the case be dismissed, this time on Time's motion for summary judgment—a pro-cedural device that authorizes the court to dismiss a case prior to trial when there are no disputed issues of material fact and the defendant is entitled to judgment, based on those facts, as a matter of law.

In his second decision in the *Pape* case, Judge Robson—in a move that had become increasingly common in the years following *Sullivan*—concluded that, even if Pape could prove to a jury all of the facts he had alleged in his complaint against Time, he would nevertheless have failed to amass the clear and convincing evidence of actual malice necessary to secure an award of damages against the magazine. In the wake of *Sullivan*, and of Brennan's observation there that "would be critics of official conduct" could be "deterred from voicing their criticism . . . [for] fear of the expense" of having to prove it true in court, media defendants had begun to urge trial court judges to dismiss defamation action governed by the *Sullivan* standard prior to trial in just this manner and thereby spare them the significant expense they would necessarily incur in vindicating their publications before a jury.

The Seventh Circuit, however, reversed for a second time and instructed Judge Robson that there needed to be a trial adjudicating whether Time's failure to specify that the details it reported about Pape were only allegations constituted actual malice within the meaning of *Sullivan*. Undeterred, after the jury heard the evidence, Judge Robson granted a directed verdict for the magazine, which meant that he again deemed the evidence insufficient to establish actual malice, regardless of what the jury might conclude it showed. For a third time, the Sev-enth Circuit reversed and again said the jury must decide if actual malice was present. Rather than make a fourth trip to the district court, Time sought review in the Supreme Court.

In *Ocala Star-Banner Co. v. Damron*, a small daily newspaper in Ocala, a town in north-central Florida south of Gainesville, published a story reporting that Leonard Damron, then the mayor of nearby Crystal River and a candidate for county tax assessor, had been charged with perjury in a federal court and that the case against him had been carried over to the court's next term. The article also reported some details of what allegedly prompted the perjury charge. As it turned out, the story was false—in fact, Damron faced no such charges and never had. Rather, his brother James was then facing perjury charges, and an editor at the newspaper had changed the name to Leonard, thinking the reporter must have made an error and not knowing of the brother's existence. Leonard Damron sued the newspaper for defamation and, in something of a mirror image of what had happened in *Pape*, a Florida trial judge granted a directed verdict as to liability for Damron at the end of a jury trial, and the jury then awarded him $22,000 in compensatory damages. In support of his liability verdict, the trial judge said that *Sullivan* did not apply because the article was not about Damron's performance of his official duties as mayor or as a candidate for elected office. A Florida appeals court affirmed the verdict, similarly concluding that the article reported on Damron's private conduct and that no showing of actual malice was therefore necessary. For its part, the Florida Supreme Court declined to hear the newspaper's appeal.

The stage was set for the three cases to be argued and decided together, and the arguments brought some big guns before the Supreme Court. In *Roy*, the *Concord Monitor* was represented by famed Washington litigator and criminal defense lawyer Edward Bennett Williams. Williams rested much of his argument on what he described as the trial judge's erroneous instruction to the members of the jury that it was up to them to decide if the "bootlegger" comment was a libel about Roy's private conduct such that, despite his status as a candidate for elected office at the time of the article's publication, the actual malice standard did not apply. Specifically, Williams asserted:

> It is our contention, if the Court please that the logical sequel to *New York Times against Sullivan* is that defamations against candidates for public office, so long as they relate to the fitness of the candidate for office, so long as they are within the ambit

of public discourse and dialogue regarding the qualifications and background of the candidate, have a constitutional protection unless uttered maliciously.

Chief Justice Burger asked Williams if a candidate for office was a public official or a public figure. Williams opted for public official, arguing that a candidate's life and personal background are "appropriate for public discourse." A short time later, however, he backpedaled a bit, suggesting that a candidate does not lose all claim to privacy the moment he announces for public office. When Justice Marshall asked if this were not "an imaginary line," Williams responded there might be some private details of a candidate's life about which the public was not entitled to be informed.

Roy was represented by Stanley Brown of Manchester, New Hampshire, the same lawyer who had also argued in 1965 for Frank Baer, the former manager of the ski resort who was the plaintiff in *Rosenblatt v. Baer*. Brown contended that he had proven that Roy was not a bootlegger, but Justice White wanted to know if the jury could award damages under New Hampshire law even if they believed that he was. When Brown replied that the jury could not, White pressed the point repeatedly, apparently in an effort to probe Brown's contention that, because the bootlegger allegation related to Roy's private conduct, the First Amendment did not apply at all and the state was therefore free to impose liability on even a truthful statement. Ultimately, Brown responded only that extending the actual malice requirement to statements about the private affairs of public officials would go too far: "I don't think that you can take the position as argued by my brother Williams that whatever anybody wants to write about anybody who stands for public office is . . . automatically subject to the strictures of *New York Times and Sullivan*."

In *Pape*, the magazine was represented by the colorful media lawyer Don Reuben, a well-known figure in the Chicago legal community. Reuben contended that the *Time* reporter consciously omitted the word *alleged* from the description of police brutality against the Monroe family because he in fact believed, albeit erroneously, that the Civil Rights Commission had verified the accuracy of the details from Monroe's complaint that it had included in its report. "He knew exactly what he was doing?" Justice White asked. "Absolutely," Reuben replied. Justices Brennan, Harlan, and White then took turns asking, in one fashion or another, whether the magazine's report was false—whether the allegations in Monroe's complaint, as recounted by the Civil Rights Commission, were in fact untrue. Reuben responded that, while there was no finding to that effect by Judge Robson, the justices could

assume falsity to decide whether the trial judge correctly determined that there
was insufficient evidence of actual malice in any event. Relying on the Court's
newly minted decision in *St. Amant*, with its emphasis on the subjective nature of
the actual malice standard and its requirement that the defendant have published
despite "a high degree of awareness" of the "probable falsity" of the alleged defamation, Reuben argued:

> There is not one thing in this record that indicates that this author or this researcher
> or Time Incorporated had any knowledge of falsity or had any awareness of falsity.
> Rather what we believe and what the District Judge held and what two judges or
> at least the first dissenting Circuit Court judge held was that a fair reading of the
> Civil Rights material alone could lead to the conclusion that the report about Pape
> in the Civil Rights Commission was true.

Patrick Dunne, another Chicago lawyer representing Pape, argued to the justices
that the *Time* article's failure to include the word *alleged* in its description of the
facts underlying the Monroe case was critical. "The omission of words, we submit,
is a known falsity and meets the test of malice in *New York Times*," he contended,
adding that this was so because, as Reuben had expressly conceded, the omission
was an intentional choice, not an inadvertent act. Dunne asserted that the Civil
Rights Commission report itself discussed the details of the Monroe case in the
context of a complaint having been filed that contained the referenced allegations, while the *Time* article reported those allegations as if they were established
fact. At this juncture, Brennan asked Dunne whether, even if *Time* could prove
that the reported details of the Monroe incident were true, he would nevertheless
contend that the magazine published with actual malice because its article falsely
represented that the Civil Rights Commission had endorsed their accuracy. Dunne
agreed that he would still endeavor to prove actual malice in that circumstance.

In *Damron*, Harold Wahl of Jacksonville, Florida, another well-regarded media
lawyer, argued for the newspaper. He conceded at the outset that his client made
a mistake when it referred to Leonard Damron, rather than to his brother. Nevertheless, Wahl contended, Leonard Damron was a public official because he served
as mayor and was then a candidate and that, much like Reuben had argued on
behalf of the *Time* reporter in *Pape*, there was no evidence that the *Star-Banner*
editor had inserted Leonard's name in the article knowing that, by doing so, he

had likely rendered its account of the perjury charge false. Of the reporter, Wahl
said, "he was negligent, but he certainly wasn't guilty of express malice or a calculated lie with an intent to harm." And, Wahl continued, the newspaper ran a
retraction the next day and published at least two subsequent letters to the editor
correcting its mistake.

Wallace Dunn of Ocala argued for Damron. He contended that the trial judge
had properly directed a verdict for his client because the newspaper had admitted
its liability. According to Dunn, the newspaper had effectively conceded that there
was sufficient evidence of actual malice. When Brennan questioned whether the
paper had really made that concession, and other justices wondered why the Florida appeals court had addressed the *Sullivan* rule at all if liability had already been
admitted, Dunn confessed that he had failed to argue in the Florida appeals court
that the newspaper had conceded liability, including the existence of actual malice.

The justices took up all three cases at the same conference. There is little
in Brennan's files memorializing the discussion there or the Court's subsequent
deliberations, likely because, as noted, none of the cases had been assigned to him.
Justice Douglas, however, debated whether he could vote in the cases at all. In
another defamation case being considered at about the same time, *Rosenbloom v.
Metromedia*, one of the lawyers was Tom Clark's son Ramsey, who was no longer
attorney general and was now in private practice. Clark was part of a team of
lawyers representing Douglas in a threatened impeachment by the House of Representatives. Since Douglas could therefore not take part in the *Rosenbloom* case,
he wondered if he should recuse himself in the three other pending cases as well.
Shortly before they were decided, however, Douglas wrote privately to Black, "I
thought I would not sit in these three if they were controlled by or substantially
influenced by *Metromedia*. I talked to Bill Brennan and he said they are not so I
thought I would in due course cast my vote in these three cases in which Potter
Stewart has written."

All three decisions were announced on February 24, 1971, with three separate
majority opinions, each written by Justice Stewart. In *Monitor Patriot Co. v. Roy*,
the Court held that allegations about the criminal conduct of a political candidate are directly relevant to his fitness for office and, therefore, are subject to the
actual malice standard, as defined in *Sullivan*, should they become the subject of
a defamation action by that candidate. "We therefore hold as a matter of constitutional law that a charge of criminal conduct, no matter how remote in time or

place, can never be irrelevant to an official's or a candidate's fitness for office for purposes of application of the 'knowing falsehood or reckless disregard' rule of *New York Times Co. v. Sullivan*," Stewart wrote for a majority that included seven justices. Although Black and Douglas would have entered judgment for the newspaper, based on their by-then familiar view that the First Amendment precluded all defamation actions brought by public officials and candidates for public office (a view they reiterated applied in *Pape* and *Damron* as well), their colleagues sent the case back to the lower courts to apply the actual malice standard.

In *Time, Inc. v. Pape*, the Court determined that the omission of the word *alleged* constituted a plausible reading of the otherwise ambiguous report issued by the Civil Rights Commission and, as a result, could not provide the evidence of actual malice necessary to sustain a libel judgment in favor of a public official such as Pape. Justice Stewart's opinion cautioned that the Court's decision should not be read to render the word *alleged* a "superfluity" in good news reporting practices, and took some pains to emphasize that "neither lies nor false communications serve the ends of the First Amendment, and no one suggests their desirability or further proliferation." Nevertheless, he concluded—in an opinion that represented the views of all but one of his colleagues—that the *Time* reporter's "rational interpretation" of an ambiguous document, even though concededly knowing and deliberate, was insufficient to support a jury finding of actual malice, and that Judge Robson was correct in granting the magazine's request for a directed verdict (and presumably its earlier motion for summary judgment prior to trial as well). Both of those conclusions would prove to have far reaching ramifications. Not only would the so-called "rational interpretation" doctrine come before the justices twice more in the years ahead, in *Bose Corp. v. Consumers Union* and in *Masson v. New Yorker Magazine*, but the Court's implicit endorsement of what Judge Robson had done in *Pape*—dismiss a defamation case on its merits before it could be considered by a jury—would embolden the lower courts to formulate and adopt something of a "preference" for such summary dispositions in all defamation cases governed by the actual malice standard. The propriety of this practice would soon enough come to occupy the justices' attention as well.

Only Justice Harlan dissented from the Court's decision in *Pape*, asserting that, while he supported the *Sullivan* rule, the Court had gone too far in evaluating the facts of the case itself. No doubt concerned both by the number of defamation cases in which the Court had granted review following *Sullivan*, and mindful of

the quagmire in which it had immersed itself in obscenity cases where it had similarly felt obliged to grant review in and consider on their facts a parade of cases
finding a particular book or film to be obscene, Harlan argued that "it is almost
impossible to conceive how this Court might continue to function effectively
were we to resolve afresh the underlying factual disputes in all cases containing
constitutional issues."

Finally, in *Damron*, the Court again held, as it had in *Roy*, that reports about
a candidate's qualifications for office require protection under the actual malice
standard. As Stewart wrote for a unanimous (save for Black and Douglas) Court,
"[p]ublic discussion about the qualifications of a candidate for elective office presents what is probably the strongest possible case for application of the *New York
Times* rule. And under any test we can conceive, the charge that a local mayor and
candidate for a county elective post has been indicted for perjury in a civil rights
suit is relevant to his fitness for office." Accordingly, the Court reversed the damage award in *Damron* and, as it had in *Roy*, sent the case back to the state courts
to apply the liability standard required by the First Amendment.

For Brennan, despite the fact that he had not been assigned to write them, the
Court's decisions in *Roy*, *Pape*, and *Damron* had to be gratifying. After all, in all
three, the Court had applied the actual malice standard he had created in *Sullivan*
to reverse lower court rulings in favor of defamation plaintiffs. And the Court had
done so by large majorities, which included both the new chief justice and Justice
Blackmun, who had joined the Court the previous June. Nevertheless, even beyond
the fact that Burger appeared determined to deny him the authority to speak for
the Court in such cases, there was a more serious storm brewing, although it is
doubtful that Brennan was aware of it at the time. In both *Roy* and *Damron*, although
he joined Stewart's opinions in both cases, Byron White felt the need to submit
a single, one paragraph concurring opinion of his own. In it, the justice who had
been perhaps Brennan's single most consistent ally on the Court in *Sullivan* and
thereafter, took pains to emphasize, obviously with some regret, that, although it
was required by the First Amendment, application of the actual malice standard

will result in extending constitutional protection to lies and falsehoods which, though
neither knowing nor reckless, do severe damage to personal reputation. The First
Amendment is not so construed, however, to award merit badges for intrepid but
mistaken or careless reporting. Misinformation has no merit in itself; standing alone

it is as antithetical to the purposes of the First Amendment as the calculated lie.... Its substance contributes nothing to intelligent decisionmaking by citizens or officials; it achieves nothing but gratuitous injury. The sole basis for protecting publishers who spread false information is that otherwise the truth would too often be suppressed.

The significance of this observation, though at best obscure at the time, would become all too apparent in the years ahead.

CHAPTER 4

LOSING CONTROL

After the onslaught of defamation cases that ended the 1960s and spilled over to the beginning of the new decade, the justices might have hoped for a respite. The Court is known generally to subscribe to the "percolation" approach to judicial decision making—after it decides an important case, especially one like *Sullivan* creating a new body of constitutional law, the justices typically prefer to let the lower state and federal courts wrestle with the new doctrine for a while to see how it works and whether it needs to be refined. Plainly, *Sullivan* proved to be an exception. After it was decided, a steady stream of cases worked their way through the Court in short order, many of them seemingly necessitated by the justices' perceived need to be vigilant in reviewing the way judges were applying their newly minted actual malice standard, others a function of the Court's apparent desire to grapple with how far that standard should extend, if at all, beyond defamation actions instituted by "public officials."

With respect to the first issue, state courts in some parts of the country had proven somewhere between reluctant and recalcitrant in their acceptance of *Sullivan*. As a result, Justice Brennan was not alone in believing that the Court had to thrash out the details of how the actual malice standard ought to be applied in concrete cases and correct those lower courts that had confused the knowledge of "probable falsity" he defined it to require with the kind of hatred, ill will, or a desire to harm that had been the hallmarks of common law "malice" under state law for decades. As for the second, Brennan increasingly came to wonder about whether the distinction he and the Court had drawn between public officials and "public figures," on the one hand, and all other libel plaintiffs, on the other, was the constitutionally appropriate one and whether it would make more sense for application of the actual malice standard turn instead on the subject matter of the alleged defamation. Having witnessed how the question of extending *Sullivan* to public figures had divided his colleagues, Brennan might reasonably have thought that focusing the constitutional inquiry on whether or not the publication before the Court addressed a matter of public concern, without regard to who brought the case, might be a better way to promote the First Amendment interest in free expression. As Brennan would learn soon enough as the new decade began in earnest, and the Court's membership continued to change, he was about to embark on what proved to be a tortuous path for him, for his colleagues, and for *Sullivan* itself.

Rosenbloom v. Metromedia, Inc.

George Rosenbloom was a Philadelphia-based distributor of magazines published by nudist groups. In October 1963, he had contracts to provide his publications to multiple newsstands. By any measure, before October 1, 1963, Rosenbloom was a private person operating a private business. On that fateful day, however, Captain Clarence Ferguson, head of the Special Investigations Squad of the Philadelphia Police Department, launched a crackdown on pornography, which included a series of raids on local newsstands. Rosenbloom was arrested while making a delivery of his magazines during one such raid. Within a couple of days, police had searched his home and a barn that he used as a warehouse and had seized his entire inventory. Based on the evidence so acquired, he was arrested again.

Rosenbloom's libel suit grew out of news accounts of Captain Ferguson's pornography crackdown that were broadcast on WIP, a Philadelphia radio station owned by Metromedia, Inc. The station, apparently relying on information supplied by Ferguson, reported that police had seized one thousand "allegedly obscene books" at Rosenbloom's home and another "3,000 obscene books" from his barn. The radio report added that the captain "believes they have hit the supply of a main distributor of obscene material in Philadelphia." In a later broadcast of the same story, the word *reportedly* was inserted before the reference to the three thousand obscene books. Meanwhile, Rosenbloom, contending that the books seized from him were not obscene, filed a lawsuit seeking an injunction to prevent further police interference with his business and to stop Ferguson from publicizing his arrest. When WIP reported on the lawsuit, its broadcast again referred to

Rosenbloom, albeit not by name, but described those filing the lawsuit as involved in the "smut literature racket" and as "girlie-book peddlers." Rosenbloom thereafter paid a personal visit to the station, where he complained about its coverage of him. Seven months after his arrests, Rosenbloom was acquitted of obscenity charges in state court, the trial judge finding that the magazines he distributed were not obscene in the first place.

Armed with his acquittal, Rosenbloom filed a defamation action against WIP in federal district court. In his complaint, he contended that he was libeled both by the station's failure to make clear that the three thousand books seized from his barn had not been adjudicated to be obscene and by its subsequent description of him as a "smut" distributor and "peddler" of "girlie books." A jury awarded Rosenbloom $25,000 in compensatory damages and $725,000 in punitive damages. In August 1968, the trial judge reduced the punitive damages award to $250,000.

In September 1969, the U.S. Court of Appeals for the Third Circuit reversed the judgment for Rosenbloom in its entirety. Judge Collins Seitz, whose daughter, Virginia, would serve as Brennan's law clerk some years later, wrote the opinion for a unanimous three-judge panel. Seitz and his colleagues conceded that Rosenbloom was neither a public figure nor a "public man," as Brennan and his colleagues had used that term. But the appeals court determined that the broadcasts nevertheless involved matters of significant public interest and also constituted "hot news" that required timely reporting. In Judge Seitz's view, both of these conditions triggered application of the actual malice standard, despite the fact that Rosenbloom was a private person. In addition, the court of appeals explained, there was insufficient evidence presented to the jury to support a finding of actual malice.

Rosenbloom took his case to the Supreme Court. The opening lines of the narrative account of the dispute in Brennan's term history dramatically framed its importance:

> Was it the "little man" against the media barons? [O]r was it a chilling fear of libel judgments dampening the ardor and willingness of the press to pursue news? Those conflicting views of extending the requirement of *New York Times v. Sullivan* to libel cases involving private individuals were the substance of this case.

The Court had agreed, over Brennan's objection, to hear Rosenbloom's case. Brennan thought the Third Circuit had gotten it right and that the justices could simply decline to review its decision. According to Brennan's term history, the vote was five-to-three in favor of hearing the case. Those voting yes were Chief Justice Burger and Justices Black, Harlan, White, and Marshall. Voting against were Justices Brennan, Douglas, and Stewart. Justice Blackmun would not join the Court until the following June.

Oral argument began on the afternoon of December 7, 1970, and carried over to the morning of December 8. This was just over a week before the Court heard arguments in *Monitor Patriot Co. v. Roy*, *Time, Inc. v. Pape*, and *Ocala Star-Banner Co. v. Damron*, although those three cases would be decided some three months before *Rosenbloom*. The argument in *Rosenbloom* presented a battle of legal giants. Representing Rosenbloom was Ramsey Clark, the former U.S. Attorney General and son of retired Justice Tom Clark. Metromedia's lawyer was Bernard G. Segal, a prominent Philadelphia lawyer and the immediate past president of the American Bar Association.

In his opening words, Clark framed the issue starkly. The question before the Court, he said, was whether the actual malice standard created in *Sullivan* "is to be extended to the very private individual, to the two hundred million Americans who are not famous, who are not public officials and who are not public figures such as Coach Butts or General Edwin Walker, but just plain people engaging in ordinary life." Clark asserted that WIP's broadcasts about Rosenbloom had caused him to lose more than half of his sixty newsstand clients and had forced him out of business. In addition, Clark touched on an issue that would arise often in the Court's later decisions exploring whether a particular plaintiff was or was not a public figure—how much access does that person have to the news media to try to refute reports that are damaging his reputation. Clark asserted that Rosenbloom did not have the same access to the media that public figures like Butts and Walker enjoyed.

Justice Brennan asked Clark if the Court had already decided the issue he was presenting when it extended the reach of the *Sullivan* rule in *Time Inc. v. Hill*. Clark responded that the issue remained an open one because *Hill* involved invasion of privacy but not defamation, a distinction, he said, that made a difference. As Clark explained it, James Hill had not been the subject of a false report that destroyed his reputation. For someone like Rosenbloom, Clark said, "we're going to have to look at the powerlessness of the individual in mass society and the great power of the concentration of the media because of technology in the area of free speech."

Clark was also pressed about whether he thought the First Amendment applied at all to libel cases involving private individuals. He conceded that it did but argued that a private citizen should nonetheless be able to recover from a media defendant in a defamation case when the defendant had failed to exercise "reasonable care." Although neither he nor any of the justices knew it at the time, Clark's proposal would prove prophetic.

When his turn came to address the justices, Segal felt compelled to refute Clark's sweeping opening statement, asserting that the issue before the Court was more about the facts specific to the case than what legal standard should govern defamation suits by those two hundred million Americans engaged in "ordinary life." He said Rosenbloom was the subject of extensive media coverage in Philadelphia immediately after his arrests, including in newspaper and television news reports, and that he did not learn about the WIP broadcasts for several weeks thereafter. In fact, Segal said, Rosenbloom did not even mention WIP in his previous lawsuit seeking to prevent further adverse publicity about his arrests. Segal asserted that the crux of the case, as in *Time, Inc. v. Pape*, was the omission of the word *allegedly* before *obscene* when the news report referred to the seizure of Rosenbloom's three thousand books. As Segal parsed WIP's broadcast, which did use the word *allegedly* in an earlier reference to the charges against Rosenbloom, that reference should be inferred to cover the three thousand books as well. Moreover, Segal argued that the omission was corrected about an hour later when the news report was next broadcast. For Segal, it was also significant to his fact-based analysis of the case that WIP did not identify Rosenbloom by name in its broadcast about his lawsuit against the police and the media and that, at trial, Rosenbloom's lawyers presented no evidence that anyone had actually listened to the WIP broadcasts and thought less of Rosenbloom as a result.

In addition to all of that, Segal argued, Clark had changed his client's argument in the Supreme Court. Segal asserted that, in the lower courts, Rosenbloom's lawyers had contended that "plaintiff is protected by Pennsylvania libel laws without First Amendment strictures. . . . Now, here he's shifted his argument, he's said you are entitled to constitutional protection, but only for reasonable care." Then, returning again to the facts, Segal maintained that Rosenbloom had access to the news media to tell his side of the story, but he did not take advantage of it because, Segal advised the justices, individuals who are arrested and charged with crimes are usually advised by their lawyers not to make public comments. "That is why he did not come on the radio here, that is why he never complained," Segal said. Without a rule like the *Sullivan* actual malice standard governing libel suits brought by persons, like Rosenbloom, who become involved in public controversies, Segal said, the news media would have to "find some other way to meet the public's right and need to know if the public is to meet the obligations of a modern society today."

As Segal used up his argument time and started to sit down, Justice Harlan asked for clarification. Apparently left unsatisfied by Segal's largely fact-bound argument, Harlan wanted to know whether he was asking the Court to extend the actual malice standard to suits brought by plaintiffs like Rosenbloom, who were not public figures. Segal replied that, in essence, the Court had already done so, hence his focus during his presentation on the facts of the case. When the Court "left the post of public official and went to public figure, you were in effect saying that the public's right to know extended to public issues of important, significant matters," Segal said. That contention prompted a new round of questioning and a telling exchange between Justice Stewart and Segal:

> Justice Stewart: Then that means, Mr. Segal, doesn't it, that any newspaper or radio station can pick out any one of the 200 million Joe Dokes in the United States and just by the fact of picking him out and printing a news story about him that is false, a false news story, so long as it's not malicious within the terms of *New York Times*, that newspaper's absolutely protected though it falsely defamed him. Doesn't it follow?
>
> Segal: No I would not say that, your Honor.
>
> Justice Stewart: Because the newspaper itself can create the public figure in your submission, take any little Joe Dokes in the country and create immunity for itself by the very fact of publishing a false story about him.
>
> Segal: . . . Now I say that if your Honors could show that in order to involve an individual, they created a public issue, I think probably that might demonstrate actual malice. But if you have an individual who becomes involved in something the public has the right to know, then freedom of the press under the First Amendment demands that it be held for fault but that that fault be calculated falsehood or reckless disregard.
>
> Justice Stewart: Under our system of free enterprise and a free press, it is up to each newspaper publisher to decide what he thinks the public has a right to know, including I suppose how many showers Joe Dokes took this afternoon or when he brushed his teeth.

Segal: . . . I would accept the . . . language that Mr. Justice Harlan used in which
he said that it had to be a matter of significant and important interest to the public.
I think that is right. I think backyard gossip is not. I think if you want to engage in
backyard gossip, it may be even about a public figure, you may be liable. . . .

At the mention of his name, Justice Harlan asked Segal what would happen to
his case if the *Sullivan* rule did not apply. Segal replied that "I start with a cer-
tainty . . . that . . . under present conditions where half a million verdicts, million
dollar, and three-quarter of a million have become par for the course, no station
and no newspaper can operate as it today operates." And, Segal added, some recent
jury verdicts for libel "are more than some newspapers cost. They are more than
most radio stations cost." If a lesser standard than actual malice applied, he asserted,
a radio station would have to give up "hot news," because it would otherwise be
overwhelmed by the duty to investigate. Such a result would run counter, Segal
concluded, to the reality that "news is more important today than ever."

In a rebuttal argument that was extended because Segal had been questioned
for several minutes longer than his time allotment, Clark responded:

[W]here you come to the individual, the private person, who has no chance to
engage really in robust or wide open discussion of these issues with Metromedia,
that the power of technology and communication, the power to debate these issues
in the marketplace of public opinion for private citizens in this country is very, very
limited, and they can be crushed, as was Mr. Rosenbloom.

When the justices considered the case in conference, they voted five-to-three to
affirm the Third Circuit's ruling in favor of Metromedia, although the composition
of the eight-member Court had changed since the justices first voted to hear the
case. Justice Douglas, who had voted to deny review, now felt obliged to recuse
himself because of the appearance on behalf of Rosenbloom of Clark, a member
of Douglas's own legal team in the ongoing impeachment efforts against him. Justice Blackmun, who had not yet taken his seat on the Court when Rosenbloom's
petition for review was granted, joined Chief Justice Burger and Justices Black,
Brennan, and White in voting to affirm Judge Seitz's decision. Justices Harlan,
Stewart, and Marshall, however, all voted to reverse.

According to Blackmun's notes from the conference, Burger set the tone of the discussion by referring to Rosenbloom as a "smut peddler." The most impassioned comments, however, appeared to come from those justices who wanted to rule in his favor. Blackmun's notes indicate that Justice Marshall, usually Brennan's reliable ally across a broad range of constitutional issues, expressed the strongest view, asserting that the "press creates its own public figures here" and that, as he saw it, the "First Amendment has no place at all" in limiting Rosenbloom's right to recover damages from WIP. According to Brennan's notes, Harlan asserted that the case was "not *New York Times*" and ought therefore to be judged by a "different First Amendment standard," which he suggested (as Clark had at argument) ought to be "negligence." And Stewart, according to Brennan's notes, said he would "limit [the *Sullivan*] rule to punitive damages and otherwise allow state tort law full sway."

On December 29, 1970, Chief Justice Burger sent the other justices the assignment sheet showing who he had designated to write which opinions in the cases that had been heard most recently, including not only *Rosenbloom* but also *Pape*, *Roy*, and *Damron*, which had been argued together the previous week. There is no definitive explanation for what happened that day, but Burger assigned all four cases, including *Rosenbloom*, to Justice Stewart. Stewart, however, was in dissent in *Rosenbloom*. Was this an inadvertent by-product of Burger treating the four libel cases together by mistake? Did Burger's own notes from the conference erroneously show Stewart in the majority? Or was Burger trying so hard to keep all of the majority opinions away from Brennan that it caused him to overlook the voting lineup in *Rosenbloom*? There is no way to know which is the correct explanation for Burger's otherwise inexplicable assignment. In any event, Stewart wrote to Burger the same day, copying the other justices, and gently suggested that he had "some difficulties with the assignment list circulated today." Mentioning *Rosenbloom*, Stewart wrote in politely understated fashion, "I should probably not be assigned to write the opinion for the Court. I was one of the three (the others being John and Thurgood) who voted to reverse the judgment in this case. There were 5 votes to affirm, with Bill Douglas not participating." At this point, Burger reluctantly assigned the majority opinion in *Rosenbloom* to Brennan, his first—and last—assignment to write an opinion for the Court in a defamation action during the entirety of Burger's tenure as its chief justice.

According to Brennan's narrative history of the term, he doubted right from the start that he could craft an opinion that would command a majority. Brennan perceived that Burger and Blackmun were both more interested in ruling against Rosenbloom because he was a "smut peddler" than they were in extending the reach of the actual malice standard beyond libel suits brought by public figures. And Brennan knew that Black continued to believe libel laws were inherently unconstitutional and that he would not endorse any application of the actual malice standard, in any context. Of the four other justices in Brennan's putative majority, only Byron White had consistently supported him in such matters. Nevertheless, Brennan was determined to seize the moment and redirect the focus of the body of constitutional law he had created in *Sullivan* away from the status of the putatively injured plaintiff and toward the subject matter of the allegedly defamatory publication, specifically whether what was broadcast or published addressed a matter of public concern.

Brennan circulated a draft of his opinion to the other justices on February 17, 1971, and awaited their feedback. Ominously, none was forthcoming. In other chambers, the Brennan draft was being scrutinized carefully. Blackmun's law clerk wrote in a memorandum to his justice that same day, "Generally, I think the opinion is unnecessarily long and rather clumsily written." Nevertheless, he said, the Brennan approach was "defensible." The absence of response frustrated Brennan and, at some point during the ongoing silence, he and Blackmun must have discussed the case. Blackmun's own files contain a March 9 letter to Brennan saying he would concur in the result and "substantially all that is said in the opinion for this case." But a handwritten note on the page says, "not used," and it appears Blackmun never sent it.

Among the other signs that such discussions were taking place is a Blackmun letter of March 22, 1971, sent privately to Brennan and not shared with the other justices. In it, Blackmun said, "I fully understand your concern about not having had a response from anyone. . . ." He added that he was "about ready to join" Brennan's opinion, but had "mild reservations," which he proceeded to share. First, Blackmun told Brennan he was troubled by this passage in Brennan's draft that appeared on the eleventh page of his twenty-four-page opinion:

> The guarantees secured by the First and Fourteenth Amendments for speech and
> press constitute the cornerstone of a government "of the people, by the people, and
> for the people," ensuring a free flow of information and a free marketplace of ideas

competing for popular acceptance. See generally Meiklejohn, "The First Amendment is an Absolute," 1961 Sup. Ct. Rev. 245.

Blackmun's March 22 letter expressed concern about Brennan's citation to Meiklejohn's famous explication of his theory of free expression in a democracy, not so much because of its content, but rather its title. "I suspect I am not an absolutist so far as the First Amendment is concerned, and I am not sure the First Amendment is the cornerstone of our government," Blackmun explained. "It is important, but there are others." He said he would be "happier" if Brennan would delete the quotation entirely.

Blackmun had a second request. On page twenty-one of Brennan's draft, in what Blackmun characterized as the "heart" of the opinion, he was troubled by Brennan's description of the Court's holding, which read:

> We thus hold that a libel action by a private individual for a defamatory falsehood relating to his involvement in an event of legitimate public concern may be sustained only upon clear and convincing proof that the defamatory falsehood was published with knowledge that it was false or with reckless disregard of whether it was false or not.

Blackmun's concern, which he said "bothers me somewhat," was that:

> The sentence as written is unlimited so far as the identity of a defendant is concerned. If it could be confined to an action "against a defendant which qualifies as a genuine segment of the communications media" or some language to this general effect, I believe I would be satisfied. I am disinclined to have the central sentence of the opinion left completely wide open at this point, for I feel there is still some room for the operation of state libel laws against private individuals or non-genuine segments of the media.

Although Blackmun shared this thought only with Brennan, it appears to be the first occasion in which a member of the Court introduced a new variable in the constitutional calculus—the status of the *defendant*. The significance of that issue, for the Court generally and for Brennan specifically, would become all too apparent in due time.

While some justices might have regarded Blackmun's points as minor ones, to Brennan this kind of give-and-take aimed at trying to secure a majority was the heart of the lawmaking process at the Supreme Court. In that spirit, he responded privately to Blackmun the next day. Brennan easily accommodated Blackmun's first request, telling Blackmun he would drop the entire sentence and the foot-note that accompanied it from his next draft. Accommodating Blackmun's second request was a trickier proposition. As Brennan noted in his term history, he did not want to start down the path of defining what was "genuine" news media and determining whether application of the actual malice standard would ultimately turn on such a definition. Thus, while thanking Blackmun for his "helpful note," especially because—as Brennan confided in his new colleague—he "had begun to feel completely isolated," Brennan proposed recasting the sentence embodying the Court's holding in a manner that would limit its immediate reach (Brennan's proposed additions to the sentence are italicized): "We thus hold that a libel action, *as here*, by a private individual *against a licensed radio station* for a defamatory false-hood *in a newscast*" relating to his involvement in an event of legitimate public concern is governed by the actual malice standard. Blackmun accepted Brennan's proposal later the same day and, after Brennan circulated a new draft to the full Court incorporating it on March 25, Blackmun joined the opinion, without res-ervation, on March 29.

Still, Blackmun's vote left Brennan three short of a majority for his formulation of the constitutional standard. The day that Brennan circulated his new draft, Chief Justice Burger wrote to him and to the full Court, saying he had "considerable trouble with the proposed opinion." Burger's letter left Brennan somewhat mysti-fied. In it, the chief justice said, first, that regardless of whether one applied state or federal libel law, the statements about which Rosenbloom complained were not defamatory. In this, Burger appeared to misstate the allegations of Rosenbloom's complaint, addressing neither the radio station's failure to qualify its reference to the three thousand seized magazines as "obscene" or its characterization of the plaintiff as a "smut peddler." Instead, the chief justice appeared to assume that Rosenbloom had objected to the radio station's accurate report that his property was raided, that he was arrested, and that one thousand allegedly obscene maga-zine were confiscated from the newsstands he serviced. Brennan politely replied on March 29 that he too had considered simply concluding that the broadcast contained no defamatory falsehoods, but determined that he was unable to do so because Rosenbloom's complaint focused "narrowly" on the description of him as a "smut peddler" and on the seizure of three thousand "obscene" books without qualification. "This seems to me to foreclose," Brennan suggested, the conclusion that there were no false, defamatory statements alleged.

Burger's letter raised a second concern. He wrote that, while "I agree with the general proposition that participation in any activity that is affected with important public interest draws the participants somewhere in the 'target zone' the Court has given public officials and public figures," he feared that so holding would make book publishers and distributors "fair game" just as much as "public figures." Brennan's reply, evidencing his befuddlement at what Burger was trying to say, diplomatically offered the following: "The third paragraph of your note states concisely the precise proposition that I was seeking to embody in my draft opinion." He continued that, since Burger agreed with the premise of his opinion, if the chief justice nevertheless felt that it was "not clear enough," he "would welcome any suggestions you might have." For six weeks thereafter, Brennan heard nothing further from Burger.

Finally, on April 19, Burger joined Brennan's opinion, without qualification. Eight days later, however, the chief justice proposed a one-paragraph concurring opinion explaining that, if he had reservations or questions about the Court's decision, they "relate to the need of every man to protect his own reputation." He added that, "[w]ith a majority of the Court I would, on a proper showing, allow recovery for knowingly false or reckless assaults on reputation." A month later, on May 25, following a personal meeting with Brennan in which he pledged his support, Burger withdrew his concurring opinion and simply joined Brennan's in its entirety. As Brennan's term history recounted their personal meeting, which took place in the chief justice's chambers, Burger "rejected the major argument" of what the term history described as "the Marshall-Harlan position," specifically that the Brennan opinion "involved too much attention by the Court to evaluations of the record—constitutionalizing the fact-finding process." According to Brennan, Burger told him that "the Marshall-Harlan approach involved as much scrutiny of the record, albeit to resolve different issues."

As Brennan's focus on the so-called Marshall-Harlan approach suggests, on May 19, some three months after he had circulated his first draft and a few days before his meeting with the chief justice, Harlan and Marshall had each circulated dissenting opinions. It must have been especially strange for Brennan to have Marshall, his frequent ally and friend, on the other side. Marshall had been supportive of extending *Sullivan* in his initial votes after joining the Court nearly four years earlier. But, for reasons that—beyond the analysis contained in his dissenting opinion— remain something of a mystery, Marshall broke ranks with Brennan in *Rosenbloom*.

In his own opinion, Marshall wrote that, in his view, extending *Sullivan* to libel suits brought by private individuals was unfair to "millions of Americans who live their lives in obscurity." Marshall was himself a very private person and that may have been a factor in his thinking. Moreover, as a civil rights leader in the 1940s and 1950s, Marshall sometimes found the news media, especially the local and regional press, to be hostile; in later years, he liked to tell the story of a local news outlet in the South that gave out the name of the motel at which he was stay-ing, as if to invite angry segregationists to find him. And Marshall had witnessed firsthand the impact the news media can have on private lives and reputations, including the public's fascination with the divorce and subsequent marriage to a white woman of NAACP Executive Secretary Walter White in 1949. Whatever the life lessons that informed his views, in his draft dissent in *Rosenbloom*, Marshall warned that, if the determination whether the actual malice standard applies in a given case turns on whether the challenged article or broadcast addressed a matter of legitimate "public interest," the Court would inevitably become the ultimate arbiter of which subjects were of sufficient importance to justify informing the public about them, and which were not. "The danger such a doctrine portends for freedom of the press," Marshall wrote, "seems apparent."

Although he had initially indicated his intention to write his own dissenting opinion, Marshall's views apparently proved attractive to Justice Stewart, who joined his colleague's dissenting opinion in its entirety and did not add anything of his own. In fact, Brennan's term history suggests that Stewart worked actively with Marshall to secure Harlan's support for Marshall's opinion as well.

That, however, was not to be. In the end, Harlan wrote his own dissent. Before he circulated it to the other justices in mid-May, he and Marshall had exchanged views in private correspondence. Brennan's term history makes clear that both dissents had been through multiple drafts during "a battle we had not known was going on." A significant point of disagreement between Harlan and Marshall was apparently that Marshall, with Stewart's support, proposed precluding the award of punitive damages in defamation actions as a way of protecting the press from crippling damage awards and the consequent potential for media self-censorship.

Harlan, however, believed the States should be able to award punitive damages in those cases in which the defamation plaintiff could prove actual malice as defined in *Sullivan*.

At this juncture, Brennan's opinion, in virtually its final form, continued to hold that there was no constitutionally valid reason to distinguish between "public men" and private citizens in deciding defamation cases, and that the actual malice standard should apply to both, provided that they were the subjects of news reports addressing matters of legitimate public concern. As Brennan's term history later explained it, his "principal objective" in *Rosenbloom* was "to obtain agreement upon the principle that within a sphere of public interest, the press's freedom to publish cannot be abridged by libel judgments based on the uncertain and wavering line of a jury's determination of negligence." In doing so, however, he was cognizant of the fact that this "result and conclusion do not flow ineluctably from *New York Times* or indeed any earlier case, but rather are reached independently on the basis of principles and arguments canvassed in the opinion."

Whatever its constitutional basis, Brennan's opinion concluded that the actual malice standard properly governs every libel claim in which the offending publication or broadcast involved a matter of "public or general interest." In this, Brennan made a conscious choice to replace the references to matters of "legitimate public interest" in his initial draft and instead borrow a phrase from a famous 1890 article in the *Harvard Law Review* written by a Boston lawyer named Samuel Warren and his then law partner and future Supreme Court Justice, Louis Brandeis. As Brennan's term history explained, by doing so he hoped to blunt Marshall's criticism that his opinion "placed courts in the position of saying what it was legitimate for the public to know." In Brennan's view, this change in language "had the advantage of adopting a test of some authority, as well as making clear that [the] thrust of the test—to divide the public from the private" would "allow the press full play in the former area."

In addition to formulating a "public or general interest" test, Brennan's opinion rejected the rationale, offered by Harlan and the now departed Warren in *Butts* and *Walker*, that the reputations of private citizens deserve more protection because they are less able to correct the record or otherwise gain access to the media to have their say. "In the vast majority of libels involving public officials or public figures, the ability to respond through the media will depend on the same complex factors on which the ability of a private individual depends: the unpredictable event of the media's continuing interest in the story," Brennan wrote. He argued that it is a "legal fiction" to say that public figures have exposed their entire lives to scrutiny while everyone else has chosen to remain entirely out of view. Such an artificial distinction, Brennan contended, threatened to interfere with public discussion of important issues and controversies. In that regard, his opinion suggested without further elaboration, new state laws creating a right of reply or to a retraction might redress any concern about a "private" plaintiff's putative lack of access to the media.

Much of Brennan's opinion was devoted to refuting the alternative to the actual malice standard proffered by Marshall and Harlan. The thrust of what they both proposed, as Brennan saw it, was that a private person claiming injury to reputation would only have to show a publisher's negligent failure to ascertain the truth in order to prevail in a defamation action, although they would be limited to actual, not punitive damages (unless, in Harlan's formulation, they could carry their burden of proving actual malice). In his own opinion, Brennan warned that such a standard of "reasonable care" would leave the media subject to the whims of juries and would, in turn, produce too much self-censorship by reporters and editors fearful of large and unpredictable jury verdicts. Thus, Brennan concluded, "the negligence standard gives insufficient breathing space to First Amendment values. Limiting recovery to actual damages has the same defects. . . . [T]hat standard, too, leaves the First Amendment insufficient elbow room within which to function." The threat to freedom of the press is not simply from damages, Brennan wrote, but from "the very possibility of having to engage in litigation, an expensive and protracted process" that he recognized was "threat enough" to engender self-censorship. The reality of defamation litigation that formed the foundation of this observation would also become a subject of the Court's attentions in the years ahead, as lawyers and judges alike began to grapple with the practical ramifications of the body of constitutional law Brennan and the Court had crafted.

In May 1971, however, Brennan was more focused on a different practical issue—namely, where would he find a fourth and fifth vote for his opinion in *Rosenbloom*. For one thing, Brennan knew that Douglas, who had proved somewhat receptive in years past to a certain flexibility in providing a necessary vote for an extension of *Sullivan* that fell somewhat short of the absolute construction of the First Amendment he favored, had recused himself. He also knew that Black, who held the same absolute substantive views as Douglas, lacked his colleague's willingness to compromise them. Sure enough, in *Rosenbloom*, Black refused to budge from his standard opinion concurring only in the judgment, in which he asserted that the First Amendment protects the press from libel judgments even when the published statements at issue in a given case are knowingly false.

What proved surprising was that Justice White, who had been Brennan's reliable ally—indeed, his co-conspirator in crafting a working majority in support of an analogous "public concern" standard in *Time, Inc. v. Hill*—had begun, it appeared, to lose his enthusiasm for extending *Sullivan's* reach any further. Some three months after he submitted his cryptic, one-paragraph concurring opinion in *Roy* and *Damron*, in which he appeared to lament what he described as *Sullivan's* deleterious consequences for individual reputation, White voted to affirm the Third Circuit's decision in favor of WIP but, instead of joining Brennan's opinion as he had in the past, White said he would concur only in the Court's judgment and in a separate opinion that expressly questioned the need to afford the media the broad protection in suits by private individuals that Brennan's formulation would require. Signaling that he may have reached what for him were the limits of *Sullivan*, White wrote:

> Some members of the Court seem haunted by fears of self-censorship by the press and of damage judgments that will threaten its financial health. But technology has immeasurably increased the power of the press to do both good and evil. Vast communication combines have been built into profitable ventures. My interest is not in protecting the treasuries of communicators but in implementing the First Amendment by insuring that effective communication which is essential to the continued functioning of our free society. I am not aware that self-censorship has caused the press to tread too gingerly in reporting "news" concerning private citizens and private affairs or that the reputation of private citizens has received inordinate protection from falsehood.

Nevertheless, White remained willing to rule against Rosenbloom on the theory that it was official conduct—the police raids and arrests that were the focus of the news reports that formed the basis of his claim—that brought him into the public eye and made reporting about him fair game. As White explained it, the press was entitled to the protections of the actual malice standard whenever it reported about official conduct, regardless of whether the plaintiff before the Court was himself a public official or public figure. Thus, White's difference with Brennan was, at least at this juncture in the evolution of his thinking, incremental—while Brennan would extend the protection of the actual malice standard to all reports about matters of legitimate public interest, White would extend it only so far as news reports about the conduct of government.

After receiving White's draft opinion in late May, Brennan tried, according to his term history, to persuade his colleague that "his shift in focus from the person involved to the *issue*, really put him in Justice Brennan's camp." Brennan's efforts, however, proved unsuccessful for, as his term history described what ensued, White "remained firm on his opinion." As a result, Brennan reluctantly came to grips with the reality that his opinion would speak for only a plurality of the Court—himself, the chief justice, and Justice Blackmun.

The Court's decision, announced in Brennan's plurality opinion on June 7, 1971, was accompanied by the concurring opinions of Black and White (which, though not quite that stark in their contrasts, approached the issue before the Court from markedly different perspectives nonetheless) as well as by the separate dissenting opinions of Harlan and Marshall. If Brennan had hoped to eliminate the unpredictability and disagreement within the Court that had begun to characterize its decisions in defamation cases by shifting the focus of such litigation to the subject matter of the alleged libel rather than the status of the plaintiff, he had failed miserably. And if he had hoped to use his first opportunity to write for the "Burger Court" on these matters to reassert his leadership in crafting the constitutional law of defamation, Brennan had done himself no favors either. The Court not only remained deeply divided in *Rosenbloom*, but Brennan would never again succeed in attracting a majority of his colleagues to such an opinion bearing his name. The extent to which he would become marginalized, however, did not become apparent for another three years when, after an uncharacteristic respite from defamation cases, a newly constituted Court took up *Gertz v. Robert Welch, Inc.*

Still, at the time it was decided, *Rosenbloom v. Metromedia, Inc.* had an undeniable and immediate impact on the litigation of defamation cases. Although Brennan's opinion spoke only for three justices, courts, like nature, abhor a vacuum. As a result, judges throughout the country largely embraced Brennan's reasoning and required the defamation plaintiffs before them to satisfy the actual malice standard in all cases, including those in which the plaintiff was not a public figure, in which the alleged libel addressed a subject of public concern. *Gertz v. Robert Welch, Inc.* was one of those cases.

Gertz v. Robert Welch, Inc.

The period from June 7, 1971, to February 20, 1973, was by far the longest stretch since *Sullivan* in which the justices did not have a libel case on their docket awaiting either argument or decision. In one sense, the hiatus was not surprising given the divisiveness of and Brennan's inability to form a majority in *Rosenbloom*. Finally, on February 20, 1973, the Court agreed to hear arguments in *Gertz*, which would prove to be its most significant decision applying the First Amendment to the law of defamation after *Sullivan*.

During the intervening period, the makeup of the Court changed yet again, as it had so often since President Johnson made his fateful decision to replace Arthur Goldberg with Abe Fortas some seven years earlier. Already, those years had witnessed the departures of Warren, Clark, and Fortas himself as well as the arrivals of Marshall, Burger, and Blackmun. Following the Court's announcement of its decision in *Rosenbloom* in June 1971, the Court that decided *Sullivan* would lose two more of its members. Justice Black, who had been a reliable vote for Brennan's results, if not his reasoning, in *Sullivan* and all of the cases that followed it, resigned from the Court on September 17, 1971, and died just eight days later. He had served as an associate justice for more than three decades. Justice Harlan, who had inherited the role of the Warren Court's principal dissenter from Felix Frankfurter and had increasingly opposed Brennan's efforts to expand the reach of *Sullivan*, retired one week after Black, on September 24, 1971. Although in the hospital and gravely ill himself, Harlan reportedly delayed his announcement to permit Black, his longtime friend and intellectual adversary, to announce his resignation first and receive the undistracted public acclaim Harlan believed he deserved. Harlan himself passed away on December 29.

The departures of Black and Harlan meant that the Court that had decided *Sullivan* now retained only four of its members. With Richard Nixon in the White House, and undoubtedly still smarting from the bruising nomination process that had ultimately resulted in the appointment of Harry Blackmun, Brennan could only guess how the President's next two appointees would view the conception of the First Amendment he had fashioned in *Sullivan* and thereafter. As a general proposition, Brennan knew that, whomever Nixon appointed, the two new justices were likely to be antagonistic to much of the work of the Warren Court—Nixon had based his election campaign in large measure on appointing judges who would not be "activists" like Warren and Brennan. Still, when it came to *Sullivan*, Brennan had cause for cautious optimism. After all, the only two justices to join his plurality opinion in *Rosenbloom* were Burger and Blackmun, Nixon's first two appointees.

This time around, the President appointed Richmond, Virginia, lawyer and former American Bar Association President Lewis Powell and one-time Phoenix, Arizona, lawyer William Rehnquist, who was then serving as an assistant attorney general in the Justice Department. It was generally known that Powell had declined Nixon's attempt to appoint him two years earlier to the Fortas seat that was eventually filled by Blackmun. And the conventional wisdom was that, of the two, Rehnquist was considerably more likely to be hostile to the perceived judicial "activism" of the Warren Court. What could not have been known at the time was that, beginning with *Gertz v. Robert Welch, Inc.*, and continuing through Brennan's own retirement from the Court more than fifteen years later, these two justices, more than any others, would effectively control the fate of *New York Times Co. v. Sullivan* and that they would do so in a manner that would, in the end, defy that conventional wisdom.

The case that the newly constituted Court chose for its maiden voyage into the recently stormy waters surrounding the law of defamation was, in many ways, a typical example of how the lower courts had reacted to libel claims in the wake of *Rosenbloom*. The plaintiff, Elmer Gertz, was a prominent Chicago lawyer who by his own description had a sterling reputation in the Illinois bar, appeared from time to time on radio and television, wrote books, articles and reviews with a wide following, and was actively involved in public affairs, most notably serving as counsel in cases pressing civil rights claims. In 1968, Gertz was hired to bring one such action—he represented the family of a Chicago teenager, Ronald Nelson, who had been shot and killed by Chicago police officer Richard Nuccio. Nuccio was tried and convicted of second-degree murder. On the Nelson family's behalf, Gertz attended the coroner's inquest to determine how the teenager died and filed a civil suit for damages against Nuccio. According to the record evidence in his subsequent defamation action, that was the extent of Gertz's involvement in the events surrounding the Nelson shooting.

In March 1969, *American Opinion*, a monthly magazine published by Robert Welch, Inc. to serve as an outlet for the views of the John Birch Society, ran an article describing Nuccio's conviction as a "frame-up" and part of a nationwide conspiracy to undermine police authority so that Communists could take over the country without significant resistance from law enforcement. Although Gertz had no connection to the Nuccio prosecution, the article depicted him as the architect of the frame-up. Among other things, it reported that the Chicago police file on Gertz was so thick it could only be lifted by a "big, Irish cop," and that Gertz was a "Leninist" and a "Communist-fronter" who had been a member of the Marxist League for Industrial Democracy and a leader of the National Lawyers Guild, which the article described as a Communist organization. There was precious little evidence to support any of this. In fact, Gertz had no criminal record or police file and there was nothing to suggest that he was a Communist, much less the architect of a Leninist-inspired "frame-up." About the only accurate statement in the article's description of Gertz was its reference to his membership in the National Lawyers Guild, albeit some fifteen years earlier, but the connection between his membership in that organization and Communist activity was dubious at best.

Gertz sued the article's publisher for defamation in federal district court in Chicago. At the outset, the trial judge ruled that Gertz's complaint had properly alleged libel per se under the law of Illinois, a form of defamation involving statements so inherently injurious to one's reputation that the plaintiff need not prove that he sustained any harm in order to recover damages. Rather, such damages were presumed from the mere fact of publication. Apparently, at the time, calling a respected lawyer a Communist was enough to constitute libel per se under Illinois law. In the face of this construction of state law, the publisher responded that the actual malice standard should apply both because Gertz was a public figure within the meaning of *Butts* and *Walker* and because the article addressed a matter of public concern. The trial judge, however, initially refused to grant summary judgment on this basis and sent the case to the jury, which awarded $50,000 in damages to Gertz. But, in December 1970, the judge changed his mind. He now concluded that Gertz was indeed a public figure and that the actual malice standard should govern the case. Applying that standard to the record evidence, the court threw out the jury's verdict and granted judgment for Robert Welch, Inc.

On August 1, 1972, the U.S. Court of Appeals for the Seventh Circuit unanimously affirmed. The appeals court's decision was written by Judge John Paul

Stevens who would, in a few short years, replace William O. Douglas on the Supreme Court. In his opinion, Stevens agreed with the trial judge that the subject matter of the article in *American Opinion* was of substantial public interest and that it was therefore protected by the First Amendment, as construed by Justice Brennan in *Rosenbloom*, in the absence of clear and convincing evidence that it had been published with actual malice. Judge Roger Kiley joined Stevens's opinion, but wrote a short concurrence to express his concern that the ruling "pushed through what I consider the outer limits of the First Amendment protection against liability for libelous statements" and "further eroded the interest of non-'public figures' in their personal privacy."

Gertz petitioned the Supreme Court to review Stevens's decision, and the justices agreed to do so on February 20, 1973. Chief Justice Burger and Justices White, Marshall, Blackmun, Powell, and Rehnquist all voted to hear the case, according to Brennan's handwritten docket sheet. Only Justices Douglas, Brennan, and Stewart would have denied review. Powell's handwritten notes on the case summary prepared by his law clerk give an indication of the battle that lay ahead. "This libel case is probably controlled by *Rosenbloom*—which I think extends *Sullivan* too far," Powell wrote. "If there is sentiment to review this area of the law, I will join in a grant." Elsewhere, on his docket sheet for the case, Powell wrote in reference to Justice Stewart, "Potter is willing to reconsider *Rosenbloom*, but until we do he feels bound by it."

Normally, Brennan's views about the case, both before and after the Court decided to hear it, would be revealed in the narrative history of the Court's term prepared at its conclusion by the justice and his law clerks. In the decade that began with *Sullivan* and concluded with *Gertz*, virtually all of the defamation cases decided by the Court during that period are addressed in the annual term history, often at some length. There is, however, not a word about *Gertz* in the narrative history of the October 1973 term, apparently because the law clerk in Brennan's chambers who the justice assigned to work with him on the case never prepared a draft for Brennan's consideration. As a result, we are left without a key roadmap for assessing Brennan's views about the case, the Court's internal deliberations in it, and the constitutional law that emerged from it. To be sure, we can reconstruct at least some of this from the materials that survive in Brennan's files as well as from the views expressed about it in subsequent term histories (especially in the history describing *Time, Inc. v. Firestone*, which the Court decided shortly after *Gertz*).

Nevertheless, we are left to wonder about the extent to which Brennan came to feel marginalized during the Court's deliberations in *Gertz* while they were ongoing.

The case itself was not argued until November 14, 1973. Gertz was represented by Wayne Giampietro, his friend and a fellow Chicago lawyer. The defendant, Robert Welch, Inc., was represented by Clyde Watts, the same lawyer who had argued on behalf of a defamation plaintiff, General Edwin Walker, a few years earlier. As Giampietro began to describe to the Court what the *American Opinion* article had said about Gertz, Justice Rehnquist—hearing his first argument in a defamation case—asked if it would be libelous per se under Illinois law to say that someone was a member of the American Civil Liberties Union. Giampietro responded that a reference to membership in the ACLU, standing alone, would not be defamatory, but that adding that its members were Communists could be. Gertz's counsel then devoted his attention to arguing that his client was neither a public official nor a public figure, defining the latter as "a person whose very existence and presence would require public comment." He also insisted that Gertz's activities in connection with the Nuccio case were "not a part of any matter of public interest or importance." As he explained it, Gertz had nothing to do with the criminal case against Officer Nuccio, although he conceded under questioning that his client did file and win a $20,000 civil damage judgment for the Nelson family against the police officer.

During his presentation, Giampietro observed that some justices had expressed concern about press self-censorship if the risk of defamation liability was too great. But he said, "I think, in some areas, however, that such self-censorship is not entirely a bad thing. I think in some areas the press ought to have to stop and consider what they are about to do to an individual." At one juncture in Giampietro's argument, Justice Powell, also sitting on his maiden defamation case, noted that the lawyer had asserted that there was no public interest in the civil suit filed by Gertz against Nuccio. "Who determines whether or not there is a public or general interest in a libelous statement," Powell asked, clearly reflecting the concerns on that score expressed most notably by Justice Marshall in *Rosenbloom*. The courts, Giampietro replied, "and certainly, ultimately this Court."

Powell then asked Giampietro whether there had been press coverage of the civil suit that Gertz had initiated on behalf of the Nelson family. The lawyer responded that there had been very little, and conceded that the constitutional question might well be a closer one if there had been. With that, Powell asked a question that had also been raised in the *Rosenbloom* argument: "Well doesn't this enable the press to decide, in almost every case, what you said might be a Constitutional question, that is whether or not a particular story is or is not a matter of general or public interest?" Recognizing a rhetorical softball when he saw it come across home plate, Giampietro readily agreed that, under such a standard, the press may effectively be able to insulate itself from defamation liability by creating a previously nonexistent public controversy. At this point, Justice Stewart, one of the *Rosenbloom* dissenters, chimed in as well—"But isn't that just about what the lead opinion in [*Rosenbloom*] adds up to?" After Giampietro agreed with this assertion as well, Stewart asked whether his only effective answer was that there had been no majority opinion for the Court in *Rosenbloom* and that the question therefore remained open for reconsideration in *Gertz*. Once again, Giampietro both embraced Stewart's suggested "answer" and added, for good measure, that this case might provide a good opportunity to do so.

After listening to this exchange, Brennan tried to turn the tide a bit, focusing a series of questions on the evidence that was actually before the trial judge. Brennan observed that the judge had first found that the killing of a citizen by a policeman was a matter of public interest, especially because it came at a time when there was considerable scrutiny of police misconduct in Chicago. Then, Brennan asserted, the judge found that Gertz had "thrust himself into the vortex" of that controversy by representing the family in the civil suit. Giampietro, however, told the justice that he did not need to dispute the first finding, because there was no evidence to support the second. In short, Giampietro said, the evidence showed that Gertz had not involved himself in the larger controversy surrounding police misconduct.

During his own argument, Watts staked out the somewhat bizarre position that the case was really about the absence of "equal justice under law," the phrase that sits over the entrance to the Supreme Court building. What he apparently meant was that, in his view, Gertz was asking the Court to treat the John Birch Society and Robert Welch, Inc. differently than it would *Time* magazine or the *New York Times*. When Justice Powell asked if it had been conceded at trial that the article was false, Watts seemed unsure. And when Powell then suggested that the statement about the police file needing a "big Irish cop" to lift was itself libelous per se, Watts disputed Powell's point with another curious assertion, responding that, if there was a police file on Gertz, it was likely to have reflected criminal activity. As he proceeded to attempt to explain away the defamatory import of other aspects of the article, including whether it in fact suggested that Gertz was a Communist, a mystified Rehnquist observed that he was arguing points of Illinois law "that I think this Court would be disinclined to review." Surprisingly, Watts agreed with Rehnquist's assessment and returned to his earlier argument, that the real issue in the case was whether the courts should apply "the same rule with respect to this *American Opinion* that it would have applied with any other publisher."

Attempting to return the argument to a discussion of the issues that had actually been decided in the court of appeals, Justice White asked Watts if the question before the Court was whether the *Sullivan* rule should apply to the case. Watts, however, did not seem to understand the question, which White then repeated twice more. When Watts finally figured out what White was asking, Brennan immediately interrupted. Trying to clarify the point, Brennan asked if Watts conceded that Gertz was not a public official. Watts undoubtedly surprised Brennan by refusing to concede the point, asserting that when Gertz appeared at the coroner's inquest, he became a "de facto public official." White then returned to his own question and asked yet again whether the *Sullivan* rule would apply if Gertz were neither a public official nor a public figure. To this, Watts finally replied that Gertz was involved in a matter of public interest. But, before he could complete his answer—presumably with the contention that, as a result, he was obliged by Brennan's opinion in *Rosenbloom* to satisfy the actual malice standard—Brennan interjected again, this time suggesting that the focus of the inquiry should be whether Gertz had thrust himself into the vortex of that public issue. When Watts responded that the issue was more complicated, White was prompted to remark, "why didn't you just say yes to Justice Brennan's question?" At this juncture, Watts actually told White that his answer was no, although he proceeded to expound on it in a manner that appeared to agree with Brennan's contention—that Gertz had indeed played an active role in the relevant public controversy.

In this exchange, it appeared that Brennan was attempting to press the point that Gertz was a "public figure" in the mold of General Walker, Watts's client in that earlier case. There is no written explanation of Brennan's strategy in doing so, though it seems likely that he recognized, even at the time of argument in *Gertz*, that he would be unable to secure the additional votes he needed to turn his plurality in *Rosenbloom* into a majority for the "public or general interest" standard he had advocated in that case. Accordingly, through his questions to Watts, Brennan may have been hoping to build support for an opinion affirming the decision below on the ground that Gertz was a public figure and that, as a result, the Court need not reach the *Rosenbloom* issue at all.

If this was indeed Brennan's strategy, it is safe to say that Watts did not appreciate it. As his time ran down, Watts argued again that Gertz was a public official simply because he had asked questions at the coroner's inquest. This time, Watts's contention apparently got under the skin of Justice Marshall, who had been silent up to that point. He asked if Gertz had a right to ask questions at the inquest and how the article (and Watts) could seriously contend that Gertz had somehow influenced its outcome when the inquest itself was inconclusive as to what caused the teenager's death. "Well I don't consider that great influence, would you?" Marshall asked. Before Watts could fashion his answer, Marshall added, "you keep talking about the persecution of this police officer . . . is this the same police officer that was found guilty?" Watts said it was, and Marshall shot back, "And you call that persecution?"

Although he may well have wished he were, Watts was not finished yet. Pummeled with additional questions about why the actual malice standard should apply, Watts said to Justice White, "I feel so incapable of riding the perimeters of this rule that about all I can do is raise questions." And when Watts attempted to press Brennan's suggestion that Gertz had become a public figure because he had thrust himself into the center of a public controversy, Marshall recoiled again. "How can you use the word inject?" Marshall asked. "Any lawyer once he gets in a lawsuit, even going to the coroner's inquest, loses all of his rights under *New York Times*. . . . [H]e loses all of those rights, it doesn't pay to be a lawyer does it?" With that, Watts finally retreated to the argument that publishers should be protected by *Sullivan* and its actual malice standard whenever they write about "controversies in matters in which the public is vitally interested." Rehnquist, for one, was not moved. "By your test," he said, "everything in a newspaper except the funnies would be under *New York Times*." Undeterred, Watts countered that even the comics might sometimes implicate the *Sullivan* rule.

At conference following the argument, the votes went in three directions. The overall tally was eight-to-one to reverse the judgment against Gertz, with Justice Douglas alone in voting to affirm. According to Douglas's notes, six justices— Burger, Stewart, White, Marshall, Powell, and Rehnquist—wanted to reverse the judgment that the court of appeals had entered in favor of the publisher and reinstate the original jury verdict for Gertz. Justices Brennan and Blackmun preferred to reverse the judgment but to order a new trial. During the discussion, the chief justice, as always, spoke first and, according to Douglas's notes, pressed the point that "a lawyer who takes a case does not become a public figure because his client was one." Douglas's notes indicate that, at conference, Brennan defended his position in *Rosenbloom* and said the *Sullivan* standard should apply, though he favored returning the case for a new trial to give Gertz a chance to prove actual malice. Justice Stewart reportedly said that he continued to reject Brennan's formulation in *Rosenbloom* and that Gertz, who he had concluded was not a public figure, was entitled to the jury verdict he had received under state law. Justice White, according to Douglas's notes, indicated that he did not want to expand the reach of *Sullivan* beyond public figures. Blackmun, however, said he was prepared to stick with *Rosenbloom* and that he, like Brennan, would reverse for a new trial on the issue of actual malice. Finally, the two new justices both indicated that they would not only reverse, but would reinstate the jury verdict that Gertz had secured. In a subsequent letter he sent to Burger memorializing his own understanding of the justices' various positions at conference, Powell described them as follows:

> My notes indicate that only Bill Douglas voted to affirm. You were clear that Gertz was not a public figure, and you expressed doubt whether his connection with any matter of public or general interest was close enough to be meaningful. Potter, Thurgood and I agreed that Gertz was not a public figure, although I understood that Potter and Thurgood thought that the Rosenbloom plurality opinion could not be avoided on the ground of the remoteness of Gertz's connection with the controversy. Bill Rehnquist voted to reverse without fully articulating his reasons. Byron, while indicating that he thought Gertz might be a public figure, expressed his "total disagreement" with Rosenbloom and stated that he would reverse the holding below. Harry Blackmun expressed a tentative view that Rosenbloom was indistinguishable in principle. He joined Bill Brennan in thinking that the case should be reversed, but only because of the trial court's failure to give the jury an opportunity to find knowledge of falsity or reckless disregard of the truth.

In explaining his own vote at conference, Powell reportedly told his new colleagues that he rejected the "public interest" standard that Brennan had crafted in *Rosenbloom* because, as his questions at argument suggested, it permitted the press to decide for itself what is of interest to the public. As he later described those views in his letter to Burger, Powell asserted that the Court's adoption of the "public or general interest" standard Brennan had devised in *Rosenbloom* "would destroy entirely the law of libel, for anything a newspaper thinks important enough to print is arguably a matter of public or general interest."

Although Burger ended up writing what was denominated a dissenting opinion, his vote to reverse and reinstate the verdict at conference presumably allowed him to select who would write the Court's opinion in *Gertz*. In what would prove to be a noteworthy decision, he assigned it to Powell.

During the summer after the Court had agreed to hear the case, but before it was argued, Powell had written a memorandum to himself reflecting on the issues it raised. In it, he said, "[t]he Court has gone too far already in protecting the First Amendment rights of the media as against the individual rights." His law clerk, he wrote, should therefore try to "find a more rational adjustment between the competing interests." Armed with the assignment to write an opinion that could command a majority of the Court, Powell now proceeded to do just that. On December 28, 1973, some six weeks after the argument, he circulated a twenty-seven page draft that attempted to assess the competing interests anew and recalibrate them in the cause of arriving at a "more rational adjustment."

Powell's draft, like his final opinion, left few stones unturned in his quest to strike what he considered the appropriate balance. In Part III of his draft, Powell began with what he described as "the common ground." In an effort to explain why, in *Sullivan* and thereafter, the Court had held that the "First Amendment requires that we protect some falsehood in order to protect speech that matters," his opinion asserted that "[u]nder the First Amendment, there is no such thing as a false idea. However pernicious an opinion may seem, we depend for its correction not on the conscience of judges and juries but on the competition of other ideas." This passage, which survived unaltered in Powell's final opinion for the Court, would prove to be among its most significant. In short order, it inspired an impressive body of precedent in the lower courts, holding that the First Amendment provides absolute protection from defamation liability for the expression of "opinion." The Court would ultimately pass on the validity of that analysis in *Milkovich v. Lorain Journal Co.*, the last defamation case on which Brennan would sit as a member of the Supreme Court.

Arrayed against the First Amendment interest in "'uninhibited, robust, and wide-open' debate on public issues" identified by Brennan in *Sullivan*, Powell's draft opinion asserted, were two countervailing considerations. First, he observed, "there is no constitutional value," standing alone, "in false statements of fact." Second, there is "the legitimate state interest underlying the law of libel"—specifically, "the compensation of individuals for the harm inflicted on them by defamatory falsehoods." Embracing Justice Stewart's description of that interest in his concurring opinion in *Rosenblatt v. Baer*, Powell's draft incorporated it verbatim, putting the weight of the full Court behind Stewart's observation that the law of defamation "'reflects no more than our basic concept of the essential dignity and worth of every human being—a concept at the root of any decent system of ordered liberty.'" This passage as well, which reflected a view with which Brennan demonstrated considerable sympathy in other contexts, survived in Powell's final opinion.

Having thus placed what he described as the competing interests on roughly equal footing, Powell wrote that when a libel claim is asserted by a plaintiff who is neither a public official nor a public figure, the standard of liability required by the First Amendment is negligence, not actual malice. In this portion of his opinion, Powell rejected Brennan's extension of the actual malice standard in *Rosenbloom* to all cases involving matters of public interest. Rather, he returned the focus to the status of the plaintiff, embracing the holding in *Butts* and *Walker* that only public officials and public figures should be obliged to prove actual malice in a defamation action. As Powell described it, however, the several states would nevertheless be bound to require a showing of negligence in libel cases in which a private individual was the plaintiff.

Powell based his rejection of the *Rosenbloom* standard on two distinct grounds. First, he concurred in the views expressed by Marshall in *Rosenbloom*, which he had pressed at argument, namely that the standard Brennan had articulated in that case would require "judges to decide on an *ad hoc* basis which publications address issues of 'general or public interest' and which do not." As Powell explained it, the majority for which he was ostensibly writing "doubt[ed] the wisdom of committing this task to the conscience of judges."

In addition, Powell determined that application of the actual malice standard in defamation actions brought by plaintiffs who were not "public person[s]" undervalued the states' interest in protecting their reputations. In this, Powell relied on the assumption, which Brennan had sought to refute in *Rosenbloom*, that private persons enjoy less access to the media than public officials and public figures to rebut defamatory falsehoods. Powell distinguished between those "who, by reason of the notoriety of their achievements or the vigor and success with which they seek the public's attention, are properly classified as public figures," and those who "are not only more vulnerable to injury than public officials and public figures," but "are also more deserving of recovery." As Powell explained it, those "classed as public figures," like public officials, "usually enjoy significantly greater access to the channels of effective communication and hence have a more realistic opportunity to counteract false statements than private individuals normally enjoy." As a result, he wrote, such public figures may reasonably be required to prove actual malice in order to recover damages in a defamation action.

To this point in his analysis, Powell had avoided providing lower courts with any guidance in distinguishing public defamation plaintiffs from private ones, beyond his contention that the former "enjoy significantly greater access to the channels of effective communication" and his reference to what he described as the "compelling normative consideration" that a public figure, like a public official, "must accept certain necessary consequences of . . . involvement in public affairs." Toward the end of Part III of his draft, however, he included a single paragraph that undertook to describe the public figure in somewhat more detail:

> Hypothetically, it may be possible for someone to become a public figure through no purposeful action of his own, but the instances of truly involuntary public figures must be exceedingly rare. For the most part those who attain this status have assumed roles of especial prominence in the affairs of society. Some occupy positions of such persuasive power and influence that they are deemed public figures for all purposes. More commonly, those classed as public figures have thrust themselves to the forefront of particular public controversies in order to influence the resolution of the issues involved.

It is unclear whether, in drafting this passage, Powell intended to provide the lower courts with a working definition of the "public figure." Whether he did or not, both the lower courts and the Supreme Court itself would seize on this language in the years ahead as they turned to the task of determining whether a particular libel plaintiff was a public figure who, as a result of that status, was required to assume the burden of proving actual malice in order to prevail.

In Part IV of his draft opinion, Powell undertook to adjust the constitutional calculus further, this time by focusing on the issue of damages. Here, Powell's draft limited the ability of his newly created class of private plaintiffs to recover either punitive or presumed damages, the latter category encompassing those damages of the kind available in states like Illinois, in cases of libel "per se," even in the absence of evidence of any actual injury. As Powell explained it, although the Court had determined that a private person could prevail in a defamation action on proof of mere negligence, that plaintiff may not recover either presumed or punitive damages based on such a showing. In reaching this conclusion, Powell asserted that a state's interest in protecting individual reputation "extends no further than compensation for actual injury" and that, as a result, it "is necessary to restrict defamation plaintiffs who recover on a showing of negligence to compensation for actual injury." Even so, Powell expressly declined to define "actual injury," except to observe that "the more customary types of actual harm inflicted by defamatory falsehood include impairment of reputation and standing in the community, personal humiliation, and mental anguish and suffering." And Powell's discussion of presumed and punitive damages was less than clear with respect to under what circumstances, if ever, a defamation plaintiff could recover presumed or punitive damages. With respect to the former, his draft was silent on the subject; with respect to the latter, he included only a somewhat cryptic citation to the Court's decision in *Garrison*, accompanied by the assertion that "[b]ecause punitive damages perform much the same functions as criminal penalties, the incidence of their imposition should be governed" by that case.

In Part V of his draft, Powell applied this new regime to the facts of the *Gertz* case, rejecting the contention that Gertz himself was either a public official or a public figure. Powell easily brushed aside Watts's contention that Gertz had become a "de facto public official" by virtue of his presence at the coroner's inquest. More significantly, he reiterated the description of the "public figure" set out in Part III of his draft and concluded that Gertz had neither become "a public figure for all purposes" or "for a limited range of issues." As Powell explained it, although Gertz was "well known in some circles, he had achieved no general fame or notoriety in the community." Moreover, he played only a minor role in the coroner's inquest, and his involvement in the Nuccio matter "related solely to his representation of a private client." Accordingly, Powell wrote, tracking the language of the questions Brennan had posed at argument and that William Rogers had first uttered during his argument to the Court in *Walker*, Gertz had not "thrust himself into the vortex of this public issue, nor did he engage the public's attention in an attempt to influence its outcome."

In crafting this last portion of his draft opinion, Powell was apparently concerned that his analysis of whether Gertz was a public figure not cost him one of the three other votes (Stewart, Marshall, and Rehnquist) he thought he could count on. He appeared to be particularly concerned about Stewart's reaction to this portion of his draft, and he asked his law clerk, John Jeffries, who would go on to become a distinguished law professor and the author of a compelling biography of the justice, "to determine whether Mr. Justice Stewart's prior opinions in this area are in any way inconsistent with the discussion of the public figure doctrine in Part V." After reviewing Stewart's opinions for the Court in *Bresler, Roy, Pape,* and *Damron,* Jeffries reported that "I find nothing in these four cases even arguably inconsistent with Part V of the draft."

Powell's draft, which concluded—despite the apparent sentiments of a majority of the justices at conference—that a new trial was necessary because Gertz had not been required to prove negligence the first time around, included another feature that went largely unnoticed at the time. As reflected in his final opinion for the Court, Powell described the issue before the Court as whether "*a newspaper or broadcaster* that publishes defamatory falsehoods about an individual who is neither a public official nor a public figure may claim a constitutional privilege against liability for the injury inflicted by those statements." Throughout his draft, as well as in the ultimate opinion itself, Powell appeared to limit its scope in the manner that Blackmun had first suggested to Brennan during the Court's deliberations in *Rosenbloom*—to libels disseminated by the "media" or by "publishers or broadcasters." In one memorable passage, Powell wrote that "[o]ur decisions recognize that a rule of strict liability that compels a publisher or broadcaster to guarantee the accuracy of his factual assertions may lead to intolerable self-censorship. Allowing the media to avoid liability only by proving the truth of all injurious statements does not accord adequate protection to First Amendment liberties." There appeared to be no discussion of this aspect of Powell's draft during the Court's deliberations in *Gertz* though, as we shall see, it would come to dominate the justices' attentions soon enough.

As the new year dawned, Powell waited for reaction to his draft. Rehnquist joined Powell's opinion on January 2, and Marshall and Stewart both signed on to a slightly revised draft on January 14. Not unexpectedly, Brennan told his colleagues on January 10 that he planned to write a dissent. Chief Justice Burger sent a private note to Powell on January 3, saying that he doubted he could join Powell's opinion and questioned whether it even accurately reflected the discussion and votes at the Court's conference. Burger concluded his one paragraph note with the observation that, "I write to you now, without copy to the conference, to let you know my concern."

While Burger's note was terse, Powell's response was lengthy. In it, he wrote that he was "disappointed" that Burger was "not initially taken" with the draft's attempt to "work the Court out of its present dilemma." And he confessed that he did "find it difficult to reconcile all views and to judge how far a majority of the Court would be willing to go in reversing the strong tide toward near-total abrogation of the individual's opportunity to recover for libel in favor of the stringent demands of the *New York Times* rule." Nevertheless, Powell told Burger, he believed a clear majority of the Court wanted to abandon the Brennan position in *Rosenbloom* and afford some measure of additional protection to private individuals who are libeled. He said he had chosen negligence as the "constitutional minimum" because it was a "familiar" standard, although he conceded that the conference discussion gave him little guidance on that point. In addition, Powell explained that he had compromised his own views on damages—which he did not otherwise explain—in an attempt to achieve consensus around the idea of limiting awards of presumed and punitive damages in some meaningful fashion. His goal, he said, was "what seemed possible in obtaining agreement among five justices on a coherent theory of the law of libel and the First Amendment."

Finally, Powell offered Burger an intriguing piece of intelligence. He advised the chief justice that Blackmun, who had supported the Brennan approach in *Rosenbloom* and in conference in *Gertz*, might join Powell's opinion for the sake of coherence if his vote were needed. Nevertheless, Powell added, "I think it is too speculative to count Harry as part of a majority for this case."

On January 5, Burger called Powell to discuss the case. According to Powell's notes of their conversation, the chief justice made several points. First, he told Powell that he had not altered his view that the Court had carried *Sullivan* "way too far." Then, he described *Rosenbloom* as an "aberration" and described his own vote to join Brennan's opinion in that case as a function of the "monstrous injustice" of awarding significant damages to a "smut peddler." In addition, Burger suggested that Rosenbloom may even have been a public figure because "he may have been guilty of criminal conduct." And he told Powell that he was not persuaded by how his draft treated punitive damages. Finally, Burger said he agreed with Powell that "we must try hard to get a Court" and that he would therefore "reexamine carefully" his own views. Still, Powell emphasized in his notes of the conversation, Burger, "while generally encouraging," had made "*no* commitment."

White wrote to Powell on January 10, expressing his own reservations with his colleague's draft. In his letter, White wrote that, while he agreed "that the plaintiff in this case should not be required to prove knowing falsehood or reckless disregard, . . . neither would I interpose a federal negligence standard that he must satisfy before he can recover under state libel law." In what appears to be his first explicit statement on the subject, White made plain to Powell what he had only hinted at in his separate opinions in *Roy*, *Damron*, and *Rosenbloom* and how far he had now come in parting company with Brennan, his longtime ally. White wrote to Powell that, "[a]side from situations involving public officials or public figures, I would leave libelous speech in its historic legal position—that is, unprotected by the First Amendment." As a result, White said, "I thus will be in dissent from your remand for a new trial."

On January 11, Powell circulated a new draft. In it, he altered somewhat his description of the constitutional rules he had formulated. In this draft, rather than expressly stating that such a plaintiff must prove at least "negligence" in order to prevail, Powell described the Court's holding as providing that, "so long as they do not impose liability without fault, the States may define for themselves the appropriate standard of liability for a publisher or broadcaster of defamatory falsehood injurious to a private individual." In addition, in explaining the limitations his opinion placed on awards of punitive and presumed damages in such circumstances, Powell's new draft made it explicit that such damages were impermissible "at least when liability is not based on a showing of knowledge of falsity or reckless disregard for the truth."

Less than a week later, White wrote to Powell again, apparently in response to his latest draft. This time, White told Powell that the changes he had made to his opinion, especially in the section describing the liability standard, did not alter its substance. As White correctly asserted, although Powell's new draft did not expressly "say what showing of fault may be required, by way of negligence or otherwise, you still require fault beyond the damaging circulation of the falsehoods. This pretty well forces the States to revise their libel laws substantially." In addition, White noted, "requiring that the private plaintiff prove actual injury to reputation imposes a substantial federal limitation on state libel laws, and pretty well scuttles

the ingrained idea that there are certain statements that are *per se* libelous." Once
again, White told Powell that he "would dissent from the remand for a new trial."

At least as far as can be discerned from his own files and those of other justices,
Brennan communicated his own views to his colleagues for the first time since
the conference discussion the previous November when he circulated his draft
dissenting opinion on January 17. His draft spoke only for himself and therefore
changed little from its initial circulation to the version that appears in the official
reports of the case. In it, despite his apparent attempt to at least probe the efficacy
of the contrary position during argument, Brennan agreed with Powell's conclusion that Gertz was neither a public official nor a public figure. Brennan could
not, however, bring himself to "agree . . . that free and robust debate—so essential
to the proper functioning of our system of government—is permitted adequate
'breathing space' when, as the Court holds, that States may impose all but strict
liability for defamation if the defamed party is a private person." Rather, Brennan
continued to believe, as he had in *Rosenbloom*, "that we strike the proper accommodation between avoidance of media self-censorship and protection of individual
reputations only when we require States to apply the *New York Times Co. v. Sullivan*,
knowing-or-reckless-falsity standard in civil libel actions concerning media reports
of the involvement of private individuals in events of public or general interest."

Quoting liberally from his opinions in both *Rosenbloom* and *Time, Inc. v. Hill*,
in both of which he had applied the actual malice standard in cases brought by
persons who were not public figures but were otherwise involved in matters of
public concern, Brennan again rejected the notions that "private" plaintiffs have
a greater stake in protecting their reputations and that courts are ill-equipped
to identify those publications that address a subject of legitimate public interest.
With respect to the former, Brennan asserted that "[s]ocial interaction exposes all
of us to some degree of public view," quoting his own observation for the Court
in *Hill* that "[t]he risk of this exposure is an essential incident of life in a society
which places a primary value on freedom of speech and of press." With respect to
the latter, he rebutted Powell's contention, itself borrowed largely from Marshall's
dissent in *Rosenbloom*, that his own "view improperly commits to judges the task
of determining what is and what is not an issue of 'general or public interest.'"
Although he conceded, as he had in *Rosenbloom*, "that performance of this task
would not always be easy," Brennan expressed his ongoing confidence that "the
courts, the ultimate arbiters of all disputes concerning clashes of constitutional

values, would only be performing one of their traditional functions in undertaking this duty." Although neither of them knew it at the time, eventually even Powell would come to embrace Brennan's views about the constitutional necessity of just such a judicial role.

At the time, however, the only other justice who appeared to be attracted to Brennan's position was Blackmun. Upon reviewing Brennan's draft, Blackmun's law clerk told his justice that Brennan had written a "good dissent," indeed one that offered "a better resolution of the competing values than the majority." Nevertheless, the law clerk counseled Blackmun that he ought to keep his options open. "[I]t is most important for a majority position to be carved out," the law clerk wrote, "so my recommendation would still be to join Justice Powell if your vote is needed for a 5th. If the Chief joins Justice Powell, it would probably be best to stick with Justice Brennan."

Meanwhile, on January 18, Powell advised Jeffries about an ominous conversation he had had the previous day with Rehnquist. As Powell explained it to his law clerk, Rehnquist had warned him that he might change his mind "on the basis of Byron's views." Apparently, White had also told Rehnquist that Powell's opinion did not follow the conference, at which there was a majority vote—as he recorded it—to reinstate the judgment of the district court. Concerned that he was losing his grip on the majority opinion, Powell drafted a five-page double-spaced letter to White that same day. In it, after acknowledging that some of the issues he had addressed in his draft were never discussed by the justices in conference, Powell attempted to walk White through his thought process, likely in yet another effort to win him over.

Although Powell ultimately decided not to send the letter, it serves as an informative guidebook of sorts that is, if nothing else, useful in parsing the Court's ultimate decision. Powell began his letter by explaining his belief, that in crafting his opinion in *Gertz*, he "assumed we were addressing only First Amendment rights of the press. As I understand *New York Times* and its progeny," Powell wrote, "these decisions do not control the application of the law of defamation to libelous statements made by non-media speakers." Thus, he added, the "balancing of public and private interests may be different where the defendant may not fairly be deemed a part of the media, especially where the non-media defendant is not a public official or candidate for public office."

Because he never sent this letter to White, however, there is no indication that Powell ever shared this insight with any of the other justices during the Court's deliberations in *Gertz*. Ten years later, however, Powell, White, Brennan, and the rest of the Court would become embroiled in attempting to resolve precisely that question—whether the First Amendment protections crafted in *Sullivan* and in *Gertz* applied only to media defendants. In this early writing on the subject, as would be the case a decade later, Powell apparently was unaware, or had forgotten, that *Sullivan* itself extended the protections of the actual malice standard to the four ministers sued by Sullivan, nonmedia defendants who were neither public officials nor candidates for public office.

In his unsent letter to White, Powell identified as his central challenge in crafting an opinion that could garner the support of a majority of the Court, the fact that, "[a]lthough the conference decided not to follow the *Rosenbloom* plurality, it did not decide what constitutional doctrine to announce in its place." In formulating that doctrine, he wrote that he was guided, in significant part, by his belief that most of the justices who might form a majority in *Gertz* would not support "a return to the common law rule of strict liability for defamation, at least as applied to the press and the broadcast media." By the same token, he concluded "on the basis of the record that a majority of the Court would favor, in a Gertz or Rosenbloom type situation, allowing the states to apply such rule of liability as they respectively deem appropriate, short of making the media guarantee the truth of publications often written or broadcast under exigent time pressures with little or no opportunity for careful verification." Thus, he concluded that leaving the fault standard to the states as long as it did not permit strict liability "was the only hope for a majority position."

Assessing why he thought each of the other justices might be expected to support his position, Powell took pains—in a footnote to his unsent letter—to emphasize that he had not bothered to mention "my very senior colleagues, Bill Douglas and Bill Brennan, as their views—although not entirely in accord with each other—are well known." In this passage, Powell effectively acknowledged what had become increasingly obvious: that his fellow justices, with the exception of Blackmun, considered Brennan's views—specifically, that the actual malice standard should govern all defamation actions involving speech about a matter of public concern—to be the functional equivalent of the idiosyncratic and generally rejected "absolutist" position now espoused only by Douglas. For the majority

of the justices that comprised the Supreme Court in 1974, the fact that Brennan
had formulated the actual malice standard in *Sullivan* precisely so as to reserve to
public officials some ability to vindicate their reputations and that he did so in
the face of the staunch opposition of Douglas, Black, and Goldberg to such a perceived erosion of the First Amendment's protections, was, at best, ancient history.

Finally, in his unsent letter to White, Powell turned his own attentions to explaining his reasons for venturing beyond the applicable liability standard and limiting
as well the right of a defamed plaintiff to recover punitive and presumed damages.
As Powell saw it, since the jury in *Gertz* had been instructed that it could properly award presumed damages, addressing the issue in his draft opinion "seemed
unavoidable." In addition, although he asserted that his own "preference" was "for a
broad damage rule in libel cases," including awards of "punitive damages in accordance with the common law," Powell professed to have limited their availability
only because he perceived it necessary to do so to secure the votes of Marshall
and Stewart. Somewhat ironically, Powell concluded his letter by reminding White
that "a majority position is highly desirable if this can be reached without sacrifice
of a principled view of a Justice."

On January 22, Burger wrote to Powell that he planned to wait and see what
the dissents looked like. At the same time, he wrote separately to Blackmun to ask
to discuss *Gertz* and the Powell opinion with him. "Lewis is treating this too much
like an ordinary negligence case," Burger complained to Blackmun. And although
the chief justice acknowledged to Blackmun that there were also "problems with
Byron's view," he was hopeful that White's anticipated dissent "might lead Lewis
to clarify his proof-of-damage concept."

On February 20, Rehnquist wrote privately to Powell, apologizing for having
"already orally burdened you with my misgivings about this case" and characterizing his letter as "an effort on my part to fish or cut bait." Rehnquist pronounced
himself torn between his sympathy for White's position—that Powell's opinion purported to constitutionalize too much of the law of defamation—and his "strongly"
held belief that "as an institutional matter it is very desirable that there be a Court
opinion in the case." In the end, he told Powell that he was prepared to endorse his
opinion if Powell would add language to it emphasizing that, in assessing whether
there was competent evidence of "actual injury" in a given case, "there need be
no evidence which assigns an actual dollar value to the injury." If Powell made
the requested change, Rehnquist said, "and if your opinion becomes the opinion

of the Court, I will stay put. If not, I will in any event do nothing until Byron circulates, and do not know exactly what I will do after that."

Two days later, Powell responded, advising Rehnquist that he "ever so much appreciate[d]" his letter and declaring "without hesitation that the change which you suggest is entirely agreeable to me." He also told Rehnquist that, in "an accidental conversation with Harry [Blackmun] yesterday afternoon, and in response to his inquiry as to where matters stood on Gertz, I advised Harry of your letter." As Powell related the conversation, Blackmun "expressed satisfaction and reiterated his present intention to join the four of us if necessary for a Court." Nevertheless, Powell explained, Blackmun remained "troubled by the inconsistency with his vote in Rosenbloom and will await all circulations before voting here."

On February 26, Powell circulated another draft opinion incorporating the change that Rehnquist had requested. Thereafter, internal communications about the case ground to a virtual halt. It appeared that the next step was White's to take, since he had not circulated his promised dissenting opinion and, in what had all the makings of a game of dominos, the reaction within the Court to whatever White had to say would likely govern how the remaining tiles would fall. Indeed, at that juncture, Burger had advised Powell that he would wait for White's opinion before casting his own vote, Rehnquist had conditioned his own support on Powell otherwise securing a majority, and Blackmun had indicated he would join Powell only if necessary to form one.

The waiting ended on April 1, when White circulated his draft dissent. It was a blistering document, recalling at its outset that, for "some 200 years—from the very founding of the Nation—the law of defamation and the right of the ordinary citizen to recover for false publication injurious to his reputation has been almost exclusively the business of state courts and legislatures." Now, however, White contended, the Court, using the First Amendment "as its chosen instrument . . . in a few short pages has federalized major aspects of libel law by declaring unconstitutional in important respects the prevailing defamation law in all or most of the 50 states." And then, in a direct rebuke of Powell, White offered the following:

> I assume these sweeping changes will be popular with the press, but this is not the
> road to salvation for a court of law. As I see it, there are wholly insufficient grounds
> for scuttling the libel laws of the States in such wholesale fashion, to say nothing of
> deprecating the reputation interest of ordinary citizens and rendering them powerless

to protect themselves. I do not suggest that the decision is illegitimate or beyond the bounds of judicial review, but it is an ill-considered exercise of the power entrusted to this Court, particularly when the court has not had the benefit of briefs and argument addressed to most of the major issues which the Court now decides.

"Lest there be any mistake about it," White scolded, "the changes wrought by the Court's decision cut very deeply." Thereafter, in page after page, White proceeded to catalogue the many ways in which Powell's opinion had abrogated the common law, pausing at each one to explain why he perceived the change to be both ill-advised and of dubious legitimacy as a rule of constitutional law. Aiming his rhetorical guns at Powell's requirement that all defamation plaintiffs henceforth prove both some level of fault by the defendant and that they had sustained "actual injury," White's salvos were particularly explosive:

The impact of today's decision on the traditional law of libel is immediately obvious and indisputable. . . . No longer will the plaintiff be able to rest his case with proof of a libel defamatory on its face or proof of a slander historically actionable *per se.* In addition, he must prove some further degree of culpable conduct on the part of the publisher, such as intentional or reckless falsehood or negligence. And if he succeeds in this respect, he faces still another obstacle: recovery for loss of reputation will be conditioned upon "competent" proof of actual injury to his standing in the community. This will be true regardless of the nature of the defamation and even though it is one of those particularly reprehensible statements that have traditionally made slanderous words actionable without proof of fault by the publisher or of the damaging impact of his publication. The Court rejects the judgment of experience that some publications are so inherently capable of injury, and actual injury so difficult to prove, that the risk of falsehood should be borne by the publisher, not the victim. Plainly, with the additional burden on the plaintiff of proving negligence or other fault, it will be exceedingly difficult, perhaps impossible, for him to vindicate his reputation interest by securing a judgment for nominal damages, the practical effect of such a judgment being a judicial declaration that the publication was indeed false. Under the new rule the plaintiff can lose, not because the statement is true, but because it was not negligently made.

And just in case what preceded it had not been sufficiently clear, White characterized Powell's opinion as working "radical changes in the law" that constituted "severe invasions of the prerogatives of the States." Accordingly, White asserted, they "should at least be shown to be required by the First Amendment or necessitated by our present circumstances." Nonetheless, he concluded, "[n]either has been demonstrated."

Not surprisingly, Powell hurriedly circulated a brief memorandum to the other justices that same day announcing his intention to "make some response" to White's missive as well as his promise "to give this some priority." After reading it a second time, Powell dictated his thoughts about White's opinion in a lengthy memorandum that bears his handwritten notation "as dictated and not edited." In it, he catalogued several of White's more acerbic descriptions of his opinion, observing that it constituted "[q]uite a mouthful for a page and a half!" And at one juncture, he paused to consider how it was that White came to author such a document in the first place. White's dissent, Powell observed, "ignores—quite literally almost entirely—the relevant decisions of this Court over the past ten years." In addition, Powell wrote, "the tone of the dissent reflects (despite a disclaimer) a deep dissatisfaction with *New York Times* even though the author of that dissent joined in the decision." This, Powell said, was "[e]ven more remarkable" given the fact that White had "joined Chief Justice Warren in the opinion which extended" the actual malice requirement to public figures in *Butts* and *Walker.*

Meanwhile, Powell attempted to regroup his forces. The following day, April 2, he told Jeffries that he had just gotten off the "hot line" with Stewart, who—like Jeffries himself—had pronounced the dissent "powerful" and allowed that there was "a good deal of 'merit' to it." Nevertheless, Powell reported that, following a "lengthy telephone talk, Justice Stewart stated that he is staying with us 100% on the standard of liability, but would like for us to relax our position as to damages." Apparently, as Powell recounted it, Stewart now wanted him to attempt to make some distinction between punitive and presumed damages—in which direction was not immediately clear—warning that, otherwise, "he thinks our 'Court' may be in real jeopardy."

All of this angst over White's dissent led to the drafting a few days later of what eventually became footnote 10 of the Court's opinion, a refutation of White's broadside and a defense of Powell's position that, by repudiating the liability standard advocated by the *Rosenbloom* plurality, the Court was actually easing the restraints on state libel law considerably even if stopping short of permitting continuation of the kind of strict liability that White advocated. Powell first shared footnote 10 as part of a revised draft he circulated on April 12. On April 25, however, Rehnquist wrote to Powell saying that the footnote "reaffirms *New York Times* much more emphatically than the body of the opinion does, and much more emphatically than I would be willing to do." Because of this, Rehnquist again threatened to change his vote. In short order, therefore, Powell revised the footnote, shrinking it, and according to a note in Powell's file, securing Rehnquist's approval before he circulated it to the other justices. In the new, slimmed down version, Powell deleted from the footnote the adamant contention that White's view "accords no weight whatever to the First Amendment values implicated by a rule requiring the media to guarantee the accuracy of all factual assertions and contradicts the essential premise underlying *New York Times* and every subsequent decision of this Court. This fundamental precept is that the prospect of liability for innocent error will induce a cautious and restrictive exercise of the constitutionally guaranteed freedoms of speech and press." Powell also removed a quotation from and citation to *Sullivan* that immediately followed this passage.

Beyond the addition of footnote 10, Powell made few other substantive changes to his opinion in response to White's attack. Despite his earlier discussion with Stewart about the need to alter his treatment of presumed and punitive damages in a fashion that distinguished between them, Powell ultimately left the relevant portions of Part IV of his draft largely intact. Powell's files contain no clear explanation for this, except for a cryptic handwritten note on his copy of the February 26 draft (the version that immediately preceded White's dissent), which reads, in its entirety, "after discussion with J. Stewart I decided to leave Part IV substantially as written in this draft—at least pending further reaction from the Justices."

For his part, Brennan apparently concluded that White's dissent did not require significant changes to his own opinion. To be sure, White's opinion was directed almost entirely to decrying the unprecedented changes to the law of defamation that Powell had crafted, changes that Brennan had neither advocated himself nor endorsed. Moreover, White's dissent included a pledge of allegiance to both *Sullivan* and *Butts*, in which he expressly proclaimed that he "continue[d] to subscribe to the *New York Times* decision and those decisions extending its protection to defamatory falsehoods about public persons." Although Powell had privately referred to this passage somewhat derisively as a "disclaimer" and perceived in White's opinion a fundamental hostility to the premises of *Sullivan* itself, at the time, Brennan had little reason to believe, at least unless he was looking for one, that White meant anything different than what he said.

Thus, in the wake of White's dissent, Brennan added only a brief paragraph to a footnote in his own opinion in which he addressed, "parenthetically," White's complaint that, by requiring a "private" defamation plaintiff to prove some level of fault, both Powell and Brennan had prevented such a plaintiff "from vindicating his reputation by securing a judgment that the publication was false." To this, Brennan responded that White's argument "overlooks" the ability of states to enact legislation establishing a cause of action "for retraction or for publication of a court's determination of falsity if the plaintiff is able to demonstrate that false statements have been published concerning his activities." This, of course, reiterated the same point that Brennan had included in his opinion in *Rosenbloom*.

Brennan closed his newly added paragraph by acknowledging that "questions could be raised concerning the constitutionality of such statutes," an aside undoubtedly prompted by another case, *Miami Herald Publishing Co. v. Tornillo*, which the Court was considering at the same time as *Gertz* and which was ultimately decided on the same day. *Tornillo* was not a libel case, and it came up much later in the term than *Gertz*. Nevertheless, the justices found some important connections between *Tornillo* and the *Sullivan* line of cases, some of which influenced the deliberations in and the ultimate resolution of *Gertz* itself.

Pat Tornillo was the executive director of a Florida teachers' union when he decided to run for the Florida legislature in 1972. In two editorials in September 1972, the *Miami Herald* criticized Tornillo's candidacy. The first mocked Tornillo's attacks on his opponent for failing to file a campaign expenditure report, referring to him as "Czar Tornillo," and reminding voters that he had led a teachers strike in 1968. "Call it whatever you will, it was an illegal act against the public interest and clearly prohibited by the statutes," the editorial said. The second editorial referred, among other criticisms of Tornillo's candidacy, to his "shakedown statesmanship." Tornillo demanded that the *Herald* publish a reply he had submitted to the newspaper and, when he was rebuffed, he sued, invoking a Florida law that afforded candidates for public office a right to have their replies published by a newspaper that impugned their personal character and integrity. After a Florida trial court held that the statute violated the First Amendment, the Florida Supreme Court reversed, concluding that the law enhanced public information and, therefore, served the purposes of the First Amendment.

When the case reached the U.S. Supreme Court, Brennan in particular was intrigued by the interplay between it and the issues with which the justices were then grappling in *Gertz*. As the footnote he added to his own dissent in *Gertz* suggested, Brennan saw the potential of the kind of retraction statute he described there and in *Rosenbloom* to provide some redress for libel plaintiffs, including private persons, and thereby ease the concerns, expressed within the Court and elsewhere, about the inability of those plaintiffs who could not prove actual malice as required by his opinion in *Rosenbloom* to vindicate their reputations. Accordingly, on June 4, Brennan wrote to Burger, who had assigned himself to write the majority opinion in *Tornillo*, and pointed the chief justice to the footnote he had added to his dissent in *Gertz*. He asked Burger to add a footnote to his own opinion in *Tornillo* making it clear that the fact that right-of-reply statutes, like the one at issue in that case, violate the First Amendment does not necessarily speak to the constitutionality of the kind of retraction statute Brennan envisioned.

The overlap between the issues before the Court in *Gertz* and *Tornillo* was also on the mind of White, who crafted a concurring opinion in the latter in which he took yet another shot at Powell's opinion in the former. Agreeing with the Court's determination that the First Amendment precludes the government from telling a newspaper what to publish, White hastened to add that, by "[r]eaffirming the rule that the press cannot be forced to print an answer to a personal attack made by it," *Tornillo* had thrown "into stark relief the consequences of the new balance forged by the Court in the companion case also announced today." As White saw it, Powell's opinion in *Gertz* "goes far toward eviscerating the effectiveness of the ordinary libel action, which has long been the only potent response available to the private citizen libeled by the press." And, White added, "it is a near absurdity to so deprecate individual dignity, as the Court does in *Gertz*, and to leave the people at the complete mercy of the press, at least in this stage of our history when the press, as the majority in this case so well documents, is steadily becoming more powerful and much less likely to be deterred by threats of libel suits."

Ultimately, after consulting with Blackmun, Powell decided to respond to White in kind, adding a paragraph to footnote 10 of his opinion in *Gertz* objecting to White's suggestion that, in *Gertz*, the Court had "trivialize[d] and denigrate[d] the interest in reputation." On June 20, Powell circulated the eighth draft of his opinion, in which he took White on directly, complaining that "[i]n light of the progressive extension of the knowing-or-reckless-falsity requirement" from *Sullivan* through *Rosenbloom,* "one might have viewed today's decision allowing recovery under any standard save strict liability as a more generous accommodation of the state interest in comprehensive reputational [*sic*] injury to private individuals than the law presently affords."

After Brennan circulated his own revised dissent in *Gertz* referencing the prospect of state legislation creating a right to a retraction, White added a footnote to his own opinion backing his play. In it, White seized yet another opportunity to poke at Powell, this time complaining that his opinion for the Court "does not even consider this less drastic alternative to its new 'some fault' libel standards."

As the month of April 1974 wore on, Powell continued his quest for votes in support of his opinion in *Gertz.* On April 24, following further discussions between them in the wake of White's dissent, Blackmun sent to Powell a draft of a concurring opinion, which he said he would not circulate to the other justices "until I have your reaction." In it, Blackmun acknowledged that he had joined the *Rosenbloom* plurality and explained that he did so because he considered Brennan's analysis in that case to be both "logical and inevitable." By the same token, Blackmun allowed that he "sense[d] some illogic" in the approach that Powell had taken in *Gertz.* Nevertheless, Blackmun's draft concluded:

> The Court was sadly fractionated in *Rosenbloom.* A result of that kind inevitably leads to uncertainty. I feel that it is of profound importance for the Court to come to rest in the defamation area and to have a clearly defined majority position that eliminates the unsureness engendered by *Rosenbloom*'s diversity. If my vote were not needed to create a majority, I would adhere to my prior view. A definitive ruling, however, is paramount.

The following day, presumably after securing Powell's approval for his own proposed opinion, Blackmun shared it with the chief justice. In his cover note, Blackmun reminded Burger that "you and I are the holdouts on this." Although he did not expressly ask Burger to follow him in joining Powell's opinion, Blackmun's note suggested to the chief that "[p]erhaps this will prompt discussion of the case so that some decision on it will be made." And in that regard, Blackmun reminded

Burger that this "case, I believe, is holding up disposition of . . . *Old Dominion Branch v. Austin*."

Austin was another defamation case that had been argued the same day as *Gertz*. It arose from a dispute in Richmond, Virginia, between nonunion letter carriers and certain local and national unions representing postal workers. Since the case was overshadowed by *Gertz*, there is relatively little record of the Court's deliberations in those of the justices' internal files that have been made public. The plaintiffs, a nonunion letter carrier named Henry Austin and several of his coworkers, complained that they had been defamed by the local union's newsletter, the *Carrier's Corner*, which included them in a list of "scabs" who had not yet joined the union. A subsequent issue of the newsletter included a very negative description of what the term *scab* means, concluding with a paragraph generally attributed to the author Jack London, which read, "Esau was a traitor to himself; Judas was a traitor to his God; Benedict Arnold was a traitor to his country; a SCAB is a traitor to his God, his country, his family and his class.'"

Relying on the Supreme Court's decision in *Linn v. Plant Guard Workers Local 118*, a Virginia trial judge declined to dismiss the suit, concluding that it could proceed under state law as long as any liability was based on actual malice, although he appeared to suggest as well that a finding of actual malice could be based on the publication of insulting words motivated by hatred, spite, or ill-will and made with deliberate indifference to the rights of the plaintiffs. A jury awarded each of three plaintiffs $10,000 in compensatory damages and $45,000 in punitive damages, for a total of $165,000. The Virginia Supreme Court affirmed the judgment.

The U.S. Supreme Court heard the union's appeal the same day as the *Gertz* argument. Ultimately, the justices reversed the Virginia Supreme Court's ruling by a six-to-three vote on June 25, 1974, the same day the Court finally announced its decision in *Gertz*. Justice Marshall wrote the Court's opinion, holding that the Virginia courts' definition of actual malice was in error. Applying the correct iteration of the standard, Marshall's opinion concluded that it "should be clear that the newsletter's use of the epithet 'scab' was protected under federal law and cannot be the basis of a state libel judgment. Rather than being a reckless or knowing falsehood, naming the appellees as scabs was literally and factually true." In so holding, Marshall quoted from Powell's assertion in *Gertz* that "there is no such thing as a false idea," lending further credence to the conclusion subsequently reached by a litany of courts that, in *Gertz* itself, the Court had thereby exempted all expressions of "opinion" from defamation liability.

Marshall's opinion in *Austin* did not garner the support of Douglas, who concurred based on his consistent view that all such defamation actions were precluded by the First Amendment, or Powell, who wrote a dissenting opinion that was joined by Burger and Rehnquist. Powell's dissent was based largely on his concern that the Court's extension of the *Sullivan* requirement of actual malice to virtually all statements made in the context of a labor dispute went beyond *Linn* and afforded workers little protection from statements made against them by employers or unions in the context of a such a dispute. And turning to the merits of the defamation claim itself, Powell disagreed with Marshall's characterization of the alleged libel as a mere epithet. "It is one thing to say that lawyers are shysters and that doctors are quacks," Powell wrote, but "it is quite another matter—indeed, it is libelous per se, to publish that lawyer Jones is a shyster or that Dr. Smith is a quack."

While the justices completed their work on *Austin*, Chief Justice Burger was still trying to reconcile *Gertz* and *Tornillo*, in which he was then crafting the Court's opinion. On June 5, he wrote to Powell and advised him of Brennan's willingness to join his opinion in *Tornillo* provided that "we do not reach nor decide the question of the validity or constitutionality of right-to-reply laws generally." Burger described himself as "a little puzzled" by Brennan's request, since "it seems to me that as it now stands," the majority opinion in *Tornillo* "does not leave much room for right-to-reply statutes which are mandatory." In his letter to Powell, Burger observed—incorrectly—that Powell's draft opinion in *Gertz* eliminated punitive damages and wondered whether Powell would be willing to include in his *Gertz* opinion language to the effect that "nothing in the holding impairs the right of the states to have statutes . . . allowing a newspaper to avoid all but compensatory damages by publishing a retraction."

Powell replied the next day, politely reminding the chief justice that "*Gertz*, as written, does not eliminate punitive damages in a libel action against a newspaper where malice is proved in conformity with the *New York Times* standard." Accordingly, Powell said it "would seem to me to be appropriate to add a note to your opinion along the lines you suggest." But, Powell added, "[a]s *Gertz* does not get into this area at all, it would be awkward and gratuitous—it seems to me—to make a reference to retraction statutes in that case."

Following this exchange with Powell, Burger wrote to Brennan and told him that he would "amplify to meet your memo" in the next draft of his *Tornillo* opinion, which he said he would circulate later that day. It appears, however, that no such amplification was ever made. As a result, Brennan ultimately wrote a brief, one-paragraph concurring statement in *Tornillo*, joined by Rehnquist, in which he underscored his understanding that the Court was taking no position on the constitutionality of the kinds of retraction statutes he envisioned.

In contrast to the ongoing deliberations in *Gertz*, the Court's decision in *Tornillo* came together relatively quickly. In his opinion for the Court, Burger used the occasion to discourse at length about the dangers of concentrated media ownership and to lament the fact that, in his view, the press presented more diverse points of view when the First Amendment was ratified in 1791. "The result of these vast changes has been to place in a few hands the power to inform the American people and shape public opinion," Burger wrote, adding that the "monopoly of the means of communication allows for little or no critical analysis of the media except in professional journals of very limited readership." Nevertheless, when it came to actually deciding the case, the chief justice concluded forcefully that compelling newspapers to publish replies was too intrusive into the processes of editors and therefore violated the First Amendment. In the opinion's most frequently quoted passage, Burger wrote:

> Even if a newspaper would face no additional costs to comply with a compulsory access law and would not be forced to forgo publication of news or opinion by the inclusion of a reply, the Florida statute fails to clear the barriers of the First Amendment because of its intrusion into the function of editors. A newspaper is more than a passive receptacle or conduit for news, comment, and advertising. The choice of material to go into a newspaper, and the decisions made as to limitations on the size and content of the paper, and treatment of public issues and public officials— whether fair or unfair—constitute the exercise of editorial control and judgment. It has yet to be demonstrated how governmental regulation of this crucial process can be exercised consistent with First Amendment guarantees of a free press as they have evolved to this time.

In his own concurring opinion in *Tornillo*, White amplified Burger's point, asserting that the Florida law "runs afoul of the elementary First Amendment proposition that government may not force a newspaper to print copy which, in its journalistic discretion, it chooses to leave on the newsroom floor."

On June 20, Burger finally turned back from *Tornillo* and circulated his own proposed dissent in *Gertz*, which he characterized to the other justices as "very 'ragged.'" In it, he expressed sympathy for "much" of what White had said in his own dissenting opinion, although he added—without much explanation—that he did "not read the Court's new doctrinal approach in quite the way [White] does." Burger then focused his attention on Gertz himself, who the chief justice described as performing his "professional representative role as an advocate in the highest tradition of the law," and proceeded to emphasize the potential adverse impact of libels directed at lawyers, an impact that he said could "gravely jeopardize[]" the "important" public policy underlying "the right to counsel" itself. Accordingly, Burger wrote, he would reinstate the verdict that Gertz had secured in the trial court.

The Court's decision in *Gertz* was finally announced five days later, on June 25, along with its rulings in *Austin* and *Tornillo*. In the end, there were six separate opinions in *Gertz*; the majority opinion, written by Powell for five justices (himself, Marshall, Stewart, Rehnquist, and Blackmun), along with the aforementioned concurring opinion by Blackmun and separate dissenting opinions by Brennan, White, Burger, and Douglas (reiterating his view that the First Amendment permitted no libel suits against the press at all). When he announced the decision that day in open court, Powell summarized the Court's holding as follows:

> We decline today to extend *New York Times* to a case where neither a public official nor a public figure is the plaintiff merely because the publication is a matter of public interest. We recognize that the State's interest in protecting the reputation of private individuals must be balanced against the First Amendment interests. Accordingly we hold that the states may allow compensatory damages for libel which causes injury to the reputation of private individuals without applying the strict *New York Times* test. But we would not approve the imposition of liability without fault as we think this would unduly burden a free press. Thus with regard to libel suits by private individuals, the states will be free to apply any standard which does not impose liability without fault, such as a negligence standard. Accordingly we reverse the Court of Appeals and remand the case for a new trial.

Following the decision, Powell received considerable praise in private quarters for his efforts. His files include a letter from *New York Times* columnist and Pulitzer Prize-winning Supreme Court reporter Anthony Lewis, who had become a personal friend of Brennan and who would go on to write *Make No Law*, the highly acclaimed, definitive work on *Sullivan* itself. In his letter, Lewis lauded Powell's opinion in *Gertz*, proclaiming not only that it "resolved the tensions in an intellectually most satisfying way" but that, in Lewis's view, "it is the right way for the press, too." Powell also received a "fan letter" from Professor John Wade of Vanderbilt Law School who had recently replaced the legendary scholar William Prosser as Reporter for the American Law Institute's influential *Restatement (Second) of Torts*. Wade told Powell that *Gertz* "restores a needed sense of perspective to the problem, with a reasoned and unemotional balancing of the conflicting interests." He predicted the decision would "straighten out the tort law of defamation while giving due respect to the principles of constitutional law."

Within days of receiving it, Powell shared Wade's letter with the justices who had joined his majority in *Gertz*. In his cover note, he told them that, "[i]n view of our 'long winter of discontent'" grappling with the constitutional law of defamation, "perhaps those of us who joined—with varying degrees of reluctance—the Court's opinion in *Gertz*, will derive some satisfaction from Professor Wade's enclosed letter."

Although Powell's note was not addressed to Brennan, its description of the Court's "long winter of discontent" in *Gertz* surely would have struck a responsive chord with the author of *Sullivan*. In the end, Brennan stood alone in advocating the position he had staked out in *Rosenbloom*, a position he firmly believed was the inevitable consequence of the First Amendment theory he had championed in *Sullivan* itself. By now, Brennan could have no doubt that the most recent changes in the Court's composition had not only deprived him of the power to speak on its behalf when it addressed the meaning and scope of that decision but also had taken from him the working majority that had supported his views on those subjects for much of the previous decade. Most of his newest colleagues were not only inclined to construe *Sullivan* less expansively but one of them, Justice Powell, also appeared to be both keen on taking the law in a very different direction and fully prepared to engage in the kind of internal lobbying and horse trading necessary to achieve his goals. And it began to appear more clearly that Brennan had lost the full-throated support of Justice White, who had been perhaps his most consistent ally on the Court in *Sullivan* and in the decisions that followed it. Although

White continued to voice support for *Sullivan* in his dissenting opinion in *Gertz*, the bases for his attack on the new constitutional rules devised by Powell seemed to apply with equal force to the alternative liability rule crafted by Brennan in *Rosenbloom* and, at least to some extent, in *Sullivan* itself.

There are two postscripts to the *Gertz* story. First, although the Court held that Elmer Gertz was not a public figure at the time of his lawsuit, things might have looked different some years later. In 1992, Gertz published a 295-page book in which he told the story of the case in detail and reflected on the experience. And in 2000, the Illinois State Bar Association initiated the annual Elmer Gertz Human Rights Award to honor "unsung heroes" who as lawyers have made a commitment to human rights.

Second, whether it is because he mellowed with age or simply came to accept the outcome in *Gertz*, Brennan years later came to think of the decision as something of a victory in one important respect: it extended the reach of the First Amendment to defamation actions brought by private plaintiffs, even if only as to the availability of presumed and punitive damages and the requirement that such plaintiffs bear the burden of proving at least some level of fault. In an interview with his biographer in his Supreme Court chambers on December 17, 1986, Brennan observed:

> And indeed, *Gertz* itself is only an extension in the sense that, in the case of a private individual, the idea that there were any First Amendment restraints simply hadn't occurred to anybody, but when Powell came up with *Gertz* and said there ought to be if he wants to get punitive damages, and then he can't have compensatory damage without proving some fault on the part of the defendant, he's got to prove fault.

Unfortunately, because Brennan did not address *Gertz* in his narrative history of the October 1973 term, or apparently in other private correspondence that year, we are left to wonder about the extent to which he pondered these matters at the time. There would, however, be plenty of opportunities for Brennan to revisit these issues in the years to come as the justices began to confront the ramifications of the new rules Powell had announced on their behalf in *Gertz*. And the first of those opportunities would not be long in coming.

CHAPTER 5

UNPACKING *GERTZ*

Much as the decade after *Sullivan* was dominated on the Supreme Court's docket by a series of cases setting the boundaries of the constitutional doctrine articulated by Justice Brennan in *Sullivan* itself, the five years immediately following *Gertz* featured an analogous spate of decisions exploring the implications of Justice Powell's handiwork there. Thus, just as the period between *Sullivan* and *Gertz* focused on assessing the reach and contours of the actual malice standard, the period immediately following *Gertz* was devoted, in significant part, to exploring the dimensions of the public figure standard Powell had constructed in that case as well as the consequences of the Court's pronouncements that even so-called private plaintiffs are required to show that the defendant had published a defamatory falsehood with at least some degree of fault and sustained some actual injury as a result. And in the years following *Gertz*, the Court also began to grapple with the practical ramifications—both for the press and for the subjects of its reporting—of the constitutional scheme it had created in *Sullivan* and *Gertz* and the extent to which the actual litigation of defamation actions had, for better or for worse, been transformed as a result.

Cox Broadcasting Corp. v. Cohn

The Court's first post-*Gertz* opportunity to revisit the issues addressed in that case came in *Cox Broadcasting Corp. v. Cohn*, which was decided the following term. It arrived at the Court in December 1973, before *Gertz* had even been decided. The case arose from the August 1971 gang rape in Georgia of 17-year-old Cynthia

Cohn, who did not survive the attack. Six men were indicted for her rape and
murder and, when they appeared for trial the following April, all but one pled
guilty and the trial of the sixth was postponed to a later date. In the eight months
that passed between the attack and the guilty pleas, the incident received significant press attention. None of the stories, however, identified Ms. Cohn.

During the April trial call, a reporter for WSB-TV reviewed the indictments,
which were contained in the public record of the case and available for inspection
in the courtroom. The indictments identified Ms. Cohn by name, and the reporter
included that information in a story that was broadcast by the television station
both that evening and the following day:

> Six youths went on trial today for the murder-rape of a teenaged girl. The six Sandy
> Springs High School boys were charged with murder and rape in the death of seven-
> teen year old Cynthia Cohn following a drinking party last August 18th. The tragic
> death of the high school girl shocked the entire Sandy Springs community. Today
> the six boys had their day in court.

In May 1972, Ms. Cohn's father brought a suit seeking damages against Cox
Broadcasting Corp., which owned the station, as well as against the reporter. His
complaint relied, in part, on a Georgia criminal statute that made it a misdemeanor
to publish or broadcast the identity of a rape victim. He also purported to assert a
common law claim for invasion of privacy. The trial court rejected the defendants'
contention that both claims were precluded by the First Amendment and, holding
that the criminal statute did indeed create a private right to sue for money damages, entered a judgment in Mr. Cohn's favor with respect to liability.

On appeal, the Georgia Supreme Court, in the first of two decisions, disagreed
with the trial judge that the criminal statute gave rise to a damages claim, but
concluded that Mr. Cohn could proceed to trial on his common law claim for
invasion of privacy, the First Amendment notwithstanding. On rehearing, the court
again rejected the defendants' First Amendment-based arguments, holding both
that the criminal statute demonstrated, as a matter of state law, that the identity of
a rape victim does not constitute a matter of legitimate public concern and that
the statute itself was therefore "a legitimate limitation on the right of freedom of
expression contained in the First Amendment."

The Supreme Court heard argument in the defendants' appeal on November 11, 1974, a few short months after it announced its decision in *Gertz*. Not surprisingly, therefore, the defendants' counsel, Kirk McAlpin, a prominent Atlanta lawyer and later President of the Georgia State Bar, began his argument by attempting to fit the case within the analytical framework that Justice Powell had erected there. He asserted that the *Cohn* case, unlike *Gertz*, "does not involve any false statements," "does not involve any defamation," but rather concerned the imposition of civil liability on what was "clearly a truthful, non-defamatory statement of a reporting of a public trial in the State of Georgia." When pressed by Justice Brennan whether he was arguing for a "limited" First Amendment right "truthfully to report [on a] judicial proceeding," McAlpin demurred, asserting that, following *Gertz*, "it may be that truthful reporting of non-defamatory matter has absolute privilege." After Brennan secured McAlpin's agreement that he did indeed want the Court "to go that far," Justice Stewart sounded what appeared to be a word of caution, suggesting that the most the Court could do in the case before it was "deal with the constitutional validity of this Georgia statute." Undeterred, Brennan interjected that "this is probably the first case, as I recall, since I've been here, where we dealt with [a] concededly truthful report . . . and the question of the extent to which at least where the press is concerned, . . . under the First Amendment [there is] protection to publish that no matter where it comes from."

For his part, Justice Powell, the author of *Gertz*, appeared troubled by McAlpin's contention that the statute violated the First Amendment simply because publication of the victim's name addressed a matter of legitimate public interest. Although he did not say so expressly, McAlpin's proposition may have struck Powell as uncomfortably close to Justice Brennan's formulation in *Rosenbloom*. Thus, when Powell asked McAlpin, "[w]ho decides what is a matter of public interest?" the lawyer answered that the Court's decision in *Tornillo* suggested that "you may have a rule that would say that . . . it's an editor's judgment unless [there] is clear and extreme abuse." In response, Powell asked, "[i]f it's the editor's decision then the judiciary would have no further function in this area?'" to which McAlpin replied, "Your Honor, it may be."

When Mr. Cohn's counsel, Georgia lawyer Stephen Land, sought to argue that the statute was entirely consistent with the First Amendment, leaving for trial only the issue of whether his client's privacy had been invaded, Brennan picked up on Powell's colloquy with McAlpin and asked Land whether, at trial, "the defendant is stripped of any defense that this was a matter of public interest?" When Land equivocated, Brennan asked him whether the television station and reporter could also defend themselves by arguing "the mere fact that they were reporting a court proceeding involving pleas to an indictment which named this young lady was itself evidence that this was a matter of public interest?" After Land responded in the negative, White pressed him further, leading the lawyer to confirm both that "there would be no defense rooted in the Constitution" and that he could "see no way [the] Fulton [County] Superior Court could turn around and say that the identity of a rape victim is a matter of general public interest."

Brennan then seized on Land's response, initially in an effort to attempt to establish that the Georgia courts had indeed purported to decide the First Amendment issue:

> Suppose we disagree with the Supreme Court of Georgia and we're to say that no this is the report of a judicial proceeding namely the plea proceedings and the rest of it and that out of which came the report that the indictment named Cynthia Cohn and we would say that this kind of publication has First Amendment protection. That issue is before us, isn't it?

After Land gave what he himself characterized as "a weasel sort of answer"—neither agreeing nor disagreeing with Brennan's proposition—the justice shifted gears, inquiring whether there might be a valid distinction, at least for constitutional purposes, between "the report of a judicial trial which disclosed the name of the victim and a report from some other source?" To this question, Land gave a direct response, opining that he did not believe that the proffered "distinction is valid."

Land's answer led Brennan to pick up on his earlier line of questioning, asking Mr. Cohn's counsel if his position was, "if there's any First Amendment protection for this report at all, it would extend to a report as long as it's truthful without regard to the source?" After first professing not to "follow the question," Land ultimately agreed with Brennan's description of his position: "You would say if there's any First Amendment protection, it has to cover the whole spectrum and can't be limited to the report of a judicial proceeding." This exchange appeared to stir Justice White, prompting him to ask Land to concede that "historically" the press "has enjoyed a qualified privilege" to report on "judicial proceedings" that it "hasn't . . . in other contexts." Ultimately, Land took White's point—that "it has been [a] characteristic of libel law to distinguish between the reports of judicial proceedings and other kinds of reports."

At conference following the argument, according to Brennan's notes, much of the discussion was directed to the extent to which the Georgia statute was in fact implicated by the decision below. Most of the justices appeared to conclude that it was and, more importantly, that it could not be squared with the First Amendment. Stewart, for example, reportedly opined both that the statute was "directly implicated" and that "on its face its [sic] unconstitutional." White agreed, asserting (as Brennan noted it) that, to the extent the statute was implicated, it is unconstitutional "as applied to report of a public trial," a proposition with which Marshall apparently concurred as well. Blackmun similarly concluded that a state "can't handle [the] press constitutionally this way." As Brennan recorded his comments, Blackmun asserted that, "as [a] practical matter, [you] have to rely on [the] self restraint of [the] press in these cases." For his part, Powell asserted (again, according to Brennan's rendition of his comments) that the case would "require reversal as truthful reporting of public trial." Ultimately, all of the justices except Rehnquist (who concluded that the Georgia Supreme Court had not rendered a final judgment that was properly before the justices for review) voted to reverse the Georgia Supreme Court, and Chief Justice Burger assigned the Court's opinion to White.

Like his brief comments at argument, White's draft opinion focused its constitutional analysis closely on a First Amendment right to report accurately about judicial proceedings. On January 14, 1975, after White had circulated his first draft, Powell sent a note to him (with copies to the other justices) indicating his intention to draft "a brief concurring opinion to record my understanding of the 'truth' issue, which differs somewhat from yours." Powell's draft was circulated the next day. In it, he disputed White's identification as "an 'open' question the issue of 'whether the First and Fourteenth Amendments require that truth be recognized as a defense in a defamation action brought by a private person as distinguished from a public official or a public figure.'" In Powell's "view, our recent decision in *Gertz* . . . resolves that issue." Thus, Powell wrote, "I think that the constitutional necessity of recognizing a defense of truth is equally implicit in our statement of the permissible standard of liability for the publication or broadcast of defamatory statements whose substance makes apparent the substantial danger of injury to the reputation of a private person." Put differently, "[i]t is fair to say that if the statements are true, the standard contemplated by *Gertz* cannot be satisfied."

Powell circulated a revised draft of his concurring opinion two days later. In this version, he appeared to narrow the focus of his comments to "media publications of allegedly false statements that are claimed to defame a private individual," a tweak that would have substantive ramifications for Powell and the Court a decade later. He also cut back somewhat on the reach of his first draft in another way—recognizing, as his original draft had not, that the "Constitution may permit a different balance to be struck" where "state actions that are denominated actions in defamation . . . in fact seek to protect citizens from injuries that are quite different from the wrongful damage to reputation flowing from false statements of fact." In his revised draft, Powell acknowledged that "causes of action grounded in a State's desire to protect privacy generally implicate interests that are distinct from those protected by defamation actions." Still, Powell concluded, "in cases in which the interests sought to be protected are similar to those considered in *Gertz*, I view that opinion as requiring that the truth be recognized as a complete defense."

There is no indication in Brennan's files as to why Powell made the referenced alterations to his concurring opinion. Nor is there any indication as to what Brennan thought of either Powell's initial draft or his final product, beyond the fact that he did not seek to join either of them. Instead, Brennan, without further explanation, gave his unqualified "join" to White's opinion for the Court.

In that opinion, White explained that the First Amendment precluded the case Mr. Cohn sought to pursue in the Georgia courts. In so holding, White acknowledged that "powerful arguments can be made, and have been made, that however it may be ultimately defined, there is a zone of privacy surrounding every individual, a zone within which the State may protect him from intrusion by the press, with all its attendant publicity." Nevertheless, White explained, even the "strong tide running in favor of the so-called right of privacy" was insufficient to overcome the right of the press and public to repeat what they learned in a public judicial proceeding.

Although White's analysis began by describing the evolution of the Court's defamation jurisprudence from *Sullivan* through *Gertz*, including the observation that, in such cases, "the defense of truth is constitutionally required where the subject of the publication is a public official or public figure," his opinion stopped well short of holding that the truth of a published report secured its constitutional protection. Rather, he expressly rejected the defendants' invitation that the Court issue "the broad holding that the press may not be made criminally or civilly liable for publishing information that is neither false nor misleading but absolutely accurate, however damaging it may be to reputation or individual sensibilities" and emphasized instead that the "Court has . . . carefully left open the question whether the First and Fourteenth Amendments require that truth be recognized as a defense in a defamation action brought by a private person as distinguished from a public official or public figure." Accordingly, White's opinion articulated the Court's precise holding narrowly:

> In this sphere of collision between claims of privacy and those of the free press, the interests on both sides are plainly rooted in the traditions and significant concerns of our society. Rather than address the broader question whether truthful publications may ever be subjected to civil or criminal liability consistently with the First and Fourteenth Amendments, or to put it another way, whether the State may ever define and protect an area of privacy free from unwanted publicity in the press, it is appropriate to focus on the narrower interface between press and privacy that this case presents, namely, whether the State may impose sanctions on the accurate publication of the name of a rape victim obtained from public records—more specifically, from judicial records which are maintained in connection with a public prosecution and which themselves are open to public inspection. We are convinced that the State may not do so.

In other words, White explained, "[o]nce true information is disclosed in public court documents open to public inspection," even if that information is the name of the victim of a violent rape, "the press cannot be sanctioned for publishing it. In this instance as in others reliance must rest upon the judgment of those who decide what to publish or broadcast."

Burger, without further elaboration, concurred only in the Court's judgment. Douglas also concurred in the judgment, advocating for the broader holding that he had pressed at argument, specifically that "there is no power on the part of government to suppress or penalize the publication of 'news of the day.'" Only Rehnquist dissented, and solely on the ground that he did not believe the Court had before it an appealable final judgment. His opinion concluded by warning his colleagues that its decision to treat the Georgia Supreme Court's decision in *Cohn* as an appealable order may well have implications for another case lurking on the Court's docket that had a similarly convoluted procedural history. That case,

Time Inc. v. Firestone, was not only next up on the Court's roster of post-*Sullivan* decisions, but it provided the first glimpse of Brennan's private views of Powell's opinion in *Gertz*.

Time, Inc. v. Firestone

In stark contrast to the 1973–1974 term, when his narrative history does not even mention *Gertz*, two years later Brennan devoted substantial attention to *Time, Inc. v. Firestone*, the Court's first pure defamation decision after Powell's reformulation of the constitutional law governing such claims. Especially when considered in conjunction with the available materials from the files of other justices with respect to *Gertz* itself, Brennan's own papers addressing *Firestone* lead to the disquieting conclusion that, by 1976, Brennan had all but lost the authority within the Court to spearhead what was to become of the constitutional law of defamation he had effectively founded in *Sullivan*.

Firestone arose from a single paragraph published in the "Milestones" section of *Time* magazine, which reported on the divorce of Russell and Mary Alice Firestone—he the wealthy heir to the then-ubiquitous tire company and she his socialite spouse. The *Time* report read, in its entirety:

> DIVORCED. By Russell A. Firestone Jr., 41, heir to the tire fortune: Mary Alice Sullivan Firestone, 32, his third wife; a onetime Palm Beach schoolteacher; on grounds of extreme cruelty and adultery; after six years of marriage, one son; in West Palm Beach, Fla. The 17-month intermittent trial produced enough testimony of extramarital adventures on both sides, said the judge, "to make Dr. Freud's hair curl."

In fact, during the divorce proceedings, which had been instituted by the husband, the judge had made the aforementioned reference to the parties' "extramarital adventures," although he did so in a sentence referencing "certain testimony" elicited on behalf of Mr. Firestone. What the judge had not done, however, was clearly describe the grounds on which he had granted Mr. Firestone his requested divorce. And, unfortunately for Time, Inc., the magazine's corporate publisher, although Mr. Firestone had sought a divorce on the grounds of "extreme cruelty and adultery," the court had granted Mrs. Firestone's request for alimony, which, under Florida law, should not have happened if her husband had indeed been allowed to end the marriage on the ground of "adultery." Nevertheless, the judgment did conclude with the Florida court's pronouncement that "it is abundantly clear from the evidence of marital discord that neither of the parties has shown the least susceptibility to domestication, and that the marriage should be dissolved."

Time learned of the divorce and the court's judgment from a wire service report and from an item in a New York newspaper. It secured further information regarding the circumstances surrounding the divorce from its Miami Bureau Chief and from a "stringer" it regularly engaged to assist it with stories emanating from south Florida. After the item appeared in the magazine, Mrs. Firestone sued the corporate publisher for defamation. Following a jury trial, in which she disclaimed any intention to recover damages for injury to her reputation, a jury awarded her $100,000 for the emotional distress she alleged she had suffered in the wake of the publication. The resulting judgment was ultimately affirmed by the Florida Supreme Court.

Shortly after its decision in *Cohn*, during the deliberations in which Justice Rehnquist had noted that the *Firestone* case had made its way to the Supreme Court, the justices granted Time, Inc.'s petition for review. Justice Brennan's term history begins by characterizing *Firestone* as having "presented the Court with its first full opportunity to clarify several of the uncertainties created by" *Gertz* with respect to "the constitutionality under the First Amendment of the application of state libel laws to persons other than public figures." It goes on to describe how, "unfortunately" in Brennan's view, "the Court left the law in an even worse state than before," due "partly to the peculiar nature of the case and partly to the internal Court processes in handling the case."

As Brennan's term history explained it, the Florida Supreme Court's final decision was written "shortly after *Gertz* was decided," and included an "obviously tacked-on paragraph at the end of" its opinion "finding" that Time had been negligent in not recognizing that, due to the award of alimony, Mr. Firestone could not have been granted a divorce on the ground reported. Brennan was plainly skeptical of both the Florida court's reasoning and its motive. The term history noted that, "[l]ying in the background of the case at the time it was before us was the public scandal enveloping the State Supreme Court respecting alleged bribery of certain Justices and rumors that the instant case was one involved in the scandal."

The case was argued on October 14, 1975. At the outset of his presentation, Time's counsel, John Pickering, a prominent Washington, D.C., lawyer, was asked by Justice Rehnquist to "concede that the article was inaccurate," a concession the advocate declined to make. Brennan then questioned Pickering concerning the source of the magazine's colorful quotation of the judge's reference to Freud's hair. When he responded that the quote came to Time's attention from the wire service report it had received, Pickering hastened to add that it was nevertheless "an exact quote from the language of the divorce decree itself." This led to a mild rebuke from Justice Stewart, who reminded Pickering both that he had already conceded that Time had never "seen the divorce decree itself" and that "my brother Brennan's question" was therefore "where did [the magazine] get this quote." Justice Marshall followed suit, forcing Pickering to concede that Time did not actually review the document in which the quote was contained until "[a]fter [this] lawsuit was filed." Marshall proceeded to ask whether a "cautious editor [would] ask a cautious reporter or stringer that I want the inside information on a Court decree, would not both of them assume that somebody would go to the guess what, Court . . . . Would not that be normal?" Pickering's rejoinder that it would not, and his suggestion that it would be "normal" for a reporter simply to consult with one of the parties' lawyers to confirm the accuracy of his information, did not elicit a further response from any of the justices.

Later in his argument, Pickering was confronted by Chief Justice Burger with an article published in the Miami Herald prior to the Time report, in which the newspaper had quoted a portion of the divorce court's judgment in which the judge noted that "'he discounted much of the testimony in the case as unreliable.'" When Pickering responded that the judge had nevertheless concluded that neither party was "domesticated," Brennan asked him what that phrase meant, specifically whether it "mean[s] that she is guilty of adultery?" Following Pickering's suggestion that the phrase's meaning was "not clear" from the face of the judgment, Brennan himself proffered something of a definition gleaned from Florida precedent (specifically a case called Chesnut v. Chesnut that had been quoted by the Florida courts in the underlying Firestone divorce case). His reading of the precise quotation—"when the bride and groom are both devoid of a yen for domestication, the marital bark puts out to sea with its jib pointed to the rocks"—predictably elicited laughter from the gallery. Brennan then turned serious, however, pointedly asking Pickering whether he was contending that the divorce had in fact been granted on the ground of adultery, leading Time's counsel to respond that, although "I am not suggesting that necessarily comes from lack of domestication," it does follow from the fact that Mr. Firestone had been granted a divorce and had sought it on "the grounds of extreme cruelty and adultery."

At this juncture, Justice Blackmun directed Pickering's attention to the legal arguments, asking him whether Time was entitled to a new trial because the jury had not been instructed on fault. Pickering responded in the negative, asserting that the magazine was in fact entitled to judgment in its favor under the "malice standard." When Blackmun pressed and asked whether Time had "abandoned any position that you are protected in part by the thesis of *Gertz*," Pickering regrouped and contended that "liability without fault" had in fact been imposed in violation of the rules set out in *Gertz* for three separate reasons—that *Time* had accurately published a report of a judicial proceeding within the meaning of *Cohn*, that there was no finding of fault by the Florida courts "of any kind," and that the applicable standard was "actual malice" in any event. Following a further colloquy with Blackmun, in which the justice again attempted to gauge whether "you feel you are entitled to an instruction on fault," a reluctant Pickering ultimately conceded he did after Blackmun urged it on him as "at least . . . a secondary position."

Pickering then turned to explaining why he contended that the actual malice standard properly applied, basing his argument alternatively on Justice White's concurring opinion in *Rosenbloom* (that all reports about the conduct of public officials—including presumably judges—are governed by the actual malice standard, regardless of the status of the plaintiff) and on the notion that Mrs. Firestone was indeed a public figure under *Gertz*. This prompted Brennan to ask "what is it that makes . . . Mrs. Firestone a public figure in the *New York Times* sense?" Before Pickering could answer, Blackmun added to the question "[o]ther than the journalism profession itself made her such." When Pickering referred to the plaintiff as a "very prominent wealthy individual," Blackmun again interjected that she had "received nationwide notoriety because the media itself gave her that notoriety." And, after Pickering wondered aloud "how does one become a public figure other than coming to the attention of the press in some way," Blackmun himself responded, "oh, by becoming President of the United States, the United States Senator, maybe."

When Palm Beach lawyer Edna Caruso, Mrs. Firestone's counsel, took the podium, she seized on the exchange between Blackmun and her adversary concerning the issue of a new trial in which the jury could be instructed on negligence.

She reminded the justices that "throughout the appellate process in the case Time, Inc. has never ever argued until today that it is entitled to any trial. The briefs that have been filed throughout the appellate courts in Florida and the briefs that are filed today solely urge that they are entitled to a judgment as a matter of law."

Caruso was questioned by several justices about Mrs. Firestone's abandonment of any claim for recovery based on injury to reputation. White took up her cause on this issue, effectively cross-examining her to emphasize that there "apparently is [a] basis for recovery under Florida law" for damages limited to emotional distress, a proposition established by the fact that the "Supreme Court of Florida affirmed. You won, did you not?" This exchange led Blackmun to wonder aloud "how can you separate really mental anguish and impingement upon reputation?"

At this point in Caruso's argument, Justice Powell turned the discussion to the standard of care. He asked her "what standard do you think the Supreme Court of Florida [applied] in support of liability under the *Gertz* standard?" When Caruso hesitated, Powell added that "[t]he only specific evidence that I recall was that since under Florida law, alimony could not be granted an adulteress that a sort of a per se result, the Supreme Court of Florida found negligence, is that your read-ing of the case?" Surprisingly, Caruso seemed entirely unprepared for the question, responding "I do not frankly recall the specific things pointed to in the Florida Supreme Court's decision." Once again, however, White stepped in, asserting that "well, the Court said that if anybody looked at the decree that had been claimed on the grounds [of extreme cruelty and adultery] and that the careful examina-tion" of the decree required the conclusion that it had been granted on "grounds of cruelty, . . . that was what the Supreme Court ruled." Caruso quickly agreed with White's analysis.

This exchange led Justice Brennan to ask Caruso specifically whether she was contending that "the failure of [Time's] New York Home Office of those involved in the publication, particularly the failure to spot the word adultery, satisfies the premise of negligence?" When Caruso began to disagree, by relying on record evidence establishing the failure of *Time's* fact checker to mark off the word *adul-tery* as having been specifically "checked" during her review, Brennan continued by noting that "[t]he [Florida] Supreme Court did not say anything about that, did they? . . . . [Y]our Supreme Court did not rely on that fact, did it?" This time, Brennan's comment prompted Rehnquist to come to Caruso's assistance, assert-ing that "I suppose the Supreme Court of Florida has occasion on more than one appeal to simply summarily say there is sufficient evidence of negligence and we disallow that point without going into great detail as to why they think there is sufficient evidence of negligence." That observation, however, apparently did not sit well with Justice Stewart, who asked "[w]hy, if they are reversing another appellate court would they—do they often do that cryptically? Because there is one thing when you are affirming, it is something else when you are reversing." Rehnquist again responded on Caruso's behalf, asserting "[c]ertainly, there is nothing in the federal constitution [that] would prevent them from doing it anyway."

At the time, Brennan expressed some frustration with the argument in *Firestone*. He responded to a letter from his friend, *New York Times* columnist Anthony Lewis who had attended the session, by noting, "I was glad that you could witness first hand our latest annoyance, *Firestone*, although the argument was hardly enlightening."

Following the argument, and likely as a consequence both of it and of the outcome in *Gertz*, Brennan thought that a "majority of the Brethren would affirm on the ground that the *Gertz* fault standard applied, that the State Supreme Court had sloppily adopted the *Gertz* standard, and that the record would support a finding of negligence (although not necessarily on the ground stated by the State Supreme Court)." To his surprise, however, "the Brethren were badly fragmented" and "there was no majority for any disposition." As had been the case in *Gertz*, Brennan and Douglas, the two "senior" justices (as Powell somewhat disparagingly had referred to them during the internal deliberations in *Gertz*), believed that the First Amendment precluded liability—Brennan on the ground that this was a protected report of a judicial proceeding within the holding the previous term in *Cohn*; Douglas, who resigned from the Court before the decision in *Firestone* was announced, but nevertheless "participated in the conference and cast his standard vote regarding the unconstitutionality of state libel laws under the First Amendment." The Brennan position, for which he noted he "got no takers," is memorialized in his dissenting opinion, in which he argues that inaccurate reports of judicial proceedings (as opposed to the accurate reports at issue in *Cohn*) should be adjudicated under the actual malice standard. This position—as John Pickering noted in his argument—drew its inspiration from White's concurring opinion in *Rosenbloom*.

It is, therefore, worth noting that among those who failed to embrace Brennan's position in *Firestone* was White. In one sense, this is not surprising given White's strongly worded dissent in *Gertz* and all that preceded it during the Court's deliberations in that case. Still, White was both the author of *Cohn* and, as Brennan pointed out in his dissent in *Firestone*, had premised his own vote in *Rosenbloom* on his conclusion that "the First Amendment gives the press and broadcast media a privilege to report and comment upon the official actions of public servants in full detail," a conclusion which (especially in the wake of *Cohn*) could reasonably have been expected to include reporting about the operations of the judicial branch. By this point, however, White had apparently become so disenchanted with what he viewed as *Gertz's* expansion of the reach of the First Amendment in defamation cases that he was prepared to abandon his position in *Rosenbloom*, albeit *sub silentio*—his only direct discussion of the case in his own opinion in *Firestone* is his conclusion that neither it nor *Gertz* should apply retroactively to a news report published in 1967.

With "no takers" for either the Brennan or Douglas positions, the rest of the Court split in several different directions. Stewart voted to reverse, according to Brennan's term history, on the ground that the *Time* report was not false in any material sense and that, "in any event liability in this case had been imposed without a finding of fault in violation of *Gertz*." Powell agreed with him but, as Brennan noted it, on the latter ground only. Blackmun also concurred "that liability had been imposed without a finding of fault" but, unlike Stewart and Powell, was not convinced there was insufficient evidence for the standard to be met and therefore favored a remand for the state courts to consider "whether there was evidence supporting a finding of fault in the record." White, Marshall, and Rehnquist all voted to affirm, according to Brennan, on the ground that the *Gertz* negligence standard applied, that the Florida Supreme Court had adopted it, and that there was sufficient evidence of negligence in the record to support the jury's verdict. As noted, White was also of the view that *Gertz* should not be applied retroactively. Finally, as was apparently often the case, Burger "passed," although, as Brennan noted, "it seemed apparent that he was in sympathy with the views of those who wished to affirm."

Even though Burger's vote would not have created a majority in favor of affirming the judgment below, he nevertheless assigned the opinion to Rehnquist to see if he could garner a majority based on a remand to the state courts to apply the *Gertz* standard. Brennan had "heard indirectly" that Burger had first attempted to assign the opinion to both Powell and Blackmun, but that they had each declined. In the wake of this uncertainty, Brennan "set to work immediately to prepare a memorandum to the conference," again advocating his view that *Cohn* ought to provide the basis for a decision. The memorandum was ready for circulation before Rehnquist had completed his own draft and Brennan "still had some hope of gaining adherents to my view."

The Rehnquist draft was circulated on December 11, 1975, and was very similar to the ultimate opinion he delivered for the Court. Like the final version, it concluded that Mrs. Firestone was a not a public figure because she had not voluntarily injected herself into a "public controversy" as required by *Gertz*, and remanded the case back to the state courts for further consideration of the fault issue. Brennan thought the opinion was "clearly written in a manner very antagonistic to the publisher and favorable to an ultimate judgment of liability." In Brennan's view, the remand "was premised on the disingenuous ground that the State Supreme Court had not made a 'conscious' determination of fault." What troubled Brennan the most about the Rehnquist opinion was that it did not preclude, and in fact seemed to invite, "a finding of fault on exactly the same ground" on which the Florida Supreme Court had premised its initial decision—"that alimony could not have been awarded if the divorce was granted on the basis of adultery and that Time should have discovered that fact."

Brennan circulated his own draft on December 12, "but it stirred no interest." The next day, Powell distributed a memorandum indicating that, while a remand was "not his first choice," he would go along with that result "in the interest of having a Court." Nevertheless, because he believed that Rehnquist's opinion "'lean[ed]' rather strongly in favor of Firestone, with the probable result that the Florida Court will conclude that Time, Inc. was guilty of fault (negligence)," Powell indicated that he would write a concurring opinion in order "at least to alert our friends in Florida that some of us here lean the other way on the evidence." On December 15, Stewart weighed in, indicating that he would await Powell's opinion.

Powell circulated his draft concurring opinion, which looked much the same as the final version (except in one significant respect discussed below), on December 23, and Stewart joined it the following week. White circulated a dissent, arguing both that *Gertz* should not be applied retroactively and that the Florida Supreme Court had indeed made the requisite finding of negligence in any event. On New Year's Eve, Blackmun joined Rehnquist's opinion. After the holiday, on January 5, Burger circulated a memorandum to the conference indicating that he was inclined to join the Rehnquist opinion, but that he had some "observations" that he would pass on to him. "Typically," Brennan's term history later noted, Burger "never stated what these 'observations' were and no changes were made in the Court opinion at his request."

All was then quiet for nearly a month when, apparently out of nowhere, the dynamic changed. Marshall, who had dissented in *Butts* and *Walker*, had been an early ally of Powell in *Gertz*, and had voted to affirm the judgment in *Firestone* at conference, dropped "something of a minor bombshell on the rest of the Court"—he circulated a dissenting opinion in which he argued that Mrs. Firestone was a public figure and that the actual malice standard therefore applied to her. In his term history, Brennan confessed that he "was prepared for this dissent as my law clerk had worked with TM's on it." Apparently, Marshall's about-face was particularly disturbing to Stewart because, as Stewart recognized, if Marshall had so voted at conference, there would have been five votes to reverse and, as Brennan's term history later put it, "the Court would not now be stuck with WHR's very one-sided opinion."

According to Brennan's term history, Marshall's change of heart was motivated by Rehnquist's invocation of Marshall's dissent in *Rosenbloom* in his own opinion—specifically, Marshall's rejection of the notion that judges should properly make judgments concerning what constitutes a matter of public concern and what does not. In his *Firestone* dissent, Marshall "flushed" what Brennan's term history described as "the logical contradiction" in Rehnquist's opinion, which was "really a continuation of the same contradiction in *Gertz* itself under one possible reading of that opinion"—namely, while "*Gertz* had rejected the plurality opinion in *Rosenbloom* on the ground that judges should not be picking and choosing 'what information is relevant to self-government' under the 'matters of general or public concern' standard," Rehnquist's opinion in *Firestone* "reintroduced this feature under the heading of 'public controversy,'" which Rehnquist emphasized was required in order for a defamation plaintiff to deemed a public figure. In his term history, Brennan recounted that he had decided "not to treat with the issue" in his own memorandum in *Firestone* because he did not "want to distract attention from the main point I was trying to make"—presumably the expansion of the *Cohn* rationale—"but I was happy that TM had done so." Unfortunately, at least from Brennan's perspective, no other justice picked up on Marshall's point, including Powell who, as Brennan's term history theorized, "could not reject" Rehnquist's analysis of the "public controversy" requirement, "whether or not" he intended that result when he wrote *Gertz*, and still join Rehnquist's "attempt to write an opinion for the Court." (In this sense, *Firestone* was something of a precursor of the difficulties the court would face nearly a decade later when it considered whether to reintroduce the "matter of general or public concern" concept on a far broader scale in *Dun & Bradstreet v. Greenmoss Builders*).

Nevertheless, Marshall's dissent did spur further consideration among the justices of whether "the ground stated by the State Supreme Court as supporting a finding of negligence—the failure of Time to see the significance of the alimony award—could on remand continue to support a finding of fault." In his opinion, in addition to making the case that Mrs. Firestone was a public figure, Marshall had taken issue with the Florida Supreme Court's conclusion that *Time* had published a negligent falsehood, writing that "if the trial court awarded alimony while basing the divorce on a finding of adultery by the wife, Time cannot be faulted for reporting that fact." Moreover, Marshall asserted, "[u]nless there is some basis for a finding of fault other than that given by the Supreme Court of Florida, I think it clear there can be no liability."

According to Brennan's term history, Rehnquist's failure to respond to Marshall on this issue "proved to be too much" for Stewart, who circulated yet another concurring opinion on February 23 in which he agreed with Marshall on this aspect of the fault issue. As a result, Brennan noted, this "created the rather silly situation" of six separate opinions in what, in the wake of Douglas's intervening resignation, was now an eight-member Court. This proved "too much for Powell" (there appeared to be a lot of "too much proving" going on in *Firestone*) who had the announcement of the decision in the case delayed so that he could incorporate Stewart's most recently stated views in his own opinion (which ultimately led Stewart to withdraw his separate concurrence).

In the end, Rehnquist's opinion for the Court, announced on March 2, 1976, vacated the Florida Supreme Court's decision and remanded so that the lower courts could address the fault issue directly. Along the way, Rehnquist rejected both alternative grounds for application of the actual malice standard raised by Time, and championed in dissent by Brennan and Marshall respectively. First, his opinion concluded that Mrs. Firestone was not a public figure despite the fact that her divorce had been characterized by the lower courts as a "cause célèbre," she had held press conferences during the course of the proceedings, and she even retained a clipping service to monitor press reports of her activities within Palm Beach society. In Rehnquist's view, "[d]issolution of a marriage through judicial proceedings is not the sort of 'public controversy' referred to in *Gertz*, even though the marital difficulties of extremely wealthy individuals may be of interest to some portion of the reading public." Second, Rehnquist declined to read either *Rosenbloom* or *Cohn*, or the two in combination, as extending the actual malice standard to inaccurate press reports of judicial proceedings. As Rehnquist explained, "[w]hatever their general validity, use of such subject-matter classifications to determine the extent of constitutional protection afforded defamatory falsehoods may too often result in an improper balance between the competing interests in this area. It was our recognition and rejection of this weakness in the *Rosenbloom* test which led us in *Gertz* to eschew a subject-matter test for one focusing upon the character of the defamation plaintiff."

Next, Rehnquist's opinion turned to Time's contentions that its report was neither false nor published with fault, as well as the consequences of Mrs. Firestone's decision not to seek damages for injury to reputation. With respect to falsity, Rehnquist relied on the Florida Supreme Court's conclusion that *Time* had falsely attributed the grounds on which Mr. Firestone had been granted a divorce to include adultery and, though he acknowledged Time's argument that "the meaning of the trial court's decree was unclear," he concluded that fact did not "license it to choose from among several conceivable interpretations the one most damaging" to Mrs. Firestone. And, Rehnquist professed "little difficulty" in concluding that Florida retained ample authority, even after *Gertz*, "to permit recovery for other injuries without regard to measuring the effect the falsehood may have had upon a plaintiff's reputation. This does not transform the action into something other than an action for defamation as that term is meant in *Gertz*."

Finally, although Rehnquist returned the case to the Florida courts for further consideration of whether Time had negligently published the defamatory falsehood that formed the basis of the jury's $100,000 award, his opinion quoted the Florida Supreme Court's observation that a "careful examination of the final decree prior to publication would have clearly demonstrated that the divorce had been granted on the grounds of extreme cruelty, and thus the wife would have been saved the humiliation of being accused of adultery in a nationwide magazine. This is a flagrant example of 'journalistic negligence.'" Not only that, but Rehnquist further indicated that "[i]t may well be that petitioner's account in its 'Milestones' section was the product of some fault on its part, and that the libel judgment against it was, therefore, entirely consistent with *Gertz*."

It was this last observation that formed the basis of Powell's concurring opinion, which was joined by Stewart. In it, Powell took pains to assert that a "clear majority of the Court adheres to the principles of *Gertz*," but nevertheless confessed that there remained substantial differences among the justices concerning "the proper application of such principles to this bizarre case." Powell explained his own decision to join Rehnquist's opinion as premised entirely on his hope "to avoid the appearance of fragmentation of the Court on the basic principles involved." The bulk of his own opinion, however, devoted itself to recounting what Powell described as "substantial evidence, much of it uncontradicted, that the editors of Time exercised considerable care in checking the accuracy of the story prior to its publication." As Powell explained:

> My point in writing is to emphasize that, against the background of a notorious divorce case, and a decree that invited misunderstanding, there was substantial evidence supportive of Time's defense that it was not guilty of actionable negligence. At the very least the jury or court assessing liability in this case should have weighed these factors and this evidence before reaching a judgment. There is no indication in the record before us that this was done in accordance with *Gertz*.

And, in a footnote, Powell took apparent pains to distance himself (and Stewart) from Rehnquist's quotation of the Florida Supreme Court's reference to Time's "journalistic negligence," asserting in the identical words used by Marshall in his dissent that "[u]nless there exists some basis for a finding of fault other than that given by the Supreme Court of Florida there can be no liability" under *Gertz*.

In all, there were ultimately three dissenting opinions. Brennan, as noted, rested on what he saw as the logical extension of *Cohn*—application of the actual malice standard to all reports of judicial proceedings. In so doing, he could not resist reminding his colleagues (and especially Justice White) that *Gertz* had not purported to overrule *Rosenbloom* on its facts and that, at the very least, that case's result, as circumscribed by White's concurring opinion, called for application of the actual malice standard in all cases of allegedly "erroneous reporting of the public actions of public officials." And, Brennan included a footnote that bemoaned the Court's reformulation of *Gertz*'s "actual injury" requirement to include compensation for emotional distress even in the absence of asserted injury to reputation.

White's own dissenting opinion, to say the least, came at the case from a different perspective. Although he ostensibly dissented on the ground that neither *Rosenbloom* nor *Gertz* should be applied to a defamation action filed before either of those cases was decided, White succinctly offered his own observation on the issues addressed in his colleagues' multiple opinions:

> I would affirm the judgment of the Florida Supreme Court because First Amendment values will not be furthered in any way by application to this case of the fault standards newly drafted and imposed by *Gertz v. Robert Welch, Inc.*, upon which my Brother REHNQUIST relies, or the fault standards required by *Rosenbloom v. Metromedia, Inc.*, upon which my Brother BRENNAN relies; and because, in any event, any requisite fault was properly found below.

Finally, Marshall's separate dissent focused largely on his contention that Mrs. Firestone was indeed a public figure within the meaning of *Gertz* and his concomitant and "more fundamental[]" criticism of Rehnquist for attributing "to the term 'public controversy' used in *Gertz*" a meaning that "resurrects the precise difficulties that I thought *Gertz* was designed to avoid." Thus, Marshall asserted that, having "rejected the appropriateness of judicial inquiry into 'the legitimacy of interest in a particular event or subject,' *Gertz* obviously did not intend to sanction any such inquiry by its use of the term 'public controversy.' Yet that is precisely how I understand the Court's opinion to interpret *Gertz*."

The result, as Brennan's term history counted the votes, "was that the Court, distributed among five different opinions, was split four to four on whether the ground relied upon by the State Supreme Court could on remand support a finding of fault no matter how 'conscious' the determination" of negligence made by that court. For Brennan, this "unfortunate" result "clearly revealed some of the weaknesses of the *Gertz* opinion" and afforded him an opportunity, which he had curiously not expressed, at least in that form during the Court's internal consideration of *Gertz* itself, to set out in his term history his own criticism of the constitutional framework the Court had erected in that case. For one thing, Brennan rejected Powell's contention, in his own opinion in *Firestone*, that the Court's fragmentation was a function of the "bizarre" nature of the case. In Brennan's view, "it seems clear that *Gertz* of necessity constitutes the determination of 'fault' [as] a matter of constitutional fact, and there may be severe difficulty in any given case in obtaining a majority of those justices adhering to *Gertz* for a common view respecting constitutionally-sufficient 'fault' in the circumstances.'"

As a result, Brennan suggested, in a prophecy that proved to be spot on, "this fact may make the Court less willing to hear such cases, as is happening on the current Court with the issue of obscenity under *Miller* standards." In its 1973 decision in *Miller v. California*, the Court had reformulated the constitutional standards cabining the law of obscenity that Brennan had largely crafted in a series of decisions beginning with *Roth v. United States*. In the years following *Miller*, the Court had largely gotten out of the business of hearing obscenity cases, a marked departure from its previous practice of regularly reviewing lower court decisions finding various publications and films to be obscene. And, as we shall see, although the Court continued to consider various aspects of the *Gertz* regime for several years after *Firestone*, it has not decided a defamation case in the last two decades. Indeed, but for *Masson v. New Yorker Magazine* in 1991, it has not decided such a case on the merits since Brennan left the Court.

Finally, Brennan suspected, a suspicion that has also proven largely correct, that "the facet of the *Firestone* opinion that will prove the most destructive to First Amendment values is its effective abolition of the supposed 'protective' restriction of *Gertz* limiting damage awards in libel suits to 'actual injury.'" Brennan made this point in a footnote to his dissenting opinion, which, his term history noted, "drew not so much as a comment from any member of the *Gertz* majority."

It is difficult to read Brennan's own files relating to *Gertz* and *Firestone* and not come to the conclusion that, by the time the latter was decided, he had not only lost his position as the Court's unquestioned leader and driving force with respect to formulating the constitutional law of defamation, but had become effectively marginalized as the Court proceeded to build a very different body of law on the foundation set out by Powell in *Gertz*. In one sense, this is obvious from the Court's rejection in *Gertz* of Brennan's expansion, for a plurality of the Court in *Rosenbloom*, of the zone of protection afforded by the actual malice standard to all matters of public concern. Still, the internal record of the Court's deliberations document not only his lack of any meaningful involvement in the internal debate that resulted in *Gertz* (including Powell's pointed indication early on in that case that Brennan's views had become as irrelevant to the Court's deliberations as the absolutist position advocated by Douglas), but also his own recognition that his efforts to draw support for his views in *Firestone* (from an expansion of the holding in *Cohn* to include application of the actual malice standard to false speech to his criticism of the Court's expansion of the concept of "actual injury") were met with indifference by his colleagues, as well as the unsettling fact that he apparently felt it necessary to channel his fundamental attack on the validity of the *Gertz* "public figure" standard (its resurrection, in the context of the "public controversy" requirement, of the same judicial inquiry that had led it to reject the "matter of public concern" standard in *Rosenbloom*) through Marshall by having their clerks collaborate on a dissenting opinion to be issued in Marshall's name.

Landmark Communications, Inc. v. Virginia

The Court took a brief hiatus from the law of defamation following *Firestone* and, in fact, did not return to the subject directly until the October 1978 term when it heard *Herbert v. Lando.* Nevertheless, in the intervening years, the justices did decide *Landmark Communications, Inc. v. Virginia*, a nondefamation case in which *Sullivan* played a central role. Brennan, however, took no part in the deliberations in that case, so his views with respect to it (if any) remain unknown. He had undergone treatment for throat cancer in January 1978, missed the oral argument sessions that month, and did not participate in the Court's decisions for that period. Justice Powell also recused himself in *Landmark Communications* and, as a result, the authors of *Sullivan* and *Gertz* were both on the sidelines when the Court again took up the question, first raised in *Cohn*, of whether criminal or civil sanctions imposed on truthful speech about a matter of public concern can be squared with the First Amendment.

The case arose from an article in the *Virginian Pilot*, a newspaper published in Norfolk by the corporate defendant, which identified by name a judge who was the subject of a pending inquiry by the Virginia Judicial Inquiry and Review Commission. The article was accurate in all relevant respects. A Virginia statute not only mandated that the commission's proceedings and records be kept confidential but also made "unlawfully divulge[ing] the identification of a Judge" as the "subject of an investigation and hearing" by the commission a crime. Landmark was convicted of violating the statute following a jury trial and was fined $500. After the Virginia Supreme Court affirmed the conviction, the Supreme Court, in an opinion by Chief Justice Burger, unanimously reversed. Although Brennan did not participate in the case, it is worth noting some aspects of the Court's decision, and the deliberations that preceded it, both because they illustrate how the other justices interpreted *Sullivan* and *Gertz* in this context and because it presages the Court's subsequent decisions in *Smith v. Daily Mail Publishing Co.* and *Florida Star v. BJF*, on which Brennan sat and cast a vote.

In his opinion for the Court in *Landmark Communications*, the chief justice purported to reject the "categorical approach" urged on him by the newspaper, which was represented by Floyd Abrams, the renowned First Amendment advocate. Specifically, as White had with respect to the analogous issue in *Cohn*, Burger deemed it "unnecessary" for the Court to decide whether "truthful reporting about public officials in connection with their public duties is always insulated from the imposition of criminal sanctions by the First Amendment." Rather, his opinion concluded that, because "the publication that Virginia seeks to punish under its statute lies near the core of the First Amendment, and the Commonwealth's interests advanced by the imposition of criminal sanctions are insufficient to justify the actual and potential encroachments on freedom of speech and of the press," the newspaper's conviction could not stand. In making this determination, Burger relied on *Sullivan* to support the Court's conclusions both that the newspaper's reporting about public officials "clearly served those interests in public scrutiny and discussion of governmental affairs which the First Amendment was adopted to protect" and that "injury to official reputation is an insufficient reason 'for repressing speech that would otherwise be free.'"

For whatever reason, Brennan did maintain a file of sorts on the case and retained in it a portion of the materials that passed among the justices during their deliberations. Thus, for example, he retained a memorandum that Justice Marshall circulated to the conference explaining his vote to reverse the decision below. In it, Marshall asserted that, "[w]hen the State seeks to punish criminally the making of truthful statements about public officials relating to their performance of their official duties, it must meet a very stringent burden of justification," a burden Virginia "has failed to meet" in the case at bar. Marshall went on to urge the Court "not to place too much weight on the fact that this case involves a newspaper. The statute at issue applies to any person who divulges Commission information, so that, for example, an individual who reads about a Commission proceeding in the newspaper and repeats it to a friend has apparently violated the statute. I would hold that such an individual is as much protected as is the newspaper, rather than giving the press any special protection in the circumstances of this case." This latter issue would come to occupy the Court's full attention less than a decade later in *Dun & Bradstreet v. Greenmoss Builders.*

Brennan also retained a letter written by Justice Rehnquist to Burger, after the chief justice had circulated his initial draft of the Court's opinion. In it, Rehnquist indicated his willingness to join Burger's opinion "if you can see your way clear to make what seems to me a relatively small addition." Rehnquist was troubled by Burger's reference to the question "explicitly reserved in *Cox" Broadcasting Corp. v. Cohn*—"whether the publication of truthful information withheld by law from the public domain is . . . privileged"—because it could be read to imply that the Court in *Cohn* had not reserved the issue of "the constitutionality in other circumstances of governmental efforts to prohibit the publication of information which has been mandated to be confidential." Accordingly, he asked Burger to consider revising the passage to add, "While we need not decide that broader question here, either, we conclude that in the circumstances of this case Landmark's publication is entitled to constitutional protection." Burger accommodated Rehnquist's request, and the opinion as issued contains, in substantial part, the language Rehnquist had requested.

Finally, Brennan's file contains a short concurring opinion, in typescript (rather than prepared by the Court's printer), circulated by Justice John Paul Stevens, who had taken Douglas's seat on the Court in December 1975. In it, the Court's then-junior justice rejected the Virginia Supreme Court's application of a "clear and present danger" test for reasons that "differ somewhat from the Court's." Specifically, Stevens wrote, "[e]ven if these kinds of injury were inevitable, . . . I believe that the First Amendment would protect the third party from punishment for publishing this accurate news story. The mere fact that speech creates a clear and present danger of adverse opinion cannot justify its abridgment. Favorable opinion cannot be guaranteed, nor unfavorable opinion prevented, by legislative fiat." Stevens never filed this opinion and it is unclear from Brennan's papers whether Burger made changes to address Stevens's concerns. It is, however, evident from Burger's opinion itself that the Court's treatment of the "clear and present danger" test, which had been invoked by the Virginia courts, began by expressly "question[ing] the relevance of that standard here" and asserting that the Court could not, in any event, "accept" the Virginia Supreme Court's "mechanical application of the test" to affirm the newspaper's conviction.

Herbert v. Lando

Following *Firestone*, the Court's next opportunity to address directly the constitutional law of defamation came during the October 1978 term in *Herbert v. Lando*. How that case came before the justices, and how it was decided, at once illustrates the role that the news media itself played during this period in affecting the law's evolution, the continued diminution of Brennan's influence in that cause, and the first signs of the impact of *Sullivan* on the practical reality of defamation litigation.

As Brennan's term history noted, *Herbert* "was billed as a press case of major constitutional significance" even before it reached the Supreme Court. It arose from a *60 Minutes* broadcast, reported by legendary CBS News Correspondent Mike Wallace, about Colonel Anthony Herbert, a military officer who had garnered significant media attention for exposing what he said were war crimes and civilian atrocities committed by U.S. forces in Vietnam. A *60 Minutes* investigation, however, suggested that Herbert had fabricated significant aspects of his claims in an effort to explain his own relief from command.

Following the broadcast, Herbert sued CBS for defamation, and his counsel began an aggressive discovery campaign designed to uncover the kind of circumstantial evidence of actual malice that the Court in *Butts* and *St. Amant* had indicated would be necessary to support such a finding. Among other things, CBS witnesses, including Wallace and his producer Barry Lando, were subjected to depositions lasting days, even weeks at a time. In all, Lando's deposition continued intermittently for more than a year and ultimately consumed nearly three thousand pages of transcript accompanied by some 240 exhibits.

In the wake of Herbert's discovery campaign, CBS began instructing witnesses such as Lando to decline to answer deposition questions, based on what its lawyers came to describe as an "editorial process privilege." The theory was that the First Amendment protected a reporter's right to shield unpublished journalistic work product and the thought processes attendant to it as well as prepublication interactions with editors and colleagues from discovery lest he or she refrain from aggressively pursuing stories of public interest for fear of the consequent need to endure such scrutiny. The trial judge largely rejected the novel claim, but CBS succeeded in convincing the United States Court of Appeals for the Second Circuit in New York to hear the case and address the issue before further discovery could continue. In the Second Circuit (and later in the Supreme Court), CBS was represented by Floyd Abrams, fresh off his victory in *Landmark Communications*.

The Second Circuit panel that heard the case was presided over by Chief Judge Irving R. Kaufman who, over the preceding decade, had carefully cultivated a reputation as a champion of the First Amendment and of the press. It helped that the opinions he wrote in favor of the press were routinely the subject of favorable reports in the *New York Times*, which also took to publishing magazine length articles and op-ed columns the judge wrote on the subject. The Second Circuit's decision in *Herbert* took this phenomenon to another level. The *Times* indeed treated Kaufman's opinion which, along with a separate opinion written by Judge James Oakes, recognized the privilege advocated by CBS, as "a press case of major constitutional significance," affording it front-page treatment under an ample headline. The article quoted at length from Kaufman's opinion, most prominently his characterization of Herbert's inquiries in discovery as a "strike to the heart of the vital human component of the editorial process."

The *Times's* prominent treatment of the pretrial discovery dispute at issue in *Herbert* was, in significant part, likely a reaction by the institutional press to what it then perceived as a material change in the complexion of defamation litigation in the few short years following *Gertz* and *Firestone*. Prior to the Court's decision in *Gertz*, defamation actions against the press had increasingly been resolved on dispositive motions made by media defendants following minimal or no discovery. As a rule, it appeared that judges generally assumed that the actual malice standard was virtually impossible to satisfy in cases brought against the mainstream media and that defamation plaintiffs, typically represented by lawyers who did not specialize in the field, were at a loss to figure out how to make the requisite showing. Moreover, prior to *Gertz*, the courts generally did not view the "public figure" issue as a terribly complicated one to be determined based on the application of the kind of multifactor tests that became the norm following that decision and especially following *Firestone*. And, of course, the universe of cases to which the actual malice standard applied expanded significantly following Brennan's plurality opinion in *Rosenbloom*, which did not even require courts to consider whether the plaintiff was a public figure at all.

In the years following *Gertz* and *Firestone*, however, the litigation landscape began to change. For one thing, defamation plaintiffs and their lawyers came to understand the importance of contesting and "winning" the "public figure" issue, and the Court's decisions in those cases gave them the ammunition to do so. For another, *Gertz* and *Firestone* offered skilled members of the bar hope that the courts might become more hospitable to defamation claims, even those brought by public figures. And, perhaps most significantly, those lawyers began to find, in cases like *Butts* and *St. Amant*, previously untapped support for the notion that the actual malice hurdle could in fact be scaled, especially if they used the rules of discovery to examine both the journalists who prepared the publications and broadcasts that allegedly defamed their clients and the documents those reporters generated and gathered in the course of their work. As a result, in increasingly lengthy pretrial depositions, journalists came to be questioned extensively about whether they relied on biased sources and why they did not credit in a published story information in their possession that contradicted its allegedly defamatory sting. In addition, media defendants were increasingly called upon to produce large quantities of internal documents that might reflect expressions of doubt voiced by editors or even the existence of the aforementioned biased or exculpatory sources. The net result was that defamation cases became exponentially more expensive to defend, the imposition on the time and attention of reporters and editors became notably more significant, and the perceived risk that such a case would survive until trial and result in a verdict for the plaintiff rose demonstrably.

Thus, although it did involve an extremely popular television program (*60 Minutes*), a very high-profile reporter (Wallace), a plaintiff who had already gained a measure of fame himself, and a story about perhaps the overarching news event of the era (the Vietnam War), the *Times's* prominent treatment of the Second Circuit's decision in *Herbert* may have had less to do with the case itself than with what it had come to represent, from the media's perspective, about the process of defamation litigation. In many ways, *Herbert v. Lando* had become a poster child for what the mainstream media increasingly viewed as a litigation process that had gone seriously off the rails.

Against this backdrop, when Herbert sought Supreme Court review of the Second Circuit's decision, five justices (Burger, White, Powell, Rehnquist, and Stevens) voted to grant his request. The argument, held on October 31, 1978, focused largely on the justices' struggle to understand precisely the scope of the privilege that had been crafted by Judges Kaufman and Oakes as well as how to divine the line between those inquiries to which CBS had asserted the privilege and those to which it had not. With respect to the latter, at one point in the argument, the chief justice skeptically inquired whether CBS in fact had responded to inquiries about its editorial processes "when it helped the defendant's case, but not when conceivably it might harm the defendant's case?" When Rehnquist playfully added that "it wouldn't be the first time in a deposition that that sort of thing had happened," Herbert's counsel, New York lawyer Jonathan Lubell, responded, to the laughter of the gallery, that he did not "believe so." Burger seemed to sum up the frustrations of a number of justices when he asked Abrams "[h]ow do you probe for the presence or absence of malice if you can't ask what was the state of mind at the time this or that was done?" Abrams's response, that "the way it has been done in libel cases, and the way it is routinely done in criminal cases, and securities act cases, and antitrust cases, is for a jury to infer a particular state of mind from a particular set of facts," did not appear to assuage those concerns.

Brennan focused his own questions at argument on the state of the record with respect to the issue of falsity, securing from Lubell a concession that Lando had answered all questions put to him regarding the truth of the allegedly false, defamatory meaning that Herbert attributed to the broadcast. Brennan's inquiries also led Lubell to concede that "the issue of falsity is [still] in the case, very much in the case" and that CBS had not "conceded that the statements made on the program are false." And, when Brennan asked Lubell whether there was "ever any suggestion that the issue of falsity should be determined before you get into the question of malice," because, as Brennan put it, "unless something was false, I gather you wouldn't have a case," Lubell acknowledged that "there was no [such] suggestion." This led Brennan to ask, with respect to the "issue of so-called editorial privilege" that was before the Court, "I take it that [issue] wouldn't even be in the case unless there was first the finding of falsity of something about this program, would there?" Likely sensing where Brennan was going, Rehnquist joined the conversation, securing Lubell's ready agreement that, "in an ordinary lawsuit, in the discovery stage of the case, you have to do your discovery, for all of the issues that you think will be necessary to prove at trial before you ever get to trial."

During Abrams's argument, when Burger asked CBS's counsel whether "the privilege of a reporter is different from the privilege of some other witness," Abrams noted both that the "Court has yet to rule on whether the *Gertz* case, first of all, applies alone to the press and the media or to other entities" and that CBS did "not take the position that individual speakers cannot get the protection." After Burger pointedly observed that "there are many libel cases brought against people

who have nothing to do with journalism," Abrams suggested that, although he
was not advocating for a privilege that would protect only the press, "there are
particular reasons why the press needs the protection because of the nature of the
process it is engaged in, the regularity of it and the like." The issue at the core
of this exchange—whether the First Amendment rights articulated in *Gertz* are
reserved to the media or apply more broadly to all defamation defendants (which
Marshall had raised most recently in his memorandum to the conference in *Landmark Communications*)—would come to assume increasing significance within the
Court, culminating in the internal debate surrounding the Court's decision in
Dun & Bradstreet v. Greenmoss Builders.

Near the conclusion of Abrams's argument, in response to a question from Marshall about how exactly inquiry into the editorial process would "chill" newsroom
discussions between reporters and editors, the lawyer saw an opening to make
what appeared to be his central contention:

> I know of no case in which discovery has gone on for 26 days and 2900 pages in
> a libel case. If this case is lost, Mr. Justice Marshall, or if I may say so, if there is no
> protection at all here, I think it is fair to predict that questions like this will, for the
> first time, become routine, that public officials and public figures, the very people set
> out by this Court in *Sullivan* as being, for a variety of societal reasons, people who
> will receive less protection against defamatory falsehoods than other people, will be
> able to commence libel actions and immediately plunge into the core questions at
> issue here, why did you write these bad things about me, why didn't you put in the
> good things about me?

This led White to interject that "of course, this never happened under the old
libel law," precisely because the elements of the common law tort did not involve
any requirement of actual malice or intent of any kind. White's observation had
also begun to occur to reporters and editors as well, some of whom had started to
wonder whether, in the real world in which they operated, the First Amendment
rights they had won in *Sullivan* had proven to be a victory at all.

At conference, it appeared that the justices were, if anything, put off by all the
hoopla that had accompanied the case as it made its way to the Court. Not only
did they "not view it as particularly difficult," as Brennan's term history recounted,
but Marshall (according to that account) told his colleagues that, "[t]his is a non-case,

deliberately fashioned to get press protection," and White reportedly added that "[t]he case is a tempest in a teapot." According to Brennan's term history, White "expressed what seemed to be a general feeling when he said that he would 'hate to be pressured into a major First Amendment case.'" In all, at conference, seven justices agreed with White that the First Amendment afforded no special protection to the editorial process. Brennan's notes reflect that all nine justices concurred that the decision below should at least be "modified."

That said, as Brennan saw it, several justices were troubled by the wide-ranging discovery to which Herbert's counsel had subjected CBS and its journalists. Accordingly, Brennan's term history reported, "[t]here was some sentiment to use the First Amendment as grounds for requiring a stricter relevance for discovery questions directed at the press." Justice Stevens, sitting on his first pure defamation case since joining the Court following Douglas's retirement, suggested, according to Brennan's notes, that the First Amendment should operate to strike questions of only marginal relevance, a suggestion with which Stewart appeared to agree.

Brennan himself advocated recognizing a limited privilege of the kind ultimately described in his separate opinion in the case and presaged by his questions to Lubell during the argument. Specifically, Brennan advocated a privilege that would protect defamation defendants from inquiry into their prepublication editorial discussions until and unless the plaintiff had first made a showing that the allegedly defamatory statement was indeed false. As Brennan ultimately put it in his separate opinion dissenting in part, "the First Amendment requires predecisional communications among editors to be protected by an editorial privilege, but that this privilege must yield if a public-figure plaintiff is able to demonstrate to the prima facie satisfaction of a trial judge that the publication in question constitutes defamatory falsehood."

According to Brennan's term history, at conference, Marshall was prepared to support such an approach. As had been the case in *Firestone*, however, Brennan's views did not move any of the other justices, who rejected them as either too burdensome for plaintiffs or too difficult to administer. Thus, as Brennan's conference notes reflect, Stewart asserted that he, for one, was "sorry we used 'malice' in Sullivan" and, although he viewed the Brennan proposal as "tempting," he predicted "we'd run into intractable problems of determining defamatory falsehood." Powell, the author of *Gertz*, dismissed Brennan's approach as "too complex." According to Brennan's notes, Powell too opposed a "special privilege" for the press and asserted that he could discern "no legal principle" supporting "Kaufman's distinction between [the] editing process and what's published." In Powell's view, as Brennan recorded it, "once [you] put aside any privilege, this is just a discovery call." In the end, however, because Powell had doubts that all of the categories of questions permitted by the district judge were "entirely proper," he was "not sure" a trial court should be limited to deciding only "relevance and materiality" in adjudicating media "claims of confidentiality."

As Brennan recounted them, Rehnquist said that his views were "closest to Lewis," adding that he would "be loathe to go WJB['s] way" because the "plaintiff already has [a] heavy burden and I wouldn't add to it." Moreover, Rehnquist reportedly noted that, "as practical matter too, [I] don't think [you] can segregate issues between defamatory falsehood on one hand and malice on [the] other." For his part, Burger picked up on his colloquy with Abrams at argument and wondered whether the Court could "distinguish[ ]" between "press" and "non-press defendants" in articulating rules of discovery. In addition, according to Brennan's notes, Burger questioned whether, "if *Sullivan* spoke of state of mind, why wouldn't that heavy burden allow discovery?" Thus, Burger indicated that he believed that the Second Circuit's decision should at least be "modif[ied]," in part because it appeared to recognize a "difference . . . between press and individual" defendants and "to give special status to press."

Despite all this, Brennan "retained some hope" that his formulation of a limited privilege might "acquire some support," so he wrote it up and circulated it virtually simultaneously with the first draft of the Court's opinion, which Burger had assigned to White. In his book describing his interactions with the last five chief justices, Justice Stevens described how Burger, much like the Second Circuit's Kaufman, appeared to court the press's favor by assigning the pro-First Amendment opinions he joined to himself (see, e.g., *Nebraska Press Association v. Stuart, Landmark Communications, Inc. v. Virginia, Richmond Newspapers v. Virginia, Press-Enterprise Co. v. Superior Court*), but delegating that task to White or Rehnquist in cases in which the press did not prevail. By the time *Herbert* was decided, Rehnquist had already written *Firestone* (although Brennan understood that the chief justice had originally offered that assignment to both Powell and Blackmun) and White had already written *Branzburg v. Hayes*, rejecting another privilege advocated on behalf of the press—a First Amendment-based privilege to protect the identities of confidential news sources from an inquiring grand jury.

In his own draft opinion in *Herbert*, Brennan agreed with the majority of the other justices to a point—he concurred that no "privilege insulates factual matters that may be sought during discovery, and that such a privilege should not shield" the press's "mental processes" from discovery. Nevertheless, as his questions at argument and his comments at conference suggested, Brennan wrote that, in his view, "the First Amendment requires predecisional communication among editors to be protected by an editorial privilege," albeit one that "must yield if a public-figure plaintiff is able to demonstrate to the prima facie satisfaction of a trial judge that the publication in question constitutes defamatory falsehood." Analogizing to the executive privilege with which the Court had famously grappled five years earlier in *United States v. Nixon*, Brennan explained in the final version of his opinion in *Herbert*:

> The same rationale applies to respondents' proposed editorial privilege. Just as the possible political consequences of disclosure might undermine predecisional communication within the Executive Branch, so the possibility of future libel judgments might well dampen full and candid discussion among editors of proposed publications. Just as impaired communication "clearly" affects "the quality" of executive decision making, so too muted discussion during the editorial process will affect the quality of resulting publications. Those editors who have doubts might remain silent; those who would prefer to follow other investigative leads might be restrained; those who would otherwise counsel caution might hold their tongues. In short, in the absence of such an editorial privilege the accuracy, thoroughness and profundity of consequent publications might well be diminished.

Brennan's "hope" that he might attract five votes for his limited privilege was quickly dashed when, as his term history recounted, it "became immediately apparent" that his efforts had been "in vain." White circulated his own first draft on February 8, 1979, and it was quickly joined by Rehnquist that same day, by Powell the following day, by Stevens and Burger the next week, and by Blackmun on February 22. The centerpiece of White's opinion was its rejection of the First Amendment-based privilege articulated by Judges Kaufman and Oakes below. As White's opinion explained, "*New York Times* and its progeny make it essential to proving liability that the plaintiffs focus on the conduct and state of mind of the defendant" and that, "[i]nevitably, unless liability is to be completely foreclosed, the thoughts and editorial processes of the alleged defamer would be open to examination." Thus, White asserted, "contrary to the views of the Court of Appeals, according an absolute privilege to the editorial process of a media defendant in a libel case is not only not required, authorized, or presaged by our prior cases, but would tend to frustrate the expectations evidenced by the prior opinions of this Court." In sum, White's opinion explained:

> Permitting plaintiffs such as Herbert to prove their cases by direct as well as indirect evidence is consistent with the balance struck by our prior decisions. If such proof results in liability for damages which in turn discourages the publication of errone-ous information known to be false or probably false, this is no more than what our cases contemplate and does not abridge either freedom of speech or of the press.

Moreover, responding to the suggestion that the "costs and burdens" of defama-tion litigation had "escalated and become much more troublesome for plaintiffs and defendants" and that "the large costs of defending lawsuits will intimidate the press and lead to self-censorship," White asserted both that "[c]reating a constitu-tional privilege foreclosing direct inquiry into the editorial process . . . would not cure this problem for the press" and that "mushrooming litigation costs, much of it due to pretrial discovery, are not peculiar to the libel and slander area." Accord-ing to White, "until and unless there are major changes in the present rules of civil procedure, reliance must be had on what in fact and law are the ample powers of the district judge to prevent abuse."

In a second draft of his opinion circulated on February 28, White took direct aim at Brennan's proposed modification of the Second Circuit's decision. White asserted that, if Brennan's proposal that "answers to relevant questions about in-house conversations" be excused "until the plaintiff has made a prima facie case of fal-sity . . . contemplates a bifurcated trial, first on falsity and then on culpability and injury, we decline to subject libel trials to such burdensome complications and intolerable delay." By the same token, White wrote, "if, as seems more likely, the prima facie showing does not contemplate a mini-trial on falsity, no resolution of conflicting evidence on this issue, but only a credible assertion by the plaintiff, it smacks of a requirement that could be satisfied by an affidavit or simple verifica-tion of the pleadings," which White nevertheless indicated, "[w]e are reluctant to imbed . . . in the Constitution."

A few days earlier, Stewart had circulated his own dissenting opinion. Like the final version that appears in the official reports, it mirrored, to a significant extent, the views he had expressed at conference, including his "regret" over the Court's adoption of the phrase "actual malice" in *Sullivan*. Marshall also circulated his own dissent. In it, he focused on the scope of discovery that had been permitted by the trial court and, as reflected in the published version released along with White's opinion for the Court, asserted that the "potential for abuse of liberal discovery procedures is of particular concern in the defamation context" because "many self-perceived victims of defamation are animated by something more than a rational calculus of their chances of recovery" and, as a result, their "pre-trial maneuvers may be fashioned more with an eye to deterrence or retaliation than to unearthing germane material." Accordingly, Marshall wrote that he "would require that district courts superintend pretrial disclosure in such litigation so as to protect the press from unnecessarily protracted or tangential inquiry" and, unlike Brennan who was prepared to permit some such inquiry if the plaintiff could make a *prima facie* showing of falsity, "would foreclose discovery in defamation cases as to the substance of editorial conversations" entirely.

Responding to the last portion of White's draft concerning the escalating scope and burden of discovery in defamation actions, Powell informed White, shortly after receiving the first draft of his colleague's opinion, that he would undertake a concurring opinion of his own. As Powell explained to White, he had thought the Court's own opinion, "after deciding the constitutional question," would more directly address the "scope of discovery on remand." Because it did not—indeed, White's opinion concluded by expressly stating that the issue was "not before us"—Powell circulated his own draft concurring opinion on March 28. In it, he emphasized his view, which he asserted was "not . . . inconsistent with the Court's opinion," that "in supervising discovery in a libel suit brought by a public figure, a district court has a duty to consider First Amendment interests as well as the private interests of the plaintiffs." Thus, as Powell understood White's opinion, it required a district judge to "ensure that the values protected by the First Amendment, though entitled to no constitutional privilege in a case of this kind, are weighed carefully in striking a proper balance." In each case, Powell wrote, a district judge should properly "measure the degree of relevance required in light of both the private needs of the parties and the public concerns implicated."

In addition to providing this guidance to district judges concerning their power to control discovery in defamation cases, Powell's first draft also took some pains to emphasize his disagreement with Brennan. The resulting exchange between the authors of *Gertz* and *Sullivan* demonstrates that Brennan remained able to secure at least small victories and, more significantly, how his intervention in this way continues to have a real, if previously unappreciated, impact on the litigation of defamation cases today.

In his draft opinion, Powell included a footnote in which he expressly rejected Brennan's view that "the First Amendment requires that discovery into the exchange of views among press employees must be postponed until a preliminary determination of the falsity of the publication is made." Powell explained that he did not "believe the issues of falsity and belief of falsity always will be separable" and proceeded to endorse the fundamental premise of White's opinion—that affording protection to the editorial process in defamation cases would both deprive plaintiffs of necessary evidence and constitute a form of "double counting," providing the press with additional protections beyond those afforded by *Sullivan* itself with respect to the ultimate issue of liability. On April 9, Brennan responded, by adding the following to his own draft opinion:

> My Brother POWELL writes separately to emphasize that district courts must carefully weigh "the values protected by the First Amendment" in determining the relevance of discovery requests.... At the same time, however, he concludes that there should not be an evidentiary privilege which protects the editorial process because he is unpersuaded "that court-supervised inquiry into [editorial] exchanges is likely to exert a significant effect on future publications," and because "[n]ewsroom conversations... enjoy no special First Amendment protection other htan [*sic*] what they derive from that accorded to published speech." But if the exposure of predecisional editorial discussions will not affect the nature of subsequent publications, I have difficulty understanding exactly what First Amendment values my Brother POWELL expects district courts to place in the balance.

Three days later, Powell deleted his footnote. As a practical matter, this deletion has had tangible consequences. Media defendants regularly cite Powell's concurring opinion to soften the hard edge of White's in the cause of emboldening trial judges to exercise their discretion, in the name of "the values protected by the

First Amendment," to limit the scope of discovery in defamation cases. Most significantly, as Judge Robert D. Sack has noted in his authoritative treatise on the
subject, trial judges and appellate courts have invoked the Powell concurrence as
both a limitation on the scope of the majority opinion and as support for the stag-
ing of discovery in defamation cases—including the adoption of discovery plans
in which discovery proceeds first on the issue of material falsity, to be followed by
discovery of the defendant's unpublished journalistic work product and editorial
process only if the plaintiff is first able to survive a motion for summary judgment
directed to the issue of substantial truth. Needless to say, if Brennan had not persuaded Powell to withdraw his footnote, with its express rejection of the concept
of staged discovery, the law would likely have evolved in a very different direction.

The decision in *Herbert* was announced on April 18. As Brennan's term history
noted, White's opinion for the Court "provoked a thunderstorm of press condemnation." Brennan's reaction was twofold and at least arguably contradictory. First,
in a speech he delivered the following fall at the Newhouse Law Center at Rutgers University, he chided the press for its overreaction and attempted to send it
something of a signal that such behavior could prove, as it did in *Herbert*, counter-
productive. Ironically, Judge Kaufman, who had befriended publishing magnate S.I.
Newhouse (as well as *Times* publisher Arthur Sulzburger), spoke at the same event.

Second, Brennan's term history ended its discussion of the case by pointing out,
with an obvious measure of satisfaction, that the *Washington Post*, the newspaper he
undoubtedly read each morning, had editorialized that "[i]t would have been far
better if the court had taken the suggestion of Justice William J. Brennan," and that
its columnist Charles Seib had opined that "a court less cool toward the press might
have accepted the position of one of the dissenting justices, William J. Brennan, Jr."

Smith v. Daily Mail Publishing Co.

Herbert was not the only decision implicating *Sullivan* that the Court decided
during the October 1978 term. It also took the opportunity to revisit the line of
cases it had begun in *Cox Broadcasting Corp. v. Cohn* and continued in *Landmark
Communications, Inc. v. Virginia*, when it decided *Smith v. Daily Mail Publishing Co.*
The case arose from a February 1978 shooting at a school in St. Albans, West Virginia, about a dozen miles from Charleston. A fourteen-year-old boy, who was

identified by seven eyewitnesses, was taken into custody and appeared at a juvenile hearing, where he was declared a delinquent under West Virginia law. That same day, two daily newspapers published in Charleston, the *Gazette* and the *Daily Mail*, learned about the incident by scanning a police band radio frequency and dispatched reporters and photographers to the school, where they proceeded to interview witnesses, several of whom identified the boy as the shooter by name. The newspapers confirmed his identity with police officers and an assistant prosecuting attorney present at the scene.

The next day, both newspapers published the boy's name, in violation of a West Virginia law that made it a crime for a newspaper (and only a newspaper) to publish the name of a juvenile who was under arrest or pending a hearing without securing a "written order of the court." The same information was broadcast by at least three different radio stations. Nevertheless, both newspapers were subsequently indicted by a grand jury. Before they could be tried on those charges, however, they sought appellate review of their contention that the statute violated their rights under the First and Fourteenth Amendments. The West Virginia Supreme Court, reasoning that the statute operated as a prior restraint on the newspapers' right to publish, held that it violated the freedom of the press. West Virginia thereafter sought review in the Supreme Court, and the required four justices (Brennan, White, Marshall, and Blackmun) voted to grant its request on the eve of the term.

Much of the argument in the case, which was held on March 20, 1979 (barely a month before the Court announced its decision in *Herbert*), centered on the justices' evident interest in exploring the validity of the West Virginia Supreme Court's conclusion that the statute operated as a prior restraint. The task was complicated by the fact that Cletus Hanley, a Special Assistant Attorney General representing West Virginia, initially conceded the point, leaving it largely to the justices to debate the issue among themselves. Hanley further conceded that the statute would likely prohibit the publication of a juvenile's name, even when it was already common knowledge in the community. For his part, Floyd Abrams, again appearing for the press as he had in *Landmark Communications* and in *Herbert*, argued that the statute in fact imposed a regime of prior restraint "because the essence of it and the essence of the crime alleged here is that you must seek written permission of the judge before you can print the name of the child." By the same token, in response to a question from Justice Blackmun, Abrams made clear that, but for the requirement that a newspaper seek judicial permission to publish a juvenile's name, "it

would not be a prior restraint statute." Even so, Abrams explained, in response to
a question from Justice Rehnquist, "if instead of a licensing statute,... you have a
flat ban on any kind of publication,... it would likely be unconstitutional but it
wouldn't be a prior restraint." Or, as Abrams put it in response to a question from
Justice Stewart, "the statute is so clearly unconstitutional for a variety of reasons
that whether or not it is a prior restraint or a subsequent punishment statute [it]
would be just as unconstitutional."

When the case came before the justices for conference following argument,
seven of them voted to affirm. Rehnquist initially voted to reverse and Powell
did not participate. At conference, Burger, perhaps searching for a way to retain
assignment authority, appeared—according to Brennan's notes—to favor a narrow ground on which the judgment below might be affirmed, suggesting that
the "narrowest basis is to say [that the] name [was already in the] public domain
from TV and radio report[s]." Although Brennan left no record of his own stated
views at conference, it appears that he urged a broader ground for decision—that
the statute was unconstitutional on its face because, as Abrams had contended
at argument, it operated as a prior restraint. In response, according to Brennan's
notes, several other justices, including Stewart and Marshall, endorsed his broader
approach, while several others, including White, Rehnquist, Stevens, and Blackmun,
expressed various degrees of support for a narrow holding. Blackmun apparently
opined that the statute bore a "superficial resemblance to prior restraint but it's
for me just a flagrant restriction on speech," while Rehnquist warned that, if the
court opted for the so-called broader ground, "prior restraint would be robbed of
all analytical content." Finally, Brennan noted that Stevens said he, too, "wouldn't
decide" the prior restraint issue but would hold instead that the newspapers "just
got information lawfully and [West Virginia therefore] can't penalize [the] paper
[for] publishing it."

Burger assigned the opinion to himself and circulated his first draft on May 18,
1979. In it, as in his final opinion, he relied largely on Stevens's formulation of the
"narrow ground" but also included strains of the prior restraint analysis that had
been advocated by Abrams and, apparently, by Brennan at conference. After noting that West Virginia did "not dispute that the statute amounts to a prior restraint
on speech," precisely because "the prior-approval requirement acts in 'operation
and effect' like a licensing scheme," Burger wrote that the "resolution of this case
does not turn on whether the statutory grant of authority to the juvenile judge

to permit publication of the juvenile's name is, in and of itself, a prior restraint" because "[w]hether we view the statute as a prior restraint or as a penal sanction for publishing lawfully obtained, truthful information" it nevertheless "requires the highest of state interest to sustain its validity." As Burger explained it, because "state action to punish the publication of truthful information seldom can satisfy constitutional standards," the First Amendment requires that, "if a newspaper lawfully obtains truthful information about a matter of public significance then state officials may not constitutionally punish publication of the information, absent a need to further a state interest of the highest order." And, Burger wrote, the only state interest advanced by West Virginia in support of the statute—the protection of the anonymity of the juvenile offender—did not constitute such an interest. Moreover, even if it did, it "does not accomplish its stated purpose" because it applies only to newspapers and "does not restrict the electronic media, or any form of publication except 'newspapers.'"

Stevens and White both joined Burger's opinion on May 22, as did Blackmun on May 25. On June 11, Brennan wrote to Burger to inform him (and the other justices) that "I am with you on this and would be happy to join your opinion if you could see your way clear of dropping" the following sentence, which appeared in the section of Burger's draft addressing whether the West Virginia statute furthered a state interest of the "highest order":

> The values embodied in the First Amendment are generally of comparable importance to those rights guaranteed by the Sixth Amendment. See *Nebraska Press Association v. Stuart,* 427 U.S. 539, 561.

Burger responded that same day, resisting Brennan's suggestion but offering an alternative for "changing it to a neutral cast":

> The important values embodied in the First Amendment must be considered along with the rights of defendants guaranteed by the Sixth Amendment.

The chief justice closed his letter by asking Brennan, "Doesn't this accomplish your objective?" On his copy of the letter, Brennan apparently tried his hand at editing it, crossing through the words "values embodied" and handwriting over them "rights created." The next day, Brennan wrote only to Burger (with no copies to

the other justices as he had in his initial request) and said "I appreciate your willingness to accommodate my suggestions. May I make one last one: could 'rights
created by' be used in the first line for 'values embodied in'? With that change,
I'm happy to join." Burger circulated another draft on June 13, incorporating this
language, and Brennan promptly joined his opinion that same day.

Stewart joined Burger's opinion on June 13 as well and Marshall did so on
the 20th. In the end, Rehnquist decided to concur in the judgment which, he
explained in a short opinion, was based on his view that, although West Virginia's
interest in protecting the anonymity of juveniles did indeed constitute an interest
of the "highest order," it did not "accomplish its stated purpose" for the reasons
articulated by Burger toward the end of his opinion for the Court. The decision
was announced on June 26, 1979.

Hutchinson v. Proxmire, Wolston v. Reader's Digest Association

The October 1978 term also featured two other decisions that, though less
celebrated than *Herbert v. Lando* when decided, proved to be equally significant—
Hutchinson v. Proxmire and *Wolston v. Reader's Digest Association*. In *Firestone*, although
the Court's attention was in significant measure focused on the kind of evidence
that would support a finding of "fault" within the meaning of *Gertz*, Justice
Rehnquist's opinion also invoked *Gertz*'s description of the so-called "limited
purpose public figure" and determined that Mary Alice Firestone was not such a
plaintiff and was therefore not obliged to prove actual malice in order to prevail.
Rehnquist's effort to flesh out this aspect of the *Gertz* decision had been, in significant part, a subject of Marshall's dissent in that case, including most especially
its emphasis on the role of judges in determining whether the alleged defamation
in a given case addressed a "public controversy." It was not, however, until *Hutchinson* and *Wolston* that the Court focused its post-*Gertz* attentions squarely on the
often pivotal question of who constitutes a public figure.

Hutchinson was brought by a research scientist who, after receiving a government
grant through the state of Michigan to conduct studies on monkeys assessing their
reaction to stress, was the subject of a tongue-in-cheek "Golden Fleece Award,"
regularly presented at the time by United States Senator William Proxmire, a

Wisconsin Democrat, to persons and organizations he deemed to have wasted taxpayer money. The "award" was actually presented to the federal agencies— including NASA and the National Science Foundation—that had awarded the $500,000 grant because of the potential of Dr. Hutchinson's research for resolving problems associated with confining humans in close quarters for extended periods in space and undersea. Most of the senator's ire, however, which he expressed in a speech placed in the Congressional Record, in a newsletter sent to approximately one hundred thousand people, in a press release circulated to two hundred seventy-five media entities, in subsequent television and radio appearances, and in follow-up telephone calls made on his behalf to the "award winning" agencies, was reserved for Dr. Hutchinson himself. Among other barbs, Proxmire wrote that "Dr. Hutchinson's studies should make the taxpayers as well as his monkeys grind their teeth" and that "the good doctor has made a fortune from his monkeys and in the process made a monkey out of the American taxpayer." In fact, Dr. Hutchinson contended, he received only a modest salary from the state institutions for which he worked, and the grant itself was paid not to him but to the state.

Hutchinson thereafter instituted a defamation action against Proxmire, which a federal district court sitting in Wisconsin dismissed on a motion for summary judgment filed by the senator. The district court offered multiple grounds for its decision, including that the Constitution's Speech or Debate Clause (which generally protects statements made by members of Congress in the course of performing their legislative duties) granted Proxmire immunity from defamation liability, that the First Amendment protected his allegedly defamatory statements because Dr. Hutchinson was both a public official and a public figure who could not prove actual malice, and that the scientist had failed to state a viable claim for defamation under state law in any event. That decision was, in turn, affirmed by the United States Court of Appeals for the Seventh Circuit, albeit on narrower grounds. The court of appeals held that most of Proxmire's statements were protected by the Speech or Debate Clause and that those that were not, such as what the senator said on television and radio, were protected by the First Amendment because Dr. Hutchinson was a public figure who had failed to come forward with sufficient evidence, in response to the senator's summary judgment motion, to ground a finding of actual malice. The Seventh Circuit did not reach either the public official or common law issues on which the district court had alternatively based its decision.

The case was argued on March 17, 1979, the same day as *Wolston* and three days after the Court had heard argument in *Daily Mail*. Most of the argument in *Hutchinson* was devoted to the Speech or Debate Clause issue, but the justices did pose some questions directed at the First Amendment-based aspects of the Seventh Circuit's decision. At one juncture in his argument, Chief Justice Burger asked Michael Cavanaugh, a Lansing, Michigan, lawyer appearing on behalf of Dr. Hutchinson, whether his client's status as a public figure "is a jury issue which cannot be resolved by the court on summary judgment." When Cavanaugh endorsed that position, Burger added that "well then, you must mean that among other things that that's an issue which cannot be resolved, that's a factual issue which cannot be resolved on affidavits but only by a trial of the issues."

Later, Justice Stewart asserted that the public figure and public official designations had only "been deemed important in the decisions and opinions of this Court when the alleged false defamatory material has been published by some instrumentality of the public news media" and pointedly asked Cavanaugh "is there any case here that holds that the so-called *New York Times* rules are applicable when the defamatory statement has been made by an individual person, human being?" When Cavanaugh responded in the negative, Stewart persisted, asserting that "it may be that whether or not your client is a public figure is totally irrelevant." But, after Stewart then pressed him on why "you don't brief or argue this basic question," Cavanaugh politely explained that he did not do so because "*New York Times* involved both media defendants and non-media defendants" and it would therefore "appear from the ruling in *New York Times* that there was an assumption that the same rule would apply to both types of defendants." Still, Cavanaugh conceded, "since that time in *Gertz* and in other public figure cases, the Court seems to have rather carefully indicated that the defendant was a media defendant." Once again, Stewart's inquiry and Cavanaugh's response had touched on an issue—whether *Sullivan* and *Gertz* applied only in suits instituted against media defendants—that would come to occupy the justices' attentions five years later in *Dun & Bradstreet v. Greenmoss Builders.*

During his own argument, Alan Raywid, counsel for Senator Proxmire, did not receive a single question about the First Amendment issues raised by the case; the entirety of his presentation, and the justices' questions to him, were directed to the applicability of the Speech or Debate Clause. But, when Cavanaugh rose for his rebuttal, Justice Stevens asked him about an issue that the Seventh Circuit had not reached—whether by virtue of his position as a state employee, Dr. Hutchinson was a public official within the meaning of *Sullivan*. When Cavanaugh contended that he was not, largely because he had only "ten or eleven" employees under his supervision, Stevens asked whether it was appropriate to "measure" a defamation plaintiff's public official status "by the number of persons under his supervision?" "Is that the test," Stevens wondered, "or was it the importance of his responsibilities?" At this juncture, Justice Marshall joined the debate, asserting pointedly that Hutchinson "was an officer of the state, wasn't he?"

Like the argument, most of the Court's internal debate in the *Hutchinson* case was ultimately devoted not to the defamation issues, but rather to the applicability of the Speech or Debate Clause. Nevertheless, Brennan's notes indicate that, at conference, the chief justice began the discussion by identifying three issues that he believed were before the Court—specifically, whether the Speech or Debate Clause "protect[s] newsletters and press releases;" whether Hutchinson "is a public figure;" and whether, "if so, should there have been summary judgment." Brennan left no record of how he responded to the chief's comments beyond a somewhat cryptic handwritten note in which he appears to question his vote at conference to affirm the decision below—apparently because of doubts with respect to the proper resolution of the Speech or Debate Clause issue. Stewart, as Brennan recorded his views, attempted to supplement Burger's formulation of the relevant issues, adding that, if the Speech or Debate Clause did not apply to any of Proxmire's various publications (and he said he believed it did not apply to protect the Senator's newsletters), another issue would then be presented—whether those publications were defamatory. That question, Stewart contended, would have to be answered before reaching the separate issue of whether the "*N. Y. Times* rule applies to plaintiff." Nevertheless, Stewart asserted, the Court's review should "stop" with resolution of the Speech or Debate issue and the justices should remand to the lower courts for further consideration of whether Proxmire's otherwise unprotected publications "were defamatory and, if so, whether [Hutchinson was a] public figure." And, Stewart placed yet another issue on the lower court's prospective agenda, whether, even if he was a public figure, Hutchinson was obliged to prove "actual malice" in order to prevail in a case in which the defendant he had "sued [was] not [a] member of [the] media."

As Brennan recounted it in his conference notes, although White and Marshall disagreed with Stewart to some extent on the number of Proxmire's publications that should enjoy immunity under the Speech or Debate Clause, they appeared to endorse his views with respect to remanding the defamation issues. Blackmun too reportedly said that the Court "need not decide" the defamation issues, although he added that he did not "think plaintiff is either [a] public official or public figure." Powell, however, opined that the Court "should reach the public figure issue" and Rehnquist added that he "could agree" with Stewart on the remand issue "except" for the fact that, in *Wolston*, which had been argued the same day as *Hutchinson*, the justices would have to grapple with the issue of whether "summary judgment is especially appropriate in libel cases" in any event. Finally, at least according to Brennan's notes, Stevens confined his comments at conference to the Speech or Debate issue.

On May 26, 1979, Burger, who had assigned the majority opinion in the case to himself, circulated a memorandum in which, somewhat curiously given Brennan's notes of his comments there, the Chief asserted that, during the conference, he had entirely "overlooked calling attention to the 'public figure' issue in this case." As a result, the draft opinion he circulated that day did not address the issue at all, concluding, as Stewart had urged at conference, with the holding only that "the Speech and Debate Clause does not protect newsletters or press releases," reversing the contrary portion of the judgment below, and remanding the case for further proceedings "consistent with this opinion." In his accompanying memorandum, however, Burger reported that his "notes indicate a substantial number—but perhaps not five—thought respondent was not a public figure. I agree but am not sure as to the votes." He added that, if "four others so vote, it will be a simple matter to add this holding."

Two days later, on May 28, Powell wrote to Burger and questioned the scope of the "holding" reflected in the chief justice's draft. According to Powell, "a majority of the conference thought we should vacate the judgment of [the court of appeals] in its entirety, and remand the case to it to consider first the state-law issue (which could be decisive), and thereafter—if reached—the 'private person' issue under federal law." Nevertheless, Powell informed his colleagues that his "own view" was somewhat different—"in addition to deciding the Speech or Debate Clause issue, we should hold that Hutchinson is a private rather than a public person, and resolve that issue. Otherwise," Powell wrote, the court of appeals "may well reaffirm its decision that Hutchinson *was* a public figure if it gets by the state law question. We then will probably be called upon to review the case again." Still, Powell conceded, "my view did not prevail at Conference," which left him "willing to join your opinion for the Court if the entire judgment . . . is vacated, and the remand is limited to the state law issue," specifically, whether the publications not protected by the Speech or Debate Clause were defamatory. Burger responded the following day reiterating his willingness to "to add a section to hold that Hutchinson was not a public figure, if there are five votes for that position." He added that, if there were to be a remand of the kind reflected in his initial draft, "Bill Rehnquist's opinion in *Wolston v. Reader's Digest* may well have an influence on the [Seventh Circuit's] view on remand." This possibility, he wrote, he would "take into account when *Wolston* comes around."

Burger's memorandum prompted Powell to circulate his own, later that same day, urging the court "to reach and decide the 'public figure' issue." "It has been argued," he wrote, "and I think it was before us." Four other justices (Blackmun, Stevens, Stewart, and Rehnquist—the author of the still-to-come opinion for the Court in *Wolston*) thereafter all indicated their willingness to hold that Hutchinson was *not* a public figure as well. Blackmun reminded his colleagues that he had so opined at conference, Stevens indicated merely that he would "also join" an opinion so holding, and Rehnquist wrote that he had "no objection to reaching the 'public figure' issue if it can be done without violating the traditional maxim that we avoid constitutional adjudication unless it is necessary." He cautioned, however, that "it might be a trickier job to reach the 'public figure' issue in the case." Stewart was even more emphatic. Despite his advocacy of a remand on the issue at conference, he advised Burger not only that, in his view, Hutchinson was not a public figure but also expressed his "hope that in this opinion we can hold that he is not."

At about the same time that the last of these justices (Rehnquist) weighed in on June 5, Brennan circulated a brief dissent, addressing only the Speech or Debate Clause issue. The following day, Burger circulated a new draft, in which he tackled the public figure issue for the first time. His revised draft included an expanded factual recitation, which recounted additional information relevant to Hutchinson's putative public figure status, recited the basis for the lower courts' holdings that he so qualified, added a paragraph explaining—in light of Rehnquist's expressed concerns—why it was appropriate to reach this constitutional issue, and appended a final section holding that Hutchinson was indeed not a public figure.

In so doing, the chief justice confined his analysis to the Seventh Circuit's "holding that Hutchinson is a public figure for the limited purpose of comment on his receipt of federal funds for research projects" which, Burger explained, "was based ... upon two factors: first, Hutchinson's successful application for federal funds and the reports in local newspapers of the federal grants" and "second, Hutchinson's access to the media, as demonstrated by the fact that some newspapers and wire services reported his response to the announcement of the Gold[en] Fleece Award." Burger rejected this analysis, largely on the ground that "[n]either of these factors demonstrate that Hutchinson was a public figure prior to the controversy engendered by the Golden Fleece Award" and that "Hutchinson did not thrust himself or his views into public controversy to influence others" before that time. In addition, Burger's opinion chastised the Senator's counsel for failing to identify a "particular controversy" into which Hutchinson had thrust himself, and asserted that any expressed "concern about general public expenditures" was not only "shared by most" citizens but "relates to most public expenditures." Characterizing such a concern as a "public controversy" within the meaning of *Gertz*, Burger wrote, would mean that "everyone who received or benefited from the myriad public grants for research could be classified as a public figure." Moreover, the chief justice asserted, Hutchinson had "at no time assumed any role of public prominence in the broad question of concern about expenditures" in any event. Finally, Burger added, the Court could not "agree that Hutchinson had such access to the media that he should be classified as a public figure" because his "access" was "limited to responding to the announcement of the Golden Fleece Award."

The chief justice's opinion for the Court also contained three footnotes of some significance. In one of them, footnote 8 in the final opinion, he noted that the district court had held that Hutchinson was a "public official" as defined in *Sullivan*. To this, Burger wrote that the Court would "express no opinion" because it had not been addressed by the Seventh Circuit, but added that, although "Court has not provided precise boundaries for the category of 'public official'; it cannot be thought to include all public employees." In another, footnote 16 of the final opinion, Burger noted that neither court below had "considered whether the *New York Times* standard can apply to an individual defendant rather than to a media defendant." After noting that, at argument, counsel for Dr. Hutchinson had not conceded the point, he asserted that "[t]his Court has never decided the question [and] our conclusion that Hutchinson is not a public figure makes it unnecessary to do so in this case." Burger's assertion that the Court had "never decided the question" was, at the very least, difficult to square with its decisions in *Sullivan, St.*

Amant, Garrison, and *Henry v. Collins,* all of which applied *Sullivan* to "individual" defendants unaffiliated with the media.

Most significantly, in footnote 9, Burger took on the lower courts' decision that, if the actual malice standard applied, Proxmire was entitled to summary judgment on that issue. In language that would have a discernible impact on the litigation of defamation cases in the years that followed, the chief justice asserted that the Court was "constrained to express some doubt about the so-called 'rule,'" on which lower courts had increasingly relied in disposing of defamation actions brought by public figures and public officials prior to trial, to the effect that "in determining whether a plaintiff had made an adequate showing of 'actual malice,' summary judgment might well be the rule rather than the exception." As Burger saw it, the "proof of 'actual malice' calls a defendant's state of mind into question" and, citing *Herbert* as well as *Sullivan,* it "does not readily lend itself to summary disposition. In the present posture of the case," he hastened to add, "the propriety of dealing with such complex issues by summary judgment is not before us." As noted, Brennan did not take issue with any of these aspects of the Court's opinion. And, as his expressed views in subsequent cases would reveal, he was in fact more sympathetic to the positions staked out by the chief justice than might have been expected.

Like *Hutchinson, Wolston* was brought by an otherwise obscure plaintiff who had nevertheless achieved a measure of notoriety. Ilya Wolston, the nephew of convicted Soviet agents Jack and Myra Sobel, had been called to testify before a grand jury investigating Soviet espionage in 1957. He failed to comply with the subpoena, citing ill health. For that failure, he was cited for contempt, a charge he declined to contest after his wife broke down on the witness stand during the contempt hearing. He subsequently testified as ordered. Wolston's initial failure to appear and the resulting contempt proceedings were the subjects of contemporaneous news reports. In the decades that followed, he largely faded from public view. In 1974, however, Reader's Digest published a book entitled *KGB: The Secret Work of Soviet Agents,* which identified Wolston as a Soviet agent, an allegation he claimed was both false and defamatory. During discovery in Wolston's defamation action against the publisher and author, the latter testified that he had based the allegedly defamatory statements on an FBI report, which he had in his possession and which did indeed purport to implicate Wolston in espionage on behalf of the Soviet Union.

Wolston brought his defamation action in the federal court for the District of Columbia, where it was dismissed on a pretrial motion for summary judgment. The trial court, affirmed by the court of appeals, held that Wolston was a public figure who had failed to come forward with the requisite evidence of actual malice. These conclusions, which mirrored those of the lower courts in *Hutchinson*, formed the basis of Wolston's petition for review by the Supreme Court. His case, unlike Hutchinson's, was unencumbered by other issues such as the potential applicability of the Speech or Debate Clause.

Wolston was argued on April 17, 1979, the same day as *Hutchinson*. At the outset of his argument, Wolston's counsel, Washington, D.C., lawyer Sidney Dickstein, was peppered with questions by Justice Rehnquist, not about the public figure issue, but rather (as he later reminded his colleagues at conference in *Hutchinson*) about the district court's decision to grant summary judgment on the question of actual malice. In an exchange that laid the groundwork for footnote 9 to Chief Justice Burger's opinion for the Court in *Hutchinson*, Rehnquist asked, "[i]sn't it the rule on summary judgment that where a party defendant makes an affidavit that he's not only got—you have [the] right to depose him—but that the District Court has to resolve issues against him if they are triable issues of fact?" Dickstein responded that, although that was the "normal rule of course," it was not followed in the District of Columbia Circuit in "matters involving libel." And, after Dickstein explained that the district court had credited the author's affidavit, in which he described how he said he gathered the information about Wolston contained in his book and the basis for his subjective belief that it was accurate, Rehnquist asked whether the trial judge "chose to believe his statement without a trial of fact?" To that question, Dickstein responded, "[t]hat is correct, precisely."

During his questioning of John Buckley, who argued on behalf of the defendants as his law partner Edward Bennett Williams had for the defendant in *Monitor Patriot Co. v. Roy* several years earlier, Rehnquist similarly asked him to confirm that "the District Court simply accepted at its face value the affidavit of an interested defendant that he intended no malice and granted judgment on that basis?" Buckley, however, would not do so, asserting that "it was undisputed that [the author] relied upon an official report of the FBI which so identified" Wolston, "so there was no evidence here of knowledge of falsity or reckless disregard." Rehnquist appeared unmoved, responding that "there's no reason why the District Court has to—should believe that on a motion for summary judgment" because "an interested party's testimony can always be disbelieved by a jury." When Buckley argued that a court could properly do so when there was corroborating evidence—such as the referenced FBI report itself—Rehnquist resisted, reminding Buckley that "the burden is on the party moving for summary judgment and the credibility of an interested witnesses [is] for the jury." This led Buckley to ask "how can reliance upon an official report of the FBI unequivocally, categorically identifying some-one as a Soviet agent constitute proof in any sense of actual malice?" If it were, he continued, "then historians and newscasters would report the official findings of such agencies at their peril because under petitioner's view, there must always be a costly trial irrespective of the evidence."

When Dickstein rose for his rebuttal, Justice Stevens returned to the issue, ques-tioning Wolston's counsel as to how he had "discharged [his] affirmative burden" to come forward with evidence of actual malice sufficient to avoid summary judg-ment. When Dickstein suggested that a jury was entitled to disbelieve the author's testimony on that score, Justice White asserted that "just because the jury can disbelieve and disregard his affidavit doesn't mean they have to conclude or that he absolutely knew or suspected that something was false." White then reminded Dickstein that, in *St. Amant*, his opinion for the Court had pointed to objective evidence from which a jury could infer actual malice and asked him, in this case, "what obvious reasons were there for the defendant to doubt the accuracy of his information objectively?" When Dickstein identified a number of them, largely relating to the fact that Wolston had never been indicted for espionage and the source on which the FBI report was largely based "had been characterized as a liar by one who knew him best," White appeared satisfied, summing up Dick-stein's argument by stating "so you say at least there was a jury question about that."

During Dickstein's opening argument, the chief justice turned the questioning to the public figure issue, asking him if "the issue of whether or not a person is a public figure invariably [is] a fact issue for the jury?" In response, Dickstein threw Burger something of a curve ball, asserting that "this is a case in which Wolston cannot be classified as a public figure and hence no fact issue arises which . . . a jury would have to consider." Blackmun then pressed Wolston's counsel, asking whether, even if his client had been a public figure in 1958, he had "ceased to be one in 1974?" Again, Dickstein threw his curve, advising Blackmun that he had abandoned any such contention because, "upon reflection" he had become "per-suaded" on that point "by the views expressed by the courts below" that "if one

were a public figure in 1958, one would remain a public figure for the purpose
of commenting upon those same events in a historical work published in 1974."
This concession, however, did not stop Justice Stevens from asking Buckley, the
defendants' counsel, whether it was "reasonable to say that a historian should have
the same latitude when he has plenty of time to research and presumably writes
something that has a stamp of careful research . . . as opposed to the reporter who
has to meet a deadline to get in before 4:30 or whatever time the story has to be
filed?" Stevens's comment led Blackmun to explain to Buckley and presumably
to his colleagues that "this is why I asked your opponent why he abandoned the
passage of time argument."

Throughout Buckley's argument, the questions were decidedly less sympathetic than those received by his opponent. Both the chief justice and Justice
White expressed discomfort with Buckley's position that someone who engages in
criminal conduct—in this case the failure to appear that earned Wolston a criminal contempt citation—automatically becomes a public figure. White responded
to the contention by asking, "you wouldn't suggest that a person who's convicted
of burglary or armored car robbery in 1958 is necessarily a public figure if he's
accused of doing the same thing in 1979?" And Justice Marshall joined the questioning as well, quizzing Buckley about "how many people are usually arrested in
New York City in any one day" and extracting the concession that, under Buckley's theory, "they would all be public figures." That led Marshall to ask, "[h]ow do
they become a public figure [if] nobody ever heard of them?"

Later in his argument, Chief Justice Burger returned to the subject, expressing
his own doubts about whether "just an ordinary citizen, secretary, clerk" who is
"accosted on the street by a policeman who wants to arrest him and has no reason"
would be a public figure. And, when White asked Buckley "would you say he is a
public figure if he hadn't been convicted for contempt," the lawyer conceded "that
would create a much more difficult question." This ultimately led Justice Powell
to suggest that "it seems to me that you spent a good deal of your time defending
an issue that's not even before us, as I understand it. You don't need to defend the
position that anyone convicted of any crime at any time becomes a public figure." As Powell saw it, the lower courts had held that "this man became a public
figure . . . only because he was convicted of contempt in the context of the great
furor in this country that existed at the time with respect to communist espionage."

When Rehnquist asked whether Wolston had "inject[ed] himself into a controversy intentionally," Buckley suggested that, by becoming an "activist" when he declined to appear before the grand jury voluntarily, Wolston had "invited defamatory comments as to have opened the door to speculation on the basis for his refusal to comply with the subpoena." Buckley's response led Burger to ask skeptically, "who invites defamatory comments?," and Marshall to wonder how Wolston can be said to "invite somebody to tell a lie?" Later in his argument, when Buckley responded to Stevens's request that he identify the "public controversy or the public question that this man had prominence in," by pointing to "the controversy over Soviet espionage," Stevens pointedly asked "what was the controversy? Everybody is against Soviet espionage. There aren't pros and cons about that, are there?" At this point, after Buckley retrenched and identified the controversy more precisely as "the propriety of the actions by the public officials running the investigation, by the grand jury conducting it," Stevens inquired what Wolston "had to do with that controversy?" And, when Marshall then asked Buckley when he had "first heard" of Wolston and effectively challenged him "to name one other one that was involved" in Soviet espionage, Stevens remarked that "it's ironic, you know, to think of someone trying to conceal his activities as a spy being a public figure."

Brennan retained no notes memorializing the justices' discussion at conference in *Wolston*, leaving only those clues about it that can be gleaned from his rendition of the colloquy in *Hutchinson*, which was discussed the same day and, of course, Rehnquist's draft opinion for the Court, which was circulated near the end of May. In his opinion, Rehnquist focused on the public figure issue and concluded that "the undisputed facts do not justify the conclusion that . . . [Wolston] 'voluntarily thrust' or 'injected' himself into the forefront of the public controversy surrounding the investigation of Soviet espionage in the United States." Relying on his own opinion for the Court in *Firestone*, Rehnquist wrote:

> It would be more accurate to say that petitioner was dragged unwillingly into the controversy. The government pursued him in its investigation. Petitioner did fail to respond to a grand jury subpoena, and this failure, as well as his subsequent citation for contempt, did attract media attention. But the mere fact that petitioner voluntarily chose not to appear before the grand jury, knowing that his action might be attended by publicity, is not decisive on the question of public-figure status.

Rather, Rehnquist's opinion explained, because "[i]t is clear that petitioner played only a minor role in whatever public controversy there may have been concerning the investigation of Soviet espionage," the Court could not "hold that his mere citation for contempt rendered him a public figure for purposes of comment on the investigation of Soviet espionage." In addition, Rehnquist picked up on Stevens's questions at argument, asserting in a footnote that "[i]t is difficult to determine with precision the 'public controversy' into which petitioner is alleged to have thrust himself," especially since "there was no public controversy or debate in 1958 about the desirability of permitting Soviet espionage in the United States; all responsible United States citizens understandably were and are opposed to it."

Rehnquist also addressed Buckley's alternative contention—that the public controversy "involved the propriety of the actions of law enforcement officials in investigating and prosecuting suspected Soviet agents." His opinion, however, concluded that Wolston had not "engaged the attention of the public in an attempt to influence the resolution" of that issue. As Rehnquist explained it, a "private individual is not automatically transformed into a 'public figure' just by becoming involved in or associated with a matter that attracts public attention. To accept such reasoning would in effect reestablish the doctrine advanced by the plurality" in *Rosenbloom*. Not surprisingly, therefore, Rehnquist's opinion also rejected Buckley's contention "that any person who engages in criminal conduct automatically becomes a 'public figure' for purposes of comment on a limited range of issues relating to his conviction." And, finally, in another footnote, Rehnquist noted Dickstein's concession on the passage-of-time issue and explained that, since Wolston was not a public figure in 1958 in any event, the Court did not have to reach the issue.

By May 31, Powell had indicated to the conference his agreement with Rehnquist's analysis that Wolston was not a public figure, but added two suggestions of some note. First, Powell expressed concern that, in a footnote, Rehnquist had implied that summary judgment had been improper for the additional reason that "the court below denied the jury the right to assess credibility and draw inferences." This troubled Powell because, he wrote Rehnquist, "I believe summary judgment here could have rested on the ground that Wolston's [*sic*] failed to produce any evidence to rebut [the author's] assertion that he had substantial reasons to believe the charge of espionage was accurate." He therefore suggested that Rehnquist revise the footnote to remove the implication.

Second, Powell opined that it would be "useful to flag an issue not raised by Reader's Digest"—that "[s]ome of our cases indicate that the accurate reporting of libelous accusations made by a governmental agency is protected by the First Amendment," citing *Time, Inc. v. Pape*—because "Reader's Digest may be in a position to argue here that the statements . . . are nothing more than accurate reporting of the charges made in the FBI document published by the Senate." Accordingly, Powell suggested that Rehnquist add the following footnote to his opinion for the Court:

> Neither do we reach the question, arguably presented by this case although not addressed by the court below, whether respondent's conduct amounts to anything more than accurate reporting of defamatory statements made by a governmental body in its official capacity, and if not, whether the First Amendment protects such reporting. Cf. *Time, Inc. v. Pape*, 401 U.S. 279 (1971).

Rehnquist responded the next day, noting that Powell had been "generous enough not to condition your 'join' letter . . . on either of the suggestions which it contained." As a result, Rehnquist indicated that he had "taken the liberty of adopting the first but not the second" of Powell's two suggestions. He rejected the second because, he wrote Powell, he understood the issue had indeed been raised below and that he "would guess that Edward Bennett Williams and his firm do not need any coaching from us to the effect that they should renew it on remand." As for Powell's first suggestion, Rehnquist revised footnote 3 of his opinion to state simply that, "[i]n view of our disposition of the public-figure issue, we need not and do not reach the question" of the propriety of summary judgment with respect to the actual malice issue and cited footnote 9 of the chief justice's opinion for the Court in *Hutchinson*. The issues of the propriety of summary judgment in defamation cases, as well as the ability of a reviewing court to assess witness credibility or draw inferences from the record evidence with respect to actual malice—both of which Rehnquist had addressed in his original version of the footnote—would nevertheless return to the Court's docket in a series of cases in the years that followed, specifically in *Bose Corp. v. Consumers Union*, *Anderson v. Liberty Lobby, Inc.*, and *Harte-Hanks Communications, Inc. v. Connaughton*.

Brennan joined the fray on June 18, when he circulated his very brief dissenting opinion. On the one hand, Brennan disagreed with Rehnquist's holding that

Wolston was not a public figure as well as Blackmun's view, contained in his concurring opinion first circulated three days earlier, that Wolston had lost whatever public figure status he had attained in 1958 by the time the book was published in 1974. In Brennan's view, the "mere lapse of time is not devisive [sic]," and the "issue of Soviet espionage in 1958 and of Wolston's involvement in that operation continues to be a legitimate topic of debate today, for that matter concerns the security of the United States." Brennan also took issue with Powell's first point in his memorandum to Rehnquist several weeks earlier, asserting—albeit without further explanation—that summary judgment was nevertheless inappropriate because "the evidence raised a genuine issue of fact respecting the existence of actual malice."

With this dissent in *Wolston*, Brennan did, at least as a technical matter, get the last word in the Court's last opinion of the fifteenth term following *Sullivan*. In it, he stood alone in defending a construction of the public figure standard that tracked most closely the broader "public interest" test he had championed in *Rosenbloom*. And, curiously, although he had premised *Sullivan* in significant part on the self-censorship engendered by the threat of litigation and the potentially crippling attorneys' fees and costs such litigation can entail, and had specifically decried it yet again earlier in the year in *Herbert*, he went out of his way in *Wolston* to speak to an issue not addressed by the Court itself and assert that, even though Wolston was a public figure, he was entitled to take his case to trial. The apparent contradiction in Brennan's views in this regard would continue in the terms to come, as the Court increasingly turned its attentions to some of the myriad procedural issues that *Sullivan* had spawned in cases like *Calder v. Jones, Keeton v. Hustler Magazine, Inc., Bose Corp. v. Consumers Union,* and *Anderson v. Liberty Lobby, Inc.*

CHAPTER 6

SUBSTANCE OR PROCEDURE?

The Court took what at the time was a rare break from defamation-related cases following the October 1978 term. At least to some extent, however, this hiatus was not by design. In fact, during the October 1981 term, the Court granted review in two defamation cases decided by the United States Court of Appeals for the Sixth Circuit in opinions written by Judge Gilbert Merritt, who like Irving Kaufman, had built a reputation as a judicial advocate of the press's First Amendment rights. In one of them, *Street v. National Broadcasting Co.*, the court of appeals had held that the plaintiff, the prosecutrix and main witness in the infamous rape trial of the "Scottsboro boys" in Alabama some forty years earlier, was and remained a public figure for purposes of a defamation action she brought against the producers of a television "docudrama" about the case. Thus, *Street* afforded the Court an opportunity to revisit the issues it had addressed in *Hutchinson* and, especially, in *Wolston*. In the other, *Wilson v. Scripps-Howard Broadcasting Co.*, Judge Merritt wrote an opinion for his court holding that a defamation plaintiff who was not a public figure bore the burden of proving that the purportedly defamatory statements at issue were false. The Court that was primed to hear *Street* and *Wilson* featured a new member—in September 1981, Justice Sandra Day O'Connor, the first female justice, replaced the retired Justice Stewart who, although often solicitous of a defamation plaintiff's interest in protecting his reputation, had voted with Justice Brennan in defamation-related cases more often than not.

Justice O'Connor would, however, have to wait a bit longer than her first term to consider on its merits an issue arising from a defamation case decided under the constitutional regime established in *Sullivan* and *Gertz*. Although they had prevailed in the Sixth Circuit, the defendants in both *Street* and *Wilson* settled their cases shortly after the Court granted review. There is no public record explaining why they did so. Still, it is at least arguable that the results reached by the Court in *Hutchinson, Wolston,* and *Herbert,* coupled with the then-fresh change in the Court's make up, were weighed in the calculus. The media defendants in *Street* and *Wilson* may well have thought it prudent to let some additional time pass before the "new" Court again tackled the kinds of issues raised in those cases. As it turned out, the Supreme Court has not revisited the public figure issue since its decisions in *Hutchinson* and *Wolston,* leaving it entirely to the lower courts to refine and apply the constitutional standard for determining when a defamation plaintiff is obliged to prove actual malice in order to recover. But, as we shall see in chapter 8, it did not take long for the Court to grapple with the question raised in *Wilson*—less than five years later, in an opinion written by Justice O'Connor, it decided the issue in *Philadelphia Newspapers, Inc. v. Hepps.*

In all, it was not until two years after O'Connor joined the Court that the justices reentered the defamation arena. When they did so during the October 1983 term, they heard argument in no less than four such cases, *Bose Corp. v. Consumers Union, Keeton v. Hustler Magazine, Inc., Calder v. Jones,* and *Dun & Bradstreet v. Greenmoss Builders.* Three of them—*Bose, Keeton,* and *Calder*—were all argued the same day, November 8, 1983. The fourth—*Greenmoss Builders*—was first heard the following March and proved to be sufficiently vexing to the justices that it was ultimately held over for reargument the following term. The extensive internal deliberations that led to the Court's decision in *Greenmoss Builders,* which itself came at the close of the October 1984 term, are chronicled in the chapter that follows. This chapter addresses the three cases heard on November 8, 1983, each of which, in its own way, considered the impact of the First Amendment principles articulated in *Sullivan* on the procedural rules governing the litigation of defamation claims.

Keeton v. Hustler Magazine, Inc.

The first case the Court heard on the morning of November 8 was *Keeton v. Hustler Magazine, Inc.* It arose in the context of a defamation action brought by Kathy Keeton, a senior executive at Penthouse, the "adult" magazine publisher, who shared a personal relationship with Bob Guccione, the company's colorful founder and CEO. As her counsel, the equally colorful New York lawyer Norman Roy

Grutman put it at argument, her suit centered on "a series of unprovoked calumnies and vilifications heaped upon [her] accusing her of among other things licentious promiscuity and having a venereal disease which in any jurisdiction would be tantamount of libel per se." These "calumnies and vilifications" were contained in the adult magazine *Hustler*, published by the defendant and its even more colorful founder and CEO Larry Flynt.

The case was originally filed by Keeton, a New York resident, in Ohio, where the corporate defendant was incorporated. After several years of pretrial and appellate maneuvering in the Ohio courts, it was dismissed, albeit without prejudice to its reinstitution at a later date. By that time, however, the only state in which the statute of limitations had not run was New Hampshire, so Keeton refiled the action in federal district court there, although she herself had never visited the state and had no discernible connection to it. Hustler did, however, have subscribers there and, in all, sold some 10,000 copies of its magazine in New Hampshire each month. Nevertheless, the New Hampshire court dismissed the case for lack of personal jurisdiction, a decision affirmed by the United States Court of Appeals for the First Circuit, in an opinion by future Justice Stephen Breyer. In that opinion, then-Judge Breyer concluded that the "New Hampshire tail is too small to wag so large an out-of-state dog."

Keeton is the only one of the three cases heard on that November day that is treated in Brennan's history of the October 1983 term, although for reasons entirely unrelated to its jurisprudential significance. Discussion of the case in the term history begins by acknowledging that, on its "merits, this was a relatively uncontroversial personal jurisdiction case" in which "[a]ll of the Justices agreed that the district Court for the District of New Hampshire could constitutionally exercise jurisdiction over Hustler in this libel suit, and accordingly voted to reverse the First Circuit."

Hustler and Flynt had retained respected Yale Law School Professor Lea Brilmayer to argue on his behalf in the Supreme Court. Two months before the scheduled argument, Flynt sent to each of the justices, as well as to several members of Congress, President Reagan and Vice President Bush, a complimentary subscription to his magazine. The first issue received by each justice was accompanied by a personal letter from Flynt, in which he explained that they would each be delivered "on a regular, monthly basis the world's greatest porn magazine" and proceeded to inform them that he was "as committed to my pornography as the Pope is to his celibacy."

Brennan's term history notes that the justices "responded to the subscription in various fashions." Brennan said he "thought it best" simply to "ignore" the matter. O'Connor, as Brennan's term history recounted it, wrote back to Flynt and asked him to send no further issues. "Rehnquist reportedly gave the magazine to his messenger." For her part, Brilmayer, who was obviously unaware of Flynt's plans, withdrew as counsel for Hustler. According to the term history, there also "were rumors around the Court that Flynt had written a highly offensive letter to O'Connor, and that this letter caused Brilmayer to withdraw."

On November 3, 1983, five days before the argument, Flynt, through his remaining counsel, informed the Court by telegram that he would argue the case on his own behalf. His corporate counsel—David L. Kahn—wrote to the Office of the Clerk: "I regret to inform you that my client, Larry Flynt, has discharged me as his attorney in the above case. As a result, I will be unable to participate in the oral argument of this case on Tuesday, November 8, 1983." Kahn's telegram continued: "Mr. Flynt has asked me to advise the Court (1) that he will argue the case on his own behalf . . . and (2) that he will be fully informed as to both the relevant facts in the record and the applicable law since he has read all of the briefs (including those of amici) and has been advised by counsel as to the applicable law." On the same day, Flynt wrote to each of the justices himself. His stationary was captioned "Larry Flynt for President" in large red, white and blue letters and featured an illustration of a woman's spread legs embracing the capitol dome. As recounted in Brennan's term history, the "tasteful man's missive" included the following:

> I trust for the sake of justice and the judicial system you will permit me to argue this case in the spirit of the grand American tradition of allowing me to retain counsel of my choice—namely me.

That same day, the chief justice forwarded to the rest of the conference the telegram along with a letter the clerk had received from Ms. Keeton's counsel opposing Flynt's request. In his cover memorandum, Burger indicated argument in the case had deliberately been scheduled "in tandem" with *Calder v. Jones* "because of the parallel issues" and noted that a "third case to be argued [that day]—*Helicopteros, etc. v. Hall*, also involves an *in personam* jurisdiction issue." Burger ended by asserting, "I see no motions or even a request from any authorized representative of Mr. Flynt to argue his own case. However, this matter can be discussed at our Conference tomorrow as an agenda item." For his part, the clerk advised Burger that "the Court is not required to hear from" Flynt and, "[i]n the alternative, the Court could appoint an amicus curiae to argue." In that regard, the Clerk informed Burger that three such amicus or "friend of the court" briefs had indeed been filed by interested third parties in support of Flynt and suggested that he "be authorized to inform general counsel for Hustler Magazine, Inc. (1) that he need not appear (2) Mr. Flynt will not be allowed to argue (3) that Mr. _____ counsel for amicus curiae will present oral argument." As a "P.S.," the Clerk informed Burger that "Mr. Stephen Shapiro recently of the Solicitor General's Office is counsel on the *amicus curiae* brief for the Motor Vehicle Manufacturers Assn. in support of affirmance. Counsel for the other *amici curia* [*sic*] have not argued before this Court. Miss Brilmayer who prepared respondents' brief has not previously argued here."

Needless to say, the Court did not grant Flynt's request and instead appointed Shapiro to argue "in support of the judgment below." With Flynt seated in the gallery in his gold-plated wheelchair (he had lost the use of his legs in a shooting incident some years earlier), Shapiro rose to argue the case on Hustler's behalf. During the argument, however, Flynt began to shout at the assembled justices. Among other things, his tirade included the following:

"Fuck this Court. I am being denied the counsel of my choice all because of one token cunt. Goddamm motherfuckers."

At his authoritative best, the chief justice loudly instructed courtroom security personnel to take Flynt into custody, which the Court police promptly did. According to Brennan's term history, Burger followed this order by muttering under his breath, "sonofabitch if that isn't contempt." Soon after, Flynt was taken in front of a magistrate judge and charged with impeding the administration of justice, a misdemeanor carrying a maximum penalty of a $5,000 fine and a one-year prison term. He later pled guilty to using "threatening and abusive language before the United States Supreme Court."

The argument itself proceeded, as best it could under the circumstances, without further incident. With Grutman at the podium, Justice Rehnquist pressed him about the extent to which Judge Breyer's decision for the First Circuit was grounded in the First Amendment as opposed to an application of New Hampshire law. In response, Grutman focused on New Hampshire's interest in redressing the harm suffered by Keeton, which prompted Brennan to ask what injury she had actually sustained in New Hampshire. Grutman replied that "the harm occurs in the defamation itself. . . . There is no requirement when you speak of harm, Mr. Justice Brennan . . . that the plaintiff has to demonstrate that she suffered her principal injury or loss in that particular state, so long as some harm occurred there, and the harm by definition . . . under the law of New Hampshire would be the circulation." And, when Justice Stevens asked whether that would be so "even if the plaintiff was totally unknown in the jurisdiction before the magazine was circulated," Grutman asserted that it would.

During his own argument, Shapiro fended off a host of questions probing whether, in reality, his "client's" concern was not so much with the exercise of personal jurisdiction in New Hampshire as with whether a New Hampshire court would then apply its own statute of limitations to allow Keeton to recover damages she alleged she had sustained in all fifty states. Shapiro responded that, "[i]f the suit was focused solely on damages in the state of New Hampshire, we say it would be [a] different case" and that he was, at the moment, "a fence sitter" as to how such a case should be resolved. When asked, to the laughter of the gallery, "which side are you going to fall off of," Shapiro conceded "in that case . . . there may well be jurisdiction over that particular limited cause of action, although it is not at all clear."

As they had at the outset of Grutman's argument, the justices pressed Shapiro about the extent to which the decision below had been premised on the First Amendment. Shapiro resisted the suggestion that it had been and, when he was asked to assume otherwise, he responded "[w]ell, in that situation, if the Court were disposed to look at the case as one seeking both one percent of the damages in New Hampshire and ninety nine percent of the damages in another jurisdiction, if the Court were to do that, the correct constitutional result would be that only one percent of the damages in the local jurisdiction could be collected because collection of the ninety nine percent from the rest of the jurisdictions would infringe the statutes of limitations in those states." To this, Rehnquist responded, "[b]ut that is not a reason for dismissing the whole suit."

At conference, all nine justices voted to reverse the First Circuit. According to Brennan's notes of the discussion, Burger began by observing that "Keeton had to sue in New Hampshire because the statute of limitations ran elsewhere." Burger added that he would "reject [the] argument that [a] plaintiff can't take advantage of [a] state's very long statute of limitations."

The memorandum that Brennan had his clerks prepare for him for use at conference indicates that he told his colleagues that he did "not think that there is any doubt that there is jurisdiction in this case." Not only did "Hustler purposefully distribute[] its product in the forum state," but Brennan thought it was "clear that New Hampshire has an interest in compensating the plaintiff for her New Hampshire damages and in preventing the distribution of a libelous publications [sic] within its borders." As Brennan saw it, Flynt's "real argument stems from an objection to the application of New Hampshire's statute of limitations to the damages that were not suffered in New Hampshire." With respect to that, Brennan asserted, "this is a choice of law question that has no place in the analysis of whether due process rights are violated by the exercise of jurisdiction." In addition, Brennan concluded that, Flynt's objections notwithstanding, "I do not think that there is any constitutional prohibition against forum shopping." And, most importantly, Brennan wrote, "I also do not think that first amendment considerations should form a part of [the] due process analysis that is required to determine whether there is jurisdiction. . . . Certainly, the exercise of jurisdiction is not itself a violation of the first amendment."

After Brennan spoke, White indicated, according to Brennan's notes, that he had "nothing to add." In his view, the "Constitution doesn't prevent New Hampshire from exercising jurisdiction." Marshall reportedly said that he "wouldn't address damages until [the] lower courts do." And, Blackmun suggested that the First Circuit had "collapsed personal jurisdiction and choice of law" and that was "wrong—[it] must decide personal jurisdiction first." According to Brennan's notes, Blackmun said "there's enough here for that and [the] due process clause doesn't bar it. . . . Choice of law should be left to remand." After Powell agreed, Rehnquist emphasized, according to Brennan, that the "First amendment radiation" argument—the contention that the First Amendment required additional protections against the exercise of personal jurisdiction in a defamation action—"is simply wrong." Stevens and O'Connor reportedly concurred in these prevailing sentiments as well.

Ultimately, in an opinion by Rehnquist for a unanimous Court, the justices reversed Judge Breyer's decision for the First Circuit. It did so, however, by focusing virtually exclusively on the due process issues that inform the law of personal

jurisdiction, rather on the First Amendment issues about which Rehnquist had
inquired at argument. Thus, Rehnquist's opinion embraced Grutman's contention
that "[f]alse statements of fact harm both the subject of the falsehood *and* the readers
of the statement. New Hampshire may rightly employ its libel laws to discourage
the deception of its citizens." Moreover, he wrote, the "reputation of the libel victim
may suffer harm even in a State in which he has hitherto been anonymous. The
communication of the libel may create a negative reputation among the residents
of a jurisdiction where the plaintiff's previous reputation was, however small, at
least unblemished." Accordingly, the Court concluded that the potentially more
difficult "question of the applicability of New Hampshire's statute of limitations to
claims for out-of-state damages presents itself in the course of litigation only after
jurisdiction over respondent is established, and we do not think such choice-of-law
concerns should complicate or distort the jurisdictional inquiry."

For his part, Brennan submitted a brief opinion concurring in the judgment
in which he expressly agreed with the Court's holding that Hustler's "'regular
circulation of magazines in the forum State is sufficient to support an assertion of
jurisdiction in a libel action based on the contents of the magazine.'" Although
Brennan had expressed similar views in his conference memorandum, his separate
opinion did not purport to endorse the single footnote in Rehnquist's opinion
that there "is no [constitutional] justification for restricting libel actions to the
plaintiff's home forum," and, citing his own opinion in the second case argued
on November 8, *Calder v. Jones*, emphasizing that the Court "reject[ed] categorically the suggestion that invisible radiations from the First Amendment may defeat
jurisdiction otherwise proper under the Due Process Clause."

Calder v. Jones

In *Calder*, the justices considered the exercise of personal jurisdiction by the California courts over the editor and a reporter for the *National Enquirer*, which was
published in and disseminated from Florida where they both resided, in a defamation action initiated against them in California by an actress, Shirley Jones, and
her actor husband Marty Engels. In all, 600,000 copies of the *Enquirer* circulated
in California, almost twice the number of the next highest state. In addition, the
reporter regularly traveled there for his job, albeit not necessarily in connection

with the story about which the plaintiffs had sued. The editor never traveled to California except once for vacation and once to testify in an unrelated case. He did, however, approve the idea for the story and, after it was written, edited and otherwise prepared it for publication.

The case was argued for the reporter and editor by John Kester, another partner in Edward Bennett Williams's law firm about which Rehnquist had corresponded with Powell during the Court's deliberations in *Wolston*. In his argument, Kester emphasized that the corporate publisher of the *Enquirer* had consented to jurisdiction in California and that the only reason that the plaintiffs had seen fit to sue the individual employees as well was to enhance their opportunity to be awarded punitive damages. Nevertheless, Kester was forced to concede that, although the reporter did not travel to California to work on the story, he did make several telephone calls into the state to gather the information he ultimately included in it. When Brennan asked him whether the Court had "ever said" that "First Amendment considerations may argue against or for [personal] jurisdiction," Kester conceded that the justices had "never said it." And, when Justice Powell asked if it would "make any difference with respect to whether the individuals could be sued in California" if the corporate defendant "had been bankrupt," Kester agreed that it would, prompting Powell to wonder "[w]hy would it, from the viewpoint of jurisdiction of the California court?"

After California lawyer Paul Ablon, counsel for Jones and Engels, received a series of almost uniformly friendly and relatively infrequent questions from the justices, Kester was pressed on rebuttal by Powell, who asked, somewhat incredulously, "you are not suggesting that one who knowingly publishes libel doesn't anticipate harm, are you?" Kester responded by asserting that "metaphorically we can say that a libelous article is launched and causes harm, but the harm is much more difficult to define." Powell quickly responded, "[b]ut doesn't that cut the other way? When you come down to the standard of liability in a First Amendment case, you have *New York Times* and *Gertz* that afford very substantial protection that perhaps isn't available in a products liabilities case." Ultimately, Kester asserted that "it is not necessary to decide this case even to reach the First Amendment." Rather, he argued, "[t]his case can be decided under the standard jurisdictional principles of the Fourteenth Amendment as they always have been applied." As he sought to explain why, his time expired and, in mid-sentence, the chief justice interrupted and said, "Thank you counsel, thank you. The case is submitted."

Following argument, as in *Keeton*, all nine justices agreed on the outcome, this time voting unanimously to affirm the decision of the California Court of Appeal. According to Brennan's notes, the chief justice first noted that the article had been "distributed where [the] actress lives," which, Burger believed, was "more than enough contact with [the] forum." In Burger's view, the defendants' First Amendment argument had "no merit." Brennan agreed with the Chief, explaining—in the written memorandum his clerks had prepared for his use at conference—that "I have little trouble affirming the California Court of Appeal and finding personal jurisdiction in this case. The state of California's interests in protecting its citizens from defamations, invasions of privacy, and intentional inflictions of emotional distress is quite strong. And the plaintiff's connections to the forum are also quite compelling—she both lives and works primarily in California, and the importance of her reputation in that state is self-evident." Brennan's memorandum noted that he similarly had "little trouble" in finding the individual defendants' "connections with the forum" sufficient for personal jurisdiction:

> The reporter, it was found, made various investigative phone calls into the state, made a specific call to one of the plaintiffs below in which he read the disputed article, and made at least one trip into the state for the purpose of this article. The editor/president was charged with general supervision of the magazine, edited the particular article in question, and later refused to retract the article. Most importantly, both defendants knew that the article would have a substantial impact in California, and thus the foreseeable effect of the article supports California's jurisdiction in this case.

At the conclusion of the memorandum, Brennan added, as he had in the analogous writing prepared for *Keeton*, that, "assuming the issue must be reached, I do not believe that the first amendment should require any different analysis of the due process issue."

White concurred, adding (according to Brennan's notes) that, "for me, anyone who participated in writing the story could be sued knowing it was to be circulated in California where plaintiff lived." After Marshall agreed with White, Brennan's notes indicate that Blackmun said that he also believed that there was jurisdiction over the defendants because "they intended to communicate with these readers in California." Blackmun added that he too had "no interest in First Amendment argument." As Brennan recounted it, Powell then said he had "nothing to add," except that, in his view, the "First Amendment argument is frivolous." Rehnquist also had "nothing to add." After Stevens raised an issue about the Court's appellate jurisdiction, O'Connor indicated that she concurred with her colleagues on the merits as well as with their conclusion that the Court should "reject [the] First Amendment argument."

Burger assigned the opinion to Rehnquist for him to prepare along with the Court's decision in *Keeton*. In his initial draft as well as in his final opinion, Rehnquist was brief, dispatching Kester's arguments swiftly and in turn. On the Fourteenth Amendment issue, he wrote:

> The allegedly libelous story concerned the California activities of a California resident. It impugned the professionalism of an entertainer whose television career was centered in California. The article was drawn from California sources, and the brunt of the harm, in terms both of respondent's emotional distress and the injury to her professional reputation, was suffered in California. In sum, California is the focal point both of the story and of the harm suffered. Jurisdiction over petitioners is therefore proper in California based on the "effects" of their Florida conduct in California.

And, with respect to Kester's invocation of the First Amendment, Rehnquist's opinion "reject[ed] the suggestion" that such "concerns enter into the jurisdictional analysis." Not only would the "infusion of such considerations . . . needlessly complicate an already imprecise inquiry" but, citing both *Sullivan* and *Gertz*, "the potential chill on protected First Amendment activity stemming from libel and defamation actions is already taken into account in the constitutional limitations on the substantive law governing such suits." Thus, Rehnquist explained, "[t]o reintroduce those concerns at the jurisdictional stage would be a form of double counting" and, citing *Herbert* as well as footnote 9 in *Hutchinson*, he said the Court had "already declined in other contexts to grant special protection to defendants in libel and defamation actions in addition to the constitutional protections embodied in the substantive laws."

On December 8, Brennan wrote to Rehnquist about his draft opinions in both the *Calder* and *Keeton* cases, explaining that "[w]hile I fully agree with your result in both of these cases, I may want to write something of my own. My problem is that I am the only dissenter in . . . *Helicopteros Nacionales de Columbia, S.A. v. Hall*," the other personal jurisdiction case heard by the Court on November 8, "and I'm not quite sure what to write in these cases until I have seen what Harry [Blackmun] will circulate later in *Helicopteros*."

On March 16, 1984, however, Brennan joined Rehnquist's opinion for the Court in *Calder*. In his letter doing so, he extended "my apologies for postponing release of the Court opinion, but until now I was uncertain whether my separate writing in *Helicopteros* would affect my decision in this case." To the extent it did, of course, Brennan limited himself to the short concurring opinion he submitted in *Keeton* and did not otherwise qualify his support for Rehnquist's opinion for the Court in *Calder*. The unanimous decision in *Calder* was announced on March 20, 1984, the same day as *Keeton*.

Bose Corp. v. Consumers Union

As it happened, *Bose Corp. v. Consumers Union*, the last of the three media-related cases to be argued on November 8, as well as the last of them to be decided that term, proved to be the most significant. Even so, it is addressed not at all in Brennan's term history and is not, technically speaking, a "defamation" case. Rather, *Bose* was a product disparagement claim that, like *Keeton*, came to the Court from the First Circuit. That court had reversed the entry of a judgment of liability in Bose's favor following a 19-day bench trial of its claim that a published review of audio speakers it manufactured had falsely disparaged the product.

Although Bose had based its claim on several aspects of the review that it considered false and that had allegedly caused it injury, the trial court's judgment was premised on its finding that *Consumer Reports* magazine had falsely disparaged the speakers by writing that they spread sound "about the room" in which they were played, rather than along a wall. Most significantly, the trial judge held that Bose, a corporation it deemed to be a public figure (a determination that was not before the Supreme Court), had demonstrated by clear and convincing evidence that the author of the offending statement had published it with actual malice—that he and his colleague who had tested the Bose speakers (and therefore his employer, Consumers Union) knew that the review's description of the sound produced by the speakers was false at the time the magazine published it. The trial judge's conclusion in this regard was based largely on (a) testimony he credited that it is scientifically impossible for sound to spread "about" a room (as opposed to "along" a wall) and

(b) his determination that, as a result, the author's testimony to the contrary—that he in fact perceived the sound in the manner he described it in the review—was not credible. In short, the district court determined that the speakers in fact produced sound "along the wall" rather than "about the room" and, as a result, the author must have been lying when he contended he heard something different.

The First Circuit reversed. Although it accepted the trial judge's conclusion that the published statement was disparaging, and assumed without deciding that it was false, it undertook what it termed an "independent review" of the record evidence of actual malice, as the Supreme Court had done in *Sullivan*, and concluded that, the trial judge's findings of facts notwithstanding, the record did not establish actual malice by the requisite clear and convincing evidence. In so holding, the First Circuit rejected Bose's contention that Rule 52(a) of the Federal Rules of Civil Procedure limited the scope of its review of the trial judge's factual findings to a determination of whether they were "clearly erroneous." Instead, it determined that it was obliged by *Sullivan* to "perform a de novo review, independently examining the record to ensure that the district court has applied properly the governing constitutional law and that the plaintiff has indeed satisfied its burden of proof." Based on that review, the court of appeals determined:

> The evidence presented merely shows that the words in the article may not have described precisely what the two panelists heard during the listening test. [Consumers Union] was guilty of using imprecise language in the article—perhaps resulting from an attempt to produce a readable article for its mass audience. Certainly, it does not support an inference of actual malice.

Although Bose sought review of the First Circuit's decision in the Supreme Court in January 1983, the case, as noted, was not argued until the following November. It had been relisted at Justice White's request in mid-April, and the Court voted to grant review later that month. The company's petition received the votes of the chief justice and Justices White, Rehnquist, and O'Connor. Brennan's handwritten notes indicate that O'Connor may have changed her mind at some point in the process to provide the fourth vote necessary to take the case.

The case was finally heard on the afternoon of November 8, following the arguments in *Keeton* and *Calder*. During his argument on behalf of Bose, Boston intellectual property lawyer Charles Hieken received several questions addressing what precisely an appellate judge is obliged to do when reviewing a trial court's finding of actual malice. At turns, he was asked whether *Sullivan* contemplates "any different review of factual findings than in any other kind of case" (he ultimately agreed that "in a First Amendment case under *New York Times v. Sullivan*" appellate courts have "a special duty to look at the record more closely than we normally would"); whether the First Circuit was correct that it was required to "independently examine the whole record" (he conceded that it was); whether the court of appeals was bound by the trial judge's findings of fact (he asserted that it was unless they were "clearly erroneous"); whether the appellate court could set such findings aside "by relying on testimony from a witness that the district Court said he did not believe" ("[a]bsolutely not"); and whether the First Circuit was bound by the trial judge's findings on credibility (it was "absolutely bound by the rulings on credibility unless the findings on credibility were clearly erroneous"). When Hieken was pressed on whether he was asking the Court to "cut back on" *Sullivan*, he responded that he was not, but nevertheless rejected Justice Stevens's suggestion that, as a result, "there really is not any question of law of any particular significance at stake" in the case beyond his request that the Court "take a good hard look at the record here and be sure that the Court of Appeals did its job correctly." To the contrary, Hieken asserted, the constitutional issue before the Court was whether the First Circuit was correct when it held that it was "not bound by the 'clearly erroneous' rule of Rule 52(a)" and therefore proceeded to "make de novo findings."

At the conclusion of his opening argument, Hieken was asked by Justice Blackmun whether he had any comment on the Court's 1944 decision in *Baumgartner v. United States,* which, the justice noted, Hieken had not cited in his brief but had been "cited extensively by your opposition." Indeed, Consumers Union had relied heavily on *Baumgartner* in which, the magazine contended, Justice Frankfurter, writing for the Court, had explained that the "clear and convincing" evidence standard, when applicable (as it is under *Sullivan* with respect to findings of actual malice), obligated reviewing courts to make an independent assessment of the record evidence. When Hieken asked if he could "comment on it after in my rebuttal period," Blackmun reiterated "I do want to hear from you on it because I find nothing in your briefs about it." In fact, Hieken did address *Baumgartner* during his rebuttal, asserting that the case "deal[t] with an ultimate finding of fact . . . which is really a . . . mixed question of law and fact." As a result, he contended, "the Court can always look at the evidence to see if there is enough evidence to be clear and convincing to the trier of fact."

Consumers Union's counsel, Michael Pollet, began his argument by taking a pass at convincing the Court that the review's reference to speakers that moved sounds "about" a room was not disparaging in the first place, leading to several questions from skeptical justices about whether that issue was properly before them. Early on, therefore, the questioning turned to the issue of independent review and, specifically, whether Pollet was contending that "the clearly erroneous standard of review just does not apply in a First Amendment case." When Pollet replied that it does not govern review of the "ultimate fact"—the "question of law" whether or not there was actual malice—but that it does apply to the trial court's findings of "historical facts," Justice White asked him to "assume that the question of knowledge is a historical fact" and, based on that assumption, whether "the clear erroneous standard would apply to that." When Pollet resisted the assumption, White sharpened the inquiry, focusing on the case in which "the claim is that the person who wrote the article or made the defamatory statement knew that it was false, just knew. Let's assume that is a historical fact. Would the clearly erroneous standard apply to that?" When Pollet replied that it would not, because that "historical fact" was actually the "ultimate fact" in issue, he also amended his earlier response and asserted that the clearly erroneous standard does not apply in "First Amendment cases" at all. This led Justice Rehnquist to ask Pollet "what principle of the First Amendment suggests that it is desirable to allow a Court of Appeals such as it did in this case to simply second-guess a trial judge's finding that a witness whom the trial judge heard testify was not credible?" Pollet responded, "with all due deference," that "the facts of this case as you have posed them are not as they occurred." Rather, Pollet explained, in his case, the trial judge "plainly and clearly articulated his reason, his sole rationale for the finding of so-called incredibility . . . was that the author was too intelligent to have made an honest mistake. That is not a credibility finding. That is an erroneous application of law." To that, Rehnquist responded simply, "each is entitled to his own opinion."

Later in Pollet's argument, White again returned to the fact that there are "two ways of finding malice"—"[o]ne is to find that there was a knowing falsehood and the other is that there is a reckless disregard for truth." After he got Pollet to concede that "[i]f you find . . . knowing falsehood you have satisfied the burden of proof" under *Sullivan*, White asked why a reviewing court "ought to look behind what the particular finding is?" Pollet's response centered on his contention that "[m]alice is a legal construct derived specifically from the Constitution" and that, as a result, "it is an ultimate fact" that is subject to independent review by appellate courts.

Despite the probing and often skeptical questioning during the argument, at the conference later that week, seven justices voted to affirm the court of appeals. According to Brennan's notes, Burger ultimately voted to affirm, after first indicating that he would reverse at the conference itself. As Brennan recorded it, the chief justice initially opined that the *Sullivan* standard "of falsity and recklessness deals with fact finding" and that the "court of appeals [was] wrong in saying that [it was] not bound [by] Rule 52," which subjects appellate review of such finding to a "clearly erroneous" standard. Following the conference, however, Burger mysteriously circulated a memorandum to his colleagues indicating that "[f]urther consideration . . . persuades me to vote to affirm."

As a result, at that juncture, the only justices left in dissent were White and Rehnquist. At the conference, White had told his colleagues, as Brennan recounted it, that the court of appeals had "meant" to perform a "de novo" review and "that's wrong." In White's view, the Court should instruct appellate judges to "apply [the] right standard" and emphasize, as he did during his questioning at argument, and as he ultimately would in his separate opinions in both *Bose* and in *Harte-Hanks Communications, Inc. v. Connaughton*, that the "clear and convincing" standard recognized in *Sullivan* is "not as applicable to actual knowledge [of falsity] as it is to recklessness." For his part, Rehnquist asserted that, although "some of [the] language in *Baumgartner* [*v. United States* and *Sullivan* itself] is obscure" on the point, he believed that "historical facts must be subject to a clearly erroneous standard." According to Brennan's notes, Rehnquist said that Justice Frankfurter's opinion in *Baumgartner* "doesn't stand up as carefully reasoned" and that, in the last analysis, the First Circuit "here did not give sufficient deference" to the fact finder.

The rest of the justices, however, were not moved. Brennan's notes record that Marshall said he was not prepared to "cut back on *Sullivan*." And, according to Brennan, Blackmun asserted that whether actual malice was described as an "ultimate" fact or a "mixed question of law and fact," it was subject to independent review. Brennan's notes indicate that O'Connor too agreed that the judgment should be affirmed because "'independent' *NY Times* [review] is different from 'clearly erroneous'" review. As Powell saw it, at least as recounted by Brennan, the trial judge's "purely factual findings" had been "accepted" by the First Circuit and the only issue it had actually decided was "whether actual malice existed." Stevens, to whom the chief justice would ultimately assign the majority opinion, told the conference that the question raised by *Bose* was whether "we [are] going to look at First Amendment cases as federal courts to the extent we do in state cases" such as *Sullivan* itself. The answer to that question, as recounted in Brennan's notes of Stevens's remarks, was that independent review of federal court decisions "must be at least as broad and probably broader" than in cases coming from a state court.

Brennan's own views were set forth in a four-page "Conference Memo." In it, he asserted that the "answer" to the question presented "is controlled by *New York Times v. Sullivan* and its progeny, which on numerous occasions have recognized that an appellate court must undertake *an independent review of the evidentiary basis* for the lower court's findings of actual malice." According to Brennan, this "consistent practice . . . is justified by several interdependent reasons":

> First and most importantly, in cases applying the *New York Times* standard, we have properly imposed a "clear and convincing" burden of proof on the plaintiff. As Justice Frankfurter explained for the Court in *Baumgartner v. United States* (1944), "the importance of 'clear, unequivocal, and convincing' proof . . . would be lost if the ascertainment by the lower courts whether the exacting standard of proof had been satisfied on the whole record were to be deemed a 'fact' of the same order as all other 'facts,' not open to review here." Whether the proof offered by a plaintiff is sufficient to meet a clear and convincing standard, therefore, is an issue of law subject to review on appeal. Second, the actual malice standard, as well as the knowledge of falsity which is equated with that standard, are issues of ultimate fact (i.e., mixed questions of law and fact) which also deserve heightened scrutiny from appellate courts. . . . Finally, when applying the *New York Times* standard, we are concerned with potential infringement of first amendment rights. The solicitude we pay to first amendment values is most evident in the application of the clear and convincing standard, and is another interrelated reason for subjecting the findings made below to careful scrutiny.

In Brennan's view, the *Bose* case, "because it combines each of these factors—a clear and convincing burden of proof, the actual malice standard, and review of

constitutional facts—is quite simple, and is directly controlled by *New York Times*."
As a result, Brennan's memorandum concluded:

> I would affirm the First Circuit because it properly undertook an independent review
> of the evidentiary basis for the finding of actual malice. In so doing, the court may
> have misspoke when it stated that a *de novo* review was in order. But it properly
> noted that, at least to the extent that the independent review mandated by *New York
> Times* is inconsistent with the "clearly erroneous" standard, then Rule 52 does not
> apply. Moreover, the court properly recognized that it must pay due regard to cred-
> ibility determinations made by the trial judge, and that these should control unless
> they are clearly erroneous.

In a footnote to his memorandum, Brennan took on the concerns expressed by
White and Rehnquist about the First Circuit's reference to the propriety of "de
novo" review. According to the memorandum:

> If de novo review was appropriate, the appellate court would start with the evidence
> and make its own findings of fact and conclusions of law. Under the "independent
> review" standard, the appellate court starts with the findings of fact and conclusions
> of law made by the trial judge, and simply ensures that there is record evidence to
> support those findings by, in this case, clear and convincing proof. Moreover, when
> doing independent review, the appellate court must pay due regard to credibility
> findings unless they are clearly erroneous.

There is some reason to believe that, following the conference, the chief justice
joined the majority in order to control the assignment of the opinion, which—as
noted—he gave to Stevens. Burger not only expressed his apparently strong opposition to affirming at conference (at least according to Brennan's notes), at argument,
one can hear in the audio recording (albeit not reflected in the official transcript),
Burger dismissively mutter under his breath that Pollet's preferred distinction
between a credibility finding and an erroneous application of law "sound[ed] like
a play on words." After the assignment, Brennan complained privately that Burger
had not assigned the case to him, suggesting that, as the author of *Sullivan*, it should
have been his to write. It appears at least arguable therefore that, if Burger had
remained in dissent, Brennan would have assigned the opinion to himself.

There is additional circumstantial support for this view. *Bose* was decided in 1984, which was the 20th anniversary of *Sullivan,* and it was the subject of several retrospective conferences celebrating its importance and impact on modern First Amendment jurisprudence generally and on the press specifically. One such conference was sponsored by the Practising Law Institute and held in New York, at the Waldorf Astoria hotel. It was chaired by Richard M. Winfield, William Rogers's longtime law partner, outside counsel to the Associated Press and, a fierce advocate for its First Amendment rights. In Brennan's papers on the *Bose* case, nestled between drafts of the circulating draft opinions and the memoranda exchanged by the justices, are two pieces of thick cardboard, which form a protective cover over a copy of an advertisement for Winfield's program, a memento that Brennan apparently wished to preserve. In fact, Brennan told his biographer that he had been invited to give the keynote address at the Waldorf, but concluded it would be inappropriate for him to do so.

Stevens circulated the first draft of his majority opinion on March 13, 1984. Like the final version, its constitutional analysis began by quoting Rule 52(a)'s express admonitions that "[f]indings of fact shall not be set aside unless clearly erroneous" and that "due regard shall be given to the opportunity of the trial court to judge the credibility of the witnesses" as well as the concession that it "surely does not stretch the language of the Rule to characterize an inquiry into what a person knew at a given point in time as a question of 'fact.'" Still, Stevens asserted, in First Amendment cases, including most especially *Sullivan* from which he quoted, "we have repeatedly held that an appellate court has an obligation to 'make an independent examination of the whole record' in order to make sure 'that the judgment does not constitute a forbidden intrusion on the field of free expression.'" In fact, Stevens wrote, the "conflict between the two rules is in some respects more apparent than real" because, while *Sullivan* "emphasizes the need for an appellate court to make an independent examination of the entire record; Rule 52(a) never forbids such an examination." Moreover, while Rule 52(a) "commands that 'due regard' shall be given to the trial judge's opportunity to observe the demeanor of witnesses; the constitutionally-based rule of independent review permits this opportunity to be given its due."

Nevertheless, Stevens concluded, the "difference between the two rules . . . is more than a mere matter of degree. For the rule of independent review assigns to judges a constitutional responsibility that cannot be delegated to the trier of fact."

Thus, Stevens explained, "the constitutional values protected by the rule make it imperative that judges—and in some cases judges of this Court—make sure that it is correctly applied." Accordingly, echoing Brennan's views both in *Sullivan* itself and in his conference memorandum in *Bose*, Stevens wrote for the Court that

> [w]hen the standard governing the decision in a particular case is provided by the Constitution, this Court's role in marking out the limits of the standard through the process of case-by-case adjudication is of special importance. This process has been vitally important in cases involving restrictions on the freedom of speech protected by the First Amendment, particularly in those cases in which it is contended that the communication in issue is within one of those few classes of "unprotected" speech [such as defamation]."

In such cases, Stevens explained, "the limits of the unprotected category, as well as the unprotected character of particular communications, have been determined by the judicial evaluation of special facts that have been deemed to have constitutional significance" and, as a result, the "Court has regularly conducted an independent review of the record both to be sure that the speech in question actually falls within the unprotected category and to confine the perimeters of any unprotected category within acceptably narrow limits in an effort to ensure that protected expression will not be inhibited." It has done so, Stevens wrote, because simply "[p]roviding triers of fact with a general description of the type of communication whose content is unworthy of protection has not, in and of itself, served sufficiently to narrow the category, nor served to eliminate the danger that decisions by triers of fact may inhibit the expression of protected ideas." And, it has done so in recognition of the fact that, "[a]t some point, the reasoning by which a fact is 'found' crosses the line between application of those ordinary principles of logic and common experience which are ordinarily entrusted to the finder of fact into the realm of a legal rule upon which the reviewing court must exercise its own independent judgment." In the last analysis, Stevens's draft concluded:

> The requirement of independent appellate review reiterated in *New York Times Co. v. Sullivan* is a rule of federal constitutional law. It emerged from the exigency of deciding concrete cases; it is law in its purest form under our common law heritage. It reflects a deeply held conviction that judges—and particularly members of

this Court—must exercise such review in order to preserve liberties established and ordained by the Constitution. The question whether the evidence in the record in a defamation case is of the convincing clarity required to strip the utterance of First Amendment protection is not merely a question for the trier of fact. Judges, as expositors of the Constitution, must independently decide whether the evidence in the record is sufficient to cross the constitutional threshold that bars the entry of any judgment that is not supported by clear and convincing proof of "actual malice."

Turning to the application of the independent review standard in *Bose* itself, Stevens's opinion affirmed the First Circuit's conclusion that "the difference between hearing violin sounds move around the room and hearing them wander back and forth fits easily within the breathing space that gives life to the First Amendment." In this case, he wrote, "[w]e may accept all of the purely factual findings of the District Court and nevertheless hold as a matter of law that the record does not contain clear and convincing evidence" that the defendants "prepared the loud-speaker article with knowledge that it contained a false statement, or with reckless disregard of the truth." Stevens's draft (as well as the opinion for the Court that it ultimately became) closed with the following:

> [T]he central legal question before us may seem out of place in a case involving a dispute about the sound quality of a loudspeaker. But though the question presented reaches us on a somewhat peculiar wavelength, we reaffirm the principle of independent appellate review that we have applied uncounted times before. We hold that the clearly erroneous standard of Rule 52(a) . . . does not prescribe the standard of review to be applied in reviewing a determination of actual malice in a case governed by *New York Times Co. v. Sullivan*. Appellate judges in such a case must exercise independent judgment and determine whether the record establishes actual malice with convincing clarity.

Brennan promptly joined Stevens's opinion in its entirety the following day. Rehnquist's dissent was first circulated a month later, on April 12. In it, he began by noting that there "is more than irony in this 'Case of the Wandering Instruments,' which subject matter makes it sound more like a candidate for inclusion in the 'Adventures of Sherlock Holmes' than in a casebook on constitutional law"— most prominently "that a constitutional principle which originated in *New York*

Times Co. v. Sullivan because of the need for freedom to criticize the conduct of public officials is applied here to a magazine's false statements about a commercial loudspeaker system." Turning to the substance, Rehnquist put flesh on the views he expressed in conference and which undergirded his sharp questioning of the magazine's counsel at argument. Specifically, he asserted that "the facts dispositive" of the actual malice inquiry—"actual knowledge or subjective reckless disregard for truth—involve no more than findings about the mens rea of an author, findings which appellate courts are simply ill-prepared to make in any context, including the First Amendment context." In Rehnquist's view, "[u]nless 'actual malice' now means something different from the definition given to the term 20 years ago by this Court in *New York Times*, I do not think that the constitutional requirement of 'actual malice' properly can bring into play any standard of factual review other than the 'clearly erroneous' standard."

Two days later, Rehnquist circulated a revised draft that included what became footnote 1 in the final version, in which he took on Stevens's reliance on the Court's practice of reviewing *de novo* lower court decisions concerning whether the speech at issue in a given case fell within one of the multiple exceptions to the First Amendment—such as obscenity, incitement, and fighting words. In Rehnquist's view, these cases were different because, unlike those in which courts are called on to apply the actual malice standard, they do not distinguish protected from unprotected speech by reference to findings of what he characterized as "pure historical fact."

On April 17, O'Connor changed her mind. She wrote to Stevens that, "[a]fter reading the dissent, I have decided to join it rather than the Court's opinion." The following day, Stevens wrote to Rehnquist that, upon reviewing that dissent, he had decided to add the following footnote to his own opinion:

> The intermingling of law and fact in the actual malice determination is no greater in state or federal jury trials than in federal bench trials. . . . And, of course, the limitation on appellate review of factual determinations under Rule 52(a) is no more stringent than the limitation on federal appellate review of a jury's factual determination under the Seventh Amendment, which commands that "no fact tried by jury, shall be otherwise re-examined in any Court of the United States, than according to the rules of the common law."

As Stevens explained in his letter to Rehnquist, the point needed to be made because "the logic of the argument you make" to the contrary "requires overruling not only *Time, Inc. v. Pape*," in which the Court had independently reviewed evidence of actual malice adduced before a federal court, "but *New York Times v. Sullivan* as well."

On April 20, White circulated his own, one-paragraph dissent, repeating the view he expressed at argument and at conference that, while a finding of "reckless disregard" is not an issue of historical fact, a finding of "actual knowledge of falsity" is and therefore should not be subject to independent appellate review. Finally, on April 26, Burger purported to change his mind yet again and wrote Stevens that, because Rehnquist's dissent "has given me a good deal of trouble," he had concluded that "I will join only in the judgment." This maneuver provides further support for the theory that Burger had initially joined the majority, at least in part, in order to keep the assignment power away from Brennan, who the chief may well have feared would have taken the case for himself. As we shall see in the next chapter, Burger expressed analogous concerns about giving Brennan the power to speak for the Court in defamation cases at the very same time in the context of the Court's then-ongoing deliberations in *Dun & Bradstreet v. Greenmoss Builders*.

The Court's decision in *Bose* was announced on April 30, 1984. Although the majority opinion did not carry Brennan's name, it unambiguously reflected the views he had expressed in his conference memorandum and, more importantly, represented an unmistakable reaffirmation, by a 7–2 majority, of the actual malice standard, of the "obligation" of appellate courts to vindicate that standard by independent review of the record evidence in every case purporting to deprive speech of constitutional protection on that basis, and of his decision for the Court, twenty years earlier, in *Sullivan* itself. Whatever satisfaction Brennan derived that day, however, would prove to be short-lived. Within a matter of months, as the Court continued its deliberations in the *Greenmoss Builders* case into the following term, Brennan would come to believe that *Sullivan* itself was in danger of being reconsidered and even overruled.

THE LANDMARK THAT WASN'T

In all, *Dun & Bradstreet v. Greenmoss Builders* consumed the Court's attention for two full years, from the beginning of the October 1983 term, when it first considered the petition for review filed in the case, through the last day of the October 1984 term, when the decision was finally announced. As a result, the justices left behind one of the most detailed records of the Supreme Court's internal deliberations on a single case in recent memory, certainly in a case involving the competing interests of free expression and individual reputation. And that record tells a tale that at times resembles the maneuverings of battlefield commanders, in this case seeking strategic advantage in a constitutional war of ideas while simultaneously defending against the salvos of their ideological adversaries. At bottom, however, Justice Brennan's papers, and those of several of his colleagues, reveal an internal struggle for the very survival of *Gertz* and *Sullivan*, in which three members of the Court—Justices Brennan, Powell, and White—advocated profoundly different visions of the role of a free press in a democracy and of the proper responsibility of government to place limits on that freedom.

Greenmoss Builders was not an obvious candidate for the articulation of fundamental First Amendment principles. It did not, like *Sullivan*, spring from a raging public controversy over civil rights or even from a publication addressing any public issue at all. Rather, it arose from a credit report issued to its paid subscribers by Dun & Bradstreet, which falsely informed them that the plaintiff company had filed for bankruptcy. The Vermont Supreme Court had ruled for the plaintiff, concluding that the constitutional limitations on an award of damages in a defamation action set out in *Gertz* did not apply in a case brought against a nonmedia defendant such as Dun & Bradstreet and that, as a result, the plaintiff could recover both presumed and punitive damages without a showing of either fault or actual injury. As a technical matter, the precise issue raised before the Court was whether Greenmoss Builders could recover such damages without satisfying the actual malice standard erected as a barrier to such awards in *Gertz*.

Initially, Brennan assumed that *Greenmoss Builders* would be a simple case. As framed by the Vermont Supreme Court and the petition for review, it squarely raised only one issue: whether the First Amendment protections identified in *Gertz* applied to nonmedia defendants. The only justice who had ever indicated publicly that the First Amendment applied more robustly to media (as opposed to nonmedia) speakers was Potter Stewart, who had retired from the Court before *Greenmoss Builders* and had been replaced by Justice O'Connor. That debate had already played itself out in academia and in a number of nondefamation cases (most notably the Court's 1978 decision in *First National Bank of Boston v. Bellotti*), with justices at both ends of the Court's ideological spectrum (including Brennan) rejecting Stewart's idea that the First Amendment protects media speech most robustly.

Brennan's narrative history for the October 1984 term later recounted that he expected *Greenmoss Builders* to be an "easy" case but that, for a number of reasons, it turned out to be more "complicated." For one thing, Dun & Bradstreet itself proved to be arguably less popular with the justices than the gallery of media defendants that had come before them in previous defamation cases (less popular even than Larry Flynt and the John Birch Society, not to mention *Time Magazine* and the *New York Times*). The way Brennan's term history explained it, "[m]any of the Justices had had personal experience in private practice with Dun & Bradstreet and were not especially enamored of what they thought of as a large, often irresponsible, company that could easily ruin small businesses." In addition, a number of justices expressed concern that a reversal would place in doubt the constitutionality of the federal Fair Credit Reporting Act, which regulated the dissemination of credit-related information by entities such as Dun & Bradstreet.

Most importantly, as Brennan's term history noted, the deliberations in *Greenmoss Builders* revealed deep "hostility" within the Court "to the *New York Times v. Sullivan* line of cases generally and to *Gertz* in particular." As a result, the case was "fiercely fought out" in a manner largely unseen by the public, but nevertheless of substantial significance to an informed appreciation of the Court's defamation jurisprudence after *Sullivan*.

When the request for review in *Greenmoss Builders* was first discussed by the justices in conference in early October 1983, only Brennan, White, and Powell expressed serious interest in it. Thereafter, both White and Powell had it relisted several times. Still, in the preliminary memorandum prepared for the "cert. pool" (then serving six of the nine justices), a law clerk advised those justices that, in essence, the Vermont Supreme Court had gotten it right—"[o]n its face, *Gertz* does not apply to a non-media defendant, and this Court has never so extended it."

As had become evident in *Gertz* and increasingly clear in following terms, by the time the *Greenmoss Builders* case arrived at the Court, Justice White had come to harbor serious reservations about the Court's development, following *Sullivan*, of a constitutional law of defamation. Those reservations become even more apparent in an October 13, 1983 dissent that White circulated from what then appeared to be a denial of review in the *Greenmoss Builders* case. In that never-issued dissent, White argued that the issue "whether the First Amendment actual malice standard applies in a defamation action brought by a private plaintiff against a non-media defendant" was both "important and unsettled" and therefore "deserves our attention." White correctly acknowledged that the Court had "several times, without discussion, applied *New York Times* in cases involving public figure plaintiffs and nonmedia defendants," specifically citing *Garrison v. Louisiana* and *Henry v. Collins*, and noted as well that "*New York Times* was decided along with *Abernathy v. Sullivan*, which involved four individual petitioners to whom the same standards were applied as to the newspaper." However, he also observed that, in *Hutchinson v. Proxmire*, the Court asserted that it had "'never decided' whether *New York Times* extends to nonmedia defendants, thus indicating that the question remains open."

In addition, White contended that *Greenmoss Builders* raised what he described as the "related question" of *Gertz's* applicability "in a case involving a private plaintiff and a nonmedia defendant." In White's view, these issues are "especially appropriate for consideration by this Court because of [their] implications for First Amendment jurisprudence as a whole." And citing Chief Justice Burger's opinion in *Bellotti*, White wrote, "this issue intersects with another difficult issue: the extent to which the institutional press perhaps enjoys unique privileges" under the First Amendment.

Brennan, as noted, believed that *Greenmoss Builders* was an "easy" case and should be disposed of on the simple ground that the constitutional rules set out in *Sullivan* and *Gertz* protected all defamation defendants, not just those affiliated with the media. Accordingly, he arrived at each of the Court's conferences in the fall of 1983 prepared to vote to grant the petition and, thereafter, to reverse the decision of the Vermont Supreme Court. By the end of October, Chief Justice Burger had joined White and Brennan in voting to grant review. Powell, however, had the case relisted again and, finally, on November 4, 1983, voted to grant as well.

The October 1983 Term

The case was heard on March 21, 1984. During the argument of Atlanta lawyer Gordon Garrett, counsel for Dun & Bradstreet, Justice O'Connor observed that "[t]here are federal laws in the securities fields, such as Section 10(b)(5), that govern statements that are made in connection with the sale of securities," and asked him whether he believed that "there's a First Amendment right for people who are publishing information about securities that has to be considered every time we have a 10(b)(5) action?" When Garrett responded that there would have to be a "different analysis" in the Rule 10(b)(5) context because "we would be talking about individuals publishing matters who are subject to the control of the SEC, as being licensed," O'Connor nevertheless persisted in "wondering" aloud whether recognizing First Amendment protection in the context of credit reports "wouldn't lead us to having to recognize First Amendment rights in a 10(b)(5) situation or an ordinary fraud situation, anything?"

During his argument, Thomas Heilmann, counsel for Greenmoss Builders, faced a number of questions when he asserted that the case involved "commercial speech" and that, as a result, was entitled to no First Amendment protection at all under the Supreme Court's so-called commercial speech doctrine, because the credit report before the Court was concededly false. In response to Heilmann's assertion, White recognized that "if you're right about your commercial speech ground you never get at all to" the media/nonmedia defendant issue and proceeded to characterize Heilmann's contention as one vindicating the principle that "there's no constitutional objection to the suppression of commercial messages that do not accurately inform the public" regardless of whether the defendant is affiliated with the media. And, White continued, "if it's conceded this report was false, they have conceded themselves out of First Amendment protection" if, in fact, "this is commercial speech."

Toward the end of Heilmann's argument, Justice Stevens invoked the hypothetical case of "a newspaper of general circulation that has a column on the
back: Recent legal developments, subhead bankruptcies, and they mistakenly say
your company went into bankruptcy, the same facts" and asked, "what happens
with that?" When Heilmann responded by invoking the specter of unacceptable
"self-censorship" in that scenario, and opined that "if the newspaper is going to say
they won't publish the fact because of presumed damages, and if they won't publish
that for that reason, for the reason of presumed and punitive damages, then the
news will just be pabulum, and that's the fear that the Court has, obviously," the
justices became confused. And when Heilmann was asked whether he was in fact
"saying a different rule would apply to that case than to this case," he responded
in the affirmative, asserting that the dispositive distinction ought to be that Dun
& Bradstreet, unlike a newspaper, is not going to "be chilled."

From Brennan's perspective, the argument provided few clues about the internal
fireworks to come. Although, as Brennan saw it, Justice Rehnquist appeared "to
push strongly for an affirmance," the other justices "seemed resigned, with varying degrees of enthusiasm, to a reversal," which would overturn the jury verdict
against Dun & Bradstreet. Following the argument, and even after both White and
Powell "seemed to grow intrigued with the idea that the case could be affirmed
on commercial speech grounds," the "betting" in Brennan's chambers before the
conference was that Powell (the author of *Gertz*) would vote to reverse and White
(the "vigorous" dissenter in that case) would vote to affirm. What transpired thereafter, Brennan would note later, "demonstrated the folly of such predictions."

According to Brennan's term history, and confirmed by his handwritten notes
at conference on March 23, 1984, the discussion of *Greenmoss Builders* that day
was "surprisingly spirited and tentative." As had become his custom "in difficult
cases in which he wishes to maintain his assignment power" regardless of whether
he ultimately joined the majority, Burger voted to avoid a decision on the merits
entirely by dismissing the writ "as improvidently granted," while at the same time
expressing his opposition both to invocation of the commercial speech doctrine
and to a media/nonmedia distinction in the allocation of First Amendment rights.
Taking the issue as framed by the Vermont Supreme Court, Burger, according to
Brennan's account, again expressed his disagreement with Justice Stewart's views
that the First Amendment reflected an "institutionalized dichotomy" that gave the
"press special First Amendment protection."

After Burger had spoken, Brennan set out his view that the judgment should be reversed on the ground that the *Gertz* standard necessarily applied. According to Powell's notes of the conference, Brennan specifically urged the Court to "address [the] commercial speech issue and reject it." Invoking Stevens's hypothetical at argument, Brennan reportedly said that "D&B is like [the] Wall Street Journal reporting a bankruptcy."

White then surprised at least Brennan by joining his vote to reverse, calling the case a "clear reversal." White, in Brennan's account, explained that, although he was "no fan of *Gertz*," he rejected both the notion that the speech at issue was "commercial" (according to Powell, White said the speech at issue was "like all financial reporting") and any media/nonmedia distinction in applying the law of defamation. Justices Marshall and Blackmun expressed essentially the same views, although the former added that he would not be averse, as the chief justice had suggested, to dismissing the writ as improvidently granted. After Powell passed, Rehnquist voted to affirm. He reportedly told his colleagues that, although he considered all of the alternative arguments for deciding the case "singularly unattractive," he believed *Gertz* to be "a last minute compromise," which he said he would not join again (although he had provided the fifth vote for Powell's opinion in that case) and did not wish to extend any further.

Stevens, who (as Brennan noted in his term history) was "author of the Seventh Circuit opinion that had been reversed in *Gertz*," said he considered *Greenmoss Builders* to be an extremely "difficult" case and, like Marshall, expressed some sympathy for Burger's proposal simply to dismiss it. If the Court were to decide the case, Stevens said, he was inclined to reverse, although he was particularly concerned that a decision to do so would call into question the constitutionality of the Fair Credit Reporting Act. On the one hand, Stevens suggested, the kind of speech regulated by that statute might be considered "commercial;" on the other, the Vermont Supreme Court had been wrong to hold that *Gertz* is "inapplicable" to all nonmedia defendants.

For her part, O'Connor also expressed some interest in dismissal but offered an alternative theory to affirm. In her view, *Gertz* ought not to be held to apply to "purely private speech." Rather, only speech concerning public affairs ought to be protected by the First Amendment in the defamation context. In other words, she reportedly told her colleagues, the "*Gertz* standard applies to some non-media" defendants but only if the purposes of *Gertz* are "engaged."

Justice William Brennan's official
portrait as a member of the 1976
U.S. Supreme Court.

The March 29, 1960, *New York
Times* "Heed Their Rising Voices"
advertisement. The advertisement
led to the landmark Supreme
Court decision in *New York
Times v. Sullivan.*

Group photo of 1964 Supreme Court,
which decided *New York Times v. Sullivan.*
First Row: Tom C. Clark, Hugo Black,
Earl Warren, William O. Douglas, John
M. Harlan **Second Row:** Byron White,
William J. Brennan Jr., Potter Stewart,
Arthur J. Goldberg

New Orleans District Attorney Jim Garrison, who was at the center of *Garrison v. Louisiana*.

Richard Nixon, counsel for the plaintiff in *Time, Inc. v. Hill*.

University of Georgia athletic director and football coach Wally Butts being carried off the field on his teams' shoulders. Butts filed a libel lawsuit against the *Saturday Evening Post* after it ran an article alleging he conspired to fix games.

Retired General Edwin Walker. Fighting back against various media outlets for their negative accounts of him, Walker filed numerous libel lawsuits, one of which was appealed to the Supreme Court in *Associated Press v. Walker.*

Civil rights lawyer Elmer Gertz, who
brought the libel action *Gertz v. Robert
Welch, Inc.* against the John Birch Society
for accusing him of being part of a
Communist conspiracy. The Supreme
Court eventually ruled in Gertz' favor.

Portrait of Justice Lewis
F. Powell by George
Augusta. Powell wrote the
majority opinion in *Gertz
v. Robert Welch, Inc.*

Group photo of 1974 Supreme Court, which
decided *Gertz v. Robert Welch, Inc.* **First Row:**
Potter Stewart, William O. Douglas, Warren E.
Burger, William J. Brennan Jr., Byron White
Second Row: Lewis F. Powell Jr., Thurgood
Marshall, Harry Blackmun, William Rehnquist

Legal scholar and former director of the American Law Institute Herbert Wechsler argued *New York Times v. Sullivan* before the Supreme Court.

William Rogers, attorney general under President Eisenhower and secretary of state under President Nixon, represented the AP in *Associated Press v. Walker*.

Famed Washington litigator and criminal defense lawyer Edward Bennett Williams represented the *Concord Monitor* in *Monitor Patriot Co. v. Roy*.

Renowned lawyer and First Amendment advocate Floyd Abrams represented the press in *Landmark Communications v. Virginia*, *Herbert v. Lando*, and *Smith v. Daily Mail Publishing Co.*, among other cases.

Justice Byron White, who
served on the Supreme Court
from 1962 to 1993, became
a pivotal figure in the years
following *Sullivan*.

Portrait of Earl Warren, who
served as Chief Justice of
the United States from 1953
to 1969.

Warren E. Burger, who served as
Chief Justice of the United States
from 1969 to 1986.

William Rehnquist, who served as
Chief Justice of the United States
from 1986 to 2005.

Jerry Falwell talks about his first time.*

FALWELL: My first time was in an outhouse outside Lynchburg, Virginia.

INTERVIEWER: Wasn't it a little cramped?

FALWELL: Not after I kicked the goat out.

INTERVIEWER: I see. You must tell me all about it.

FALWELL: I never *really* expected to make it with Mom, but then after she showed all the other guys in town such a good time, I figured, "What the hell!"

INTERVIEWER: But your mom? Isn't that a bit odd?

FALWELL: I don't think so. Looks don't mean that much to me in a woman.

INTERVIEWER: Go on.

FALWELL: Well, we were drunk off our God-fearing asses on Campari, ginger ale and soda—that's called a Fire and Brimstone—at the time. And Mom looked better than a Baptist whore with a $100 donation.

INTERVIEWER: Campari in the crapper with Mom . . . how interesting. Well, how was it?

FALWELL: The Campari was great, but Mom passed out before I could come.

INTERVIEWER: Did you ever try it again?

FALWELL: Sure . . .

lots of times. But not in the outhouse. Between Mom and the shit, the flies were too much to bear.

INTERVIEWER: We meant the Campari.

FALWELL: Oh, yeah. I always get sloshed before I go out to the pulpit. You don't think I could lay down all that bullshit *sober*, do you?

© 1983—Imported by Campari U.S.A. New York, NY 48°proof Spirit Aperitif (Liqueur)

Campari, like all liquor, was made to mix you up. It's a light, 48-proof, refreshing spirit, just mild enough to make you drink too much before you know you're schnockered. For your first time, mix it with orange juice. Or maybe some white wine. Then you won't remember anything the next morning. **Campari. The mixable that smarts.**

CAMPARI® You'll never forget your first time.

*AD PARODY—NOT TO BE TAKEN SERIOUSLY

Parody advertisement featuring prominent fundamentalist minister Jerry Falwell that ran in *Hustler* magazine in 1983. The ad led to the Supreme Court's decision in *Hustler Magazine v. Falwell*.

Group photo of 1990 Supreme Court, which decided
Milkovich v. Lorain Journal. **First Row:** Thurgood
Marshall, William J. Brennan Jr., William Rehnquist,
Byron White, Harry Blackmun **Second Row:** Antonin
Scalia, John Paul Stevens, Sandra Day O'Connor,
Anthony Kennedy

Supreme Court Justice William Brennan gives a commencement
speech at Loyola Marymount law school in 1986.

When Powell finally spoke, he revealed—apparently for the first time and with surprising candor—that he had come to regret what he described as the "unnecessarily broad language" that he had employed in *Gertz*. He said that he had now concluded that his "sins" in *Gertz* had returned to "haunt" him. Having reconsidered the issue, Powell had determined, according to Brennan's account, that "*Gertz* must be read in" and limited to the "context of media defendants."

Because four justices (Burger, Powell, Stevens, and O'Connor) had not cast final votes, the case was scheduled for a second conference on March 30, 1984. On March 26, Stevens notified the other justices that he too would vote to reverse, having satisfied himself that a narrowly crafted opinion would not threaten the Fair Credit Reporting Act. Two days later, however, O'Connor circulated a memorandum in which she announced her vote to affirm on the ground she had advanced at the first conference, that the speech at issue in *Greenmoss Builders* "related to commercial credit and the marketplace of money, not the marketplace of ideas." In her view, "[s]uch information is marketed more as a commodity than as speech and deserves only the most modest First Amendment protection."

Within hours of his receipt of O'Connor's memo, Powell—who had apparently received an early copy of it—informed the other justices that he agreed with it and would also vote to affirm. Although (as Brennan's term history described him) Powell was no "friend of punitive damages," he remained troubled by "what he saw as Dun & Bradstreet's enormous unchecked power to harm small businesses." Hence, Brennan believed Powell had been struggling to find a way to "avoid his own opinion in *Gertz*," which he otherwise "had no desire to overrule."

In his own memorandum to the conference, Powell included large portions of a private letter that he had drafted but not sent to Stevens and O'Connor the previous week. In it, he described the *Greenmoss Builders* case as "a 'sport' in the law of libel." He noted that Dun & Bradstreet is a "business" that "has some of the characteristics of the financial page of newspapers, but is essentially different" because "its business is narrowly specialized." At this juncture, however, Powell appeared to change his mind about the consequences of this distinction. Specifically, although Powell said in his unsent letter that he would "agree cheerfully" to a decision that granted the credit reporting service the protections of the actual malice standard, he now told the conference that "in view of the nature of D&B's business and its capability to destroy the credit of other businesses (particularly small businesses), it would not be irrational to hold D&B to strict liability." Accordingly, Powell asserted, it would be "unfortunate" if the Court were to "choose this case as a vehicle for constitutionalizing the entire law of libel" and agreed with O'Connor's proposal that the justices treat "D&B as belonging to a special category of disseminators of information" who traffic in a "type of commercial speech."

At the March 30 conference, therefore, five justices (Brennan, White, Marshall, Stevens, and Blackmun) voted to reverse, while three (Powell, Rehnquist, and O'Connor) voted to affirm. Burger indicated that, although he "might vote to affirm," he was not yet "at rest." Accordingly, the chief justice had no choice but to relinquish to Brennan, the senior associate justice in the majority, the authority to assign the case. Although he gave some thought to assigning the majority opinion to White in order to keep him on board, Brennan assumed that White's vote was secure since he had not altered his position following receipt of the O'Connor and Powell memoranda. Thus, according to his term history, Brennan "considered it safe" to keep the opinion for himself and thereby take advantage of his first opportunity since his plurality opinion in *Rosenbloom* in 1971 to write the Court's controlling opinion in a defamation case. Needless to say, it would also be his first opportunity to lead the Court in a reexamination of *Gertz* and its implications.

Brennan's colleagues appeared to sense the potential significance of this assignment as well. After it was made, Powell and Rehnquist received a private letter from Burger in which the chief justice confided that he did not believe it "feasible to assign a dissent until we see how far Bill [Brennan] goes. He will, I assume, want to push out some 'new frontiers' on *Sullivan*." The following week, Powell wrote Burger to agree, and suggested that he share his views with O'Connor as well.

Brennan circulated his draft majority opinion on May 29. In it, he squarely held that *Gertz's* prohibition of "awards of presumed or punitive damages for false and defamatory statements absent a showing of knowing falsity or reckless disregard for the truth" extends to nonmedia defendants. He characterized the Court's decision in *Rosenbloom*, "[d]espite the variety of views on liability" expressed in that case, as reflecting a "clear consensus for the conclusion that, at the very least, the First Amendment limits the availability of punitive damages awards in defamation actions brought by private parties." And hoping that his words would speak for the Court, Brennan endeavored to re-explain the relevant holding in *Gertz*. He wrote that, although the Court in *Gertz* "had no occasion to consider" whether "presumed and punitive damages in defamation actions are invariably incompatible with the First Amendment," it did hold that "such damages could not be awarded" absent a showing of actual malice. Building on the multiple reasons that Powell had articulated in *Gertz* for this limitation, Brennan concluded that "when the threat of unpredictable and disproportionate damages induces potential speakers to refrain from speaking, both the speaker and society as a whole are the losers." His opinion proceeded to reject the notion that there is any relevant distinction to be made between media and nonmedia speakers in this regard, noting (apparently in anticipation of a dissent from Powell) that "the fact that petitioner's information is 'specialized' or that its subscribers pay 'substantial fees' hardly distinguishes these reports from articles in many publications to which respondent would presumably attach the label 'media.'"

Brennan then turned to the heart of the matter, explaining why and how the First Amendment simultaneously protects the press and nonmedia speakers. "Recognizing the critical historical role played by the press in gathering and disseminating information for the benefit of the public, we have often emphasized the need for careful judicial scrutiny of government actions that impede the exercise of that function or that single out the press for different treatment." By the same token, Brennan asserted, by "guaranteeing equal liberty of expression, the First Amendment furthers a central object of our constitutional scheme, to assure every member of society an equal right to dignity, respect, and the opportunity to participate in self-government." As a result:

> [T]he constitutional protections afforded speech depend on the nature, context, and function of the expressive activity at issue, not on the status or identity of the speaker. Accordingly, the rights of the institutional press, however defined, are no greater and no less than those enjoyed by other individuals or organizations engaged in the same activities.

Finally, Brennan's opinion rejected the contention that the "character or content" of the speech at issue—that is, its putative status as "commercial speech"—deprived it of the First Amendment's protections. Here, Brennan reminded his readers that "apart from identifying those limited types of unprotected expression" famously catalogued in *Chaplinksy v. New Hampshire*, the Court had been quite clear that "judges, like other government officials, are not free to decide on the basis of their content which sorts of protected expression are in their judgment less 'valuable' than others." In addition, he rejected the "commercial speech" argument on the

ground that "the mere fact that petitioner's speech concerns commerce or business in itself provides no basis for altering the constitutional analysis." The so-called
"commercial speech" doctrine, in contrast to the publication at issue in *Greenmoss
Builders*, encompasses only expression that, by its terms, purports to "propose" a
"commercial transaction" by relating "facts uniquely within the speaker's knowledge."

The opinion was classic Brennan. He used the occasion of having what he
thought was a solid five-vote majority to underscore the major values undergird-
ing First Amendment protection in defamation cases and to bolster the foundations
of *Sullivan* that had, perhaps, eroded some in *Gertz* and thereafter. Two years shy
of his 80th birthday and less often in command of majorities than earlier in his
tenure, Brennan seemed mindful that he would not be on the Court forever and
that opportunities to advance important constitutional values should not be missed.

Marshall promptly joined Brennan's opinion, as did Stevens who, at least according to his clerks, had "become solidly convinced" to do so by Brennan's "excellent
opinion." He did, however, privately ask Brennan to modify the sentence, quoted
above, in which Brennan wrote that "judges, like other government officials, are
not free to decide on the basis of their *content* which sorts of protected expression are in their judgment less 'valuable' than others." Stevens wrote to Brennan
that he feared the sentence could be viewed as inconsistent with the view he had
championed in cases such as *Young v. American Mini-Theatres* and *FCC v. Pacifica Foundation*, which envisioned judges doing just that in many circumstances.
Although Brennan had crossed swords with Stevens on the latter's reasoning in
this regard in the past, he thought it best not to confront him again and offered
to change the word "content" to "message." This accommodation satisfied Stevens,
who promptly joined the Brennan opinion on June 4, 1984.

White, however, was another matter. After returning from the Fifth Circuit
Judicial Conference in early June (which he had attended with Brennan), White
circulated a memorandum to his colleagues that Brennan's chambers described
"as something of a bombshell." Having learned that Powell was planning to write
a dissent, and that O'Connor had said she would wait for it before announcing
her own intentions, White did the same—he said that he would await Powell's
draft before casting his own vote. Brennan's chambers learned that White's clerks
"as usual, had no idea what was bothering" their justice, which further perplexed
Brennan, especially because White "had pushed to get the case granted in the first
place" and had called it a "clear reversal" at conference.

Brennan was moved to pick up the phone and call White, who explained that he "hated" *Gertz* and had been "startled" to learn that Powell was planning to write a dissent. As Brennan described the conversation, White said he "could not imagine what Powell would write but would be sympathetic to any reasonable way to get around" *Gertz*. After the call, Brennan described himself as "fairly confident" that White would "ultimately go along" with his opinion.

Unbeknownst to Brennan, however, there was a wild card in the process that would prompt White to withhold his vote. Specifically, Brennan was unaware of the degree to which Powell himself now harbored doubts about his own decision in *Gertz*. Indeed, on June 1, 1984, Powell dictated a memorandum in which he considered his options. After reminding himself that, in *Sullivan*, the Court "draws no distinction between 'damages' of various kinds," and noting "as a matter of interest" that *Sullivan*, "in several places, indicates that truth or falsity is really irrelevant to any constitutional consideration, a position *Gertz* rejected," Powell acknowledged that Brennan's proposed holding in *Greenmoss Builders* was "limited to presumed and punitive damages" and did not purport to address either the standard of liability or the availability of compensatory damages in such cases. Nevertheless, he remained concerned that "much" of the Brennan opinion "can be read—and perhaps will be—as limiting even actual damages to proof of malice when that issue is before the Court."

Accordingly, Powell set out his options. There were two suggested by his law clerk: (1) concurring in the result and writing separately to emphasize that, although "there is a difference between private speech and public speech," the government "interest in both presumed and punitive damages is so minimal that states cannot impose them at all except under constitutional standards," or (2) dissenting in an opinion that "'back[s] away slightly from *Gertz's* statement that there is no state interest in presumed and punitive damages.'" Powell himself added a third—"make a distinction between presumed and punitive damages"—an option that he wrote "would appeal to me because I think a malice standard may well be justified before punitive damages are awarded even in a suit by a private person against a private person." In assessing this last alternative, Powell returned to the language of his "holding" in *Gertz*—"the states may not permit recovery of presumed or punitive damages, at least when liability is not based on a showing of knowledge of falsity of [sic] reckless disregard for the truth." This, he recognized, "may not be easy to reconcile in terms of drawing a distinction between presumed and punitive damages." Later that same day, Powell notified the other justices that he would "try my hand at a dissent."

Powell circulated the first draft of that dissent on June 15. In it, he relied both on the identity of the speaker and on the content of the speech at issue to distinguish *Greenmoss Builders* from *Sullivan* and *Gertz*, which were otherwise endorsed in all respects. The opinion's opening paragraph framed the discussion of *Sullivan* as limiting "the reach of state laws of libel and slander in suits against media defendants," ignoring entirely the minister defendants in that case, and asserted that "[a]ll of the Court's decisions since then that have considered the constitutional role in defamation law also have involved suits against a media defendant arising out of an article or broadcast on an issue of public concern and importance," despite the presence of cases like *Garrison v. Louisiana, Henry v. Collins,* and *St. Amant v. Thompson* among the Court's defamation decisions. It included a footnote warning that, while Brennan's "opinion discusses only the questions of presumed and punitive damages, its effect is broader," and its "logic . . . apparently would require that the rule announced in *Gertz* . . . barring liability without fault in cases involving media discussion of public issues, be applied in all defamation actions." *Gertz* did not support such a result, Powell wrote, both because in that case there "was a libel suit against a media defendant" and because the "article in question discussed a question of undoubted public importance." *Greenmoss Builders,* in contrast, involved "a purely private defamation action against a commercial credit reporting agency." In the end, Powell asserted that Brennan's result "unnecessarily repudiates the common law and trivializes the First Amendment. There is nothing in *Gertz* that requires it." At this point, the opinion contained another footnote that addressed Powell's previously expressed concerns about the express "holding" in *Gertz*:

> There is language in *Gertz* that can be read broadly to the effect that presumed and punitive damages have no place in the law of defamation. It is necessary, however, to view this language in the context of the only issue before the Court. The suit was by a private person against a media defendant. It was the presence of the media defendant that primarily caused the Court in *Gertz* to limit recovery to "actual injury."

As to the damages question, Powell added:

Presumed and punitive damages were deemed—for the reasons first articulated in
New York Times—to threaten the historic role of the media in a representative democracy. No such threat is present when one private party is libeled by another private
party—at least where the libel is circulated in the course of, and is solely concerned
with, both parties' businesses. In weighing the interests that may be at issue, it is well
also to repeat that there is a significant public interest "in compensating private individuals for wrongful injury to reputation."

Powell's draft was apparently enough for Blackmun to cement his own views—he
joined Brennan's opinion that same day. O'Connor and Rehnquist, however, joined
Powell. With a tally of four for Brennan and three for Powell, that left Burger and
White. Although Brennan's chambers had been led to believe that Burger's own
clerk had "pushed him hard" to join the Brennan-crafted majority opinion, the
chief justice reportedly could not "bring himself" to do so and, on June 19, 1984,
told his colleagues that, "as of now," he would vote only to dismiss the case.

At this juncture, therefore, Brennan knew he needed White but that further
efforts to persuade him might backfire. So, although Brennan was known as the
master of discerning and accommodating the concerns of other justices to forge
majority opinions, he held back and awaited further word from White. Powell, however, was more proactive. Following what appears to have been some one-on-one
discussion with White, Powell wrote to him privately on June 18 to address White's
apparent suggestion that the case be reargued because Powell's opinion "would
decide an issue not decided below or argued here"—whether all of the First
Amendment-based protections set out in *Gertz* applied in suits against nonmedia
defendants. Powell disagreed, telling White that the "question of whether the entire
law of defamation should be constitutionalized clearly is before us and needs to
be decided." That said, he invited White to make "suggestions" for revisions to
his opinion, which Powell said he would "welcome the opportunity to consider."

On June 20, Powell wrote a second private letter, this one to Burger, with copies
to Rehnquist and O'Connor. In it, he told the chief justice that his vote to dismiss
the case "came as a surprise." He then proceeded to "review[] the 'bidding,'" for
Burger's benefit, emphasizing that the chief justice had not only previously indicated an inclination to join him, O'Connor, and Rehnquist, but also that he had
subsequently written to them to express concern about "how far Bill Brennan"
would go in his own opinion. Powell pushed hard to define the contours of the

debate, adding that "I note at this point that Bill could not have gone any farther than he has in his opinion for the Court." Powell concluded with the following:

> In view of this rather clear record, I wrote a full dissenting opinion on the assump-
> tion that there were four of us who could not go with Bill Brennan. His opinion
> overrules two centuries of the common law and the present defamation laws of
> most of the states. As a vote to [dismiss] at this time would have no significance, I
> hope that in due time—when you have an opportunity to take another look—you
> will "stay with us."

Upon receiving her copy, O'Connor wrote a handwritten note to Powell, thanking him "for writing to the Chief to refresh recollections of the history of this
important case."

Powell's letter got Burger's attention. Later that same day, the Chief wrote to
Powell, with copies to Rehnquist and O'Connor, indicating that "[i]f you think
it will help 'institutionally,' I will go along with you. I would want to see what, if
anything, Byron [White] does." Thus, it became even more apparent to both Powell
and Brennan that White's vote would almost certainly determine the outcome of
the case. For his part, Powell took renewed aim at Brennan's opinion in an effort
to win White's vote and garner his own majority. He launched what Brennan's
term history described as a "battle of footnotes" in which the authors of *Sullivan*
and *Gertz* appeared to fight for the legacy of their signature cases, each invoking
"increasingly strong language through several drafts on both sides."

As the term wound down, the waiting continued. White left town again, this
time for his daughter's wedding. Nevertheless, both Brennan and Powell continued
to court his vote, informally sending typewritten versions of additional footnotes
for his consideration. Still, White remained silent. When he returned to the Court
on June 25, 1984, White visited Powell and asked him directly whether he was
prepared to overrule *Gertz*. Powell reportedly told him that, although he had no
intention of overruling *Gertz*, he did hope to cut back on the implications of
some of the broad dicta in his opinion. White was not satisfied. Indeed, he subsequently confided in Brennan that, if Powell had only made some changes in his
dissenting opinion, he might have joined it, thereby creating a majority to affirm
the Vermont Supreme Court.

After his meeting with Powell, White broke his silence, in a memorandum he addressed to Brennan and circulated to all the justices later that same day. He said that he was "up in the air" about the case on a number of fronts:

> As you might suspect, Lewis' opinion strikes a responsive chord in me; but because it appears to narrow *Gertz v. Welch*, or at least to withdraw somewhat from the rationale of that case, I am unprepared to take that step without a reargument. On the other hand, there is substance to his views, and I will not join your opinion with its reaffirmation of *Gertz*. If there is not reargument, which I am prepared to move, I shall concur in the judgment with the following few words:
>
> Justice White concurring in the judgment.
>
> I am unprepared to join either Justice Brennan's or Justice Powell's opinion and believe that the case should be reargued. That view not having prevailed, I join the Court's judgment of reversal, which I think is more consistent with existing precedent than an affirmance would be.

The irony in all of this was palpable. Brennan, the author of *Sullivan* and *Rosenbloom*, who had been effectively marginalized by Powell as he crafted the Court's majority and opinion in *Gertz*, had been placed in the position of defending Powell's work product and reaffirming it. White, who had joined Brennan in *Sullivan*, had been his loyal ally in most of the decade that followed, and had railed against Powell's opinion in *Gertz*, was sufficiently moved by Powell's reasoning (and troubled by Brennan's defense of *Gertz*) to withhold his vote from Brennan. And Powell, who had withstood White's withering attack in *Gertz* and had dismantled the plurality Brennan had cobbled together in *Rosenbloom*, had apparently managed to curry at least some favor with White by disclaiming at least some aspects of his own reasoning in *Gertz*.

White's memorandum provoked Brennan to telephone his colleague again, this time to inquire whether White's cryptic reference to Brennan's opinion being "more consistent with existing precedent" might lead him to join the Brennan opinion if additional changes were made. It was then that White told Brennan that, if anything, Powell was more likely to secure his vote if changes were made in Powell's opinion. Nevertheless, White continued to advocate reargument, perhaps in the hope that he could thereby garner sufficient support to overrule at least significant portions of *Gertz*.

It might have been expected that Burger, who had by this time twice voted to dismiss the case, would be opposed to reargument. Nonetheless, perhaps because White had provided him with a fifth vote for reargument in *Garcia v. San Antonio Metropolitan Transit Authority* at about the same time, the other justices were not surprised when Burger wrote to White on June 25 that "I had voted to [dismiss] but I will give you a 'consolation vote' to join your vote to re-argue." Brennan had written to Burger earlier that day and, after noting that the chief had "voted to deny cert in this case and . . . twice voted to" dismiss it, assumed that "Byron's suggestion that the case be argued again will not have much appeal for you." Accordingly, Brennan asked, "Is there anything I can do in the way of changing my opinion that might enable you to join it so that we can avoid burdening the Court with another argument in this case?" In a handwritten note to Brennan scrawled across the bottom of the latter's letter, Burger replied, "Dear Bill, I want to relieve your worries about the December calendar—hence I will vote to reargue." Even before Burger had announced his intentions, Stevens privately predicted as much to his clerks: "He didn't think the case should be argued, but he'll probably think that since it was argued, it should be argued twice!"

Just before the conference voted 5–4 to rehear the case, Powell made one last attempt to secure White's vote on the merits, repeating his contention that Brennan's opinion would overrule "centuries" of common law. Upon hearing this, Rehnquist was moved to say, "Why, Lewis, I thought *you* did that in *Gertz*."

Brennan and Powell then put down their swords long enough to collaborate on the questions that the parties would be asked to reargue the following term. On June 26, 1984, Powell's law clerk proposed four separate questions, each reflecting a different permutation of the media/nonmedia distinction and the nature of the speech, which was variously referred to as "speech of an economic nature" and "reports on the financial condition of private parties." By the following day, however, Powell had reduced the questions to two, which he proposed to Brennan in a private letter:

1. Whether, in a defamation action, the constitutional rule of *New York Times* and *Gertz* with respect to presumed and punitive damages should apply where the suit is against a non-media defendant?

2. Whether, in a defamation action, the constitutional rule of *New York Times* and
Gertz with respect to presumed and punitive damages should apply where the speech
is of a commercial or economic nature?

In his letter, Powell told Brennan that he believed these questions were both appropriate because, while the "reasoning of your opinion applies to all defamation
actions against media and nonmedia defendants and without regard to the type
of speech," Powell's "would leave open the question whether the constitutional
rule applies with equal force regardless of the nature of speech," and "[t]here may
be a different balance where the speech relates solely to an economic matter (as
in this case) or to an accusation that a lady is sleeping with the wrong gentleman."

Brennan apparently agreed, because later that same day, Powell adapted his letter to Brennan as a memorandum to the entire conference, which included both
the questions he had proposed to Brennan as well as the rationale for posing them.
O'Connor, White, and Burger all concurred in what was now the Powell-Brennan
formulation.

And there it stood on the term's final day, when the justices returned from lunch
to announce that both *Greenmoss Builders* and *Garcia* would be reargued the following fall. At the time, Brennan did not suspect that the case would ultimately
"number among the great disappointments" of the October 1984 term or that it
would "presage difficulties for Justice Brennan's doctrines of First Amendment
limitations on state defamation law" for years to come.

The October 1984 Term

The reargument was held on October 3, 1984. At the outset, Gordon Garrett, again
appearing for Dun & Bradstreet, was peppered with questions about whether the
defendant was a media company and whether that made a difference in the constitutional calculus. Brennan, for one, asked Garrett "if you would tell me your
definition of the difference between media and non-media," and asserted that "I can
understand it clearly if a private individual writes a letter and makes the statement.
That person as an individual is probably non-media. But what is your definition of
non-media generally?" When Garrett responded that "the media could be defined
as one who uses a medium to communicate information, and Dun and Bradstreet,
much like a newspaper, does that. We hire reporters to obtain information which

our subscribers will want," Brennan observed that, "in Washington" we have "I don't know how many, but I suppose it must be a great number of letters, like The Kiplinger Letter, that goes out every week or periodically, sometimes on a broad range of subjects, sometimes on a limited subject like labor law." This led Garrett to suggest that, while "the Kiplinger Letter, like Dun and Bradstreet, may not be considered the traditional media, it is certainly media in that it is an organization that communicates information to its readers which have a reason to know that." White then questioned whether Dun & Bradstreet could properly even raise the issue of whether it was a "media" defendant, because it had not sought review in the Supreme Court of the Vermont courts' conclusion that it was not. Ultimately, Garrett appeared to do his best to have it both ways, asserting that "we have never taken the position that Dun and Bradstreet was part of the traditional media like the *New York Times* or CBS, but we certainly are media in the sense that we communicate information to our subscribers." And, he contended, in any event, "the constitutional prohibitions against presumed and punitive damages don't depend on the nature of the speaker or the subject matter of his speech."

During his argument, Thomas Heilmann, appearing again on behalf of Greenmoss Builders, received multiple questions from, among others, Justice Stevens, inquiring whether, if he had to do so, he could prove at trial that his client had sustained actual damages. When he responded that he thought "we could prove actual damages," Heilmann was asked whether he thought "most libel plaintiffs" could do so, "if they have to?" Heilmann attempted to sidestep the question, asserting instead that a "presumption" of damages "is necessary to assist private plaintiffs to bridge several causation gaps," before ultimately suggesting that "many private plaintiffs may be able to prove some form of actual injury." After this initial exchange, however, Heilmann was permitted to present his argument in long stretches without interruption from any member of the Court.

In his term history, Brennan and his clerks described the reargument itself as revealing "little new." The subsequent conference, however, was—as Brennan's term history put it—"another story." Burger began the discussion by once again declining to take a firm position. According to Powell's notes, the chief justice asserted that "D&B, & Kiplinger, & others who give advice are different from media," and they "inflict more damage." By the same token, Burger said he would "not extend *Gertz*," which, he added, he "didn't agree [with] then, & don't agree [with] now," because the "[r]ationale of media cases does not apply to private defendant[s]." Thus, although the case had now been argued twice on its merits, Burger reiterated that he would prefer to dismiss it entirely, but "will not reverse."

That left the field open for the combatants from the previous term to launch their initial salvos, proceeding as always in order of seniority. Brennan began by reiterating the views expressed in his previous, albeit ill-fated opinion. According to a memorandum his clerks prepared for him, and he likely read at conference as was by then his custom, Brennan was unusually blunt. After noting that "[n]othing presented on reargument has changed my mind," he limited his "remarks to three items that I believe to be of particular significance." First, he explained:

> [T]his Court has never accepted the distinction between media and non-media defendants. Are we now prepared to announce that we have changed our minds and that the billion dollar media industry in this country is deserving of greater first amendment protection than the individual citizen or the "lonely pamphleteer"? I hope not.

Second, Brennan asserted, even if the Court were to attempt to make such a distinction, "there is no principled way to draw a line between Dun & Bradstreet and innumerable other corporations and organizations, including the *Wall Street Journal* and the *New York Times*, that publish for financial gain and rely upon the accuracy of those publications to attract subscribers." Third, Brennan argued that "the distinction between public and non-public speech" that Powell had proposed the previous term "does not sufficiently protect the values behind the first amendment," which is "concerned not only with furthering self-government but also with guaranteeing the dignity of the individual." In Brennan's view, "[e]conomic, social, and religious information plays a critical role in that process."

For his part, White offered a new twist on the position he had announced in June. Not unexpectedly, he began by saying he was prepared to overrule *Gertz*. According to Powell's notes, White said that, "*Gertz* is dead wrong," but had been "accepted . . . as a precedent." If "we still accept *Gertz*," he added, "it is not easy to avoid it here." Thus, he said, he would vote to affirm if the Court were prepared to overrule *Gertz* but, if not, he would vote to reverse, but would join only in the judgment, "probably" in a separate opinion. And although the comment apparently and somewhat remarkably escaped Brennan's attention at the time (since it is not noted in his term history or taken into account in his subsequent strategy),

Powell's notes indicate that White also told his colleagues that, "[*Sullivan*] also was [a] mistake."

After Marshall and Blackmun reaffirmed their support for Brennan, Powell, as Brennan's term history described it, "stirred the soup." While voicing his continued support for a media/nonmedia distinction, he floated the proposal that presumed and punitive damages be treated differently—that the former be permitted in nonmedia cases, but that the latter be prohibited in all cases absent a showing of actual malice. As Brennan's term history put it, this proposal not only came "out of the blue," but it had not been considered by the court below, by the litigants in their briefing or at argument, or by any member of the Court the previous term.

Powell described his own vote at conference as one "to affirm in part and reverse in part." While he emphasized that he was "not entirely at rest," he asserted that he would "not agree a non-media defendant is entitled to the same protection as media." Powell then set forth what he described as his "tentative" thinking. He again asserted (albeit incorrectly) that "all prior cases applying the First Amendment in defamation cases have involved media defendants," and that "*Gertz* involved a *private* plaintiff and the same First Amendment concerns identified in *New York Times* for media defendants existed." According to Powell, "at risk [in *Gertz*] was freedom of the *press* to express views on *public issues*." In Powell's view, "none of these concerns is present when one private person is libeled by another private person." If the Court were to adopt Brennan's view, Powell said, "we are talking about changing the common law—centuries old." Thus, Powell asserted, "*Gertz* must be read in the context of a *media* defendant" and, "if it can be read otherwise, it is dicta."

At this point, Powell proceeded to explain that his dissent the previous term "adhered to [the] common law" by concluding that "only falsity and publication need be shown to be entitled to presumed and punitive damages." Now, he said, he was advocating a "possible modification of the common law," one which recognized what he perceived as "a major difference between *presumed* and *punitive* damages," that would reflect the fact that "the purpose of one [is] to *compensate*" while "the purpose of the other [is] to *punish*." After pointing to the criticism of punitive damages contained in Brennan's opinion from the previous term, Powell said he "would consider" erecting a regime that would "allow *presumed* damages against non-media defendants without proof of malice" because, in cases such as *Greenmoss Builders*, "proof of actual damages is often impossible" and "many *private* persons libeled can't *afford* to prove malice." But, he said, his construct would "allow *punitive* [damages] only on proof of malice as defined" in *Sullivan*.

From Brennan's perspective, Powell's strategy was, to say the least, unclear. Although his negative views of punitive damages were by this time well known, Powell's proposal did not appear to be designed to command a majority. It would appear especially unlikely to appeal to White, who particularly abhorred Powell's extensive renovations of the common law in the name of the First Amendment in *Gertz* itself. Brennan speculated that Powell might have thought the approach would solidify the votes of Rehnquist and O'Connor, both of whom had similarly expressed disdain for punitive damages more generally, as well as Brennan and at least some of his allies, who disapproved of them in defamation cases. It is also conceivable that Powell thought his proposal would be attractive to White, who had generally suggested in his *Gertz* dissent that the First Amendment's focus should be on limiting damage awards, not on further tinkering with common law liability rules.

Regardless of its motivation, the Powell proposal was, as Brennan's term history put it, "dead on arrival" at the conference. No member of the Court embraced it. Rehnquist appeared satisfied to leave the common law where it was in all respects. According to Powell's notes, Rehnquist reiterated that he had only "joined *Gertz* because he thought it was [the] least objectionable view at the time." Addressing Powell's latest proposal, Rehnquist said that, "if punitive damages are ok in other types of litigation, they are ok in libel cases." Powell's notes of Rehnquist's comments also include two parenthetical remarks. In one, Powell indicated that, "Bill [Rehnquist] said to me privately (at a break) that as of now he would not abolish punitive damages here unless we [overrule] *Gertz*." In another, which may or may not have reflected what Rehnquist actually said at conference, Powell noted that, "Bill agrees with [White] that *New York Times* was a mistake."

Stevens, at least according to Powell's notes, said he "agree[d] with some" of what Powell had said "about punitive damages." In addition, Stevens reportedly expressed some sympathy for "clarify[ing] presumed damages to hold that a plaintiff can't rely on the presumption alone" but must introduce "some evidence" of harm. Still, Stevens asserted, at the end of the day, "D&B should get as much protection" as a media defendant.

O'Connor continued to focus on distinctions drawn based on the identity of the speaker and the content of the speech. Although Powell noted that she too said she was "not at rest," O'Connor emphasized that "we have distinguished different types of speech—commercial, fire in crowded theater, obscenity" in past cases and that, in her view, "D&B is more akin to private speech than to media."

As Brennan saw it, the result of the conference appeared to be that, since Powell had not indicated a willingness to overrule *Gertz*, Brennan had retained White's vote and the majority. Accordingly, on October 30, 1984, Brennan recirculated his putative majority opinion from the previous term, with only minor modifications. Within forty-eight hours, Stevens, Blackmun, and Marshall joined it. O'Connor, not surprisingly, promptly responded that she would "await further writing" before "deciding what action to take," and Powell wrote Brennan that, "[a]s you would expect, my position remains basically in dissent. I may make some changes, however, in the draft I circulated last term." He added that it "may take me a while to get this done."

Indeed, Powell spent several weeks working on his new opinion, which he finally circulated on November 23, denominating it, as he had indicated he would at conference, one "affirming in part and reversing in part." When he circulated it to Burger, Rehnquist, and O'Connor, he added a cover letter. In it, Powell told them that the opinion "adhere[d] to my view of last term that the entire law of libel should not be constitutionalized" because that "would be an unprecedented extension of *New York Times* and *Gertz.*" At the same time, Powell advised his colleagues that:

> After considerable thought, I have concluded that punitive damages should be *abolished* except where authorized by a statute that prescribes appropriate standards. The imposition of punishment is a function of the state, not of lay juries without standards or statutory limitations. I do not see how permitting a jury to impose private fines can be reconciled with the Fifth and Fourteenth Amendments. Also, the purpose of tort recovery is to compensate—not to confer a windfall.

He concluded by noting that his "opinion is divided into parts so that you may, if you wish, join it in part. You would be welcome."

Powell's new approach fell largely on deaf ears. White, Rehnquist, and O'Connor did not respond to it, at least in communications shared with the rest of the Court. Something, however, did appear to be afoot, albeit unbeknownst to Brennan. The first hint came on November 29, when Burger wrote to his colleagues that, because he was "hav[ing] some problems with the case," he would "await Byron's views which, I gather, he may write out." Brennan had not previously been informed that White had taken up his pen. That same day, again unbeknownst to Brennan, Rehnquist wrote to Powell with copies to Burger and O'Connor, similarly to advise him that "I agree more with your separate opinion in this case than I do with Bill Brennan's proposed opinion, but I have enough reservations about yours so I think that I will wait and see what Byron writes. I am not yet ready to prohibit punitive damages in defamation cases."

On December 14, Brennan circulated a second draft of his own opinion, in which he responded, albeit briefly and only in footnotes, to Powell's new proposal. With respect to Powell's proposed treatment of presumed damages, Brennan confined himself largely to criticizing once again the distinction between media and nonmedia defendants on which it was premised, citing a host of cases in which state courts had not distinguished between them in adjudicating defamation cases. With respect to Powell's call to abolish punitive damages, Brennan pointed out that Powell had articulated the same rationale in *Gertz* itself for limiting, but not abolishing, both punitive *and* presumed damages. In addition, Brennan took aim at Powell's contention that presumed damages should be available "in the realm of commercial expression" despite the fact, as Brennan saw it, in such cases "proving that actual damages occurred is relatively easy."

In Powell's chambers, Brennan's minimal treatment of his opinion was viewed as "surprising[]." In response to Brennan's use of Powell's own language in *Gertz* to undermine his newly minted distinction between presumed and punitive damages, Powell himself drafted a rejoinder, also as a footnote:

My opinion for the Court in *Gertz*, as the Court today notes, did not distinguish between presumed and punitive damages in libel suits against media defendants. Upon the more mature reflection, required in this case in which the Court constitutionalizes the entire law of libel, I find both historic and logical reasons for the distinction I now make.

Building on that logic, Powell added:

The purpose of presumed damages essentially is compensatory. As I have noted in the text above, they are appropriate where it is clear from the nature of the libel that injury occurred and where proving a dollar amount for the injury often is impossible. This compensatory rationale for allowing presumed damages is wholly different from allowing a private litigant to punish a defendant by awarding punitive damages without due process of any kind.

Powell's chambers also reviewed all of the state cases Brennan had cited, and undertook additional research concerning the comparative fates of media and nonmedia defendants at common law. In the course of doing so, Powell's law clerk was obliged to make an embarrassing admission to the justice. On December 18, 1984, the clerk wrote to Powell that, "in going through all the state cases I was pushed into rereading *New York Times* and [a] few of this Court's other pre-*Gertz* cases. I noticed that several of them, including *New York Times* itself, apply the actual malice standard to nonmedia defendants."

In writing at least, Powell took the clerk's discovery in stride. In handwritten notes in its margins, he pronounced the memo "perceptive" and expressed "surprise" both by the "string of new cases" Brennan had cited and by the fact that "apparently WJB and I both missed" the Court's own prior cases applying the actual malice standard to nonmedia defendants. Over the following days, therefore, Powell and his clerk worked to revise his opinion, inserting multiple references to "public expression" in those places where its predecessor had referred to "suits against a media defendant." They also recrafted the opinion's characterization of *Greenmoss Builders*, referring to it as a case involving "private expression" rather than a "nonmedia defendant." Isolated references to the "press clause" of the First Amendment were also jettisoned. And Powell responded to Brennan's string cite of state cases by pointing out that, "though not invariably clear, these cases involved *public* expression pertaining to 'public questions.'" This, Powell now discovered, "is a critical distinction" because "[t]he case before us today involves a privately communicated libel by one private party against another on a subject of little First Amendment concern."

Powell circulated his revised draft on December 21. With it, the major premise for the petition for review and the central issue over which the justices had skirmished the entire preceding term, not to mention the central issue the Court had asked the parties to address at reargument—whether the constitutional rules announced in *Sullivan* and *Gertz* applied in defamation actions instituted against nonmedia defendants—ceased to be an issue at all, at least for Powell's purposes.

On December 26, White wrote to Brennan that it would be "some time before I am ready in this case," which led to virtual silence from all quarters over the next month, at least from the perspective of Brennan's chambers. Shortly thereafter, moreover, Powell was diagnosed with prostate cancer and his treatment and recovery would keep him away from the Court for several months. Although he continued to remain involved in cases, including *Greenmoss Builders*, in which he had participated in the argument, dozens of others that were argued in January and February 1985 after he took ill were either resolved by 4–4 votes, decided without him, or held over for argument to the following term.

On January 25, 1985, White sent Brennan a note shortly before noon. It read, in its entirety:

Dear Bill,

It will not surprise you, I am sure, to learn that I am voting to affirm in this case.
I shall circulate shortly indicating my position. Neither am I joining Lewis [Powell]
at this point. Having said this, I am fleeing the city for a week or two.

And there things stood at high noon on January 25, 1985. By then, the *Greenmoss Builders* case had been on the Court's calendar for nearly two years, had spawned two sets of briefs and arguments on the merits, and had consumed literally hundreds of pages of opinions that had yet to be issued. Still, at that moment, the case was no closer to decision than it was when White first drafted a dissent from what he believed was the Court's wrong-headed inclination to deny review in the first place. Now, it appeared that it was effectively up to White to determine the outcome.

As it turned out, Brennan did not have long to wait to learn White's "position," how it differed from Powell's, at least for the moment, and why White had felt obliged to give Brennan some (albeit minimal) advance warning both that he was voting to affirm and that he was about to "flee" the city. White's dissent was circulated during the lunch hour that very day. It was, as Brennan's term history would later describe it, a full "frontal assault" on *Sullivan* itself. It did not differ materially from the opinion that White ultimately filed in the case and included essentially the same proclamation, made by a justice who had joined, without reservation, Brennan's landmark opinion twenty years earlier:

> I have . . . become convinced that the Court struck an improvident balance in the *New York Times* case between the public's interest in being fully informed about public officials and public affairs and the competing interest of those who have been defamed in vindicating their reputation.

In White's newly formulated view, *Sullivan* "countenances two evils: first, the stream of information about public officials and public affairs is polluted and often remains polluted by false information; and second, the reputation and professional life of the defeated plaintiff may be destroyed by falsehoods that might have been avoided with a reasonable effort to investigate the facts." To White, "these seem grossly perverse results." On reflection, White had come to conclude that, in *Sullivan*, "instead of escalating the plaintiff's burden of proof to an almost impossible level, we could have achieved our stated goal by limiting the recoverable damages to a level that would not unduly threaten the press. . . . Had that course been taken and the common-law standard of liability been retained," White wrote, "the defamed public official, upon proving falsity, could at least have had a judgment to that effect" such that his "reputation would then be vindicated."

Perhaps most cutting, in a later draft of his opinion, White characterized the celebrated analytical underpinnings of Brennan's opinion in *Sullivan*—his equation of a "private" defamation action by a public official with the law of seditious libel— as an analogy that "substitutes hyperbole for an analysis of the interests actually at stake." Moreover, White contended, "other commercial enterprises in this country must pay for the damages they cause as a cost of doing business, and it is difficult to argue that the United States did not have a free and vigorous press before the rule in *New York Times* was announced." As a result, White simply was not prepared to "assume that the press, as successful and powerful as it is, will be intimidated into withholding news that by decent journalistic standards it believes to be true."

That afternoon, Brennan was, as his term history described his reaction to White's opinion, "crestfallen." He had expected an attack on *Gertz* but "the gratuitous attack on *Times* itself could not reasonably have been anticipated in a case presenting no question of criticism of government officials." Brennan not only feared that other justices, most notably Rehnquist, O'Connor, and Burger, might now join White, he found "deeply troubling" what his term history later characterized as "the notion of a fissure in the very foundation of the doctrine of constitutional limits on state defamation law," which he considered one of his "most important contributions to the advancement of constitutional law." From Brennan's perspective, "[n]o Justice in twenty years had objected in an opinion to the fundamental premises of *Times* itself." And although his term history did not mention it, Brennan must have remembered that, just the previous term, the full Court had reaffirmed *Sullivan* in emphatic terms in *Bose* (a decision, however, from which White dissented).

Shortly after he received it, Brennan wrote to the other justices to say that White's opinion "requires a considered response," which he said he would "undertake to make as soon as I can." While he waited for word from other chambers, Brennan and his clerks considered his options. They devoted most of the morning of January 28, 1985, to doing just that. Although the consensus in Brennan's chambers was that a direct response to White's "jeremiad against *Times*" was imperative, he and his clerks recognized that the vehicle that White had chosen to launch it—a case involving credit reporting, not speech criticizing public officials for the performance of their official duties—made the task a difficult one. Ultimately, Brennan agreed with his clerks' proposal that they try their hand at an opinion that began with a defense of *Sullivan*, proceeding as it must from "Meiklejohnian premises and stress[ing] the chilling effect on speech crucial to public affairs and self-government," and moving from there to the issue of affording constitutional protection to credit reporting, a subject concededly "far" from the "political speech that first gave rise to constitutional limits on state defamation law."

As for Powell, he finally circulated his new draft opinion on February 22. In it, he gave up entirely on his efforts to preclude punitive damages awards, arguing instead that both presumed and punitive damages should be available where, as in *Greenmoss Builders*, the speech at issue constituted "private expression involving purely a matter of private concern." He did not circulate a separate opinion addressing the presumed/punitive damages issue. Express reference to a media/nonmedia distinction had also disappeared although, at least in Brennan's view, it lingered in the analysis nonetheless.

More significantly, Powell's new draft retained its dual focus on "purely private expression on a matter of private concern." It characterized *Sullivan* as a case "involving public expression on matters of public concern" and contrasted it with the facts in *Greenmoss Builders*, which Powell said involved "private expression between a construction company and a commercial credit reporting agency on an issue of purely private concern." And in a footnote responding to Brennan's survey of state law cases declining to make a media/nonmedia distinction, Powell pointed out that "though not invariably clear, these cases do not involve private expression on essentially private matters. This, not a defendant's media or non-media status, is the critical distinction." In the opinion's concluding section, Powell asserted that, while "[i]n this case there is no need to define precisely what constitutes private expression on matters of private concern," in his view, "the libelous speech at issue here implicates the First Amendment at most tangentially," primarily because it was "private expression" distributed "to only five subscribers, who were not allowed under the subscription agreement to disseminate it any further."

As winter turned to spring in 1985, therefore, the Court appeared no closer to a resolution than it had been in October 1983, when it first considered taking the case. Far from having clarity or developing consensus with the passage of time, the Court was more splintered than ever, with the fate of *Gertz* very much still up in the air and that of *Sullivan* not far behind.

On March 4, 1985, still recuperating and "handicapped here in the apartment without books and face-to-face discussion with justices as well as" his clerks, Powell dictated a "MEMO TO MYSELF," in which he once again attempted to sort out his options. In it, he made a telling, albeit private, concession:

> As I view it now, my opinion in *Gertz* is an example of overwriting a Court opinion.
> I said much that was unnecessary to a decision of that case. A large part of *Gertz* is *dicta*.

Thus, Powell wrote that he found himself "left in something of a dilemma particularly in view of what I wrote (perhaps unnecessarily) in *Gertz*."

As Powell continued to assess his options, his clerk talked to Rehnquist's and learned that Rehnquist wanted Powell "to drop entirely the private expression prong of your 'private expression on a matter of private concern' test." On March 7, therefore, Powell sketched out by hand the contours of a "possible compromise." He could, he wrote, "de-emphasize" his previous reliance on the concept of "private expression," retain his "emphasis on 'private concern' but leave open when *expression* may be viewed as *public*." Thus, in *Greenmoss Builders*, "where there was no *public* interest in the [*Sullivan*] sense, I'd reach [the] same result if D&B had circulated to 1000 customers." Such a narrow holding, Powell thought, would leave open the question of constitutional protection in a case in which "the D&B report to 1000 had said the *only bank* in town was bankrupt," which would presumably be a matter of "*local* public concern." Powell asked himself whether this would be "the type of public concern within the *NYT/Gertz* sense of 'robust debate' on public issues?" In the end, Powell concluded, he could simply "leave open when the expression is public . . . ."

Ultimately, this is what Powell chose to do. He circulated a fourth draft of his opinion to O'Connor and Rehnquist privately. In it, he removed virtually all express references to the concept of "public expression" and focused instead solely on the distinction between "matters of public concern," on the one hand, and "expression on a matter of purely private concern," on the other. He professed "no need to define precisely what constitutes expression on matters of private concern" because "it is clear that the libelous speech at issue here implicates the First Amendment at most only tangentially." His opinion provided no further guidance beyond the assertion that "[p]etitioner's credit reporting is a matter of private concern, for it is speech solely in the individual economic interest of the speaker and its specific business audience" and a footnote suggesting that "commercial reporting dissemi-nated in the general public interest would involve different considerations." All that was left of the "public expression" concept was a sentence in another footnote, in which Powell noted that the "particular information contained in the disputed credit report, for example, was made available to only five business subscribers, who, under the terms of the subscription agreement, could not disseminate it any further." The significance of this observation was not further explained.

On March 12, before it had been circulated to the conference, Rehnquist reaf-firmed his support for Powell's new approach in a letter thanking him "for your response to my suggestions" and pronouncing himself "happy to join your fourth draft." It appears that this letter was inadvertently copied to all the other justices, since Brennan's chambers received it that day as well and Rehnquist sent a more formal "join" letter to Powell, with a copy to the other justices, the following week.

For Brennan and his clerks, who had been collectively unaware of the jockeying over Powell's now-abandoned "public expression" concept, Rehnquist's decision to join Powell was significant for a very different reason. By joining Powell, Rehnquist had effectively deprived White of any additional votes for his repudiation of *Sul-livan*, with the possible exception of Burger's. And even as Powell continued to court Burger's vote, Brennan thought he had at least some reason to believe that the unpredictable chief justice would join him, which would create a majority through which to rebut both Powell and White.

On March 20, Brennan finally circulated his own revised opinion, including his rejoinder to White and now to Powell's latest position. Still styled as an opinion for the Court, Brennan set out the question presented as he at that juncture continued to understand it—"whether *Gertz* should be restricted to cases that do not involve 'nonmedia' defendants or speech about economic and commercial matters." Once again, Brennan purported to "reject any distinction between 'media' and 'nonmedia' defendants." In the body of the opinion, however, Brennan shifted the analysis on this score slightly, ascribing the proposed media/nonmedia distinction to "Respondent" (rather than to Powell) and noting that Powell now "seeks the same result solely on the basis of the content of the speech." Brennan wrote that "both approaches" were not only "unworkable and irreconcilable with our precedents," but "[m]ore fundamentally" they "contravene basic First Amendment values." Indeed, Brennan wrote, "[o]nly legal alchemy could transform these independently insufficient rationales into a legitimate justification for denying the type of speech at issue in this case any protection from the chill of unrestrained presumed and punitive damage awards."

In addition, Brennan mounted a full-throated defense of *Sullivan*, which emphasized the difficulty of litigating the issue of truth in a courtroom as well as a self-governing society's fear of designating any branch of government—including the judiciary—as an arbiter of political truth:

> Even if the erroneous assertion were not the inevitable companion of the truthful one in robust discourse, the difficulty of litigating the question of "truth" would, we suggested in *New York Times v. Sullivan*, still stand as a daunting deterrent. Our cases in the two decades since that decision bear out this perception about the judicial risks of a judicial test of truth. Often the spoken or written word will capture a judgment, inference or interpretation the "truth" of which is not readily susceptible to adjudication. [*Bose*]. "Truth" will often be a matter of degree or context. [*Bresler*]. Particularly when we debate the unwisdom of a policy or political point of view, our perspective on "truth" will be colored by the shared assumptions of the day; often what seems truth is but fashion. . . . The amorphous essence of political "truth" creates the risk of erroneous imposition of liability, and thereby chills debate, even when a jury seeks to discharge its duty in good faith. When the speaker is unpopular and the jury hostile, a rule of law permitting the imposition of liability for mere inaccuracy gives the jury *carte blanche* to oppress.

In this portion of his opinion, Brennan took pains to elaborate the basis for his concern about making the government the final arbiter of truth:

> The aversion to a judicial test of political truth also reflects a related judgment about the propriety of vesting an organ of government with such powers to say what the truth is. . . . When we entrust to courts, to the government, the unfettered power to resolve ambiguous questions about the truth of political expression we cede a measure of our individual liberty and right of self-government and hazard a regime of imposed orthodoxy. . . . Sharp criticism and free trade in political ideas does not guarantee the discovery of political truth, but our Constitution embodies the judgment that it is far better to risk error than suffer tyranny.

Although his draft did not mention or otherwise discuss either case specifically, it seems obvious that Brennan had in mind the trials in *Westmoreland v. CBS, Inc.* and *Sharon v. Time, Inc.* These defamation cases, which had then only recently concluded in New York, had spawned much discussion and criticism of the role of *Sullivan* in those extraordinarily expensive examples of litigation viewed by many as designed to yield a definitive "verdict" on the truth of issues such as the propriety of U.S. involvement in Vietnam and the Israeli incursion into Lebanon. It is indeed difficult to read Brennan's opinion and not conclude that he was, at the same time, attempting both to rebut White's attack on *Sullivan* and to explain how the decision had since been misperceived by litigants and misconstrued by courts:

> Nor would a shift in emphasis from proof of defendant's state of mind to proof of the truth of the challenged speech reduce the chilling effect of litigation costs. Allegations of libel will often raise difficult historical or policy questions that can only be answered through complex, and consequently expensive, litigation. The would-be critic will be deterred not only by the cost of his or her own attorney fees but also by the prospect of liability for the other side's fees if the jury verdict is unfavorable. And this approach adds incremental deterrence because it encourages public officials to sue to vindicate their reputations and thereby increases the number of libel suits a would-be critic will be faced with defending. Thus the suggested alternative would result in more suits and more victories for plaintiffs and would not significantly reduce the deterrent potential of damages that could be awarded in these suits.

It is also difficult to discern how Brennan could reconcile these views with his advocacy ten years earlier, in both *Gertz* and *Tornillo*, of "retraction" statutes designed to afford the subject of allegedly false and defamatory news reporting a judicial forum in which to secure a judicial declaration of such falsity.

In crafting his new opinion, Brennan considered whether to abandon the support for *Gertz* that had characterized his earlier drafts (and effectively driven away White) and to advocate instead the position he had previously championed in *Rosenbloom*. After all, now that White was in dissent, Brennan no longer needed to defend *Gertz* to secure his vote (perverse as that logic might have been, it was actually quite right—White had earlier indicated his willingness to join Brennan's majority only if the Court were not prepared to overrule *Gertz*). In addition, Burger, whose vote Brennan now needed to cobble together a majority, had joined his plurality in *Rosenbloom*.

Upon reflection, however, Brennan determined that he was not likely to secure Burger's vote, no matter what position he took on *Gertz*. As a result, Brennan concluded that his "best course" would be to accept *Gertz* and attempt to explain its rationale and rules in a way that would further the law's development in more constructive directions. In Brennan's view, because "future debate would be about the scope of *Gertz*," no matter what his opinion in *Greenmoss Builders* said, "the most leverage could be brought to bear by staying with *Gertz* at this time, even if he thought the *Rosenbloom* approach correct." In addition, as his term history explained, Brennan feared that "Powell and White between them had so destabilized defamation law by abandoning *Gertz* and moving right" that he should not "exacerbate the uncertainty by abandoning *Gertz* and moving left." And, of course, Brennan was fairly sure that, if he too attacked *Gertz*, he would lose the votes of Marshall (who had not joined him in *Rosenbloom* and was an early supporter of Powell in *Gertz*) and Stevens.

Brennan's concerns about forming a majority were driven home within one day of the circulation of his March 20 draft when he received what his term history later described as a "dispiriting" private letter from Stevens. To Brennan's dismay, Stevens had written to express "serious misgivings" about Brennan's opening section—his pointed defense of *Sullivan* against White's attack. Stevens wrote that he found Brennan's argument "less persuasive" than *Sullivan* itself and urged him to limit himself to "nothing more than a few appropriate quotations" from *Sullivan* coupled with "a brief reference to its solid acceptance in the jurisprudence of the

Court." More significantly, Stevens rejected Brennan's contention that *Sullivan* was the "'well-spring' for the Court's First Amendment libel jurisprudence," conceding it "was indeed a great opinion and [that] it did mark the Court's first step into the field," but gently asserting that, as he had on behalf of the Court itself the previous term in *Bose*, it was "a natural development of principles that have always underlain our First Amendment jurisprudence" and that it was "presaged by a solid common law development and scholarly opinion." And the central problem of defending *Sullivan* in the context of *Greenmoss Builders* did not escape Stevens's notice:

> [T]he extensive and passionate discussion of the importance of public debate . . . strikes me as somewhat counterproductive in the context of the particular facts of this case. As I read these parts of the opinion I kept asking myself whether the arguments shed much light on the question whether commercial credit reports are entitled to special protection.

In the end, Stevens counseled, "[u]nless someone joins Byron," Brennan could and, in Stevens's view should, "safely assume that eight members of the Court (perhaps I should say seven) accept the basic holding in *New York Times*." It was then not entirely certain to Brennan to which of his colleagues Stevens was referring in the quoted parenthetical—the mystery, however, would be cleared up soon enough.

As disappointed as he was by Stevens's response, Brennan knew that he had no choice but to accommodate him. After all, as his term history later explained it, "[g]iven White's broadside," a defense of *Sullivan* that Stevens declined to join would suggest that support for the case "was crumbling on the Court." In his response to Stevens that same day, Brennan "confess[ed]" that his draft "reflects concern that Byron's propositions might attract support" and conceded it was "[p]erhaps . . . an overreaction." He told Stevens that his "suggestion that eight (or at least seven) of the Court accept the basic holding of *New York Times* is very comforting" and ended his private letter by assuring Stevens that he would "be trying to adjust the circulation along the lines that you suggest."

Although Marshall and Blackmun were advised of Brennan's plans through their law clerks, Brennan held back another draft for a time, concerned "that hasty withdrawal of the defense of *Times* would further encourage White." Thus, on March 29, White fired back at the original draft in what Brennan described as "harsh tones," specifically aiming his shots at Brennan's defense of *Sullivan*. Among other things,

White took issue with what he characterized as Brennan's suggestion "that courts, as organs of the government, cannot be trusted to discern what the truth is" in a defamation action. To this, White asserted that "[i]t is perverse indeed to say that these bodies are incompetent to inquire into the truth of a statement of fact in a defamation case" when "[w]e entrust to juries and the courts the responsibility of decisions affecting the life and liberty of persons."

In addition, White noted the changes that Powell had made to his own opinion, applauding the fact that Powell "does not rest his application of a different rule here on a distinction drawn between media and non-media defendants" and noting his agreement with Brennan that the "First Amendment gives no more protection to the press in defamation suits than it does to others exercising their freedom of speech." On this score, however, White concluded his analysis with a bow toward Powell:

> If *Gertz* is to be distinguished from this case, it should be on the ground that it applies only where the allegedly false publication deals with a matter of general or public importance. If the false publication does not deal with such a matter, the common-law rules would apply whether the defendant is a member of the media or other public disseminator or a non-media individual publishing privately.

Powell circulated a new draft of his own on April 1. "There is a good deal more that could be said in reply," he wrote to O'Connor and Rehnquist, "but I am inclined to think that our view of this case is adequately stated . . . . Bill Brennan's opinion, although 50% longer, still would constitutionalize the entire law of libel." Predictably, Powell took on Brennan's description of the sweep of *Gertz*, accusing him of "mischaracteriz[ing] that case and mistak[ing] its holding." As Powell now saw it, "[l]ike every other case in which this Court has found constitutional limits on state laws of defamation, *Gertz* involved expression directly relevant to the effective operation of our system of democratic self-government."

After receiving Powell's latest draft, Burger sent a pair of curious notes to Powell and to White, on April 9 and 10 respectively, the latter of which was copied to the other justices. To Powell, Burger wrote that he had "long struggled with this case" and reminded Powell that "[y]ou know what I think of the excess of *New York Times* and my reservations on your *Gertz*." In the end, he told Powell, "I think my views are best served by joining both you and Byron. This is a 'tight rope' to walk and I hope I can do it *sans* explanation." The next day, Burger sent a similar note to White, in which he advised him that "I have joined Lewis, but I will also join your concurring opinion."

In Brennan's chambers, Burger's proclamation was treated with derision. It did not seem to phase the chief justice, Brennan's term history asserted, that White's opinion proceeded from the premise that *Gertz* (and *Sullivan*) had been wrongly decided, while Powell's opinion endorsed both of them, and particularly *Gertz*. A Brennan clerk (and perhaps others) alerted Burger's chambers to the "problem," and the clerk thought that Burger's administrative assistant "immediately assumed a stiffly defensive posture."

In any event, Burger did clarify his position the following day, and thereby revealed himself unambiguously as the justice cryptically referenced in Stevens's parenthetical comment to Brennan, advising his colleagues that he would "add something along the following line":

> I join those parts of Justice Powell's opinion essential to the disposition of the case; I agree generally with Justice White's opinion with respect to *Gertz v. Robert Welch, Inc.* and *New York Times Co. v. Sullivan.*

With Burger's vote, there were now five justices committed to affirming the Vermont Supreme Court. On April 22, therefore, Powell again wrote to Burger to remind him that he needed to "confirm your assignment of this case to me" so that he could "convert my dissent into a plurality opinion for the four of us." Accordingly, on April 22, Burger formally reassigned the lead opinion to Powell, "with all the 'pluses' and 'minuses' that go with it!"

Burger's reassignment of the opinion to Powell, coupled with a perceived need to accommodate Stevens, led Brennan to change course yet again. Now that he was in dissent, Brennan decided that the best strategy was to "make the case seem as idiosyncratic and trivial as possible" and to stress that the Court was not speaking with a single voice even then. And, he decided, he would position the dissent less as an angry attack on the Court's abandonment of core First Amendment principles, and more as a clarification and reminder that the Court had done precisely the opposite—in other words, though he and Powell might disagree on how to deal with this "trivial" case, there was no question that the Court remained solidly committed to the fundamental constitutional doctrine laid out in *Sullivan*. Accordingly, Brennan's new draft began as follows:

> This case involves a difficult question of the proper application of *Gertz v. Robert Welch, Inc.* to credit reporting—a type of speech at some remove from that which first gave rise to explicit First Amendment restrictions on state defamation law—and has produced a diversity of considered opinions, none of which speaks for the Court. JUSTICE POWELL'S plurality opinion affirming the judgment below would not apply the *Gertz* limitations on presumed and punitive damages to this case; rather, the three Justices joining that opinion would hold that the First Amendment requirement of actual malice . . . should have no application in this defamation action because the speech involved a subject of purely private concern and was circulated to an extremely limited audience. Establishing this exception, the opinion reaffirms *Gertz* for cases involving matters of public concern and reaffirms *New York Times Co. v. Sullivan* for cases in which the challenged speech allegedly libels a public official or a public figure.

He then added a few lines to reaffirm the core principles of *Sullivan*:

> The four who join this opinion would reverse the judgment of the Vermont Supreme Court. We believe that, although protection of the type of expression at issue is admittedly not the "central meaning of the First Amendment," *Gertz* makes clear that the First Amendment nonetheless requires restraints on presumed and punitive damage awards for this expression. The lack of consensus in approach to these idiosyncratic facts should not, however, obscure the solid allegiance the principles of *New York Times v. Sullivan* continue to command in the jurisprudence of this Court. See also *Bose Corp. v. Consumer's Union of the United States, Inc.*

Brennan had successfully employed an analogous strategy in defining Powell's handiwork in the past—most notably in *Regents of the University of California v. Bakke* addressing the issue of affirmative action—and he would make use of it again in future defamation cases—most notably *Milkovich v. Lorain Journal Co.* Still, Brennan remained unsure that Stevens would go along, even though the notion of the Court's ongoing support for *Sullivan* was his. Finally, Brennan decided to press his luck with Stevens by recasting his detailed defense of *Sullivan* as a long footnote. As his term history put it, Brennan thought it was "worth a try."

On May 9, 1985, Powell delivered advance copies of his new "plurality" opinion to O'Connor and Rehnquist, explaining that he had "not changed the substance of what you have approved." He added that he had written "the Chief a personal letter and talked to him some time ago in an effort to persuade him that he could join our opinion without qualification, and still agree with Byron that *New York Times* and *Gertz* should be overruled. I do not know what he will do." Later that same day, O'Connor pronounced the Powell plurality opinion to be "splendid" and predicted that "it will be helpful in a number of First Amendment cases in the future." The new opinion was circulated to the full Court on May 10.

On May 20, Brennan circulated his revised draft, now a dissent, to his putative allies, Marshall, Blackmun, and Stevens. He hoped to gain their approval before sharing it with others, especially White. As Brennan's term history reflected on it, this tactic "proved sage" since, although Marshall and Blackmun expressed their approval, Stevens sent Brennan another private letter, this time focusing on his "concern[s]" about the newly added footnote. It ended with the somewhat ominous assertion that, "[e]ven though I am not sure I disagree with anything you have said, I am presently inclined to join all of your dissent except footnote 2."

This, in Brennan's view, was the death knell for his direct rejoinder to White. Brennan was not only "disappointed" that Stevens's objections had deprived him of that opportunity, he was also concerned that Stevens's reluctance to join reflected Stevens's own "desire to preserve substantial leeway for tinkering with the actual malice standard" in the future. Brennan's concern was not far off the mark. As we shall see in chapter 9, Stevens subsequently did just that, albeit with Brennan's concurrence, in *Harte-Hanks Communications, Inc. v. Connaughton.*

On May 22, Brennan privately advised Marshall and Blackmun of Stevens's position "that we circulate initially with footnote 2 deleted. His thought is that we don't yet know what Byron may circulate when he converts his present dissent into a concurrence." Brennan added that, "[i]f Byron repeats his attacks on the *Times/Sullivan* principles, we could then reconsider a response. If there is not to be one, I think John would wish to consider some revision of footnote 2. I have sent the draft to the printer with footnote 2 deleted." Despite Brennan's attempt to leave the door open in his letter to Marshall and Blackmun, and the arrival of a supportive note from Blackmun that same day, no version of footnote 2 would ever be reinserted. Instead, the opinion's first footnote gently observed that White's dissent "ventures some modest proposals for restructuring the First Amendment protections currently afforded defendants in defamation actions," but asserted that White "agrees with *New York Times v. Sullivan*" that "the breathing space needed to ensure the robust debate of public issues essential to our democratic society is impermissibly threatened by unrestrained damage awards for defamatory remarks."

Brennan's efforts to soften his attacks on Powell's plurality opinion, and to emphasize instead the broad areas on which they agreed, were apparently lost on Powell himself. When he read Brennan's draft on May 23, Powell told his law clerk, he did so "[w]ith an increasing rise in my blood pressure." On the Brennan draft itself, Powell sketched out by hand his proposed "answer" to Brennan's opinion: "Effect of this opinion is to extend *NYT* to entire law of libel, a result contrary to the common law, to the history of our country, and with a total disregard of the interest of the individual in his reputation." To Brennan's footnote assertion that "[o]ne searches *Gertz* in vain for a single word to support the proposition that limits on presumed and punitive damages obtained only when speech involved matters of public concern," Powell protested in the margin that this question was "not at issue in *Gertz*." And in a memorandum to his law clerk, Powell fumed that Brennan's dissent "repeatedly attributes to our opinion views we did not express." In yet another memorandum, Powell sought his clerk's views on the advisability of adding the following sentiment to his opinion:

> If the dissent were the law, a woman of impeccable character who was branded a whore would have no effective recourse unless she could prove "malice" by clear and convincing evidence—not in the ordinary meaning of that term but under the more demanding standard of *New York Times*. The dissent would, in effect, constitutionalize the entire common law of libel.

In suggesting this, it apparently had slipped Powell's mind that, when it came to both the standard of liability and the ability of a private figure plaintiff to recover actual damages for injury to reputation, Brennan's dissent deferred entirely to Powell's own formulations in *Gertz* which, among other things, did not obligate the "woman of impeccable character" to prove "malice" at all.

In the meantime, Brennan held out some hope that, having accommodated Stevens, White might soften his own assault on *Sullivan*. Alas, this was not to be. On

June 11, White circulated a new draft of his own opinion "concurring in the judgment," which retained virtually all of his attacks on *Sullivan*. In fact, in a move that was "somewhat irksome" to Brennan's chambers, White "even retained his explicit rejoinders" to Brennan's now deleted arguments in support of *Sullivan*, introducing them with the phrase "it could be argued," rather than "Justice Brennan argues."

The process by which White came to include this language in his draft is revealing. Initially, his law clerk took a crack at revising his then extant dissenting opinion in the wake of Brennan's and Powell's circulations. In addition to changing it from a dissent to an opinion "concurring in the judgment," White's clerk deleted in significant part the sharp language from the previous draft that had attacked Brennan's now-abandoned defense of *Sullivan*. In a memorandum to White dated May 29, 1985, the clerk noted that "Justice Brennan has pulled the language in defense of *New York Times v. Sullivan* that had caused you to respond," which, the clerk indicated, warranted the deletion of much of the previous draft's rejoinder. White, however, overruled the clerk, using the editing term "STET" to signify his decision to retain most of the strong language from the previous draft and substituting, in his own hand, phrases such as "it might be suggested" and "it could be suggested" for the prior draft's references to what "Justice Brennan suggests."

On May 23, the same day that Brennan circulated the latest incarnation of his dissent, Burger too circulated a new opinion, again "concurring in the judgment." In it, Burger attempted to explain himself at greater length. He reiterated his dissatisfaction with *Gertz* but explained that it "is now the law of the land, and until it is overruled, it must, under the principle of *stare decisis*, be applied by this Court." Accordingly, Burger pronounced his agreement with Powell "to the extent that it holds that *Gertz* is inapplicable in this case." Nevertheless, Burger emphasized, he agreed with White that "*Gertz* should be overruled" as well as with White's general "observations concerning *New York Times v. Sullivan*." He then took the opportunity to endeavor to rewrite the actual malice standard itself, declaring that "since *New York Times* equates 'reckless disregard of the truth' with malice, this should permit a jury instruction that malice may be found if the defendant is shown to have published defamatory material which, in the exercise of reasonable care, would have been revealed as untrue." He added that:

If this is not what *New York Times v. Sullivan* means, I agree with JUSTICE WHITE
that it should be reexamined. The great rights guaranteed by the First Amendment
carry with them certain responsibilities.

Consideration of these issues inevitably recalls the aphorism of journalism attributed to the late Roy Howard that, "too much checking on the facts has ruined many
a good news story."

On June 19, 1985, after clearing it with O'Connor and Rehnquist, Powell circulated his own revised opinion. In it, he added three footnotes rebutting specific
points in the Brennan dissent. Most notably, in footnote four, he took on the
troublesome contradiction Brennan had noted between the plurality opinion
and *Gertz*, explaining that "[g]iven the context of *Gertz*," the holding in that case
rightly applied only "in cases involving *public speech*." And, in footnote 7, he added
his hypothetical treatment of the "woman of impeccable character."

The following day, White wrote to Powell and to the rest of his colleagues to
advise them that, having reviewed the latest drafts, he would only be adding the
following "two sentences" to his own opinion:

> A legislative solution to the damages problem would also be appropriate. Moreover,
> since libel plaintiffs are very likely more interested in clearing their names than in
> damages, I doubt that limiting recoveries would deter or be unfair to them.

With these changes, White asserted, "I see no reason why the case cannot be scheduled to come down next week."

The decision was finally announced on June 26, 1985. In doing so, Powell
told the gallery in the courtroom that, unlike the Court's prior defamation cases:

> [T]he suit today—by a private party—involves only a matter of private interest to
> the parties. In a word, this is a typical common law libel suit. A majority of the Court
> declines to constitutionalize the entire law of libel.
>
> Accordingly the judgment of the Vermont Supreme Court is affirmed. There is,
> however, no Court opinion.

From Brennan's perspective, this last sentence read aloud by Powell was undoubtedly the most significant. In the end, there was "no Court opinion" that restricted

Sullivan and *Gertz* to suits brought against media defendants; there was "no Court opinion" placing speech about matters not deemed to be of "public concern" entirely outside the reach of the First Amendment; and most importantly, there was "no Court opinion" questioning, much less overruling, the constitutional balance struck in *Sullivan* itself.

After two years of ideological combat on all of these fronts, Brennan could rightfully declare this at least a small victory. In a December 17, 1986, interview with his biographer, he was asked if then-recent libel decisions like *Greenmoss Builders* were signs of efforts within the Court to overrule *Sullivan*. Brennan replied, "Oh, no, no on the contrary, the whole Court has felt that the *New York Times* and *Sullivan* basically was a very, very successful effort." Whether this was Brennan's attempt to put a happy face on a wrenching experience, or whether that is how he preferred to remember the case some eighteen months later, it is impossible to know.

On December 19, 1985, almost six months after the decision in *Greenmoss Builders* was announced, Burger wrote to the conference to explain that he was revising the last sentence of his own opinion to "accommodate a request of the estate of Roy Howard." Burger's opinion now concluded with the otherwise unattributed "aphorism of journalism that 'too much checking on the facts has ruined many a good news story.'" Apparently, Mr. Howard had never said any such thing. To the contrary, Howard *was* the author of the much quoted "Editor's Creed," taken from a letter he had written to a disgruntled reader of one of his newspapers in which he explained that journalism's mission is to "insure to readers the fullest possible access to the truth and the greatest possible divergency of viewpoint." It is not known whether the irony of the chief justice's publication of such a defamatory falsehood, which, as he put it, "in the exercise of reasonable care, would have been revealed as untrue," was ever called to his attention.

CHAPTER 8

THE LAST OF THE
BURGER COURT

The justices had barely had an opportunity to catch their collective breath following *Greenmoss Builders* when, early in the new term that commenced in October 1985, they heard arguments in two more defamation cases. Both cases required the justices to revisit the less-than-bright line that separates procedural rules surrounding the law of defamation, which do not implicate the First Amendment (like those before the Court in cases such as *Herbert*, *Keeton*, and *Calder*), and those that do (like the "clearly erroneous" evidentiary standard in *Bose*). For Brennan, the Court's deliberations and ultimate decisions in *Anderson v. Liberty Lobby, Inc.* and *Philadelphia Newspapers, Inc. v. Hepps*, which were argued together on December 3, 1985, would provide another opportunity to sort out his own, often conflicting views about the extent to which the protections for free expression he crafted in *Sullivan* required the support of procedural rules, also grounded in the First Amendment, to fulfill their constitutional mission. Perhaps more significantly, the cases offered Brennan an early indication of the extent to which, following *Greenmoss Builders*, *Sullivan* remained in jeopardy.

And, although he did not know it at the time, *Liberty Lobby* and *Hepps* would prove to be the last defamation cases considered on their merits by a Court presided over by Warren Burger, who would resign at the end of the term. His replacement as chief justice, William Rehnquist, had proven to be a persistent critic of *Sullivan*, and his elevation to the center chair created a vacancy that was filled by Antonin Scalia, who not only appeared to share Rehnquist's views with respect to *Sullivan* but, as fate would have it, had authored the D.C. Circuit's opinion in *Liberty*

Lobby reversing a trial court decision granting summary judgment to muckraker Jack Anderson.

Anderson v. Liberty Lobby, Inc.

In many ways, the *Liberty Lobby* case epitomized the kind of defamation litigation to which the institutional press had become increasingly subject in the years following *Gertz*. Like *Westmoreland* and *Sharon*, neither of which ever reached the Supreme Court, *Liberty Lobby* featured a well-funded public figure plaintiff (in this case a high-profile political organization and its controversial leader) who sought to embroil media defendants in extensive and costly pretrial discovery before they had an opportunity to argue to a court that their work was protected by the First Amendment as construed in *Sullivan*. Unlike *Westmoreland* and *Sharon*, however, the trial judge in *Liberty Lobby* had granted the defendants' motion for summary judgment, holding that the record evidence compiled largely through a voluminous affidavit submitted by the article's author, which described his news gathering and included the documents on which he relied as sources, could not lead a reasonable jury to find actual malice by the clear and convincing evidence required by *Sullivan*. As a result, at least at that juncture in the litigation, the defendants had been spared the burden and substantial expense of full-blown discovery and a jury trial. The trial court's decision, however, had been reversed on appeal, in an opinion authored by then-Judge Scalia, which relied, in significant part, on the intimations by Burger in *Hutchinson* that summary judgment of this sort was actually disfavored.

The case arose from an article in *The Investigator*, a magazine published by the well-known investigative columnist and self-described muckracker Jack Anderson. Anderson had learned his craft at the knee of Drew Pearson, the author of the column that led to *Monitor Patriot Co. v. Roy*, and had in fact succeeded Pearson as the author of his renowned "Washington Merry-Go-Round" column. The article at issue in *Liberty Lobby* reported on the activities of Liberty Lobby and its founder, Willis Carto, and related information that, if true, could lead a reader to conclude that they were neo-Nazis, fascists, anti-Semitic, and racist. The author, Charles Bermant, submitted a detailed affidavit in support of the defendants' motion for summary judgment, in which he explained that he had spent more than a month researching the article, that he had filed Freedom of Information Act requests with several government agencies as part of his research, that he had gathered and relied on a host of previously published material and other third-party documents about Liberty Lobby and Carto, and that he had conducted numerous interviews, all of which led him to believe that what he had reported was the truth. In the face of this showing, the trial judge granted the defendants' motion for summary judgment on the ground that the plaintiffs were both public figures and that the record evidence demonstrated that they could not prove actual malice by the necessary clear and convincing evidence.

The D.C. Circuit Court of Appeals, however, reversed the trial judge's decision. According to Scalia's opinion, the lower court had erred in purporting to apply *Sullivan*'s clear and convincing evidence standard at the summary judgment stage. In Scalia's view, to require clear and convincing evidence of actual malice to defeat a summary judgment motion "would change the summary judgment inquiry from a search for a minimum of facts supporting the plaintiff's case to an evaluation of the weight of those facts and (it would seem) of the weight of at least the defendant's uncontroverted facts as well." Applying what it deemed to be the appropriate standard, the court of appeals determined that, with respect to nine of the twenty-eight specific statements and two illustrations about which Liberty Lobby and Carto had complained, "a jury could reasonably conclude that [they] . . . were defamatory, false, and made with actual malice."

At argument before the Supreme Court, Anderson's counsel, Washington, D.C., litigator David Branson, invoked *Sullivan* at the outset, but took pains to limit his reliance on Brennan's opinion to its requirement that actual malice be proven by clear and convincing evidence. In the wake of *Herbert* and especially footnote 9 in *Hutchinson*, Branson did not suggest that the First Amendment independently required a preference for summary judgment in defamation cases. During his presentation, focused as it was on the requirements of Rule 56 of the Federal Rules of Civil Procedure (the rule authorizing federal courts to grant motions for summary judgment prior to trial), Branson received relatively few questions from the justices. And when he did receive one—such as how a trial court considering a summary judgment motion should sort out "a straight conflict between two sets of affidavits on a question of fact"—he was careful not to suggest any deviation from generally applicable procedural norms. Thus, in response to the inquiry about dueling affidavits, Branson said unequivocally that "the duty of the district court is to draw the inferences in favor of the person opposing the motion" and conceded that, if the question of fact was material, that meant the case "goes to trial." And, when pressed about the ongoing relevance of footnote 9 in the wake of *Bose*, Branson advanced the relatively modest proposition that the proper reading of the footnote "is that it calls for a neutral application of the summary [judgment] rules" that favors neither party in its application.

The limited reach of Branson's argument left his adversary, Mark Lane, a lawyer perhaps best known for his books and articles setting out a conspiracy theory explaining the assassination of President Kennedy, to argue largely that the record evidence did contain sufficient evidence for a reasonable jury to find actual malice, regardless of the burden of proof. At one point, Justice Stevens remarked that "as I listen to your argument, and listening to your opponent, you are in effect saying that the evidence already in the record is adequate to meet the clear and convincing standard." Lane did not disagree. And when Lane suggested that summary judgment should rarely be available because it did not afford a mechanism for assessing a live witness's credibility through the "crucible of cross-examination," he was obliged to concede, in response to a host of questions from a skeptical bench, that even if cross-examination would demonstrate that the witness was a "complete liar," it would not make a difference because "you assume that on summary judgment" in any event by requiring that "all the inferences [ ] be taken in favor of the nonmoving party."

In the course of Lane's argument, Justice White questioned him about the consequences of a decision adverse to his client. Specifically, White asked Lane whether he took the position that, if the court of appeals decision was reversed, "we shouldn't review these nine allegations . . . under the clear and convincing" standard. Ultimately, and somewhat surprisingly only after White pressed the point, did Lane agree with his suggestion that "if we disagree with you," the proper course would be to remand and "ask the Court of Appeals" to apply the proper standard. On rebuttal, Branson seized on White's questions and urged the Court to apply the "clear and convincing" standard to the record evidence itself and, hopefully, spare his clients the burden and expense of further litigation in the lower courts. When asked whether the Supreme Court had ever performed such an independent review in a case in which the lower court had simply not applied the correct standard, Branson pointed directly to *Sullivan*, which he correctly explained "was tried on the strict liability theory, and you applied the clear and convincing standard, the actual malice standard, and you made the assessment and did not send that case back to Alabama for a trial in the Alabama courts." This led Justice Rehnquist to conclude the argument by remarking:

> Well, what you say has some virtue, I suppose to say a particular standard should be applied for one court and tell another court to apply it can be a pretty abstract proposition. It may be better to have the court which is deciding which standard to apply to say what it means by applying the standard to the facts of that case.

At conference, as reflected in Brennan's notes, Burger began by posing the question before the Court, the oral argument notwithstanding, as whether, on summary judgment, "must we [apply the] 'clear and convincing' standard?" According to the chief justice, the answer was no. Then, as Brennan presaged in the typewritten statement he planned to read at conference, he agreed with Burger that "a plaintiff defeats a defendant's motion for summary judgment by producing some—i.e., any—evidence of every element which he must prove to win at trial." In Brennan's view, a plaintiff must only "make out a *prima facie* case with admissible evidence" and "is required to do no more." Thus, Brennan wrote:

> The judge does not weigh the evidence produced, for the simple reason that the factfinder is entitled to believe or disbelieve, credit or discredit the witnesses and the evidence as he sees fit. In other words, the jury may believe the admitted perjurer and disbelieve the 100 bishops. Since in my view of summary judgment the weight to be afforded the evidence is not material, the ultimate burden of proof is similarly irrelevant at that stage of the proceeding.

Nevertheless, Brennan emphasized that, if his "view of summary judgment" did not "command a Court—were we, in other words, to permit or require a judge to assess or weigh the evidence on motion for summary judgment—then, for the sake of consistency, I would think that we *would* require the ultimate burden of proof to be a part of that determination of whether a trial is necessary." In that event, Brennan explained, while he did "not think that the First Amendment should get 'special treatment' at the summary judgment phase," it "should also not be penalized." Accordingly, he said, "[i]f we 'put teeth' into summary judgment motions for the benefit of, *e.g.*, anti-trust defendants concerned with strike suits, we ought to let those teeth bite on behalf of the press as well." Finally, and in this last regard, Brennan sought to remind his colleagues that, in *Calder v. Jones*, "all nine of us joined in an opinion which suggested that to grant libel defendants special protections over and above the substantive protections provided by *New York Times, Inc. v. Sullivan, Gertz*, etc., would be a form of 'double counting,'" and, in so doing had "specifically referred to summary judgment, as we had in the *Hutchinson* footnote. I see no reason at this time to depart from that analysis."

It appears from Brennan's written statement, as well as from the dissenting opinion he ultimately wrote in *Liberty Lobby*, that he viewed the case through the prism of an injured plaintiff who, in attempting to secure justice from a well-financed corporate defendant, might be deprived of the ability to make his case to a jury if the court, as he described it, "put teeth" into the summary judgment standard. This apparently explains his express caveat that, if the court did not adopt his view, media defendants in defamation cases should receive the benefits as well as defendants in antitrust cases. It also bears emphasis that the *Liberty Lobby* case was one of three that the Court decided that same term addressing related issues, the net effect of which was to render summary judgment a more potent tool for the disposition of the entire range of civil cases in federal courts before trial. Brennan generally opposed that trend and, therefore, almost certainly viewed *Liberty Lobby* as a part of it.

Still, it is hard to understand why Brennan felt compelled to endorse *Keeton/ Calder* and the *Hutchinson* footnote, especially in the wake of his unpublished defense of *Sullivan* the previous term in *Greenmoss Builders*, in which he had specifically recognized the inhibiting effect on robust public debate occasioned by the high costs of defending defamation actions like *Westmoreland* and *Sharon*. In that regard, Brennan was undoubtedly aware of another contemporary and well-publicized side effect of the Court's pronouncements in *Herbert* and in footnote 9 with respect to the scope of discovery and the availability of summary adjudication in defamation actions—the phenomenon of well-funded and otherwise controversial groups, including the Synanon Church, the followers of perennial presidential candidate Lyndon LaRouche, and Liberty Lobby itself, filing and aggressively prosecuting defamation actions in response to published accounts of their activities in a manner that rendered reporting about their activities extremely burdensome and expensive, regardless of the ultimate merits of their claims. In a deposition in one of many such cases, this one brought by the Synanon Church against Anderson, his managing editor, Joseph Spear, testified that he and Anderson had declined to report on certain "litigious" persons and groups that "make it tremendously expensive just to print their names" because "it isn't worth the price you pay." When Synanon's counsel asked whether Spear had "ever heard that generally, that you should not do any more columns about a group that is more likely to sue?" the witness responded:

> Yes. Not just groups, individuals. In my function as editor for Mr. Anderson, I didn't mention a presidential candidate . . . during the whole election because . . . [he] is litigious. I call it censorship myself.
>
> Q. Do you believe that is bad journalism?
>
> A. No, I think it is bad law.

Despite all of this, Brennan was prepared to endorse the *Hutchinson* footnote at Conference. He explained to his biographer six months after the Supreme Court decided *Liberty Lobby* that his attitude about summary judgment was heavily influenced by an opinion he had written on the New Jersey Supreme Court in 1954. In a December 17, 1986 interview, Brennan recalled his opinion in *Judson v. Peoples Bank & Trust Co. of Westfield*, in which he emphasized that judges must be careful to limit their review on a motion for summary judgment to whether there are issues of material fact and must not decide those issues before the trier of fact gets the opportunity to assess the demeanor of witnesses. Referring to *Liberty Lobby*, Brennan said that "going back to *Judson* . . ., I couldn't take what I thought was a retreat not just from summary judgment in defamation cases but from summary judgment in general. . . . It was contrary to what I said in *Judson*, and I'm just getting too damned old to change my ways." *Judson*, he said, was one of the most widely cited opinions he wrote in New Jersey. This explanation of why Brennan felt so strongly about not tipping the summary judgment process too heavily in favor of defamation defendants is somewhat remarkable both because he described it from memory thirty-two years after the New Jersey ruling and because he never offered this explication publicly.

On this issue, at least, Brennan undoubtedly expected to draw the support of White in *Liberty Lobby*. But while White asserted at conference that he did "not see" the case as presenting a request for a "special rule for libel or First Amendment" litigation, he did advocate that the decision below be reversed. According to Brennan's notes, White recounted Scalia's concession below—that the "'clear and convincing' [standard] would apply on [a] motion for directed verdict"—and asserted that he "would do the same on summary judgment." In quick succession, Marshall and Blackmun, Brennan's typical allies in such matters, and Powell all agreed with White, the latter noting, as Brennan recorded it, that "in fraud cases, [the] clear and convincing [standard] is applied on summary" judgment as well. Rehnquist, however, agreed with Burger and Brennan, questioning, according to Brennan's notes, "what does 'clear and convincing' mean" and asserting that at the "directed verdict stage you know what [the] evidence is," at least a "lot more than" at summary judgment. Stevens lined up with White, but agreed with Rehnquist that he "can't think" the standard would "make that [much of a] difference." In his notes, Brennan recorded O'Connor as saying that she "agree[d] that [we] should have [the] same standard at [the] summary [judgment] and directed" verdict stages and that she would "therefore reverse." Brennan's notes reveal no discussion about whether the Court should or should not proceed to make an independent examination of the record evidence applying the appropriate standard.

Being the senior justice in the majority, White assigned the opinion to himself. Burger, in turn, asked Brennan if he "would be willing to take on a dissent?" Brennan, however, was having second thoughts. On December 23, he wrote to Burger, with a copy to Rehnquist, to advise them that, "[a]fter the Conference vote, I had concluded that I probably would not dissent in this case." He added that, although he would likely "be more certain of my ground after Byron circulates his proposed opinion for the Court, . . . the probabilities are that I would join it." It appears that this led Burger to turn to Rehnquist for a dissenting opinion.

White's draft opinion, which he circulated on February 25, 1986, began from the premise that, under Rule 56, "summary judgment will not lie if [a] dispute about a material fact is 'genuine,' that is, if the evidence is such that a reasonable jury could return a verdict for the nonmoving party." Thus, White wrote that, although "at the summary judgment stage the judge's function is not himself to weigh the evidence and determine the truth of the matter," the trial court is required to "to determine whether there is a genuine issue for trial." Put differently, the "inquiry performed is the threshold inquiry of determining whether there is the need for a trial—whether, in other words, there are any genuine factual issues that properly can be resolved only by a finder of fact because they may reasonably be resolved in favor of either party." For this reason, White asserted, "[W]e are convinced that the inquiry involved in a ruling on a motion for summary judgment . . . necessarily implicates the substantive evidentiary standard of proof that would apply at the trial on the merits." In resolving a summary judgment motion, White wrote,

> the judge must ask himself not whether he thinks the evidence unmistakably favors one side or the other but whether a fair-minded jury could return a verdict for the plaintiff on the evidence presented. The mere existence of a scintilla of evidence in support of the plaintiff's position will be insufficient; there must be evidence on which the jury could reasonably find for the plaintiff.

Turning specifically to "determining if a genuine factual issue as to actual malice exists in a libel suit brought by a public figure," White explained that "a trial judge must bear in mind the actual quantum and quality of proof necessary to support liability under *New York Times.*" In other words, "in ruling on a motion for summary judgment, the judge must view the evidence presented through the prism of the substantive evidentiary burden."

White's initial draft—as well as his ultimate opinion for the Court—are notable for the absence of any substantive discussion of the "double counting" principle he had championed in *Herbert* and that the Court had generally embraced in *Calder* and *Keeton.* Most significantly, in footnote 7 to his final opinion, White, speaking for the Court's majority, invoked *Calder* in what appeared to be an effort to back away from a broad reading of footnote 9 in *Hutchinson*—that summary judgment in defamation cases raising the issue of actual malice was in fact "disfavored"— which had led many lower courts to shy away from granting such motions at all. Specifically, after asserting in the text of his opinion that where a "factual dispute concerns actual malice, clearly a material issue in a *New York Times* case, the appropriate summary judgment question will be whether the evidence in the record could support a reasonable jury finding either that the plaintiff has shown actual malice by clear and convincing evidence or that the plaintiff has not," White wrote in his footnote that:

> Our statement in *Hutchinson v. Proxmire*, 443 U.S. 111, 120 n. 9, . . . that proof of actual malice "does not readily lend itself to summary disposition" was simply an acknowledgment of our general reluctance "to grant special procedural protection

to defendants in libel and defamation actions in addition to the constitutional protections embodied in the substantive laws." *Calder v. Jones*, 465 U.S. 783, 790–91, . . .

White's opinion, however, stopped short of applying the clear and convincing
standard to the record evidence, as Anderson's counsel had urged at argument.
Rather, it concluded with the assertion that "[b]ecause the Court of Appeals did
not apply the correct standard in reviewing the District Court's grant of summary
judgment, we vacate its decision and remand the case for further proceedings not
inconsistent with this opinion."

On February 26, having reviewed White's draft, Brennan wrote to him to say that
"I am attracted to your opinion," but that "since I voted the other way at Conference, I will await further writing before making up my mind." Shortly thereafter,
Rehnquist circulated a draft of what would become his dissent. In it, he rejected
the Court's characterization of the clear and convincing evidence requirement as
a "substantive standard" and asserted that "it is actually a procedural requirement
engrafted on to Rule 56, contrary to our statement in *Calder*" that the Court would
not "grant special procedural protections to defendants in libel and defamation
actions in addition to the constitutional protections embodied in the substantive
laws." That said, Rehnquist devoted the bulk of his critique to what he termed
the Court's unwarranted "concerns for intellectual tidiness" which, he contended,
manifested itself most prominently in its failure "to apply its newly announced
rule to the facts of this case." In Rehnquist's view:

> Instead of thus illustrating how the rule works, [the Court] contents itself with
> abstractions and paraphrases of abstractions, so that its opinion sounds much like a
> treatise about cooking by someone who has never cooked before and has no inten-
> tion of starting now.

Rehnquist predicted that, by creating "a standard that is different from the standard traditionally applied in summary judgment motions without even hinting as
to how its new standard will be applied to particular cases," the "primary effect
of the Court's opinion today will likely be to cause the decisions of trial judges
on summary judgment motions in libel cases to be more erratic and inconsistent
than before."

Ultimately, Brennan decided he could not join White's opinion, although he did not endorse Rehnquist's dissent either. Instead, Brennan crafted his own dissenting opinion, in which he explained his reasoning as follows:

> I simply cannot square the direction that the judge "is not himself to weigh the evidence" with the direction that the judge also bear in mind the "quantum" of proof required and consider whether the evidence is of sufficient "caliber or quantity" to meet that "quantum." I would have thought that a determination of the "caliber and quantity," *i.e.*, the importance and value, of the evidence in light of the "quantum," *i.e.*, amount "required," could *only* be performed by weighing the evidence.
>
> If, in fact, this is what the Court would, under today's decision, require of district courts, then I am fearful that this new rule—for this surely would be a brand new procedure—will transform what is meant to provide an expedited "summary" procedure into a full-blown paper trial on the merits. It is hard for me to imagine that a responsible counsel, aware that the judge will be assessing the "quantum" of the evidence he is presenting, will risk either moving for or responding to a summary judgment motion without coming forth with all of the evidence he can muster in support of his client's case. Moreover, if the judge on motion for summary judgment really is to weigh the evidence, then, in my view, grave concerns are raised concerning the constitutional right of civil litigants to a jury trial.

At the same time, Brennan was not pleased with Rehnquist's opinion, apparently in large part because of its reliance on *Calder*. In his own opinion, Brennan manifested what was apparently a change of heart on the subject, abandoning in substantial part his own reliance on *Calder* expressed in his preconference memorandum. Specifically, he wrote that he "simply do[es] not understand why JUSTICE REHNQUIST, dissenting, feels it appropriate to cite *Calder*, and to remind the Court that we have consistently refused to extend special procedural protections to defendants in libel and defamation suits. The Court today does nothing of the kind. It changes summary judgment procedure for all litigants, regardless of the substantive nature of the underlying litigation."

The Court's decision was announced on June 25, 1986. In the end, all of the justices, save Brennan, Burger, and Rehnquist, joined White's opinion. Only Burger joined Rehnquist's dissent, and Brennan wrote only for himself.

Despite both White's and Brennan's efforts to divorce the Court's decision in *Liberty Lobby* from the First Amendment protections afforded to defendants in defamation cases, and Rehnquist's prediction that White's opinion would lead to erratic results in future cases, in practice, defamation defendants have been particularly successful since *Liberty Lobby* in relying on the case to convince trial judges to pay particular attention to summary judgment motions in defamation litigation, especially in cases governed by the actual malice standard. Indeed, on June 24, the day before the decision in *Liberty Lobby* was announced, White wrote to his colleagues to discuss the proper disposition of *Synanon Church v. Reader's Digest*, another defamation case instituted by that frequent libel plaintiff that had been held for consideration pending the outcome of *Liberty Lobby*. In it, the California Supreme Court had ordered the entry of summary judgment in favor of *Reader's Digest*, which had published a critical account of the church, a drug rehabilitation enterprise turned religion, and its founder. As White noted in his memorandum, without further guidance from the justices, the California Supreme Court had attempted to come to grips with the significance of footnote 9 in *Hutchinson*, concluding that "[i]t is pointless to declare in the abstract that summary judgment is a favored or disfavored remedy. A more subtle analysis is required—one that explains how a motion for summary judgment should be decided in a defamation case under the *New York Times* test." According to White, the California Supreme Court had adopted "in essence the standard set forth in the Court's opinion in *Liberty Lobby*," which he described as a holding that "summary judgment was appropriate unless it appeared that actual malice could be proved at trial by clear and convincing evidence." Thus, White concluded, because "the standard adopted below is the standard the Court adopts in *Liberty Lobby*, and because the California Supreme Court recited the proper legal standards with respect to the other issues, I recommend that the petition be denied." The Court agreed and, as practitioners well know, the *Readers Digest* case and others coming to the same conclusion are now regularly cited for the proposition that, as a practical matter, there is indeed a preference for summary judgment in defamation actions instituted by public officials and public figures precisely because such a plaintiff bears the burden of proving actual malice by clear and convincing evidence.

Unfortunately for Anderson, the lower courts' post-*Liberty Lobby* affinity for summary judgment in actual malice cases did not extend to his own dispute with Carto and his organization. Following remand from the Supreme Court, the court of appeals (without Justice Scalia, who by this time had been confirmed to join the Court) similarly declined to apply the clear and convincing standard to the record evidence and instead sent the case back to the trial judge to reconsider his own previous decision granting summary judgment to the defendants under that same standard. This time around, however, a different judge construed the Supreme Court's decision as requiring that it withhold summary judgment as to two of the challenged statements, specifically "Allegation 19, 'the illustration suggesting that Carto emulated Hitler,' and Allegation 29, the assertion "'that Carto joined in the singing of Hitler's 'Horst Wessel Lied' and delivered a speech in an attempt to emulate Hitler's style and charisma." There ensued some five years of additional litigation, which cost Anderson a total of approximately $1 million in attorneys' fees. The case finally concluded when, on the eve of trial, the parties agreed to put down their swords. They made a joint $1,000 contribution to the Reporters Committee for Freedom of the Press and issued a joint statement, modeled no doubt on the similar device that had finally concluded the litigation hostilities between General Westmoreland and CBS some years earlier. In their joint agreement, Anderson and Carto acknowledged that they "have divergent views of the world," Anderson disclaimed any intention to communicate the defamatory "impression" about Carto's "personality" attributed to the article by the district court on remand, and Carto recognized Anderson's right, grounded in the First Amendment, "to express his views."

Philadelphia Newspapers, Inc. v. Hepps

Brennan left no written record explaining why in *Liberty Lobby*, after appearing to endorse in his preconference memorandum the Court's assertion in *Calder* that the First Amendment does not afford "procedural" protections to defendants in defamation actions beyond those provided by the "substantive" law, he ultimately not only declined to join Rehnquist's dissent, but appeared to go out of his way to criticize its reliance on *Calder* in his own. Perhaps a part of the explanation is *Philadelphia Newspapers, Inc. v. Hepps*, the case in which the Court heard argument immediately following *Liberty Lobby* on December 3, 1985.

Like *Liberty Lobby*, the *Hepps* case came to the justices from a lower court decision in favor of a defamation plaintiff. Unlike *Liberty Lobby*, the issue presented in *Hepps* had been before the Court previously, although the justices had been deprived of the opportunity to decide it two terms earlier when the parties in *Wilson v. Scripps-Howard Broadcasting* settled their dispute after the plaintiff's petition for review had been granted. In *Wilson*, the Sixth Circuit had held that, in a defamation action brought by a private person (i.e., not a public official or public figure) arising from speech about a matter of public concern, the First Amendment requires that the plaintiff bear the burden of proving falsity. In *Hepps*, the Pennsylvania Supreme Court rejected that contention. At common law and by state statute, the Pennsylvania court accurately explained, truth was an affirmative defense, and the burden of proving it rested on the defendant.

The case arose from a series of articles published in the *Philadelphia Inquirer* about Maurice Hepps, the principal shareholder of a company that operated a chain of Thrifty stores, which sold beer, soft drinks, and snacks. The articles, which were published periodically between May 1975 and May 1976, reported that Hepps and his company had ties to organized crime and had used those connections to influence governmental officials. Among other things, the articles reported about a state legislator, described as "a Pittsburgh Democrat and convicted felon," who had allegedly intervened with state government "on behalf of Hepps and Thrifty." In addition, the articles asserted that federal "investigators have found connections between Thrifty and underworld figures," that "the Thrifty Beverage chain ... had connections with ... organized crime," and that Thrifty had "won a series of competitive advantages through rulings by the State Liquor Control Board." According to the articles, a grand jury was investigating the "alleged relationship between the Thrifty chain and known Mafia figures."

At trial, Hepps testified at length that the articles' assertions that he and his company were connected to organized crime were false. The trial judge instructed the jury that, despite the Pennsylvania statutory rule to the contrary, the plaintiffs bore the burden of proving that the challenged statements were false. So instructed, the jury rendered a verdict for the newspaper and its reporters. On direct appeal from the jury's verdict, however, the Pennsylvania Supreme Court remanded the case for a new trial, holding that the trial judge should have placed the burden of proving truth on the defendants.

According to Brennan's notes, five justices voted to note probable jurisdiction in the ensuing appeal to the U.S. Supreme Court and a sixth, Marshall, voted to postpone that decision pending consideration of the merits of the appeal. Of that group of five, three—Powell, White, and O'Connor—had been in the working majority in *Greenmoss Builders*, while two others—Blackmun and Stevens—had joined Brennan's dissent. Brennan himself joined with Burger and Rehnquist in voting not to hear the case.

As noted, *Hepps* was argued on December 3, 1985, immediately following *Liberty Lobby*. During his argument, prominent Philadelphia lawyer David Marion, the newspaper's counsel, attempted to convince the Court that, although in some sense the burden of proof with respect to falsity was a "procedural" rule, it nevertheless "does rise to the constitutional level" because "falsity is the line that divides protected speech from unprotected speech." He was, however, interrupted by White, who challenged him to concede that he was asking the Court "to abrogate the common law" in an unprecedented manner by holding "that not only is truth a complete defense but the plaintiff must prove falsity. We haven't said that." When Marion attempted to suggest otherwise by citing to "Your Honor's statement in *Herbert v. Lando*," White interrupted again, as he was prone to do when advocates made the mistake of personalizing an opinion of the Court to the justice who authored it, to remind Marion that "that was a Court statement, counsel."

When Hepps's counsel, Ronald Surkin rose to argue, he was asked whether a public figure properly bears the burden of proving falsity. Surkin responded that such a plaintiff does "because in that case the issue of falsity is inextricably intertwined with the issue of actual malice." And, when asked about how "you can separate the two in a private case," he asserted that a jury could reasonably find "falsity but not negligence." The bulk of Surkin's argument, however, passed with no questions at all.

At the conference on December 6, the chief justice voted to affirm the Pennsylvania Supreme Court noting, according to Brennan's account of his comments, that *Gertz* "gives leeway to some of [the] common law," including "putting [the] burden of [proving] truth on [the] defendant." Brennan spoke next, arguing that the Pennsylvania Supreme Court's decision should be reversed. In his prepared remarks, he invoked Powell's reasoning in *Greenmoss Builders*, beginning his discussion by noting "there is no question that the contested statements were of significant public concern." Accordingly, Brennan said:

> If the Court were to affirm the Pennsylvania Supreme Court, it would approve a
> statutory scheme that permits the imposition of substantial liability on the press for

publishing some true statements and that doubtlessly deters the press from publishing other true statements, the truth of which may be difficult to prove in court.

In my view, the Constitution mandates that the burden of proving the truth or
falsity of a defamatory statement be allocated in a way that minimizes the risk that
truthful speech regarding matters of public concern will be penalized or chilled.
That means that the plaintiff must be required to prove falsity. The common-law
rule, codified by the State of Pennsylvania, is constitutionally unacceptable because
it causes close cases to be resolved in favor of the falsity of the statement. It thus
must result in the penalization of some true speech and certainly must deter far more.

White, not surprisingly, agreed with Burger, asserting (according to Brennan's
account) that *Gertz* "didn't require this," but only "that fault be proved." After
Marshall initially passed, and Blackmun agreed with Brennan, Powell offered what
sounded to Brennan like another expression of regret about the reach of his opinion in *Gertz*. According to Brennan's notes, Powell said he was "not sure" *Gertz*
was "my best." (Blackmun's notes similarly recount Powell as confessing that his
"*Gertz* opinion is too long.") Nevertheless, Powell continued, the "common law
rule of burden of [proving] truth on defendant *was* changed by [*New York*] *Times* for
public official[s]. In private figure cases, *Gertz* said [plaintiff] must prove fault—that
includes I think proof of falsity of [the] libel as part of negligence proof." Rehnquist
then expressed his agreement with Burger and White, leaving the floor to Stevens
who, despite his allegiance to Brennan in *Greenmoss Builders* and his own opinion
for the Court in *Bose*, sided with Burger as well. In Stevens's view, as recounted in
Brennan's notes, "*Gertz* didn't decide that proof of fault requires proof of falsity"
and "didn't . . . require [a] private plaintiff to do that." Blackmun's notes too reflect
that Stevens deemed *Hepps* to be a "hard case," one that Powell's opinion in *Gertz*
"did not decide." At this point, attention turned to O'Connor who, asserting that
it would be "exceedingly difficult" for a defamation plaintiff "to prove a negative,"
sided with Burger as well, albeit "very tentatively," giving him a majority. Finally,
Marshall voted to reverse on the ground, according to Blackmun's notes of the
Conference, that "*Gertz* controls."

Burger promptly assigned the majority opinion to O'Connor, no doubt in
an effort to solidify her "very tentative" vote in his favor. Brennan, meanwhile,
assigned the dissenting opinion to Blackmun. There matters stood until well into

the following year when, on February 18, 1986, O'Connor wrote to Burger, with a copy to the other justices:

> At conference on this case I explained that my vote to affirm was very tentative. You assigned the case to me to write. I have reluctantly concluded that the better view is that, in a libel case such as this against a media defendant and involving matters of public concern, the plaintiff is required to prove not only fault but also falsity. This means I am now persuaded the judgment below should be reversed. Unfortunately, the change will necessitate a reassignment of the case as the vote was 5 to 4. I am distressed to be the cause of such a change and can only offer my apologies to all.

On receiving this news, Brennan wasted little time, writing to Burger that afternoon to confirm that, in "light of Sandra's change of vote" the task of assigning the majority opinion now fell to him. As he reminded the chief, "Thurgood, Harry, Lewis and I voted to reverse at Conference and now Sandra makes the fifth." Burger responded promptly, asking Brennan to "take over the assignment in this case."

At this point, according to his term history, Brennan "moved quickly to 'reward'" O'Connor for her change of heart "with the re-assignment of the opinion." For her part, Brennan recounted, O'Connor "reportedly was surprised by and delighted with the assignment, observing that it was by far the best case she had received all Term." Thus, with a measure of satisfaction, Brennan wrote to Burger on the following day, February 19, and advised him that "Sandra will try her hand at an opinion for the Court, reversing the judgment of the Third Circuit" (Brennan had apparently forgotten that the decision below had in fact been rendered by the Pennsylvania Supreme Court).

O'Connor circulated her draft opinion in mid-March and Powell promptly joined it on March 20. In it, she relied heavily on *Sullivan* itself, including its oft-quoted observation that "[a] rule compelling the critic of official conduct to guarantee the truth of all his factual assertions—and to do so on pain of libel judgments virtually unlimited in amount—leads to . . . 'self-censorship'" and that such a rule threatened to deter would-be speakers "from voicing their criticism, even though it is believed to be true and even though it is in fact true, because of doubt whether it can be proved in court or fear of the expense of having to do so." After tracing the Court's expansion of that principle through *Gertz* and then to *Greenmoss Builders*, she asserted that the justices had already held in *Garrison v.*

Louisiana, "as one might expect given the language of the Court in *New York Times*" she had quoted at the outset, that "a public-figure plaintiff must show the falsity of the statements at issue in order to prevail in a suit for defamation." And, she wrote, "[w]e believe that the common law's rule on falsity—that the defendant must bear the burden of proving truth—must similarly fall here to a constitutional require-ment that the plaintiff bear the burden of showing falsity, as well as fault, before recovering damages." As O'Connor explained:

> There will always be instances when the factfinding process will be unable to resolve conclusively whether the speech is true or false; it is in those cases that the burden of proof is dispositive. Under a ruling forcing the plaintiff to bear the burden of showing falsity, there will be some cases in which plaintiffs cannot meet their burden despite the fact that the speech is in fact false. The plaintiff's suit will fail despite the fact that, in some abstract sense, the suit is meritorious. Similarly, under an alterna-tive rule placing the burden of showing truth on defendants, there would be some in which defendants could not bear their burden despite the fact that the speech is in fact true. Those suits would succeed despite the fact that, in some abstract sense, those suits are unmeritorious. Under either rule, then, the outcome of the suit will sometimes be at variance with the outcome that we would desire if all speech were either demonstrably true or demonstrably false.

"Where the scales are in such an uncertain balance," O'Connor concluded, "the Constitution requires us to tip them in favor of protecting true speech." Echoing Brennan's language in *Sullivan*, she wrote that, "[t]o ensure that true speech on mat-ters of public concern is not deterred, we hold that the common-law presumption that defamatory speech is false cannot stand when a plaintiff seeks damages against a media defendant for speech of public concern." Curiously, both in this passage and in another summarizing the Court's holding, O'Connor limited its reach to cases involving "media defendants." Not even a year removed from its ultimate decision in *Greenmoss Builders*, she added a footnote to her opinion (footnote 4) emphasizing that the Court need not "consider what standards would apply if the plaintiff sues a nonmedia defendant."

A week after O'Connor circulated her draft, Stevens advised the conference that he would be submitting a dissent. That opinion, which was ultimately joined by Burger, Rehnquist, and White, manifested an almost palpable sense of outrage at O'Connor's analysis that appeared out of character for a justice who had not only written the Court's decision in *Bose* but had stood by and counseled Brennan in *Greenmoss Builders*. Stevens wrote that he could "not agree that our precedents require a private individual to bear the risk that a defamatory statement—uttered either with a mind toward assassinating his good name or with careless indifference to that possibility—cannot be proven false. By attaching no weight to the State's interest in protecting the private individual's good name, the Court has reached a pernicious result." As Stevens elsewhere put it, "deliberate malicious character assassination is not protected by the First Amendment. . . . That Amendment does require the target of a defamatory statement to prove that his assailant was at fault, and I agree that it provides a constitutional shield for truthful statements. I simply do not understand, however, why a character assassin should be given an absolute license to defame by means of statements that can neither be verified nor disproven." Indeed, in a footnote, Stevens went so far as to assert that, if "the issue were properly before us," he would not place the burden of proving truth on a public figure plaintiff either, suggesting that the Court's "contrary remarks" in cases like *Garrison* "were not necessary to the decisions in those cases."

On March 28, Brennan joined O'Connor's opinion, but also offered a one-paragraph concurrence in which, in the wake of *Greenmoss Builders*, he felt compelled to speak to O'Connor's apparent reliance on the fact that the defendant in *Hepps* was a newspaper:

> I write separately only to note that, while the Court reserves the question whether the rule it announces applies to non-media defendants, . . . I adhere to my view that such a distinction is "irreconcilable with the fundamental First Amendment principle that '[t]he inherent worth of . . . speech in terms of its capacity for informing the public does not depend upon the identity of the source, whether corporation, association, union, or individual.'" *Dun & Bradstreet, Inc. v. Greenmoss Builders, Inc.*

On April 7, Marshall told O'Connor that he would join her opinion without reservation. That same day, Blackmun announced that he would join Brennan's concurring opinion. In addition, he told O'Connor that he would also join her opinion, but added that "I would feel easier if you would see fit to drop footnote 4 on page 12" (in which she purported to reserve the issue of whether a plaintiff suing a nonmedia defendant would bear the burden of proving falsity), although his "joinder is not conditioned on this." O'Connor responded that same day, advising Blackmun that she "prefer[red] to keep footnote 4, at least for the present."

In the end, O'Connor retained the footnote. When the Court announced its decision on April 21, 1986, Brennan, Blackmun, Marshall, and Powell joined her opinion for the court, subject only to Brennan's brief concurring opinion, which was endorsed by Blackmun. Thus, by a vote of five to four, the Court had resolved the issue first raised two terms earlier in *Wilson*, when O'Connor was so new to the Court that the media defendant in that case apparently settled it rather than risk jeopardizing the constitutional principle on which it was based. And the Court had done so in an opinion by O'Connor herself, who, having first voted to affirm the Pennsylvania Supreme Court's contrary decision at conference, not only changed her mind but was tapped by Brennan to memorialize the Court's holding and reasoning. One can legitimately question whether she would have revisited her initial instinct if the issue had actually come before the Court in *Wilson*.

THE END OF THE ROAD

In 1986, William Rehnquist became the Court's 16th chief justice. The 1986–87
term, the first under the new chief, looked as though it would pass without the
Court considering on its merits any cases involving the constitutional law of defamation. There was, therefore, at least some reason to believe that, following the
justices' protracted inability to come to agreement on issues large and small in
Greenmoss Builders, and the narrow majority by which it had decided *Hepps*, the
"Rehnquist Court," which included not only the new chief justice but also the
newly appointed Justice Scalia, had decided to leave further development of the
constitutional law of defamation and related claims to the lower courts, at least for
a time. Among other notable cases in which the Supreme Court denied petitions
for review during this period was *Tavoulareas v. Piro*, in which a deeply divided
United States Court of Appeals for the District of Columbia Circuit had produced
an unusual, coauthored majority opinion (by Judges J. Skelly Wright and Kenneth
Starr). In that opinion, the court affirmed a trial judge's decision to render judgment in favor of the *Washington Post* in the face of a multimillion dollar jury verdict
against the newspaper in a defamation action prosecuted against it by William
Tavoulareas, the then-President of the Mobil Oil Corporation, and his son Peter.

Near the end of the 1986–87 term, however, the Court granted a petition for
review in *Hustler Magazine, Inc. v. Falwell*. That, it turned out, was only the beginning. In all, the Court would ultimately decide four defamation-related cases in
the three terms that followed, including not only *Falwell*, but also *Harte-Hanks
Communications, Inc, v. Connaughton, Florida Star v. B.J.F.*, and *Milkovich v. Lorain Journal Co*. In both the first and the last of them—*Falwell* and *Milkovich*—the Court's
opinion would be written by the new chief justice, a fact that, standing alone, did

not bode well for the ongoing vitality or even the viability of *Sullivan*. Rehnquist, after all, had authored the Court's opinions in both *Firestone* and *Wolston*, in which he had construed Justice Powell's less than precise language in *Gertz* in a manner that Brennan, with ample reason, viewed as significantly narrowing the scope of substantive protection afforded by *Sullivan*. In addition, Rehnquist had not only joined Powell's plurality in *Greenmoss Builders*, he had dissented in every defamation decision on which he had sat in which the defendant had prevailed including, most recently, *Hepps*, *Liberty Lobby*, and *Bose*.

That Rehnquist was apparently prepared to assume a leadership role in formulating First Amendment jurisprudence in this context would come to assume especial significance because, at the same time, Brennan himself was nearing the end of his tenure on the Court. Although no one, including Brennan himself, knew this when Rehnquist became chief justice in 1986, Brennan would serve on the "Rehnquist Court" for only four terms. As a result, the decision that Rehnquist announced for the Court in *Milkovich* on June 21, 1990, was the last of *Sullivan*'s progeny in which Brennan would cast a vote. That his vote was in dissent, however, tells only part of the story of Brennan's ongoing role in preserving the legacy of *Sullivan* itself.

Hustler Magazine, Inc. v. Falwell

In *Falwell*, the United States Court of Appeals for the Fourth Circuit had divided evenly and, over a passionate dissent from Judge J. Harvie Wilkinson, had affirmed a trial verdict and damages award for the tort of "intentional infliction of emotional distress" in favor of the Reverend Jerry Falwell against *Hustler* magazine and its publisher, Larry Flynt. Needless to say, neither Flynt nor his magazine were strangers to the Court, and his remonstrations both before and during its consideration of the *Keeton* case no doubt remained fresh in at least some of the justices' minds. For his part, Falwell was at least equally prominent, a fixture on television and in the media generally as the leader of and spokesperson for the "Moral Majority," a groundbreaking political movement that sought to organize and bring to bear on the political process the faith-based views of fundamentalist Christians.

The case itself arose from an advertising parody published in *Hustler* in which Falwell was depicted as describing his first sexual experience as having been with his own mother in an outhouse. The "advertisement" was based on a then-popular marketing campaign by the makers of Campari Liqueur, in which various celebrities were depicted describing their "first time" which, despite the provocative double entendre, ultimately was revealed by the advertisement to be their initial encounter with the beverage. In the *Hustler* parody, a putative interview with Falwell revealed him and his mother, as the court ultimately described them, "as drunk and immoral" and arguably suggested that Falwell "is a hypocrite who preaches only when he is drunk." In small print, at the bottom of the page, *Hustler* included the disclaimer, "ad parody—not to be taken seriously," and the magazine's table of contents identified it as "Fiction; Ad and Personality Parody."

Falwell instituted a civil action against Hustler and Flynt in federal court in Virginia, in which he asserted claims for both defamation and the intentional infliction of emotional distress. A jury found in favor of the defendants on Falwell's defamation claim because the parody did not contain a false statement of fact, specifically concluding that it could not "reasonably be understood as describing actual facts about [Falwell] or actual events in which [he] participated." It nevertheless proceeded to award $100,000 in compensatory and $50,000 in punitive damages against each of the defendants on Falwell's alternative claim for intentional infliction. As noted, after a three-judge panel of the Fourth Circuit affirmed the jury's verdict, the entire court of appeals divided evenly on whether to rehear the case. When Hustler and Flynt then sought review in the Supreme Court, Brennan, White, Blackmun, Powell, and Stevens voted to grant their petition. By the time the case was argued the following term, however, Powell had retired and the arduous process of confirming his replacement (Justice Kennedy was confirmed only after the Senate had rejected the nomination of Judge Robert Bork and the nomination of Judge Douglas Ginsburg had been withdrawn) had not yet run its course. Thus, the Court that considered the *Falwell* case during the 1987–88 term was comprised of only eight justices.

The case was scheduled for argument on December 2, 1987. In advance of it, the justices received a host of *amicus* submissions, but one, filed on behalf of the Association of American Editorial Cartoonists, appeared to have been particularly effective. It included an appendix containing examples of the kinds of cartoons that, throughout history, had almost certainly inflicted emotional distress on the public officials and figures depicted in them. Blackmun's clerk "particularly" called his justice's "attention to the cartoons," they were discussed at the argument itself, and they featured prominently in Rehnquist's ultimate opinion for the Court.

As it turned out, the argument raised other issues for the justices. Plainly mindful of Flynt's outburst during the argument in *Keeton*, his new attorney in the *Falwell* case notified Alfred Wong, the Court's Marshal, that Flynt "requested to be present during the argument." According to the Marshal, "Mr. Flynt advised that he would withdraw his request if the Marshal disapproved." In a memorandum to Rehnquist the day before the scheduled argument, Wong told the chief justice that "inquiries" had been made and he had "found that none of the cases in which Mr. Flynt was a defendant required as a term of probation, that he not visit a Federal Court." Accordingly, Wong wrote, "it was decided that Mr. Flynt had the same rights as any other person to hear oral argument as a spectator" and his counsel "was so informed. It was agreed that there would be no bodyguards accompanying Mr. Flynt and that one attendant would be permitted in order to assist Mr. Flynt with his wheelchair." The Marshal closed his memorandum by noting, "[a]s a matter of information, the Rev. Jerry Falwell and his family are guests of the respondent's attorney for the oral argument."

The argument itself proceeded without incident, at least from Flynt. This time, Hustler and its publisher were represented by their chosen counsel, Alan Isaacman of Los Angeles. Falwell was represented by Norman Roy Grutman, the same lawyer who had argued on behalf of Kathy Keeton in her case against Flynt. Not surprisingly, Isaacman premised his argument on the contention that the advertisement before the Court was a parody and that the jury had expressly found that it could not reasonably be construed as a statement of fact. When Justice O'Connor asked if this would be a "different case if the jury had found that the allegations could be considered factual," Isaacman agreed, leading O'Connor to ask whether, under *Bose*, the Court could or should independently review the jury's conclusion in that regard. When Isaacman responded that the Court was bound by the jury's finding, Rehnquist characterized his argument as a contention that "*Bose* is a one way street."

Isaacman also placed considerable reliance on the Court's decision in *Garrison*, in which, among other things, Brennan had emphasized that the subjective state of mind that *Sullivan* required to ground a finding of actual malice was an "intent to cause harm through knowing falsehood or reckless falsehood," not an intent to harm or "ill will" more generally. Justice Scalia challenged Isaacman's premise, asserting that "all *New York Times* says is if you state falsehood with knowledge of the falsehood [and] intent to be false, the First Amendment does not prevent" a successful defamation action. Justice Scalia continued, "[a]ll I'm asking you is why can't that principle be extended to say you can cause emotional harm to your heart's content, just as you can state falsity to your heart's content, but where you intend to create that emotional harm, we have a different situation." When Isaacman resisted, and in fact asserted that no "reasonable reader of any of the speech that has occurred in the cases including *New York Times v. Sullivan, Garrison* and all the other cases that have come down . . . could ever say that the speaker did not intend to cause harm," Scalia conceded that, while "[t]hat may well be," his point was simply that *Sullivan* "doesn't speak to" the issue now before the Court; in Scalia's view, *Sullivan* "says intent is okay, is enough to get you out of" the realm of First Amendment protection.

At that juncture, Justice Stevens also questioned whether *Sullivan* "speaks to the problem we have before us in this case," which he described as "pretty much the same thing Justice Scalia" had suggested. With this, Isaacman reiterated his reliance on the absence of a false statement of fact in the parody before the Court, which prompted O'Connor to repeat her contention that "that gets us back to *Bose* and whether we have to reexamine this statement for ourselves to determine whether it is a factual statement." This time, she added that she did not think that the Court had ever decided the issue of whether the requirement of independent review was in fact a "one-way street" and suggested that Isaacman was "asking us to move on to another step beyond" the decision in *Bose.*

Perhaps the most intriguing portion of Isaacman's argument came when Scalia renewed his own line of questioning, this time asserting, "Mr. Isaacman, to contradict Vince Lombardi, the First Amendment is not everything. It's a very important value, but it's not the only value in our society, certainly. You're giving us no help in trying to balance it, it seems to me, against another value, which is that good people should be able to enter public life and public service. The rule you give us says that if you stand for public office, or become a public figure in any way, you cannot protect yourself, or indeed your mother, against a parody of your committing incest with your mother in an outhouse." He then asked Isaacman whether "George Washington would have stood for public office if that was the consequence?" When Isaacman, relying on the *amicus* brief submitted by the cartoonists, reminded Scalia of contemporary drawings depicting the first president "being led on a donkey and underneath there's a caption" describing him as an "ass," Scalia responded, "I can handle that. I think George could handle that. But that's a far cry from committing incest with your mother in an outhouse. I mean, there's no line between the two?"

The justices' questions were equally probing when Grutman rose to present his argument on behalf of Falwell. O'Connor raised the example of then-recently published photographs of presidential candidate Gary Hart apparently cavorting on a boat aptly named "Monkey Business" with a woman other than his wife and asked Grutman whether Hart would have a claim for emotional distress, even though the photographs were accurate in all respects. Grutman responded that yes, indeed, "under the theory of the intentional infliction of emotional distress, even the truth can be used in such a way if it is used in some outrageous way." Later in his argument, O'Connor deflected Grutman's descriptions of the malicious intent with which Flynt had published the Falwell cartoon, reminding him that although "there's plenty of malice here all right, . . . I don't think that's your problem. . . . [T]he jury said this can't be reasonably viewed as making a factual allegation." And Scalia, who had jousted with Isaacman about the cartoon depicting Washington and the donkey, told Grutman that, although "you've given us a lot of words to describe" the kind of expression that could give rise to liability for intentional infliction—including "outrageous, heinous, repulsive and loathsome"—"maybe you haven't looked at the same political cartoons that I have, but some of them, and a long tradition of this, not just in this country but back from English history, I mean, politicians depicted as horrible looking beasts. . . .You talk about portraying someone as committing some immoral act. I would be very surprised if there were not a number of cartoons depicting one or another political figure as at least the piano player in a bordello." To this, Grutman could respond only that, "Justice Scalia, we don't shoot the piano player. I understand that." At that juncture, Scalia turned serious, asking Grutman for "something that the cartoonist or the political figure can adhere to, other than such general words as heinous and what not. I mean, does it depend on how ugly the beast is, or what?" Grutman's substantive response, which came only after a quip about measuring "the amount of hair the beast has or how long his claws may be," was that the courts must rely on "an evolving social sensibility" in resolving such issues.

Toward the end of his argument, Grutman made the error (just as David Marion had in *Hepps*) of referring in passing to "Mr. Justice Powell's decision in *Gertz*," which led Justice White to admonish the advocate that "lawyers always personalize these opinions and they are Court opinions." After Grutman quickly apologized "to the other members of the Court [to] whom I meant no slight," and White acknowledged that "of course, I was in dissent," Grutman added that "in my view, Mr. Justice White, that dissent either is or may become, or should become the law of the land." To this, White responded tersely, "I doubt it."

Despite the close questioning of both advocates at argument, at the conference that followed, the Court was unanimous in its conclusion that the judgment for Falwell should be reversed. The new chief justice began the discussion, according to Brennan's notes, by emphasizing that Falwell was a public figure and that Hustler "intended to inflict emotional distress." As both Brennan's and Blackmun's notes of the conference reflect, moreover, Rehnquist said he saw *Sullivan* as of "only tangential" relevance. In Rehnquist's view, the jury had found that this was a "parody" that had made "no factual assertion" and "therefore" resulted in "no damage" because the "First Amendment protects cartoon[s] and parody."

Brennan's prepared statement, on which he had come increasingly to rely when speaking in conference, indicates that, although he agreed with Rehnquist about the proper result and with much of his reasoning, he differed in one significant respect. As he wrote at the time:

> [T]his case is squarely controlled by *New York Times v. Sullivan*. The point of *New York Times* is that since *false* speech has little value, we will permit libel suits to proceed, but only when the plaintiff can demonstrate that the false speech was made with "actual malice." The speech in question here could not have reasonably been understood to constitute a statement of fact. There is an unappealed jury finding holding as much. The advertisement at issue was, at worst, tasteless hyperbole. I would nevertheless find it protected by the First Amendment. If we allow this suit to proceed, I fear that every political cartoon and every parody could be scrutinized by a jury for a determination of the motive behind it. The chilling effect would be intolerable.

As had by this time become somewhat routine, White was not moved by Brennan's analysis. He began his comments at conference, according to Brennan's and Blackmun's notes, by asserting that *Sullivan* "has nothing to do with" this case which was "not a libel case." For White, the "issue is whether these statements are actionable" and, he argued, "this is so false that no one would believe" it which, presumably, rendered it incapable of causing legally cognizable injury. According to Brennan's notes, Marshall indicated that he too would reverse "subject to what my research on libel precedents produces" while Blackmun said that, although the case involved "offensive writing that makes one gag," it was not unlike "some outrageous cartoons in our past." Stevens, again according to both Brennan's and Blackmun's notes, agreed with Rehnquist and White that "*Sullivan* doesn't speak to this issue." O'Connor then sided with Brennan, asserting, as Brennan noted it, that "what *Sullivan* requires also applies to this tort." According to O'Connor, "if there was proof of falsity, we'd have [a] different case." Finally, Scalia, the newest justice, suggested that the Court "write very narrowly" and emphasize that "*Sullivan's* line between true and false facts [is] important."

Rehnquist assigned the opinion to himself and circulated a draft of it toward the end of January 1988. As the final version indicates, it relied—despite his comments at the conference—largely on *Sullivan* and expressly reaffirmed both it and its reasoning. Indeed, Rehnquist's opinion began its substantive analysis from *Sullivan's* premise that the "sort of robust political debate encouraged by the First Amendment is bound to produce speech that is critical of those who hold public office or those public figures who are 'intimately involved in the resolution of important public questions or, by reason of their fame, shape events in areas of concern to society at large.'" Then, quoting one of Brennan's most memorable passages in *Sullivan* itself, the chief justice explained that "[s]uch criticism, inevitably will not always be reasoned or moderate; pubic figures as well as public officials will be subject to 'vehement, caustic, and sometimes unpleasantly sharp attacks.'" As a result, Rehnquist continued, the Court in *Hepps* had reiterated both that "'[f]reedoms of expression require 'breathing space,'" and that such protection "is provided by a constitutional rule that allows public figures to recover for defamation only when they can prove *both* that the statement was false and that the statement was made with the requisite level of culpability."

Turning to the heart of the matter, Rehnquist's opinion flatly rejected Grutman's contention that "outrageous" expression should be exempt from these constitutional limitations and reaffirmed the essential holding of Brennan's opinion for the Court in *Garrison* that "in the world of debate about public affairs, many things done with motives that are less than admirable are protected by the First Amendment." Drawing on the illustrations depicted in the cartoonists' *amicus* brief, Rehnquist asserted that, "[w]ere we to hold otherwise, there can be little doubt that political

cartoonists and satirists would be subjected to damage awards without any showing that their work falsely defamed its subject."Thus, although there could be "no
doubt that the caricature" of Falwell "and his mother published in Hustler is at
best a distant cousin of the political cartoons" submitted by the *amici*, "and a rather
poor relation at that," the Court was "quite sure that the pejorative description
'outrageous' does not supply" what Rehnquist described as a "principled standard
to separate the one from the other." Accordingly, Rehnquist's opinion concluded,
"public figures and public officials may not recover for the tort of intentional infliction of emotional distress by reason of publications such as the one at issue here
without showing . . . that the publication contains a false statement of fact which
was made with 'actual malice'" as defined in *Sullivan* itself. For Rehnquist, such a
holding was "not merely a 'blind application'" of *Sullivan*, but rather "reflects our
considered judgment that such a standard is necessary to give adequate 'breathing
space' to the freedoms protected by the First Amendment."

As a practical matter, Rehnquist's opinion accomplished everything that Brennan had hoped to achieve in the unpublished defense of *Sullivan* he had prepared
in response to White's attack in *Greenmoss Builders*. On January 22, O'Connor
and Stevens (who had both urged Brennan not to include a defense of *Sullivan* in
his dissenting opinion in *Greenmoss* and had joined Rehnquist at conference in
rebutting the notion that it controlled the disposition in *Falwell*) promptly joined
Rehnquist's opinion without further comment or suggestion. On January 25,
Marshall, Scalia, and Blackmun joined as well. That same day, Brennan wrote to
Rehnquist to announce that he would "enthusiastically join your splendid opinion."

Brennan did, however, offer "one suggestion," but emphasized that "[w]hether
or not you accept it, my join stands." Brennan was concerned about a passage in
Rehnquist's draft explaining that, while "bad motive may be deemed controlling
for purposes of tort liability in dealings between one private individual and another,
we think the First Amendment prohibits such a result in the area of public debate."
As he explained it to Rehnquist, Brennan feared it might "be read as suggesting
that bad motive can be a ground for recovery in speech directed against private
individuals." Accordingly, Brennan suggested that such an "inference" might "be
avoided if the sentence were worded something like the following: 'Thus, at least
in the area of public debate, we think the First Amendment prohibits the imposition of tort liability on the basis of the speaker's bad motive.'"

Rehnquist responded the next day and pronounced himself "perfectly willing to try to rephrase." As an alternative to Brennan's formulation, he proposed
changing the sentence to read, "Thus, while such a bad motive may be deemed
controlling for purposes of tort liability in other areas of the law, we think the
First Amendment prohibits such a result when we deal with public debate about
public figures." That same day, Brennan informed Rehnquist that his "suggested
revision in lieu of my proposal is entirely agreeable. Thank you very much for
considering my suggestion."

The following day, January 27, White effectively conceded defeat on the *Sullivan* issue, submitting a one-paragraph opinion concurring in the judgment. It read,
in its entirety, "As I see it, the decision in *New York Times v. Sullivan*, . . . has little
to do with this case, for here the jury found that the ad contained no assertion of
fact. But I agree with the Court that the judgment below, which penalized the
publication of the parody, cannot be squared with the First Amendment."

Brennan, when asked later to reflect on whether Rehnquist was generally his
most frequent antagonist on the Court, told his biographer that he once was, "but
after *Falwell* and those, he's certainly taken a big leap my way, I must say. When I say
'my way,' I mean points of view that I've held. God, what he's done with *New York
Times* and *Sullivan*, you of the press ought just to kiss him." In an interview conducted on March 8, 1988, Brennan referred to the *Falwell* outcome as "remarkable,"
and said of Rehnquist, "now he wipes away with one opinion all the reasons for
concern that so many people have had . . . about *New York Times* and *Sullivan*. . . ."

Harte-Hanks Communications, Inc. v. Connaughton

When the Court completed its work for the 1987–88 term, it had granted review
in no defamation cases to be heard the following fall. Thus, as the justices recon-
vened after their summer recess, it appeared that no such case would be heard
that term. At its September 26 conference, however, the Court was scheduled to
take up *Harte-Hanks Communications, Inc. v. Connaughton*, a defamation action in
which the United States Court of Appeals for the Sixth Circuit, in a 2–1 decision,
had affirmed a jury verdict of $200,000 against a community newspaper in favor
of Connaughton, a candidate for the office of Municipal Judge in rural Ohio. In
so doing, the Sixth Circuit majority appeared to part company with several other

federal courts, including the D.C. Circuit in *Tavoulareas*, with respect to the scope
of the "independent" appellate review of a finding of actual malice mandated by
Sullivan and reaffirmed in *Bose*.

Specifically, in affirming the jury's verdict, the Sixth Circuit majority in *Connaughton* considered itself bound by a host of inferences it determined the jury
"could have" drawn from the record evidence. Cumulating those multiple inferences,
and performing what it described as the required "independent review" only of
them, the court determined that Connaughton had proven actual malice by the
requisite clear and convincing evidence.

Despite the apparent conflict in the circuit courts, and a "*cert* pool" memorandum recommending that the Court take the case, the justices' initial inclination
was to deny review. Nevertheless, Anthony Kennedy, the Court's newest justice,
requested that it be relisted. On October 6, however, Kennedy apparently had a
change of heart and wrote his fellow justices to say that, although the case "presents a close issue," he too would vote to deny review. Five days later, on October
11, Justice White circulated a dissent from what he understood would be the
Court's decision to do so. In it, White observed that, since *Bose*, "appellate courts
have struggled to discover the breadth and meaning of the *Bose* requirement of
de novo fact review. The Sixth Circuit decision in this case, limiting its appellate
review to the jury's ultimate finding of actual malice, is a narrower standard of
review than that adopted by some federal courts and represents one point on a
spectrum of approaches." After reviewing the apparent disarray in the lower courts,
White asserted that the "scope of appellate review required by the Constitution
in libel suits is a potential issue in practically every libel suit, of which there are a
great number in federal and state courts." Accordingly, White concluded, "the difference of opinion ... is unlikely to disappear without guidance from the Court."

White's dissent convinced Blackmun, who indicated his agreement that the
Court should take the case the next day. After it was relisted yet again, Brennan
and Marshall joined with White and Blackmun, and the Court granted the petition for review on October 17. The case was scheduled for argument on March
20, near the end of the Court's argument calendar for the 1988–89 term.

The underlying facts were voluminous and less than straightforward. Connaughton had challenged an incumbent judge, Dolan, who had become embroiled
in a bribery scandal involving his Director of Court Services, a man named Billy
New. At the heart of the case against New, and at least by association, Dolan, were

allegations made by two sisters, Alice Thompson and Patsy Stephens, that New had taken money to fix traffic offenses in Dolan's court. Of the two sisters, Stephens was a decidedly more significant witness in the case against New, and Thompson had both a prior criminal record and, at least reportedly, a history of psychological problems. The allegations received significant attention in the run-up to the election, with the Cincinnati *Enquirer*, which also circulated in the local community served by the Hamilton *Journal News*, driving much of the press coverage critical of Dolan and his court.

Shortly before the election, the *Journal News* published an article reporting on the circumstances pursuant to which Stephens and Thompson had come to make their allegations against New. According to the article, the sisters had met with Connaughton and several supporters in what it described as an "all night" session and allowed him to record it. Connaughton had then provided the information he received from the sisters to the local prosecutor who proceeded to secure testimony from both of them and to arrest New. The *Journal News* article further reported that, in a subsequent interview with the newspaper, which was also recorded, Thompson contended that she and her sister had made the allegations against New only after Connaughton had engaged in what she described as "dirty tricks," which included promising them, during portions of the meeting when the recorder was turned off, that he would, following the election, provide them with employment, take them to dinner at an expensive restaurant in Cincinnati, and bring them along on a planned vacation.

Before the article was published, the *Journal News* interviewed Connaughton about the truth of Thompson's statements concerning his alleged promises. During the course of that interview, which was also recorded, Connaughton confirmed both that the meeting with the sisters had lasted most of the night and that each of the subjects of the promises that Thompson referenced had indeed been discussed. Nevertheless, he denied that he had offered the sisters anything in return for their testimony.

As published, the article accurately recounted Thompson's allegations, presenting them as her allegations, as well as Connaughton's responses to them, which were also accurately recounted. Before its publication, the *Journal News* interviewed most of the participants in the late night meeting, all of whom denied that Connaughton had offered the sisters any inducements to provide information implicating either Dolan or New in wrongdoing. Their comments were accurately included in the article as well. The newspaper did not, however, interview Stephens and, although it had a copy of it, did not listen to the recording Connaughton and his supporters had made of his meeting with the sisters. Shortly after the article was published, the *Journal News* gave its editorial endorsement to Dolan, an endorsement that questioned Connaughton's role in generating the accusations surrounding the local court.

Dolan won reelection and, shortly thereafter, Connaughton instituted a defamation action against the corporate publisher of the *Journal News*. In it, he alleged that the article injured his reputation by falsely communicating that he had engaged in improper and unethical behavior by inducing the sisters to testify against New. When the case went to trial, the jury was provided with a special verdict form in which it was asked, among other things, to determine whether the article was published with actual malice. It unanimously responded in the affirmative and awarded Connaughton $200,000 in compensatory and punitive damages.

As noted, a divided panel of the Sixth Circuit affirmed the jury's verdict after conducting what the majority described as an "independent review" of the jury's "ultimate" finding of actual malice. It did so, however, by first crediting eleven "subsidiary" facts that it determined the jury "could" have found from the record evidence, including that "the *Journal* was engaged in a bitter rivalry with the *Cincinnati Enquirer*, for domination of the greater Hamilton circulation market," that " the *Journal* was aware of Thompson's prior criminal convictions and reported psychological infirmities and the treatment she had received for her mental condition," that "every witness interviewed by *Journal* reporters discredited Thompson's accusations," and that "the *Journal* intentionally avoided interviewing Stephens . . . even though it knew that Stephens could either credit or discredit Thompson's statements."

The Sixth Circuit majority concluded that these "subsidiary" facts that the jury "could" have found were not "clearly erroneous" and that "in the exercise of its independent judgment" based on its evaluation of the "cumulative impact of the subsidiary facts[,] . . . Connaughton proved, by clear and convincing evidence, that the *Journal* demonstrated its actual malice when it published . . . despite the existence of serious doubt which attached to Thompson's veracity and the accuracy of her reports." And, although the majority's opinion recognized, in this passage, that a finding of actual malice required the kind of "serious doubt" about the truth described by the Supreme Court in *St. Amant*, it also appeared to resurrect the less rigorous liability standard advocated by Justice Harlan in *Butts*, asserting that the cumulated, subsidiary facts it described "demonstrated highly unreasonable conduct constituting an extreme departure from the standards of investigation and reporting ordinarily adhered to by responsible publishers."

Judge Guy dissented. In his view, the admissions that Connaughton made during his interview with the newspaper concerning the subjects he had discussed with the sisters sufficiently corroborated Thompson's allegations to preclude a finding of actual malice as a matter of law.

Despite the morass of facts on which the appellate court had premised its independent review, the argument before the Supreme Court, which was held twenty-five years to the month after the Court's decision in *Sullivan*, focused largely on the legal issue on which the Court had granted review—how a reviewing Court is to assess the record evidence in conducting the "independent review" mandated by *Sullivan* and *Bose*. Washington, D.C., lawyer Lee Levine, the newspaper's counsel, argued that the Sixth Circuit had erred in not crediting undisputed evidence favoring the newspaper (including what Judge Guy had described as Connaughton's "admissions") and, most significantly, by drawing all inferences from the record evidence in favor of Connaughton. According to Levine, although the court was obliged to resolve disputed issues of historical fact in favor of the jury's verdict, it was entitled to draw its own inferences from the record evidence in the process of undertaking its own, independent review of that evidence. The justices plainly had difficulty with this contention, with several of them asking how, "if the crucial distinction [is] between fact and inference," the reviewing court is supposed to divine "the difference between an inference and a factual determination."

After Levine's argument was interrupted by the Court's lunch recess, Justice Scalia resumed the questioning by again asking how "one go[es] about separating the facts that the jury has found from the inferences?" Levine's response, that the jury's presumptive "purely factual findings"—e.g., "the testimony in the record, what the documents say, . . . did a meeting take place"—had to be credited but that inferences from those facts did not, was not addressed further because, at that juncture, the chief justice joined the discussion by asking whether the Seventh Amendment, which guarantees a civil litigant a right to trial by jury, precluded any "independent review" at all in cases tried in federal courts, as opposed to a state court as in *Sullivan*. Specifically, Rehnquist asserted that *Sullivan* "wouldn't have involved the Seventh Amendment" because "that came from a state court." In response, Levine cited the *Chicago B&Q Railroad* case in which the Court had "expressly held that, with respect to the second clause of the Seventh Amendment, the one that's at issue here, that cases coming from state courts for purposes of review are governed by the Seventh Amendment" as well. Levine continued by recounting that, during the argument in *Sullivan* itself, "Justice Goldberg asked counsel for the respondent when he raised that very issue with the Seventh Amendment—how could it apply here" and was cited to the same precedent which, in turn, led Brennan to include a footnote in his opinion for the Court in *Sullivan* "in which that proposition was rejected—the proposition that the Seventh Amendment posed any conflict with the First Amendment in [making the] actual malice determinations."

During this exchange, Brennan—who did not pose any questions of his own during the argument—leaned over to Rehnquist, who sat immediately to his left at the center of the bench, chuckled and whispered audibly, "he's right, Bill." At this, Rehnquist relented, saying "so, we've held the Seventh Amendment does apply to state courts in some situations?" When Levine responded with "Yes, we have," and then quickly corrected himself by saying "*you* have," the gallery laughed.

As his argument concluded, Levine faced a series of questions from Justice Blackmun, who appeared overtly skeptical that the newspaper's argument was premised on *Bose,* asserting "I'm a little puzzled as to why you need it, from your point of view. And maybe you do. Do you concede that the article is false?" When Levine responded that, "for purposes of this proceeding we concede that it is susceptible to a defamatory interpretation which is false," Blackmun added, "I guess what I'm saying is I think that you have a stronger case without *Bose* and you don't have to rely on *Bose,* but, go ahead, do it your own way."

During his argument, Connaughton's counsel John Lloyd, the veteran Ohio trial lawyer who tried the case, attempted to shift the Court's focus to the underlying facts, emphasizing the newspaper's reliance on the statements made by Thompson, who he described as "a lady with a psychiatric history, a criminal record, a motive to lie, . . . and other bases to believe she was undesirable." The newspaper's failure to attempt to confirm Thompson's account with her sister, Lloyd asserted, was "perverse, premeditated ignorance. I'm going to stick my head in the sand so nobody can prove I knew it because if I ask one more question, I'm going to find out something that's going to keep me from running the article I'm determined to run in order to ruin Dan Connaughton." In this manner, Lloyd endeavored to evoke the facts underlying the Court's decision in *Butts,* where Chief Justice Warren had both cast the deciding vote applying the actual malice standard and concluded that it had been satisfied by evidence that the defendant there had relied on a dubious source and failed to consult other, obvious sources who might have provided information contradicting its "exposé."

To this, Justice Stevens asked Lloyd how, in the actual malice calculus, he accounted for the newspaper's interview with his client, during which "on almost each point that tends to look unfavorably toward your client there is at least some factual basis on each of those isolated points." Among other things, Stevens noted, Connaughton had conceded discussing with the sisters "the promise of the Florida trip, and he admits they talked about going down to Hilton Head or Florida, and the promise of a job." He also challenged Lloyd's response that the promises Thompson alleged had been made are not reflected on the tape of the sisters' meeting with Connaughton and his supporters, asking "it is true, is it not, that the interview lasted much longer than the tape?"

On rebuttal, Levine turned to the facts as well, and was challenged by Justice Scalia concerning the newspaper's failure to interview Stephens. When Levine conceded both that this undisputed fact was properly weighed in the balance in an appellate court's independent review of the record evidence, and that "it would have been a better story" if Stephens had been interviewed, the justice asserted that "it would have been a non-story if you had, not a better story, because she contradicted everything her sister said." In response, Levine pointed to Stephens's trial testimony in which, he asserted, she had corroborated her sister's account of what had been discussed by Connaughton at the meeting, but testified that she did not construe his statements as promises.

At that juncture, Scalia returned to the legal issue and asked "what do we do with that testimony? Is that a fact or an inference? Do I take it to be a denial that it occurred or not a denial that it occurred? Is that something I give the jury the benefit of the doubt on or do I decide that for myself?" Levine answered that the Court should credit the fact that, "Stephens testified at trial that she did not believe she was promised anything" and weigh it along with the other material facts, including that "the article itself is a fair and accurate account both of Alice Thompson's statements and of Mr. and Mrs. Connaughton's responses to them" and that it "references conversations that Mr. Connaughton concedes took place and subjects he concedes were discussed." At this, Blackmun interjected, asking Levine, "well, then, where is the falsity?" Levine responded that he saw "no falsity in this story" which, he said, contains "nothing that I would call a material false statement." Nevertheless, he conceded that "this jury found falsity" and that the newspaper had sought "independent review only of the actual malice inquiry, so I'm here on the question of actual malice, not falsity."

At the conference following the argument, according to Blackmun's notes, Rehnquist took the position that *Bose* "requires acceptance" of facts as found by the jury. Although the chief justice indicated that, "on balance," he would affirm the Sixth Circuit's decision, he "might not" have "done it the way" the Sixth Circuit had. Brennan then voted to reverse. In his prepared remarks, he said,

> Under *New York Times* and *Bose*, the reviewing court must undertake an independent review of the entire record on the question of actual malice. This standard does not bar it from resolving disputed questions of what we have sometimes called "historical fact" in the direction of the jury verdict. But deference to hypothetical findings the jury *could have* made does not constitute the independent review that is required under *New York Times*. I think we must correct CA6 on this point and remand for application of the correct standard.

White disagreed, on the ground that the jury had been properly instructed, it proceeded to find the requisite reckless disregard for the truth, and the Sixth Circuit had employed the proper standard. Marshall, Blackmun, Stevens, and O'Connor, however, all voted to reverse. According to Brennan's notes of the conference discussion, Stevens indicated that he had already read "much of [the] transcript" and had concluded that there was "enough evidence to prove no reckless disregard," especially since the article at issue was "at best marginally false." O'Connor, according to Brennan's notes, agreed with the Sixth Circuit that an appellate court should not review "credibility facts" but believed that there was "not sufficient evidence of malice" under the applicable "clear and convincing" standard. Scalia and Kennedy, on the other hand, both voted to affirm, agreeing with the chief justice's construction of *Bose* and concluding that the newspaper's failure to interview Stephens was sufficient evidence to support the jury's verdict that there had been a "reckless disregard" for the truth.

Although it is unclear whether or the extent to which he asserted these views at conference—Brennan's notes, for example, do not reference them—Blackmun had apparently been convinced by his law clerk that the actual issue in the case was not the one on which the circuits were in conflict or on which the Court had granted review. Rather, as his questions at argument suggested, he had come to believe that the case was an "easy" one that had been rendered more complicated by the Sixth Circuit's analysis of the independent review issue and the newspaper's efforts to challenge it. As Blackmun saw it, the article had accurately presented both sides of the dispute it reported about and did so in a neutral fashion. Accordingly, Blackmun believed, the article was not false. He and his clerk were, therefore, plainly frustrated when, in response to his questions at argument, Levine had indicated that the jury's finding of falsity was not before the Court.

Still, at the close of the conference, there were five votes to reverse the Sixth Circuit (including Blackmun) and, because Rehnquist was in dissent, Brennan assumed responsibility for assigning the Court's opinion. Although he had reportedly been frustrated five years earlier when Burger assigned the opinion in *Bose* to Stevens, rather than to him, in this instance, Brennan informed the other justices on March 21 that he had asked Stevens to write for the majority in *Connaughton* as well.

Almost two months later, however, on May 11, Stevens wrote to inform his colleagues that he had changed his mind:

> I have spent a great deal of time studying the record in this case, including listening to all of the tape recordings, and I am now persuaded that the defamatory story was not only false, but that the people responsible for printing it either knew or should have known that it was false and that they surely acted recklessly in not interviewing the key witness in the case and also in not even listening to the tapes describing the corruption in the municipal court before they decided to support the incumbent judge for re-election and to publish the story that gave rise to the lawsuit. In short, although I am afraid the draft I am working on is probably a good deal longer than it should be, I am now convinced that the judgment should be affirmed.

With the end of the term approaching, Stevens said he thought it important to give the other justices "this advance notice because one or more of my former allies may have to write a dissent and I am afraid that I may not have the opinion in final form much before the deadline on June 1st."

In fact, Stevens circulated his first draft on May 31. Like the final decision in the case, it parted company with the Sixth Circuit on its interpretation of the independent review requirement under *Sullivan* and *Bose*, as well as its suggestion that the actual malice standard could be satisfied simply by a showing of "highly unreasonable conduct," as Justice Harlan had unsuccessfully urged in *Butts*. Nevertheless, following an exhaustive review of the record evidence, Stevens determined that there was clear and convincing evidence of actual malice. Stevens's draft emphasized that, in conducting the sort of independent review mandated by *Sullivan* and *Bose*, an appellate court "must consider the factual record in full" and, although "credibility determinations, if not clearly erroneous, may be left for the trier of fact," the reviewing court must nevertheless "examine for [itself] the statements in issue and the circumstances under which they were made to see . . . whether they are of a character which the principles of the First Amendment . . . protect." In the case before it, Stevens wrote, "[b]ased on our review of the entire record, we agree with the Court of Appeals that the evidence did in fact support a finding of actual malice" but that "[o]ur approach . . . differs somewhat from that undertaken by the Court of Appeals." He then proceeded to recount the Sixth Circuit's approach to independent review—specifically, its identification of "11 subsidiary facts that the jury 'could have' found" which, "when considered cumulatively . . . provide clear and convincing evidence of actual malice"—but asserted that "the case should be decided on a less speculative ground." Beyond that, Stevens's draft, and the final opinion he authored for the Court, provided little guidance with respect to either the flaws in the Sixth Circuit's approach or how an appellate court should properly conduct the independent review mandated by *Sullivan* and *Bose*.

Instead, Stevens proceeded to set out the trial record in considerable detail and, based on what he described as an independent review of "those facts not in dispute," asserted "it is evident that the jury *must* have rejected (1) the testimony of [the newspaper's] witnesses that Stephens was not contacted simply because Connaughton failed to place her in touch with the [*Journal News*]; (2) the testimony of [the newspaper's editorial director] that he did not listen to the tapes because he thought they would provide him with no new information; and (3) the testimony of those *Journal News* employees who asserted they believed Thompson's allegations were substantially true." Accordingly, Stevens's draft concluded, "[w]hen these findings are considered alongside the undisputed evidence, the conclusion that the newspaper acted with actual malice inextricably follows."

As Stevens explained it, "[a]ccepting the jury's determination" that the referenced testimony proffered by the newspaper concerning why it had not interviewed Stephens or listened to the tape was "not credible," it became "likely that the newspaper's inaction was a product of a deliberate decision not to acquire knowledge of facts that might confirm the probable falsity of Thompson's charges." And, Stevens wrote, "[a]lthough failure to investigate will not alone support a finding of actual malice," the sort of "purposeful avoidance of the truth" reflected in the trial record is sufficient to do so. As Stevens put it, the actual malice standard is "satisfied if [the] publisher 'willfully blind[ed] itself to the falsity of its utterance.'" In sum, Stevens wrote, "[t]here is a remarkable similarity between this case—and in particular, the newspaper's failure to interview Stephens and failure to listen to the tape recording of the September 17 interview at Connaughton's home—and the facts that supported the Court's judgment in *Curtis Publishing Co. v. Butts*," where the magazine had similarly failed to consult several "obvious" sources, a conclusion that vindicated Lloyd's strategy of modeling his introduction of the evidence supporting Connaughton's case after the facts of that earlier decision.

Stevens's introduction of the "willful blindness" concept into the actual malice calculus appeared to be the sort of recalibration of the constitutional standard that Brennan had feared was the motive for Stevens's refusal to join him in a full-throated defense of *Sullivan* in *Greenmoss Builders*. Nevertheless, on June 2, Brennan, without further comment, wrote to Stevens and the other justices to indicate that he would join the opinion without qualification. Thereafter, in quick succession, so did Marshall and O'Connor. Brennan's files on the case contain no indication as to how he came to his decision to change his own vote at conference.

On June 5, Scalia indicated that he would be writing separately, no doubt adapting what he had originally conceived would be a dissent into a concurring opinion defending the Sixth Circuit's narrow conception of "independent review." On June 6, White circulated his own, one-paragraph concurring opinion, in which—like he had in *Bose*—he distinguished the "knowledge of falsity" prong of the actual malice test (which he deemed a historical fact subject to review under a clearly erroneous standard) from the "reckless disregard" prong which, he agreed with Stevens, "is to be reviewed independently by the appellate court" in the manner Stevens had suggested.

Also on June 6, Scalia circulated his own opinion, concurring in the judgment. In it, he criticized Stevens for not squarely addressing the issue on which review had been granted and which had led to a conflict between the Sixth Circuit's decision in *Connaughton* and the D.C. Circuit's decision in *Tavoulareas v. Piro*—specifically, whether "the trial judge and reviewing courts must make their own 'independent' assessment of the facts allegedly establishing malice" or "as the Sixth Circuit held here (explicitly rejecting *Tavoulareas*) that they must merely make their own 'independent' assessment that, *assuming all of the facts that could reasonably be found in favor of the plaintiff were found in the favor of the plaintiff,* clear and convincing proof of malice was established." He described Stevens's resolution of the case as "peculiar" and asserted that he "would have adopted the Sixth Circuit's analysis in its entirety."

Later that same day, Stevens wrote to Scalia to take issue with his characterization of the D.C. Circuit's decision in *Tavoulareas*. Specifically, although Scalia's draft asserted that the D.C. Circuit had held that "the trial judge and reviewing courts must make their own 'independent' assessment of the facts allegedly establishing malice," Stevens pointed him to language in the opinion that "expressly disagrees with your statement of its holding." Scalia responded promptly and acknowledged that Stevens was indeed correct—"I was describing what *Tavoulareas* did rather than what, in some parts of the opinion, it said it was doing." Still, Scalia wrote:

> Of course it is irrelevant to my point whether *Tavoulareas* said it was doing this, or even, for that matter, whether *Tavoulareas* did it. Indeed, I suppose I should *prefer* to point out that even the D.C. Circuit never said or did such a silly thing. *Tavoulareas*, as (reasonably) interpreted by the Sixth Circuit, simply puts on stage the alternative interpretation of *Bose* that the petition asks us to approve: "review that examines both the subsidiary facts underlying the jury's finding of actual malice and the jury's ultimate finding of actual malice."

Thus, Scalia concluded, he would "make minor changes to correct" his "inaccuracy." In fact, his final opinion describes a conflict between the Sixth Circuit's decision in *Connaughton* and what that court "understood the District of Columbia Circuit to have held in *Tavoulareas*."

The next day, June 7, Kennedy wrote to Stevens to voice concern about the opinion's references to the "willful blindness doctrine." While serving as a judge on that court, Kennedy had written a dissent from the Ninth Circuit decision establishing the doctrine in non-defamation cases, and continued to believe that "willful blindness has proven a mischievous doctrine in that circuit" that "I would not like to import [it] into this Court's jurisprudence by its implicit approval here." In Kennedy's view, "it does not fit anyway," since the "point is not that the newspaper knew" that Thompson "was lying, but that it acted in reckless disregard by not asking" Stephens whether her sister "was lying or not. So I would have to write a special concurrence objecting to willful blindness if your opinion relies on it. I do not think your opinion needs it." Kennedy closed by advising Stevens that he was "considering a one-line concurrence indicating that I join the opinion with the understanding that it is not inconsistent with Nino [Scalia]'s separate writing." Later that same day, Stevens agreed to remove his opinion's references to "willful blindness," relying instead exclusively on the "purposeful avoidance of the truth" concept he had also employed in his initial draft. The change having been made, on June 8, Kennedy agreed to join Stevens's opinion as well, albeit with the one-sentence concurrence he had promised.

On June 12, White circulated a second draft of his own concurring opinion. In this version, beyond what he had written previously, he joined Kennedy in observing that he too read the Stevens and Scalia opinions to be "consistent." Rehnquist then promptly joined White's opinion. On June 13, Blackmun wrote to Rehnquist and asked that the decision not be announced on June 15 as planned. He said that he was still not "fully at rest and probably shall write briefly."

On June 14, Stevens wrote to the other justices to address the fate of *P.G. Publishing Co. v. DiSalle*, a petition for review that had been held pending the outcome of *Connaughton*. In *DiSalle*, in which a Pennsylvania appellate court had affirmed a jury verdict of more than $2 million, largely in punitive damages, against a newspaper, the petition had argued "that the story at issue should be protected under the 'neutral reportage' doctrine." That doctrine, which had been articulated most fully by Chief Judge Kaufman in a decision of the Second Circuit captioned *Edwards v. National Audubon Society*, held that the First Amendment protected a publisher from defamation liability for publishing a knowing falsehood provided that it did so in the context of accurately and neutrally recounting an independently newsworthy statement made by one responsible person or group about another such person or group. In his memorandum addressing the fate of *DiSalle*, Stevens concluded that the "neutral reportage" issue was not "worthy" of review:

> The Superior Court held that *if* there is a "neutral reportage" doctrine, it only protects publishers in cases in which a public figure (or public official) embroiled in a public controversy makes false allegations concerning another public figure. In addition, the publisher must have neither espoused nor concurred in the allegations. Because these requirements are not satisfied on the facts of this case, the Superior

Court concluded that it was unnecessary to resolve the question whether the doctrine is constitutionally mandated.

Then, in a passage that stands as something of a preemptive rejoinder to Blackmun's eventual concurring opinion in *Connaughton* itself, Stevens offered the following:

> This case is on the same footing with the District Court's handling of the "neutral reportage" issue in [*Connaughton*. . . .] There, the court held that because Alice Thompson was not a prominent organization or a public figure, the *Journal News* could not defend its story as a neutral account of newsworthy allegations. . . . My own opinion is that we would be well-advised to wait for a better case. In order to conclude that the knowingly false defamatory publication in this case was constitutionally protected by the neutral reportage doctrine, we would have to conclude that the protection is available even though the report was not neutral and the source of the false report was not sufficiently prominent to make his false charge newsworthy. . . . I shall vote to deny.

The Court agreed and the petition in *DiSalle* was in fact rejected.

On June 19, Blackmun finally indicated that he too would join Stevens's opinion. With the term quickly coming to an end, his law clerks "didn't think it was possible to write a dissent (at least without the kind of review of the record that is impossible at this date)" but did recommend that he submit a separate concurring opinion. Blackmun circulated a draft of that opinion—in substantially its final form—on June 19 as well. In it, he criticized the newspaper for having "abandoned the defense of truth despite the fact that there might be some support for that defense." Similarly, he asserted that, although the question had not been "squarely presented," "[w]ere this Court to adopt the neutral reportage theory, the facts of this case arguably might fit within it." More importantly, Blackmun took pains to "emphasize" that, in exercising its duty of independent review with respect to actual malice, an appellate court must keep in mind that "the form and content of the story are relevant." Accordingly, he wrote that he found "significant the fact that the article in this case accurately portrayed Thompson's allegations *as* allegations, and also printed Connaughton's partial denial of their truth." Even so, Blackmun concluded, he was "convinced that the majority has considered the article's content and form in the course of its painstaking 'review of the entire record.'"

In the days that followed, neither Brennan nor any other justice apparently indicated any interest in joining Blackmun's opinion. The decision was finally announced on June 22.

Florida Star v. B.J.F.

The day after the argument in *Connaughton*, the Court heard from the lawyers representing the parties in *Florida Star v. B.J.F.* In that case, a Florida newspaper had published the name of a rape victim as part of a compilation of reports of crimes in the local community it served. The victim's name had been included in an incident report that had been made available to reporters in the pressroom of the Sheriff's Department. A reporter trainee for the newspaper had copied the report verbatim and provided it to a reporter who, despite the newspaper's internal policy of not publishing the names of victims of sexual attacks, proceeded to prepare a one-paragraph summary, including B.J.F.'s name, that was thereafter included in the "Robberies" subsection of the newspaper's "Police Reports" feature.

Under a Florida statute, it was unlawful to "print, publish, or broadcast . . . in any instrument of mass communication" the name of the victim of a sexual offense. Invoking the statute, B.J.F. had instituted a civil action against both the Sheriff's Department and the newspaper. After the department settled, her case proceeded to trial against the newspaper alone. At trial, B.J.F. testified that she had suffered emotional distress as a result of the newspaper's publication and that her mother had received threatening phone calls from a man who asserted that he would rape B.J.F. again. As a result, she testified that she was compelled to change her telephone number, to seek police protection, and to obtain counseling.

At the close of the evidence, the trial judge granted B.J.F.'s motion for a directed verdict with respect to the newspaper's liability, finding that its publication of her name was "*per se* negligent" given the existence of the statute. The jury's deliberations were therefore limited to the issues of causation and damages, and it awarded B.J.F. a total of $75,000 in compensatory damages and $25,000 in punitive damages. The trial court's judgment was affirmed in its entirety by the Florida appellate courts.

The case initially came before the justices in the fall of 1987, but was relisted twice, first at the request of Scalia and then, in early December, at the request of

Brennan. Ultimately, all of the justices (including Kennedy, who had by then joined the Court), except Stevens, voted to hear it.

At argument, the newspaper's counsel, St. Petersburg lawyer and highly regarded media counsel George Rahdert, attempted to convince the Court that the case was controlled by *Cox Broadcasting Corp. v. Cohn*. Justice White, the author of the Court's opinion in *Cohn*, questioned Rahdert closely on the point, asking whether in *Florida Star*, unlike in *Cohn*, the newspaper had knowingly violated its own internal policies by publishing the victim's name. Other questions focused on the fact that, in *Cohn*, the name of the rape victim "came to light during [a] judicial proceeding" and that the facts in *Florida Star* would not "fall within that exception" to the legal claim, otherwise recognized under Florida law, for injury caused by the tortious publication of private facts. When Rahdert contended that the "private facts" tort had also traditionally contained an exception for "accurately reporting [the content of] government records," Justice Stevens interjected that any such exception at common law did not support Rahdert's overriding contention, i.e., that "you were covered like a blanket by the *Cox* case, and I don't think you are."

Rahdert also received several questions from justices inquiring whether his position would be different if the newspaper had acquired the information unlawfully as opposed to having it made available voluntarily by the Sheriff's Department. In response, Rahdert argued that, although a newspaper could be held liable for an act of unlawful acquisition (under, for example, the law of theft), "under the law of *Cox Broadcasting Corp. v. Cohn* and its progeny, this Court had suggested that before publication of truthful information can be punished, there has to be a state interest of the highest order and there should be an evaluation of whether there are less restrictive alternatives." And, Rahdert said, "punishing the act of theft would be a less restrictive alternative."

This contention led Justice O'Connor to question the breadth of Rahdert's position, asserting "I don't think this Court has ever adopted the rule you propose, of absolute freedom to publish true information" and asking what "would that rule do to, for example, the tort of publication of private facts," which provides for the imposition of liability based on the publication of truthful but private facts. Although his attempt to answer the question was repeatedly interrupted, O'Connor at least purported to understand Rahdert to concede that the private facts tort "would be gone" under his view of the First Amendment's protection for truthful speech. Moreover, when the questioning moved beyond privacy-based claims, to include whether the First Amendment would permit liability for publishing truthful information that endangered national security or violated the copyright laws, Rahdert replied that protecting national security had been held to constitute a governmental interest of the highest order that could overcome the First Amendment's protection of truthful expression and that the copyright laws do not prohibit the publication of facts, only the manner in which they are expressed. That answer, in turn, led O'Connor to question whether the protection of "a victim of rape from the potential of physical, further physical abuse, and physical danger" constituted a "compelling state interest," especially since the evidence before the Court indicated that "the publication here resulted in some . . . additional trauma for the victim." In response, Rahdert conceded that the state has a legitimate interest in preventing such injury but repeated that, in these circumstances, it could vindicate that interest through the less speech-restrictive means of prohibiting the unlawful acquisition of the victim's identity.

At this juncture, Justice Scalia asserted that Rahdert's response was "not really very satisfying." Invoking the Court's well-known reference to the publication during wartime of the sailing date of troop ships in *Near v. Minnesota,* which the Court there had invoked to illustrate a circumstance under which a prior restraint of expression would likely be permissible, Scalia opined that, under Rahdert's "theory, the government should be very careful not to let that information out, but once it gets out, there's nothing it can do, so long as it's true. If it were a false date that they published, that would be okay, then you could stop that." The last comment provoked laughter from the gallery, after which Rahdert explained that the publication of such information endangering national security would not be protected by the First Amendment because the government's interest in preventing such harm constituted an interest of the "highest order." This led Scalia to observe that "so, that's what this basically comes down to, to how important we think it is to prevent a rape victim from being killed by her assailant while he's . . . still out there somewhere."

Not surprisingly, Joel Eaton, the Miami lawyer representing B.J.F., began his argument by attempting to distinguish *Cohn,* largely on the same grounds suggested by the justices during their questioning of Rahdert as well as because the victim in *Cohn* "was dead. Her mental and physical security did not need to be protected at that point." Eaton also made an effort to argue that the information had been obtained by the newspaper unlawfully, largely because the Florida Public Records

Act then contained an exception for the release of such information. Even so, Justice Scalia asserted, "that doesn't mean the person to whom [the Sheriff] releases it is violating the law, any more than if somebody comes over and hands me a classified document that he's not supposed to give me, and I look at it. I haven't violated the law." When Easton responded that he was not "suggesting . . . that the newspaper violated the Florida Public Records Act," Scalia concluded "so then, it received, it acquired the information legally as far as it was concerned."

Other justices focused their questions to Eaton on the fact that the Florida statute actually before the Court "prohibits the newspaper from publishing the information no matter where it gets it" and that, although "everybody in town can know it, . . . the only person that can't talk about it is the newspaper reporter." When Eaton attempted to justify the statutory distinction on the ground that "the damage is done by mass circulation, not by this woman telling her physician, or her boss, or her mother," Justice Kennedy responded that "that would be quite a break with our precedents if we were to hold that, would it not? I really know of no precedent, correct me if I'm wrong, which puts on the press a disability, forbidding them from publishing something that it doesn't put on everybody else." That led Eaton to suggest that the "underbreadth" of the statute was not relevant since, in this case, the newspaper's violation of the statute had been invoked by the trial judge only to support his conclusion that liability could be imposed on a negligence *per se* theory. In response, Scalia remarked, "gee, there's really less to this case than meets the eye. I thought it was a really major constitutional issue here. But you're saying it's really just what the jury found is the only thing that's up. That no matter whether the statute's good or bad, this judgment stands." Ultimately, Eaton returned to *Cohn*, advising the justices that "I'm not the least bit ashamed to stand here and suggest to this Court, notwithstanding that you were unanimous in *Cox Broadcasting*, that the name of a rape victim never ought to be in a newspaper and I don't care where they get it. It serves no purpose whatsoever." With that, Justice Blackmun reminded Eaton that, nevertheless, "you do have to distinguish *Cox*," but quickly added "you have done your best."

Following argument, all of the justices but Rehnquist and White voted to reverse. At conference, according to Brennan's notes, Rehnquist began the discussion by conceding that *Cohn* was "closest on point" of the Court's precedents but argued that it was "distinguishable" because the "records here [were] not open to public inspection." Moreover, Rehnquist said he believed that the asserted "rights of privacy [are] very strong here" as was the "state interest to protect [the rape victim] from criminals."

According to his internal memorandum prepared for the conference, Brennan acknowledged that *Cohn* "does not completely control the result in this case." Nevertheless, he reasoned that "in conjunction with *Landmark* and other recent decisions, it comes close to doing so." Thus, Brennan concluded:

> I do not think we need go as far as the newspaper asks, and say that the First Amendment entails that the publication of truthful information can never be forbidden. But I do think we might follow Justice Stewart's concurring opinion in *Landmark*, where he said that "though government may deny access to information and punish its theft, government may not prohibit or punish the publication of that information once it falls into the hands of the press, unless the need for secrecy is manifestly overwhelming."

In his memorandum, Brennan asserted, the Court had come "very near to adopting that test in *Cox*, since we said that it was up to government to protect whatever privacy interests there were to be protected in judicial proceedings, not up to the press." In Brennan's view, "[t]his is a case about who should bear the liability for the harm resulting from the release of personal, embarrassing, possibly dangerous information" and the "First Amendment favors a bright-line rule holding the government accountable and leaving the press free to publish."

According to Brennan's notes of the discussion at conference, White then agreed with Rehnquist that the case before the Court is "not *Cox*" and that the "victim shouldn't have to" suffer the consequences of the "paper's negligence." Marshall, however, sided with Brennan. As Brennan recounted it, Blackmun expressed his "sympathy with [the] victim," and further indicated his view that the Court didn't "have to say truth is always punishable." Still, Blackmun concluded, the statute was "overbroad as applied." Stevens asserted, again according to Brennan's notes, that he "would maintain [a] tort action for damages here," but the "theory of liability" actually asserted "relied on [the] statute and it is plainly overbroad." Like Blackmun, however, Stevens said he "wouldn't go as far as [the] Petitioner" advocated. O'Connor too said she would recognize "no absolute right to publish." In her view, as recounted in Brennan's notes, the state has an "interest in protecting victims" and may "prohibit publication of truth lawfully" acquired. By the same token,

O'Connor asserted (at least according to Brennan's notes), the statute itself "doesn't survive scrutiny." Finally, Brennan's notes reveal that Scalia, with whom Kennedy agreed, said "where Sandra and John are is where I'm at."

With Rehnquist in dissent, Brennan assigned the Court's opinion to Marshall. The resulting opinion, which Brennan and three other justices (Blackmun, Stevens, and Kennedy) joined, began by reviewing the "trilogy" of cases addressing a perceived conflict between the First Amendment and "personal privacy," beginning with *Cohn* and extending through *Smith v. Daily Mail Publishing Co.* In so doing, however, Marshall emphasized that, "although our decisions have without exception upheld the press' right to publish, we have emphasized each time that we were resolving this conflict only as it arose in a discrete factual context." Moreover, his opinion concluded that, "[d]espite the strong resemblance this case bears to *Cox Broadcasting*, that case cannot fairly be read as controlling here" because, in *Cohn*, unlike *Florida Star*, the victim's name had been "obtained from courthouse records that were open to public inspection." And, although it is not at all clear that the newspaper ever issued it, Marshall declined to "accept" what his opinion described as its "invitation to hold broadly that truthful publication may never be punished consistent with the First Amendment." According to Marshall, the Court's previous "cases have carefully eschewed reaching this ultimate question, mindful that the future may bring scenarios which prudence counsels our not resolving anticipatorily."

Ultimately, Marshall's opinion concluded that "this case is appropriately analyzed with reference to" a more "limited First Amendment principle," specifically, the one "which we articulated in *Daily Mail* in our synthesis of prior cases involving attempts to punish truthful publication: '[I]f a newspaper lawfully obtains truthful information about a matter of public significance then state officials may not constitutionally punish publication of the information, absent a need to further a state interest of the highest order.'" In so holding, Marshall's opinion emphasized both "the overarching 'public interest, secured by the Constitution, in the dissemination of truth,'" and that, since a newspaper is protected only when it publishes information "lawfully obtain[ed]," the "government retains ample means of safeguarding significant interests upon which publication may impinge, including protecting a rape victim's anonymity." As Marshall put it, "[w]here information is entrusted to the government, a less drastic means than punishing truthful publication almost always exists for guarding against the dissemination of private facts." And, "[t]o the extent sensitive information rests in private hands, the government may under some circumstances forbid its nonconsensual acquisition, thereby bringing outside the *Daily Mail* principle the publication of any information so acquired." This paragraph ended with footnote 8 to the Court's opinion, which would assume considerable significance more than a decade later:

> The *Daily Mail* principle does not settle the issue whether, in cases where information has been acquired *unlawfully* by a newspaper or by a source, government may ever punish not only the unlawful acquisition, but the ensuing publication as well. This issue was raised in *New York Times Co. v. United States,* and reserved in *Landmark Communications,* 435 U.S. at 837. We have no occasion to address it here.

Marshall's opinion for the Court concluded that, "[a]pplied to the instant case, the *Daily Mail* principle clearly commands reversal." The newspaper's account of B.J.F.'s rape "concerned 'a matter of public significance,' in the sense in which the *Daily Mail* synthesis of prior cases used that term"—"the article generally, as opposed to the specific identity contained within it, involved a matter of paramount public import: the commission, and investigation, of a violent crime which had been reported to authorities." And, in response to the argument that the Florida statute serves the requisite state interest of the highest order—by, among other things, protecting the victim's privacy and physical safety as well as by encouraging other victims "to report these offenses without fear of exposure"—Marshall identified three problems with the Florida statutory remedy: (1) the government's own ability to safeguard such information more effectively; (2) the potential applicability of the statute "regardless of whether the identity of the victim is already known throughout the community; whether the victim has voluntarily called public attention to the offense; or whether the identity of the victim has otherwise become a reasonable subject of public concern because, perhaps, questions have arisen whether the victim fabricated an assault by a particular person[;]" and (3) the statute's "facial underinclusiveness." These factors, Marshall wrote, "raise[] serious doubts about whether Florida is, in fact, serving, with this statute, the significant interests . . . invoke[d]."

Scalia concurred in part, and in the Court's judgment, expressing his view that it is "sufficient to decide this case to reply upon" Marshall's conclusion that "a law cannot be regarded as protecting an interest 'of the highest order'" within the meaning of the *Daily Mail* principle, "and thus justifying a restriction upon truthful speech, when it leaves appreciable damage to that supposedly vital interest unprohibited." As Scalia saw it, "[t]his law has every appearance of a prohibition that society is prepared to impose upon the press but not upon itself. Such a prohibition does not protect an interest 'of the highest order.'"

White, the author of the Court's opinion in *Cohn*, dissented, in an emotional opinion joined by Rehnquist and, despite her apparent vote otherwise at conference, by O'Connor. White began by noting that, "'[s]hort of homicide, [rape] is the ultimate violation of self,'" and proceeded to assert that, for B.J.F., "the violation she suffered at a rapist's knifepoint marked only the beginning of her ordeal." In White's view, "it is not too much to ask the press, in instances such as this, to respect simple standards of decency and refrain from publishing a victim's name, address and/or phone number." His opinion further asserted that the Court had accepted the newspaper's invitation "to obliterate one of the most noteworthy legal inventions of the 20th century: the tort of the publication of private facts." For White, the Court had now "hit the bottom of the slippery slope" begun in Brennan's opinion for the Court in *Time, Inc. v. Hill* and continued in his own opinion for the Court in *Cohn*. Despite those decisions, he wrote, he "would find a place to draw the line higher on the hillside: a spot high enough to protect B.J.F.'s desire for privacy and peace-of-mind in the wake of a horrible personal tragedy."

The Court's decision was announced on June 21, 1989, the day before it issued its ruling in *Connaughton*.

Milkovich v. Lorain Journal Co

The final defamation decision in which Brennan participated as a Justice of the Supreme Court was *Milkovich v. Lorain Journal Co*, a case that—as his term history recounted—"was heard largely through the Chief Justice's efforts." Although that was undoubtedly the case, the Court's disposition of *Milkovich* speaks, one final time, to Brennan's enduring influence on the body of constitutional law he had crafted in *Sullivan*.

In *Milkovich*, a sports columnist for an Ohio newspaper had written a critical appraisal of the conduct of Milkovich, a local high school wrestling coach, during a match that had concluded in a brawl between fans of the two competing schools.

According to the columnist, Milkovich had "lied" after "having given his solemn oath to tell the truth" when he denied personal involvement in inciting the crowd during testimony about the incident he gave before a high school athletic association investigating the incident. The columnist had been present at the match.

The case, as well as a related defamation action brought by another school official mentioned in the column, had something of a tortured history in the lower courts, including previous petitions for review to the Supreme Court at other stages of the proceeding in one or another of the cases. On this occasion, the issue presented was whether the columnist's statements were protected by the First Amendment as the expression of his "opinion." That notion—that the First Amendment provided absolute protection from defamation liability to opinions—had been embraced by a host of lower state and federal courts on the basis of the passage that Powell had included at the outset of the legal analysis set out in his opinion for the Court in *Gertz*: "Under the First Amendment, there is no such thing as a false idea. However pernicious an opinion may seem, we depend for its correction not on the conscience of judges and juries but on the competition of other ideas. But there is no constitutional value in false statements of fact."

As Brennan's term history noted, the lower courts had, based on Powell's language in *Gertz*, established elaborate tests that "addressed the question of how to distinguish statements of opinion from statements of fact" with one, articulated by the D.C. Circuit in a case called *Ollman v. Evans*, having become "ubiquitous." The *Ollman* test looked at four factors to determine whether the statement at issue, considered in the context of both (1) the language of the publication itself and (2) the broader societal setting in which it was disseminated, constituted (3) a verifiable statement of fact that (4) would be understood by a reasonable reader to have been intended as such.

The Supreme Court, however, had never squarely addressed the issue, despite several opportunities, and its failure to do so had long stuck in Rehnquist's craw. As Brennan's term history explained, "[t]he Chief Justice had twice written dissents from denial of certiorari in such cases," including in *Ollman*. In *Milkovich* itself, Rehnquist asked for the coach's petition for review to be relisted, and he circulated a dissent from what he assumed would be another denial on January 18, 1990, the day before it was scheduled to be discussed at conference. In it, taking direct aim at Powell's comments in *Gertz*, Rehnquist complained that "[i]solated passages from opinions of this Court sometimes take on lives of their own when

repeatedly invoked out of context by other courts." He reiterated his view, previously expressed in his similar dissent from the denial of review in *Ollman*, that
this "dictum from *Gertz*" was "merely a reiteration of the classical view that there
is 'no such thing as a false idea' in the political sense, and that the test of truth for
political ideas is indeed the marketplace and not the courtroom." Turning to the
Ohio Court's application of the *Ollman* factors, Rehnquist was particularly blunt:

> The notion that an accusation of perjury is less a factual assertion when it appears on
> the sports page than when it appears on some other page in the newspaper is bereft
> of rational justification. I am likewise at a loss to comprehend how a perceived bias
> on the part of the speaker transforms into "opinion" an inescapably factual asser-
> tion that someone lied under oath. . . . It is not clear whether the *Gertz* dictum or
> the increasingly ubiquitous *Ollman* test, . . . is the ultimate source of the aberrational
> results produced by this purportedly constitutional "fact-opinion" analysis. The mat-
> ter, in any event, is plainly deserving of consideration by the Court.

The next day, as the justices prepared to gather for conference, Kennedy, the current
occupant of Powell's seat, wrote Rehnquist that he "would be pleased to join your
dissent from the failure to grant *certiorari*." And, at the conference itself, White and
Scalia added their votes as well, thereby placing the case on the Court's calendar.

No doubt aware that the notion that a published accusation that a witness had
perjured himself constituted an expression of "opinion" was something of a hard
sell, the newspaper's counsel, in both briefing and argument, pressed the contention that the decision below had not in fact relied on either the *Gertz* dictum or
the *Ollman* analysis. This, among other instances of counsel attempting "to defend
views not only indefensible but unnecessary to their positions," led a number of
justices, including Brennan, to conclude that case had been "poorly argued."

At the outset of his presentation on behalf of Coach Milkovich, his counsel,
Cleveland lawyer Brent English, was asked by Justice O'Connor whether the
allegedly defamatory column addressed a matter of public concern. When he
conceded that it did and that it therefore fell "under the rubric of the *Hepps* case,"
placing on the plaintiff the burden of proving falsity, O'Connor asked whether
the statements in the column about which the coach had sued were "capable of
being proven false." English responded that they were, that the "primary impact
of this article is to accuse the petitioner of committing the crime of perjury," and

that therefore—as O'Connor put it—"it doesn't much matter whether you label it fact or opinion." By the same token, in response to further questioning, English conceded that the article "is sort of a mixed assertion of fact and commentary" and urged the justices that it was of no consequence that the actual phrasing of the allegedly defamatory "fact" focused on the author's subjective belief about "what everyone who attended the meet knew in his heart."

The newspaper's counsel, Richard Panza of Lorain, Ohio, encountered a much more skeptical bench, which appeared to grow increasingly frustrated with his responses to questions. Early on, when Panza was asked whether, if the author had written "'in my opinion Milkovich perjured himself,'" such a statement "should be actionable if it can be proved false," he responded by asserting that he did not believe the author's "intentions" were "relevant." When he was then asked by Rehnquist if he could answer the question that had been put to him, and responded "Yes, I can," without further elaboration, a frustrated chief justice asked, "why don't you?" Ultimately, Panza took the position that such a statement would be protected as opinion, leading Scalia to assert, "well, that's a very handy device. I assume that all book publishers can just put on the first page, 'everything contained in this book is, of course, the opinion of the writer.' And then you can go and say anything you like? And there's no liability for libel at all. And all newspapers can have on their masthead, 'everything here is the opinion of the people who write it.'" When Panza responded that he was not "a proponent of that," and Scalia replied, "I thought you were" based on his response to Rehnquist's inquiry, Panza emphasized that "I am not up here asking the Court to agree that merely [by] putting some mystical words 'I think' and then reciting objective fact you can protect all that fact. Absolutely not." Scalia then told Panza "it's not clear to me what your position is," and asked him to "suppose . . . it's just one sentence . . . 'in my view, in my opinion, Milkovich committed perjury.' That's all." In response, Panza said that, "[i]f the reader perceives that as opinion, then that is protected," which led the justices to ask him whether the readers' perceptions should be an issue of fact for the jury. Panza again responded "absolutely not," explaining that "if you allow a jury to decide that question, you will be promoting self-censorship and not public debate."

Later in his argument, the questioning turned to whether, as Justice Kennedy put it, "it is perfectly all right . . . if I say, 'in my opinion, so and so is a child abuser; I don't have a whole lot of facts to go on but that's my opinion.'" When Panza responded by asserting that he could "imagine that there are scurrilous forms of opinion that this Court may not choose to extend constitutional protection to," Kennedy intervened, asking incredulously, "you're suggesting to us that we have different categories of subjects, some of which are protected and some of which are not? That's the position of your newspaper?" With that, Panza appeared to demur, asserting that "the way I'm answering the question is that I could imagine, with facts unrelated to my own, that there may be certain forms of private opinion submitted in situations that do not concern social controversy that this Court may choose not to protect." At another point, Stevens asked what he described as a "hard hypothetical"—i.e., "supposing in this case the fact of the matter was that Mr. Milkovich never testified at the hearing and that the author of the article knew that and nevertheless wrote the same article." Panza responded only that, "as I pointed out before, I do not see that the speaker's intention is in any way relevant."

At conference, amplifying the views expressed in his draft dissent from what he incorrectly anticipated would be the Court's decision to deny review, Rehnquist took the position that, since *Hepps* had established that unverifiable statements could not be proven false and were therefore protected by the First Amendment, there was nothing further to be accomplished by recognizing a "fact/opinion" distinction of the kind articulated in cases like *Ollman*. For his part, Brennan came to the conference armed with a four-page written response to Rehnquist, which it is assumed he read to his colleagues. He began by noting that this "was a badly argued case so permit me to explain my vote in more detail than usual." Agreeing with Rehnquist, to a point, Brennan continued that his "approach to this question is as follows: we have held that it is a constitutional requirement that the plaintiff has to prove a statement false to recover for libel." For Brennan, "[t]hat means that 'what the actual statement was' is a fact on which the defendant's constitutional right hinges." As a result, Brennan said, "the factors discussed" in *Ollman* "are useful in evaluating what a reasonable reader would think he was reading" as is the *Restatement of Torts*'s "distinction between an opinion which discloses the facts it is based on and an opinion which doesn't." In the last analysis, Brennan asserted, "to determine how the reasonable reader would understand" published statements, "it is necessary to consider them in context."

Turning to the facts of the *Milkovich* case, Brennan concluded that "the reasonable reader would view this column, read as a whole, as saying: 'I wasn't there but I figure Milkovich must have lied in court to get this result.'" Still, Brennan took pains to note, "I agree with those of you who are dismayed by unfounded character assassination. But as long as it's clear to the reader that character assassination rather than solid information is what the reader is being offered, I don't think there is any call to quash public debate."

Brennan's position fell largely on deaf ears. Aside from Marshall, no other justice purported to embrace it at conference. According to Brennan's term history, White, O'Connor, and Scalia asserted their agreement with Rehnquist and all said they did not think the context surrounding the allegedly defamatory falsehood made any difference. Moreover, at least as recounted in Brennan's term history, Kennedy, who in later years would be viewed by many as his heir as the Court's preeminent protector of First Amendment rights, said he did not agree with the decision in *Hepps* and believed that a libel defendant should properly bear the burden of proving that the alleged defamation in a given case was true.

Blackmun and Stevens, though apparently less enamored with Rehnquist's reasoning, agreed with his conclusion as well. According to Brennan's term history, Blackmun said that he was not "big" on a rigid fact/opinion distinction. And, as Brennan recounted it, Stevens said that, while he favored protection for expressions of opinion and endorsed a broad "totality of the circumstances" test as preferable to a rigid rule, he believed that, in this case, it was impossible for a judge applying such an approach to conclude, as a matter of law, whether the average reader would construe the column as fact or opinion. Thus, he believed, the issue was properly submitted to the finder of fact.

As he had in *Falwell*, Rehnquist assigned the opinion to himself, and Brennan told Marshall that he would try his hand at a dissent. When Rehnquist's first draft arrived in his chambers on May 25, however, Brennan was, as he had been in *Falwell*, surprised and to a significant extent relieved. As recounted in his term history, "it was far narrower than either oral argument or conference had led anyone to expect." As Brennan read Rehnquist's opinion:

> Instead of holding that statements of opinion are actionable, it held that only statements of opinion that imply a statement of defamatory and false facts are actionable. On its face, this was no different than the rule most lower courts were already applying. Moreover, it appeared to apply a kind of truncated *Ollman* test to the statements at issue to determine whether they implied any statements of fact. The Chief looked at the language used, at the "general tenor" of the article, at the verifiability of the statements, and at the broader social context. The Chief, however, seemed to

assume that the only statements of opinion that would not imply facts were those that were either unverifiable, evaluative statements, or else statements cast in terms of hyperbole or parody.

In fact, Rehnquist's draft, like the final opinion, began by setting out and reaffirming the contours of the Court's defamation jurisprudence from *Sullivan* through *Connaughton*. In so doing, he placed particular emphasis on the Court's holdings in *Hepps* that "'the plaintiff bear the burden of showing falsity;'" in *Bresler* and *Falwell* that there are "constitutional limits on the *type* of speech which may be the subject of state defamation actions," limits that prevent the imposition of liability on "rhetorical hyperbole" and other speech that "'could not reasonably have been interpreted as stating actual facts about" the plaintiff; and in *Bose* and *Connaughton* as well as in *Sullivan* itself that "'in cases raising First Amendment issues . . . an appellate court has an obligation to make an independent examination of the whole record in order to make sure that the judgment does not constitute a forbidden intrusion on the field of free expression." As Rehnquist's draft explained it, the newspaper in *Milkovich* "would have us recognize, in addition to the established safeguards discussed above, still another First Amendment-based protection for defamatory statements which are categorized as 'opinion' as opposed to 'fact.'"

Having defined the issue before the Court in that context, Rehnquist's draft proceeded to critique and dismiss the lower courts' reliance on the *Gertz* dictum, expressly concluding that "we do not think this passage from *Gertz* was intended to create a wholesale defamation exception for anything that might be labeled 'opinion.'" Such a "wholesale" exception, Rehnquist asserted, would not only be "contrary to the tenor and context of the passage"—which was "merely a reiteration of Justice Holmes's classic 'marketplace of ideas' concept"—"but it would also ignore the fact that expressions of 'opinion' may often imply an assertion of objective fact."

Rehnquist's draft then turned to cases like *Ollman*, which he characterized both as incorrectly relying on the *Gertz* dictum and as setting out "a number of factors" to be "considered in deciding" whether a particular statement is one of fact or of opinion. At first blush, Rehnquist purported to reject the *Ollman* factors, asserting that the necessary First Amendment protection "is adequately secured" in such circumstances "by existing constitutional doctrine without the creation of an artificial dichotomy between 'opinion' and fact.'" But then, as Brennan's term history later noted, Rehnquist's opinion proceeded to describe the Court's holdings in *Hepps* and in cases such as *Bresler* and *Falwell*, in a manner that appeared to reintroduce the *Ollman* factors in the constitutional analysis. Specifically, Rehnquist wrote that "*Hepps* stands for the proposition that a statement on matters of public concern must be provable as false before there can be liability under state defamation law," a holding that would "ensure that a statement of opinion relating to matters of public concern which does not contain a provably false factual connotation will receive full constitutional protection." Next, Rehnquist recounted that cases like *Bresler* and *Falwell* provide "protection for statements that cannot 'reasonably be construed as stating actual facts' about an individual," protection that "provides assurance that public debate will not suffer for lack of 'imaginative expression' or the 'rhetorical hyperbole' which has traditionally added much to the discourse of our Nation."

Applying these "established" protections to the column at issue, Rehnquist's draft concluded that it did not contain "the sort of loose, figurative or hyperbolic language which could negate the impression that the writer was seriously maintaining that [Milkovich] committed the crime of perjury. Nor does the general tenor of the article negate this impression." And, Rehnquist wrote, "the connotation" in the column that Milkovich "committed perjury is sufficiently factual to be susceptible of being proved true or false." Accordingly, Rehnquist's draft proceeded to reverse the judgment below and remand the case to the Ohio courts for further proceedings.

All six justices who had voted with Rehnquist at conference quickly joined his opinion. In Blackmun's chambers, the prevailing sentiment was that the opinion accurately captured "the views of those justices, including yourself, who were in the majority at Conference" that "proof of falsity and negligence is sufficient to safeguard the First Amendment values at stake in libel actions, and that no new 'opinion' category is necessary."

Rehnquist circulated a second draft of his opinion, which contained minor changes from his initial circulation, on June 5. That same day, Brennan indicated to the other justices his intention to circulate a dissent. But, as he had ultimately concluded in *Greenmoss Builders*, Brennan decided not to sound the "death knell to protection" for expressions of opinion "that an angry, despairing dissent would ring in a 7 to 2 decision," but rather, as his term history recounted, "to write a dissent that could help shape the nature and reach of the Chief Justice's opinion by showing how the Chief's own words and analysis could be as protective of statements of opinion as the rules developed in response to the *Gertz* dictum." As Brennan analyzed the situation, "[g]iven the alacrity with which state and lower federal courts translated that dictum into a new protective First Amendment doctrine, there seemed a possibility that some of them might be interested in preserving that protection if they could do so consistently with Supreme Court precedent."

Although Brennan recognized that "[s]uch an approach is, of course, far from guaranteed success," he adopted it nonetheless in the opinion that he circulated on June 15. In it, Brennan praised Rehnquist's opinion for addressing the question of the constitutional protection that the First Amendment affords to expressions of opinion "cogently and almost entirely correctly." He agreed with Rehnquist's reliance on *Hepps, Bresler,* and *Falwell,* and his opinion's consequent holding that "only defamatory statements that are capable of being proved false are subject to liability under state libel law" and "that the 'statement' that the plaintiff must prove false under *Hepps* is not invariably the literal phrase published but rather what a reasonable reader would have understood the author to have said." And, he placed the Court's analysis and result in what he considered the appropriate context: "In other words, while the Court today dispels any misimpression that there is a so-called opinion privilege *wholly in addition* to the protections we have already found to be guaranteed by the First Amendment, it determines that a protection for statements of pure opinion is dictated by *existing* First Amendment doctrine."

From this premise, Brennan's opinion proceeded to amplify how, under Rehnquist's analysis, lower courts and litigants were to determine whether the protections for opinion articulated by the Court apply in a given case. Specifically, as his term history described it, he resuscitated the *Ollman* factors within the contours of the chief justice's own analysis by noting that, "[a]mong the circumstances to be scrutinized by a court in ascertaining whether a statement purports to state or imply 'actual facts about an individual,' as shown by the Court's analysis of the statements at issue here, are the same indicia that lower courts have been relying on for the past decade or so to distinguish between statements of fact and statements of opinion: the type of language used, the meaning of the statement in context, whether the statement is verifiable, and the broader societal circumstances in which the statement was made."

Brennan did, however, "part company" with the Court in its application of such factors to the column at issue in *Milkovich*, concluding that, properly viewed, "the

challenged statement cannot reasonably be interpreted as either stating or imply-
ing defamatory facts." In Brennan's view, the column before the Court traded in
"conjecture," a form of expression that he wrote "is intrinsic to 'the free flow of
ideas and opinions on matters of public interest and concern' that is at 'the heart
of the First Amendment.'" As Brennan explained it, in what would turn out to
be the last opinion on the subject that the author of *Sullivan* wrote as a justice of
the Supreme Court:

> The public and press regularly examine the activities of those who affect our
> lives. . . . But often only some of the facts are known, and solely through insistent
> prodding—through conjecture as well as research—can important public questions
> be subjected to the "uninhibited, robust, and wide-open" debate to which this coun-
> try is profoundly committed. Did NASA officials ignore sound warnings that the
> Challenger Space Shuttle would explode? Did Cuban-American leaders arrange for
> John Fitzgerald Kennedy's assassination? Was Kurt Waldheim a Nazi officer? Such
> questions are matters of public concern long before all the facts are unearthed, if they
> ever are. Conjecture is a means of fueling a national discourse on such questions and
> stimulating public pressure for answers from those who know more.

In the last analysis, Brennan wrote, "[p]unishing such conjecture protects reputation only at the cost of expunging a genuinely useful mechanism for public debate."
   Marshall joined Brennan's opinion the same day and it was announced along
with Rehnquist's decision for the Court on June 21, 1990, one month before
Brennan announced his retirement. As we know now, Brennan's gamble paid off
in spectacular fashion. The lower courts were indeed "interested" in preserving
the protections inherent in the fact/opinion distinction and, guided by Brennan's
opinion, they have proceeded to construe Rehnquist's holding as doing little more
than disassociating the *Gertz* dictum from such protection by grounding it instead
in cases like *Hepps* (which Brennan had wisely assigned to O'Connor), *Bresler*,
and *Falwell*. As a result, in the more than two decades since *Milkovich*, the *Ollman*
factors have survived largely unscathed, and the lower courts routinely assess the
content of allegedly defamatory statements in the context in which they were
published to determine, as a matter of law, whether they constitute factual assertions on which a potentially costly defamation action can properly be premised.
Had he lived to see it, Brennan might have taken some extra satisfaction in the fact

that such protection had thrived after being unmoored from Powell's language in *Gertz*, the case in which Brennan had ostensibly lost his ability to influence the development of the constitutional law of defamation.

EPILOGUE

Brennan retired from the Supreme Court on Friday, July 20, 1990, one month after the Court on which he had served for thirty-four years rendered its decision in *Milkovich*. When he announced his retirement, Brennan was the subject of tributes and accolades rarely afforded one of the Court's associate justices. Many of them honored his singular contributions to the protection of civil liberties, including most especially those rights guaranteed by the First Amendment. Whole organizations dedicated to continuing his legacy were created in his honor, including the Brennan Center for Justice at the New York University School of Law. Other organizations, like the Media Law Resource Center, created a prestigious award in his name, honoring his commitment to a free press generally and to the constitutional protections he first articulated in *New York Times Co. v. Sullivan*.

Indeed, when Brennan left the Court, it appeared that, in cases like *Hepps*, *Falwell*, and *Milkovich*, he had succeeded in turning back the efforts of Byron White and others of his colleagues to revisit *Sullivan* or cut back on its protections in any meaningful way. Even Chief Justice Rehnquist, who had been an early critic and had succeeded, in cases like *Firestone* and *Wolston*, in construing those protections as narrowly as possible, had come to embrace and validate them in the opinions he wrote for the Court in *Falwell* and *Milkovich*. And Justice O'Connor, who had been a loyal ally of Powell and Rehnquist early in her tenure, including in depriving Brennan of a majority in *Greenmoss Builders*, had ultimately not only provided the crucial fifth for Brennan's position in *Hepps*, she had written an opinion for the Court that, in many ways, set the stage for what, in Brennan's view, had been a surprising and welcome reaffirmation of *Sullivan* in *Falwell* and *Milkovich*.

Still, when he retired in 1990, Brennan continued to have reason for concern about the fate of *Sullivan*, which he considered one of his most important judicial achievements. Not only would he no longer be there to stand guard against future assaults on his handiwork, but he was replaced on the Court by David Souter, a little-known judge who had spent most of his judicial career in the state courts of New Hampshire, where he left few clues about his views on constitutional law generally and virtually none concerning the constitutional law of defamation. In addition, the other most recently appointed justices, Antonin Scalia and Anthony Kennedy, had both expressed various degrees of antipathy toward *Sullivan* and overt sympathy for some of White's bromides against it. And, at least in later years, Scalia would not hesitate to announce publicly not only that he believed *Sullivan* had been wrongly decided but also that it was something of a poster child for what he deemed both wrong and illegitimate about the process of constitutional interpretation Brennan and his colleagues on the Warren Court had practiced. For his part, Kennedy had reportedly expressed the view in conference that *Hepps*, the product of a five-justice majority that included Powell (the justice he replaced), had been wrongly decided. Even Justice Stevens, who had often voted with Brennan in cases in which *Sullivan* was on the table, had proven an unsteady ally—he had not only written a scathing dissent in *Hepps*, he had articulated a new and seemingly less robust definition of *actual malice* in his opinion for the Court in *Connaughton* and had effectively prevented Brennan from defending *Sullivan* itself from White's attacks in *Greenmoss Builders*.

At the time, however, Brennan looked back with only one regret. Over the years since it was decided, he had come to believe that his choice of the term *actual malice* in *Sullivan* had been a mistake. To be sure, he had no problem with the definition of the term—the requirement that liability be premised on knowledge of falsity or reckless disregard for the truth. The problem, he complained to his biographer toward the end of his tenure, was that juries had a hard time distinguishing between malice as used in the phrase "actual malice" and the more common understanding of the term—hatred, ill will, or a desire to do harm. "I wish I had never used the word 'malice,'" Brennan told his biographer. "I have only confused things with that because people think of malice with its ordinary connotations, not with the special definition I gave it in *Times v. Sullivan*." He would repeat this view, telling his biographer on another occasion, "It's confused everybody. 'Malice' as I defined it is a very different thing. Oh well, you have to make some mistakes."

Brennan would not have long to wait following his retirement to begin to get some answers about the fate of *Sullivan*. In the term immediately after he left the Court, the justices heard two cases that would not only test the ongoing vigor of *Sullivan* itself but would also provide insights concerning the views of some of the Court's newest members on the constitutional rights of the press more generally. For Brennan, and indeed for *Sullivan*, the early returns were decidedly mixed. And, although he surely did not know it at the time, the Court's decisions in 1991 in *Masson v. New Yorker Magazine* and *Cohen v. Cowles Media Co.* would be the last cases to address the issue for the next decade. As it happened, it was not until four years after Brennan's death—with its decision in *Bartnicki v. Vopper*—that the Court would next add to *Sullivan's* progeny. Nor could he have known that, in the dozen years since *Bartnicki* was decided in 2001, the Court has not again seen fit to revisit the constitutional law that Brennan had crafted fifty years earlier in *Sullivan*.

Masson v. New Yorker Magazine, Inc.

When it reached the Court in the October 1990 term, the *Masson* case had already become something of a *cause célèbre*. The plaintiff was Jeffrey Masson, a loquacious and controversial psychoanalyst who had been fired as projects director of the Sigmund Freud Archives (which were then housed at Freud's London home, Maresfield Gardens) after making public comments critical of Freud's theories. The defendants included the highly respected *New Yorker* magazine and Janet Malcolm, one of its most distinguished writers and the author of the well-regarded book *The Journalist and the Murderer*, in which she had famously characterized the journalistic craft as something of a sophisticated con game that took advantage of the naiveté of unwitting sources. Amidst much fanfare, Masson sued Malcolm and the *New Yorker* for defamation. In his complaint, he alleged that, after befriending him following his provocative public statements about Freud, and seducing him to agree to sit with her for more than forty hours of tape-recorded and other interviews, Malcolm had proceeded to fabricate material portions of lengthy quotations she attributed to him in the resulting two-part profile she published in the magazine (and in a book version of those articles), and that she did so in a manner that falsely made him appear to be a braggart, an egomaniac, and a fool.

Masson vigorously denied that he had made the statements attributed to him by Malcolm and, in an ill-advised letter she wrote to the *New York Times* in response, Malcolm asserted that she had accurately quoted Masson in all respects and that each of the quotations could be verified by reference to the tape recordings she had made of her various interviews with him. In fact, however, many but not all of the quotations identified in Masson's complaint appeared on the tapes, although the rest were contained in typewritten notes that Malcolm testified she took from the tapes as well as from handwritten notes she had made of those interviews she conducted with Masson that were not recorded. Unfortunately for Malcolm, the handwritten notes had gone missing.

As a result, when discovery was completed, and Malcolm and her publishers moved for summary judgment, they could not, in the face of Masson's denials that he had in fact uttered a handful of the more incendiary words and sentences she had attributed to him, effectively argue that there were no disputed issues of material fact for a jury to resolve on the issue of truth, at least on the issue of whether Masson had actually said them. Instead, Malcolm's lawyers invoked the Court's decision in *Time, Inc. v. Pape* and argued that the quotations that Malcolm attributed to Masson in the articles were, at the very least, "rational interpretations" of other, analogous statements that he had in fact made and which were reflected in the tape recorded interviews. Thus, for example, although Masson denied that he ever used the phrase "a place of sex, women [and] fun" to describe his plans for Maresfield Gardens, where Masson aspired to take up residence after the house's current occupant—Freud's daughter Anna—died, the tapes did contain passages in which he discussed living in the Freud house and described how he and another psychoanalyst would "pass women on to each other" when he did. In another, Masson denied asserting, as Malcolm quoted him to say, that he would soon be acknowledged as the "greatest analyst who ever lived," but the tapes did reveal him boasting that "psychoanalysis stands or falls with me now," albeit in the context of discussing the impact on the discipline of "the things I discovered."

Both a federal district court in California and a divided three-judge panel of the Ninth Circuit Court of Appeals in San Francisco accepted the defendants' "rational interpretation" theory and granted summary judgment to Malcolm and her publishers. In the court of appeals, however, Judge Alex Kozinski, who had served as a law clerk for both Justice Kennedy on the Ninth Circuit and for Chief Justice Burger on the Supreme Court, and was himself then widely considered a candidate for appointment to the Supreme Court, wrote an elaborate dissent in which he argued that *Sullivan* could not be read to protect the deliberate falsification of quotations of the kind that Malcolm stood accused of. The court's decision, and especially Kozinski's dissent, which featured sharp rebukes to Malcolm and *New Yorker* (based on the judicial assumption, for purposes of summary judgment, that Masson's allegations that she had fabricated the quotations in the first place were in fact true), received considerable press attention. On October 1, 1990, less than three months after Brennan had retired from the Court, the justices granted Masson's petition that they review the Ninth Circuit's decision.

The case was decided on June 20, 1991, and the Court's opinion was written by Justice Kennedy. It reversed the Ninth Circuit's decision with respect to five of the six allegedly fabricated quotations that remained disputed, thereby reaching largely the same result that Kozinski, Kennedy's former law clerk, had advocated in his dissent below. But Kennedy did so in a manner far less hostile to the defendants' contentions and, more importantly, in an opinion that both reflected a nuanced appreciation of those contentions and articulated a constitutional rule that appeared to honor *Sullivan*'s commitment to "robust, uninhibited and wide open" expression. In that sense, although the defendants most definitely "lost" the *Masson* case in the Supreme Court, the media itself appeared to secure something of a victory, not unlike it had in Rehnquist's decision for the Court in *Milkovich* the preceding term.

Specifically, Kennedy began the substantive portion of his opinion by acknowledging that a "fabricated quotation may injure reputation in at least two senses, either giving rise to a conceivable claim of defamation." First, Kennedy explained, "the quotation may injure because it attributes an untrue factual assertion to the speaker," such as a false confession that he had committed a crime. Second, he continued, "regardless of the truth or falsity of the factual matters asserted within the quoted statement, the attribution may result in injury to reputation because the manner of expression or even the fact that the statement was made indicates a negative personal trait or an attitude the speaker does not hold."

By the same token, unlike Judge Kozinski in the court of appeals, Kennedy emphasized that not all alterations to quotations made with knowledge of their inaccuracy should properly ground a finding of actual malice. In some instances, Kennedy wrote, readers will not understand the use of quotation marks to denote that the "speaker" actually uttered the precise words attributed to him. Thus, for

example, when the challenged "work is so-called docudrama or historical fiction," or one that purports to "recreate[] conversations from memory, not from
recordings," such circumstances may dictate "that the quotations should not be
interpreted as the actual statements of the speaker to whom they are attributed."
For these reasons, Kennedy's opinion concluded, if "every alteration constituted
the falsity required to prove actual malice," as Kozinski had all but contended below,
"the practice of journalism, which the First Amendment standard is designed to
protect, would require a radical change, one inconsistent with our precedents and
First Amendment principles."

Accordingly, Kennedy articulated a different standard to govern defamation
claims based, as Masson's was, on allegedly fabricated quotations. Drawing on the
Court's decisions in *Hepps* and *Milkovich*, Kennedy explained that, in the wake of
those precedents, an allegedly defamatory statement cannot be "considered false
unless it 'would have a different effect on the mind of the reader from that which
the pleaded truth would have produced.'" As a result, he wrote, if "an author alters
a speaker's words but effects no material change in meaning, including any meaning conveyed by the manner or fact of expression, the speaker suffers no injury to
reputation that is compensable as a defamation." Put differently, even "a deliberate
alteration of the words uttered by a plaintiff does not equate with knowledge of
falsity for purposes of *New York Times Co. v. Sullivan* and *Gertz v. Robert Welch, Inc.*
unless the alteration results in a material change in the meaning conveyed by the
statement." And, although he rejected the Ninth Circuit majority's invocation of
the "rational interpretation" standard derived from the Court's decision in *Pape*,
Kennedy took pains to reaffirm the validity of that standard in appropriate cases:

> The protection for rational interpretation serves First Amendment principles by
> allowing an author the interpretive license that is necessary when relying upon
> ambiguous sources. Where, however, a writer uses a quotation, and where a reason-
> able reader would conclude that the quotation purports to be a verbatim repetition
> of a statement by the speaker, the quotation marks indicate that the author is not
> involved in an interpretation of the speaker's ambiguous statement, but attempting
> to convey what the speaker said.

In Masson's case, Kennedy continued, five of the six quotations that remained
in dispute could be construed by a reasonable jury to communicate a materially

different meaning from the other statements concededly made by Masson during the recorded interviews. The Court nevertheless concluded that one of them—Malcolm's attribution to Masson of the statement that he had changed his middle name to "Moussaieff" from Lloyd because it "sounded better," when, in a tape-recorded interview, he said that he did so because he "just liked" it—"did not materially alter the meaning of his statement."

Kennedy's opinion for the Court was joined by six other justices. In addition to Marshall and Blackmun, Brennan's longtime allies, Kennedy garnered the votes of Rehnquist, Stevens, O'Connor, and Souter, Brennan's successor. He did not, however, entirely win over either White or Scalia, the two justices most overtly hostile to *Sullivan* itself. In a dissenting opinion written by White, they rejected the Court's "material change in meaning" standard, characterizing it as "not only a less manageable one than" that proposed by Kozinski below—i.e., that disputed issues of fact with respect to any alteration in quotation, beyond changes for purposes of grammar or syntax were sufficient to get a plaintiff past summary judgment on the issues of falsity and actual malice—"it also assigns to courts issues that are for a jury to decide." Thus, they argued, "the defendants' motion for summary judgment based on lack of malice should not have been granted on any of the six quotations."

Although the Court's first post-Brennan decision was greeted with something of a sigh of relief by journalists, authors, and filmmakers, it provided little immediate solace to Malcolm and her publishers. Following the Supreme Court's remand to the Ninth Circuit, "for further proceedings consistent with" Kennedy's opinion, the case dragged on for another five years, during which they endured two jury trials and two additional appearances before the Ninth Circuit. In the first trial, the jurors found in favor of the *New Yorker* but reached a mixed verdict as to Malcolm in which they were unable to come to an agreement with respect to whether Masson had sustained any damages. At a second trial, the jury unanimously found in favor of Malcolm with respect to all of the disputed quotations. By the time that verdict was affirmed by the Ninth Circuit in June 1996, however, the defendants had incurred literally millions of dollars in attorneys fees and, despite her ultimate vindication, Malcolm was forever tied to Masson's claims that she had fabricated quotations in the manner detailed in Kozinski's initial dissent and, to a lesser extent, in Kennedy's opinion for the Supreme Court. And, in a final twist, after the second trial, while the litigation process continued in the court of appeals, Malcolm's two-year-old granddaughter, while exploring a bookcase in her grandmother's country home, found a notebook filled with handwritten notes wedged behind a shelf of books. The notebook included, in Malcolm's hand, many of the notes that she had all along sworn she had taken of the interviews she had conducted with Masson when she did not have her tape recorder. In its pages were recounted, verbatim, three of the five quotations that Masson had denied saying at trial.

Cohen v. Cowles Media Co.

Four days after it decided *Masson*, the Court announced its decision in *Cohen v. Cowles Media Co.* Like the purportedly "fabricated quotations" at issue in *Masson*, the *Cohen* case featured a set of factual allegations that placed the journalists before the Court in a decidedly less than favorable light. In *Cohen*, the plaintiff, a political operative working for a firm supporting the Republican candidate for Lieutenant Governor in Minnesota, separately approached reporters for the two major daily newspapers serving the Minneapolis-St. Paul region. In return for a promise of confidentiality, he supplied both reporters with negative information about the opposing candidate, specifically that she had once been convicted of petit theft (for leaving a store without paying for $6 worth of merchandise) and that she previously had been charged with unlawful assembly (for participating in a protest rally). When the reporters returned to their respective newspapers, their editors independently reached the same conclusion—the fact that Cohen was peddling these relatively minor allegations on behalf of the campaign for which he worked was as newsworthy as the charges themselves. Accordingly, both editors decided to identify Cohen as the source of the information in their stories, without regard to the promises of confidentiality the reporters had made to him. Shortly after the stories identifying him were published, Cohen was fired.

Unable to sue the newspapers for defamation because the facts reported about him were true, Cohen instead asserted claims against them for breach of contract and fraud, both based on the newspapers' breach of their agents' promise to keep his identity secret. He prevailed in the trial court, where a jury awarded him $200,000 in compensatory damages and $500,000 in punitive damages. An intermediate appellate court held that Cohen had failed to establish a claim for fraud under state law (and vacated the punitive damages award that was based on it), but upheld the jury's award of $200,000 for breach of contract. The Minnesota Supreme Court, however, vacated the remainder of the jury's verdict, holding that Cohen had also failed to state a claim for breach of contract under state law. In the course of its decision, however, the court wondered whether Cohen could have prevailed on a claim for promissory estoppel under state law. Although its opinion was less than clear on this point, it could be read to state that, even if such a claim were viable under Minnesota law, it would nevertheless run afoul of the First Amendment.

When Cohen sought review in the Supreme Court, the newspapers both opposed his request primarily on the ground that the Minnesota court had not decided any constitutional question—that Cohen had never asserted a claim for promissory estoppel and that the Minnesota Supreme Court's musings about the invalidity of such a claim were predicated on state law, not the First Amendment, in any event. Even after the Supreme Court accepted the case for review, the newspapers pressed this argument as their principal contention in their briefs on the merits and at argument.

Although the Supreme Court could have, in its discretion, denied review on this ground and, alternatively, could have avoided the First Amendment issue raised by Cohen on this basis even following consideration of the merits, when it announced its decision on June 24, 1990, a 5–4 majority asserted that the news-papers' contention with respect to the scope of the Minnesota Supreme Court's decision did not "merit extended discussion." Rather, in an opinion by Justice White, the Court proceeded to hold that the First Amendment did not preclude Cohen from basing a claim for promissory estoppel on the contention that the newspapers had accurately identified him as the source of the negative informa-tion about the Democratic candidate. Chief Justice Rehnquist and Justices Stevens, Scalia, and Kennedy joined White's opinion.

In the Supreme Court, the newspapers had relied on the *Daily Mail* principle, the line of cases starting with *Cox Broadcasting Corp. v. Cohn* and running through *Florida Star v. B.J.F.*, which provides that the publication of truthful information, lawfully obtained, about a matter of public concern cannot be made illegal under state law absent a need to vindicate a governmental interest of the highest order. In *Cohen*, the newspapers argued, the core of the promissory estoppel claim hypoth-esized by the Minnesota Supreme Court was that Cohen had sustained injury as a result of their publication of truthful information about him—that he had provided them with information about the opposing candidate. White's opinion, however, rejected that contention, holding that the case "is not controlled by this line of cases but, rather, by the equally well-established line of decisions holding that generally applicable laws do not offend the First Amendment simply because their enforcement against the press has incidental effects on its ability to gather and report the news."

That White relied on the "equally well established line of decisions" addressing "generally applicable laws" was hardly surprising, since he was the author of the Court's opinions in virtually all of them. From *Herbert v. Lando* in the defamation context, to the Court's decisions in *Branzburg v. Hayes* and *Zurcher v. Stanford Daily* exploring other alleged intrusions on the press's First Amendment rights to gather news, White had championed the notion that generally applicable laws, like the obligation of all citizens to testify before grand juries (*Branzburg*), to comply with search warrants (*Zurcher*), and to respond to civil discovery (*Herbert*), are fully applicable to reporters and editors even if they can be said to have an "incidental" impact on their ability to gather information for publication. In none of these prior cases, however, had the Court extended the rationale to a case, like *Cohen*, where a generally applicable law—in this case, the law of promissory estoppel—was invoked to impose liability on the actual publication of information.

In his opinion for the Court, White explained away this result on a number of grounds. First, he wrote that, as the Court had long recognized, the *Daily Mail* principle applied only in those cases in which the information itself had been "lawfully acquired" and that, in this case, the newspapers had "obtained Cohen's name only by making a promise that they did not honor." Second, he rejected the notion that, in this context, the newspapers were being penalized for publishing truthful information at all. Rather, he asserted, the "payment of compensatory damages in this case is constitutionally indistinguishable from a generous bonus paid to a confidential news source." And, third, he concluded that the *Daily Mail* principle was inapplicable because, in those cases to which it applied, the "State itself defined the content of the publications that would trigger liability," while, in this case, "any restrictions that may be placed on the publication of truthful information are self-imposed."

Finally, White's opinion brushed aside the contention that the result it reached could not be squared with the Court's decision in *Falwell*. As White saw it, Cohen was not "attempting to use a promissory estoppel cause of action to avoid the strict requirements for establishing a defamation claim." Rather, he was seeking damages "for breach of a promise that caused him to lose his job and lowered his earning capacity."

There were two dissenting opinions. In one, Justice Blackmun, on behalf of himself and Justices Marshall and Souter, rejected White's reliance on *Branzburg* and the other opinions he had authored dealing with "generally applicable laws," asserting that those "cases did *not* involve the imposition of liability based upon the content of speech." In Blackmun's view, the case was properly controlled by *Falwell*, in which a unanimous Court had held that another "generally applicable law"—the tort of intentional infliction of emotional distress—could not properly be invoked "to penalize the expression of opinion," precisely because "the law was subject to the strictures of the First Amendment." For Blackmun, "the operation of Minnesota's doctrine of promissory estoppel in this case cannot be said to have a merely 'incidental' burden on speech." Rather, as in *Falwell*, "the publication of important political speech *is* the claimed violation" and, as a result, "the law may not be enforced to punish the expression of truthful information or opinion."

Justice Souter, Brennan's successor on the Court, not only joined in Blackmun's opinion but also felt constrained to articulate his own views. His separate opinion, which was joined not only by Blackmun and Marshall but also by Justice O'Connor, similarly rejected White's reliance on the fact that the law of promissory estoppel is "generally applicable" and, citing *Falwell*, focused instead on an evaluation of the "competing interests involved" in order to "determine the legitimacy of burdening constitutional interests." In so doing, he took issue with White's contention that the Court could "dispense" with such an analysis because "the burden on publication is in a sense 'self-imposed' by the newspaper's voluntary promise of confidentiality." Instead, Souter asserted that "freedom of the press is ultimately founded on the value of enhancing [public] discourse for the sake of a citizenry better informed and thus more prudently self-governed" and, as a result, it did not necessarily matter, for First Amendment purposes, whether an individual speaker had purported to restrict his own right to disseminate information of value to that citizenry.

This last passage of Souter's opinion, with its references to the Meiklejohnian concepts of a self-governing citizenry that undergirded *Sullivan* itself, could easily have been authored by Brennan. In this sense, therefore, Brennan's presence on the Court in *Cohen*, had he not retired when he did, would not itself have altered the 5–4 vote in favor of the plaintiff. Still, one has to wonder whether, as the Court's senior justice, Brennan might not have been able to accomplish what Souter, its newest member, could not—use his vast experience in such matters to cajole Stevens, Kennedy, or even Rehnquist to join him in applying *Falwell* and the *Daily Mail* cases to protect the publication of truthful information about a matter of public concern. As it was, however, White, the Court's then-reigning senior justice, was able to garner those votes in support of his own signature theory—that the application of so-called "generally applicable laws" did not merit *any* First Amendment scrutiny, even when they operated to curtail truthful speech about public matters.

Cohen was the last defamation-related case on which Byron White would sit as a justice of the Supreme Court. With his retirement in 1993, following Brennan's three years earlier, the Court had lost two justices who, in the end, had come to hold very different views about *New York Times Co. v. Sullivan* and the body of constitutional law it had spawned over the almost three decades they served together. Even as their views of *Sullivan* diverged, however, White and Brennan remained good friends. White would regularly stop in to Brennan's chambers during the fall to bring him freshly picked apples and pies baked from them. There was a genuine warmth and affection between them. The divergence in their views on *Sullivan* is, however, well-represented in a story about how they each reacted to a *Wall Street Journal* article published on February 27, 1981.

The article, which appeared prominently on the newspaper's front page, discussed a New Jersey land dispute and a series of lawsuits between a local family and an amusement park that resulted from it. The litigation eventually ended up in the U.S. Supreme Court where Brennan, in his role as "Circuit Justice" for the federal circuit that encompassed New Jersey, denied a request for a stay of a lower court's judgment pending Supreme Court review. In its article, the *Journal* effectively accused Brennan of a conflict-of-interest, saying he singlehandedly denied the family selling the land the right to be heard in the Supreme Court when his son was a lawyer working for the amusement park. In fact, Brennan did not know—and could not have discerned from the papers filed in the Supreme Court—that his son was involved in the case and, once he learned of his son's role, he took no further part in the full Court's consideration of the matter. Nevertheless, after the article's publication, Brennan received numerous angry letters complaining about his perceived unethical conduct, some of which he shared with colleagues like White. And, when Brennan asked for a letter to the editor to be published to correct the record and clear his reputation, the *Journal* waited two full months and then ran only a short correction on page 5 of its April 27, 1981 edition.

Brennan was offended and angry. He told his biographer that the *Journal's* conduct was "indefensible." But ultimately he brushed it off and never let it affect his view of the First Amendment protections to which the media, and all other speakers, were entitled. A year or so after the *Journal* article, however, White used the occasion of a phone call about another matter with the newspaper's Supreme Court correspondent to lambast the *Journal* and the press generally. He railed against the media for several minutes for the way the *Journal* had treated Brennan and how it had not even responded to, much less published, his letter to the editor. For Brennan, the *Journal* article was a painful and embarrassing moment that passed and said nothing about whether the press was entitled to the protections of the First Amendment. For White, the same episode spoke volumes about how irresponsible journalists can be and reinforced his view that they are undeserving of the protections that Brennan advocated for them.

The narrowness of White's majority in *Cohen* suggested that, in the years ahead, the Court would continue to struggle, as it had almost annually since *Gertz*, to reconcile the robust protection of the press and other public speakers ushered into the First Amendment by Brennan in *Sullivan* with the growing antipathy to that constitutional doctrine expressed by White and, as the years progressed, Scalia. Brennan, however, would not live to see another such skirmish. After its decision in *Cohen*, the Court simply stopped hearing defamation and other cases in which the First Amendment protections fashioned in *Sullivan* and its progeny were at issue. Since 1964, rarely had a term gone by in which the Supreme Court had not adjudicated at least one such case. From its 1991 decision in *Cohen*, however, until Brennan's death in July 1997, the Court did not hear a single such case. Indeed, the Court's silence with respect to the First Amendment principles for which Brennan had fought so long and so hard would continue for another four years.

In all, an entire decade would pass before the Court would again revisit *Sullivan* and its ongoing efficacy. When it did, in its 2001 decision in *Bartnicki v. Vopper*, its composition had changed markedly. Not only were Brennan's latter-day allies Marshall and Blackmun long retired, but so was his old adversary Byron White. Their replacements, Justices Thomas, Ginsberg, and Breyer, had not, during their relatively brief tenure on the Court, taken part in a single case in which the First Amendment protections first articulated in *Sullivan* were at issue. Of all the justices

on the Court in 2001, only Chief Justice Rehnquist had participated in its deliberations in *Gertz* and only he, O'Connor, and Stevens had endured the drama that
had unfolded in *Greenmoss Builders*. As a result, how the justices would treat *Sullivan* was very much an open question up to the moment the Court announced
its decision in *Bartnicki v. Vopper* on May 21, 2001.

Bartnicki v. Vopper

Bartnicki was one of three cases which, as fate would have it, had percolated through
the lower courts in three separate federal circuits at almost precisely the same time
and raised the identical constitutional issue—as Justice Stevens ultimately put it
at the outset of his opinion for the Court in *Bartnicki*, "an important question
concerning what degree of protection, if any, the First Amendment provides to
speech that discloses the content of an illegally intercepted communication." In all
three cases, the participants in telephone conversations that had been intercepted
and recorded by a third party, in violation of the federal and analogous state wiretap laws, had sued for damages yet another party, who had not itself recorded the
conversation but had received and disseminated its contents more broadly. The
three district and three circuit courts of appeal that had considered the issue had
reached divergent results based on a variety of different constitutional theories,
which made the cases ideal candidates for Supreme Court review to resolve the
resulting "conflict" among the circuits.

In the first of the three cases to be decided by a federal appellate court, *Boehner
v. McDermott*, the District of Columbia Circuit had held that Congressman James
McDermott, the ranking Democrat on the House Ethics Committee, could be held
liable in damages for disclosing to the news media the tape of an illegally recorded
telephone conference among members of the House Republican leadership, which
he had received in his capacity as a member of the Ethics Committee from a Florida
couple that had recorded it using a scanner. A majority of the three-judge panel
that heard the case reversed the decision of a district court, which had determined
that the subject matter of the call—then Speaker of the House Newt Gingrich's
anticipated strategy in responding to charges that he had committed ethical vio-
lations—addressed an issue of public concern, and the tape was a concededly
accurate rendition of what the participants in the call had said. Accordingly, the

district court had held that the plaintiff, future Speaker and then-Congressman John Boehner (who was one of the participants in the call), was precluded by the First Amendment, and specifically by application of the *Daily Mail* principle, from successfully invoking the wiretap acts' provisions that permitted an award of civil damages against anyone who disseminated the contents of an unlawfully intercepted communication. A majority of the court of appeals disagreed, on the ground that Congress had the power, the First Amendment notwithstanding, to prohibit the dissemination of information that had been unlawfully acquired, regardless of its accuracy or public significance. One judge, David Sentelle, dissented, asserting that the *Daily Mail* principle controlled and that the First Amendment protected McDermott's right to disseminate the contents of the tape to the press.

In the last of the three cases, *Peavy v. WFAA-TV, Inc.*, the Fifth Circuit held that a Dallas television station could be held liable under the federal and the analogous Texas wiretap statute for, among other things, disseminating to its viewers information derived from cordless telephone conversations of a local school official that had been unlawfully intercepted by his neighbor. In *Peavy*, like *Boehner*, the subject matter of the recorded conversations addressed issues of public concern—the plaintiff's apparent participation in a host of questionable activities in his capacity as a public official. Rejecting the First Amendment-based arguments mounted by the defendants, the court of appeals in *Peavy* determined that the *Daily Mail* principle did not apply because the information ultimately disseminated by the defendants had been unlawfully acquired and that the media defendants had actively counseled the neighbor in connection with his unlawful conduct.

Instead, the Fifth Circuit concluded, as the D.C. Circuit had in *Boehner v. McDermott*, that because the statutes were "content neutral"—i.e., their prohibitions on speech were not justified by reference to its content—they were properly subject to only an "intermediate" level of First Amendment scrutiny. Moreover, both courts held, the statutes survived such scrutiny because they constituted a reasonable legislative attempt both to dry up the market for intercepted communications and to protect the privacy of cellular and cordless telephone users.

The *Bartnicki* case, the only one of the three that the Supreme Court chose to consider on its merits, arose from analogous facts and raised the same constitutional issue. Because it represents the first case addressing the First Amendment protections derived from *Sullivan* to be decided by the Supreme Court in the decade following *Cohen*, and remains the last case to do so as we reach the fiftieth anniversary of

CHAPTER 10

Sullivan a decade thereafter, its facts (and their relation to those before the Court in *Sullivan* itself) are worth recounting in some detail.

Bartnicki came to the Court from Northeastern Pennsylvania, an economically depressed region that has never quite recovered from the collapse of the coal mining industry that sustained it for much of the last century. That economic reality afforded little reason for the sons and daughters of Scranton, Wilkes-Barre, and the small towns that surround them to remain there when they reached adulthood, leaving the region with a population dominated by the parents and grandparents they left behind. Many of these folks were not pleased at the prospect of their property taxes going up to pay for raises for local school teachers. The teachers, however, were not happy about the local Board of Education's publicly stated refusal to offer them a meaningful pay increase.

Not surprisingly, and especially in a region that had grown up on labor strife and more than occasional violence in the coal mines, the stand-off between the Board of Education and the teachers' union in the Wyoming Valley West School District became less than pleasant. The negotiations were characterized by unexplained vandalism and threats of economic reprisals by both sides. All of this, but most especially the negotiations themselves, was major news in the local community. It spawned the creation of a taxpayer's group to oppose the teachers' demands, founded by one Jack Yocum. It also became the frequent subject of heated debate on local "talk radio" programs, including the "Fred Williams Show." Williams, whose real last name is Vopper (hence the name of the case), was something of a local Rush Limbaugh and, on his daily radio program, he was a predictable and vocal critic of the teachers. His targets often included Anthony Kane, the longtime president of the local bargaining unit of the state teacher's union and himself a teacher at Wyoming Valley West High School, and Gloria Bartnicki, a former teacher at that same high school and the teachers' chief negotiator employed directly by the union. For months, Bartnicki and Kane were the subjects of Williams's criticism, which they described as his "ranting and raving." As Kane later put it, Williams "poked fun at me; he tried to incite people. . . . I don't think anybody has to be subjected to that. He called me a goon. He said I was incompetent."

In May 1993, tensions were high. The union was about to stage a one-day strike near the close of the school term, something it had never done in all the years that Kane had been its local president. One night, he and Bartnicki discussed the situation over the telephone, he sitting in his home and she in her car using a cellular telephone. They talked about the gap between the percentage salary increase offered by the Board of Education and that demanded by the teachers. At one point in the conversation, Kane said this about the members of the school board:

> If they're not gonna move for three percent, we're gonna have to go to their, their homes . . . to blow off their front porches, we'll have to do some work on some of those guys. . . . Really, uh, really and truthfully because this is, you know, this is bad news.

The telephone conversation was tape recorded, presumably by someone using a portable scanner who was able to intercept the signal coming to and going from Bartnicki's cellular telephone. Some time later, an unknown person deposited a copy of the recording, without any markings to identify its origin, in Yocum's mailbox. Yocum promptly alerted several members of the school board to the tape's contents and played it for them. He also provided copies of the tape to several newspapers and radio stations, including to Fred Williams.

Williams played the tape on his program for three consecutive days in September 1993, at about the same time that an arbitrator had issued a nonbinding proposal to settle the dispute, one that was widely viewed as favorable to the teachers. During these three days, Williams played the tape once in its entirety, played the portion containing the "threat" repeatedly (often accompanied by sound effects of a bomb exploding), and discussed its contents with dozens of listeners and with two members of the school board, who appeared as guests on the program and claimed that they did in fact fear for their physical safety. Throughout these broadcasts, Williams expressed his strong disapproval of the tactics he believed were revealed on the tape, called for both Bartnicki and Kane—who he took to referring to as "the goon and the goonette"—to resign, and urged the school board not to be intimidated.

Immediately following Williams's initial broadcast, other local media disseminated the contents of the tape as well. Two local television stations reported stories disclosing its contents and played portions of it later that day and evening. Two local newspapers published articles in their next editions, and one even included a transcript of portions of the Bartnicki-Kane conversation. Bartnicki and Kane took no action against these other media entities, however, because—as they later testified—they "appreciated" the "fair and accurate" manner in which the other media had treated the story. Williams was another matter. Bartnicki and Kane believed that his criticism of them had injured their reputations. As Kane testified, "I feel my reputation as a professional person in the community and a citizen of this community—I've been a good citizen—has been held up to ridicule."

They did not, however, sue Williams for defamation. In fact, they could not. After *Sullivan*, they could not prevail in a defamation suit, no matter how injurious to their reputations the Williams program was, since what he reported about them—their own words as recorded on tape—was entirely accurate. Instead, they invoked both the Pennsylvania and federal wiretap laws. Both statutes, like their counterparts in Florida and Texas, provide not only for criminal penalties, they also authorize the participants in unlawfully intercepted telephone calls to sue to recover money damages, not just from the persons who intercept such a call but also from anyone who disseminates its contents with "reason to know" it had been unlawfully intercepted. Bartnicki and Kane contended that Williams had reason to know he was disseminating the contents of an unlawfully intercepted call because the tape itself revealed that Bartnicki was speaking on a cellular phone—which Williams knew could be intercepted by a radio scanner. Thus, they sued Williams and the two radio stations that broadcast his show, seeking the recovery of up to $10,000 each in damages fixed by law (regardless of whether they suffered any actual harm) as well as punitive damages to be determined by a jury.

During the early stages of the case, the plaintiffs learned that Williams had secured the tape from Yokum, their old nemesis. So, they added him to the suit as a defendant as well, since he too had disseminated the contents of the tape—to Williams, to the school board, and to the other local media—with reason to know it had been unlawfully intercepted.

In proceedings in the trial court, both plaintiffs conceded that they could not prove that they had suffered any actual damages at all because of the defendants' dissemination of their call, at least no damage beyond that to their reputations as a consequence of the public's knowledge of what they had in fact said to each other. In their lawsuit, however, they correctly argued that none of this mattered, at least for purposes of determining whether the statutes had been violated and whether they could recover damages pursuant to their terms. On their face, the wiretap statutes authorized Bartnicki and Kane to recover damages even if they in fact had no expectation that their conversation was private, even if they suffered no actual harm as a result of its public disclosure, even if the information disclosed by the defendants addressed a matter of obvious public concern, and even if the defendants played no role, of any kind, in the unlawful interception of their call in the first place.

The defendants' only real recourse, therefore, was to argue that the statutes, at least as applied to the circumstances of this case, violated the First Amendment. Accordingly, throughout the litigation, they contended that the case was controlled by *Sullivan* and the cases that followed it, specifically those cases articulating the *Daily Mail* principle. They argued that, by broadcasting the tape, they had disseminated to the public truthful information about a matter of public concern, an activity protected by the First Amendment even in the face of a law that purported to declare such information to be "private."

In the lower courts, however, not a single judge accepted the defendants' contention. The district court, for its part, held that the case was controlled not by *Sullivan*, but by *Cohen*. The wiretap statutes, it reasoned, like the law of promissory estoppel at issue in *Cohen*, were neutral laws of general application. Accordingly, they were not properly subject to any limitations imposed by the First Amendment at all. On appeal, the Third Circuit similarly rejected the defendants' claim that it should properly apply the *Daily Mail* principle, but it did not rely on *Cohen* in doing so. Rather, like the D.C. Circuit in *Boehner* and the Fifth Circuit in *Peavy*, all three members of the Third Circuit panel that heard the *Bartnicki* case concluded that, because the federal and Pennsylvania wiretap statutes are "content neutral," they were properly subject to "intermediate" constitutional scrutiny, which asked only whether they "'further[ ] an important or substantial governmental interest'" and whether their "'incidental restriction on alleged First Amendment freedoms is no greater than is essential to the furtherance of that interest.'"

Ultimately, however, the Third Circuit parted company with its sister circuits, not in its method of constitutional analysis, but rather in its application of the intermediate scrutiny test. Specifically, two of the three judges concluded that, although the general "interest in protecting privacy" of cellular telephone conversations constitutes a "significant state interest," the "connection between prohibiting third parties from using or disclosing intercepted material and preventing the initial interception is indirect at best" and the government had offered no support for its "unsupported allegation" that the statutes were likely to prevent interceptions in the first place. Accordingly, they held that the application of the statutes to Vopper, the radio stations, and Yokum violated the First Amendment. The third member of the Third Circuit panel—Judge Louis Pollack, a former dean of both the Yale

and University of Pennsylvania law schools—agreed that intermediate scrutiny
applied, but concluded, like the D.C. and Fifth Circuits, that the statutes satisfied
such scrutiny and were therefore constitutionally applied to all three defendants.

Thus, by the time *Bartnicki*, *Boehner*, and *Peavy* reached the Supreme Court, of
the nine appellate judges that had addressed the issue, eight had concluded that
the statutes were subject to only "intermediate" First Amendment scrutiny and
that neither *Sullivan* nor the *Daily Mail* principle it spawned were of any relevance
to the constitutional analysis. In all, twelve federal judges had opined on whether
the referenced provisions of the federal and state wiretap laws violated the First
Amendment—five had concluded that it did, seven that it did not. At the urging
of the solicitor general of the United States, which had intervened in all three
cases to defend the federal statute's constitutionality, the Supreme Court agreed
to resolve only *Bartnicki v. Vopper* on its merits, while holding *Boehner* and *Peavy*
in abeyance pending its decision in *Bartnicki*.

On May 21, the Court issued its decision. In an opinion by Justice Stevens
written on behalf of six justices, the Court held that the First Amendment precluded Bartnicki and Kane from pursuing their claims against Williams, Yocum,
and the radio stations. Justice Breyer, joined by Justice O'Connor, wrote a separate, concurring opinion, and Chief Justice Rehnquist, joined by Justices Thomas
and Scalia, dissented.

At the outset of its opinion, the Court agreed with the government that the
wiretap act is a "content-neutral law." Nevertheless, Justice Stevens wrote that,
even when a law is content-neutral, what he called a "naked prohibition against
disclosure is fairly characterized as a regulation of pure speech" and not a "regulation of conduct" that can coexist with the First Amendment. A prohibition on
"the publication of truthful information seldom can satisfy constitutional standards,"
Stevens noted, invoking expressly the "*Daily Mail* principle."

The Court then proceeded to address what it described as "a narrower version"
of a question "raised" but not resolved in footnote 8 in the Court's opinion in
Florida Star. According to Stevens, the "narrower" question before the Supreme
Court in *Bartnicki* "is this: 'Where the punished publisher of information has
obtained the information in question in a manner lawful in itself but from a
source who has obtained it unlawfully, may the government punish the ensuing
publication of that information based on the defect in a chain?'" The answer, Stevens wrote, is "clear"—"a stranger's illegal conduct does not suffice to remove the

First Amendment shield from speech about a matter of public concern." Rather, to overcome the First Amendment, the government carries the heavy burden of showing a "need . . . of the highest order."

Having answered the relevant portion of the question reserved in *Florida Star*, the Court undertook to apply the *Daily Mail* principle to the two interests asserted by the government in support of the law's constitutionality. It held that neither justified the wiretap statutes' application to the expression before the Court in *Bartnicki*, but for very different reasons.

The first interest, the asserted need to "dry up the market" for the fruits of unlawful interceptions, the Court concluded, simply did not rise to the level of a "'need of the highest order.'" Rather, Stevens observed, the "normal method of deterring unlawful conduct is to impose an appropriate punishment on the person who engages in it." Thus, he wrote, "if the sanctions that presently attach to a violation" of the prohibition on interception contained in wiretap laws "do not provide sufficient deterrence, perhaps those sanctions should be made more severe." In any event, the Court emphasized, "it would be quite remarkable to hold that speech by a law-abiding possessor of information can be suppressed in order to deter conduct by a non-law-abiding third party."

The second asserted interest, the Court explained, raised significantly different issues. "Privacy of communication," Stevens noted, "is an important interest," rendered more important still where "the fear of public disclosure of private conversations might well have a chilling effect on private speech." In this context, the Court indicated that *Bartnicki* "present[s] a conflict between interests of the highest order—on the one hand, the interest in the full and free dissemination of information concerning public issues, and, on the other hand, the interest in individual privacy and, more specifically, in fostering private speech." Applying the *Daily Mail* principle under such circumstances—where an articulated governmental interest is indeed of the "highest order"—required a more finely tuned consideration of the competing interests.

It is here, however, that Stevens's opinion, ostensibly written for the Court, and Breyer's concurring opinion, written for himself and O'Connor, appear to diverge, at least in their emphasis. For Stevens, "[i]n this case, privacy concerns give way when balanced against the interest in publishing matters of public importance." As Stevens asserted, "[o]ne of the costs associated with participation in public affairs is an attendant loss of privacy" and, as a result, the "'right of privacy does not prohibit any publication of matter which is of public or general interest.'" In *Bartnicki*, therefore, where the information disseminated was, in Stevens's own words, "unquestionably a matter of public concern," and the defendants "were clearly engaged in debate about that concern," the Court held that plaintiffs' privacy interest was required to yield to the First Amendment.

Although he and O'Connor purported to join in Stevens's opinion, and not simply in the Court's judgment, Breyer's concurring opinion appeared to calibrate the competing interests much more finely. For Breyer, as for Stevens, when there are interests of the highest order "'on both sides of the equation,'" as he put it, some "balancing" is required. In Breyer's view, however, that "balance" appeared to be influenced by his suggestion that the competing privacy interest was not only important, it was of constitutional dimension itself. According to Breyer, while the wiretap acts "directly interfere with free expression in that they prevent the media from publishing information," they also "directly enhance private speech" by encouraging "conversations that otherwise might not take place." Under such circumstances, he wrote, where "important competing constitutional interests are implicated," the Court must assess "whether the statutes strike a reasonable balance between their speech-restricting and speech-enhancing consequences." And, he added, "despite the statutes' direct restrictions on speech," the First Amendment "must," as a general matter, "tolerate laws of this kind because of the importance of these privacy and speech-related objectives."

Applying his balancing test in *Bartnicki*, however, Breyer concluded that the provisions of the wiretap act "applied in these circumstances, do not reasonably reconcile the competing constitutional objectives," but rather "disproportionately interfere with media freedom." On the one hand, he observed, the "broadcasters here engaged in no unlawful activity" and, on the other, the plaintiffs had little or no "*legitimate* interest in maintaining the privacy" of a conversation that raised, in Breyer's judgment, "a significant concern for the safety of others." Thus, even though it appeared that Williams did not disseminate the content of the recording for several months after he first learned about the threats, Breyer concluded, "that fact cannot legitimize the speaker's earlier privacy expectations. Nor should editors, who must make a publication decision quickly, have to determine present or continued danger before publishing this kind of threat."

Breyer's views appear to be difficult to reconcile, at least in part, with the opinion of the Court he purported to join. Despite the Court's rather explicit holding that "privacy concerns give way when balanced against the interest in publishing matters of public importance," Breyer asserted that the Court "does not create a 'public interest' exception that swallows up the statutes' privacy-protecting general rule." According to Breyer, the Court only "finds constitutional protection for publication of intercepted information of a special kind" and only in circumstances in which, as he put it, "the speakers' legitimate privacy expectations are unusually low, and the public interest in defeating those expectations is unusually high."

In dissent, the chief justice was plainly moved by the prospect of invasions of privacy arising from new technologies that "permit[] millions of important and confidential conversations to occur through a vast system of electronic networks." Accordingly, Rehnquist would have permitted Congress and state legislatures to address the problem through "content neutral" laws such as the wiretap statutes without doing violence to the First Amendment. In Rehnquist's view, the law's prohibition on the disclosure of unlawfully intercepted communications is no more extensive than necessary to serve the asserted governmental interest in "drying up the market" for them.

The week after it announced its decision in *Bartnicki*, the Court granted the petition for review in *Boehner v. McDermott*, and simultaneously sent that case back to the lower courts for further consideration in the wake of *Bartnicki*. It denied review entirely in *Peavy*, explaining in a footnote to its decision in *Bartnicki* that there appeared to be evidence that the defendants in that case had "in fact participated in the interceptions at issue." Years later, and after multiple additional proceedings in both the district court and the D.C. Circuit, the latter court held in a badly divided series of opinions that the *Daily Mail* principle did indeed apply to the dissemination of the contents of the recording in *Boehner*, but that McDermott could not invoke its protections because, as a member of the House Ethics Committee, he had, much like the defendants in *Cohen* had by their agreement not to reveal their source's identity, expressly forfeited his First Amendment rights with respect to the information he received in that capacity.

Beyond its impact on the litigants in *Bartnicki* itself as well as the parties in *Boehner* and *Peavy*, *Bartnicki* continues to represent the Court's most recent pronouncement on the ongoing validity of *Sullivan* and *its* impact on the scope of the First Amendment. After a decade of uncertainty following *Cohen*, *Bartnicki* confirmed that the Supreme Court is not prepared to abandon *Sullivan* and its progeny, including the *Daily Mail* principle, even when a "neutral law of general application" is before it. In all, six justices were of the view that the *Daily Mail* principle is the appropriate mode of constitutional analysis to be applied to laws that directly prohibit the dissemination of truthful information about matters of public concern, even when those laws are—like the wiretap acts—"content neutral" and do not purport to single out the press. In addition, six justices squarely rejected the notion that the press forfeits its First Amendment right to disseminate information it has lawfully acquired simply because someone else obtained it illegally.

In the dozen years that have now elapsed since it was decided, it appears increasingly likely that the overriding significance of *Bartnicki* is its unequivocal endorsement of the First Amendment theory nurtured by Justice Brennan and given its most eloquent expression in *New York Times Co. v. Sullivan. Bartnicki* confirms that, even in an era when the press is held in low regard and even in a case in which the federal government came before the Court championing the potent competing interest in personal privacy as justification for stripping the press of the First Amendment's protections, the principles articulated by Brennan in *Sullivan* endure. It is, in that sense, fitting that the final sentences of Stevens's opinion for the Court in *Bartnicki*, written by a justice who had not always agreed with Brennan on such matters when they served together, and who had effectively prevented him from mounting a defense of *Sullivan* when it came under attack in *Greenmoss Builders*, should contain just such a reaffirmation:

> Our opinion in *New York Times Co. v. Sullivan*, reviewed many of the decisions that settled the "general proposition that freedom of expression upon public questions is secured by the First Amendment." Those cases all relied on "our profound national commitment to the principle that debate on public issues should be uninhibited, robust and wide-open." (quoting *Sullivan*). . . . We think that parallel reasoning requires the conclusion that a stranger's illegal conduct does not suffice to remove the First Amendment shield from speech about a matter of public concern. The months of negotiations over the proper level of compensation for teachers at the Wyoming Valley West High School were unquestionably a matter of public concern, and [Fred Williams was] clearly engaged in debate about that concern. That debate may be more mundane than the Communist rhetoric that inspired Justice Brandeis . . . , but it is no less worthy of constitutional protection.

As the nation celebrates the fiftieth anniversary of Brennan's opinion for the Court in *Sullivan*, these words—the ones most recently penned by the Supreme Court on the subject—would almost certainly have brought a smile to his face.

Notes on Sources

Published opinions of the Supreme Court and lower federal and state courts are cited here to the official reporters containing those opinions or, when such citations are unavailable, to the Lexis or Westlaw databases. Similarly, statutes and regulations are cited to the official compendia in which they are contained. Briefs filed in the Supreme Court are identified by party, case name, title of the brief, and where applicable, a citation to the Westlaw database.

The draft opinions, memoranda between Justices, and other case-specific materials cited can, with few exceptions, be found in the publicly accessible papers of Justice Brennan and other referenced Justices, specifically, Chief Justice Rehnquist and Justices Douglas, Harlan, White, Marshall, Blackmun, and Powell. Brennan's papers, as well as those of Douglas, White, Marshall, and Blackmun, are all housed in the Manuscript Division of the Library of Congress in Washington, D.C.; Powell's papers are maintained at the William C. Hall Law Library, Washington and Lee University Law School in Lexington, Virginia; Rehnquist's can be found at the Hoover Institution Archives at Stanford University in Palo Alto, California; and Harlan's are at the Seeley G. Mudd Library at Princeton University in Princeton, New Jersey.

Citations to draft opinions identify the author of the opinion, the name of and citation to the case, the number of the draft, and the date on which it was circulated to other justices. Memoranda circulated between justices are identified by the author's initials, the recipient's initials (where applicable), and the date the memorandum was circulated. Other correspondence is identified by the name of the author and recipient(s) and the date. Conference notes and vote sheets are identified by the author's initials, the case name, and the date of the conference. The memoranda that Brennan and his clerks prepared in his later years for his use at Conference are identified by his initials and the case name. The term histories prepared by Brennan and his clerks are identified by the nomenclature used at the Court to identify a term. So, for example, Brennan's final year on the Court, 1989–90, is formally referred to as October Term 1989; references in notes to the term history are described as "OT '89 Term History," followed by the page number.

We have not provided citations for quotations from the interviews that Justice Brennan conducted with Steve Wermiel between 1986 and 1990, but have identified them in the text as comments Brennan made in interviews conducted by "his biographer." We have also not provided citations for interviews that one or the other of the authors conducted, either prior to publication of the biography or in connection with the preparation of this book with several of Brennan's law clerks, for the purpose of confirming or, in some cases, illuminating information gleaned from the publicly available materials that are cited.

Quotations from arguments are cited to the transcripts of those arguments and include the name of the case and the date of the argument. For cases argued prior to 1983, citations are generally to the transcripts prepared by the Oyez Project at the IIT Chicago-Kent College of Law, which are available on its website, www .oyez.org. For cases argued in the October 1983 Term and thereafter, citations are to the transcript published on the Lexis database. In either case, the actual audio recordings were reviewed to attempt to ensure both that the quoted portions are accurate and that the justice quoted is correctly identified. In those instances in which the quotation or identification here differs from the cited source, it is because a review of the audio recording reveals that that the transcription in the cited source is incorrect. In addition, although quotations are cited to the specific page on which they appear in the Lexis transcription, there are no analogous page citations to the Oyez transcripts, which do not contain them.

Citations to articles appearing in newspapers and other periodicals identify the author, the headline, the name of the publication (which is typically abbreviated), and the date. Abbreviations most frequently used are NYT (New York Times), LAT (Los Angeles Times), WSJ (Wall Street Journal) and WP (Washington Post). Law review articles, books, and other secondary sources are cited using the form set out in *The Bluebook: A Uniform System of Citation*.

In those instances in which an entire paragraph in text is based on a single source, that source is cited only once and the citation includes references to all pages in the cited source from which the information in the paragraph is drawn. For the reader's convenience, each new paragraph begins with such a citation, even if the material referenced in it is drawn from the same source as the preceding paragraph.

CHAPTER 1

Sullivan

1   To understand and: New York Times Co. v. Sullivan, 376 U.S. 254 (1964); *see* U.S. CONST. amend. I.

The first years: *See* LEONARD W. LEVY, FREEDOM OF THE PRESS FROM ZENGER TO JEFFERSON xlviii–lxxix (1966).

2   Most notably, the: New York Times Co. v. Sullivan, 376 U.S. 254, 273–74 (1964) (quoting Act of June 18, 1798, 1 Stat. 596 (Sedition Act)).

At the time: 376 U.S. at 274 (quoting Virginia Resolutions of 1798, *reprinted in* 4 Elliot's Debates on the Federal Constitution 553–54 (1876).

When he became: 376 U.S. at 276 (quoting Letter to Mrs. Adams, July 22, 1804, 4 Jefferson's Works 555–56 (Washington ed.)).

The Sedition Act: 376 U.S. at 276, n.16. *See* DAVID RABBAN, FREE SPEECH IN ITS FORGOTTEN YEARS (1999).

The exceptions largely: *See, e.g.*, Dennis v. United States, 341 U.S. 494 (1951); Abrams v. United States, 250 U.S. 616 (1919); Schenck v. United States, 249 U.S. 47 (1919).

These cases uniformly: *See, e.g.*, Pierce v. United States, 252 U.S. 239, 253–73 (1920) (Brandeis, J., dissenting); Schaefer v. United States, 251 U.S. 466, 482–95 (1920) (Brandeis, J., dissenting); Abrams v. United States, 250 U.S. 616, 624–31 (1919) (Holmes, J., dissenting); *see also* Whitney v. California, 274 U.S. 357, 372 (1927) (Brandeis, J., concurring).

3   Most notably, the: *See, e.g.*, Booker v. State, 100 Ala. 30 (1894) (criminal conviction for slander); Giles v. State, 6 Ga. 276 (1849) (criminal conviction for libel); Williams v. Karnes, 23 Tenn. 9 (1843) (civil libel action); Runkle v. Meyer, 1803 WL 773 (Pa. 1803) (same).

In addition, their: *See, e.g.*, Pennekamp v. State, 156 Fla. 227 (1945), *rev'd sub nom.*, Pennekamp v. Florida, 328 U.S. 331 (1946); Bridges v.

Superior Court of Los Angeles Cnty., 14 Cal. 2d 464 (1939), *rev'd sub nom.*, Bridges v. California, 314 U.S. 252 (1941); People v. Muller, 96 N.Y. 408 (1884).

And, their executive: *See, e.g.*, People v. Street, 20 N.Y.2d 231 (1967), *rev'd sub nom.*, Street v. New York, 394 U.S. 576 (1969); State v. Chaplinsky, 91 N.H. 310 (1941), *aff'd sub nom.*, Chaplinsky v. New Hampshire, 315 U.S. 568 (1942).

Prior to the: U.S. CONST. amend. I ("Congress shall make no law . . . ").

In addition to: U.S. CONST. amend. XIII; U.S. CONST. amend. XIV; U.S. CONST. amend. XV.

That promise, however: Slaughter-House Cases, 83 U.S 36 (1872).

In fact, it: *See, e.g.*, Gideon v. Wainwright, 372 U.S. 335 (1963); Mapp v. Ohio, 367 U.S. 643 (1961).

4   In 1925, the: Gitlow v. New York, 268 U.S. 652, 670 (1925); Near v. Minnesota, 283 U.S. 697 (1931).

That latter case: Near v. Minnesota, 283 U.S. 697 (1931); *see also* FRED W. FRIENDLY, MINNESOTA RAG (1981)

Although the state: Near v. Minnesota, 283 U.S. 697 (1931).

In one influential: Chaplinsky v. New Hampshire, 315 U.S., 568, 572 (1942).

In another, decided: Beauharnais v. Illinois, 343 U.S. 250, 255 (1952).

Thus, when, on: "Heed Their Rising Voices," advertisement published in NYT, Mar. 29, 1960, *reprinted in* New York Times Co. v. Sullivan, 376 U.S. 254, 305 app. (1964).

This fact was: ANTHONY LEWIS, MAKE NO LAW 11 (1992) [hereinafter "MAKE NO LAW"]; SETH STERN & STEPHEN WERMIEL, JUSTICE BRENNAN: LIBERAL CHAMPION 220–21 (2010) [hereinafter "JUSTICE BRENNAN"].

5   Like the laws: New York Times Co. v. Sullivan, 273 Ala. 656, 673–76 (1962).

Damages flowing from: *Id.* at 685.

Punitive damages, in: New York Times Co. v. Sullivan, 376 U.S. at 262.

The body of: "Heed Their Rising Voices," advertisement published in NYT, Mar. 29, 1960, *reprinted in* New York Times Co. v. Sullivan, 376 U.S. 254, 305 app. (1964).

The ad referred: *Id.*

6   Following its publication: JUSTICE BRENNAN at 20.

     In all, the: New York Times Co. v. Sullivan, 376 U.S. at 278 n.18; *see also* MAKE NO LAW 12–13.

     In 2013 dollars: *See US Inflation Calculator*, COIN NEWS, http://www.usinflationcalculator.com (accessed Aug. 28, 2013).

     The entire circulation: New York Times Co. v. Sullivan, 376 U.S. at 260 n.3.

     Among the plaintiffs: *Id.* at 256.

     In his complaint: *Id.* at 256, 305 app.

     Sullivan alleged that: *Id.* at 258; *see also* JUSTICE BRENNAN at 220.

     Commissioner Sullivan asserted: New York Times Co. v. Sullivan, 376 U.S. at 258–59.

7   At trial, Sullivan: *Id.* at 289 & n.28; *see also* MAKE NO LAW at 29–30.

     One witness testified: New York Times Co. v. Sullivan, 376 U.S. at 260.

     When the case: *Id.* at 262.

8   Following two hours: JUSTICE BRENNAN at 220; *see also* New York Times Co. v. Sullivan, 376 U.S. at 278 n.18; MAKE NO LAW at 35.

     The trials in: New York Times Co. v. Sullivan, 376 U.S. at 278 n.18.

     When the Times: M. Roland Nachman, Remarks at Libel Law Under the Constitution: Marking the Twentieth Anniversary of New York Times Co. v. Sullivan, Sponsored by the ABA Forum Comm. On Communications Law, et al. (Apr. 13, 1984).

     In 1962, the: *See generally* JIM NEWTON, JUSTICE FOR ALL: EARL WARREN AND THE NATION HE MADE (2007) [hereinafter "JUSTICE FOR ALL"]; BERNARD SCHWARTZ, SUPER CHIEF (1984) [hereinafter "SUPER CHIEF"].

     Seven months later: Brown v. Board of Ed., 347 U.S. 483 (1954).

     From there, the: Miranda v. Arizona, 384 U.S. 436 (1966); Baker v. Carr, 369 U.S. 186 (1962); Mapp v. Ohio, 367 U.S. 643 (1961); Cooper v. Aaron, 358 U.S. 1 (1958).

     Opponents of the: *See, e.g.,* JUSTICE FOR ALL at 393, 468–69; ALEXANDER M. BICKEL, THE MORALITY OF CONSENT (1975).

     The Court that: ROGER K. NEWMAN, HUGO BLACK: A BIOGRAPHY (1997); EDWIN P. HOYT, WILLIAM O. DOUGLAS: A BIOGRAPHY (1979).

9   For both Black: *See, e.g.,* Duncan v. Louisiana, 391 U.S. 145, 162–71 (1968) (Black, J., concurring) (joined by Douglas, J.); Adamson v.

California, 332 U.S. 46, 68–92 (1947) (Black, J., dissenting) (joined by Douglas, J.); *see also* HUGO LAFAYETTE BLACK, A CONSTITUTIONAL FAITH 34, 45 (1968).

After *Brown* and: *See, e.g.,* Gideon v. Wainwright, 372 U.S. 335 (1963); Mapp v. Ohio, 367 U.S. 643 (1961).

The other Justices: *See, e.g.,* Mapp v. Ohio, 367 U.S. at 673–86 (Harlan, J., dissenting); Malinski v. New York, 324 U.S. 401, 412–20 (1945) (Frankfurter, J., dissenting); Ashcraft v. Tennessee, 322 U.S. 143, 156–74 (1944) (Jackson, J., dissenting); *see also* JEFFREY D. HOCKETT, NEW DEAL JUSTICE (1996).

The intellectual and: *See* CLYDE E. JACOBS, JUSTICE FRANKFURTER AND CIVIL LIBERTIES (1961); *see also* SUPER CHIEF at 40 ("To Frankfurter, the law was almost an object of religious worship—and the Supreme Court its holy of holies. . . . Frankfurter saw himself as the priestly keeper of the shrine, he looked on Black and his supporters, notably Justice Douglas, as false prophets defiling hallowed ground.")

Until his retirement: *See* JUSTICE FOR ALL at 264–70, 330; *see also* SUPER CHIEF at 28–58.

By 1962, however: JUSTICE BRENNAN at 71–83.

Almost from the: *Id.* at 104–06; *see* Baker v. Carr, 365 U.S. 838 (1961); Cooper v. Aaron, 358 U.S. 1 (1958).

Brennan and Warren: JUSTICE BRENNAN at 250–52, 452–53.

10   For another thing: SUPER CHIEF at 392–93.

With that single: *Id.* at 446–50.

The other two: SUPER CHIEF at 320; *see also* JUSTICE FOR ALL at 368.

White was similarly: SUPER CHIEF at 428–30; *see also* DENNIS J. HUTCHINSON, THE MAN WHO ONCE WAS WHIZZER WHITE (1998).

Not surprisingly, given: *See, e.g.,* Miranda v. Arizona, 384 U.S. 436, 526–45 (1966) (White, J., dissenting) (dissenting from holding that "the privilege against self-incrimination forbids custody interrogation without [specified warnings] and without a clear waiver of counsel" on ground that it has "no significant support in the history of the privilege or in the language of the Fifth Amendment"); Heart of Atlanta Motel, Inc. v. United States, 379 U.S. 241 (1964) (White joined majority opinion upholding provisions of Civil Rights Act

of 1964); Massiah v. United States, 377 U.S. 201, 208–13 (1964)
(White, J., dissenting) (dissenting from decision excluding testimonial
statements made by defendants after the Sixth Amendment right
to counsel has attached); Goss v. Bd. of Ed., 373 U.S. 683 (1963)
(White joined majority opinion holding that transfer provisions of
formal desegregation order that allowed student to transfer schools
solely on basis of racial classification were unconstitutional method
of perpetuating segregation); Watson v. City of Memphis, 373 U.S.
526 (1963) (White joined majority opinion ordering immediate
desegregation of public parks).

Even so, he: JUSTICE BRENNAN at 250–52, 452–53.

In the First Amendment: Roth v. United States, 354 U.S. 476 (1957).

11   In that case: *Id.* at 488 ("The door barring federal and state intrusion
into this area cannot be left ajar; it must be kept tightly closed and
opened only the slightest crack necessary to prevent encroachment
upon more important interests. It is therefore vital that the standards
for judging obscenity safeguard the protection of freedom of speech
and press for material which does not treat sex in a manner appealing
to prurient interest.").

For his part: *Id.* at 494–96 (Warren, J., concurring in judgment).

Black and Douglas: *Id.* at 507–14 (Douglas, J., dissenting).

Harlan also dissented: *Id.* at 496–507 (Harlan, J., dissenting) (objecting
to, among other matters, the majority's "broad brush" that "may result
in a loosening of the tight reins which state and federal courts should
hold upon the enforcement of obscenity statutes").

The Court's decision: *See, e.g.,* Ginzburg v. United States, 383 U.S.
463 (1966); Manual Enters., Inc. v. Day, 370 U.S. 478 (1962); Smith
v. California, 361 U.S. 147 (1959); *see also* ALEXANDER M. BICKEL, THE
SUPREME COURT AND THE IDEA OF PROGRESS 50–54 (1978) (discussing
the "instances of ad hoc subjectivity resulting in palpable injustice to
individuals" that characterized the Court's obscenity rulings after 1966).

In large sections: JUSTICE BRENNAN at 254–55.

When *New York Times*: *Id.* at 220–21; *see also* MAKE NO LAW at 35–36.

12   In short, Brennan: JUSTICE BRENNAN at 221.

And, if Brennan: *Id.* at 222; TAYLOR BRANCH, PILLAR OF FIRE: AMERICA
IN THE KING YEARS 1963–65 (1999).

Both at argument: JUSTICE BRENNAN at 221.

At the very: *New York Times Co. v. Sullivan,* Jan. 6, 1964 (The Oyez
Project at IIT Chicago-Kent College of Law).

13   For his part: JUSTICE BRENNAN at 222.

Among other things: *New York Times Co. v. Sullivan,* Jan. 6, 1964 (The
Oyez Project at IIT Chicago-Kent College of Law).

When Wechsler continued: *Id.*

Later, when the: *Id.*

14   This contention, and: *Id.*

Toward the end: *Id.*

When Nachman rose: *Id.*; *see* U.S. CONST. amend. VII.

He was, however: *New York Times Co. v. Sullivan,* Jan. 6, 1964 (The Oyez
Project at IIT Chicago-Kent College of Law).

15   Nachman, however, was: *Id. See* Chi. B. & Q.R. Co. v. City of Chi., 166
U.S. 226, 242–43 (1897).

At this juncture: *New York Times Co. v. Sullivan,* Jan. 6, 1964 (The Oyez
Project at IIT Chicago-Kent College of Law).

This response led: *Id.*

Toward the end: *Id.*

16   In response, White: *Id.*

Three days after: JUSTICE BRENNAN at 222.

For his part: *Id.* at 223; WOD Conference Notes for *New York Times Co.
v. Sullivan,* Jan. 10, 1964.

That Brennan would: JUSTICE BRENNAN at 223.

He certainly believed: *Id.*; *see* ALEXANDER MEIKLEJOHN, FREE SPEECH
6 (1948) ("But government by consent—self-government—is not
thus simple. . . . the crux of the difficulty lies in the fact that, in such a
society, the governors and the governed are not two distinct groups of
persons. There is only one group—the self-governing people.").

17   "As money is": JUSTICE BRENNAN at 223 (quoting WJB, "Dedication
of the Samuel I. Newhouse Law Center" (speech, Rutgers University,
Newark, NJ, Oct. 17, 1979), *reprinted in* WJB, *Address,* 32 RUTGERS L.
REV. 173 (1979)).

And, in addition: JUSTICE BRENNAN at 223.

Family members aside: *Id.*

"I did put": *Id.* (quoting WJB to Luis Blanco Lugo, Feb. 21, 1962).

As he explained: JUSTICE BRENNAN at 223 (WJB to Marietta College, Oct. 1966).

Brennan's personal experience: JUSTICE BRENNAN at 223; OT '63 Term History at 1.

Over the years: JUSTICE BRENNAN at 223; *see, e.g.*, Baker v. Carr, 369 U.S. 186 (1962); Cooper v. Aaron, 358 U.S. 1 (1958).

Moreover, with his: JUSTICE BRENNAN at 223–24.

In this case: *Id.* at 224; *see also* OT '63 Term History at 3.

18   In all, Brennan: JUSTICE BRENNAN at 224; OT '63 Term History at 1–11.

For *Sullivan*, Brennan: JUSTICE BRENNAN at 224.

In that initial: OT '63 Term History at 1–2.

And, as Brennan: *Id.* at 2.

Years later, Brennan: JUSTICE BRENNAN at 224; *see* Coleman v. MacLennan, 78 Kan. 711, 98 P. 281 (1908).

In fact, that: JUSTICE BRENNAN at 224; Barnett interview, Apr. 11, 2007.

Brennan's initial draft: JUSTICE BRENNAN at 224; OT '63 Term History at 1–2.

The second draft: OT '63 Term History at 2.

19   Specifically, Brennan wrote: *Id.*

As Brennan's term: *Id.*

Both Warren and: JUSTICE BRENNAN at 224; OT '63 Term History at 3 (noting concurring opinions circulated by Goldberg (Feb. 25, 1964) and Black joined by Douglas (Feb. 26, 1964)).

But Brennan, who: JUSTICE BRENNAN at 224.

"In order to": *Id.* at 224–25; WJB interview, July 12, 1988 (41–14).

More than pragmatism: JUSTICE BRENNAN at 225.

He had repeatedly: *Id.*; Edward V. Heck, "Justice Brennan and the Changing Supreme Court" (Ph.D. thesis, Johns Hopkins University, 1978).

Brennan believed that: JUSTICE BRENNAN at 225; WJB interview, July 12, 1988 (41–14).

As Brennan explained: JUSTICE BRENNAN at 225; William J. Brennan, Jr., *The Supreme Court and the Meiklejohn Interpretation of the First Amendment*, 79 HARV. L. REV. 1 (1965) (citing David Reisman, *Democracy and Defamation: Fair Game and Fair Comment*, 42 COLUM. L. REV. 1085 (1942)).

Not only had: JUSTICE BRENNAN at 115–117 (McCarthy interaction at hearings), 14–16 (Brennan's father's experience as commissioner).

20   At sixteen, the: *Id.* at 16; WJB interview, May 30, 1990 (63–10).

Without his usual: JUSTICE BRENNAN at 225.

But the Justices: *Id.*; WJB interview, Apr. 4, 1988 (31–3).

Thus, when Brennan: OT '63 Term History at 2–3.

On February 25: *Id.* at 3.

The next day: *Id.*

Douglas quickly joined: *Id.*; JUSTICE BRENNAN at 225.

At the same: OT '63 Term History at 3.

Still, without Black: *Id.*

21   In it, he: *Id.* at 3–4.

Surprisingly, since Harlan: *Id.* at 4.

Harlan's revision addressed: *Id.*

Relying largely on: *Id.*; 28 U.S.C. § 2106 (June 25, 1948, c. 646, 62 Stat. 963).

In Harlan's view: OT '63 Term History at 4.

Harlan's approach did: *Id.*

That decision proved: *Id.* at 5.

Indeed, upon receiving: *Id.*

22   In yet another: *Id.*

On a different: *Id.*

As a result: *Id.*

Even if this: *Id.* at 5–6.

According to Brennan's: *Id.* at 6.

On March 2: *Id.*

As Brennan's term: *Id.*

23   Harlan's new proposal: *Id.* at 6–7.

Brennan did, however: *Id.*

The next day: *Id.* at 7.

24 Not surprisingly, Harlan: JUSTICE BRENNAN at 225; JMH to Conference,
Mar. 3, 1964; OT '63 Term History at 7.

Harlan circulated his: OT '63 Term History at 7–8.

Nevertheless, Harlan's draft: *Id.* at 8.

With that, Brennan: *Id.* at 8.

The chief justice: *Id.*

Still, with Clark: *Id.*

Recognizing this, Douglas: *Id.* at 8–9.

Goldberg then announced: *Id.* at 9.

25 Despite his private: *Id.*; JUSTICE BRENNAN at 225–26; HLB to WJB,
undated.

To make matters: OT '63 Term History at 9.

And, to punctuate: *Id.* at 9–10.

At this juncture: *Id.* at 10.

26 Douglas reaffirmed his: *Id.*

Meanwhile, however, Justice: *Id.*

Although Brennan thought: *Id.* at 10–11.

Brennan's gambit did: *Id.* at 11.

Thus, Brennan thought: *Id.*

During the afternoon: JUSTICE BRENNAN at 226; WJB to clerks, Mar. 5,
1964; OT '63 Term History at 11.

Moreover, Clark told: OT '63 Term History at 11.

Brennan wasted little: *Id.*; *see* New York Times Co. v. Sullivan, 376 at
284–85.

Warren, White, and: OT '63 Term History at 11.

27 On Sunday, March: *Id.* at 11–12; JUSTICE BRENNAN at 226.

In many respects: JUSTICE BRENNAN at 226.

The following morning: *Id.*

"We are required": New York Times Co. v. Sullivan, 376 U.S. at 256.

The opinion itself: JUSTICE BRENNAN at 226.

Not surprisingly, the: NYT, "Free Press and Free People," Mar. 10,
1964.

In many ways: New York Times Co. v. Sullivan, 376 U.S. at 273.

In Part II: *Id.* at 267–83.

"In deciding the": *Id.* at 269.

In short: *Id.*

28   Brennan then proceeded: *Id.* at 269–83.

He began from: *Id.* at 269.

After recounting such: *Id.* at 270–71.

With respect to: *Id.* at 271.

Then Brennan proceeded: *Id.* at 271–72.

With respect to: *Id.* at 272.

As Brennan explained: *Id.* at 273.

29   It is at: *Id.*

In the sentences: *Id.* at 273–76.

From there, Brennan: *Id.* at 279.

In saying all: MAKE NO LAW at 150.

What followed, however: 376 U.S. at 293–97 (Black, J., concurring, joined by Douglas, J.); *id.* at 297–305 (Goldberg, J., concurring, joined by Douglas, J.).

30   Brennan, knowing that: *Id.* at 278–79.

The First Amendment: *Id.* at 280.

As noted, the: *Id.* at 283–92.

In addition to: *Id.* at 285.

And, at the: *Id.* at 285 n.26 (citing Chi. B. & Q.R. Co. v. City of Chi., 166 U.S. 226, 242–43 (1897)).

31   Acknowledging that the: 376 U.S. at 285.

With that issue: *Id.* at 292.

As Brennan had: MAKE NO LAW at 160–61.

Professor Harry Kalven: Harry Kalven, Jr., *The New York Times Case: A Note on the Central Meaning of the First Amendment*, 1964 SUP. CT. REV. 191, 193–94 (1964).

And, Kalven reported: *Id.* at 221 n.125.

CHAPTER 2

Garrison v. Louisiana

34   Well before he: Max Holland, *The Power of Disinformation: The Lie That Linked CIA to the Kennedy Assassination*, STUDIES IN INTELLIGENCE, No.

11 (2001), *available at* https://www.cia.gov/library/center-for-the-st
udy-of-intelligence/csi-publications/csi-studies/studies/fall_winter
_2001/article02.html; *see also* Donald E. Wilkes, Jr., *Destiny Betrayed:
The CIA, Oswald, and the JFK Assassination*, Flagpole Magazine, Dec. 7,
2005, *available at* http://www.law.uga.edu/dwilkes_more/jfk_22destiny
.html.

First elected in: Garrison v. Louisiana, 379 U.S. 64, 65–66 (1964).

But under local: *Id.* at 66 n.2.

The District Attorney: State v. Garrison, 244 La. 787, 795–803 (1963),
rev'd sub nom., Garrison v. Louisiana, 379 U.S. 64 (1964).

Based on the: Garrison v. Louisiana, 379 U.S. at 65 & n.1 (citing La.
Rev. Stat. § 14:47 (1950)).

35   On his conviction: State v. Garrison, 244 La. at 793.

The Louisiana Supreme: State v. Garrison, 244 La. 787 (1963), *rev'd sub
nom.*, Garrison v. Louisiana, 379 U.S. 64 (1964); Garrison v. Louisiana,
375 U.S. 900 (1963) (noting probable jurisdiction).

When the appeal: WOD Conference Notes for *Garrison v. Louisiana*,
undated.

The first of: *Garrison v. Louisiana*, Apr. 22, 1964 (The Oyez Project at
IIT Chicago-Kent College of Law).

Indeed, a month: Tom Clark, *The Supreme Court Conference*, 37 Tex. L.
Rev. 273, 274 (1959) ("On our regular docket each party at argument
is allowed on hour, unless by reason of the nature of the question the
case is transferred to the 'Summary Calendar' and the time is cut in
half."); Frederick Bernays Wiener, *The Supreme Court's New Rules*, 68
Harv. L. Rev. 20, 76–77 (1954) (quoting Rule 44(3) then in effect, that
cases are placed on the summary calendar when "the court concludes
that it is of such a character as not to justify extended argument"); *see
also* ELS to WOD, Mar. 18, 1964 (recommending vote to deny motion
by Garrison to remove case from summary calendar).

After the first: WOD Conference Notes for *Garrison v. Louisiana*, Apr.
24, 1964; *see* OT '64 Term History, at 2.

Given the approach: OT '64 Term History, at 2.

In *Sullivan*, after: New York Times Co. v. Sullivan, 376 U.S. 254, 274–76
(1964).

Citing liberally to: *Garrison v. Louisiana*, No. 400 at 10 (1964), *reprinted in* OT '64 Term History, at 57.

36   Proceeding from this: *Id.* at 7–8, *reprinted in* OT '64 Term History, at 51–53 (quoting Reports on the Virginia Resolutions, 4 Elliot's Debates 570).

Recalling in this: *Garrison v. Louisiana*, No. 400 at 8 (1964) *reprinted in* OT '64 Term History, at 53.

And, he declared: *Id.* at 16, *reprinted in* OT '64 Term History, at 69.

To explain this: *Id.* at 14, *reprinted in* OT '64 Term History, at 65.

As Brennan explained: *Id.* at 10, *reprinted in* OT '64 Term History, at 57.

37   There was a: *See id.* at 14 n.15, *reprinted in* OT '64 Term History, at 65.

Brennan's draft produced: OT '64 Term History, at 2.

Douglas prepared a: *Garrison v. Louisiana*, No. 400 (June 16, 1964) (Douglas, J., concurring)*, reprinted in* OT '64 Term History, at 71–77.

Actual malice becomes: *Id.* at 2, *reprinted in* OT '64 Term History, at 73.

And, as he: *Garrison v. Louisiana*, No. 400 (May 1964) (Goldberg, J., concurring), *reprinted in* OT '64 Term History, at 125.

38   Although the reactions: OT '64 Term History, at 2.

Clark, in a: *Garrison v. Louisiana*, No. 400 (1964) (Clark, J., dissenting), *reprinted in* OT '64 Term History, at 89–105.

Pulling other free: *Id.* at 3–4, *reprinted in* OT '64 Term History, at 93–95; *see* Chaplinsky v. New Hampshire, 315 U.S. 568 (1942).

Noting that he: *Garrison v. Louisiana*, No. 400 at 6 (1964) (Clark, J., dissenting), *reprinted in* OT '64 Term History, at 99.

Somewhat surprisingly, White: OT '64 Term History, at 2; *Garrison v. Louisiana*, No. 400 (1964) (White, J., dissenting), *reprinted in* OT '64 Term History, at 107–23.

Brennan's opinion, White: *Id.* at 1.

White explained that: *Id.* at 2, *reprinted in* OT '64 Term History, at 109.

For White, therefore: *Id.* at 8–9, *reprinted in* OT '64 Term History, at 121–23.

39   The three dissents: OT '64 Term History, at 2.

At the second: *Garrison v. Louisiana*, Oct. 19, 1964 (The Oyez Project at IIT Chicago-Kent College of Law).

Brennan, perhaps trying: *Id.*

In this regard: *Id.*; *see Garrison v. Louisiana*, No. 400 at 8 (1964) (White, J., dissenting), *reprinted in* OT '64 Term History, at 121.

Brennan asserted, again: *Garrison v. Louisiana*, Oct. 19, 1964 (The Oyez Project at IIT Chicago-Kent College of Law).

40 As Deutsch concluded: *Id.*

For his part: *Id.*

When the Justices: WOD Conference Notes for *Garrison v. Louisiana*, Oct. 23, 1964.

41 Brennan spoke next: *Id.*

After Brennan spoke: *Id.*

With the opinion: OT '64 Term History, at 2.

42 "The malicious falsehood": *Garrison v. Louisiana*, No. 400 at 3 (1964) (White, J., dissenting), *reprinted in* OT '64 Term History, at 111.

Brennan's new draft: Garrison v. Louisiana, 379 U.S. at 75.

Ever the pragmatist: *Garrison v. Louisiana*, No. 400 at 8–9 (1964) (White, J., dissenting), *reprinted in* OT '64 Term History, at 121–23 (with WJB handwritten edits).

Brennan crossed out: *Id.*; Garrison v. Louisiana, 379 U.S. at 79.

43 In his new: Omitted Portion of Opinion of the Court in *Garrison v. Louisiana*, *reprinted in* OT '64 Term History, at 31–37.

In his new: OT '64 Term History, at 2.

"So long as": Omitted Portion of Opinion of the Court in *Garrison v. Louisiana*, *reprinted in* OT '64 Term History, at 35.

The conclusion that: *Id.* at n.11, *reprinted in* OT '64 Term History, at 31–33.

As had been: OT '64 Term History, at 2.

On November 18: HLB to WOD, Nov. 18, 1964.

In a handwritten: *Id.*

As a result: Garrison v. Louisiana, 379 U.S. at 80 (Black, J., dissenting); *id.* at 80–88 (Douglas, J., dissenting); *id.* at 88 (Goldberg, J., dissenting).

The concurrence by: *Id.* at 80–88 (Douglas, J., dissenting); *Garrison v. Louisiana*, No. 400 (June 16, 1964), *reprinted in* OT '64 Term History, at 71–77; Omitted Portion of Opinion of the Court in *Garrison v. Louisiana*, *reprinted in* OT '64 Term History, at 31–37.

44 In the end: Garrison v. Louisiana, 379 U.S. 64 (1964).

In addition to: *Id.* at 74.

"Speech concerning public": Garrison v. Louisiana, 379 U.S. at 74–75.

45   Brennan likely had: *See* ALEXANDER MEIKLEJOHN, FREE SPEECH 6
      (1948) ("But government by consent—self-government—is not thus
      simple. . . . the crux of the difficulty lies in the fact that, in such a
      society, the governors and the governed are not two distinct groups of
      persons. There is only one group—the self-governing people.").
      Meiklejohn passed away: ADAM R. NELSON, EDUCATION AND
      DEMOCRACY: THE MEANING OF ALEXANDER MEIKLEJOHN, 1872–1964 328
      (2009).

Henry v. Collins

The next case: Henry v. Collins, 380 U.S. 356 (1965) (per curiam).
Aaron Henry was: Aimee Edmonson, In *Sullivan's* Shadow: The Use
and Abuse of Libel Law During The Civil Rights Movement (Dec.
2008) (Ph.D. dissertation, University of Missouri) (available through
UMI Dissertation Publishing, UMI Number 3483980).

On several occasions: Henry v. Collins, 380 U.S. at 356–57.

Juries in Mississippi: Henry v. Pearson, 253 Miss. 62 (1963), *rev'd
per curiam sub nom.*, Henry v. Collins, 380 U.S. 356 (1965); Henry v.
Collins, 253 Miss. 34 (1963), *rev'd per curiam*, 380 U.S. 356 (1965).

The Justices made: Henry v. Collins, 380 U.S. 356 (1965) (per curiam).

In it, the: *Id.* at 357.

46   As they had: *Id.* at 358.

Rosenblatt v. Baer

Since both: New York Times Co. v. Sullivan, 376 U.S. 254 (1964);
Garrison v. Louisiana, 379 U.S. 64 (1964).

Frank Baer was: Rosenblatt v. Baer, 383 U.S. 75, 77 (1966).

Alfred Rosenblatt ran: Brief for Petitioner, Rosenblatt v. Baer, 383 U.S.
75 (1966) (No. 38), 1985 WL 731276 at 10.

On January 29, 1960: *Id.* at 10–11.

Baer and his: *Id.* at 14–15.

47   A jury awarded: *Id.* at 16.

Seven months after: Baer v. Rosenblatt, 106 N.H. 26 (1964), *rev'd*, 383 U.S. 75 (1966).

When Rosenblatt's appeal: OT '65 Term History, at 8–9.

In March 1965: *Id*. at 9; WJB to Conference, Mar. 1965.

At first, there: *Rosenblatt v. Baer*, No. 780 (Feb. 26, 1965) (draft per curiam); OT '65 Term History, at 9; WOD to WJB, Feb. 26, 1965; PS to WJB, Feb. 26, 1965; TCC to WJB, Feb. 20, 1965; BRW to WJB, undated.

But, according to: OT '65 Term History, at 9.

Harlan's memo led: *Id*.; WJB to Conference, Mar. 2, 1965.

In its order: Rosenblatt v. Baer, 383 U.S. at 77.

As Brennan's term: OT '65 Term History, at 9.

At the argument: *Rosenblatt v. Baer*, Oct. 20, 1965 (The Oyez Project at IIT Chicago-Kent College of Law); *see* Michael Kitch, *Legal Lion Arthur Nighswander Dies at 100*, N.H. BAR ASS'N BAR NEWS, Jan. 16, 2009, http://www.nhbar.org/publications/display-news-issue.asp ?id=4906; *see also* SETH STERN & STEPHEN WERMIEL, JUSTICE BRENNAN: LIBERAL CHAMPION 20, 22 (2010).

Perhaps of greater: *Rosenblatt v. Baer*, Oct. 20, 1965 (The Oyez Project at IIT Chicago-Kent College of Law).

48   Stanley Brown, another: *Id*.; Brief for Respondent, Rosenblatt v. Baer, 383 U.S. 75 (1966) (No. 38) 1965 WL 115707 at i.

Responding to a: *Rosenblatt v. Baer*, Oct. 20, 1965 (The Oyez Project at IIT Chicago-Kent College of Law).

Between the justices': JIM NEWTON, JUSTICE FOR ALL: EARL WARREN AND THE NATION HE MADE 456–57 (2007); Fred P. Graham, *High Court Begins a New Term Today*, NYT, Oct. 4, 1965.

When the justices: WOD Conference Notes for *Rosenblatt v. Baer*, Oct. 22, 1965.

49   At this point: *Id*.

Finally, in casting: *Id*.; *Rosenblatt v. Baer*, Oct. 20, 1965 (The Oyez Project at IIT Chicago-Kent College of Law).

With no majority: OT '65 Term History, at 9.

50   In it, he: WJB to Conference, Oct. 28, 1965.

If he was: *Id*. at 3.

Accordingly, Brennan concluded: *Id.* at 5.

And, in a: *Id.* at 8.

The discussion that: OT '65 Term History, at 9–10.

To accomplish that: *Id.; see* Rosenblatt v. Baer, 383 U.S. 75 (Jan. 7, 1966) (slip op.) (Brennan, J.) (ninth draft).

51   As Brennan explained: Rosenblatt v. Baer, 383 U.S. 75, 85 (1966) (emphasis added).

Justice Douglas quickly: WOD to WJB and AF, Nov. 19, 1965; OT '65 Term History, at 10.

"If free discussion": *Id.* at 2.

52   Brennan responded to: WJB to WOD and AF, Nov. 20, 1965.

At this juncture: OT '65 Term History, at 10.

He made no: AF to WOD, Nov. 26, 1965.

On December 8: WJB to WOD, Dec. 8, 1965.

Following his receipt: WOD to WJB, undated.

That prediction, however: Rosenblatt v. Baer, 383 U.S. at 88 (noting Clark's concurrence in the result without opinion).

53   Even as the: OT '65 Term History, at 10.

On December 7: WJB to JMH, Dec. 7, 1965.

The *Sullivan* ruling: *Id.* at 2.

The stalemate continued: OT '65 Term History, at 10–11.

"Society," Brennan wrote: Rosenblatt v. Baer, 383 U.S. at 86.

At that moment: OT '65 Term History, at 11.

In his concurring: Rosenblatt v. Baer, 383 U.S. at 92 (Stewart, J., concurring).

54   Even with Stewart's: OT '65 Term History, at 11.

First, at the: Linn v. United Plant Guard Workers of Am., Local 114, 383 U.S. 53 (1966).

The dissenters in: *Id.* at 67–69 (Black, J., dissenting); *id.* at 69–74 (Fortas, J., dissenting) (joined by Warren, C.J. and Douglas, J.).

Black in particular: *Id.* at 68 (Black, J., dissenting) ("Yet it is difficult to conceive of an element more certain to create irritations guaranteed to prevent fruitful collective bargaining discussions than the threat or presence of a large monetary judgment gained in a libel suit generating anger and a desire for vengeance on the part of one or the other of the bargaining parties. I think, therefore, that libel suits are not only 'arguably' but inevitably in conflict with the basic purpose of the Act to settle disputes peaceably—not to aggravate them, but to end them.") To underscore his: HLB to WOD, undated.

The second hurdle: OT '65 Term History, at 11–12; *see* Curtis Publ'g Co. v. Butts, 388 U.S. 130 (1967).

55   In that cause: OT '65 Term History, at 11–12; *see* Rosenblatt v. Baer, 383 U.S. at 86 n.12.

While Warren considered: OT '65 Term History, at 12.

As a result: *See* WJB to Conference, Feb. 18, 1966.

Time, Inc. v. Hill

The fragility of: Time, Inc. v. Hill, 385 U.S. 374 (1967).

The case involved: Len Garment, *Annals of Law: The Hill Case*, NEW YORKER, Apr. 17, 1989; Time, Inc. v. Hill, 385 U.S. 374–78.

56   James Hill sued: Time, Inc. v. Hill, 385 U.S. at 378–79; *see* N.Y. CIV. RIGHTS LAW §§ 50, 51 (McKinney).

A jury awarded: Time, Inc. v. Hill, 385 U.S. at 379–80.

When Time sought: OT '66 Term History, at 1–2.

When the case: *Time, Inc. v. Hill*, Apr. 27, 1966 (The Oyez Project at IIT Chicago-Kent College of Law); Len Garment, *Annals of Law: The Hill Case*, NEW YORKER, Apr. 17, 1989; *see also Harold Medina, U.S. Judge, Dies at 102*, NYT, Mar. 16, 1990.

A key issue: Len Garment, *Annals of Law: The Hill Case*, NEW YORKER, Apr. 17, 1989.

57   At argument, Nixon's: *Time, Inc. v. Hill*, Apr. 27, 1966 (The Oyez Project at IIT Chicago-Kent College of Law); *see* JIM NEWTON, JUSTICE FOR ALL: EARL WARREN AND THE NATION HE MADE (2007).

When the justices: OT '66 Term History, at 2.

Harlan wrote a: HLB to Conference, Oct. 17, 1965 at 1–2 (discussing Harlan's concurrence).

Sensing that Brennan: OT '66 Term History, at 2.

In his draft: *Id.*; *see* Hill v. Hayes, 15 N.Y.2d 986 (1965), *judgment set aside sub nom.*, Time, Inc. v. Hill, 385 U.S. 374 (1967).

58   Significantly, the concurring: Hill v. Hayes, 18 A.D.2d 485, 490–92
      (1963) (Rabin, J., concurring).
      In response to: OT '66 Term History, at 2; AF to Conference, June 14,
      1966.
      In the years: *See* Len Garment, *Annals of Law: The Hill Case*, NEW
      YORKER, Apr. 17, 1989.
      In its order: Time, Inc. v. Hill, 384 U.S. 995 (1966) (ordering
      reargument).
      The day before: OT '66 Term History, at 3; Len Garment, *Annals of
      Law: The Hill Case*, NEW YORKER, Apr. 17, 1989.
      In a classic: HLB to Conference, Oct. 17, 1966 at 3–4, 7.

59   At the second: *Time, Inc. v. Hill*, Oct. 18–19, 1966 (The Oyez Project at
      IIT Chicago-Kent College of Law) (audio recording only).
      When his turn: *Id.*
      In a somewhat: *Id.*

60   Brennan also questioned: *Id.*
      Brennan appeared to: *Id.*
      When, following the: OT '66 Term History, at 3.

61   As he set: *Id.*; *see* Spahn v. Julian Messner, Inc., 18 N.Y.2d 324 (1966),
      vacated sub nom., Julian Messner, Inc. v. Spahn, 387 U.S. 239 (1967).
      In fact, in: Spahn v. Julian Messner, Inc., 18 N.Y.2d at 328.
      For Brennan, the: OT '66 Term History, at 3.
      Thus, on December 1: Time, Inc. v. Hill, 385 U.S. 374 (Dec. 1, 1966)
      (slip op. 12) (Brennan, J.) (first draft).
      Brennan wrote that: *Id.*
      Then, in a: *Id.* at 13.

62   In such cases: *Id.* at 14.
      Initially, Brennan's opinion: OT '66 Term History, at 3; BRW to WJB,
      Dec. 1, 1966.
      On December 22: Time, Inc. v. Hill, 385 U.S. 374 (Dec. 22, 1966) (slip
      op.) (Fortas, J., dissenting) (first draft); OT '66 Term History, at 3.
      Before sharing his: AF handwritten note to WJB, undated (written on
      first page of Time, Inc. v. Hill, 385 U.S. 374 (Dec. 22, 1966) (slip op.)
      (Fortas, J., dissenting) (first draft)).
      When he finally: OT '66 Term History, at 3.

Early in the: *Id.*

63   To avoid a: *Id.*; *see* Time, Inc. v. Hill, 385 U.S. at 398–401 (Black,
J., concurring); Time, Inc. v. Hill, 385 U.S. at 401–02 (Douglas, J.,
concurring).

That gave Brennan: OT '66 Term History, at 4.

To entice Stewart: Time, Inc. v. Hill, 385 U.S. at 391 (citing Rosenblatt
v. Baer, 383 U.S. 75, 91 (1966) (Stewart, J., concurring)).

This modification proved: PS to WJB, Jan. 5, 1967; OT '66 Term
History, at 4.

In a somewhat: Len Garment, *Annals of Law: The Hill Case*, NEW
YORKER, Apr. 17, 1989.

64   There was another: Robert H. Knight to WJB, Oct. 6, 1969.

Brennan wrote back: WJB to Robert H. Knight, Oct. 9, 1969.

CHAPTER 3

Curtis Publishing Co. v. Butts, Associated Press v. Walker

66   The issue of: Curtis Publ'g Co. v. Butts, 385 U.S. 811 (1966) (granting
cert.); Associated Press v. Walker, 385 U.S. 812 (1966) (same).

In both *Rosenblatt*: Rosenblatt v. Baer, 383 U.S. 75 (1965); Time, Inc. v.
Hill, 385 U.S. 374 (1967).

The cases were: *Associated Press v. Walker*, Feb. 23, 1967 (The Oyez
Project at IIT Chicago-Kent College of Law); *Curtis Publ'g Co. v. Butts*,
Feb. 23, 1967 (The Oyez Project at IIT Chicago-Kent College of Law).

In the *Butts*: Curtis Publ'g Co. v. Butts, 388 U.S. 130, 135–37 (1967).

Butts sued for: *Id.* at 137–38.

67   The jury found: *Id.* at 138–39.

In those days: *Id.* at 139–40; *see* Curtis Publ'g Co. v. Butts, 351 F.2d 702
(5th Cir. 1965).

Judge Richard Rives: 351 F.2d at 720 (Rives, J., dissenting).

Associated Press v.: 388 U.S. 130, 140 (1967).

68   In fact, Walker: *Id.*; *see* Eric Pace, *Gen. Edwin Walker, 83, Is Dead;
Promoted Rightist Causes in 60's*, NYT, Nov. 2, 1993.

Walker sued the: 388 U.S. at 140–42.

At the trial: *Id*. at 141–42.

On October 10: *Butts*, 385 U.S. 811 (granting *cert*.); *Walker*, 385 U.S. 812 (same); OT '66 Term History, at 26.

69   At argument,: *Associated Press v. Walker*, Feb. 23, 1967 (The Oyez Project at IIT Chicago-Kent College of Law); David Stout, *William P. Rogers, Who Served as Nixon's Secretary of State, Is Dead at 87*, NYT, Jan. 4, 2001.

During his argument: *Associated Press v. Walker*, Feb. 23, 1967 (The Oyez Project at IIT Chicago-Kent College of Law).

Fortas also asked: *Id*.

70   As his argument: *Id*.

Clyde J. Watts: *Id*.

Later in his: *Id*.

71   During the argument: *Id*.

The argument in: *Curtis Publ'g Co. v. Butts*, Feb. 23, 1967 (The Oyez Project at IIT Chicago-Kent College of Law); *see* Tamar Lewin, *Herbert Wechsler, Legal Giant, Is Dead at 90*, NYT, Apr. 28, 2000.

72   For Butts, two: *Curtis Publ'g Co. v. Butts*, Feb. 23, 1967 (The Oyez Project at IIT Chicago-Kent College of Law).

Schroder followed his: *Id*.

73   On rebuttal, Wechsler: *Id*.

At Conference following: OT '66 Term History, at 26; WJB Conference Notes for *Curtis Publ'g Co. v. Butts*, Feb. 24, 1967.

On May 11: Curtis Publ'g Co. v. Butts, 388 U.S. 130 (May 11, 1967) (prefatory note for Conference) (Harlan, J.) (first draft).

74   Accordingly, in his: OT '66 Term History, at 27; *Curtis Publ'g Co.*, 388 U.S. at 155.

In response, Brennan: Curtis Publ'g Co. v. Butts, 388 U.S. 130 (May 29, 1967) (slip op. 1–3) (Brennan, J., dissenting) (first draft).

Justice White, who: Curtis Publ'g Co. v. Butts, 388 U.S. 130 (May 31, 1967) (slip op. 3) (White, J., concurring in part and dissenting in part) (first draft).

White's draft, however: *Id*.

75   White and Brennan: OT '66 Term History, at 27.

At Brennan's request: *Id*. at 27.

With that change: *Id.*; *see* Curtis Publ'g Co. v. Butts, 388 U.S. 130 (May 31, 1967) (slip op. 3) (White, J., concurring in part and dissenting in part) (second draft) (striking out statement that reckless disregard is not based on publisher's state of mind).

Justice Harlan, however: OT '66 Term History, at 27–28.

For the next: *Id.*

Warren thereafter wrote: EW to JMH, June 6, 1967.

76   Instead, Warren told: OT '66 Term History, at 28–29.

With this development: *Id.* at 29–30.

Strategic maneuvering in: *Id.* at 28–29.

77   On June 7: *Id.* at 30; *see* WJB to EW, June 7, 1967.

As Brennan's term: OT '66 Term History, at 30.

Referring to the: *Curtis Publ'g Co.*, 388 U.S. at 163.

And Warren similarly: *Id.* at 163–64.

Once Warren circulated: OT '66 Term History, at 30; *see* Butts, 388 U.S. at 133 n.* (Harlan, J.).

78   Brennan, however, prevailed: 388 U.S. at 162–65 (Warren, C.J., concurring).

There were other: *Id.* at 145 (Harlan, J.).

79   For another, the: *Id.* at 168–70 (Warren, C.J., concurring).

Finally, the Court's: *Id.* at 163–65.

It is a: Keeton v. Hustler Mag., Inc., 465 U.S. 770 (1984); Calder v. Jones, 465 U.S. 783 (1984); Time, Inc. v. Firestone, 424 U.S. 448 (1976).

80   Thus, in the: 388 U.S. at 164 (Warren, C.J., concurring).

In his own: *Id.* at 154–55 (Harlan, J.); *see* Jacobellis v. Ohio, 378 U.S. 184, 197 (1964) (Stewart, J., concurring) ("I know it when I see it, and the motion picture involved in this case is not that.").

After the justices: Fred Graham, *Justice Retiring; Step to Avoid Conflict of Interest May Hurt the Conservatives*, NYT, Mar. 1, 1967.

Beckley Newspapers Corp. v. Hanks

81   Five months later: Beckley Newspapers Corp. v. Hanks, 389 U.S. 81, 83–84 (1967).

The newspaper appealed: *Id.* at 82, 84–85.

The vote was: *Id.* at 85 (Black, J., concurring).

Although *Beckley Newspapers*: Fred Graham, *Senate Confirms Marshall as the First Negro Justice; 10 Southerners Oppose High Court Nominee in 69–11 Vote*, NYT, Aug. 31, 1967.

St. Amant v. Thompson

82   At the justices': WJB Vote Sheet for *St. Amant v. Thompson*, Jan. 12, 1968.
Phil St. Amant: St. Amant v. Thompson, 390 U.S. 727, 728–29 (1968).

83   Thompson sued St.: *Id.* at 729.
In a unanimous: Thompson v. St. Amant, 184 So. 2d 314, 323 (La. Ct. App. 1966).
One year later: Thompson v. St. Amant, 196 So. 2d 255, 261–62 (La. 1967); *id.* at 262 (Hamlin, J., dissenting); *id.* at 264 (McCaleb, J., dissenting).
But the other: 196 So. 2d at 264 (McCaleb, J., dissenting).

84   Once the case: St. Amant v. Thompson, 389 U.S. 1033 (1968) (granting *cert.*); *St. Amant v. Thompson*, Apr. 4, 1968 (The Oyez Project at IIT Chicago-Kent College of Law).
Robert Kleinpeter, a: *St. Amant v. Thompson*, Apr. 4, 1968 (The Oyez Project at IIT Chicago-Kent College of Law).

85   For his part: *Id.*
At the Conference: WOD Conference Notes for *St. Amant v. Thompson*, Apr. 5, 1968; WJB Vote Sheet for *St. Amant v. Thompson*, Apr. 5, 1968.
When it came: WOD Conference Notes for *St. Amant v. Thompson*, Apr. 5, 1968.

86   Brennan's own vote: WJB Vote Sheet for *St. Amant v. Thompson*, Apr. 5, 1968.
On April 29: 390 U.S. at 730–33.
In that regard: *Id.* at 731.

87   In this manner: *Id.* at 731–32.
By the same: *Id.* at 732.
As had become: *Id.* at 733–34 (Black & Douglas, J.J., concurring in judgment).

88   Alone in dissent: *Id.* at 734 (Fortas, J., dissenting).

Greenbelt Cooperative Publishing Association v. Bresler

On October 20: Greenbelt Coop. Publ'g Ass'n v. Bresler, 396 U.S. 874 (1969) (granting *cert.*).

According to the: WOD Conference Notes for *Greenbelt Coop. Publ'g Ass'n v. Bresler*, Oct. 8, 1969.

That was because: Special to the NEW YORK TIMES, *Fortas Quits the Supreme Court, Defends Dealings with Wolfson; Fee Is Explained*, NYT, May 16, 1968 (noting that Fortas was "the first justice in the history of the court to step down under the pressure of public criticism").

89   The series of: JOHN CALVIN JEFFRIES, JUSTICE LEWIS F. POWELL, JR., 222–32 (1994).

With the 1968: Warren's retirement letter was one sentence. It read, "Pursuant to the provisions of 28 USC, section 371(b), I hereby advise you of my intention to retire as Chief Justice of the United States effective at your pleasure." ED CRAY, CHIEF JUSTICE: A BIOGRAPHY OF EARL WARREN, 496–97 (1997). *See also* Alfonso Narvaez, *Clement Haynsworth Dies at 77; Lost Struggle for High Court Seat*, NYT, Nov. 23, 1989; Linda Greenhouse, *Ex-Justice Abe Fortas Dies at 71; Shaped Historic Rulings on Rights*, NYT, Apr. 7, 1982; Fred Graham, *Johnson Appoints Fortas to Head Supreme Court; Thornberry to Be Justice; Opposition Voiced*, NYT, June 27, 1968.

90   In June 1969: Special to the NEW YORK TIMES, *Senate Confirms Burger by 74 to 3; Vietnam War Critics Delay Vote on Chief Justice*, NYT, June 10, 1969.

Warren was also: SETH STERN & STEPHEN WERMIEL, JUSTICE BRENNAN: LIBERAL CHAMPION 104–07 (2010).

Brennan would not: *Id.* at 244–45, 318–19.

Harry Blackmun, another: TINSLEY YARBOUGH, HARRY A. BLACKMUN: THE OUTSIDER JUSTICE 115 (2008).

He would not: Fred Graham, *Blackmun Is Sworn as 98th Justice*, NYT, June 10, 1970.

A third, respected: JOHN CALVIN JEFFRIES, JUSTICE LEWIS F. POWELL, JR., 222–32 (1994).

Two years later: *Id.*

The Supreme Court's: Brief for Respondent, Greenbelt Coop. Publ'g Ass'n v. Bresler, 396 U.S. 874 (1969), 1970 WL 136277 at 2–14.

91   On October 14: *Id.*

A week later: Greenbelt Coop. Publ'g Ass'n v. Bresler, 252 A.2d 755, 761–63 (Md. 1969).

Bresler sued the: *Id.* at 763.

92   The Maryland Court: *Id.* at 770–74.

As for the: *Id.* at 774–75.

Turning to the: *Id.* at 775–78.

93   At the argument: *Greenbelt Coop. Publ'g Ass'n v. Bresler*, Feb. 24–25, 1970 (The Oyez Project at IIT Chicago-Kent College of Law).

Arguing for Bresler: *Id.*

95   At Conference, the: WOD Conference Notes for *Greenbelt Coop. Publ'g Ass'n v. Bresler*, Feb. 27, 1970.

Despite what appeared: Greenbelt Coop. Publ'g Ass'n v. Bresler, 398 U.S. 6 (Apr. 1, 1970) (slip op. 1) (Brennan, J.) (first draft).

96   Justice Harlan, too: Greenbelt Coop. Publ'g Ass'n v. Bresler, 398 U.S. 6 (Apr. 16, 1970) (slip op. 1) (Harlan, J.) (first draft).

On April 23: PS to Conference, Apr. 23, 1970.

In his new draft: Greenbelt Coop. Publ'g Ass'n v. Bresler, 398 U.S. 6, 11 (1970).

Harlan quickly accepted: JMH to PS, Apr. 23, 1970.

On May 12: WJB to PS, May 12, 1970.

That left Black: Greenbelt Coop. Publ'g Ass'n, 398 U.S. at 24 (Black, J., concurring).

Justice White also: *Id.* at 18 (White, J., concurring).

97   In the end: *Id.* at 10–11, 13–14.

Second, the Court's: *Id.* at 13; *see* Cox Broad. Corp. v. Cohn, 420 U.S. 469 (1975).

Monitor Patriot Co. v. Roy, Time, Inc. v. Pape, and Ocala Star-Banner Co. v. Damron

98   On Feburary 24: Monitor Patriot Co. v. Roy, 397 U.S. 904 (1970) (granting *cert.*).

On April 27: Time, Inc. v. Pape, 397 U.S. 1062 (1970) (granting *cert.*).

And, on May: Ocala Star-Banner Co. v. Damron, 397 U.S. 1073 (1970) (granting *cert.*).

The Court would: Monitor Patriot Co. v. Roy, 401 U.S. 265 (1971) (argued on Dec. 17, 1970; decided on Feb. 24, 1971); Time, Inc. v. Pape, 401 U.S. 279 (1971) (argued on Dec. 16, 1970; decided on Feb. 24, 1971); Ocala Star-Banner Co. v. Damron, 401 U.S. 295 (1971) (argued on Dec. 17, 1970; decided on Feb 24, 1971).

In *Monitor Patriot*: Monitor Patriot Co., 397 U.S. at 266–67; *see* Roy v. Monitor-Patriot Co, 109 N.H. 441, 441–43 (1969).

99   In *Time, Inc.*: 401 U.S. at 280–82.

In a separate: Monroe v. Pape, 365 U.S. 167 (1961); *see* Monell v. N.Y. City Dep't of Social Servs., 436 U.S. 658 (1978) (overruling *Monroe v. Pape*).

Monroe later won: Monroe v. Pape, 221 F. Supp. 635, 639 (N.D. Ill. 1963).

100 Pape's libel case: Pape v. Time, Inc., 318 F.2d 652, 653–54 (7th Cir. 1965); 401 U.S. at 282. *See also* FED. R. CIV. P. 56.

In his second: Pape v. Time, Inc., 354 F.2d 558 (7th Cir. 1965).

In the wake: 376 U.S. at 279; *see, e.g.*, Pilkenton v. Kingsport Publ'g Corp., 395 F.2d 989, 989 (4th Cir. 1968) (affirming grant of summary judgment where publisher "merely carried an accurate account of a matter of public interest"); United Med. Labs., Inc. v. Columbia Broad. Sys., Inc., 404 F.2d 706, 713 (9th Cir. 1968) (affirming grant of summary judgment where plaintiff failed to prove actual malice).

The Seventh Circuit: 354 F.2d 558 (7th Cir. 1965).

Undeterred, after the: Pape v. Time, Inc., 294 F. Supp. 1087, 1090–91 (N.D. Ill. 1969) ("The statements set forth in the article were only allowed to be published after other articles and dispatches were consulted and a good faith determination made by the writer and the researcher that the Commission had included the quoted portions with the intention that the facts be taken as 'substantially' true.").

For a third: Pape v. Time, Inc., 419 F.2d 980, 982 (7th Cir. 1969).

In *Ocala Star-Banner*: Brief for Petitioners, Ocala Star-Banner Co. v. Damron, 397 U.S. 1073 (1971), 1970 WL 136673 at 5–9; Ocala

Star-Banner Co. v. Damron, 221 So. 2d 459, 461 (Fla. Dist. Ct. App. 1969).

101 In *Roy*, the: *Monitor Patriot Co. v. Roy*, Dec. 17, 1970 (The Oyez Project at IIT Chicago-Kent College of Law); Albin Krebs, *Edward Bennett Williams, Trial Lawyer, Dead at 68; A Brilliant 'Superlawyer'*, NYT, Aug. 15, 1988.

Chief Justice Burger: *Monitor Patriot Co. v. Roy*, Dec. 17, 1970 (The Oyez Project at IIT Chicago-Kent College of Law).

102 Roy was represented: *Id.*

In *Pape*, the: *Time, Inc. v. Pape*, Dec. 16, 1970 (The Oyez Project at IIT Chicago-Kent College of Law).

Relying on the: *Id.*; *see* St. Amant v. Thompson, 390 U.S. 727, 730–32 (1968).

103 Patrick Dunne, another: *Monitor Patriot Co. v. Roy*, Dec. 17, 1970 (The Oyez Project at IIT Chicago-Kent College of Law).

In *Damron*, Harold: *Ocala Star-Banner Co. v. Damron*, Dec. 17, 1970 (The Oyez Project at IIT Chicago-Kent College of Law).

Wallace Dunn of: *Id.*

104 Justice Douglas, however: WOD to HLB, Feb. 18, 1971.

In another defamation: Rosenbloom v. Metromedia, Inc., 403 U.S. 29 (1971).

Clark was part: Fred Graham, *Impeach-Douglas Plea Raises Constitutional Question*, NYT, Aug. 24, 1970.

Since Douglas could: WOD to HLB, Feb. 18, 1971.

In *Monitor Patriot*: 401 U.S. at 277.

105 In *Time, Inc.*: 401 U.S. at 292.

Not only would: Bose Corp. v. Consumers Union, 466 U.S. 485 (1984); Masson v. New Yorker Magazine, Inc., 501 U.S. 496 (1991).

See also Wash. Post Co. v. Keogh, 365 F.2d 965, 968 (D.C. Cir. 1966) ("In the First Amendment area, summary procedures are even more essential. For the stake here, if harassment succeeds, is free debate."); Time, Inc. v. McLaney, 406 F.2d 565, 566 (5th Cir. 1969) ("[T]he failure to dismiss a libel suit might necessitate long and expensive trial proceedings").

Only Justice Harlan: 401 U.S. at 293 (Harlan, J, dissenting).

106   Finally, in *Damron*: 401 U.S. at 300–01.

       In both *Roy*: *Id.* at 301 (White, concurring).

CHAPTER 4

109   The Court is: *See, e.g.*, Maryland v. Balt. Radio Show, 338 U.S. 912,
       918 (1950) ("It may be desirable to have different aspects of an issue
       further illuminated by the lower courts. Wise adjudication has its own
       time for ripening."); William H. Rehnquist, *The Changing Role of the
       Supreme Court*, 14 FLA. ST. U. L. REV. 1, 11 (1986) ("[T]hat it is actually
       desirable to allow important questions of federal law to 'percolate' in
       the lower courts for a few years before the Supreme Court takes them
       on seems to me a very strange suggestion; at best it is making a virtue
       of necessity."); *see also* Todd J. Tiberi, *Supreme Court Denials of Certiorari
       in Conflicts Cases: Percolation or Procrastination?*, 54 U. PITT. L. REV. 861
       (1993).

Rosenbloom v. Metromedia, Inc.

110   George Rosenbloom was: Rosenbloom v. Metromedia, Inc., 403 U.S.
       29, 32–33 (1971).

       By any measure: *See, e.g.*, Rosenbloom v. Metromedia, Inc., 289 F.
       Supp. 737, 742 (E.D. Pa. 1968) ("Rosenbloom was in no sense a public
       man.").

       On that fateful: *Id.* at 739.

       Rosenbloom was arrested: Rosenbloom v. Metromedia, Inc., 403 U.S.
       at 32–33.

       Rosenbloom's libel suit: *Id.* at 32–36.

111   Armed with his: *Id.* at 36; *see* Rosenbloom v. Metromedia, Inc., 289 F.
       Supp. 737.

       In September 1969: Rosenbloom v. Metromedia, Inc., 415 F.2d 892
       (3d Cir. 1969).

       Judge Collins Seitz: *Id.*; *see Virginia Seitz, Assistant Attorney General,
       Office of Legal Counsel (since June 2011)*, WASH. POST, http://www

.washingtonpost.com/politics/virginia-seitz/gIQAX1LeKP_topic.html
(accessed Sept. 11, 2013).

Seitz and his: Rosenbloom v. Metromedia, Inc., 415 F.2d at 895–97.

Rosenbloom took his: Rosenbloom v. Metromedia, Inc., 403 U.S. 29
(1971).

The opening lines: OT '70 Term History, at 9.

The court agreed: *Id.*; Rosenbloom v. Metromedia, Inc., 397 U.S. 904
(1970) (granting cert.).

112   According to Brennan's: OT '70 Term History, at 9.

Justice Blackmun would: Linda Greenhouse, *The Evolution of a Justice*,
NYT MAGAZINE, Apr. 10, 2005.

Oral argument began: *Rosenbloom v. Metromedia, Inc.*, Dec. 7–8, 1970
(The Oyez Project at IIT Chicago-Kent College of Law).

This was just: Monitor Patriot Co. v. Roy, 401 U.S. 265 (1971) (argued
Dec. 17, 1970; decided Feb. 24, 1971); Time, Inc. v. Pape, 401 U.S.
279 (1971) (argued Dec. 16, 1970; decided Feb. 24, 1971); Ocala
Star-Banner Co. v. Damron, 401 U.S. 295 (1971) (argued Dec. 17,
1970; decided Feb. 24, 1971).

Representing Rosenbloom was: *See* David Margolick, *The Long and
Lonely Journey of Ramsey Clark*, NYT, June 14, 1991.

Metromedia's lawyer was: *See* Robert McG. Thomas Jr., *Bernard G.
Segal Dies at 89; Lawyer for Rich and Poor*, NYT, June 5, 1997.

In his opening: *Rosenbloom v. Metromedia, Inc.*, Dec. 7–8, 1970 (The
Oyez Project at IIT Chicago-Kent College of Law).

Justice Brennan asked: *Id.*

113   When his turn: *Id.*

In addition to: *Id.*

114   As Segal used: *Id.*

115   At the mention: *Id.*

In a rebuttal: *Id.*

When the Justices: OT '70 Term History, at 9.

Justice Douglas, who: Fred Graham, *Impeach Douglas Please Raises
Constitutional Question*, NYT, Aug. 2, 1970.

Justice Blackmun, who: WJB Vote Sheet for *Rosenbloom v. Metromedia,
Inc.*, Dec. 11, 1970.

116   According to Blackmun's: HAB Conference Notes for *Rosenbloom v.*
       Metromedia, Inc., Dec. 11, 1970.

       According to Brennan's: WJB Conference Notes for *Rosenbloom v.*
       Metromedia, Inc., Dec. 11, 1970.

       On December 29, 1970: WEB to Conference, Dec. 29, 1970
       (assignment sheet).

       In any event: PS to WEB, Dec. 29, 1970.

       According to Brennan's: OT '70 Term History, at 9.

117   Of the four: *See, e.g.,* Time, Inc. v. Hill, 385 U.S. 374 (1967); Rosenblatt
       v. Baer, 383 U.S. 75 (1966); Garrison v. Louisiana, 379 U.S. 64 (1964);
       New York Times Co. v. Sullivan, 376 U.S. 254 (1964).

       Nevertheless, Brennan was: OT '70 Term History, at 9.

       Brennan circulated a: Rosenbloom v. Metromedia, Inc., 403 U.S. 29
       (Feb. 17, 1971) (slip op.) (Brennan, J.) (second draft); OT '70 Term
       History, at 9.

       Blackmun's law clerk: DBE to HAB, Feb. 17, 1971.

       Blackmun's own files: HAB to WJB, Mar. 9, 1971 (unsent).

       Among the other: HAB to WJB, Mar. 22, 1971; OT '70 Term History,
       at 10.

       First, Blackmun told: Rosenbloom v. Metromedia, Inc., 403 U.S. 29
       (Feb. 17, 1971) (slip op. 11) (Brennan, J.) (second draft).

118   Blackmun's March 22: HAB to WJB, Mar. 22, 1971.

       Blackmun had a: *Id.*

       On page twenty-one: Rosenbloom v. Metromedia, Inc., 403 U.S. 29
       (Feb. 17, 1971) (slip op. 21) (Brennan, J.) (second draft).

       Blackmun's concern, which: HAB to WJB, Mar. 22, 1971.

119   While some justices: SETH STERN & STEPHEN WERMIEL, JUSTICE
       BRENNAN: LIBERAL CHAMPION 233, 455, 545 (2010).

       In that spirit: WJB to HAB, Mar. 23, 1971.

       As Brennan noted: OT '70 Term History, at 10.

       Thus, while thanking: WJB to HAB, Mar. 23, 1971.

       Blackmun accepted Brennan's: HAB to WJB, Mar. 29, 1971.

       The day that: WEB to WJB, Mar. 25, 1971.

       In it, the: WEB to WJB, Mar. 25, 1971.

       Brennan politely replied: WJB to WEB, Mar. 29, 1971.

120   Burger's letter raised: WEB to WJB, Mar. 25, 1971.

Brennan's reply, evidencing: WJB to WEB, Mar. 29, 1971.

Finally, on April 19: WEB to WJB, Apr. 19, 1971.

Eight days later: WEB to Conference, Apr. 27, 1971; Rosenbloom v.
Metromedia, Inc., 403 U.S. 29 (Apr. 27, 1971) (slip op.) (Burger, C.J.,
concurring) (first draft).

A month later: WEB to Conference, May 25, 1971; OT '70 Term
History, at 11.

As Brennan's term: OT '70 Term History, at 11.

As Brennan's focus: *Id.*; *see* Rosenbloom v. Metromedia, Inc., 403 U.S.
29 (May 19, 1971) (slip op.) (Marshall, J., dissenting) (fourth draft);
Rosenbloom v. Metromedia, Inc., 403 U.S. 29 (May 19, 1971) (slip op.)
(Harlan, J., dissenting) (third draft).

121   In his own: Rosenbloom v. Metromedia, Inc., 403 U.S. 29 (May 19,
1971) (slip op. 1) (Marshall, J., dissenting) (fourth draft).

And Marshall had: *See* Jackson Stakeman & Randy Stakeman, *Walter
White's Divorce and Remarriage,* THE WALTER WHITE PROJECT, http://scalar
.usc.edu/nehvectors/stakeman/marriage-divorce-and-remarriage
?path=walter-white-biography (accessed Sept. 12, 2013); *see also Walter
White, 61, Dies in Home Here,* NYT, Mar. 22, 1955.

Whatever the life: Rosenbloom v. Metromedia, Inc., 403 U.S. at 79
(Marshall, J., dissenting).

Although he had: PS to Conference, Mar. 11, 1971 ("I expect in due
course to write a dissenting opinion in this case."); PS to TM, May 17,
1971.

In fact, Brennan's: OT '70 Term History, at 11.

In the end: Rosenbloom v. Metromedia, Inc., 403 U.S. at 62–78
(Harlan, J., dissenting).

Before he circulated: JMH to TM, May 11, 1971.

Brennan's term history: OT '70 Term History, at 11.

A significant point: JMH to TM, May 11, 1971.

122   At this juncture: Rosenbloom v. Metromedia, Inc., 403 U.S. 29 (May
27, 1971) (slip op.) (Brennan, J.) (fourth draft).

As Brennan's term: OT '70 Term History, at 10.

Whatever its constitutional: Rosenbloom v. Metromedia, Inc., 403 U.S. 29 (May 27, 1971) (slip op. 2) (Brennan, J.) (fourth draft).

In this, Brennan: *Id.* at 2 n.2 & 13–15; *see* Samuel D. Warren & Louis D. Brandeis, *The Right to Privacy*, 4 HARV. L. REV. 193 (1890).

As Brennan's term: OT '70 Term History, at 12.

In addition to: Rosenbloom v. Metromedia, Inc., 403 U.S. 29 (May 27, 1971) (slip op. 17–18) (Brennan, J.) (fourth draft).

123   In that regard: *Id.* at 17 n.15.

Much of Brennan's: *Id.* at 23.

For one thing: *See, e.g.*, Time, Inc. v. Hill, 385 U.S. 374, 401–02 (1967) (Douglas, J., concurring); Rosenblatt v. Baer, 383 U.S. 75, 88–91 (1966) (Douglas, J., concurring).

He also knew: *See, e.g.*, Rosenblatt v. Baer, 383 U.S. at 94–96 (Black, J., concurring and dissenting) ("This case illustrates I think what a short and inadequate step this Court took in the *New York Times* case to guard free press and free speech against the grave dangers to the press and the public created by libel actions.").

124   Sure enough, in: Rosenbloom v. Metromedia, Inc., 403 U.S. at 57 (Black, J., concurring in judgment).

Some three months: Ocala Star-Banner Co. v. Damron, Monitor Patriot Co. v. Roy, 401 U.S. 295, 301 (1971) (White, J., concurring); Rosenbloom v. Metromedia, Inc., 403 U.S. at 57–62 (White, J., concurring).

Signaling that he: Rosenbloom v. Metromedia, Inc., 403 U.S. at 60 (White, J., concurring).

Nevertheless, White remained: *Id.* at 62.

125   After receiving White's: OT '70 Term History, at 11–12.

The court's decision: Rosenbloom v. Metromedia, Inc., 403 U.S. 29 (1971).

The extent to: Gertz v. Robert Welch, Inc., 418 U.S. 323 (1974).

As a result: *See, e.g.*, LaBruzzo v. Associated Press, 353 F. Supp. 979 (W.D. Mo. 1973) (news report linking plaintiff to Mafia was about matter of public concern and required plaintiff to prove actual malice); Alpine Constr. Co. v. Demaris, 358 F. Supp. 422 (N.D. Ill. 1973) (book appendix linking plaintiff and his construction company to Chicago

organized crime was about matter of public concern and required
plaintiff to prove actual malice); Kent v. Pittsburgh-Press Co., 349
F. Supp. 622 (W.D. Pa. 1972) (article about release of prison inmate
involved matter of public concern and required plaintiff to prove
actual malice).

Gertz v. Robert Welch, Inc.

126   Finally, on February 20: Gertz v. Robert Welch, Inc., 410 U.S. 925
      (1973) (granting cert.).

      Justice Black, who: SETH STERN & STEPHEN WERMIEL, JUSTICE BRENNAN:
      LIBERAL CHAMPION 353–54 (2010).

      The departures of: The justices remaining from the *Sullivan* Court
      were Brennan, White, Stewart, and Douglas. *See Members of the Supreme
      Court of the United States*, SUPREME COURT, http://www.supremecourt
      .gov/about/members.aspx (accessed Sept. 12, 2013).

127   As a general: DAVID M. O'BRIEN, STORM CENTER: THE SUPREME COURT
      IN AMERICAN POLITICS 55 (6th ed. 2003) ("Nixon vehemently opposed
      the 'liberal jurisprudence' of the Warren Court . . . .").

      This time around: SETH STERN & STEPHEN WERMIEL, JUSTICE BRENNAN:
      LIBERAL CHAMPION 359–61 (2010).

      The plaintiff, Elmer: Gertz v. Robert Welch, Inc., 322 F. Supp. 997, 998
      (N.D. Ill. 1970).

      In 1968, Gertz: Gertz v. Robert Welch, Inc., 418 U.S. 323, 325–26
      (1974).

128   In March 1969: *Id.*

      Gertz sued the: *Id.* at 327; *see* Gertz v. Robert Welch, Inc., 306 F. Supp.
      310 (N.D. Ill. 1969)

      The trial judge: *See* Gertz v. Robert Welch, Inc., 322 F. Supp. at 998.

      But, in December 1970: *Id.*

      On August 1, 1972: Gertz v. Robert Welch, Inc., 471 F.2d 801 (7th Cir.
      1972).

      The appeals court's: *Members of the Supreme Court of the United States*,
      SUPREME COURT, http://www.supremecourt.gov/about/members.aspx
      (accessed Sept. 12, 2013).

129 Judge Roger Kiley: Gertz v. Robert Welch, Inc., 471 F.2d at 808 (Kiley, J., concurring).

Gertz petitioned the: Gertz v. Robert Welch, Inc., 410 U.S. 925 (1973) (granting cert.).

Chief Justice Burger: WJB Vote Sheet for *Gertz v. Robert Welch, Inc.*, Feb. 16, 1973.

Powell's handwritten notes: LAH to LFP, Dec. 10, 1972 (handwritten note of LFP).

Elsewhere, on his: LFP Vote Sheet for *Gertz v. Robert Welch, Inc.*, Feb. 16, 1973.

130 The case itself: *Gertz v. Robert Welch, Inc.*, Nov. 14, 1973 (The Oyez Project at IIT Chicago-Kent College of Law); *see* Elmer Gertz, Gertz v. Robert Welch, Inc.: The Story of a Landmark Libel Case 94–97 (1992).

During his presentation: *Gertz v. Robert Welch, Inc.*, Nov. 14, 1973 (The Oyez Project at IIT Chicago-Kent College of Law).

Powell then asked: *Id.*

131 After listening to: *Id.*

During his own: *Id.*

132 Attempting to return: *Id.*

133 If this was: *Id.*

Although he may: *Id.*

At Conference following: WOD Conference Notes for *Gertz v. Robert Welch, Inc.*, Nov. 16, 1973.

134 In a subsequent: LFP to WEB, Jan. 4, 1974.

In explaining his: WOD Conference Notes for *Gertz v. Robert Welch, Inc.*, Nov. 16, 1973.

As he later: LFP to WEB, Jan. 4, 1974.

135 Although Burger ended: Gertz v. Robert Welch, Inc., 418 U.S. at 354–55 (Burger, C.J., dissenting).

During the summer: LFP Memorandum to File for *Gertz v. Robert Welch, Inc.*, July 6, 1973.

In it, he: *Id.* at 5–6.

On December 28, 1973: Gertz v. Robert Welch, Inc., 418 U.S. 323 (Dec. 28, 1974) (slip op.) (Powell, J.) (second draft).

Powell's draft, like: *Id.*

In Part III: *Id.* at 15.

In an effort: *Id.* at 15–16.

This passage, which: Gertz v. Robert Welch, Inc., 418 U.S. at 339–40.

In short order: *See* Chapter 9 *infra*; Milkovich v. Lorain Journal Co, 497 U.S. 1 (1990).

Arrayed against the: Gertz v. Robert Welch, Inc., 418 U.S. 323 (Dec. 28, 1974) (slip op. 15–17) (Powell, J.) (second draft) (quoting New York Times Co. v. Sullivan, 376 U.S. at 270).

136 Embracing Justice Stewart's: *Id.* at 17 (quoting Rosenblatt v. Baer, 383 U.S. 75, 92–93 (1963) (Stewart, J., concurring)).

This passage as: Gertz v. Robert Welch, Inc., 418 U.S. at 341.

Having thus placed: Gertz v. Robert Welch, Inc., 418 U.S. 323 (Dec. 28, 1974) (slip op. 18–23) (Powell, J.) (second draft).

Powell based his: *Id.* at 21–22.

In addition, Powell: *Id.* at 18–20.

137 To this point: *Id.* at 20–21.

Whether he did: *See, e.g.*, Wolston v. Reader's Digest Ass'n, Inc., 443 U.S. 157 (1979); Time, Inc. v. Firestone, 424 U.S. 448 (1976); Waldbaum v. Fairchild Publ'ns, Inc., 627 F.2d 1287 (D.C. Cir. 1980).

In Part IV: Gertz v. Robert Welch, Inc., 418 U.S. 323 (Dec. 28, 1974) (slip op. 23–25) (Powell, J.) (second draft).

138 In Part V: *Id.* at 25–27.

139 In crafting this: *See* JJ to LFP, Jan. 2, 1974; JOHN JEFFRIES, LEWIS F. POWELL: A BIOGRAPHY (2001).

After reviewing Stewart's: JJ to LFP, at 4; Ocala Star-Banner Co. v. Damron, 401 U.S. 295 (1971); Time, Inc. v. Pape, 401 U.S. 279 (1971); Monitor Patriot Co. v. Roy, 401 U.S. 265 (1971); Greenbelt Coop. Publ'g Ass'n v. Bresler, 398 U.S. 6 (1970).

Powell's draft, which: Gertz v. Robert Welch, Inc., 418 U.S. 323 (Dec. 28, 1973) (slip op.) (Powell, J.) (second draft) (emphasis added).

As reflected in: Gertz v. Robert Welch, Inc., 418 U.S. at 332.

In one memorable: *Id.* at 340.

As the new: WHR to LFP, Jan. 2, 1974; PS to LFP, Jan. 14, 1974; TM to LFP, Jan. 14, 1974.

Not unexpectedly, Brennan: WJB to Conference, Jan. 10, 1974.

Chief Justice Burger: WEB to LFP, Jan. 3, 1974.

140   While Burger's note: LFP to WEB, Jan. 4, 1974.

Finally, Powell offered: *Id.* at 3.

On January 5: LFP Notes to File for *Gertz v. Robert Welch, Inc.*, Jan. 5, 1974.

141   White wrote to: BRW to LFP, Jan. 10, 1974.

On January 11: Gertz v. Robert Welch, Inc., 418 U.S. 323 (Jan. 11, 1974) (slip op. 22–24) (Powell, J.) (third draft).

Less than a: BRW to LFP, Jan. 17, 1974.

142   At least as: Gertz v. Robert Welch, Inc., 418 U.S. 323 (Jan. 17, 1974) (slip op.) (Brennan, J., dissenting) (first draft); Gertz v. Robert Welch, Inc., 418 U.S. at 361–69 (Brennan, J., dissenting).

In it, despite: *Id.* at 361.

Quoting liberally from: *Id.* at 361–62.

With respect to: *Id.* at 364 (quoting Time, Inc. v. Hill, 385 U.S. at 388).

With respect to: 418 U.S. at 368–69.

143   At the time: RR to HAB, Jan. 17, 1974.

Meanwhile, on January 18: LFP to JJ, Jan. 18, 1974.

Concerned that he: LFP to BRW, Jan. 18, 1974 (unsent).

Although Powell ultimately: *Id.*

Powell began his: *Id.* at 1–2.

144   Because he never: *Id.* (handwritten note on page 1 reads "not used").

Ten years later: *See* Chapter 7 *infra.*

In his unsent: LFP to BRW, Jan. 18, 1974 (unsent), at 3–4.

Assessing why he: *Id.* at 3.

145   Finally, in his: *Id.* at 4–5.

On January 22: WEB to LFP, Jan. 22, 1974.

At the same: WEB to HAB, Jan. 22, 1974.

On February 20: WHR to LFP, Feb. 20, 1974.

146   Two days later: LFP to WHR, Feb. 22, 1974.

On February 26: Gertz v. Robert Welch, Inc., 418 U.S. 323 (Feb. 26, 1974) (slip op.) (Powell, J.) (fourth draft).

The waiting ended: Gertz v. Robert Welch, Inc., 418 U.S. 323 (Apr. 18, 1974) (slip op.) (White, J., dissenting) (second draft).

147   "Lest there be": *Id.* at 2.

Aiming his rhetorical: *Id.* at 6.

148   And, just in: *Id.*

Not surprisingly, Powell: LFP to Conference, Apr. 1, 1974.

After reading it: LFP to JJ, undated.

Meanwhile, Powell attempted: LFP to JJ, Apr. 2, 1974.

All of this: Gertz v. Robert Welch, Inc., 418 U.S. at 347 n.10; "Note A" in the Papers of LFP, Apr. 9, 1974.

149   Powell first shared: Gertz v. Robert Welch, Inc., 418 U.S. 323 (Apr. 12, 1974) (slip op.) (Powell, J.) (fifth draft).

On April 25: WHR to LFP, Apr. 25, 1974.

In short order: "Revised Footnote 10" in the Papers of LFP, Apr. 26, 1974 (with handwritten note "As approved by Rehnquist").

In the new: Gertz v. Robert Welch, Inc., 418 U.S. 323 (Apr. 12, 1974) (slip op. 23 n. 10) (Powell, J.) (fifth draft).

Beyond the addition: *See* Gertz v. Robert Welch, Inc., 418 U.S. at 348–50.

Powell's files contain: Gertz v. Robert Welch, Inc., 418 U.S. 323 (Feb. 26, 1974) (slip op.) (Powell, J.) (fourth draft) (handwritten note at 1).

Moreover, White's dissent: Gertz v. Robert Welch, Inc., 418 U.S. at 398 (White, J., dissenting).

Although Powell had: *See* LFP to JJ, undated, at 2 ("Moreover, the tone of [White's] dissent reflects (despite a disclaimer) a deep dissatisfaction with *New York Times*[.]").

150   Thus, in the: Gertz v. Robert Welch, Inc., 418 U.S. 323 (Apr. 19, 1974) (slip op. 8 n.3) (Brennan, J., dissenting) (third draft).

Brennan closed his: *Id.*; *see* Miami Herald Publ'g Co. v. Tornillo, 418 U.S. 241 (1974).

Pat Tornillo was: Miami Herald Publ'g Co. v. Tornillo, 418 U.S. at 243.

In two editorials: *Id.* at 243 n. 1.

Tornillo demanded that: *Id.* at 244–46.

151   As the footnote: Gertz v. Robert Welch, Inc., 418 U.S. at 368 n.3 (Brennan, J., dissenting).

Accordingly, on June 4: WJB to WEB, June 4, 1974.

The overlap between: Miami Herald Publ'g Co. v. Tornillo, 418 U.S. at 259–63 (White, J., concurring).

Ultimately, after consulting: LFP to HAB, June 18, 1974; *see* Miami Herald Publ'g Co. v. Tornillo, 418 U.S. at 262 (White, J., concurring).

On June 20: Gertz v. Robert Welch, Inc., 418 U.S. 323 (June 20, 1974) (slip op. 23 n.10) (Powell, J.) (eighth draft).

152   After Brennan circulated: Gertz v. Robert Welch, Inc., 418 U.S. 323 (Apr. 19, 1974) (slip op. 8 n.3) (Brennan, J., dissenting) (third draft); Gertz v. Robert Welch, Inc., 418 U.S. 323 (June 13, 1974) (slip op. 32 n.43) (White, J., dissenting) (fourth draft).

On April 24: HAB to LFP, Apr. 24, 1974; Gertz v. Robert Welch, Inc., 418 U.S. 323 (Apr. 24, 1974) (slip op.) (Blackmun, J., concurring) (first draft).

In it, Blackmun: Gertz v. Robert Welch, Inc., 418 U.S. 323 (Apr. 24, 1974) (slip op. 1) (Blackmun, J., concurring) (first draft).

Nevertheless, Blackmun's draft: *Id.* at 2.

The following day: HAB to WEB, Apr. 25, 1974.

153   *Austin* was another: Old Dominion Branch No. 496, Nat'l Ass'n of Letter Carriers, AFL-CIO v. Austin, 418 U.S. 264 (1974).

The plaintiffs, a: *Id.* at 266–69.

Relying on the: *See id.* at 268–70 (discussing trial court decision); *see also* Linn v. Plant Guard Workers Local 114, 333 U.S. 53 (1966).

The Virginia Supreme: Old Dominion Branch No. 496, Nat'l Ass'n of Letter Carriers, AFL-CIO v. Austin, 213 Va. 377 (1972).

The U.S. Supreme: *Old Dominion Branch No. 496, Nat'l Ass'n of Letter Carriers, AFL-CIO v. Austin*, Nov. 14, 1973 (The Oyez Project at IIT Chicago-Kent College of Law).

Ultimately, the justices: Old Dominion Branch No. 496, Nat'l Ass'n of Letter Carriers, AFL-CIO v. Austin, 418 U.S. 264 (1974).

Applying the correct: *Id.* at 282–83.

In so holding: *Id.* at 284 (quoting Gertz v. Robert Welch, Inc., 418 U.S. at 339–40). *See* Chapter 9 *infra*.

154   Marshall's opinion in: 418 U.S. at 287–91 (Douglas, J., concurring in result); *id.* at 291–97 (Powell, J., dissenting).

"It is one": *Id.* at 297 (Powell, J., dissenting).

While the justices: WEB to LFP, June 5, 1974.

Powell replied the: LFP to WEB, June 6, 1974.

Following this exchange: WEB to WJB, June 4, 1974.

155 As a result: Miami Herald Publ'g Co. v. Tornillo, 418 U.S. at 258–59 (Brennan, J., concurring).

"The result of": *Id.* at 250.

In the opinion's: *Id.* at 258.

In his own: *Id.* at 261 (White, J., concurring).

156 On June 20: Gertz v. Robert Welch, Inc., 418 U.S. 323 (June 20, 1974) (slip op. 1–2) (Burger, J., dissenting) (first draft); WEB to Conference, June 20, 1974.

The court's decision: Gertz v. Robert Welch, Inc., 418 U.S. 323 (1974); *id.* at 353–54 (Blackmun, J., concurring); *id.* at 354–55 (Burger, C.J., dissenting); *id.* at 355–60 (Douglas, J., dissenting); *id.* at 361–69 (Brennan, J., dissenting); *id.* at 369–404 (White, J., dissenting).

When he announced: Opinion Announcement for *Gertz v. Robert Welch, Inc.* in the Papers of LFP, June 19, 1974.

Following the decision: Anthony Lewis to LFP, Mar. 31, 1975.

157 Powell also received: John Wade to LFP, July 3, 1974.

Within days of: LFP to PS, TM, HAB and WHR, July 10, 1974.

158 There are two: ELMER GERTZ, GERTZ V. ROBERT WELCH, INC.: THE STORY OF A LANDMARK LIBEL CASE (1992); *Human Rights Section Gertz Award*, ILL. STATE BAR ASS'N, http://www.isba.org/awards/humanrights (accessed Sept. 13, 2013). *See also* RONALD COLLINS & SAM CHATALAN, WE MUST NOT BE AFRAID TO BE FREE 208–37 (2011).

CHAPTER 5

Cox Broadcasting Corp. v. Cohn

159 The Court's first: Cox Broad. Corp. v. Cohn, 420 U.S. 469 (1975).

It arrived at: WJB Vote Sheet for *Cox Broad. Corp. v. Cohn*, Dec. 17, 1973.

The case arose from: 420 U.S. at 471–74.

160 During the April: *Id.* at 474 n. 5.

In May 1972: *Id.* at 474–75 (citing GA. CODE ANN. § 26–9901 (1972)).

On appeal: 420 U.S. at 474–75 (quoting 231 Ga. 60, 68 (1973)).

161 The Supreme Court: *Cox Broad. Corp. v. Cohn*, Nov. 11, 1974 (The Oyez Project at IIT Chicago-Kent College of Law).

For his part: *Id.*

Thus, when Powell: *Id.* (discussing Miami Herald Publ'g Co. v. Tornillo, 418 U.S. 241 (1974)).

When Mr. Cohn's: *Cox Broad. Corp. v. Cohn*, Nov. 11, 1974 (The Oyez Project at IIT Chicago-Kent College of Law).

162 Brennan then seized: *Id.*

Land's answer: *Id.*

163 At conference following: WJB Conference Notes for *Cox Broad. Corp. v. Cohn*, Nov. 15, 1974.

Ultimately, all of: Cox Broad. Corp. v. Cohn, 420 U.S. 469, 501–12 (1975) (Rehnquist, J., dissenting).

Like his brief comments: Cox Broad. Corp v. Cohn, 420 U.S. 469 (Jan. 3, 1975) (slip. op.) (White, J.)

On January 14: LFP to BRW, Jan. 14, 1975.

Powell's draft was: Cox Broad. Corp. v. Cohn, 420 U.S. 469 (Jan. 15, 1975) (slip op. 1–3) (Powell, J., concurring) (first draft).

164 Powell circulated a: Cox Broad. Corp. v. Cohn, 420 U.S. 469 (Jan. 17, 1975) (slip op. 3–4) (Powell, J., concurring) (second draft); *see* Chapter 7 *infra* (discussing Dun & Bradstreet, Inc. v. Greenmoss Builders, 472 U.S. 749 (1985)).

Instead, Brennan, without: A "join" letter is the way a justice expresses intent to sign on to another's draft opinion that has been circulated among them. The letter literally says, "Please join me" in the opinion. The custom has long persisted despite the odd syntax, which seems to suggest that the opinion author is joining the letter-writer, rather than the letter-writer joining the opinion author.

In that opinion: 420 U.S. at 487–88.

Although White's analysis: *Id.* at 489–91, 496.

165 Burger, without further: 420 U.S. at 496 (Burger, C.J., concurring in judgment).

Douglas also concurred: *Id.* at 500–01 (Douglas, J., concurring).

Only Rehnquist dissented: *Id.* at 511 (Rehnquist, J., dissenting) ("A further aspect of the difficulties which the Court is generating is illustrated by a petition for certiorari recently filed in this Court, *Time, Inc. v. Firestone*, No. 74–944.").

Time, Inc. v. Firestone

166   In stark contrast: OT '73 Term History; OT '75 Term History, at 1–7.
       Firestone arose from: Time, Inc. v. Firestone, 424 U.S. 449, 452 (1976) (quoting *Time*, Dec. 22, 1967).
       In fact, during: 424 U.S. at 450.
       What the judge: *Id.* at 458 (citing Firestone v. Firestone, 263 So. 2d 223 (Fla. 1972)).
       And, unfortunately for: 424 U.S. at 463 (quoting Firestone v. Time, Inc., 305 So. 2d 172 (Fla. 1974)).

167   Nevertheless, the judgment: 424 U.S. at 451 (quoting Firestone v. Time, Inc., 305 So. 2d 172 (Fla. 1974)).
       Time learned of: 424 U.S. at 451–52.
       Shortly after its: Time, Inc. v. Firestone, 421 U.S. 909 (1975) (granting petition).
       As Brennan's term: OT '75 Term History, at 1.
       The term history noted: *Id.* at 2; *see* MARTIN A. DYCKMAN, A MOST DISORDERLY COURT: SCANDAL AND REFORM IN THE FLORIDA JUDICIARY (2008) (describing series of bribery and other scandals in Florida courts that percolated throughout the first half of the 1970s, peaking in the spring and summer of 1975 with impeachment proceedings against three Florida Supreme Court Justices).

168   The case was argued: *Time, Inc. v. Firestone*, Oct. 14, 1975 (The Oyez Project at IIT Chicago-Kent College of Law).
       Later in his argument: *Id. See* Mona Morris, *Firestone Gets His Divorce; She Promises a Court Fight*, MIAMI HERALD, Dec. 16, 1967.
       Following Pickering's suggestion: Firestone v. Time, Inc., 271 So. 2d 745, 747 n.1; Chesnut v. Chesnut, 160 Fla. 83, 85 (1948).

169   At this juncture: *Time, Inc. v. Firestone*, Oct. 14, 1975 (The Oyez Project at IIT Chicago-Kent College of Law).

Pickering then turned: *Id.*; *see* Rosenbloom v. Metromedia, Inc., 403 U.S. 29, 57–62 (1971) (White, J., concurring in judgment).

When Palm Beach: *Time, Inc. v. Firestone*, Oct. 14, 1975 (The Oyez Project at IIT Chicago-Kent College of Law).

170 Caruso was questioned: *Id.*

At this point: *Id.*

This exchange led: *Id.*

171 He responded to: WJB to Anthony Lewis, Oct. 21, 1975.

Following the argument: OT '75 Term History, at 2.

The Brennan position: *Id.*; 424 U.S. at 471–81 (Brennan, J., dissenting).

This position: *Time, Inc. v. Firestone*, Oct. 14, 1975 (The Oyez Project at ITT Chicago-Kent College of Law).

It is, therefore, worth: OT '75 Term History, at 3 ("BRW, TM and WHR all voted to affirm on the reasoning that the *Gertz* fault standard applied, that the State Supreme Court had adopted it, and that there was sufficient evidence to support a finding of fault.")

Still, White was: 424 U.S. at 476 (Brennan, J., dissenting).

172 By this point: 424 U.S. at 481–84 (White, J., dissenting).

Stewart voted: OT '75 Term History, at 2–3.

Finally, as was: *See* Lee Levine & Stephen Wermiel, *The Landmark That Wasn't: A First Amendment Play in Five Acts*, 88 WASH. L. REV. 1, 18 & n.73 (2013) (discussing Chief Justice Burger's custom of passing on voting in cases in which he wished to retain assignment power).

Even though Burger's: OT '75 Term History, at 3.

173 The Rehnquist draft: Time, Inc. v. Firestone, 424 U.S. 449 (Dec. 11, 1975) (slip op.) (Rehnquist, J.) (first draft).

Like the final: *Id.*

Brennan thought the: OT '75 Term History, at 3–4.

Brennan circulated his: *Id.*

The next day: LFP to WHR, Dec. 13, 1975.

On December 15: OT '75 Term History, at 4.

Powell circulated: Time, Inc. v. Firestone, 424 U.S. 449 (Dec. 23, 1975) (slip op.) (Powell, J., concurring) (first draft); PS to LFP, Dec. 29, 1975.

White circulated: Time, Inc. v. Firestone, 424 U.S. 449 (Dec. 30, 1975) (White, J., dissenting) (slip. op.) (second draft).

On New Year's: OT '75 Term History, at 4–5.

After the holiday: *Id.* at 5; *see* WEB to Conference, Jan. 5, 1976.

174   Marshall, who had: OT '75 Term History, at 5; *see* Time, Inc. v. Firestone, 424 U.S. 449 (Feb. 3, 1976) (Marshall, J., dissenting) (slip op.) (first draft).

In his term: OT '75 Term History, at 5.

According to Brennan's: *Id.* at 5–6; *see* Rosenbloom v. Metromedia, Inc., 403 U.S. 29, 78–87 (1971) (Marshall, J., dissenting).

In his *Firestone*: OT '75 Term History, at 6 (citing 424 U.S. at 484–93 (Marshall, J., dissenting)).

In his term: OT '75 Term History, at 6.

In this sense: Dun & Bradstreet, Inc. v. Greenmoss Builders, 472 U.S. 749 (1985).

175   Nevertheless, Marshall's dissent: OT '75 Term History, at 6.

In his opinion: Time, Inc. v. Firestone, 424 U.S. 448, 484–93 (1976) (Marshall, J., dissenting).

According to Brennan's: OT '75 Term History, at 6; *see* Time, Inc. v. Firestone, 424 U.S. 449 (Feb. 23, 1976) (Stewart, J., concurring) (slip op.) (first draft).

As a result: OT '75 Term History, at 6.

In the end: 424 U.S. 449, 454–56 (1976).

176   Next, Rehnquist's opinion: *Id.* at 457–60.

Finally, although Rehnquist: *Id.* at 463–64 (quoting Firestone v. Time, Inc., 305 So. 2d 172, 178 (Fla. 1974)).

177   It was this: Time, Inc. v. Firestone, 424 U.S. 448, 464–70 (1976) (Powell, J., concurring).

And, in a: *Id.* at 470 n.9; *see* Time, Inc. v. Firestone, 424 U.S. 448, 493 (1976) (Marshall, J., dissenting).

Brennan, as noted: Time, Inc. v. Firestone, 424 U.S. 448, 471–81 (1976) (Brennan, J., dissenting).

And, Brennan included: *Id.* at 475 n.3.

178   White's own: Time, Inc. v. Firestone, 424 U.S. 448, 481–84 (1976) (White, J., dissenting).

Finally, Marshall's: Time, Inc. v. Firestone, 424 U.S. 448, 484–93 (1976) (Marshall, J., dissenting).

The result, as: OT '75 Term History, at 5–6.

179   As a result: *Id.* at 7.

In its 1973 decision: Miller v. California, 413 U.S. 15 (1973); Roth
v. United States, 354 U.S. 476 (1957). *See also* A Book Named "John
Cleland's Memoirs of a Woman of Pleasure" v. Att'y Gen. of Mass.,
383 U.S. 413 (1966); Ginzburg v. United States, 383 U.S. 463 (1966);
Mishkin v. New York, 383 U.S. 502 (1966); Jacobellis v. Ohio, 378 U.S.
184 (1964).

In the years: *See* ALEXANDER M. BICKEL, THE SUPREME COURT AND
THE IDEA OF PROGRESS 50–54 (1978) (discussing the "instances of *ad
hoc* subjectivity resulting in palpable injustice to individuals" that
characterized the Court's obscenity rulings after 1966).

Indeed, but for: Masson v. New Yorker Magazine, Inc., 501 U.S. 496
(1991).

Finally, Brennan suspected: OT '75 Term History, at 7.

Landmark Communications, Inc. v. Virginia

180   The Court took: Herbert v. Lando, 441 U.S. 153 (1979).

Nevertheless in the: Landmark Commc'ns, Inc. v. Virginia, 435 U.S.
829 (1978).

Brennan, however, took: *Id.* at 846.

He had undergone: SETH STERN & STEPHEN WERMIEL, JUSTICE BRENNAN:
LIBERAL CHAMPION 449–50 (2010).

Justice Powell also: 435 U.S. at 846.

The case arose: *Id.* at 831–32 (citing VA. CODE § 2.1–37.13 (1973)).

Although Brennan did: Smith v. Daily Mail Publ'g Co., 443 U.S. 97
(1979); Fla. Star v. B.J.F., 491 U.S. 524 (1989).

181   In his opinion: 435 U.S. at 838–42; *see* FLOYD ABRAMS, SPEAKING FREELY
63–80 (2005); *see also* RONALD K. L. COLLINS, NUANCED ABSOLUTISM:
FLOYD ABRAMS & THE FIRST AMENDMENT (2013).

Thus, for example: TM to Conference, Jan. 16, 1978.

182   Brennan also retained: WHR to WEB, Mar. 20, 1978.

Burger accommodated: 435 U.S. at 840 ("We need not address
all the implications of that question here, but only whether in the

circumstances of this case Landmark's publication is protected by the
First Amendment.")
Finally, Brennan's file: Landmark Commc'ns, Inc. v.Virginia, 435 U.S.
829 (Apr. 12, 1978) (Stevens, J., concurring) (typewritten draft).
It is, however: 435 U.S. at 842.

Herbert v. Lando

183   Following *Firestone*: Herbert v. Lando, 441 U.S. 153 (1979).
As Brennan's term: OT '78 Term History, at 49.
It arose from: 441 U.S. at 155–56; *see id.* at 180–81 (Brennan, J.,
dissenting).
Following the broadcast: *Id..* at 155–57.
Among other things: *Herbert v. Lando*, Oct. 31, 1978 (The Oyez Project
at IIT Chicago-Kent College of Law).
In all: 441 U.S. at 176 n. 25.
In the wake: *Herbert v. Lando*, Oct. 31, 1978 (The Oyez Project at IIT
Chicago-Kent College of Law).
The theory was: Herbert v. Lando, 441 U.S. 153, 180–98 (1979)
(Brennan, J., dissenting); Herbert v. Lando, 568 F.2d 974, 983–84 (2d
Cir. 1977).
The trial judge: Herbert v. Lando, 73 F.R.D. 387, 395–96 (S.D.N.Y.
1977); 568 F.2d at 983–84.

184   In the Second: 568 F.2d at 975; 441 U.S. at 155; 435 U.S. at 830.
The Second Circuit: *See, e.g.*, Edwards v. Nat'l Audubon Soc'y, 556
F.2d 113 (2d Cir. 1977); Russo v. Cent. School Dist. No. 1, 469 F.2d
623 (2d Cir. 1972) (holding that teacher's First Amendment rights
were violated when school officials discharged her for refusing to
recite pledge of allegiance); New York Times Co. v. United States, 444
F.2d 544 (2d Cir. 1971) (Kaufman, J., dissenting); Wolin v. Port Auth. of
New York, 392 F.2d 83 (2d Cir. 1968) (holding that distributing leaflets
and discussing antiwar views with passersby at bus terminal were
activities protected by First Amendment).
It helped that: *See, e.g.*, Edward Ranzal, *Parody of Songs Upheld by Court*,
NYT, Mar. 24, 1964; Irving R. Kaufman, *A Free Speech for the Class
of '75*, NYT, June 8, 1975; Irving R. Kaufman, *Judges Must Speak Out*,

NYT, Jan. 30, 1982; Irving R. Kaufman, *Keeping Politics Out of the Court*, NYT, Dec. 9, 1984; Irving R. Kaufman, *The Creative Process and Libel*, NYT, Apr. 5, 1987.

The *Times* indeed: Arnold H. Lubasch, *Court Decision in Libel Suit Bars Inquiry Into Journalist's Thoughts*, NYT, Nov. 8, 1977.

Prior to the: *See, e.g.*, Davis v. Nat'l Broad. Co., 320 F. Supp. 1070, 1072 (E.D. La. 1970) (granting defendant's motion for summary judgment primarily on grounds of "fundamental defense under the First Amendment"), *aff'd*, 447 F.2d 981 (5th Cir. 1971); Bon Air Hotel, Inc. v. Time, Inc., 295 F. Supp. 704, 710 (S.D. Ga. 1969) (granting defendant's motion for summary judgment based on review of three affidavits), *aff'd*, 426 F.2d 858 (5th Cir. 1970).

Moreover, prior to: *Compare* Rose v. Koch, 278 Minn. 235, 256–61 (1967) (determining university professor was public figure), *and* Gibson v. Maloney, 231 So. 2d 823, 824 (1970) (noting simply that there "can be little doubt" plaintiff was public figure), *with* Waldbaum v. Fairchild Publ'ns, Inc., 627 F.2d 1287, 1295 (D.C. Cir. 1980) (noting "several factors" that govern public figure analysis), *and* Wilson v. Daily Gazette Co., 214 W. Va. 208, 216–17 (2003) (applying four-factor test to determine whether plaintiff was "all-purpose" public figure and three-factor test to determine whether plaintiff was "limited purpose" public figure).

And, of course: *See, e.g.*, Alexander v. Lancaster, 330 F. Supp. 341, 349 (W.D. La. 1971) (noting that, after *Rosenbloom*, there was no longer "serious question" that the court must apply "actual malice" standard); Priestley v. Hastings & Sons Publ'g Co. of Lynn, 360 Mass. 118, 119 (1971) (reversing trial court decision not to apply "actual malice" standard based on *Rosenbloom*); Hensley v. Life Magazine, Time, Inc., 336 F. Supp. 50, 54 (N.D. Cal. 1971) (noting that *Rosenbloom* required application of "actual malice" standard rather than "mere negligence").

185   As a result: *See, e.g.*, Vandenburg v. Newsweek, Inc., 507 F.2d 1024, 1027–28 (5th Cir. 1975) (considering reasonableness of reporter's faith in his sources for allegedly libelous article); Carey v. Hume, 390 F. Supp. 1026, 1030 (D.D.C. 1975) (denying defendants' summary judgment motion where pretrial discovery revealed "controverted issue

of material fact as to whether [defendants] misrepresented or distorted the report of their source"); Rosanova v. Playboy Enters., Inc., 411 F. Supp. 440 (S.D. Ga. 1976) (granting defendants' summary judgment motion following extensive questioning at depositions regarding reporters' decision to rely on sources).

In addition, media: *See, e.g.*, Westmoreland v. CBS Inc., 601 F. Supp. 66 (S.D.N.Y. 1984) (granting defendants' motion objecting to proposed admission of report by senior executive producer regarding the preparation of broadcast at issue in defamation action); Sharon v. Time, Inc., 599 F. Supp. 538, 543, 556 (S.D.N.Y. 1984) (noting that parties had engaged in "extensive discovery" and that plaintiff had "been able to bring to light the process by which the allegedly offending statement came to be written, including evidence of the possible motivations and truthfulness of its author"); McCoy v. Hearst Corp., 42 Cal. 3d 835, 847 (1986) (reviewing extensive factual record regarding actual malice and noting "that evidence concerning appellants' investigations and discoveries was . . . introduced . . . as it related to the state of mind of the appellants").

The net result: Lee Levine, *Judge and Jury in the Law of Defamation: Putting the Horse Behind the Cart*, 35 AM. U. L. REV. 3, 29–30 (1985).

Against this backdrop: WJB Vote Sheet for *Herbert v. Lando*, Feb. 6, 1978.

The argument: *Herbert v. Lando*, Oct. 31, 1978 (The Oyez Project at IIT Chicago-Kent College of Law).

186   Brennan focused his: *Id.*

During Abrams's argument: *Id.*

187   The issue at: TM to Conference, Jan. 16, 1978 ("I would hold that . . . an individual is as much protected as is the newspaper, rather than giving the press any special protection in the circumstances of this case."); Dun & Bradstreet, Inc. v. Greenmoss Builders, 472 U.S. 749 (1985); *see* Chapter 7 *infra*.

Near the conclusion: *Herbert v. Lando*, Oct. 31, 1978 (The Oyez Project at IIT Chicago-Kent College of Law).

White's observation had: Sidney Zion, "*High Court vs. The Press,*" NYT, Nov. 18, 1979.

At Conference, it: OT '78 Term History, at 49–50.

188 Brennan's notes reflect: WJB Vote Sheet for *Herbert v. Lando*, Nov. 3, 1978.

That said, as: OT '78 Term History, at 50.

Brennan himself advocated: *Id.*

As Brennan ultimately: Herbert v. Lando, 441 U.S. 153, 181 (1979) (Brennan, J., dissenting).

According to Brennan's: OT '78 Term History, at 50.

Thus, as Brennan's: WJB Conference Notes for *Herbert v. Lando*, Nov. 3, 1978.

189 As Brennan recounted: *Id.*

Despite all this: OT '78 Term History, at 50. *See* Herbert v. Lando, 441 U.S. 153 (Feb. 8, 1979) (White, J.) (slip op.) (first draft). The copies of Brennan's first and second drafts retained in his papers are both undated, however his third draft is dated February 22, 1979.

In his book: JOHN PAUL STEVENS, FIVE CHIEFS 236 (2011); *see* Neb. Press Ass'n v. Stuart, 427 U.S. 539 (1976); Landmark Commc'ns, Inc. v. Virginia, 435 U.S. 829 (1978); Richmond Newspapers v. Virginia, 448 U.S. 555 (1980); Press-Enter. Co. v. Superior Ct., 478 U.S. 1 (1986).

By the time: OT '75 Term History, at 3; Branzburg v. Hayes, 408 U.S. 665 (1972).

190 In his own: Herbert v. Lando, 441 U.S. 153 (undated) (Brennan, J., dissenting) (slip op. 1) (first draft).

Analogizing to the: Herbert v. Lando, 441 U.S. 153, 194 (1979) (Brennan, J., dissenting) (citing United States v. Nixon, 418 U.S. 683, 705 (1974)).

Brennan's "hope" that: OT '78 Term History, at 50.

White circulated his: Herbert v. Lando, 441 U.S. 153 (Feb. 8, 1979) (White, J.) (slip op.) (first draft); WHR to BRW, Feb. 8, 1979; LFP to BRW, Feb. 9, 1979; JPS to BRW, Feb. 12, 1979; WEB to BRW, Feb. 14, 1979; HAB to BRW, Feb. 22, 1979.

The centerpiece of: Herbert v. Lando, 441 U.S. 153 (Feb. 8, 1979) (White, J.) (slip op.) (first draft).

As White's opinion: *Id.* at 5–6.

191 Thus, White asserted: *Id.* at 14.

In sum, White's: *Id.* at 17.

Moreover, responding to: *Id.* at 24.

White asserted both: *Id.* at 21.

According to White: *Id.* at 22.

In a second draft: Herbert v. Lando, 441 U.S. 153 (Feb. 28, 1979) (White, J.) (slip op. 20 n.23) (second draft).

192 A few days: Herbert v. Lando, 441 U.S. 153 (Feb. 23, 1979) (Stewart, J., dissenting) (slip op. 1) (first draft).

Marshall also circulated: Herbert v. Lando, 441 U.S. 153 (Apr. 6, 1979) (Marshall, J., dissenting) (first draft).

In it, he: Herbert v. Lando, 441 U.S. 153, 204–06, 209 (1979) (Marshall, J., dissenting).

Responding to the: OT '78 Term History, at 50; LFP to BRW, Feb. 9, 1979.

Because it did: Herbert v. Lando, 441 U.S. 153 (Feb. 28. 1979) (White, J.) (slip op. 23) (second draft); Herbert v. Lando, 441 U.S. 153 (Mar. 28, 1979) (Powell, J., concurring) (first draft).

In it, he: Herbert v. Lando, 441 U.S. 153 (Mar. 28, 1979) (Powell, J., concurring) (slip op. 1–2) (first draft).

193 In addition to: OT '78 Term History, at 51.

In his draft: Herbert v. Lando, 441 U.S. 153 (Mar. 28, 1979) (Powell, J., concurring) (slip op. 1–2 n.1) (first draft).

On April 9: Herbert v. Lando, 441 U.S. 153 (Apr. 9, 1979) (Brennan, J., dissenting) (slip op. at 15 n.14) (fifth draft).

Three days later: OT '78 Term History, at 51; *see* Herbert v. Lando, 441 U.S. 153 (Apr. 12, 1979) (Powell, J., concurring) (third draft).

Media defendants regularly: Herbert v. Lando, 441 U.S. 153, 179 (1979) (Powell, J., concurring).

194 Most significantly as: ROBERT D. SACK, SACK ON DEFAMATION: LIBEL, SLANDER AND RELATED PROBLEMS §§ 14:7, 16:3.4 (4th ed. 2010); *see, e.g.*, Weyrich v. New Republic, Inc., 235 F.3d 617, 628 (D.C. Cir. 2001); Foretich v. Chung, 1994 WL 716606 (D.D.C.), *aff'd*, 1994 WL 773751 (D.D.C. Dec. 5, 1994).

The decision in: 441 U.S. 153 (1979).

As Brennan's term: OT '78 Term History, at 52. *See, e.g.*, Deidre Carmody, *Ripple Effect Is Feared in Press Ruling*, NYT, Apr. 20, 1979;

Tom Wicker, *A Chilling Court*, NYT, Apr. 20, 1979; *see also* Erik Ugland, *Newsgathering, Autonomy, and the Special-Rights Apocrypha: Supreme Court and Media Litigant Conceptions of Press Freedom*, 11 U. PA. J. CONST. L. 375, n. 4–5 (2009) (citing contemporary press reports).

First, in a: WJB, Address at the Dedication of the Samuel I. Newhouse Law Center at Rutgers University (Oct. 17, 1979), *in* 5 MEDIA L. REP. 1837 (1979).

Ironically, Judge Kaufman: Irving R. Kaufman, "Dedication of the Building," Dedication, S.I. Newhouse Center for Law and Justice 12 (Oct. 17, 1979); *see also* JAMES C. GOODALE, FIGHTING FOR THE PRESS 122 (2013) (noting Judge Kaufman's friendship with Sulzberger).

Second, Brennan's term: OT '78 Term History, at 52.

Smith v. Daily Mail Publishing Co.

It also took: Smith v. Daily Mail Publ'g Co., 443 U.S. 97 (1979).

The case arose: *Id*. at 99.

A fourteen-year-old: *Smith v. Daily Mail Publ'g Co.*, Mar. 20, 1979 (The Oyez Project at IIT Chicago-Kent College of Law).

195 That same day: 443 U.S. at 99.

The next day: *Id*. at 99–100 (citing W. VA. CODE § 49–7-3 (1976)).

The West Virginia Supreme Court: 443 U.S. at 100 (citing 161 W. Va. 684 (1978)).

West Virginia thereafter: WJB Vote Sheet for *Smith v. Daily Mail Publ'g Co.*, Sept. 21, 1978.

Much of the: *Smith v. Daily Mail Publ'g Co.*, Mar. 20, 1979 (The Oyez Project at ITT Chicago-Kent College of Law).

196 When the case: WJB Conference Notes for *Smith v. Daily Mail Publ'g Co.*, Mar. 23, 1979.

Rehnquist initially voted: Powell was hospitalized in March 1979 for intestinal surgery. *Notes on People: Justice Powell May Miss Hearing the Weber Case*, NYT, Mar. 13, 1979.

At Conference, Burger: WJB Conference Notes for *Smith v. Daily Mail Publ'g Co.*, Mar. 23, 1979.

Burger assigned the: Smith v. Daily Mail Publ'g Co., 443 U.S. 97 (May 18, 1979) (slip op.) (first draft).

197   Stevens and White: JPS to WEB, May 22, 1979; BRW to WEB, May 22, 1979; HAB to WEB, May 22, 1979.

On June 11: WJB to WEB, June 11, 1979.

Burger responded that: WEB to WJB, June 11, 1979.

The next day: WJB to WEB, June 12, 1979.

198   Burger circulated another: Smith v. Daily Mail Publ'g Co., 443 U.S. 97 (June 13, 1979) (Burger, C.J.) (slip op. 7) (fourth draft); WJB to WEB, June 13, 1979.

Stewart joined Burger's: PS to WEB, June 13, 1979; TM to WEB, June 20, 1979.

In the end: Smith v. Daily Mail Publ'g Co., 443 U.S. 97, 106–10 (1979) (Rehnquist, J., concurring).

The decision was: 443 U.S. 97.

Hutchinson v. Proxmire, Wolston v. Reader's Digest Association

The October 1978: Hutchinson v. Proxmire, 443 U.S. 111 (1979); Wolston v. Reader's Digest Ass'n, 443 U.S. 157 (1979).

In *Firestone,* although: Time, Inc. v. Firestone, 424 U.S. 448 (1976).

Rehnquist's efforts to: *Id.* at 484–93 (Marshall, J., dissenting).

Hutchinson was brought: 443 U.S. at 114–18.

199   In fact, Dr.: *Hutchinson v. Proxmire,* Apr. 17, 1979 (The Oyez Project at IIT Chicago-Kent College of Law).

Hutchinson thereafter instituted: 443 U.S. at 118–20 (citing 431 F. Supp. 1311 (W.D. Wis. 1977)).

The district court: 431 F. Supp. at 1322–24, 1327–28, 1331–32.

That decision was: 443 U.S. at 120–22 (citing 579 F.2d 1027 (7th Cir. 1978)).

The court of: 579 F.2d at 1033–35.

200   The case was: *Hutchinson v. Proxmire,* Apr. 17, 1979 (The Oyez Project at IIT Chicago-Kent College of Law).

Later, Justice Stewart: *Id.*

During his own: *Id.*

201   Like the argument: WJB Conference Notes for *Hutchinson v. Proxmire,* Apr. 20, 1979.

As Brennan recounted: *Id.*

202   On May 26: WEB to Conference, May 26, 1979.

As a result: Hutchinson v. Proxmire, 443 U.S. 111 (May 26, 1979) (slip op. 20) (Burger, J.) (first draft).

In his accompanying: WEB to Conference, May 26, 1979.

Two days later: LFP to WEB, May 28, 1979.

203   Burger responded the: WEB to LFP, May 29, 1979.

Burger's Memorandum prompted: LFP to WEB, May 29, 1979.

Four other justices: HAB to WEB, May 29, 1979; JPS to WEB, May 29, 1979; PS to WEB, May 30, 1979; WHR to WEB, June 5, 1979.

At about the: Hutchinson v. Proxmire, 443 U.S. 111 (June 5, 1979) (slip op.) (Brennan, J., dissenting) (first draft).

The following day: Hutchinson v. Proxmire, 443 U.S. 111 (June 6, 1979) (slip op.) (Burger, J., for the Court) (second draft).

In so doing: *Id.* at 22–24.

204   In one of them: 443 U.S. at 119 n.8.

In another, footnote: *Id.* at 133 n. 16.

205   Most significantly, in: *Id.* at 120 n.9 (and accompanying text). Burger's characterization of the "so-called rule" was drawn from the district court's opinion, 431 F. Supp. at 1130, which cited as support: Oliver v. Village Voice, Inc., 417 F. Supp. 235 (S.D.N.Y. 1976); Guitar v. Westinghouse Elec. Corp., 396 F. Supp. 1042 (S.D.N.Y. 1975), *aff'd*, 538 F.2d 309 (2d Cir. 1976); Perry v. Columbia Broad. Sys., Inc., 499 F.2d 797 (7th Cir.), *cert. denied*, 419 U.S. 883 (1974); Cervantes v. Time, Inc., 464 F.2d 986 (8th Cir. 1972), *cert. denied*, 409 U.S. 1125 (1973); and Wash. Post Co. v. Keogh, 365 F.2d 965 (1966), *cert. denied*, 385 U.S. 1011 (1967).

Like *Hutchinson, Wolston*: 443 U.S. at 159–63.

During discovery in : *Wolston v. Reader's Digest Ass'n*, Apr. 17, 1979 (The Oyez Project at IIT Chicago-Kent College of Law).

206   Wolston brought his: 443 U.S. at 159–60.

The trial court: Wolston v. Reader's Digest Ass'n, 429 F. Supp. 167 (D.D.C. 1977), *aff'd*, 578 F.2d 427 (D.C. Cir. 1978).

Wolston was argued: *Wolston v. Reader's Digest Ass'n*, Apr. 17, 1979 (The Oyez Project at IIT Chicago-Kent College of Law).

During his questioning: *Id.*

207   When Dickstein rose: *Id.*

    During Dickstein's opening: *Id.*

208   Throughout Buckley's argument: *Id.*

    Later in his argument: *Id.*

209   When Rehnquist asked: *Id.*

    Brennan retained no: Wolston v. Reader's Digest Ass'n, 443 U.S. 157
(May 30, 1979) (first draft)

    In his opinion: *Id.* at 8.

    Relying on his: *Id.* at 9.

210   In addition, Rehnquist: *Id.* at 8 n. 8.

    Rehnquist also addressed: *Id.*

    Not surprisingly, therefore: *Id.* at 10.

    And, finally in: *Id.* at 8 n. 7.

    By May 31: LFP to WHR, May 31, 1979.

211   Second, Powell opined: *Id.*

    Rehnquist responded the: WHR to LFP, June 1, 1979.

    As for Powell's: 443 U.S. at 161 n.3.

    The issues of: Bose Corp. v. Consumers Union, 466 U.S. 485 (1984);
Anderson v. Liberty Lobby, Inc., 477 U.S. 242 (1986); Harte-Hanks
Commc'ns, Inc. v. Connaughton, 491 U.S. 657 (1989).

    Brennan joined the: Wolston v. Reader's Digest Ass'n, 443 U.S. 157
(June 18, 1979) (slip op. 1) (Brennan, J., dissenting) (first draft); Wolston
v. Reader's Digest Ass'n, 443 U.S. 157 (June 15, 1979) (slip op. 1–2)
(Blackmun, J., concurring) ("Assuming *arguendo* that petitioner gained
public-figure status when he became involved in the espionage
controversy in 1958, he clearly had lost that distinction by the time
respondents published 'KGB' in 1974.").

212   The apparent contradiction: Calder v. Jones, 465 U.S. 783 (1984);
Keeton v. Hustler Magazine, Inc., 465 U.S. 770 (1984); Bose Corp. v.
Consumers Union, 466 U.S. 485 (1984); Anderson v. Liberty Lobby,
Inc., 477 U.S. 242 (1986).

CHAPTER 6

213 In fact, during: Wilson v. Scripps-Howard Broad. Co., 642 F.2d 371
(6th Cir. 1981) (Merritt, J.); Street v. Nat'l Broad. Co., 645 F.2d 1227
(6th Cir. 1981) (Merritt, J.); Orr v. Argus-Press Co. (6th Cir. 1978)
(Merritt, J.).
In one of them: *Street*, 645 F.2d at 1229.
In the other: *Wilson*, 642 F.2d at 374–76.
The Court that was: Linda Greenhouse, *Senate Confirms Judge
O'Connor; She Will Join the High Court Friday*, NYT, Sept. 22, 1981.
Although they had: Wilson v. Scripps-Howard Broad. Co., 454 U.S.
1130 (1981) (dismissing cert.); Street v. Nat'l Broad. Co., 454 U.S. 1095
(1981) (same).

214 As it turned: Foretich v. Capital Cities/ABC, Inc., 37 F.3d 1541 (4th
Cir. 1994); Silvester v. Am. Broad. Cos., Inc., 839 F.2d 1491, 1493 (11th
Cir. 1988); Waldbaum v. Fairchild Publ'ns, Inc., 627 F.2d 1287, 1296,
(D.C. Cir. 1980).
But, as we: Philadelphia Newspapers, Inc. v. Hepps, 475 U.S. 767
(1986).
When they did: Bose Corp. v. Consumers Union, 466 U.S. 485 (1984);
Keeton v. Hustler Magazine, Inc., 465 U.S. 770 (1984); Calder v. Jones,
465 U.S. 783 (1984); Dun & Bradstreet. Inc. v. Greenmoss Builders,
Inc., 472 U.S. 749 (1985).
Three of them: *Keeton v. Hustler Magazine, Inc.*, Nov. 8, 1983 (1983 U.S.
Trans. Lexis 37); *Calder v. Jones*, Nov. 8, 1983 (1983 U.S. Trans. Lexis 38);
Bose Corp. v. Consumers Union, Nov. 8, 1983 (1983 U.S. Trans. Lexis 40).
The fourth—*Greenmoss*: *Dun & Bradstreet. Inc. v. Greenmoss Builders,
Inc.*, Oct. 3, 1984, (1984 U.S. Trans. Lexis 19); Lee Levine & Stephen
Wermiel, *The Making of Modern Libel Law: A Glimpse Behind the Scenes*,
29 COMM. LAW 1, 36–39 (2012).

Keeton v. Hustler Magazine
It arose in: *Keeton*, 465 U.S. at 772–73.
As her counsel: *Keeton v. Hustler Magazine, Inc.*, Nov. 8, 1983 (1983 U.S.
Trans. Lexis 37, 1).

215   These "calumnies and: 465 U.S. at 781 n.13.

The case was: Guccione v. Hustler Magazine, Inc., 413 N.E.2d 860
(Oh. Ct. Com. Pl. 1977).

By that time: 465 U.S. at 772–75.

Nevertheless, the New Hampshire: Keeton v. Hustler Magazine, Inc.,
682 F.2d 33, 36 (1st Cir. 1982) (Breyer, J.).

Keeton is the: OT '83 Term History, at 72–74.

Hustler and Flynt: *Id.*

216   Brennan's term history: *Id.*

On November 3: David Kahn to Alexander Stevas, Nov. 3, 1983.

On the same day: Larry Flynt to WJB, Nov. 3, 1983.

As recounted in: OT '83 Term History, at 73–74.

That same day: Norman Roy Grutman to Alexander Stevas, Nov. 3,
1983.

In his cover: WEB to Conference, Nov. 3, 1983; *see* Helicopteros
Nacionales de Colombia, S.A. v. Hall, 466 U.S. 408 (1984).

217   For his part: Alexander Stevas to WEB, Nov. 3, 1983. The other *amici
curiae* were represented by R. Bruce Rich, a prominent New York
media lawyer, and Robert D. Sack, then also a New York media
lawyer and author of the authoritative modern treatise on the law of
defamation and later a distinguished appellate judge on the Second
Circuit. *Id. See* 465 U.S. at 771; ROBERT D. SACK, SACK ON DEFAMATION:
LIBEL, SLANDER AND RELATED PROBLEMS (4th ed. 2012).

Needless to say: OT '83 Term History, at 74.

With Flynt seated: *Supreme Court Ejects Flynt after Outburst*, MILWAUKEE
JOURNAL, Nov. 8, 1983.

Among other things: OT '83 Term History, at 74.

At his authoritative best: *Id.*

He later pled: *Larry Flynt Pleads Guilty*, NYT, Feb. 13, 1985.

With Grutman: *Keeton v. Hustler Magazine, Inc.*, Nov. 8, 1983 (1983 U.S.
Trans. Lexis 37, 10–14).

218   During his own: *Id.* at 26–28.

As they had: *Id.* at 30, 38–39.

At Conference, all: WJB Vote Sheet for *Keeton v. Hustler Magazine, Inc.*,
Nov. 11, 1983.

219   The memorandum that: WJB Conference Memo for *Keeton v. Hustler Magazine, Inc.*, (undated), 1–2.
      After Brennan spoke: WJB Conference Notes for *Keeton v. Hustler Magazine, Inc.*, Nov. 11, 1983.
      Ultimately, in an: 465 U.S. at 776–78.
220   For his part: *Id.* at 782 (Brennan, J., concurring).
      Although Brennan had: WJB Conference Memo for *Keeton v. Hustler Magazine, Inc.*, (undated), 2 ("I do not think that there is any constitutional prohibition against forum shopping."); 465 U.S. at 780, 780 n.12.

Calder v. Jones

      In *Calder*, the: 465 U.S. at 784–86.
221   The case was: *Calder v. Jones*, Nov. 8, 1983 (1983 U.S. Trans. Lexis 38, 1–5, 13, 21–22).
      After California lawyer: *Id.* at 23–41 (he spoke for over seven minutes without interruption before Justice Rehnquist asked him his first question); *id.* at 41–45.
      Following argument, as: WJB Conference Notes for *Calder v. Jones*, Nov. 11, 1983.
222   Brennan agreed with: WJB Conference Memo for *Calder v. Jones*, (undated), 1.
      White concurred, adding: WJB Conference Notes for *Calder v. Jones*, Nov. 11, 1983.
223   Burger assigned the: Calder v. Jones, 465 U.S. 783 (Dec. 7, 1983) (Rehnquist, J.) (slip op. 5, 7) (first draft) (citing Herbert v. Lando, 441 U.S. 153 (1979); Hutchinson v. Proxmire, 443 U.S. 111, 120 n.9 (1979)). On December 8: WJB to WHR, Dec. 8, 1983. *Helicopteros Nacionales de Colombia, S.A. v. Hall*, 466 U.S. 408 (1984), was a wrongful death suit arising from a helicopter crash in Peru, where a consortium had leased several helicopters for a project. Relatives of those who died in the crash brought a suit against Helicopteros, the foreign corporation that owned the crashed helicopter, in Texas state court where the consortium was headquartered. Helicopteros had previously sent its CEO to Texas on one occasion, purchased helicopters and supplies

from another Texas company, and sent pilots to be trained in Texas. It had no other contacts with the jurisdiction. The Court was presented with the question of whether Helicopteros's contacts were sufficient for Texas courts to exercise general *in personam* jurisdiction over it. Justice Blackmun, writing for the Court, held that they were not. *Id.* at 416.

224 On March 16: WJB to WHR, Mar. 16, 1984.

Bose Corp. v. Consumers Union

As it happened: 466 U.S. 485 (1984); Lee Levine, *Judge and Jury in the Law of Defamation: Putting the Horse Behind the Cart*, 35 Am. U. L. Rev. 3, 32 (1985).

Rather, *Bose* was: Bose Corp. v. Consumers Union, 692 F.2d 189 (1st Cir. 1982).

That court had: Bose Corp. v. Consumers Union, 508 F. Supp. 1249 (D. Mass. 1981).

Although Bose had: *Id.* at 1267, 1271–74.

225 The First Circuit: 692 F.2d at 195–97.

Although Bose sought: WJB Vote Sheet for *Bose Corp. v. Consumers Union*, Nov. 11, 1983; Bose Corp. v. Consumers Union, 461 U.S. 904 (1983) (granting petition).

It had been: WJB Conference Notes for *Bose Corp. v. Consumers Union*, Nov. 11, 1983. His handwritten notes appear to show that Brennan had marked "D" for denying review next to O'Connor's name. He later scratched it out and ticked the box for "G" to indicate O'Connor's vote to grant review.

The case was: *Bose Corp. v. Consumers Union*, Nov. 8, 1983 (1983 U.S. Trans. Lexis 40, 10–14).

226 At the conclusion: *Id.* at 17–18, 40; Baumgartner v. United States, 322 U.S. 665, 670–71 (1944). The Supreme Court decided *Baumgartner* just six days after the Allied Invasion of Normandy. At issue in the case was whether a German-born man and Nazi sympathizer, Carl Baumgartner, who became a naturalized American citizen in 1932, could have his citizenship revoked for "consciously with[holding] complete renunciation of his allegiance to Germany and entertain[ing]

reservations in his oath of allegiance to his country." *Id.* at 667. The
district court found in favor of the government by making a "finding
of fact," which is normally accepted on appeal absent clear error, that
Baumgartner had failed to forswear his allegiance to the Weimar
Republic in 1932, and the court of appeals affirmed. *Id.* at 666. The
Supreme Court refused to follows the clearly erroneous standard
despite the argument that the ultimate issue in the case was a purely
factual one. In an opinion by Justice Frankfurter, the Court explained,
"[d]eference properly due to the findings of a lower court does not
preclude the review here of such judgments. This recognized scope
of appellate review is usually differentiated from review of ordinary
questions of fact by being called review of a question of law, but that
is often not an illuminating test, and is never self-executing. Suffice it
to say that the emphasis on the importance of [compelling] proof on
which to rest the cancellation of a certificate of naturalization would
be lost if the ascertainment by the lower courts whether that exacting
standard of proof had been satisfied on the whole record were to be
deemed a 'fact' of the same order as all other 'facts' not open to review
here." *Id.* at 671.

227   Consumers Union's counsel: *Bose Corp. v. Consumers Union*, Nov. 8,
      1983 (1983 U.S. Trans. Lexis 40, 18–22).
      Later in Pollet's: *Id.* at 28–29.

228   Despite the probing: WJB Vote Sheet for *Bose Corp. v. Consumers Union*,
      Nov. 11, 1983; WJB Conference Notes for *Bose Corp. v. Consumers
      Union*, Nov. 11, 1983.
      Following the Conference: WEB to Conference, Nov. 11, 1983.
      As a result: WJB Conference Notes for *Bose Corp. v. Consumers Union*,
      Nov. 11, 1983.
      In White's view: *Id.*; 466 U.S. at 515 (White, J., dissenting);
      Harte-Hanks Commc'ns, Inc. v. Connaughton, 491 U.S. 657, 694
      (1989) (White, J., concurring).
      For his part: WJB Conference Notes for *Bose Corp. v. Consumers Union*,
      Nov. 11, 1983.
      The rest of: *Id.*

229   Brennan's own views: WJB Conference Memo for *Bose Corp. v.
      Consumers Union,* (undated), 1–2.
      In Brennan's view: *Id.* at 2.
230   In a footnote: *Id.* at 2 n.1.
      There is some: WJB Conference Notes for *Bose Corp. v. Consumers
      Union,* Nov. 11, 1983; *Bose Corp. v. Consumers Union,* Nov. 11, 1974
      (The Oyez Project at IIT Chicago-Kent College of Law), at 33:30.
231   It was chaired: *Richard Winfield Biography,* COLUMBIA LAW SCHOOL,
      http://www.law.columbia.edu/fac/Richard_Winfield.
      Stevens circulated the: Bose Corp. v. Consumers Union, 466 U.S. at
      515 (Mar. 13, 1984) (Stevens, J.) (slip op. 12–13) (first draft).
      Nevertheless, Stevens concluded: *Id.* at 14–15, 17.
232   In such cases: *Id.* at 18–19, 15 n.17.
233   Turning to the: *Id.* at 27–28.
      Brennan promptly joined: WJB to JPS, Mar. 14, 1984.
      Rehnquist's dissent was: Bose Corp. v. Consumers Union, 466 U.S. 485
      (Apr. 12, 1984) (Rehnquist, J., dissenting) (slip op. 1–2) (first draft).
234   Two days later: 466 U.S. 485 (Apr. 14, 1984) (Rehnquist, J., dissenting)
      (slip op. 3 n.1) (second draft); *see* Chaplinsky v. New Hampshire, 315
      U.S. 568 (1942) (fighting words); Roth v. United States, 354 U.S.
      476 (1957) (obscenity); Brandenburg v. Ohio, 395 U.S. 444 (1969)
      (incitement to violence).
      On April 17: SOC to JPS, Apr. 17, 1984.
      The following day: JPS to WHR, Apr. 18, 1984.
235   On April 20: Bose Corp. v. Consumers Union, 466 U.S. at 515 (Apr.
      20, 1984) (White, J., dissenting) (slip op. 1) (first draft).
      Finally, on April 26: WEB to JPS, Apr. 26, 1984.
      The Court's decision: 466 U.S. 485 (1984).

CHAPTER 7

237   In all, Dun: Dun & Bradstreet, Inc. v. Greenmoss Builders, Inc., 472
      U.S. 749 (1985).

Rather, it arose: Greenmoss Builders, Inc. v. Dun & Bradstreet, Inc., 461 A.2d 414, 415–17 (Vt. 1983).

238   Initially, Brennan assumed: OT '83 Term History, at 82.

As framed by: Petition for a Writ of Certiorari to the Supreme Court of the State of Vermont, Greenmoss Builders, Inc. v. Dun & Bradstreet, Inc., 461 A.2d 416 (No. 83–18), 1983 U.S. S. Ct. Briefs Lexis 1118.

The only justice: Potter Stewart, *Or of the Press*, 26 HASTINGS L.J. 631 (1975).

That debate had: Randall Bezanson, *The New Free Press Guarantee*, 63 VA. L. REV. 731 (1977) (citing other scholarly articles); First Nat'l Bank of Boston v. Bellotti, 435 U.S. 765, 797–803 (1978) (Burger, C.J., concurring).

Brennan's narrative history: OT '83 Term History, at 82.

Most importantly, as: *Id.*

239   When the request: *Id.* at 82–83.

Still, in the: Preliminary Memo from LFP to the Cert. Pool, Sept. 26, 1983, 6 (with handwritten notes from Powell, J.).

As had become: DENNIS J. HUTCHINSON, THE MAN WHO ONCE WAS WHIZZER WHITE: A PORTRAIT OF JUSTICE BYRON R. WHITE 421–23 (1998).

Those reservations become: *Dun & Bradstreet, Inc.*, 472 U.S. 749 (Oct. 13, 1983) (White, J., dissenting from denial of cert.) (slip op. 3) (first draft) (citing Garrison v. Louisiana, 379 U.S. 64 (1964); Henry v. Collins, 380 U.S. 356 (1965); Hutchinson v. Proxmire, 443 U.S. 111, 133 (1979); Abernathy v. Sullivan, 376 U.S. 254 (1964)).

In addition, White: Dun & Bradstreet, Inc. v. Greenmoss Builders, Inc., 472 U.S. 749 (Oct. 13, 1983) (White, J., dissenting from denial of cert.) (slip op. 4–5) (first draft) (citing First National Bank of Boston v. Bellotti, 435 U.S. 765, 793 n.3 (1978) (Burger, C.J., concurring)).

Brennan, as noted: OT '83 Term History, at 83.

The October 1983 Term

240   The case was: *Dun & Bradstreet, Inc. v. Greenmoss Builders, Inc.*, Mar. 21, 1984 (1984 U.S. Trans. Lexis 80, 10–11). "Section 10(b)(5)" is a securities law regulation that makes it unlawful to make "any untrue

statement of a material fact . . . in connection with the purchase or sale of any security." 17 C.F.R. § 240.10b-5.

During his argument: *Dun & Bradstreet, Inc. v. Greenmoss Builders, Inc.*, Mar. 21, 1984 (1984 U.S. Trans. Lexis 80, 27–35). As a general rule, commercial speech is protected to a lesser degree than other speech, such as speech about public affairs. The Supreme Court subjects laws inhibiting such speech to a test first developed in *Central Hudson Gas & Electric Corp. v. Public Service Commission*, 447 U.S. 557 (1980), which denies First Amendment protection to speech proposing a commercial transaction if it is false.

241   Toward the end: *Dun & Bradstreet, Inc. v. Greenmoss Builders, Inc.*, Mar. 21, 1984 (1984 U.S. Trans. Lexis 80, 42–45).

From Brennan's perspective: OT '83 Term History, at 83.

According to Brennan's: *Id.*

Taking the issue: WJB Conference Notes for *Dun & Bradstreet, Inc. v. Greenmoss Builders, Inc.*, Mar. 23, 1983.

242   After Burger had: LFP Conference Notes for *Dun & Bradstreet, Inc. v. Greenmoss Builders, Inc.*, Mar. 23, 1983.

White then surprised: OT '83 Term History, at 82–83.

White, in Brennan's: *Id.*; LFP Conference Notes for *Dun & Bradstreet, Inc. v. Greenmoss Builders, Inc.*, Mar. 23, 1983.

Justices Marshall and: OT '83 Term History, at 84.

Stevens, who (as: OT '83 Term History, at 84; *see* Gertz v. Robert Welch, Inc., 471 F.2d 801 (7th Cir. 1972).

If the Court: WJB Conference Notes for *Dun & Bradstreet, Inc. v. Greenmoss Builders, Inc.*, Mar. 23, 1983. The Fair Credit Reporting Act, 15 U.S.C. § 1681, was passed by Congress in 1970 to give citizens control and privacy with respect to consumer reporting agencies that collect credit information about them by establishing a private right of action against consumer reporting agencies that violate the Act's provisions.

For her part: OT '83 Term History, at 84.

In her view: LFP Conference Notes for *Dun & Bradstreet, Inc. v. Greenmoss Builders, Inc.*, Mar. 23, 1983.

243   When Powell finally: OT '83 Term History, at 84.

Because four justices: *Id.*

Two days later: SOC to WEB, Mar. 28, 1984.

Within hours of: OT '83 Term History, at 85.

In his own: LFP to Conference, Mar. 28, 1984; LFP to JPS & SOC, Mar 24, 1984 (unsent).

244   At the March: OT '83 Term History, at 86.

Brennan's colleagues appeared: *Id.*

The following week: LFP to WEB, Apr. 6, 1984.

Brennan circulated his: Dun & Bradstreet, Inc. v. Greenmoss Builders, Inc., 472 U.S. 749 (May 29, 1984) (Brennan, J.) (slip op. 1–12) (first draft).

245   Brennan then turned: *Id.* at 13–14.

Finally, Brennan's opinion: *Id.* at 15, 19.

Here, Brennan reminded: *Id.* (citing Chaplinsky v. New Hampshire, 315 U.S. 568, 571–72 (1942)).

246   Two years shy: Linda Greenhouse, *Vacancy on the Court; Brennan, Key Liberal, Quits Supreme Court; Battle for Seat Likely*, NYT, July 21, 1990. Just a year before his retirement, Brennan had marshaled a majority in *Texas v. Johnson*, 491 U.S. 397 (1989), where the Court overturned the conviction of a man for burning an American flag. *Id.* at 420. Indeed, just over a month before his retirement, Brennan wrote the Court's opinion declaring unconstitutional a federal law passed in response to *Johnson*, explaining that "[p]unishing desecration of the flag dilutes the very freedom that makes this emblem so revered, and worth revering." United States v. Eichman, 496 U.S. 310, 319 (1990). *See* SETH STERN & STEPHEN WERMIEL, JUSTICE BRENNAN: LIBERAL CHAMPION 525–27 (2010).

Marshal promptly joined: OT '83 Term History, at 86.

Stevens wrote to: *Id.*; Young v. Am. Mini Theatres, 427 U.S. 50 (1976); Fed. Commc'ns Comm'n v. Pacifica Found., 438 U.S. 726 (1978).

Although Brennan had: OT '83 Term History, at 86. *Compare Young*, 427 U.S. at 70 (Stevens, J.) ("[A] line may be drawn on the basis of content without violating the government's paramount obligation of neutrality in its regulation of protected communication."), *with Pacifica Found.*, 438 U.S. at 777 (Brennan, J., dissenting) ("[T]he Court's

decision may be seen for what, in the broader perspective, it really
is: another of the dominant culture's inevitable efforts to force those
groups who do not share its mores to conform to its way of thinking,
acting, and speaking.").

White, however, was: OT '83 Term History, at 86–87.

247   Brennan was moved: *Id.* at 87.

Indeed, on June 1: LFP Conference Memo for *Dun & Bradstreet, Inc. v.
Greenmoss Builders, Inc.*, June 1, 1984, 2.

Accordingly, Powell set: *Id.* at 2–5.

248   Later that same: LFP to Conference, June 1, 1984.

Powell circulated the: *Dun & Bradstreet, Inc. v. Greenmoss Builders, Inc.*,
472 U.S. 749 (June 15, 1984) (Powell, J., dissenting) (slip op. 1) (first
draft). *See* New York Times Co. v. Sullivan, 376 U.S. 254 (1964)
(consolidated with *Abernathy v. Sullivan*, in which defendants were
individual ministers and others who had endorsed advertisement
at issue); Garrison v. Louisiana, 379 U.S. 64 (1964) (defendant was
District Attorney); Henry v. Collins, 380 U.S. 356 (1965) (defendant
was President of NAACP of Mississippi); St. Amant v. Thompson, 390
U.S. 727 (1968) (defendant was candidate for office).

It included a: Dun & Bradstreet, Inc. v. Greenmoss Builders, Inc., 472
U.S. 749 (June 15, 1984) (Powell, J., dissenting) (slip op. 2, 5, 10–11)
(first draft) (quoting Gertz v. Robert Welch, Inc., 418 U.S. 323, 348–49
(1974)).

249   Powell's draft was: OT '83 Term History, at 87.

At this juncture: *Id.*

So, although Brennan: SETH STERN & STEPHEN WERMIEL, JUSTICE
BRENNAN: LIBERAL CHAMPION 223 (2010).

Powell, however, was: LFP to BRW, June 18, 1984.

On June 20: LFP to WEB, June 20, 1984. A case will be dismissed as
improvidently granted if, in hindsight, five justices believe that review
should have not been granted in the first place.

250   Upon receiving her: SOC to LFP, June 20, 1984.

Powell's letter got: WEB to LFP, June 20, 1984.

Thus, it became: OT '83 Term History, at 87.

As the Term: *Id.* at 88.

251   After his meeting: BRW to WJB, June 25, 1984.

The irony in: Lee Levine & Stephen Wermiel, *The Making of Modern Libel Law: A Glimpse Behind the Scenes*, 29 Comm. Law 1, 4 (2012).

White's memorandum provoked: OT '83 Term History, at 88–89.

252   It might have: WEB to BRW, June 25, 1984. In *Garcia v. San Antonio Metropolitan Transit Authority*, 469 U.S. 528 (1985), the Court overruled it prior holding in *National League of Cities v. Usery*, 426 U.S. 833 (1976), which had limited Congress's power under the Commerce Clause to force state and local governments to pay their employees a federally mandated minimum wage insofar as doing so would invade on states' "traditional government functions."

Brennan had written: WJB to WEB, June 25, 1984.

In a handwritten: WEB to WJB, June 25, 1984.

Even before Burger: OT '83 Term History, at 89.

Just before the: *Id.*

On June 26: Joseph Neuhaus to LFP, June 26, 1984.

By the following: LFP to WJB, June 27, 1984.

253   Brennan apparently agreed: LFP to Conference, June 27, 1984.

O'Connor, White, and: WEB to LFP, July 2, 1984; BRW to LFP, June 28, 1984; SOC to LFP, June 27, 1984.

At the time: OT '84 Term History, at 91.

October 1984 Term

The reargument was: *Dun & Bradstreet, Inc. v. Greenmoss Builders, Inc.*, Oct. 3, 1984 (1984 U.S. Trans. Lexis 19, 1–5). The Kiplinger Letter is a weekly financial newsletter, published by a company specializing in finance. *The Kiplinger Letter*, Kiplinger, https://www.kiplinger.com/orders/kwl/intro-web-offer.html.

254   During his argument: *Dun & Bradstreet, Inc. v. Greenmoss Builders, Inc.*, Oct. 3, 1984 (1984 U.S. Trans. Lexis 19, 24–25).

In his term: OT '84 Term History, at 92.

Burger began the: WJB Conference Notes for *Dun & Bradstreet, Inc. v. Greenmoss Builders, Inc.*, Oct. 5, 1984.

According to Powell's: LFP Conference Notes for *Dun & Bradstreet, Inc. v. Greenmoss Builders, Inc.*, Oct. 5, 1984.

255   Brennan began by: WJB Conference Memo for *Dun & Bradstreet, Inc. v.*
      Greenmoss Builders, Inc. (undated), 1.
      For his part: LFP Conference Notes for *Dun & Bradstreet, Inc. v.*
      Greenmoss Builders, Inc., Oct. 5, 1984.

256   After Marshall and: OT '84 Term History, at 92.
      Powell described his: LFP Conference Notes for *Dun & Bradstreet, Inc. v.*
      Greenmoss Builders, Inc., Oct. 5, 1984.
      At this point: *Id.*

257   From Brennan's perspective: OT '84 Term History, at 92–93.
      It is also conceivable: *Gertz*, 418 U.S. at 391–92 (White, J., dissenting).
      Regardless of its: OT '84 Term History, at 93.
      According to Powell's: LFP Conference Notes for *Dun & Bradstreet, Inc.*
      v. Greenmoss Builders, Inc., Oct. 5, 1984.
      Stevens, at least: *Id.*
      O'Connor continued to: *Id.*

258   As Brennan saw: OT '84 Term History, at 93.
      O'Connor, not surprisingly: SOC to WJB, Oct. 30, 1984; LFP to WJB,
      Oct. 30, 1984.
      Indeed, Powell spent: Dun & Bradstreet, Inc. v. Greenmoss Builders,
      Inc., 472 U.S. 749 (Nov. 23, 1984) (Powell, J., affirming in part and
      reversing in part) (slip op.) (first draft).
      When he circulated: LFP to WEB, WHR & SOC, Nov. 23, 1984.
      The first hint: WEB to Conference, Nov. 29, 1984.
      That same day: WHR to LFP, Nov. 29, 1984.

259   On December 14: Dun & Bradstreet, Inc. v. Greenmoss Builders, Inc.,
      472 U.S. 749 (Dec. 14, 1984) (Brennan, J.) (slip op. 22–23, 15 n.9, 21
      n.9) (second draft).
      In Powell's chambers: Daniel Ortiz to LFP, Dec. 17, 1984.
      In response to: LFP Memo for *Dun & Bradstreet, Inc. v. Greenmoss*
      Builders, Inc. (Dec. 17, 1984), 1.

260   Powell's chambers also: Daniel Ortiz to LFP, Dec. 18, 1984, 2.
      In writing at: *Id.* at 1.
      Over the following: Dun & Bradstreet, Inc. v. Greenmoss Builders, Inc.,
      472 U.S. 749 (Dec. 21, 1984) (Powell, J., affirming in part and reversing
      in part) (slip op. 1, 3, 5, 9–10) (second draft).

Powell circulated his: *Id.*

On December 26: BRW to WJB, Dec. 26, 1984.

Shortly thereafter, moreover: *Powell Back in Hospital; May Go Home Today*, WP, Mar. 16, 1985.

261 Although he continued: Michael S. Serrill, *An Illness Ties Up the Justices: The Second Oldest Court Shows the First Signs of Age*, TIME, Apr. 8, 1985.

On January 25: BRW to WJB, Jan. 25, 1985.

As it turned out: OT '84 Term History, at 96; *id.* (quoting White, J.).

It did not differ: Dun & Bradstreet, Inc. v. Greenmoss Builders, Inc., 472 U.S. 749 (Jan. 25, 1985) (White, J., dissenting) (slip op. 5–7) (first draft).

262 In White's newly: *Id.*

Perhaps most cutting: Dun & Bradstreet, Inc. v. Greenmoss Builders, Inc., 472 U.S. 749 (Mar. 29, 1985) (White, J., dissenting) (slip op. 8, 11) (fourth draft).

That afternoon, Brennan: OT '84 Term History, at 96.

263 Shortly after he: WJB to Conference, Jan. 25, 1985.

And, although his: *Bose Corp.*, 466 U.S. at 515 (White, J., dissenting).

While he waited: OT '84 Term History, at 97.

As for Powell: Dun & Bradstreet, Inc. v. Greenmoss Builders, Inc., 472 U.S. 749 (Feb. 22, 1985) (Powell, J., dissenting) (slip op. 2–8) (third draft).

More significantly, Powell's: *Id.*

264 On March 4: LFP Memo for *Dun & Bradstreet, Inc. v. Greenmoss Builders, Inc.*, (Mar. 4, 1985), 1–2, 5.

As Powell continued: Daniel Ortiz to LFP, Mar. 5, 1985.

On March 7, therefore: LFP Notes for *Dun & Bradstreet, Inc. v. Greenmoss Builders, Inc.*, (Mar. 4, 1985).

265 Ultimately, this is: Dun & Bradstreet, Inc. v. Greenmoss Builders, Inc., 472 U.S. 749 (Mar. 13, 1985) (Powell, J., dissenting) (slip op. 3–9) (fourth draft).

On March 12: WHR to LFP, Mar. 12, 1985.

For Brennan and: OT '84 Term History, at 98.

266   In addition, Brennan: *Id.* at 7–9.

On March 20: Dun & Bradstreet, Inc. v. Greenmoss Builders, Inc., 472 U.S. 749 (Mar. 20, 1985) (Brennan, J.) (slip op. 1, 3, 20–21) (fourth draft).

267   Although his draft: Westmoreland v. CBS Inc., 601 F. Supp. 66 (S.D.N.Y. 1984); Sharon v. Time, Inc., 599 F. Supp. 538 (S.D.N.Y. 1984). These defamation cases: *See, e.g.,* RENATA ADLER, RECKLESS DISREGARD: WESTMORELAND V. CBS ET AL., SHARON V. TIME (1986).

It is indeed: Dun & Bradstreet, Inc. v. Greenmoss Builders, Inc., 472 U.S. 749 (Mar. 20, 1985) (Brennan, J.) (slip op. 1, 3, 11–12) (fourth draft).

268   In crafting his: OT '84 Term History, at 98–99.

Upon reflection, however: *Id.* at 99.

Brennan's concerns about: *Id.* at 100.

To Brennan's dismay: JPS to WJB, Mar. 21, 1985.

269   As disappointed as: OT '84 Term History, at 101.

In his response: WJB to JPS, Mar. 21, 1985.

Although Marshall and: OT '84 Term History, at 101.

Among other things: Dun & Bradstreet, Inc. v. Greenmoss Builders, Inc., 472 U.S. 749 (Mar. 29, 1985) (White, J., dissenting) (slip op. 5 n.2) (fourth draft).

270   In addition, White: *Id.* at 9–10.

Powell circulated a: Dun & Bradstreet, Inc. v. Greenmoss Builders, Inc., 472 U.S. 749 (Apr. 1, 1985) (Powell, J., dissenting) (slip op. 5) (sixth draft).

"There is a: LFP to SOC & WHR, Mar. 28, 1985.

Predictably, Powell took: Dun & Bradstreet, Inc. v. Greenmoss Builders, Inc., 472 U.S. 749 (Apr. 1, 1985) (Powell, J., dissenting) (slip op. 1, 3, 11–12) (sixth draft).

After receiving Powell's: WEB to LFP, Apr. 9, 1985; WEB to BRW, Apr. 10, 1985.

271   In Brennan's chambers: OT '84 Term History, at 101.

In any event: WEB to Conference, Apr. 11, 1985.

On April 22: LFP to WEB, Apr. 22, 1985.

Accordingly, on April: WEB to LFP, Apr. 22, 1985.

Burger's reassignment of: OT '84 Term History, at 102.

Accordingly, Brennan's new: Dun & Bradstreet, Inc. v. Greenmoss Builders, Inc., 472 U.S. 749 (May 23, 1984) (Brennan, J., dissenting) (slip op. 1–2) (first draft).

272   Brennan had successfully: Regents of Univ. of Cal. v. Bakke, 438 U.S. 265, 324 (1978) (Brennan, J., concurring in judgment in part and dissenting in part); Milkovich v. Lorain Journal Co., 497 U.S. 1, 23 (1990) (Brennan, J., dissenting).

Still, Brennan remained: OT '84 Term History, at 102.

273   On May 9: LFP to WHR & SOC, May 9, 1985.

Later that same: SOC to LFP & WHR, May 9, 1985.

The new opinion: Dun & Bradstreet, Inc. v. Greenmoss Builders, Inc., 472 U.S. 749 (May 10, 1985) (Powell, J.) (plurality opinion) (slip op.) (first draft).

On May 20: OT '84 Term History, at 103.

As Brennan's term: *Id.*

This, in Brennan's: *Id.*

On May 22: WJB to TM & HAB, May 22, 1985.

Despite Brennan's attempt: HAB to WJB, May 22, 1985.

Instead, the opinion's: Dun & Bradstreet, Inc. v. Greenmoss Builders, Inc., 472 U.S. 749 (May 23, 1984) (Brennan, J., dissenting) (slip op. 2 n.1) (first draft).

274   Brennan's efforts to: LFP to Daniel Ortiz, May 27, 1985.

On the Brennan: Dun & Bradstreet, Inc. v. Greenmoss Builders, Inc., 472 U.S. 749 (May 23, 1984) (Brennan, J., dissenting) (slip op. 1, 11) (first draft) (with handwritten notes from Justice Powell).

And, in a: LFP to Daniel Ortiz, May 27, 1985.

In yet another: LFP to Daniel Ortiz, May 28, 1985.

In suggesting this: *Gertz*, 418 U.S. at 343–47.

In the meantime: OT '84 Term History, at 104.

Alas, this was: Dun & Bradstreet, Inc. v. Greenmoss Builders, Inc., 472 U.S. 749 (June 11, 1985) (White, J., concurring in judgment) (slip op. 10) (first draft).

In fact, in: OT '84 Term History, at 104.

275   Initially, his law: Dun & Bradstreet, Inc. v. Greenmoss Builders, Inc.,
      472 U.S. 749 (June 11, 1985) (White, J., concurring in judgment) (slip
      op. 10) (first draft).
      In a memorandum: Dean Gloster to BRW, May 29, 1985.
      White, however, overruled: Dun & Bradstreet, Inc. v. Greenmoss
      Builders, Inc., 472 U.S. 749 (Mar. 29, 1985) (White, J., dissenting) (slip
      op. 5, 8) (fourth draft).
      On May 23: Dun & Bradstreet, Inc. v. Greenmoss Builders, Inc., 472
      U.S. 749 (May 23, 1985) (Burger, C.J., concurring in judgment) (slip
      op. 1–2) (first draft).

276   On June 19: Dun & Bradstreet, Inc. v. Greenmoss Builders, Inc., 472
      U.S. 749 (June 19, 1985) (Powell, J.) (plurality opinion) (slip op. 7 n.4,
      11 n.7) (fourth draft).
      The following day: BRW to LFP, June 20, 1985.
      The decision was: Statement of Bench Announcement for Dun &
      Bradstreet, Inc. v. Greenmoss Builders, Inc., 472 U.S. 749 (June 26,
      1985), 2.

277   On December 19: WEB to Conference, Dec. 19, 1985.
      To the contrary: Walter Williams, *The Journalist's Creed*, MISSOURI
      SCHOOL OF JOURNALISM, http://journalism.missouri.edu/jschool/
      #creed.

CHAPTER 8

279   For Brennan: Anderson v. Liberty Lobby, Inc., 477 U.S. 242 (1986);
      Philadelphia Newspapers, Inc. v. Hepps, 475 U.S. 767 (1986).
      And, although he: Bernard Weinraub, *Burger Retiring, Rehnquist Named
      Chief; Scalia, Appeals Judge, Chosen For Court*, NYT, June 18, 1986.
      His replacement as: *Id.*; Liberty Lobby, Inc. v. Anderson, 746 F.2d 1563
      (D.C. Cir. 1984).

Anderson v. Liberty Lobby, Inc.
280   In many ways: Westmoreland v. CBS, Inc., 601 F. Supp. 66 (S.D.N.Y
      1984); Sharon v. Time, Inc., 599 F. Supp. 538 (S.D.N.Y. 1984).

Unlike *Westmoreland* and: Liberty Lobby, Inc. v. Anderson, 562 F. Supp. 201, 209–10 (D.D.C. 1983).

The trial court's: Liberty Lobby, Inc. v. Anderson, 746 F.2d 1563, 1570 (D.C. Cir. 1984) (citing *Hutchinson*, 443 U.S. at 120 & n.9).

The case arose: MARK FELDSTEIN, POISONING THE PRESS: RICHARD NIXON, JACK ANDERSON, AND THE RISE OF WASHINGTON'S SCANDAL CULTURE (2010).

The article at: *Liberty Lobby*, 477 U.S. at 244–47.

The author, Charles: Affidavit of Charles Bermant, Liberty Lobby v. Anderson, ¶¶ 9–21 (Aug. 19, 1982).

281   In the face: Liberty Lobby, Inc. v. Anderson, 562 F. Supp. 201, 207–10 (D.D.C. 1983).

The D.C. Circuit: 746 F.2d at 1570–79.

At argument before: *Anderson v. Liberty Lobby, Inc.*, Dec. 3, 1985 (1985 U.S. Trans. Lexis 138, 1–3, 7–8, 13–15).

282   The limited reach: MARK LANE, RUSH TO JUDGMENT: A CRITIQUE OF THE WARREN COMMISSION'S INQUIRY INTO THE MURDERS OF PRESIDENT JOHN F. KENNEDY, OFFICER J. D. TIPPIT AND LEE HARVEY OSWALD (1966); *Anderson v. Liberty Lobby, Inc.*, Dec. 3, 1985 (1985 U.S. Trans. Lexis 138, 31–37).

In the course: *Anderson v. Liberty Lobby, Inc.*, Dec. 3, 1985 (1985 U.S. Trans. Lexis 138, 33, 43).

283   At conference, as: WJB Conference Notes for *Anderson v. Liberty Lobby, Inc.*, Dec. 6, 1985.

Thus, Brennan wrote: WJB Conference Memo for *Anderson v. Liberty Lobby, Inc.* (undated).

Nevertheless, Brennan emphasized: *Id.*

284   Finally, and in: *Id.* (quoting Calder v. Jones, 465 U.S. 783, 790 (1984) ("To reintroduce [First Amendment] concerns at the jurisdictional stage would be a form of double counting.").

It appears from: *Id.*; *Liberty Lobby*, 477 U.S. at 257 (Brennan, J., dissenting).

It also bears: Matsushita Elec. Indus. Co. v. Zenith Radio Corp., 475 U.S. 574 (1986) (antitrust); Celotex Corp. v. Catrett, 477 U.S. 317 (1986) (tort liability).

Still, it is: Dun & Bradstreet, Inc. v. Greenmoss Builders, Inc., 472 U.S.
749 (Mar. 20, 1985) (Brennan, J.) (slip op. 7–12) (fourth draft).
In that regard: *See, e.g.*, LaRouche v. Nat'l Broad. Co., 780 F.2d 1134
(4th Cir. 1986) (defamation action by Lyndon LaRouche against
NBC); Liberty Lobby, Inc. v. Pearson, 390 F.2d 489 (D.C. Cir. 1967)
(defamation action by Liberty Lobby against syndicated columnist);
Liberty Lobby, Inc. v. Dow Jones & Co., Inc., 638 F. Supp. 1149
(D.D.C. 1986); Reader's Digest Ass'n v. Superior Court, 690 P.2d 610
(Cal. 1984) (defamation action by Synanon founder against Reader's
Digest); Seth Goodchild, *Media Counteractions: Restoring the Balance
to Modern Libel Law*, 75 GEO. L.J. 315 (1986) ("The number of libel
suits filed against news organizations increased dramatically during the
1980's. . . . [P]laintiffs appear motivated [to bring defamation actions to]
punish[] the press, obtain[] free publicity, intimidate[e] the media, or
employ[] the courthouse as a forum for response."); David E. Sanger,
Tension on the Frontiers of Libel, NYT, Dec. 18, 1983 ("Conflict between
news room and board room has intensified at a time when several
important libel cases—many initiated years ago—are near resolution in
the nation's highest courts.").
In a deposition: Lee Levine, *Judge and Jury in the Law of Defamation:
Putting the Horse Behind the Cart*, 35 AM. U. L. REV. 3, 30 n.125 (1985).

285 Despite all of: WJB Conference Notes for *Anderson v. Liberty Lobby, Inc.*,
Dec. 6, 1985.
In a December: Justson v. Peoples Bank & Trust of Westfield, 17 N.J. 67
(1954).
On this issue: WJB Conference Notes for *Anderson v. Liberty Lobby Inc.*,
Dec. 6, 1985.

286 Being the senior: *Liberty Lobby*, 477 U.S. at 244.
Burger, in turn: WEB to WJB, Dec. 20, 1985.
On December 23: WJB to WEB, Dec. 23, 1985.
White's draft opinion: Anderson v. Liberty Lobby, Inc., 477 U.S. 242
(Feb. 25, 1986) (White, J.) (slip op. 5, 7–9, 11) (first draft).

287 White's initial draft: *Liberty Lobby*, 477 U.S. at 255–56 n.7.

288 White's opinion, however: *Id*. at 257.
On February 26: WJB to BRW, Feb 26, 1986.

Shortly thereafter, Rehnquist: Anderson v. Liberty Lobby, Inc., 477 U.S.
242 (Mar. 20, 1986) (slip op. 1, 5) (Rehnquist, J., dissenting) (first draft).

289 Ultimately, Brennan decided: 477 U.S. at 266–67 (Brennan, J.,
dissenting).

Specifically, he wrote: *Id*. at 258 n.1.

290 Despite both White's: *See, e.g.*, Spacecon Specialty Contractors, LLC v.
Bensinger, 713 F.3d 1028, 1041 (10th Cir. 2013) ("To meet its burden
of showing actual malice [on summary judgment], Spacecon must
show by clear and convincing evidence Bensinger published the film
with knowledge of its falsity or in reckless disregard of the truth.");
Stepnes v. Ritschel, 663 F.3d 952, 964 (8th Cir. 2011) (affirming
summary judgment in favor of defendant reporter and CBS); Hatfill
v. New York Times Co., 532 F.3d 312 (4th Cir. 2008) (affirming
summary judgment for defendant newspaper).

Indeed, on June: BRW to Conference, June 24, 1986 (discussing
Reader's Digest Ass'n, 690 P.2d 610).

In it, the: *Reader's Digest Ass'n*, 690 P.2d at 612–13; *Synanon Suit Against
TV Station Settled Out of Court*, NYT, June 4, 1982.

As White noted: BRW to Conference, June 24, 1986, 2 (quoting
Reader's Digest Ass'n, 690 P.2d at 614).

The Court agreed: *See, e.g.*, D.A.R.E Am. v. Rolling Stone Magazine,
101 F. Supp. 2d 1270, 1278 (C.D. Cal. 2000); Masson v. New Yorker
Magazine, Inc., 832 F. Supp. 1350, 1376 (N.D. Cal. 1993).

Following remand from: Liberty Lobby, Inc. v. Anderson, No. 81–2240,
1991 WL 186998 (D.D.C. May 1, 1991).

291 This time around: *Id*. at 8.

The case finally: *Anderson Throws in the Towel*, THE SPOTLIGHT, May 27,
1991, at 1, 3. *See also* M.A. Farber, *A Joint Statement Ends Libel Action by
Westmoreland*, NYT, Feb 19, 1985.

Philadelphia Newspapers, Inc. v. Hepps

Perhaps a part: Philadelphia Newspapers, Inc. v. Hepps, 475 U.S. 767
(1986); *Philadelphia Newspapers, Inc. v. Hepps*, Dec. 3, 1985 (1985 U.S.
Trans. Lexis 139).

Like *Liberty Lobby*: Hepps v. Philadelphia Newspapers, Inc., 485 A.2d
374, 377 (Pa. 1984).

Unlike *Liberty Lobby*: Wilson v. Scripps-Howard Broad. Co., 642 F.2d
371 (6th Cir. 1981); *see* Chapter 6 *supra*.

292   In *Wilson*, the: 642 F.2d at 376.

In *Hepps*, the: 485 A.2d at 387.

The case arose: 475 U.S. at 769.

At trial, Hepps: *Id*. at 770–71.

According to Brennan's: WJB Vote Sheet for *Philadelphia Newspapers, Inc.
v. Hepps*, June 24, 1985.

293   As noted, *Hepps*: *Philadelphia Newspapers, Inc. v. Hepps*, Dec. 3, 1985
(1985 U.S. Trans. Lexis 139).

During his argument: *Id*. at 11–12.

When Hepps's counsel: *Id*. at 28.

At the conference: WJB Conference Notes for *Philadelphia Newspapers,
Inc. v. Hepps*, Dec. 6, 1985.

In his prepared: WJB Conference Memo for *Philadelphia Newspapers, Inc.
v. Hepps*, Dec. 6, 1985.

294   White, not surprisingly: WJB Conference Notes for *Philadelphia
Newspapers, Inc. v. Hepps*, Dec. 6, 1985.

Blackmun's notes similarly: HAB Conference Notes for *Philadelphia
Newspapers, Inc. v. Hepps*, Dec. 6, 1985.

Nevertheless, Powell continued: WJB Conference Notes for
Philadelphia Newspapers, Inc. v. Hepps, Dec. 6, 1985.

Blackmun's notes too: HAB Conference Notes for *Philadelphia
Newspapers, Inc. v. Hepps*, Dec. 6, 1985.

At this point: WJB Conference Notes for *Philadelphia Newspapers, Inc. v.
Hepps*, Dec. 6, 1985.

Finally, Marshall voted: HAB Conference Notes for *Philadelphia
Newspapers, Inc. v. Hepps*, Dec. 6, 1985.

Burger promptly assigned: SOC to WEB, Feb. 18, 1986.

Brennan, meanwhile, assigned: WJB to HAB, TM & LFP, Dec. 17, 1985.

There matters stood: SOC to WEB, Feb. 18, 1986.

295   On receiving this: WJB to WEB, Feb. 18, 1986.

Burger responded promptly: WEB to WJB, Feb 18, 1986.

At this point: OT '85 Term History, at 63.

Thus, with a: WJB to WEB, Feb. 19, 1986.

O'Connor circulated her: Philadelphia Newspapers, Inc. v. Hepps, 475 U.S. 767 (Mar. 15, 1986) (O'Connor, J.) (slip op. 5, 8–9, 12) (first draft); LFP to SOC, Mar. 20, 1986.

296 A week after: JPS to SOC, Mar. 27, 1986.

That opinion, which: Philadelphia Newspapers, Inc. v. Hepps, 475 U.S. 767 (Mar. 15, 1986) (Stevens, J., dissenting) (slip op. 2) (second draft).

297 On March 28: WJB to SOC, Mar. 28, 1986; Philadelphia Newspapers, Inc. v. Hepps, 475 U.S. 767 (Apr. 21, 1986) (Brennan, J., concurring) (slip op. 1) (first draft).

On April 7: TM to SOC, Apr. 7, 1986.

That same day: HAB to WJB, Apr. 7, 1986.

In addition, he: HAB to SOC, Apr. 7, 1986.

298 O'Connor responded that: SOC to HAB, Apr. 7, 1986.

In the end: 475 U.S. at 779 n.4.

CHAPTER 9

299 In 1986: Stuart Taylor, Jr., *Rehnquist and Scalia Take Their Places on Court*, NYT, Sept. 26, 1986.

Among other notable: Tavoulareas v. Piro, 817 F.2d 762 (D.C. Cir. 1987) (en banc), *cert. denied*, 484 U.S. 870 (1987); *id.* at 804–06 (Wald, J., concurring in judgment).

Near the end: Hustler Magazine v. Falwell, 480 U.S. 945 (1987).

In all, the: Harte-Hanks Commc'ns, Inc. v. Connaughton, 491 U.S. 657 (1989); Fla. Star v. B.J.F., 491 U.S. 524 (1989); Milkovich v. Lorain Journal Co., 497 U.S. 1 (1990).

300 Although no one: Linda Greenhouse, *Vacancy on the Court; Brennan, Key Liberal, Quits Supreme Court; Battle for Seat Likely*, NYT, July 21, 1990.

Hustler Magazine v. Falwell

In *Falwell*, the: Falwell v. Flynt, 797 F.2d 1270 (4th Cir. 1986), *rev'd*, 485 U.S. 46 (1988); Falwell v. Flynt, 805 F.2d 484, 484–89 (4th Cir. 1986) (Wilkinson, J., dissenting from denial of rehearing en banc).

For his part: Peter Applebome, *Jerry Falwell, Moral Majority Founder, Dies At 73*, NYT, May 16, 2007.

The case itself: Hustler Magazine v. Falwell, 485 U.S. 46, 48 (1988).

301   Falwell instituted a: *Id.* at 48–49.

When Hustler and: WJB Vote Sheet for *Hustler Magazine v. Falwell*, Dec. 4, 1987.

By the time: Stuart Taylor, Jr., *Powell Leaves High Court; Took Key Role on Abortion and on Affirmative Action*, NYT, June 27, 1987; Steven V. Roberts, *Ginsburg Withdraws Name as Supreme Court Nominee, Citing Marijuana "Clamor"*, NYT, Nov. 8, 1987; Linda Greenhouse, *Senate, 97 To 0, Confirms Kennedy to High Court*, NYT, Feb. 4, 1988.

The case was: *Hustler Magazine v. Falwell*, Dec. 2, 1987 (1987 U.S. Trans. Lexis 148).

In advance of: Brief for Ass'n of Am. Editorial Cartoonists, et al. as Amici Curiae Supporting Petitioners, Hustler Magazine v. Falwell, 485 U.S. 945 (1988) (No. 86–1287), 1987 WL 864186.

Blackmun's clerk "particularly: Emily Buss to HAB, Dec. 1, 1987, at 11–12; *Hustler Magazine v. Falwell*, Dec. 2, 1987 (1987 U.S. Trans. Lexis 148, 34); 485 U.S. at 53–55.

302   Plainly mindful of: Memorandum from Alfred Wong, Office of the Marshal for the Supreme Court, to WHR, Dec. 1, 1987.

The argument itself: *Hustler Magazine v. Falwell*, Dec. 2, 1987 (1987 U.S. Trans. Lexis 148, 6–7).

Isaacman also placed: *Id.* at 10–12; *see* Garrison v. Louisiana, 379 U.S. 64 (1964).

303   At that juncture: *Hustler Magazine v. Falwell*, Dec. 2, 1987 (1987 U.S. Trans. Lexis 148, 13–14).

Perhaps the most: *Id.* at 20–21.

304   O'Connor raised the: *Id.* at 27–28; *see, e.g.*, E.J. Dionne, Jr., *Courting Danger: The Fall of Gary Hart*, NYT, May 9, 1987; Madison Gray & S. James Snyder, *Sinful Statesmen: Gary Hart*, TIME, June 8, 2011.

Grutman responded that: *Hustler Magazine v. Falwell*, Dec. 2, 1987 (1987 U.S. Trans. Lexis 148, 34–25, 38).

Toward the end: *Id.* at 45.

305   Despite the close: WJB Vote Sheet for *Hustler Magazine v. Falwell*, Dec. 4, 1987.

The new Chief: WJB Conference Notes for *Hustler Magazine v. Falwell*, Dec. 4, 1987; HAB Conference notes for *Hustler Magazine v. Falwell*, Dec. 4, 1987.

Brennan's prepared statement: WJB Conference Memo for *Hustler Magazine v. Falwell*, Dec. 4, 1987.

As had by: WJB Conference Notes for *Hustler Magazine v. Falwell*, Dec. 4, 1987; HAB Conference Notes for *Hustler Magazine v. Falwell*, Dec. 4, 1987.

According to Brennan's: WJB Conference Notes for *Hustler Magazine v. Falwell*, Dec. 4, 1987.

306   Stevens, again according: *Id.*; HAB Conference Notes for *Hustler Magazine v. Falwell*, Dec. 4, 1987.

O'Connor then sided: WJB Conference Notes for *Hustler Magazine v. Falwell*, Dec. 4, 1987.

Rehnquist assigned the: Hustler Magazine v. Falwell, 485 U.S. 46 (Jan. 22, 1988) (Rehnquist, J.) (slip op.) (first draft).

As the final: 485 U.S. at 51 (citations to internal quotation omitted).

Then, quoting one: *Id.* (quoting New York Times Co. v. Sullivan, 376 U.S. 254, 270 (1964)).

As a result: 485 U.S. at 52 (quoting Philadelphia Newspapers, Inc. v. Hepps, 475 U.S. 767, 772 (1986)).

Turning to the: 485 U.S. at 53–56.

307   On January 22: SOC to WHR, Jan. 22, 1988; JPS to WHR, Jan. 22, 1988.

On January 25: TM to WHR, Jan. 25, 1988; AS to WHR, Jan. 25, 1988; HAB to WHR, Jan. 25, 1988.

That same day: WJB to WHR, Jan. 25, 1988.

Brennan did, however: *Id.*

Rehnquist responded: WHR to WJB, Jan. 26, 1988.

308   That same day: WJB to WHR, Jan. 26, 1988.

The following day: Hustler Magazine v. Falwell, 485 U.S. 46 (Jan. 27, 1988) (White, J., concurring in judgment) (slip op.) (first draft).

Harte-Hanks Communications, Inc. v. Connaughton

At its September 26: Preliminary Memorandum to Conference for *Harte-Hanks Commc'ns, Inc. v. Connaughton*, Aug. 1, 1988; Harte-Hanks Commc'ns, Inc. v. Connaughton, 842 F.2d 825 (6th Cir. 1988).

In so doing: Tavoulareas v. Piro, 817 F.2d 762 (D.C. Cir. 1987).

309   Specifically, in affirming: 842 F.2d 825, 833–34 (6th Cir. 1988).

Cumulating those multiple: *Id.* at 846.

Despite the apparent: Preliminary Memorandum to Conference for *Harte-Hanks Commc'ns, Inc. v. Connaughton*, Aug. 1, 1988.

Nevertheless, Anthony Kennedy: AK to Conference, Oct. 6, 1988.

On October 6: *Id.*

Five days later: BRW to Conference, Draft Dissent From Denial of Certiorari in *Harte-Hanks Commc'ns, Inc. v. Connaughton* (slip op. 1–2) (first draft), Oct. 11, 1988 (White, J.).

White's dissent convinced: HAB to BRW, Oct. 12, 1988.

After it was: WJB Vote Sheet for *Harte-Hanks Commc'ns, Inc. v. Connaughton*, Oct. 17, 1987.

The case was: *Harte-Hanks Commc'ns, Inc. v. Connaughton*, Mar. 20, 1989 (1989 U.S. Trans. Lexis 160).

The underlying facts were: Harte-Hanks Commc'ns, Inc. v. Connaughton, 491 U.S. 657, 668–69 & n.36 (1989).

310   The allegations received: 842 F.2d at 831.

Shortly before the: *Id.* at 849–51 (Guy, J., dissenting). The full text of the JOURNAL-NEWS article is included as Appendix B to Judge Guy's dissent.

Before the article: *Id.* at 853.

As published, the: *Id.*

Before its publication: 491 U.S. at 682–83.

Shortly after: 842 F.2d at 837; 491 U.S. at 675–76.

311   Dolan won reelection: 491 U.S. at 660–61.

As noted, a: 842 F.2d at 843–44.

The Sixth Circuit: *Id.* at 846; *see* St. Amant v. Thompson, 390 U.S. 727 (196); Curtis Publ'g Co. v. Butts, 388 U.S. 130, 155 (1967) (plurality opinion of Harlan, J.).

312   Judge Guy dissented: 842 F.2d at 849–57 (Guy, J., dissenting).

Despite the morass: *Harte-Hanks Commc'ns, Inc. v. Connaughton,* Mar. 20, 1989 (1989 U.S. Trans. Lexis 160); Brief for Petitioner, Harte-Hanks Commc'ns, Inc. v. Connaughton, 491 U.S. 657 (1989), 1988 WL 1026348 at i.

According to Levine: *Harte-Hanks Commc'ns, Inc. v. Connaughton,* Mar. 20, 1989 (1989 U.S. Trans. Lexis 160, 3–4).

The justices plainly: *Id.* at 6–7.

After Levine's argument: *Id.* at 9–14.

In response, Levine: Chi., B. & Q.R. Co. v. City of Chi., 166 U.S. 226 (1897); *New York Times Co. v. Sullivan,* Jan. 6–7, 1964 (The Oyez Project at IIT Chicago-Kent College of Law).

313   During this exchange: *Harte-Hanks Commc'ns, Inc. v. Connaughton,* Mar. 20, 1989 (1989 U.S. Trans. Lexis 160, 14).

As his argument: *Id.* at 19–21.

During his argument: *Id.* at 27–28; Curtis Publ'g Co. v. Butts, 388 U.S. 130, 162 (1967) (Warren, C.J., concurring in judgment).

314   To this, justice: *Harte-Hanks Commc'ns, Inc. v. Connaughton,* Mar. 20, 1989 (1989 U.S. Trans. Lexis 160, 32–35).

On rebuttal, Levine: *Id.* at 37–38.

At that juncture: *Id.* at 38–40.

315   At the conference: HAB Conference Notes for *Harte-Hanks Commc'ns, Inc. v. Connaughton,* Mar. 22, 1989.

Brennan then voted: WJB Vote Sheet for *Harte-Hanks Commc'ns, Inc. v. Connaughton,* Mar. 22, 1989.

In his prepared: WJB Conference Memo for *Harte-Hanks Commc'ns, Inc. v. Connaughton,* Mar. 22, 1989.

White disagreed, on: HAB Conference Notes for *Harte-Hanks Commc'ns, Inc. v. Connaughton,* Mar. 22, 1989; WJB Conference Notes for *Harte-Hanks Commc'ns, Inc. v. Connaughton,* Mar. 22, 1989.

Marshall, Blackmun, Stevens: WJB Vote Sheet for *Harte-Hanks Commc'ns, Inc. v. Connaughton,* Mar. 22, 1989.

According to Brennan's: WJB Conference Notes for *Harte-Hanks*
Commc'ns, Inc. v. Connaughton, Mar. 22, 1989.

Although it is: Ned Foley to HAB, Mar. 20, 1989.

316   He and his: *See id.* ("Perhaps petr has sensible reasons for its litigation
       strategy, but I must confess that they escape me. Rather, petr's approach
       makes a hard case out of what should be an easy one . . ."); *see also*
       Harte-Hanks Commc'ns, Inc. v. Connaughton, Mar. 20, 1989 (1989 U.S.
       Trans. Lexis 160, 20–21) (Justice Blackmun: "I guess what I'm saying is
       I think you have a stronger case without Bose and you don't have to
       rely on Bose. But go ahead, do it your own way.").

       Still, at the: WJB Vote Sheet for *Harte-Hanks Commc'ns, Inc. v.*
       Connaughton, Mar. 24, 1989.

       Although he had: WJB to WHR, Mar. 31, 1989.

       Almost two months: JPS to Conference, May 11, 1989.

       In fact, Stevens: Harte-Hanks Commc'ns, Inc. v. Connaughton, 491
       U.S. 657 (May 31, 1989) (slip op.) (first draft).

       Stevens's draft emphasized: *Id.* at 30–32.

317   Instead, Stevens proceeded: *Id.* at 32.

       As Stevens explained: *Id.* at 33–34.

318   As Stevens put: *Id.* at 34 n.38.

       Stevens's introduction of: *see* Chapter 7 *supra*.

       Nevertheless, on June: WJB to JPS, June 2, 1989.

       Thereafter, in quick: TM to JPS, June 5, 1989; SOC to JPS, June 6,
       1989.

       On June 5, Scalia: AS to JPS, June 5, 1989.

       On June 6, White: Harte-Hanks Commc'ns, Inc. v. Connaughton, 491
       U.S. 657 (June 6, 1989) (White, J., concurring) (slip. op.) (first draft).

       Also on June: Harte-Hanks Commc'ns, Inc. v. Connaughton, 491 U.S.
       657 (June 6, 1989) (Scalia, J., concurring in judgment) (slip. op. 2, 5)
       (first draft) (citing Tavoulareas v. Piro, 817 F.2d 762 (D.C. Cir. 1987)).

319   Later that same: JPS to AS, June 6, 1989.

       Specifically, although Scalia's: Harte-Hanks Commc'ns, Inc. v.
       Connaughton, 491 U.S. 657 (June 6, 1989) (Scalia, J., concurring in
       judgment) (slip. op. 2, 5) (first draft).

       Scalia responded promptly: AS to JPS, June 6, 1989.

In fact, his: 491 U.S. at 697 (Scalia, J., concurring in judgment).

The next day: AMK to JPS, June 7, 1989; *see* United States v. Jewell, 532 F.2d 697, 705–08 (9th Cir. 1976) (Kennedy, J., dissenting).

320   Later that same: JPS to AMK, June 7, 1989.

The change having: AMK to JPS, June 8, 1989.

On June 12: Harte-Hanks Commc'ns, Inc. v. Connaughton, 491 U.S. 657 (June 12, 1989) (White, J., concurring) (slip. op.) (second draft).

Rehnquist then promptly: WHR to BRW, June 12, 1989.

On June 13, Blackmun: HAB to WHR, June 13, 1989.

On June 14, Stevens: JPS to Conference, June 14, 1989 (citing DiSalle v. P.G. Publ'g Co., 375 Pa. Super. 510 (1988)).

That doctrine, which: Edwards v. Nat'l Audubon Soc'y, Inc., 556 F.2d 113 (2d Cir. 1977).

In his memorandum: JPS to Conference, June 14, 1989.

321   The Court agreed: P.G. Publ'g Co. v. DiSalle, 492 U.S. 906 (1989) (denying petition).

On June 19: HAB to JPS, June 19, 1989.

With the term: Ned Foley to HAB, June 15, 1989.

Blackmun circulated a: Harte-Hanks Commc'ns, Inc. v. Connaughton, 491 U.S. 657 (June 19, 1989) (Blackmun, J., concurring) (slip. op. 1–2) (first draft).

Even so, Blackmun: *Id.* at 3.

The decision was: Harte-Hanks Commc'ns, Inc. v. Connaughton, 491 U.S. 657 (1989).

Florida Star v. B.J.F.

322   The day after: *Fla. Star v. B.J.F.*, Mar. 21, 1989 (1989 U.S. Trans. Lexis 130).

In that case: Fla. Star v. B.J.F., 491 U.S. 524, 527–28 (1989).

Under a Florida: FLA. STAT. § 794.03 (1987).

Invoking the statute: 491 U.S. at 528.

At the close: *Id.*

The case initially: WJB Vote Sheet for *Florida Star v. B.J.F.*, Mar. 24, 1989. Justice Kennedy joined the Court in February 1988. *See* Linda

Greenhouse, *Senate, 97 to 0, Confirms Kennedy to High Court*, NYT, Feb. 4, 1988.

At argument, the: *Fla. Star v. B.J.F.*, Mar. 21, 1989 (1989 U.S. Trans. Lexis 130, 4–5, 21).

323 Rahdert also received: *Id.* at 5–7.

This contention led: *Id.* at 7–11.

324 At this juncture: *Id.* at 12–13; *see* Near v. Minnesota, 283 U.S. 697, 716 (1931) ("No one would question but that a government might prevent actual obstruction to its recruiting service or the publication of the sailing dates of transports or the number and location of troops.").

Not surprisingly, Joel: *Fla. Star v. B.J.F.*, Mar. 21, 1989 (1989 U.S. Trans. Lexis, 130, 23–24, 29).

325 Other justices focused: *Id.* at 31–34, 39–40.

Following argument, all: WJB Vote Sheet for *Fla. Star v. B.J.F.*, Mar. 24, 1989.

At conference, according: WJB Conference Notes for *Fla. Star v. B.J.F.*, Mar. 24, 1989.

According to his: WJB Conference Memo for *Fla. Star v. B.J.F.*, Mar. 24, 1989 (quoting Landmark Commc'ns, Inc. v. Virginia, 435 U.S. 829, 849 (1978) (Stewart, J., concurring in judgment)).

326 According to Brennan's: WJB Conference Notes for *Fla. Star v. B.J.F.*, Mar. 24, 1989.

327 With Rehnquist in: WJB to WHR, Mar. 31, 1989.

The resulting opinion: 491 U.S. at 530–32.

Ultimately, Marshall's opinion: 491 U.S. at 533–35 (quoting Smith v. Daily Mail Publ'g Co., 443 U.S. 97, 103 (1979)).

328 Marshall's opinion for: 491 U.S. at 536–40.

Scalia concurred in: *Id.* at 541–42 (Scalia, J., concurring in part and concurring in judgment).

329 White, the author: *Id.* at 542–43, 547, 550, 553 (White, J., dissenting).

The Court's decision: Fla. Star v. B.J.F., 491 U.S. 524 (1989).

Milkovich v. Lorain Journal Co.

The final defamation: Milkovich v. Lorain Journal Co., 497 U.S. 1 (1990); OT '89 Term History, at 81.

In *Milkovich*, a: 497 U.S. at 4.

330   The case as: The Court had previously denied review on two occasions.
Lorain Journal Co. v. Milkovich, 449 U.S. 966 (1980); Lorain Journal
Co. v. Milkovich, 474 U.S. 953 (1985).

On this occasion: Petition for a Writ of Certiorari from the Ohio
Court of Appeals for the Eleventh Appellate District (Lake County,
Ohio), Milkovich v. Lorain Journal Co., 65 Ohio App. 2d 143 (Lake
Co. 1979) (No. 89–645), 1989 WL 1174075 at 1.

That notion—that: *Id.* at 23 (quoting Gertz v. Robert Welch, Inc.,
418 U.S. 323, 339–40 (1974) (footnote omitted)). *See also id.* at 25–35
(noting lower court decisions that had grappled with fact/opinion
distinction).

As Brennan's term: OT '89 Term History, at 81 (citing Ollman v. Evans,
750 F.2d 970 (D.C. Cir. 1984)).

The *Ollman* test: 750 F.2d at 979.

The Supreme Court: OT '89 Term History, at 81.

In *Milkovich* itself: WHR to Conference, Dissent From Denial of
Certiorari in *Milkovich v. Lorain Journal Co.* (slip. op. at 1, 5) (second
draft), Jan. 19, 1990 (Rehnquist, C.J.).

331   The next day: AK to WHR, Jan. 19, 1990.

And, at the: WJB Vote Sheet for *Milkovich v. Lorain Journal Co.*, Apr. 27,
1990.

No doubt aware: *Milkovich v. Lorain Journal Co.*, Apr. 24, 1990 (1990
U.S. Trans. Lexis 200).

This, among others: OT '89 Term History, at 82.

At the outset: *Milkovich v. Lorain Journal Co.*, Apr. 24, 1990 (1990 U.S.
Trans. Lexis 200, 2–3, 13–15). *See also* Philadelphia Newspapers, Inc. v.
Hepps, 475 U.S. 767 (1986).

332   Early on, when: *Milkovich v. Lorain Journal Co.*, Apr. 24, 1990 (1990 U.S.
Trans. Lexis 200, 23).

Ultimately, Panza took: *Id.* at 25–27.

Later in his: *Id.* at 29–31.

333   At another point: *Id.* at 34–35.

At conference, amplifying: 475 U.S. 767 (1986); WJB Conference
Notes for *Milkovich v. Lorain Journal Co.*, Apr. 27, 1990.

For his part: WJB Conference Memo for *Milkovich v. Lorain Journal Co.*, Apr. 27, 1990.

Turning to the: *Id.*

334 Brennan's position fell: OT '89 Term History, at 81–82.

Blackmun and Stevens: *Id.*

As he had: WJB to TM, Apr. 27, 1990.

When Rehnquist's first: OT '89 Term History, at 82–83.

335 In fact, Rehnquist's: Milkovich v. Lorain Journal Co., 497 U.S. 1 (May 25, 1990) (slip. op. 12–15) (first draft) (quoting *Hepps*, 475 U.S. at 776; *Falwell*, 485 U.S. at 50–51; *Bose*, 466 U.S. at 499).

As Rehnquist's draft: Milkovich v. Lorain Journal Co., 497 U.S. 1 (May 25, 1990) (slip. op. 15) (first draft).

Having defined the: *Id.* at 16.

Rehnquist's draft then: *Id.* at 17.

336 Applying these established: *Id.* at 19.

All six justices: PS to WHR, May 29, 1990; SOC to WHR, May 29, 1990; AS to WHR, May 31, 1990; HAB to WHR, May 31, 1990; BRW to WHR, June 5, 1990; AK to WHR, June 5, 1990.

In Blackmun's chambers: Vikram Amar to HAB, May 29, 1990.

Rehnquist circulated a: Milkovich v. Lorain Journal Co., 497 U.S. 1 (June 5, 1990) (second draft).

That same day: WJB to Conference, June 5, 1990.

But, as he: OT '89 Term History at 83.

337 Although Brennan recognized: *Id.*; Milkovich v. Lorain Journal Co., 497 U.S. 1 (June 15, 1990) (Brennan, J., dissenting) (slip. op. 1) (first draft).

From this premise: *Id.* at 2.

Brennan did, however: *Id.* at 3.

338 Marshall joined Brennan's: TM to WJB, June 15, 1990; Milkovich v. Lorain Journal Co., 497 U.S. 1 (1990); Linda Greenhouse, *Vacancy on the Court; Brennan, Key Liberal, Quits Supreme Court; Battle for Seat Likely*, NYT, July 21, 1990.

The lower courts: *See generally* Partington v. Bugliosi, 56 F.3d 1147 (9th Cir. 1995); Moldea v. New York Times Co., 22 F.3d 310 (D.C. Cir.

1994); Phantom Touring, Inc. v. Affiliated Publ'ns, 953 F.2d 724 (1st Cir. 1992).

CHAPTER 10

341   Brennan retired from: Linda Greenhouse, *Vacancy on the Court; Brennan, Key Liberal, Quits Supreme Court; Battle for Seat Likely*, NYT, July 21, 1990.

When he announced: *See, e.g.*, Anthony Lewis, *Mr. Justice Brennan*, NYT, July 24, 1990.

Whole organizations dedicated: *About*, BRENNAN CENTER FOR JUSTICE, www.brennancenter.org/about.

Other organizations, like: *William J. Brennan, Jr. Defense of Freedom Award*, MEDIA LAW RESOURCE CENTER, www.medialaw.org/about-mlrc/awards/193-brennan-award.

342   Still, when he: OT '84 Term History, at 96.

Not only would: David Margolick, *Bush's Court Choice; Ascetic at Home but Vigorous on the Bench*, NYT, July 25, 1990; James Gerstenzang & David Lauter, *Little-Known Judge Named to Replace Brennan on Court: Judiciary: David Souter served as New Hampshire justice and attorney general. He has no clear record on abortion*, LAT, July 24, 1990.

And, at least: Erik Wemple, *Antonin Scalia hates 'N.Y.T. v. Sullivan'*, WP, Dec. 4, 2012.

For his part: WJB Conference Notes for *Milkovich v. Lorain Journal Co.*, Apr. 27, 1990.

343   Brennan would not: Masson v. New Yorker Magazine, Inc., 501 U.S. 496 (1991); Cohen v. Cowles Media Co., 501 U.S. 663 (1991).

As it happened: Bartnicki v. Vopper, 532 U.S. 514 (2001).

Masson v. New Yorker Magazine, Inc.

When it reached: 501 U.S. at 499–501.

The defendants included: JANET MALCOLM, THE JOURNALIST AND THE MURDERER 3 (1990) ("Every journalist who is not too stupid or full of himself to notice what is going on knows that what he does is morally indefensible. He is a kind of confidence man, preying on people's vanity, ignorance, or loneliness, gaining their trust and betraying them without remorse.").

Amidst great fanfare: Eleanor Randolph, *Malcolm Convicts All Journalists of Her Crime*, CHI. TRIB., Mar. 26, 1989; *Journalists—And Con Artists*, NYT, Mar. 19, 1989.

In his complaint: 501 U.S. at 499–507; *see* JANET MALCOLM, IN THE FREUD ARCHIVES (1983); Janet Malcolm, *I—Trouble in the Archives*, NEW YORKER, Dec. 5, 1983; Janet Malcolm, *II—Trouble in the Archives*, NEW YORKER, Dec. 12, 1983.

344   Masson vigorously denied: 501 U.S. at 501; Janet Malcolm, *Portrait of Masson*, NYT, July 8, 1984.

As a result: Brief for Respondent, Masson v. New Yorker Magazine, Inc., 501 U.S. 496 (1991), 1990 WL 10012728 at 24–29.

Thus, for example: 501 U.S. at 503–07.

Both a federal: Masson v. New Yorker Magazine, Inc., 686 F. Supp. 1396 (N.D. Cal. 1987); Masson v. New Yorker Magazine, Inc., 895 F.2d 1535 (9th Cir. 1989).

In the court: *Id.* at 1548. *See* Ben Franklin, *Senate Confirms Appellate Judge*, LAT, Nov. 8, 1985; *History of the Federal Judiciary*, FEDERAL JUDICIAL CENTER, http://www.fjc.gov/history/home.nsf/page/judges _milestones.html; Evan Thomas, *The Bush Court*, NEWSWEEK (July 29, 1990), http://www.thedailybeast.com/newsweek/1990/07/29/ the-bush-court.html.

345   The court's decision: *See, e.g.*, Albert Scardino, *Appeals Court Turns Down Suit Against Author*, NYT, Aug. 5, 1989.

On October 1: Masson v. New Yorker Magazine, Inc., 498 U.S. 808 (1990).

The case was: 501 U.S. at 510–11.

Specifically, Kennedy began: *Id.* at 511.

By the same: *Id.* at 512–14.

346   Accordingly, Kennedy articulated: *Id.* at 516–19.

In Masson's case: *Id.* at 521–25.

347   Kennedy's opinion for: *Id.* at 499.

In a dissenting: *Id.* at 525 (White, J., dissenting).

Although the Court's: Linda Greenhouse, *Justices Refuse to Open a Gate for Libel Cases*, NYT, June 21, 1991.

Following the Supreme: Masson v. New Yorker Magazine, Inc., 960 F.2d 896 (9th Cir. 1992); Masson v. New Yorker Magazine, Inc., 85 F.3d 1394 (9th Cir. 1996).

In the first: 85 F.3d at 1397; Seth Mydans, *Second Trial of Libel Case Is Under Way*, NYT, Sept. 29, 1994; Jane Gross, *Masson Over Malcolm; The Libel Case Longer than a* New Yorker *Series Grows*, NYT, June 6, 1993.

At the second: 85 F.3d at 1397.

By the time: *Id.* at 1400.

And, in a final: David Stout, *Malcolm's Lost Notes and a Child at Play*, NYT, Aug. 30, 1995.

Cohen v. Cowles Media Co.

348   Four days after: 501 U.S. at 665–66.

Unable to sue: *Id.* at 666–67.

He prevailed in: Cohen v. Cowles Media Co., 15 MEDIA L. REP. 2288, (Minn. Dist. Ct. Nov. 19, 1988).

An intermediate appellate: Cohen v. Cowles Media Co., 445 N.W.2d 248, 254 (Minn. Ct. App. 1989).

349   When Cohen sought: Brief for Respondent Cowles Media Co., Cohen v. Cowles Media Co., 501 U.S. 663 (1991), 1991 WL 11007830 at 10–14; Brief for Respondent Northwest Publications, Inc., Cohen v. Cowles Media Co., 501 U.S. 663 (1991), 1991 WL 11007831 at 19–26; Cohen v. Cowles Media Co., 498 U.S. 1011 (1990).

Although the Supreme: 501 U.S. at 667–70.

In the Supreme: *Id.* at 668–69.

350   That White relied: *Id.* at 669–670.

From *Herbert v.*: Herbert v. Lando, 441 U.S. 153 (1979); Branzburg v. Hayes, 408 U.S. 665 (1972); Zurcher v. Stanford Daily, 436 U.S. 547 (1978).

In none of: The one arguable exception is *Zacchini v. Scripps-Howard Broad. Co.*, 433 U.S. 562 (1977), in which the Court, in another opinion by Justice White, held that a "human cannonball" could maintain a claim against a television station under Ohio law for broadcasting the entirety of his performance without his permission. In his opinion: 501 U.S. at 670–71.

Finally, White's opinion: *Id.* at 671.

351   There were two: *Id.* at 672 (Blackmun, J., dissenting); *id.* at 676 (Souter, J., dissenting).

In one, justice: *Id.* at 674–676 (Blackmun, J., dissenting).

Justice Souter, Brennan's: *Id.* at 676–78 (Souter, J., dissenting).

352   The divergence in: Johnathan Kwitny, *Great Adventure: How a New Jerseyite Stands to Lose Fortune Over His Sale of Land*, WSJ, Feb. 27, 1981. The article, which: *Id.* At the time, Steve Wermiel was the JOURNAL'S Supreme Court correspondent and had the referenced telephone conversation with Justice White.

353   Brennan, however, would: Linda Greenhouse, *William Brennan, 91, Dies; Gave Court Liberal Vision*, NYT, July 25, 1997.

When it did: *Bartnicki v. Vopper*, 532 U.S. 514 (2001).

Not only were: Andrew Rosenthal, *Marshall Retires from Court; Blog to Liberals*, NYT, June 28, 1991; *The Supreme Court; Blackmun Retires, With Tribute from the Court*, NYT, July 1, 1994; Linda Greenhouse, *The Supreme Court; White Announces He'll Step Down from High Court*, NYT, Mar. 20, 1993.

Bartnicki v. Vopper

354   *Bartnicki* was one: 532 U.S. at 517–22; Boehner v. McDermott, 191 F.3d 463, 464–66 (D.C. Cir. 1999); Peavy v. WFAA-TV, Inc., 221 F.3d 158, 163–66 (5th Cir. 2000). When lower courts' decisions on the same issue conflict with each other, the courts below are said to be "split." The Supreme Court often grants review to resolve the conflict.

In the first: *Boehner*, 191 F.3d at 464–66.

A majority of: *Id.* at 471–77; Boehner v. McDermott, No. 98–594, 1998 WL 436897 at 6 (D.D.C. July 28, 1998).

355   One judge, David: 191 F.3d at 480 (Sentelle, J., dissenting).

In the last: 221 F.3d at 191–93.

Instead, the Fifth: *Id.*

356   *Bartnicki* came to: 532 U.S. at 517–22.

Not surprisingly, and: Brief for Respondents Frederick W. Vopper, Keymarket of Nepa, Inc. and Lackazerne, Inc., Bartnicki v. Vopper, 532 U.S. 514 (2001), 2000 WL 1614392 at 6–11.

In May 1993: *Id.*; 532 U.S. at 519.

357 The telephone conversation: 532 U.S. at 518–19.

Williams played the: Brief for Respondents Frederick W. Vopper, Keymarket of NEPA, Inc. and Lackazerne, Inc., Bartnicki v. Vopper, 532 U.S. 514 (2001), 2000 WL 1614392 at 8–9, 10 n.12.

Immediately following Williams's: *Id.* at 9–11.

358 They did not: Bartnicki v. Vopper, 200 F.3d 109, 113 (3d Cir. 1999).

Both statutes, like: 18 U.S.C. § 2511(c); 18 Pa. Cons. Stat. § 5725(a).

During the early: Brief for Respondent Jack Yocum, Bartnicki v. Vopper, 2000 WL 1617966 at 3–4.

In proceedings in: Brief for Respondents Frederick W. Vopper, Keymarket of Nepa, Inc. and Lackazerne, Inc., Bartnicki v. Vopper, 532 U.S. 514 (2001), 2000 WL 1614392 at 11.

On their face: 18 U.S.C. § 2520(c)(2); 18 Pa. Cons. Stat. § 5725(a).

359 Accordingly, throughout the: Brief for Respondents Frederick W. Vopper, Keymarket of NEPA, Inc. and Lackazerne, Inc., Bartnicki v. Vopper, 532 U.S. 514 (2001), 2000 WL 1614392 at 18–34, 48 ("Even laws of general application cannot properly be invoked . . . to circumvent the First Amendment protections articulated in *New York Times Co. v. Sullivan*, 376 U.S. 254 (1964), and its progeny.").

In the lower: 532 U.S. at 519–22.

The district court: Bartnicki v. Vopper, No. 94–1201, 1996 U.S. Dist. LEXIS 22517 at 10–11 (M.D. Pa. June. 14, 1996).

On appeal, the: 200 F.3d at 119–23.

Ultimately, however, the: *Id.* at 125–26, 129.

The third member: 200 F.3d at 130 (Pollack, J., dissenting). *See* Dennis Hevesi, *Louis H. Pollak, Civil Rights Advocate and Federal Judge, Dies at 89*, NYT, May 12, 2012.

360 At the urging: Reply Brief for Intervener the United States of America, United States v. Frederick W. Vopper, 2000 WL 33979558 at 1; Bartnicki v. Vopper, 530 U.S. 1260 (2000) (granting petition).

On May 21: 532 U.S. 514.

Justice Breyer, joined: *Id.* at 535 (Breyer, J., concurring); *id.* at 541 (Rehnquist, C.J., dissenting).

At the outset: *Id.* at 526–27.

The Court then: *Id.* at 529 (quoting Boehner v. McDermott, 191 F.3d at 484–85 (Sentelle, J., dissenting)), 535, 528 (quoting Smith v. Daily Mail Publ'g Co., 443 U.S. 97, 103 (1979)).

361 Having answered the: 532 U.S. at 529–30.

The second asserted: *Id.* at 532, 518.

It is here: *Id.* at 534–35.

362 Although he and: *Id.* at 535–38 (Breyer, J., concurring).

Applying his balancing: *Id.* at 538–39.

Breyer's views appear: *Compare id.* at 534 *with id.* at 540 (Breyer, J., concurring).

363 In dissent, the: *Id.* at 541, 548–53 (Rehnquist, C.J., dissenting).

The week after: McDermott v. Boehner, 532 U.S. 1050 (2001).

It denied review: Peavy v. WFAA-TV, Inc., 532 U.S. 1051 (2001); 532 U.S. at 522 n.5.

Years later, and: Boehner v. McDermott, 484 F.3d 573, 578 (D.C. Cir. 2007).

364 In the dozen: 532 U.S. at 534–35.

INDEX